The Documentary History
of the
First Federal Elections
1788–1790

VOLUME III

The Documentary History of the First Federal Elections 1788–1790

VOLUME III

Gordon DenBoer, Editor
Lucy Trumbull Brown, Associate Editor
Charles D. Hagermann, Editorial Assistant

The University of Wisconsin Press

Published 1986

The University of Wisconsin Press
114 North Murray Street
Madison, Wisconsin 53715

The University of Wisconsin Press, Ltd.
1 Gower Street
London WC1E 6HA, England

First printing

Printed in the United States of America

The Documentary History of the First Federal Elections, 1788–1790 *is sponsored by the National Historical Publications and Records Commission and the University of Wisconsin-Madison. Preparation of this volume was also made possible in part by grants from the Program for Editions of the National Endowment for the Humanities, an independent federal agency, and from the Rennebohm Foundation, Madison, Wisconsin. Publication was made possible in part by a grant from the National Historical Publications and Records Commission.*

Library of Congress Cataloging-in-Publication Data
(Revised for vol. 3)
The Documentary history of the first
Federal elections, 1788–1790.
On spine: The first Federal elections, 1788–1790.
Vols. 2– : Gordon DenBoer, editor,
Lucy Trumbull Brown, associate editor,
Charles D. Hagermann, editorial assistant.
Includes bibliographies and indexes.
1. Elections—United States—History—Sources.
2. United States—Politics and government—1789–1797—
Sources. I. Jensen, Merrill. II. Becker, Robert A.,
1943– . III. DenBoer, Gordon, 1933–
IV. First Federal elections, 1788–1790.
JK171.A1D6 324.973'03 74-5903
ISBN 0-299-06690-8 (v. 1)

Contents

PREFACE

The editors of the First Federal Elections project have incurred obligations to many institutions and individuals who collected documents, answered questions, and made the documents available for publication. Those who contributed to the project during its early years and assisted in the production of Volumes I and II are acknowledged in those volumes. The many institutions that have generously contributed material to Volume III are noted in the "List of Symbols for Manuscript Depositories," in the notes on sources for each state chapter, and in the editorial notes which follow each document.

Special thanks are due to the individuals who have contributed to Volume III: John P. Kaminski, Ratification of the Constitution project, for his review of the New York chapter; Kenneth R. Bowling and Charlene N. Bickford, First Federal Congress project, for their help in providing the congressional proceedings concerning the contested New Jersey Representatives election; Professor Richard P. McCormick for reviewing the New Jersey chapter and suggesting answers to questions posed by the editors; and Professor Robert A. Becker, coeditor of Volume I, for his research notes and preliminary work on the New York chapter. The editors also acknowledge a continuing debt to Merrill Jensen for his many contributions to the project as its first editor.

The National Historical Publications and Records Commission has continued to provide the major financial support for the project. The editors appreciate this continuing support, as well as the encouragement from the Commission, its Executive Director, Frank G. Burke, and its staff members Roger A. Bruns, Mary A. Giunta, Richard N. Sheldon, and George L. Vogt. Preparation of this volume was also made possible in part by grants from the Program for Editions of the National Endowment for the Humanities, an independent federal agency, and from the Rennebohm Foundation, Madison, Wisconsin. The History Department of the University of Wisconsin-Madison has provided a congenial working environment and support services for the project, for which the editors thank Richard H. Sewall, department chairman, and the members of the department faculty and administrative staff.

The editors also thank Elizabeth Steinberg, chief editor for the University of Wisconsin Press, for her continuing guidance and encouragement, and the librarian and staff of the State Historical Society of Wisconsin for providing ready access to the many resources of their fine institution.

EDITORIAL POLICIES AND PROCEDURES

The texts of the documents are reproduced literally, with minor exceptions. Superscripts have been lowered to the line, and in a few cases obvious slips of the pen and inadvertent repetition of words have been silently corrected. Terminal punctuation has occasionally been added within paragraphs to clarify meaning; such punctuation is enclosed in brackets. Brackets also enclose all editorial insertions. Conjectural readings are enclosed in brackets with a question mark, while illegible words are indicated by three dashes within brackets. Crossed-out words and phrases are included when they seem to be significant.

The formats of the documents are retained, with several exceptions. Salutations, complimentary closings, endorsements, and addresses of letters are generally omitted. Where they provide information important for the understanding or identification of a letter, they are included or explained in the editorial notes. Datelines of letters are not printed; information contained therein is incorporated into the document headings. Columning in legislative roll calls is standardized into two columns. The format of official documents that include a seal has been altered slightly, because the seal often took up much of the document or was stamped over the writing. To indicate that a document was sealed, the designation [SEAL] is centered at the top or bottom of our printing of the document, whichever corresponds more closely to the actual position of the seal.

Contemporary footnotes are printed after the text of the document and immediately preceding any editorial notes. Symbols, such as stars, asterisks, and daggers, have been replaced by superscripts "(a)," "(b)," "(c)," etc. All signed official documents are indicated by the designation "[signed]" before the name or names of the signers.

All document headings have been provided by the editors. The heading for a letter includes the names of the writer and the recipient, the place where the letter was written, and the date. Any questions or conjectures about this information are included in the editorial notes to the letter. The heading for a newspaper article includes the name, place of publication, and date of the newspaper, as well as the author's name (when the article is signed) or any pseudonym that may have been used by the author. When more than one item came from the same newspaper on the same date, the items are placed in the order in which they appeared in the newspaper. Headings given to broadsides and pamphlets are shortened forms of the original titles, which appear in full in the documents themselves or in the editorial notes. If the broadside or pamphlet had no title, a heading has been devised by the editors.

Only material relevant to the first federal elections is included in this volume. When such material is only a portion of a longer item, the heading identifies it as an excerpt, and information about the printing in other sources of longer extracts or of the complete item is given in the notes. Excerpts from the proceedings of the state legislatures are not marked as excerpts, even though only those actions relating to the first federal elections are printed here. During the course of their sessions the legislatures usually spent far more time on other business than they did on the first federal elections.

When both houses of a state legislature acted on the same day on a matter concerning the first federal elections, the proceedings are arranged in the order of action, so that the progress of the legislation through the two houses can be followed in the order it occurred. Bills, messages, reports, resolutions, and other actions were often copied into the journals of the house to which they were sent. To avoid repetition, editorial notes, enclosed in brackets, often summarize these actions in the proceedings of the receiving house.

The official documents within each state chapter are arranged by topic, e.g., passage of the election laws, the election of Representatives, the election of Senators. In general, within each state chapter the topics are arranged in the order they occurred in that particular state. Comments about the elections, primarily from personal correspondence and newspapers, are printed in the relevant topical part.

Cross-references to documents within the same chapter part are indicated by "above" and "below." Cross-references to documents within the same chapter but in a different part, are indicated by a reference to the part, e.g., "Part Five." Cross-references to documents in Volumes I and II are indicated by volume and page.

At the end of each state chapter the political careers of the principal candidates for office in the first federal elections are sketched. A principal candidate is defined arbitrarily as a person who declared his candidacy, who was mentioned frequently as a candidate, or who received at least one hundred votes in the elections for either Representatives or presidential Electors (according to the election statistics available). Other candidates, the writers and recipients of letters, and individuals mentioned in the documents are identified when their names first appear in the documents. For some individuals, little or no biographical data has been located—even though it is often apparent from the documents that they were prominent in their own day. Individuals listed only in legislative roll calls and persons mentioned in passing, in the context of a particular document, are not identified. The biographical data has been collected from many sources; most useful have been biographical dictionaries and directories, biographies and collected writings of individuals, civil lists, genealogies, and town and county histories.

Virtually all significant official documents, e.g., legislative records, proclamations, credentials/commissions of elected officials, are printed. Routine official documents, such as pay or expense vouchers and legislative and executive directives, are not printed. However, any useful information contained in official documents that are not printed is included in editorial notes. Unofficial documents, such as private correspondence, diaries, broadsides, pamphlets, and newspaper articles, are printed if they provide information about, or insight into, the elections.

DESCRIPTIVE SYMBOLS FOR MANUSCRIPTS

DS	Document signed. An official signed document, e.g., proclamation, credential/ commission of an elected official.
FC	File copy. Copy of a letter retained by the writer.
MS	Manuscript. Broadly defined to include all manuscripts except letters.
RC	Recipients copy. Copy of a letter intended for the addressee.
Tr	Transcript. Copy of a manuscript or a document.

LIST OF SYMBOLS FOR MANUSCRIPT DEPOSITORIES

CtHi	Connecticut Historical Society, Hartford
CtY	Yale University, New Haven, Connecticut
DLC	Library of Congress, Washington, D.C.
DNA	National Archives, Washington, D.C.
DeHi	Historical Society of Delaware, Wilmington
MB	Boston Public Library, Massachusetts
MHi	Massachusetts Historical Society, Boston
MeHi	Maine Historical Society, Portland
MiU-C	William L. Clements Library, University of Michigan, Ann Arbor
N	New York State Library, Albany
NAII	Albany Institute of History and Art, New York
NCmM	Museum Manor of Saint George, Center Moriches, New York
NHi	New-York Historical Society, New York City
NHpR	Franklin D. Roosevelt Library, Hyde Park, New York
NN	New York Public Library, New York City
NNC	Columbia University, New York City
Nc-Ar	North Carolina State Department of Archives and History, Raleigh
NcD	Duke University, Durham, North Carolina
Nj	New Jersey State Library, Archives and History, Trenton
NjHi	New Jersey Historical Society, Newark
NjMoW	Washington Headquarters Library, Morristown, New Jersey
NjP	Princeton University, Princeton, New Jersey
NjR	Rutgers-The State University, New Brunswick, New Jersey
PHC	Haverford College, Haverford, Pennsylvania
PHarH	Pennsylvania Historical and Museum Commission, Harrisburg
PHi	Historical Society of Pennsylvania, Philadelphia
PPL	Library Company of Philadelphia, Pennsylvania
PPRF	Rosenbach Foundation, Philadelphia, Pennsylvania
ViHi	Virginia Historical Society, Richmond
ViW	College of William and Mary, Williamsburg, Virginia
WHi	State Historical Society of Wisconsin, Madison

The symbols are those adopted by the Library of Congress, *Symbols of American Libraries* (10th ed., Washington, D.C., 1969).

SHORT TITLE LIST

Boyd

Julian P. Boyd and Charles T. Cullen et al., eds., *The Papers of Thomas Jefferson* (Princeton, N.J., 1950——).

Burnett, *Letters*

Edmund C. Burnett, ed., *Letters of Members of the Continental Congress* (8 vols., Washington, D.C., 1921–1936).

Butterfield, *Rush*

Lyman H. Butterfield, ed., *Letters of Benjamin Rush* (2 vols., Princeton, N.J., 1951).

DHFFC

Linda Grant DePauw and Charlene N. Bickford et al., eds., *Documentary History of the First Federal Congress of the United States of America* (Baltimore, 1972——).

DHFFE

Merrill Jensen, Robert A. Becker, and Gordon DenBoer et al., eds., *The Documentary History of the First Federal Elections, 1788–1790* (Madison, Wis., 1976——).

DHRC

Merrill Jensen, John P. Kaminski, and Gaspare J. Saladino et al., eds., *The Documentary History of the Ratification of the Constitution* (Madison, Wis., 1976——).

Hening

William Waller Hening, ed., *The Statutes at Large; Being a Collection of All the Laws of Virginia . . .* (16 vols., Richmond, Va., and Philadelphia, 1819–1823).

Johnston

Henry P. Johnston, ed., *The Correspondence and Public Papers of John Jay* (4 vols., New York and London, 1890–1893).

King, *Life*

Charles R. King, ed., *Life and Correspondence of Rufus King . . .* (6 vols., New York, 1894–1900).

McCormick, *Experiment in Independence*

Richard P. McCormick, *Experiment in Independence: New Jersey in the Critical Period, 1781–1789* (New Brunswick, N.J., 1950).

Rutland, *Madison*

Robert A. Rutland et al., eds., *The Papers of James Madison* (Chicago and Charlottesville, Va., 1973——).

Syrett

Harold C. Syrett et al., eds., *The Papers of Alexander Hamilton* (27 vols., New York and London, 1961–1985).

Thorpe

Francis N. Thorpe, comp. and ed., *The Federal and State Constitutions, Colonial Charters, and Other Organic Laws of the States, Territories, and Colonies, Now or Heretofore Forming the United States of America* (7 vols., Washington, D.C., 1909).

WMQ

William and Mary Quarterly.

Young, *Democratic-Republicans.*

Alfred F. Young, *The Democratic-Republicans of New York: The Origins, 1763–1797* (Chapel Hill, N.C., 1967).

CHRONOLOGY OF THE ELECTIONS WITH NAMES OF MEN ELECTED

Date	*State*	*Office*	*Men Elected*
1788			
30 September	Pennsylvania	Senators	Robert Morris, William Maclay
15–16 October	Connecticut	Senators	Oliver Ellsworth, William S. Johnson
25 October	Delaware	Senators	George Read, Richard Bassett
8 November	Virginia	Senators	Richard Henry Lee, William Grayson
11–12 November	New Hampshire	Senators	John Langdon, Josiah Bartlett (declined)
21–22, 24 November	Massachusetts	Senators	Caleb Strong, Tristram Dalton
24–25 November	South Carolina	Representatives (Five districts)	Aedanus Burke, Daniel Huger, William Loughton Smith, Thomas Sumter, Thomas Tudor Tucker
25 November	New Jersey	Senators	Jonathan Elmer, William Paterson
26 November	Pennsylvania	Representatives (Statewide)	George Clymer, Thomas FitzSimons, Thomas Hartley, Daniel Hiester, Frederick A. Muhlenberg, John Peter Muhlenberg, Thomas Scott, Henry Wynkoop
9–10 December	Maryland	Senators	Charles Carroll, John Henry
15 December	New Hampshire	Representatives (Statewide)	No decision.
18 December	Massachusetts	Representatives (Eight Districts)	Fisher Ames (Suffolk), George Partridge (Plymouth and Barnstable), George Thacher (York, Cumberland, and Lincoln), George Leonard (Bristol, Dukes, and Nantucket). No decision in four districts.
22 December	Connecticut	Representatives (Statewide)	Benjamin Huntington, Roger Sherman, Jonathan Sturges, Jonathan Trumbull, Jr., Jeremiah Wadsworth
1789			
1, 3 January	New Hampshire	Senator	Paine Wingate
7 January	Delaware	Representative (Statewide)	John Vining
7 January	All states (except R.I., N.C., N.Y.)	Presidential Electors	72 men elected.
7–10 January	Maryland	Representatives (Statewide)	Daniel Carroll, Benjamin Contee, George Gale, Joshua Seney, William Smith, Michael Jenifer Stone

Chronology of the Elections

17 January	Georgia	Senators	William Few, James Gunn
22 January	South Carolina	Senators	Pierce Butler, Ralph Izard
29 January	Massachusetts	Representatives (Second election)	Elbridge Gerry (Middlesex), Benjamin Goodhue (Essex). No decision in two districts.
2 February	New Hampshire	Representatives (Second election)	Nicholas Gilman, Samuel Livermore, Benjamin West (declined)
2 February	Virginia	Representatives (Ten districts)	Theodorick Bland, John Brown, Isaac Coles, Samuel Griffin, Richard Bland Lee, James Madison, Andrew Moore, John Page, Josiah Parker, Alexander White
4 February	All states (except N.Y., R.I., N.C.)	President and Vice President	George Washington, John Adams
9 February	Georgia	Representatives (Statewide)	Abraham Baldwin, James Jackson, George Mathews
11 February–18 March*	New Jersey	Representatives (Statewide)	Elias Boudinot, Lambert Cadwalader, James Schureman, Thomas Sinnickson
2 March	Massachusetts	Representatives (Third election)	Jonathan Grout (Worcester). No decision in Hampshire-Berkshire District.
3–6 March	New York	Representatives (Six districts)	Egbert Benson, William Floyd, John Hathorn, John Laurance, Jeremiah Van Rensselaer, Peter Silvester
30 March	Massachusetts	Representatives (Fourth election)	No decision in Hampshire-Berkshire District.
11 May	Massachusetts	Representatives (Fifth election)	Theodore Sedgwick (Hampshire-Berkshire)
22 June	New Hampshire	Representatives (Third election)	Abiel Foster
15–16 July	New York	Senators	Rufus King, Philip Schuyler
26 November, 2–3, 5, 8 December	North Carolina	Senators	Benjamin Hawkins, Samuel Johnston
1790			
4–5 February	North Carolina	Representatives (Four districts)	John Baptista Ashe (Roanoke), Timothy Bloodworth (Cape Fear), John Steele (Yadkin), Hugh Williamson (Edenton and Newbern)
8–9 March	North Carolina	Representatives (One district)	John Sevier (Western)
12 June	Rhode Island	Senators	Theodore Foster, Joseph Stanton
31 August	Rhode Island	Representative (Statewide)	Benjamin Bourne

*On 18 March, Privy Council determined winners on basis of returns to date.

PRESIDENTIAL ELECTORS AND THEIR VOTES, 4 FEBRUARY 1789

New Hampshire

Benjamin Bellows		
John Pickering		
Ebenezer Thompson	George Washington	5 votes
John Sullivan	John Adams	5 votes
John Parker		

Massachusetts

Caleb Davis		
Samuel Phillips, Jr.		
Francis Dana		
Samuel Henshaw		
William Sever	George Washington	10 votes
David Sewall	John Adams	10 votes
Walter Spooner		
Moses Gill		
William Cushing		
William Shepard		

Connecticut

Samuel Huntington		
Richard Law		
Matthew Griswold	George Washington	7 votes
Erastus Wolcott	John Adams	5 votes
Thaddeus Burr	Samuel Huntington	2 votes
Jedidiah Huntington		
Oliver Wolcott, Sr.		

New Jersey

David Brearley		
James Kinsey	George Washington	6 votes
John Neilson	John Jay	5 votes
David Moore	John Adams	1 vote
John Rutherfurd		
Matthias Ogden		

Delaware

Electors	Candidate	Votes
Gunning Bedford, Sr.	George Washington	3 votes
George Mitchell	John Jay	3 votes
John Baning		

Pennsylvania

Electors	Candidate	Votes
James Wilson	George Washington	10 votes
James O'Hara	John Adams	8 votes
David Grier	John Hancock	2 votes
Samuel Potts		
Alexander Graydon		
Collinson Read		
Edward Hand		
George Gibson		
John Arndt		
Laurence Keene		

Maryland

Electors	Candidate	Votes
John Rogers	George Washington	6 votes
William Tilghman	Robert H. Harrison	6 votes
Alexander Contee Hanson		
Philip Thomas		
Robert Smith		
William Matthews		
George Plater*		
William Richardson*		

Virginia

Electors	Candidate	Votes
John Pride, Jr.	George Washington	10 votes
John Harvie	John Adams	5 votes
Zachariah Johnston	George Clinton	3 votes
John Roane, Jr.	John Hancock	1 vote
David Stuart	John Jay	1 vote
William Fitzhugh		
Anthony Walke		
Patrick Henry		
Edward Stevens		
Warner Lewis*		
James Wood, Jr.		

South Carolina

Christopher Gadsden		
Henry Laurens		
Edward Rutledge	George Washington	7 votes
Charles Cotesworth Pinckney	John Rutledge	6 votes
John F. Grimké	John Hancock	1 vote
Thomas Heyward, Jr.		
Arthur Simkins		

Georgia

George Handley	George Washington	5 votes
John King	John Milton	2 votes
George Walton	James Armstrong	1 vote
Henry Osborne	Edward Telfair	1 vote
John Milton	Benjamin Lincoln	1 vote

*Did not vote.

CALENDAR FOR THE YEARS 1788–1790

1788

JANUARY

		1	2	3	4	5
6	7	8	9	10	11	12
13	14	15	16	17	18	19
20	21	22	23	24	25	26
27	28	29	30	31		

FEBRUARY

					1	2
3	4	5	6	7	8	9
10	11	12	13	14	15	16
17	18	19	20	21	22	23
24	25	26	27	28	29	

MARCH

						1
2	3	4	5	6	7	8
9	10	11	12	13	14	15
16	17	18	19	20	21	22
23	24	25	26	27	28	29
30	31					

APRIL

		1	2	3	4	5
6	7	8	9	10	11	12
13	14	15	16	17	18	19
20	21	22	23	24	25	26
27	28	29	30			

MAY

				1	2	3
4	5	6	7	8	9	10
11	12	13	14	15	16	17
18	19	20	21	22	23	24
25	26	27	28	29	30	31

JUNE

1	2	3	4	5	6	7
8	9	10	11	12	13	14
15	16	17	18	19	20	21
22	23	24	25	26	27	28
29	30					

JULY

		1	2	3	4	5
6	7	8	9	10	11	12
13	14	15	16	17	18	19
20	21	22	23	24	25	26
27	28	29	30	31		

AUGUST

					1	2
3	4	5	6	7	8	9
10	11	12	13	14	15	16
17	18	19	20	21	22	23
24	25	26	27	28	29	30
31						

SEPTEMBER

	1	2	3	4	5	6
7	8	9	10	11	12	13
14	15	16	17	18	19	20
21	22	23	24	25	26	27
28	29	30				

OCTOBER

			1	2	3	4
5	6	7	8	9	10	11
12	13	14	15	16	17	18
19	20	21	22	23	24	25
26	27	28	29	30	31	

NOVEMBER

						1
2	3	4	5	6	7	8
9	10	11	12	13	14	15
16	17	18	19	20	21	22
23	24	25	26	27	28	29
30						

DECEMBER

	1	2	3	4	5	6
7	8	9	10	11	12	13
14	15	16	17	18	19	20
21	22	23	24	25	26	27
28	29	30	31			

1789

JANUARY

				1	2	3
4	5	6	7	8	9	10
11	12	13	14	15	16	17
18	19	20	21	22	23	24
25	26	27	28	29	30	31

FEBRUARY

1	2	3	4	5	6	7
8	9	10	11	12	13	14
15	16	17	18	19	20	21
22	23	24	25	26	27	28

MARCH

1	2	3	4	5	6	7
8	9	10	11	12	13	14
15	16	17	18	19	20	21
22	23	24	25	26	27	28
29	30	31				

APRIL

			1	2	3	4
5	6	7	8	9	10	11
12	13	14	15	16	17	18
19	20	21	22	23	24	25
26	27	28	29	30		

MAY

					1	2
3	4	5	6	7	8	9
10	11	12	13	14	15	16
17	18	19	20	21	22	23
24	25	26	27	28	29	30
31						

JUNE

	1	2	3	4	5	6
7	8	9	10	11	12	13
14	15	16	17	18	19	20
21	22	23	24	25	26	27
28	29	30				

JULY

			1	2	3	4
5	6	7	8	9	10	11
12	13	14	15	16	17	18
19	20	21	22	23	24	25
26	27	28	29	30	31	

AUGUST

						1
2	3	4	5	6	7	8
9	10	11	12	13	14	15
16	17	18	19	20	21	22
23	24	25	26	27	28	29
30	31					

SEPTEMBER

		1	2	3	4	5
6	7	8	9	10	11	12
13	14	15	16	17	18	19
20	21	22	23	24	25	26
27	28	29	30			

OCTOBER

				1	2	3
4	5	6	7	8	9	10
11	12	13	14	15	16	17
18	19	20	21	22	23	24
25	26	27	28	29	30	31

NOVEMBER

1	2	3	4	5	6	7
8	9	10	11	12	13	14
15	16	17	18	19	20	21
22	23	24	25	26	27	28
29	30					

DECEMBER

		1	2	3	4	5
6	7	8	9	10	11	12
13	14	15	16	17	18	19
20	21	22	23	24	25	26
27	28	29	30	31		

1790

JANUARY

					1	2
3	4	5	6	7	8	9
10	11	12	13	14	15	16
17	18	19	20	21	22	23
24	25	26	27	28	29	30
31						

FEBRUARY

	1	2	3	4	5	6
7	8	9	10	11	12	13
14	15	16	17	18	19	20
21	22	23	24	25	26	27
28						

MARCH

	1	2	3	4	5	6
7	8	9	10	11	12	13
14	15	16	17	18	19	20
21	22	23	24	25	26	27
28	29	30	31			

APRIL

				1	2	3
4	5	6	7	8	9	10
11	12	13	14	15	16	17
18	19	20	21	22	23	24
25	26	27	28	29	30	

MAY

						1
2	3	4	5	6	7	8
9	10	11	12	13	14	15
16	17	18	19	20	21	22
23	24	25	26	27	28	29
30	31					

JUNE

		1	2	3	4	5
6	7	8	9	10	11	12
13	14	15	16	17	18	19
20	21	22	23	24	25	26
27	28	29	30			

JULY

				1	2	3
4	5	6	7	8	9	10
11	12	13	14	15	16	17
18	19	20	21	22	23	24
25	26	27	28	29	30	31

AUGUST

1	2	3	4	5	6	7
8	9	10	11	12	13	14
15	16	17	18	19	20	21
22	23	24	25	26	27	28
29	30	31				

SEPTEMBER

			1	2	3	4
5	6	7	8	9	10	11
12	13	14	15	16	17	18
19	20	21	22	23	24	25
26	27	28	29	30		

OCTOBER

					1	2
3	4	5	6	7	8	9
10	11	12	13	14	15	16
17	18	19	20	21	22	23
24	25	26	27	28	29	30
31						

NOVEMBER

	1	2	3	4	5	6
7	8	9	10	11	12	13
14	15	16	17	18	19	20
21	22	23	24	25	26	27
28	29	30				

DECEMBER

			1	2	3	4
5	6	7	8	9	10	11
12	13	14	15	16	17	18
19	20	21	22	23	24	25
26	27	28	29	30	31	

CHAPTER XII

The Elections in New Jersey

New Jersey Counties, 1788–1789

INTRODUCTION

In the early seventeenth century the Dutch and Swedish were the first Europeans to settle on the lands of present-day New Jersey. The English claimed the area, however, and in 1664 Great Britain seized control of New Netherland, which included New Jersey. The English divided the colony into East and West Jersey in 1676 to accommodate a group of English Quakers who wanted to purchase West Jersey for a colony of their own. The dividing line separating East and West Jersey was surveyed in 1687. Although the two sections were politically reunited in 1702, the dividing line remained a potent symbol of the geographic, economic, and social differences that divided East and West Jersey throughout the eighteenth century.

West Jersey, settled principally by English Quakers, was more homogeneous and conservative than East Jersey. It was basically agricultural and rural, and it was oriented to Philadelphia and that city's strong Quaker influence. East Jersey, by contrast, was more diverse in virtually all respects. It was settled mainly by New Englanders (although it also had a substantial Dutch population), and its economy was more balanced between agriculture, commerce, and mining. East Jersey gravitated into New York City's orbit. Presbyterians, the largest single religious group in the overwhelmingly Protestant colony, were more numerous in East Jersey; Anglicans, relatively few in number, were concentrated in East Jersey and wielded political power far out of proportion to their numbers.

New Jersey, like the other colonies, began the transition from colony to independent state well before the Declaration of Independence. The bridge was provided in 1774–1775 by a succession of extralegal mass meetings, committees of correspondence, and committees of observation that culminated in the meeting of the first provincial congress in May 1775. The congress quickly usurped the duties of the moribund colonial assembly (which did not formally adjourn for the last time until late in 1775), and the second provincial congress completed the transition at sessions in October 1775 and January 1776. The third congress, which convened on 10 June 1776, authorized its delegates to the Continental Congress to vote for independence, and—at the urging of Congress—wrote a state constitution to reflect the new realities. The constitution was drafted by a ten-man committee, approved by the provincial congress on 2 July, and declared in effect without ratification by the people. It was to endure until 1844.

The constitution provided for a bicameral legislature, composed of a General Assembly and a Legislative Council. Members of the Assembly (three from each of the state's thirteen counties) and the Council (one from each county) were to be elected annually on the second Tuesday in October. Assemblymen had to be inhabitants of the county for which they were elected for at least one year before the election and own real and personal property in the county worth at least £500 "proclamation money"; councillors were required to be inhabitants and freeholders of the county for which they were chosen for at least one year before the election, and possessors of real and personal property worth at least £1000 "proclamation money." County sheriffs and coroners were elected annually by the voters; they were limited to a maximum of three successive one-year terms, after which they were ineligible for the office for three years. Although the state could have no established church, the constitution implied that only Protestants were entitled to hold public office: "no Protestant inhabitant of this Colony shall be denied the enjoyment of any civil right, merely on account of his religious principles; but that all persons, professing a belief in the faith of any Protestant sect, . . . shall be capable of being elected to any office. . . ."

The legislature was virtually supreme under the constitution. All state officials were appointed by joint session of the legislature: the governor, for a one-year term; supreme court judges, for seven-year terms; judges of the county inferior courts, justices of the peace, clerks of the various courts, the attorney general, and the state secretary, for five-year terms; the state treasurer, for a one-year term; and all field and general officers of the state militia (captains and lesser officers were to be chosen by the militia companies). Either house could originate legislation, except money bills, which the Council could not originate or amend; the governor had no veto power over legislation.

Although the governor's powers were sharply limited, he was the supreme executive authority. He was president of the Legislative Council (and could, at any time, convene any three or more councillors as a Privy Council to advise him), chancellor, commander in chief of the state's military forces, surrogate general, and, with the Council, the Court of Appeals in legal cases.

Voters had to be inhabitants "of full age," residents of the county in which they voted for at least one year before the election, and owners of a "clear estate" worth at least £50 "proclamation money." Voting by ballot (instead of the customary *viva voce*) was first introduced in state elections in 1777; in 1788 only Bergen, Cape May, Essex, Morris, and Sussex counties voted *viva voce*. The first federal elections for Representatives were the first elections in New Jersey to be conducted entirely by ballot. After 1797 ballots were required in all elections in the state.

By the time New Jersey's constitution took effect in mid-1776, large scale military operations were already commonplace in the northern colonies. By late 1776 they reached New Jersey, and the state's strategic location ensured that it would be at the center of military operations throughout the Revolutionary War. The campaigns of the American, British, and French armies, as well as the internecine warfare between loyalists and patriots, were enormously destructive. East Jersey, situated astride the major land routes between New York City and Philadelphia, suffered more severely than West Jersey, which was more remote from the scenes of action and whose large pacifist, Quaker population was less involved in the war. This uneven participation deepened the historic cleavage between East and West Jersey.

The financial problems which plagued the state in the immediate postwar period also contributed to the sectional rivalry. A sharp economic downturn was triggered at war's end by deflationary monetary policies and an unfavorable balance of trade. Especially galling to Jerseyites (both East and West) was the fact that most foreign trade funneled in and out of the state through New York City and Philadelphia—with little economic benefit to the state treasury. Also, the state had incurred substantial debts during the war, which it attempted to pay off after the war by levying heavy taxes on the state's citizens.

By the mid-1780s many Jerseyites began to view paper money as the panacea for the state's economic ills, and political factions quickly coalesced around the issue in the ensuing public debate. Demand for paper money was strongest in East Jersey, where Abraham Clark headed the dominant political faction. Opposition, led by Governor William Livingston, was centered in the more conservative, creditor-oriented western counties. The East Jersey paper money forces prevailed in the state elections in October 1785, and the legislature, following a spirited public debate, enacted a loan-office bill in May 1786. The legislation provided for the issuance of £100,000 of loan-office certificates, which were to be lent out to state residents (£100 limit) on the security of real property. The certificates were to be lent out for twelve years at 6 percent annual interest; beginning in the eighth year the certificates had to be paid back in five annual installments, with the state destroying the certificates as they were received. The certificates were legal tender for all debts. The political factions sparred over other issues during the 1780s, but none had the divisive sectional effect that economic (especially paper money) matters did.

However much Jerseyites quarreled among themselves on domestic affairs, they were largely united on continental matters. They favored a stronger central government; one that would have control over western lands and trade and that would be able to levy duties on imported goods. Such advocacy reflected New Jersey's status as a "landless" state (i.e., it claimed no western lands) and the fact that the duties its citizens paid on imported goods went largely into the coffers of New York and Pennsylvania. Jerseyites reasoned that if Congress controlled, and could dispose of, western lands and could collect import duties, it would not have to reply on requisitions from the states for income. That, in turn, would allow state officials to reduce taxes.

New Jersey made its position clear on these matters at the outset of the Confederation when the Articles of Confederation were submitted to the states for ratification. In a "Representation" to Congress in June 1778, the state legislature asserted that Congress should have "the sole and exclusive Power of regulating the Trade of the United States with foreign Nations," with the revenue arising therefrom to be used "for the common Benefit of the States." The legislature also urged that Congress should have control over the western lands gained during the Revolution (excluding those legitimately claimed by the individual states) and be able to dispose of them "for defraying the Expences of the War, and for other such public and general Purposes." Without such congressional control over trade and western lands, the legislature asserted, states like New Jersey—which had no western lands—would "be left to sink under an enormous Debt . . ." (DHRC, I, 113–17).

Congress rejected the amendments to the Articles proposed by New Jersey, and the state legislature, not wishing to hold up creation of the Confederation, approved the act of ratification on 20 November 1778. Nevertheless, the legislature informed Congress that it continued to view the Articles "in divers Respects unequal and disadvantageous to this State," and that it ratified "in firm Reliance that the Candour and Justice of the several States will, in due Time, remove, as far as possible, the Inequality which now subsists" (DHRC, I, 128–29).

Congress acted to eliminate some of New Jersey's complaints when it proposed an amendment to the Articles of Confederation giving Congress the power to levy a duty of 5 percent on imported goods to pay war debts (the Impost of 1781). New Jersey readily approved in June 1781. When the impost failed to win the required unanimous approval of the states (Rhode Island and Virginia refused to ratify it), Congress proposed the modified Impost of 1783 as part of a comprehensive revenue plan. The plan also reiterated Congress' earlier requests that those states which claimed western lands should cede them to Congress. New Jersey quickly approved again in June 1783, but this time New York's ultimate refusal (in 1787) to approve the impost doomed the entire revenue plan.

When prospects for approval of the congressional revenue plan had not improved by late 1785, New Jersey expressed its exasperation by refusing to honor its share of the congressional requisition of 1785. The move had been foreshadowed by the legislature's approval in December 1783 of a plan whereby New Jersey, rather than Congress, would pay the principal and interest of debts due from the United States to citizens of New Jersey; the sum earmarked, $83,358, was equal to the state's share of the national total of $1,500,000 recommended by Congress in its comprehensive revenue plan of 1783 (which also was never approved by the states). The legislature reinforced its stand in December 1784 by prohibiting the state treasurer from paying any more money to Congress until the states had approved the congressional impost and the funds requested by Congress in its comprehensive revenue plan.

When the congressional requisition of 1785 reached the legislature in November, Abraham Clark led a movement to defer action until the legislature's next session. At that session, in February 1786, the legislature rejected the requisition request, repeating again New Jersey's determination not to comply with congressional requests for funds until the impost and revenue plans of 1783 were approved by the states. Congress sent a three-man delegation to New Jersey to persuade the legislature to relent, and although the legislature rescinded its rejection, its resolution of approval was little more than a face-saving device. In practice, New Jersey's policy of denying financial support to Congress, begun in 1783, was not altered during the remainder of the Confederation.

A new approach to strengthening Congress developed when Virginia issued a call on 21 January 1786 for a convention to meet in Annapolis in September to consider measures to expand Congress' commerce powers. New Jersey quickly accepted the invitation; the state's delegates (Abraham Clark, William C. Houston, and James Schureman) were authorized to consider, in addition to trade, "other important Matters." Only five states were represented at Annapolis, however, and the convention could therefore not act conclusively. In its official report of 14 September it recommended that an expanded convention be convened in Philadelphia in May 1787, and that the states, in empowering their delagates to that convention, should follow New Jersey's example and provide for consideration of subjects other than commerce.

New Jersey appointed delegates to the proposed convention even before Congress issued its call for the Constitutional Convention on 21 February 1787. David Brearley, William C. Houston, John Neilson, and William Paterson were appointed by the legislature on 23 November 1786, and the next day were empowered to take "into consideration the state of the Union as to trade and other important objects, and of devising such further provisions as shall appear necessary to render the Constitution of the federal government adequate to the exigencies thereof" (DHRC, I, 195–96). Governor William Livingston and Jonathan Dayton subsequently replaced Houston and Neilson in the delegation.

In the Convention, the New Jersey delegates opposed efforts to devise a strong central government with coercive powers over the states and their citizens, as envisioned in the ambitious Virginia plan. They preferred, instead, a modest amendment of the Articles of Confederation which would give Congress an adequate independent income, but which would, at the same time, protect the interests of the "small" states. The New Jersey approach came to be known as the Paterson plan, named after one of its chief spokesmen, William Paterson. Although defeated on most major points, the New Jersey delegates found in the compromises (especially that which provided for equality of representation in the Senate) enough merit to allow them to sign the finished Constitution on 17 September 1787.

Most Jerseyites seemed to share the view of their Convention delegates that the proposed Constitution provided the stronger central government that New Jersey had sought since the beginning of the Confederation. There was consequently little opposition to the Constitution in the state. On 29 October the legislature provided for a state convention of three delegates from each county to consider the Constitution. The Convention met on 11 December and ratified the Constitution unanimously on 18 December 1787; New Jersey was the third state to ratify.

Although sectional and personal rivalries played little part in the ratification process, they began to surface again on domestic matters during 1788. West Jersey conservatives had chafed under the inflationary, debtor-oriented policies enacted by the dominant East Jersey legislative faction in the mid-1780s, and, in the wake of the ratification of the Constitution, they initiated a challenge to that dominance. The effort culminated in the state elections in October 1788, which shifted political power in the legislature from East Jersey to a coalition composed of West Jerseyites and a few East Jersey allies. The first federal elections were conducted in the context of this shift of political power.

Despite the intense sectional sparring on domestic issues, there was little carryover to the election of United States Senators and presidential Electors. On 25 November 1788 the legislature elected Jonathan Elmer and William Paterson as the state's first Senators, and on 7 January 1789 the governor and Privy Council chose David Brearley, James Kinsey, David Moore, John Neilson, Matthias Ogden, and John Rutherfurd as presidential Electors. All were prominent citizens and at least nominal Federalists, and they were about equally split between East and West Jersey. In the balloting for President on 4 February, the Electors cast six votes for George Washington, five for John Jay, and one for John Adams.

There was nothing placid, however, about the elections for Representatives, which began in all thirteen counties on 11 February, and which finally ended in Essex County on 27 April. The elections, marred by fraud and manipulation, revolved around personal and sectional rivalries; the Constitution and the need for amendments were of secondary importance. The Junto ticket of Federalists Elias Boudinot, Lambert Cadwalader, Thomas Sinnickson, and James Schureman was declared elected by Governor Livingston on 19 March on the basis of returns from twelve of the thirteen counties (earlier, on 3 March, the governor had refused to declare winners as only seven counties had reported). The election was appealed to the House of Representatives by supporters of Abraham Clark and Jonathan Dayton, but on 2 September 1789 the House upheld the election of Boudinot, Cadwalader, Sinnickson, and Schureman.

NOTE ON SOURCES

The proceedings of the General Assembly are taken from the manuscript "Votes and Proceedings of the General Assembly," preserved at the Bureau of Archives and History, New Jersey State Library, Trenton. These proceedings were printed as *Votes and Proceedings of the Thirteenth General Assembly of the State of New Jersey . . .* (Trenton, 1788). The proceedings of the Legislative Council are from the *Journal of the Proceedings of the Legislative-Council of the State of New Jersey . . .* (Trenton, 1788). No manuscript journal of the Legislative Council is extant. Privy Council proceedings are from the manuscript "Minutes of Governor's Privy Council of New Jersey," I (1777–1796), at the Bureau of Archives and History, New Jersey State Library. The proceedings of the United States House of Representatives are from the *Journal of the House of Representatives of the United States* (New York, 1789).

Two weekly newspapers were published regularly in New Jersey during the period of the first federal elections: *The New-Jersey Journal, and Political Intelligencer* was published in Elizabethtown by Shepard Kollock, and *The Brunswick Gazette, and Weekly Monitor* was published by Shelly Arnett in New Brunswick. A third newspaper, *The Federal Post,* was published in Trenton by Frederick C. Quequelle and George M. Wilson, but only a few issues are extant, and it expired in early 1789. Philadelphia and New York

City newspapers, which printed many articles about New Jersey politics, were widely read in New Jersey. The wide distribution of these out-of-state newspapers in New Jersey was recognized by the state legislature when it ordered that the nomination list for Representatives "be published in the News-Papers printed in this State, and in two or more printed in the Cities of New-York and Philadelphia" (New Jersey Election Law, 21 November 1788, Part One).

The first federal elections in New Jersey were widely discussed in personal correspondence. The notes to the documents reflect the wide range of manuscript collections from which the documents were drawn. The richest collection is the William Livingston Papers at the Massachusetts Historical Society, Boston; it contains personal and official letters and copies of official documents concerning the elections. Among the many collections at the New Jersey Historical Society, Newark, two were especially useful: the Stevens Family Papers and the Dayton Miscellany. At the Historical Society of Pennsylvania, Philadelphia, the Wallace Papers and the Gratz Collection were good sources of documents. Several collections at the Rutgers University Library also provided documents. Other collections with particularly useful material include the Jonathan Dayton Papers, William L. Clements Library, University of Michigan, Ann Arbor, and the Lloyd W. Smith Collection, Morristown National Historical Park, Morristown, New Jersey.

For background on the history of the period and the first federal elections, several works by Richard P. McCormick are especially useful: "New Jersey's First Congressional Election, 1789: A Case Study in Political Skulduggery," WMQ, 3d ser., VI (1949), 237–50; *Experiment in Independence: New Jersey in the Critical Period, 1781–1789* (New Brunswick, 1950); and *The History of Voting in New Jersey: A Study of the Development of Election Machinery, 1664–1911* (New Brunswick, 1953). For the ratification of the Constitution in New Jersey, see Merrill Jensen, ed., *The Documentary History of the Ratification of the Constitution*, III (Madison, Wis., 1978).

CHRONOLOGY, 1788–1789

1788

27 August-9 September	Special session of the state legislature at Trenton.
13 September	Confederation Congress adopts Election Ordinance for first federal elections.
14 October	State elections for Legislative Council and General Assembly.
28 October	State legislature convenes at Trenton (moves to Princeton, 3 November).
11 November	Council committee submits bill for first federal elections to the Council.
14 November	Council approves election bill; sends it to Assembly.
21 November	Election law for first federal elections approved.

25 November	Jonathan Elmer and William Paterson chosen United States Senators by joint session of Council and Assembly.
1 December	State legislature adjourns.

1789

7 January	David Brearley, James Kinsey, David Moore, John Neilson, Matthias Ogden, and John Rutherfurd chosen presidential Electors by governor and Privy Council.
12 January	Deadline for nominations for Representatives by voters.
19 January	Governor William Livingston proclaims 54 nominees for Representatives.
4 February	New Jersey Electors at Trenton cast 6 votes for George Washington, 5 for John Jay, and 1 for John Adams.
11 February	Polls open for election of Representatives in all 13 counties.
3 March	Privy Council meets to count votes for Representatives; Governor William Livingston defers decision to 18 March because returns from only 7 counties available.
4 March	First federal Congress convenes in New York.
18–19 March	Privy Council meets to count votes for Representatives; Essex County return still missing; Council declares election closed.
19 March	Governor William Livingston proclaims Elias Boudinot, Lambert Cadwalader, Thomas Sinnickson, and James Schureman elected United States Representatives.
27 April	Poll for Representatives closed in Essex County.
3 May	Governor William Livingston receives election return from Essex County.
14 May	United States House of Representatives refers petitions concerning contested Representatives election in New Jersey to Committee of Elections
21 May	Committee of Elections reports to House of Representatives on contested election in New Jersey.
15 July	House of Representatives debates procedures for investigating the New Jersey election.
18 August	Committee of Elections reports its conclusions on the New Jersey election to the House of Representatives.
2 September	House of Representatives votes to seat the "sitting" members: Elias Boudinot, Lambert Cadwalader, Thomas Sinnickson, and James Schureman.

THE DOCUMENTS

PART ONE

PASSAGE OF THE ELECTION LAW

Governor William Livingston called the state legislature into special session when it was clear that the required nine states had ratified the Federal Constitution. The legislature, meeting in Trenton from 27 August to 9 September 1788, received official notices of ratification from the governors or state conventions of Georgia, New York, South Carolina, and Virginia. It also received a copy of the journal of the New Jersey Convention, which had unanimously ratified the Constitution on 18 December 1787. Responding to a resolution of the state Convention, the legislature's principal action at its special session was approval of an act ceding to Congress a tract of land ten miles square for the seat of the new federal government. The act passed both houses unanimously.

The legislature did not pass any enabling legislation for the first federal elections at its special session. The election law for those elections was approved at the annual fall session of the legislature, which began on 28 October 1788 in Trenton and moved to Princeton on 3 November. Jonathan Elmer and William Paterson were chosen United States Senators at the same session.

Assembly Proceedings, Thursday, P.M., 30 October 1788[1]

A Message from his Excellency the Governor by Mr. Secretary Reed accompanied with the following Papers. . . .

No. 5, 13th September 1788, Resolution of Congress for carrying into Operation the Constitution now ratified by eleven States. . . .[2]

The Paper marked No. 5 was read and ordered to be transmitted to Council for their Information by Mr: Wade

1. MS, Votes and Proceedings of the General Assembly, Nj. Hereafter the Assembly proceedings are cited by date only.

2. Congress' Election Ordinance (DHFFE, I, 132–33) had been sent to Governor William Livingston by Charles Thomson, secretary of Congress, with a cover letter, also dated 13 September 1788 (RC, William Livingston Papers, MHi).

Council Proceedings, Friday, A.M., 31 October[1]

Mr. Wade, from the House of Assembly, brought to this House the Resolution of Congress for carrying into Operation the Constitution now ratified by eleven States for their Information, which was read, and thereupon,

Ordered, That Mr. Chetwood, Mr. Kitchel and Mr. Thompson, be a Committee to prepare and bring in a Bill for carrying into Operation the said Constitution.

1. *Journal of the Proceedings of the Legislative-Council of the State of New-Jersey* (Trenton, 1788). Hereafter the Council proceedings are cited by date only.

Council Proceedings, Tuesday, A.M., 11 November

Mr. Kitchel, from the Committee appointed to bring in a Bill for carrying into Operation the said Constitution, reported a Bill, intitled, "An Act for carrying into Effect, on the Part of the State of New-Jersey, the Constitution of the United States, assented to, ratified and confirmed by this State, on the eighteenth Day of December, in the Year of our Lord One Thousand Seven Hundred and Eighty-seven," which was read, and ordered a second Reading.[1]

1. No copy of the Council bill has been located.

Robert L. Hooper to Jonathan Dayton, Princeton, 11 November[1]

Since Mr. Chetwood[2] returned, we find some of our *Bretherin* in are wavering, & that *District* Elections will be the mode, if the present Opinion prevails—as the Opinions now stand, I begin to suspect a majority in Council will be against the *general* mode—

I beg of you to come to Princeton[3] as soon as posseble—do not loose a day—Delecasy is out of the Question—It is thought unnecessary to appoint Members to keep up the representation in Congress[4]—I can not find one that will listen to it—

I am in haist

1. RC, Miscellaneous Manuscript Collection, NN. The letter was addressed to Dayton in Elizabethtown.
2. John Chetwood and Hooper were both members of the Legislative Council at this time; Hooper was its vice president. Chetwood (1736–1807), an Elizabethtown lawyer, represented Essex County in the state Convention in 1787 and in the Council in 1788. From 1789 until his resignation in 1797, he was an associate justice of the state Supreme Court.
3. On 30 October 1788 the Assembly voted to move from Trenton to Princeton following its meeting on 31 October and to convene at Princeton on 3 November. The Council concurred the next day.
4. Dayton, Abraham Clark, and Jonathan Elmer were elected to the Confederation Congress by the legislature on 25 November 1788 and were to serve until 4 March 1789.

Council Proceedings, Thursday, A.M., 13 November

The Bill, intitled, "An Act for carrying into Effect, on the Part of the State of New-Jersey, the Constitution of the United States, assented to, ratified and confirmed by this State, on the eighteenth Day of December, in the Year of our Lord One Thousand Seven Hundred and Eighty-seven," was read a second Time, debated, and ordered to be engrossed.

Assembly and Council Proceedings, Friday, A.M., 14 November

The Council

The engrossed Bill, intitled, "An Act for carrying into Effect, on the Part of the State of New-Jersey, the Constitution of the United States, assented to, ratified and confirmed by this State, on the eighteenth Day of December 1787," was read and compared; on the Question, Whether the said Bill do pass? It was carried in the Affirmative, as follows:

Yeas.

Mr. Chetwood,	Mr. Eldridge,
Mr. Manning,	Mr. Kitchel,
Mr. Smith,	Mr. Ogden,
Mr. Ellis,	Mr. Thompson.

Nays.

Mr. Haring,	Mr. Martin,
Mr. Holmes,	Mr. Mayhew.

Ordered, That the Vice-President do sign the said Bill.

Ordered, That Mr. Eldredge do carry the said Bill to the House of Assembly, and request their Concurrence therein.

Mr. Eldredge reported, that he had obeyed the Order of the House.[1]

The Assembly

[The Assembly received the election bill from the Council.]

Which Bill was read, and ordered a second Reading

1. No copy of the Council bill has been located.

Jonas Wade to Jonathan Dayton, Princeton, 16 November[1]

expected before this time to have been able to informed of the decision of the important Eliction Bill, it came into our House from Council on Friday last & has laid very silent since that time, believe we shall postpone the Consideration thereof for some Days, unless, the Interest for General Mode should increase beyond my expectation, which has in some Measure taken place, as a Number of the Assembly appears to have softned down and believe had not the Question been taken rather untimely, should not met with so powerfull an Oposition, have at times nearly dispaired of passing the Bill this sitting, but begin to be encouraged and hope to have it in my power to inform you of its passing by the last of this or beginning of next Week, no business of Publick Concern is yet finished worth Noteing its possible the appointments of Senate & Members of Congress may take place this Week but rather doubt it—however shall inform at every change of publick concern, am Sir with due Respect your Obedient & very Hble. Servt.

P.S. the minds of Members stand nearly the same with Respect to Senate.

1. RC, Jonathan Dayton Papers, MiU-C. Wade (d. c. 1823), Essex County coroner, 1783–1785, served in the Assembly, 1787–1790 and 1794–1797.

Assembly Proceedings, Wednesday, A.M., 19 November

The Bill intituled "An Act to carry into Effect, on the Part of the State of New Jersey, the Constitution of the United States, assented to, ratified and confirmed by this State on the 18th. Day of December in the Year of our Lord, One Thousand seven Hundred and Eighty seven" was read a second Time, and after some Time spent thereon—

Ordered, That the further Consideration thereof be postponed. . . .

The House resumed the Consideration of the Bill intituled "An Act for carrying into Effect on the Part of the State of New Jersey, the Constitution of the United States, assented to, ratified and confirmed by this State on the Eighteenth Day of December in the Year of our Lord, One Thousand seven Hundred and Eighty seven" and after having gone through the same and made sundry Amendments thereto.

Ordered, That the said Amendments be engrossed and that the said Bill be read a Third Time—[1]

1. No explanation of the amendments has been located. They possibly involved a change from district to at-large elections for the House of Representatives (see Robert L. Hooper to Jonathan Dayton, 11 November 1788, and Jonas Wade to Dayton, 16 November 1788, both above). The approved election law provided for at-large elections.

Assembly and Council Proceedings, Thursday, 20 November

The Assembly, A.M.

The Bill intituled "An Act for carrying into Effect, on the Part of the State of New Jersey, the Constitution of the United States, assented to, and ratified by this State on the Eighteenth Day of December in the Year of our Lord, One Thousand seven Hundred and Eighty seven" was read The Third Time with the Amendments; on the Question, Whether the same as amended do pass, It was carried in the Affirmative as follows

Yeas

Mr. Outwater	Mr. Cooper
Mr. Benson	Mr. Hall
Mr. Wade	Mr. Holme
Mr Combs	Mr. Whilden
Mr. Schureman	Mr E. Townsend
Mr. Freeman	Mr R Townsend
Mr. Rogers	Mr Lambert
Mr Hardenbergh	Mr Taylor
Mr. Jones	Mr. Sheppard
Mr Clark	Mr. Hankinson
Mr Davenport	Mr. Nicoll[1]

Nays

Mr. Nicoll	Mr Little
Mr. Garritse	Mr. Bunn
Mr. Condit	Mr. Blair
Mr Stillwell	Mr. Biddle

Mr. Sinnickson
Mr Cook
Mr Starke
Mr. Kitchel
Mr. Burgin
Mr Elmer
Mr Longsteet

Ordered, That the Speaker do sign the same with the Amendments

Ordered, That Mr. Bunn do carry the said Bill to the Council and request their Concurrence, in the said Amendments.

The Council, P.M.

[The Council received, in the morning, the election bill and amendments from the Assembly.]

The House took into Consideration the Bill, intitled, "An Act for carrying into Effect, on the Part of the State of New-Jersey, the Constitution of the United States," &c. with the Amendments made thereto by the House of Assembly,

Resolved, That the House agree to the said Amendments.

Ordered, That the said Bill be re-engrossed with the said Amendments.

1. Isaac Nicoll is recorded with both the "yeas" and "nays"; in the printed journal, *Votes and Proceedings of the Thirteenth General Assembly of the State of New-Jersey* . . . (Trenton, 1788), he is listed only as "nay."

Assembly and Council Proceedings, Friday, A.M., 21 November

The Council

The re-engrossed Bill, intitled, "An Act for carrying into Effect, on the Part of the State of New-Jersey, the Constitution of the United States," &c. was read and compared,

Resolved, That the same do pass.

Ordered, That the Vice-President do sign the same.

Ordered, That Mr. Martin do carry the said re-engrossed Bill to the House of Assembly, and acquaint them that the same is passed by this House with their Amendments.

Mr. Martin reported, that he had obeyed the Order of the House.

The Assembly

[The Assembly received the amended election bill from the Council.]

Which was read and Compared—

Ordered,—That the Speaker do sign the same—

The New Jersey Election Law, 21 November[1]

An ACT for carrying into Effect, on the Part of the State of New-Jersey, the Constitution of the United States, assented to, ratified and confirmed by this State, on the eighteenth Day of December, in the Year of our LORD One Thousand Seven Hundred and Eighty-seven.

WHEREAS the good People of this State, on the said eighteenth Day of December, in and by a Convention of Delegates chosen by the Citizens thereof, agreeably to an Act of the Legislature for that Purpose made and provided, did, on the Part of this State, assent to, ratify and confirm, a Constitution for the United States, agreed to and recommended, in the Name of the People of the United States, by the unanimous Consent of the said United States in Convention assembled at Philadelphia on the seventeenth Day of September, in the said Year of our LORD One Thousand Seven Hundred and Eighty-seven: AND WHEREAS, in and by the said Constitution, it is, among other Things, provided and directed, "That all Legislative Powers therein granted shall be vested in a Congress of the United States, which shall consist of a Senate and House of Representatives: That the House of Representatives shall be composed of Members chosen every second Year by the People of the several States, and the Electors in each State shall have the Qualifications requisite for Electors of the most numerous Branch of the State Legislature: That no Person shall be a Representative who shall not have attained to the Age of twenty-five Years, and been seven Years a Citizen of the United States, and who shall not when elected be an Inhabitant of that State in which he shall be chosen: That this State, until other Provision in the said Constitution mentioned is made, shall have four Representatives in said Congress: That the Senate of the United States shall be composed of two Senators from each State chosen by the Legislature thereof for Six Years: That no Person shall be a Senator who shall not have attained the Age of Thirty Years, and been nine Years a Citizen of the United States, and who shall not when elected be an Inhabitant of that State for which he shall be chosen: That the Times, Places and Manner, of holding Elections for Senators and Representatives shall be prescribed in each State by the Legislature thereof: That the Executive Power shall be vested in a President of the United States of America, and, together with the Vice-President, be elected as follows—Each State shall appoint, in such Manner as the Legislature may direct, a Number of Electors equal to the whole Number of Senators and Representatives to which the State may be entitled in the Congress, but no Senator or Representative, or Person holding an Office of Trust or Profit under the United States, shall be appointed an Elector: That the Electors shall meet in their respective States, and vote by Ballot for two Persons, of whom one at least shall not be an Inhabitant of the same State with themselves; and they shall make a List of all the Persons voted for, and of the Number of Votes for each, which List they shall sign and certify, and transmit sealed to the Government of the United States, directed to the President of the Senate: That no Person, except a natural born Citizen, or a Citizen of the United States, at the Adoption of the said Constitution, shall be eligible to the Office of President; neither shall any Person be eligible to that Office, who shall not have attained to the Age of thirty-five Years, and been fourteen Years a Resident within the United States." AND ALSO WHEREAS the United States, so met in Convention as aforesaid, did resolve that it was the Opinion of that Convention, that, as soon as the Convention of nine States shall have ratified the said Constitution, the said United States in Congress assembled should fix a Day on which Electors should be appointed by the States which shall have ratified the same; and a Day on which the Electors should assemble to vote for the President, and the Time and Place for commencing Proceedings under the said Constitution: That, after such Publication, the Electors should be appointed, and the Senators and Representatives elected: That the Electors should meet on the Day fixed for the Election of the President, and should transmit to the Government of the United States their Votes certified, signed, sealed and directed, as aforesaid: AND ALSO WHEREAS, in Conformity to the Directions of the said Constitution, and the Recommendation aforesaid, the United States in Congress assembled, on the thirteenth Day of September last past, did resolve (after reciting that the said Constitution had been ratified by the Convention of nine States, and such Ratifications duly authenticated, had been received by Congress and were filed in the Secretary's Office) that the first Wednesday in January next be the Day for appointing of Electors in the several States, which before said Day shall have ratified the said Constitution: That the first Wednesday in February next be the Day for the Electors to assemble in their respective States, and vote for a President; and that the first Wednesday in March next be the Time, and the present Seat of Congress be the Place, for commencing Proceedings under the said Constitution: AND ALSO WHEREAS it is not only the Interest, but the Wish of the good People of this State, to carry into Effect the several Requisitions, Provisions and Recommendations aforesaid, on the Part of this State, to be observed, done and performed, in Order to expedite and carry on the Government so established by the said Constitution; therefore,

Sect. 1. BE IT ENACTED *by the Council and General Assembly of this State, and it is hereby Enacted by the Authority of the same,* That it shall and may be lawful for every Inhabitant of this State, who is or shall be qualified to vote for Members of the State Legislature, to nominate four Candidates to the Choice of the People, as Representatives in the said Congress of the United States, by writing on one Ticket or Piece of Paper the Names of four Persons to be voted for as Representatives, which said Ticket or Piece of Paper shall be subscribed by the Person nominating, with the Date of doing the same, and that at any Time at least thirty Days previous to the Day of Election of said Representatives, delivering the said Ticket or Piece of Paper so subscribed and dated to the Clerk of the Court of Common Pleas of the County in which such Inhabitant may reside, which Clerk is hereby directed and required to receive and carefully to file the same, provided it be delivered within the Time aforesaid.

2. *And be it Enacted by the Authority aforesaid,* That each and every Clerk of the Court of Common-Pleas in the respective Counties of this State is and hereby are directed and required, at the Expence of the State, twenty-four Days previous to the Day of Election of the said Representatives, to transmit, by a careful and trusty Person, a true Copy of all and every such Nomination as shall be delivered to him as aforesaid to the Governor of this State for the Time being, who is hereby directed and required, at least eighteen Days previous to the said Day of Election for Representatives, to cause the same to be published in the News-Papers printed in this State, and in two or more printed in the Cities of New-York and Philadelphia; and also to transmit a true List of the Names of every Candidate so returned to him as aforesaid to each and every Sheriff of the respective Counties in this State, who is hereby required immediately to put up, in at least five of the most publick Places in his County, a true List of the Names of the said Candidates.

3. *And be it further Enacted by the Authority aforesaid,* That the Persons so nominated, and whose Names shall be transmitted to the several Sheriffs as aforesaid, shall exclusively be the Candidates from whom four Representatives shall be voted for in each of the Counties of this State; and that no Person whatever shall be set up as a Candidate on the said Day of Election, but the Persons so nominated and returned as aforesaid.

4. *And be it further Enacted by the Authority aforesaid,* That the said Election for Representatives for this State shall be had by Ballot of the Citizens of this State in like Manner as in those Counties where the Elections by Law are directed to be held by Ballot,[2] by the same Officers, and under the same Regulations (except where Provision

is otherwise made by this Law) as Members for the State Legislature shall be by Law annually chosen, and that on the second Wednesday in February next, at such Place in each County as the Election for Members in the State Legislature is by Law directed to be opened at, which may be adjourned from Day to Day, and from Place to Place, within each respective County, as shall be directed by the said Act, until the same shall be legally closed.[3]

5. *And be it further Enacted by the Authority aforesaid*, That the Sheriff of each County in this State shall give at least twelve Days Notice in his County of the Time of the said Election, by advertising the same in at least five of the most publick Places of the County; and all and every Person and Persons whose Duty it shall or may be to hold, direct, attend, inspect and govern, the general Election for the State Legislature by the Laws of this State, are hereby required and fully authorized and empowered to hold, direct, attend, inspect and govern, the Election to be held as aforesaid for Representatives of this State, and that on the second Wednesday in February next as aforesaid; and each and every of the said Person and Persons are hereby vested with the like Powers for the Purposes aforesaid (except where other Provision is made by this Law) as they shall or may be vested with in and by the Laws of this State for the Election of Members for the State Legislature, in as full and ample a Manner as if the said Powers were herein specially and particularly set forth and recited, for all which Services they and each of them shall receive the daily Pay and other Allowance as shall be granted by the Law for governing the general Election for the State Legislature.

6. *And be it further Enacted by the Authority aforesaid*, That, after the said Election shall be duly closed, the Judges and Inspectors of the said Election shall without Delay proceed to take an Account of, and cast up the Votes given in for, each Candidate; and, when ascertained, shall make a List of all the Persons voted for, and of the Number of Votes taken for each, which List the said Judges and Inspectors, or a Majority of them, shall sign, certify, seal up and direct, to the Governor of the State for the Time being, and deliver the same to the Sheriff of the County within four Days after closing the said Election, first causing a Duplicate thereof to be made and certified by them, and delivered to the Clerk of the Court of Common Pleas of the County, who is hereby required to file the same without Fee or Reward; and the said Sheriff shall, within ten Days thereafter, at the Expence of the State, transmit the same List, so delivered to him as aforesaid, to the Governor of the State for the Time being.

7. *And be it further Enacted by the Authority aforesaid*, That the Governor of the State for the Time being, shall, within four Days after receiving the said Lists from the several Counties in this State, lay the same before the Privy-Council of this State, to be summoned for that Purpose, and, after casting up the whole Number of Votes from the several Counties for each Candidate, the said Governor and Council shall determine the four Persons who shall have the greatest Number of Votes from the whole State, to be the Persons duly chosen to represent this State in the said Congress of the United States; and the said Governor shall commission each and every of them under the Great Seal of this State for the Purpose aforesaid, and also make known their Names to the Publick by Proclamation without Delay.

8. *And be it further Enacted by the Authority aforesaid*, That, until further Provision shall be made by Law for the nominating and appointing the Electors to be chosen by this State for the Purpose of voting for two Persons as is mentioned in the first Section of the second Article of said Constitution, it shall and may be lawful for the Governor and Council of this State to meet on the first Wednesday in January next at Princeton,

unless the Legislature of the State shall be sitting elsewhere, and then at such Place, and then and there, by Plurality of Votes, to nominate, elect and appoint, six Citizens of this State, being Freeholders and Residents in the State, and otherwise qualified to be the Electors for the Purposes mentioned in the said Constitution, whom the Governor for the Time being shall commission under the Great Seal of the State, and make known the same by Proclamation; and the said Electors, so chosen and appointed as aforesaid, shall meet together at Trenton, in the County of Hunterdon, on the first Wednesday in February next, and then and there proceed to vote by Ballot for two Persons mentioned in the first Section of the second Article of the said Constitution, in the Manner and agreeably to the Directions therein contained, and the true Intent and Meaning of the said Constitution, and further to do and perform all other the Duties enjoined on them by the said Constitution; for all which Services the said Electors and each of them shall receive the daily Pay and other Allowance as is granted by Law to the Council of this State for their Services, to be paid by the Treasurer of this State on Warrants signed by the President or Chairman of the said Electors, or a Majority of the said Electors, other than the Person in whose Favour the said Warrant shall be drawn.

9. *And be it further Enacted by the Authority aforesaid*, That if any Person or Persons appointed to conduct the said Election for Representatives, and also any of those who are appointed to do and perform the other Duties required of him or them by this Law respecting the said Election, shall wilfully neglect or refuse to do and perform the same, he or they, so wilfully neglecting or refusing, shall forfeit and pay to the State the Sum of Fifty Pounds, to be recovered by the Treasurer of the State for the Time being, in his own Name, by Action of Debt in any Court of Record in this State where the same may be cognizable, but to and for the Use of the State.

10. *And be it further Enacted*, That, in further Compliance with the said Constitution, two Citizens of this State, qualified as the Constitution directs, shall be chosen by the Legislature of this State in Joint-Meeting assembled, to represent this State in the Senate of the United States, in Manner and Form as is prescribed by the said Constitution; and on such Choice the Governor of the State shall commission the Persons so chosen, under the Great Seal of the State accordingly.

Passed at Princeton, November 21, 1788.

1. *Acts of the Thirteenth General Assembly of the State of New Jersey* . . . (Trenton, 1788), chapter 241, pp. 477–82. The election law was printed in the following New Jersey newspapers: *Brunswick Gazette*, 2 December 1788; *New Jersey Journal*, 3 December; and *Federal Post*, 23 December. It was widely reprinted and summarized in out-of-state newspapers. It was also printed as a broadside by Isaac Collins, the state printer. He was directed to print 200 copies of the law, "to be distributed in the different Counties of this State," by resolution of the legislature on 21 November 1788.

2. The first federal elections for Representatives were the first elections in New Jersey to be conducted entirely by ballot. The state election laws of 1777 and 1783 had prescribed ballot voting for some counties, while the remainder were to vote *viva voce*. The 1777 election law had provided for ballot voting in seven counties, and the 1783 law in five counties. Even in the 1788 supplemental state election law, the legislature continued to prescribe *viva voce* voting in state elections for five of the state's thirteen counties: Bergen, Cape May, Essex, Morris, and Sussex. After 1797 ballots were required in all elections in New Jersey. For the history of these developments, see McCormick, *Voting in New Jersey*.

3. The state election law in effect at the time of the first federal elections was "A Supplement to the Act, intitled, 'An Act for regulating the Election of Members of the Legislative-Council and Assembly, Sheriffs and Coroners of the State of New-Jersey, and of Delegates to represent the

said State in the Congress of the United States,' " passed 29 November 1788. The basic law which it supplemented had been passed 16 December 1783; the 1788 supplement greatly increased the number of polling places. Section 2 listed them: "*And be it further Enacted*, That the Sheriff or other Person conducting the Election as mentioned in the said recited Act, with a Majority of the Inspectors, shall have full Power to adjourn the Election, from Time to Time, as Occasion may require, and also to close the same when the Votes or Tickets of all the Electors present are delivered in, or a reasonable Time for that Purpose shall have been allowed. *Provided always*, That the Sheriff or other Person conducting the Election in the County of Bergen shall, when a Majority of the Inspectors of the County think it expedient, adjourn the Poll to Hopper's Town at any Time during the said Election; and the Poll in the County of Essex may be adjourned in like Manner to the House where Thomas Prentice now lives in Elizabeth-Town, and to where Manning Force now lives near Acquackanack Bridge; and the Poll in the County of Middlesex may be adjourned in like Manner to Cranberry, and the City of Amboy, and the Poll in the County of Monmouth may be adjourned in like Manner to Covenhoven's Tavern in the Township of Middletown, to Hagerman's Tavern in Shrewsbury, to Britton's Tavern in Upper-Freehold, and to Tom's River Bridge in the Township of Dover; and the Poll in the County of Somerset may be adjourned in like Manner to the House of Benjamin Skillman in Gregg's Town, to Flagg's Tavern in Hillsborough, to Pluck'emin in the Township of Bedminister, and to the House of Captain Bayard in Bernard's Town; and the Poll in the County of Burlington shall be adjourned in like Manner to the House of Joseph Douglass in Crosswicks, to the Sign of the Crosskeys in Evesham, to Pennyhill, New-Mills, Moorestown, Lumberton, and Clamtown; and the Poll shall be adjourned in like Manner in the County of Gloucester to Haddonfield, Swedesborough, May's Landing, Wrangleborough Mills, and Absecom; and the Poll shall be adjourned in like Manner in the County of Salem to Henry Louderback's Tavern in Pilesgrove, and to the House or Tavern now kept by Forman Mulford in Pittsgrove; and the Poll in the County of Hunterdon may be adjourned in like Manner to Bunnell's Tavern, the Whitehouse in Reading-Town, to Quaker-Town, Pennington and Trenton; and the Poll in the County of Morris may be adjourned in like Manner to the House late of Joshua Douglass in the Township of Roxborough, and to the Tavern late of Henry Howell in Troy; and the Poll in the County of Cumberland may be adjourned in like Manner to Manamuskin Landing, in the Township of Maurice River; and the Poll in the County of Cape-May may be adjourned in like Manner to the usual Places of holding the Town-Meetings in the Upper and Lower Precincts; and the Poll in the County of Sussex may be adjourned in like Manner to Hardiston, to Jacob Rosecrant's in the Township of Walpack, and to Oxford: And it shall and may be lawful for the Poll to be closed at any one of the said Places, where the Elections are directed to be opened at or adjourned to" (*Acts of the Thirteenth General Assembly of the State of New Jersey* . . . [Trenton, 1788], chapter 253, pp. 502–04).

[John Stevens, Jr.,] to Benjamin Van Cleve, Hoboken, 21 November[1]

I had no opportunity of conversing with you on political matters during my short Stay at Princeton—I am informed the Assembly have taken a vote on that clause of the election Bill prescribing the mode of chusing representatives—This clause as it now stands I conceive to be liable to several weighty objections some of which are the following—As every man throughout the State intitled to a vote will also as I apprehend by this Bill be intitled to hand forward to the clerk of the county in which he resides such nomination for representatives as he may think proper, the natural result will be that the nomination will be very numerous, from which two inconveniences arises, first—thus public attention will be so much divided and distracted by the great multiplicity of characters thus held up to public view that the very purpose which this previous nomination was intended to serve, will a great measure be defeated. It will be impossible that a proper scrutiny can be made into the conduct and general character of each candidate—The information of the public, therefore, respecting the men they are to vote for will necessarily be very vague and uncertain. But this is not all it may possibly put it in the power of a combination, which may not amount to more then one-tenth part of the whole number of votes throughout the state, to send representatives to congress.

For as a majority in each county from personel motives may be induced to vote for some favourites residing within the same the votes in this case would be so split and divided that a man might happen to be returned who had not perhaps more than a twentieth part of the votes of the whole State. To obviate these inconveniences I would propose to adopt a mode similar to the one prescribed in the Draft of a constitution I herewith send for your perusal—by this mode you will readily perceive that no candidate can be elected by less than a majority of the whole number of votes given in. And the number of candidates is also so limited that [it] is in the power of every man to become sufficiently acquainted with their general Characters. The success of the new constitution will depend very much on the wisdom and virtue of the men who are in the first instance to set it in motion—according [to] the [dir?]ection which *they* may happen to give it, it's future operations may become misschievous or salutary.—In the Present case therefore we are more especially called upon, in framing an election law, to do every thing we can to lessen the chances in favour of men not duly qualified being returned upon us

To form a code of Laws adapted to the exigencies of empire so extensive, the various parts of which differing so widely from each other in respect to climate soil and product as well as in the manners of the inhabitants, to make laws, I say, embracing such a variety of circumstances, is a task which few amongst us are qualifyed to execute—There is another important consideration which should make us particularly attentive and circumspect with regard to the qualifications of our representatives to congress. Jersey sends but four members whilst some other States send 8 and 10. We should endeavour therefore to make up by the weight of influence our deficiency with regard to numbers. It is not enough that our representatives are wise men, they should be also men of such property integrity and standing in life, as would insure to them an extensive influence over the public councils, and at the same time place them above the reach of temptation. I feel myself deeply interested in this business, not from patriotic motives only, but from considerations too of a more private nature, what little property I have is altogether within this state, and as the latter prospers the former of course be advanced.

The draft of the Constitution I have herewith enclosed was put together at different times during this fall as an amusement at leasure hours. As the Constitution of this State is certainly very defective and in every point of view it would be sound policy to call a new convention as soon as possible to prune away the rotten and untoward branches and that new shutes may spring up vigourously and so directed as to form a beautiful and flourishing tree. A well ordered government, energetic yet not tyranical, free yet not licentious, is of all human blessings the greatest. The credit and reputation of our new fœderal government will undoubtedly induce numbers of foreigners to settle among us, many of whom, we may [accurately?] conclude, will be possessed of considerable pro[perty?] and therefore become valuable acquisitions to the State they may fix their abode in. No State, perhaps, in the union possesses so many advantages in point of [situ?]ation soil, climate, and improvements as does this—Nothing, in short, is wanting to turn the Scale in our favour but a Good Government.

I have taken the liberty of directing to your care a number of pamphlets, which tho they may not contain a great many new and just "observations on government", were however written with the [sincerest?] intentions of promoting the public welfare.[2] Be pleased, sir, to present them [in] my name, to such of the members of the legislature, as you think proper.[3] They were written and sent to the press about a year ago. You are at liberty to communicate the contents of this as well as the draft of a new Constitution, to as many of the members as you please—When you have done with the Draft be so kind as to leave it in the care of Mr. S. Stockton, as I have no copy—

1. FC, Stevens Family Papers, NjHi. The letter is unsigned, but its contents and location indicate John Stevens, Jr., as the author (see John Stevens, Jr., to [John Stevens, Sr.], 4 December 1788, Part Four).

2. Probably Stevens's *Observations on Government, Including Some Animadversions of Mr. Adams's Defence of the Constitutions of Government of the United States of America; And on Mr. DeLolme's Constitution of England* (New York, 1787), written under the pseudonym "A Farmer of New Jersey."

3. Van Cleve was Speaker of the Assembly, which was meeting at this time. See also Stevens to John Stevens, Sr., 4 December 1788, Part Four.

PART TWO

THE ELECTION OF SENATORS

John Chetwood to William Paterson, Elizabethtown, 17 October 1788 (excerpt)[1]

Upon reading the first paragraph of your Letter[2] I found myself sensibly affected, to find, you should think yourself so circumstanced, as that you could not accept of the Appointment, to which I must think you would be unanimously elected. If to any, surely to such Men, the Country under peculiar circumstances, ought, and have a right to look up [to]—The Sacrifice on your part will be great, but I hope not so great, as to be Death to your Business—Should you be absent a couple of years, even in that case, upon your return, (I would not wish to flatter) I am persuaded from your Character, and distinguished Abilities you must be immediately introduced into Business;—Besides a grateful Country cannot forget you—My good Friend, I hope you will reconsider this matter—and that this State may yet have your able Assistance in settling a happy plan of Government under that Constitution, which was agreed upon to "form a more perfect Union, establish Justice, ensure domestik Tranquility, provide for the common Defense, promote the general Welfare, and secure the Blessings of Liberty to ourselves and our posterity."[3]

1. RC, William Paterson Papers, NjR. The letter was addressed to Paterson in New Brunswick.
2. Paterson's letter of 15 October 1788, which Chetwood had referred to earlier in this letter, has not been located.
3. Paterson's reply to this letter of Chetwood has not been located, but Paterson did authorize Chetwood to put him in nomination for Senator (see Robert L. Hooper to Jonathan Dayton, 7 November 1788, immediately below).

Robert L. Hooper to Jonathan Dayton, Princeton, 7 November[1]

My stay in N. York was short—not more then six hours. I wrote to Colo: Ogden[2] some time last week and urged him to press you to take a look at Us. I wished to have Members appointed in the last joint meeting to serve in Congress, but the necessety was not generally seen. I think on Monday or Tuesday next, the Senators & Members will be chosen—as soon as the Time is mentioned I will write you—

Yesterday Mr. Patterson authorised Mr. Chetwood to Nominate him for one of the senators—This fixes one beyond any doubt, but as to the other, I am at a loss to say or even to gess on whom the choice will fall—Boudinot, Clark, Elmore, Dickinson & Scureman are talked of, and I think the four first named will be in nomination—Great pains is takeing by some Persons here to bring General Dickinson forward, but it will not do.[3]

I have received a Letter from Major Lloyd,[4] who resides in Sussex, and he is sanguine in the *Confidential* business—you shall see the Letter—his report exceeds my expectations—I will assist Capt. Quigly—

1. RC, Gratz Collection, PHi. The letter was addressed to Dayton in Elizabethtown.

2. Probably Abraham Ogden (1743–1798), a Newark lawyer, who represented Essex County in the Assembly in 1790 and served as a United States district attorney (New Jersey district) from 1791 until his death.

3. Elias Boudinot, Abraham Clark, Jonathan Elmer, Philemon Dickinson, and James Schureman were frequently mentioned as candidates for Senator. Dickinson (1739–1809), a lawyer and landowner, was a younger brother of John Dickinson of Delaware. He was a brigadier general of New Jersey militia in the Revolutionary War and represented Delaware in Congress, 1782–1783. He later represented Hunterdon County in the Council, 1783–1784. Dickinson was a Senator, 1790–1793.

4. Richard Lloyd, a major in the Continental Army, was active in the Grand Lodge of Free Masons in New Jersey and was sheriff of Monmouth County, 1823–1825.

Elias Boudinot to James Kinsey, Trenton, 20 November (excerpt)[1]

Matters at Princeton go tolerably well; the great object is carried—I mean the general Election—as to Senators I am easy about, provided C——[2] is kept out—This altogether depends on West Jersey—We have placed the Game entirely in their hands & they can do as they please—

1. RC, New Jersey Manuscripts, NjHi. The letter was addressed to Kinsey in Burlington.
2. Abraham Clark, a resident of Elizabethtown, Essex County (East Jersey).

Assembly and Council Proceedings, Saturday, A.M., 22 November

The Council

Ordered, That Mr. Mayhew do wait on the House of Assembly, and acquaint them that Council propose going into a Joint-Meeting on Tuesday next three o'Clock in the Afternoon, at the College Library Room, for the Purpose of electing Senators and other Officers, if agreeable to them. . . .

Mr. Mayhew reported, that he had obeyed the Order of the House.

The Assembly

[The Assembly received the Council's message.]

Ordered, That Mr Clark do wait on the Council, and acquaint them that this House will be ready to go into a Joint Meeting on Tuesday next at Three OClock in the Afternoon, at the College Library Room—

Assembly and Council Proceedings, Monday, A.M., 24 November

The Council

Mr. Clark, from the House of Assembly, acquainted this House that they would be ready to go into a Joint-Meeting for the Purpose mentioned in the Message from this House on Saturday last, at the Time and Place therein mentioned.

The Assembly

Mr Clark reported, that he had obeyed the Order of the House

Proceedings of the Joint Meeting of the Legislature, Tuesday, P.M., 25 November[1]

The Council and Assembly met at the College Library Room in Princeton. . . .[2]

The Meeting proceeded to the Appointment of Senators to represent this State in the Senate of the United States, pursuant to Law, when the Honourable

William Paterson,
Jonathan Elmer, } Esquires, were duly elected; therefore,

Resolved, That the said William Paterson and Jonathan Elmer, Esquires, be empowered to represent, and vote in Behalf of, this State, in the Senate of the United States, for and during the Time limited in the Constitution of the said United States.

1. "Minutes and Proceedings of the Joint-Meeting," in *Journal of the Proceedings of the Legislative-Council of the State of New-Jersey* (Trenton, 1788), 33–34.
2. This meeting also elected Abraham Clark, Jonathan Dayton, and Jonathan Elmer to represent the state in the Confederation Congress until 4 March 1789, when the first Congress under the Federal Constitution was to meet.

Credentials of the New Jersey Senators, 25 November[1]

[SEAL]

The State of New-Jersey

To the Honorable Jonathan Elmer[2] Esquire.

Greeting.

The Council and Assembly, reposing especial Trust and Confidence in your Integrity, Prudence and Ability, have, at a Joint-Meeting, Appointed You the said Jonathan Elmer—to represent and vote in behalf of this State in the Senate of the United States of North America, for and during the Time limited in the Constitution of the said United States—

In Testimony Whereof the Great Seal of the State is hereunto Affixed. Witness William Livingston Esquire Governor Captain General and Commander in Chief in and over the State of New-Jersey and Territories thereunto belonging Chancellor and Ordinary in the same at Princeton the Twenty fifth day of November in the Year of our Lord One thousand seven hundred and eighty eight and of our Sovereignty and Independence the thirteenth—

[signed] Wil: Livingston

By His Excellency's Command

[signed] Bowes Reed Secy

1. DS, RG 46, DNA.
2. The name of William Paterson was substituted for Jonathan Elmer in the other copy of the credentials.

Joseph Bloomfield to William Paterson, Burlington, 29 November (excerpt)[1]

It is with great satisfaction, I hear of Your very honourable appointment to represent this State, in the Senate of the American *Empire*.

Mr. Sheppard[2] (who has just passed through Burlington on his return home from Princeton) has given this agreable information.

I beg leave most sincerely to congratulate You on this occasion, and the more so, as I well know, it meets with the universal approbation of the good People of this State.

1. RC, Lloyd W. Smith Collection, NjMoW. Bloomfield (1753–1823), a Burlington lawyer, was a register of the admiralty court, 1779–1783; state attorney general, 1783–1792; a presidential Elector, 1792; mayor of Burlington, 1795–1800; governor of New Jersey, 1801–1802 and 1803–1812; a brigadier general in the United States Army during the War of 1812; and a member of the House of Representatives, 1817–1821.

2. John Sheppard (1730–1805), a prosperous merchant from Greenwich Township, Cumberland County, represented the county in the colonial assembly, 1772–1775, and in the General Assembly, 1785–1788.

New Jersey Journal (Elizabethtown), 3 December

A correspondent from Princeton has favored us with the following extract from the Journals at a joint-meeting of the legislature to nominate federal senators for this state, viz. For

		Paterson.	Clark.	Elmer.	Boudinot.
[Legislative Council]					
	Mr. Haring,	1	1		
	Chetwood,	1			1
	Manning,	1		1	
	Holmes,	1		1	
	Martin,	1	1		
	Smith,	1		1	
	Ellis,	1		1	
	Mayhew,	1		1	
	Eldridge,	1		1	
	Ketchel,	1	1		
	Ogden,	1		1	
[General Assembly]					
	Vancleve. [Speaker]	1			1
Bergen.	Outwater,		1		1
	Nichol,		1		1
	Benson.		1	1	
Essex.	Garritse,		1		1
	Wade,	1	1		
	Condict.		1		1
Middlesex.	Combes,	1		1	
	Schuurman,	1	1		
	Freeman.	1		1	

		Paterson.	Clark.	Elmer.	Boudinot.
Monmouth.	Stillwell,	1	1		
	Little,	1		1	
	Rogers.	1			1
Somerset.	Bunn,	1	1		
	Blair,	1	1		
	Hardenburgh.	1		1	
Burlington.	Biddle,	1		1	
	Jones,	1		1	
	Newbold.	1		1	
Gloster.	Clark,	1		1	
	Davenport,	1		1	
	Cooper.	1		1	
Salem.	Sinickson,	1		1	
	Hall.	1		1	
	Holme.	1		1	
Cape May.	Wilden,	1		1	
	Townsend,	1		1	
	Townsend.	1		1	
Hunterdon.	Lambert,	1		1	
	Taylor.	1		1	
Morris.	Cook,	1	1		
	Stark,	1	1		
	Ketchel.	1	1		
Cumberland.	Shepard,	1		1	
	Burgen,	1		1	
	Elmer.	1		1	
Sussex.	Hankinson,	1	1		
	Beardslee,	1	1		
	Longstreet.	1	1		
		45	19	29	7[1]

1. This report was also printed in the *Federal Post*, 23 December 1788, with the notation that it had been received by the printer on 18 December. Both printers refer to this as an "extract from the Journals" of the joint meeting of the legislature, yet no votes appear in the official record of that meeting on 25 November 1788.

Pennsylvania Gazette (Philadelphia), 1 April 1789

Cumberland County, New-Jersey, March 26th, 1789.

Tuesday last the Honorable JONATHAN ELMER set out for New-York, to take his seat in the Fœderal Senate.[1]

Previous to his departure he was invited, by a number of the most respectable gentlemen of the county, to partake of an elegant entertainment provided at the house of Major Daniel Maskell. After supper the following toasts were drank.

1. The new Fœderal Constitution, may it be speedily put in operation.
2. His Excellency General Washington.
3. The Hon. John Adams.
4. The Senate of the United States.
5. The Fœderal House of Representatives.
6. The Governor and State of New-Jersey.
7. The Promoters of Public Happiness.
8. May the Liberties of the People be the principal Object of the Rulers.
9. Success to Agriculture, Manufactures and Commerce.
10. Honour, Virtue and Patriotism.
11. A speedy Reformation to Rhode-Island and North-Carolina.

At the close of the entertainment, which was conducted with the greatest order and decorum, the following address was presented to Dr. Elmer, in the name of all the gentlemen present, by Ephraim Seely, Esquire.

SIR,

As you are shortly to set out for New-York, to take your seat in the Fœderal Senate, we embrace this opportunity to take leave of you, by expressing our entire approbation of the choice of our Legislature in appointing you one of the Senators of Congress for this state.

Your literary acquirements, the early and active part you took in the cause of liberty and your country in the late revolution, your knowledge and experience in the science of government, and in the affairs of the United States, and the many public characters which you have sustained with honor and reputation, for a series of years, have procured you the esteem and confidence of your fellow citizens, and are evidences of your integrity and abilities to serve your country in the high and important station in which you are now placed. Having long experienced the inconveniences arising from the weakness and instability of our old fœderal government, we rejoice in the prospect of a speedy relief from many of those evils by the operation of the new constitution, which is now to be put in execution.—The full effects of any system of government we apprehend can only be known with certainty by experience; we wish, therefore, to see the new government tried in its present form before any alterations are attempted in it; and we feel a satisfaction in believing, that your sentiments on this subject coincide exactly with ours, and with those of every good citizen of this state.

To which the Doctor returned the following answer.

Gentlemen,

Be pleased to accept of my sincerest thanks for the favorable opinion you entertain of my public conduct, and for the marks of personal respect with which you have seen fit to honor me this evening.

I acknowledge with gratitude the high trust and confidence reposed in me by my country, in appointing me a Senator for this state in the Fœderal Legislature.

Sensible of my inability, and fully convinced from past experience of the difficulty and importance of the business in which I am about to engage, give me leave to assure you, gentlemen, that I enter upon it with the greatest diffidence and reluctance. I conceive it however to be my duty, at this critical period, to sacrifice personal and private considerations to the public good. In making this sacrifice, I feel myself actuated by a sense of the obligation I am under to my fellow citizens, for the honor they have conferred on me, and an earnest desire to promote the general welfare and interest of my country.

To make a fair experiment of the new Fœderal Constitution, by putting it into execution immediately, is an object which I have much at heart. The success of the experiment will depend, greatly, upon the manner in which this grand machine is first put in motion. Many of its supposed defects may, I humbly conceive, be much easier and more safely remedied, by a due attention to the arrangement of its various parts, than by any previous amendments, founded only on theoretic reasoning. These are the principles by which I mean to govern my conduct in this business. In so doing I flatter myself I shall meet your approbation, and contribute my mite towards the good of the union. And while I endeavor faithfully to serve my country in general, I shall make it my constant study to promote the honor and interest of the state to which I belong, and that part of it in particular, with which I am more immediately connected.[2]

1. The *Brunswick Gazette*, 17 March 1789, had informed its readers that Elmer was in "ill health" and thus delayed in taking his seat in the Senate.

2. This article was reprinted in full in the Charleston *Columbian Herald*, 22 April 1789, and in part in the Philadelphia *Pennsylvania Journal*, 2 April, and *New Jersey Journal*, 8 April.

PART THREE

THE ELECTION OF PRESIDENTIAL ELECTORS

AND THEIR VOTES

The election law authorized the "Governor and Council" to appoint presidential Electors. The state constitution of 1776 provided that the governor could convene any three or more members of the Legislative Council as a Privy Council at any time. It was thus in their capacity as privy councillors that eleven of the thirteen members of the Legislative Council met with the governor on 7 January 1789 to choose presidential Electors.

Neither the election of the Electors nor their votes for President on 4 February caused much public stir. Among the Electors, however, there was some fear that John Adams, the choice for Vice President, might finish ahead of George Washington, the choice for President, in the national balloting. To forestall that possibility, prominent Federalists such as Tench Coxe and Alexander Hamilton suggested privately that some Electors cast their second votes for someone other than Adams. On 19 January, Benjamin Rush—while advocating Adams for Vice President—had told Tench Coxe that "the Jersey federalists are alarmed without reason for the honor & fate of genl Washington. Do try to prevent their throwing away their Votes" (Philadelphia, RC, Tench Coxe Papers, PHi; printed: DHFFE, I, 384–85). Coxe replied on 2 February that the New Jersey and Maryland Electors were "undecided" about Adams; "they wish no other man but fear to hazard the General's election" (to Rush, New York, RC, Rush Papers, PPL. For other excerpts from this letter, see Chapter XIII, Part Two, and Chapter XIV). On 31 January, Coxe sent a letter to David Brearley (a New Jersey Elector), which, according to Brearley, "contained much necessary information and I can only regret that it did not arrive a day earlier" (Brearley to Coxe, 7 February 1789, Chapter XIII, Part Two). Brearley received the letter on 5 February—the day after the balloting for President. For Hamilton's efforts to ensure that Adams finished second to Washington in the balloting for President, see Chapter XIV.

Jeremiah Eldredge to Joseph Ellis, Cape May, 1 January 1789[1]

I set of[f] from home this Day with an Intention to Meet Council next Wednesday at Princetown but Returned, finding my Constitution to weakly for performing such a Journey at this cold Season of the year and now take the Liberty to wish you to Address Council on my behalf to Excuse my none Attendance—[2]

The Gentlemen on Nomination[3] with us is those as proposed with the addition of Mr Shephard and Mr— Bloomfield. Conclude with my best Respects wishing you a happy New Year—give my Respects to the Governor Mr Chatham Mr. Read.

1. RC, William Livingston Papers, MHi. The letter was addressed to Ellis in Gloucester. Eldredge (1745–1795), a lawyer, represented Cape May County in the Assembly, 1777–1778 and 1780; in the Council, 1784 and 1786–1793; and in the state Convention in 1787. Ellis (d. 1796) represented Gloucester County in the Assembly, 1778 and 1781–1785, and in the Council, 1787–1794. He was also a county judge and a justice of the peace from 1785 until his death.

2. Neither Eldredge nor Ellis attended the Council session on 7 January 1789, at which time the presidential Electors were chosen.

3. For Representatives.

Joseph Phillips to Governor William Livingston, Maidenhead, 7 January[1]

Our most profound Politicians are those that know the signs of the Times, and a select, or rather an elect part are already engaged in the service of the public: A great number more perhaps of inferior sagacity are (I understand) in Nomination for Representatives in the New proposed Congress, and at present remain in suspence, consequently are ineligible to another appointment respecting this new business.

At this Crisis, it is natural enough for our Governor's to cast about and see, what materials they have left to work upon; with leave (if you please) I will endeavour to assist a little. *There is a certain person in this Township of some modesty and ambition* (who in this dearth of admissable clever fellows) that may *perhaps do for an Elector*[2] because I verily believe [Washington?] for President &c. will not only be agreeably to his own [wish but?] to that of *All Friends.*

I dare not give [you?] another hint of this extraordinary Personage, for I am under [the?] strongest ties of honour, not to speak more openly, to avoid [the?] imputation of Egoity.—

Be pleased to forgive [– – –] & folly—And believe me to be your Excellency's devoted and most obedient Servant[3]

1. RC, William Livingston Papers, MHi. Eighteenth-century Maidenhead, in Hunterdon County, is now Lawrenceville, Mercer County. Phillips (c. 1718-c. 1789) served as a major, a lieutenant colonel, and a colonel in the New Jersey militia, 1776–1780.

2. Probably David Brearley, also of Maidenhead, who was chosen a presidential Elector on the day this letter was written.

3. For more comments to Governor Livingston about the choice of Electors, see John Mehelm to Livingston, 20 February 1789, Part Five:I.

Privy Council Proceedings, Wednesday, 7 January[1]

At a Council held at Princeton January 7th. 1789 for the purpose of choosing Electors pursuant to Law

Present

His Excellency Wm. Livingston &

The Vice president[2]

Mr Martin	Mr. Kitchel
Mr. Mayhew	Mr. Ogden
Mr. Chetwood	Mr. Manning
Mr. Smith	Mr. Holmes
Mr. Thomson	Mr. Harring

The following persons were appointed Electors for the purpose of choosing a president & Vice president of the United States agreeably to the Constitution of the said United States—

David Brearly
James Kinsey
Jno. Neilson
David Moore
John Rutherford
Matthias Ogden } Esquires

1. MS, Minutes of Governor's Privy Council of New Jersey, I (1777–1796), Nj. Printed: David A. Bernstein, ed., *Minutes of the Governor's Privy Council, 1777–1789* (Trenton, 1974).

2. Robert L. Hooper was vice president of the Legislative Council.

Proclamation by Governor William Livingston, 7 January[1]

BY HIS EXCELLENCY
WILLIAM LIVINGSTON, Esq.

Governor, Captain-General, and Commander in Chief in and over the State of New-Jersey and the Territories thereunto belonging, Chancellor and Ordinary in the same:

PROCLAMATION.

To all to whom these Presents shall come,
or may in any-wise concern:

BE IT MADE KNOWN, That on this day, the honourable DAVID BREARLEY, JAMES KINSEY, JOHN NEILSON, DAVID MOORE, JOHN RUTHERFORD and MATTHIAS OGDEN, Esquires, were duly appointed by the Governor and Council of this state, according to an act of the Legislature thereof, Electors on behalf of this state, for the purpose of choosing a President and Vice-President of the United States, agreeably to the Constitution of the said United States.

GIVEN under my Hand and Seal at Arms, in Princeton, the seventh Day of January, in the Year of our Lord one thousand seven hundred and eighty-nine.

William Livingston.

By his Excellency's command,
BOWES REED, Sec'ry.

1. *Brunswick Gazette*, 13 January 1789. The proclamation was also printed in the *New Jersey Journal*, 14 and 21 January; Philadelphia *Pennsylvania Packet*, 16 January; Philadelphia *Independent Gazetteer*, 17 January; and *Carlisle Gazette*, 4 February.

Commissions of the New Jersey Presidential Electors, 7 January[1]

[SEAL]

The State of New Jersey
To the Honble. David Brearly Esquire[2]
Greeting—

The Governor and Council reposing especial Trust and Confidence in your Integrity, Prudence and Ability, have appointed you the said David Brearly—an Elector, for the purpose of choosing a President and Vice President of the United States pursuant and agreeably to the Constitution of the said United States, and the Law of this State—You the said David Brearly—are therefore by these Presents commissioned to be an Elector on behalf of this State for the purpose aforesaid—

In Testimony Whereof the Great Seal of the State is hereunto affixed Witness William Livingston Esquire Governor Captain General and Commander in Chief in and over the State of New Jersey and Territories thereunto belonging Chancellor and Ordinary in the same at Princeton the seventh day of January in the Year of our Lord One Thousand Seven hundred and eighty nine—

By His Excelly's Command [signed] Wil: Livingston
[signed] Bowes Reed secy

1. DS, RG 46, DNA.
2. Similar commissions, dated 7 January 1789, were also prepared for James Kinsey, David Moore, John Neilson, Matthias Ogden, and John Rutherfurd.

Federal Gazette (Philadelphia), 10 January

The following are the names of the federal electors lately chosen for the state of New-Jersey.

ALL FEDERALISTS.

Gen. Ogden; chief justice Brearly; capt. David Moore; James Kinsey, esq. John Rutherfurd, esq. and colonel John Nelson.[1]

1. The names of New Jersey's Electors were widely reprinted in the newspapers.

[Walter Rutherfurd] to John Rutherfurd, New York, 12 January (excerpt)[1]

As you wished to be in Nomination as Representative, I have spoke to several Bergen men, Judge Harring &c. and wrote to Peter Wilson.[2] I expect you will run pretty generally in that County. I have also spoke to some Essex men, and wrote to Capt. Rickets[3] to influence his Friends. I expect Mr. L. will stir. I have since heard that you are appointed an Elector, by what Means I know not, I suppose you cannot now stand, but conclude the other is more honourable. I expect to see or hear from you before you set off homewards where you will find this by a Man Sproul is to send to me.

1. RC, Rutherfurd Papers, NHi. Another excerpt from this letter is printed in Chapter XIII, Part Two. The letter is unsigned, but it is in the handwriting of Walter Rutherfurd, John's father. The letter was addressed to John at "Tranquillity," his farm in present-day Allamuchy Township, Warren County. Walter Rutherfurd (1723–1804), a wealthy import merchant, had moved to New York City from Hunterdon County after the Revolution. He was a loyalist sympathizer during the Revolution.
2. Peter Haring represented Bergen County in the Council, 1784–1790 and 1792–1795; Wilson (1746–1825), a prominent Scottish-born educator, represented Bergen County in the Assembly, 1778–1781 and 1787.
3. Probably James Rickets, a loyalist officer during the Revolution and a resident of Elizabethtown after the war.

Votes of the New Jersey Presidential Electors, 4 February[1]

We the Electors on behalf of the State of New Jersey, appointed for the purpose of choosing a President and Vice President of the United States of America, pursuant to the Constitution of the United States and an Act of the Legislature of the said State, entitled, "An Act for carrying into effect on the part of the State of New Jersey the Constitution of the United States assented to ratified and confirmed by this State on the eighteenth day of December in the year of our Lord one thousand seven hundred and eighty seven"—Do hereby certify that having proceeded to vote by ballot for two persons to hold the Offices of President and Vice President of the United States of America, the following is a true list of all the Persons voted for and of the number of Votes for each—Vizt.—

George Washington Esqr.	Six Votes
John Jay Esqr.	Five Votes
John Adams Esqr.	One Vote

In Testimony whereof we have hereto subscribed our names and annexed our several Commissions under the great Seal of the State of New Jersey, this fourth day of February in the Year of our Lord one thousand seven hundred and eighty nine, and of the Independence of the United States of America the thirteenth.

[signed] David Brearley
J. Kinsey
John Neilson
David Moore
John Rutherfurd
M: Ogden

1. DS, RG 46, DNA.

David Brearley to Secretary Charles Thomson, Trenton, 4 February[1]

You have herewith enclosed, the Votes of the Electors of the State of New-Jersey, for a President and Vice President of the United States of America.

1. RC, RG 46, DNA. Brearley signed the letter as "Chairman of the Electors of New Jersey." Thomson was Secretary of Congress.

Q, Brunswick Gazette, 31 March

The following petition is offered to the inhabitants of the county of Middlesex for their consideration, and if approved, will be drawn in form that it may be signed and presented in due season.

Q.

To the worshipful ____________ ____________ Esq.[(a)]

The petition of the subscribers, INHABITANTS and FREEMEN of the county of *Middlesex*, Most humbly sheweth,

That your petitioners, in years past, together with a great number of their fellow subjects in New-Jersey, and the other, then, British provinces in North America imagined themselves to be greatly aggrieved and oppressed by, their then sovereign, his Britanic Majesty, his ministers and parliament; and also imagined that still greater grievances and oppressions were by them machinated, contrived and prepared, whereby when exercised upon them, they would be reduced to a state of the most abject slavery; that by force of these imaginations, and because they could not obtain the wished for redress, the said provinces refused obedience to the powers of Britain, declared themselves free and independent states, and entered into a league to support, protect and defend each other; that these bold and daring measures being taken, some of the most wise and prudent in the province of New-Jersey (of whom your worship had the honor to be among the foremost) and, as your petitioners believe, in some of the other provinces also, well knowing the danger of such hazardous attempts, and the hardships and miseries necessarily attendant upon a revolution of the government, and also to guard and protect their honors and offices, and to save the same harmless, whatsoever might be the event, left the public stage and hid themselves in private retirement until quietude and peace should again return; that notwithstanding your petitioners and their fellow subjects were thus deserted by those whom they had been accustomed to look upon as the first in influence and power, yet headed by some dauntless, interprising spirits and imflamed by an enthusiasm for liberty, after a nine year's war, in which their substance was consumed and the blood of thousands spilt, they shook off the chains of British tyranny, compelled their former sovereign to acknowledge their freedom and independence, and thus have become a great and extensive empire; that being thus deserted by the wise and prudent, they were compelled to commit the formation of their government, their league of confedaracy and their matters of legislation to raw and unexperienced politicians, to men, in the most humble walks of life, whose names had never reached the public ear, yet who, from having sacrificed the hard earnings of a laborious life, in the common cause, and from standing foremast in the day of danger (wonderful to tell!) obtained the confidence of an enthusiastic people; that from the ignorance and inexperience of the framers not only the general league of confederacy but also the constitution of this state particularly, has been found insufficient to answer the purposes and afford the benefits which were designed and expected from them; nor indeed has the administration of them been better than the constitutions themselves; that notwithstanding a former assembly of this state in the height of their frenzy enacted a law disabling certain descriptions of men from electing and being elected into any office of power or profit therein, and that for no other cause than that they were too wise to risk their lives and fortunes with the common herd of subjects in a dubious contest, yet the present (to the praise of their wisdom be it spoken) have repealed that law and set all men on the same footing, so that now your worship may as legally be elected, and all that train of followers, who listened to your wise and prudent advice, may as legally elect to places of honor and profit, as other citizens of this state;[1]

And for as much as the honorable the council of this state, in the exercise of the powers *they assumed* to themselves with respect to the choice of electors, by their example have taught us that places of honor are not to be lavished on the fool-hardy who exposes his life in the field of battle, and sacrifices his all at the shrine of liberty, but given to the prudent who in the day of death conseals himself that when the danger is over he may again come forth a blessing to the world;[2] and forasmuch as we are convinced that those who have heretofore been distinguished by the appellation of WHIGS, tho' they had intrepidity and courage to gain, yet have not wisdom and virtue to preserve the liberties of their country; and therefore are constrained to implore the assistance of those whom we have heretofore called by the, then, opprobrious and hateful, but now, honorable and endearing name of TORY, and to clothe them with those honors and offices which, we confess, we are unworthy to wear; and forasmuch as one of the members of the legislature for this county is now appointed to another trust;[3] and we, having the fullest evidence from your past conduct, of your warm attachment to the principles of this free republican government established under the authority of the people, and the fullest confidence in your integrity and ability; Therefore we most humbly pray that your worship will condescend to accept of our suffrages as our representative in the general Assembly of this state, and therefore as and on our behalf, as our representative, to do, perform and execute all those things which you in your great wisdom and prudence, for our benefit and for our peace and security shall think best to be done, performed and executed.

And your humble petitioners as in duty bound will ever pray, &c,

(a) It is supposed that the distinguished patriotism and ability of the gentleman, to whom the petition is to be presented, will on first sight suggest to every elector the name with which this blank is to be filled up, and at the same time, that his diffidence and excessive modesty will conceal it from himself. That the delicacy of his feelings, therefore, should not be hurt, it has been thought best to offer it to the public in this form.

1. In 1783 all persons convicted of treason, or who had sought the protection of the British during the war, or who had been imprisoned or fined for refusing to take an oath of allegiance to the state, were barred from voting. These disqualifications were repealed in 1788 (see McCormick, *Experiment in Independence*, 37–39).

2. Of the six New Jersey Electors, four (David Brearley, John Neilson, David Moore, and Matthias Ogden) were active patriots during the Revolution. John Rutherfurd, only sixteen in 1776, studied law with Richard Stockton and William Paterson during the war. John's father, Walter Rutherfurd, was a loyalist sympathizer. The sixth Elector, James Kinsey, was a Quaker and withdrew from politics during the Revolution.

3. James Schureman was elected to the House of Representatives.

PART FOUR

NOMINATIONS FOR REPRESENTATIVES

The election law, passed 21 November 1788, permitted each qualified voter to nominate four persons for Representatives. Before the legislature adjourned on 1 December, a group of West Jersey assemblymen (supported by a few assemblymen from East Jersey) agreed to support the nominations of Elias Boudinot (East Jersey), James Schureman (East Jersey), Thomas Sinnickson (West Jersey), and Lambert Cadwalader (West Jersey). During the ensuing election campaign this slate of candidates was variously referred to as the "Junto," "West Jersey," "Federal," "Western," "Assembly," or "Princeton" ticket. For the sake of convenience, this ticket will be referred to as the Junto ticket in editorial notes.

A number of other tickets emerged, but no unified opposition. Abraham Clark and Jonathan Dayton (both East Jerseyites) had many active supporters, and their names were consequently included on many tickets. Also frequently mentioned were John Witherspoon (East Jersey), Thomas Henderson (East Jersey), and Robert L. Hooper (West Jersey). Tickets frequently included local favorites, and in several instances Schureman's name was on the same ticket with Clark's and Dayton's.

Contemporaries apparently defined "ticket" broadly, to mean a list of recommended candidates—in any form. No formal printed tickets have been located, although evidence in the documents below indicates that they probably did exist.

Samuel W. Stockton to Elisha Boudinot, Trenton, 27 June 1788 (excerpt)[1]

I sincerely congratulate you & the rest of the advocates for a change of government on the prospect's approaching so rapidly—

The determination of New hampshire will make the deliberations of the remaining States not of that consequence, that I beleive some of them wish to be thought in the Union—The Antifederalists of Virga. make no hesitation to declare, it seems, that it wd be most advantageous to that State to be seperated from the Union & stand by herself—I take it that "*the Dominion*["] (Antient as it is), soon would be in a situation to fall, but she cannot be supposed to have foundation, (if we might Judge of her resources shewn during the war) to *stand alone.*[2]

I have heard several times, our broth Elias[3] spoken of for a member of our federal governmt.—and it is beleived he would be easiest elected for the House of Representatives—You must think of these things in Time & consult him & other friends.

1. RC, Stimson-Boudinot Collection, NjP. The letter was addressed to Boudinot in Newark. Stockton (1751–1795), a Trenton lawyer, was secretary of the state Convention in 1787 and was secretary of state from 1794 until his death. Elisha Boudinot (1749–1819), a Newark lawyer, was a younger brother of Elias Boudinot. He was a clerk of the circuit court, 1776–1777 and 1780–1782, and an associate justice of the state Supreme Court, 1798–1804.

2. The New Hampshire Convention ratified the Constitution on 21 June 1788; the Virginia Convention, which had been meeting since 2 June, ratified on 25 June.

3. Elias Boudinot was married to Hannah Stockton, Samuel's sister.

Brunswick Gazette, 15 July

The adoption of the new form of government, by the ten United States, has inspired the most lively joy in every patriotic and rational mind; and must serve to convince its mistaken and deluded enemies and opponents, that their conjectures were altogether groundless and visionary in the commencement, as well as events. Nothing (continues our correspondent) is now wanting, but an active cultivation of political harmony, unison, and concord, to fulfil the designs of heaven, which were calculated to make us a great and happy people.

Respected by all the nations abroad, and contented, heart-feltedly contented at home, *America* has every felicity at her command, which any young rising empire could expect or desire. What hath she to fear, but her God? Yet in vain do we view our blessed situation, without it tends to make the people better men and good citizens. The best government is of no consequence, when it falls to the fatal management of bad ministers and indifferent rulers. Nor are laws, the most salutary, any security in themselves when they are inverted and abused.

Let it, therefore, be our inflexible aim, to trust our federal affairs to men of approved probity and talents, upon whose skill we may rely with safety. For virtuous and intelligent representation is the mainspring of social happiness, and the only proper path of American glory.

W.E.I., Federal Post (Trenton), 3 October

To the Freemen and Electors of the County of Monmouth

If our country perishes, (said Haerocles) it will be as impossible to save an individual, as to preserve one of the fingers of a mortified hand.

FRIENDS and COUNTRYMEN,

I think, and I trust you must all think with me, that the present crisis of our political affairs, is a very important one:—Perhaps it may not be amiss, if I should observe, that the present situation of the *American States* is somewhat like unto a ship at sea, which is drifting and driving about at the mercy of the waves; some of the people, no doubt, and perhaps some of the legislatures too, are like some of the mariners on board of a ship, asleep, as it were, between decks, whilst others again are upon deck, keeping watch, and looking out for the time when a favorable breeze may spring up, and when Congress, our present commanders, may give the word for placing some able pilot at the helm, in order to direct our course, and some skilful and active seamen to set and trim the sails, that we may hereafter pass through the ocean of the numberless political events which may await us, under snug and easy sail. No doubt, my friends, but we are all anxiously waiting for the time when the wheels of our New Federal Constitution shall be put in motion, and the springs thereof acted upon:—Much has been said and written both for and against this constitution, and, I expect, ample justice has been done to both sides of the question, by able speakers and able writers: I shall, therefore, not attempt to enter into its merits or demerits, but only observe, that a very learned and sensible man (Mr. Wilson of Philadelphia)[1] has been bold to assert, *That*, taking it altogether, and in every point of view, *it is the best form of Government which has ever been offered to the World:* I hope, my friends, that upon trial the event will prove it so,—Yea, permit me, to hope further, permit me to hope, that to posterity, when they shall look back and trace the origin of this our noble constitution, and the noble system of laws which may be built thereon, by good and wise legislators, it shall afford a beautiful prospect, like to an old venerable oak, which raises its lofty head to the skies, whose spreading leaves may be seen from afar, and, upon a nearer approach, its trunk may be perceived, but the root cannot be discerned, the ground must be dug up to discover it: If this should be the case, we, my friends, must undoubtedly have the chance to reap the first fruits of the advantages flowing from this *glorious government*, But, my countrymen, I trust you cannot be ignorant that the best constitution in the world may be perverted, may be infringed upon, yea, may be violated, and utterly subverted, by bad men; for it is well known, that the forms of a constitution may long remain, after its spirit has been entirely extinguished, and the wisest establishment that ever was formed of a free government, may shrink and degenerate into a monarchal, an aristocratical, or democratical faction, by means of artful, designing and wicked men. It is an observation of Mr. Montesquieu's, (a writer of very great authority) that the laws always meet the passions and prejudices of the law makers, that sometimes they pass through and only imbibe a tincture, but that sometimes they make a full stop, and are incorporated with their very passions and prejudices: how careful then ought we to be who we elect unto the honorable and important trust of legislation; from impure fountains impure waters generally flow; if we do not endeavour to get good men into the grand council of the union, we can have no right to expect good federal laws: I much fear if a majority of bad men should get in there, the law will be too much like cobwebs, calculated only to catch the little flies, while the great ones will continually break through. When I speak of good men in a political sense, I mean men of independence—men of morality and integrity—men of wisdom and political knowledge—men of candour, steadiness, firmness and moderation. In order to get good men into the grand council of the union, much depends upon electing good men into the different State Legislatures; for they must, at least, intervene in the choice of the President, and they will have the whole and sole appointment of the Senators; and, I think, it is reasonable to suppose, that those men, who have influence enough to get themselves elected into the state legislatures, will also have influence with the people, when they come to elect the Representatives for the Federal Representation. The public can never have a firm existence, unless all the different ranks of men co-operate to its preservation, not faintly, but with the utmost spirit and vigour; for if among those in high stations, there is not an affection which warmly embraces the honor and interest of the Commonwealth, and if the same genius does not universally possess the people at large, such supine negligence and giddy administration will creep into the state, as must be attended at last with sudden ruin *(Burgh's Political Disquisitions).* I could almost wish, for the sake of the County of Monmouth, that there was a law of this state, to compel a man, when chosen by the voice of the people, to serve his country, for virtue is certainly the principle of a republican government, and when a man is chosen by the people, it is an attestation for his virtue, and when his virtue is thus attested, I think it is his duty to serve. It was a rule among the ancient Greek republics, that, that man who had not a hand in an insurrection, was deemed infamous—why, because the moderate part of the community stepping forth and mixing with the tumultuous at such a time, is like cool water poured into boiling hot, or like a few drops of one kind of liquor poured into another, which immediately stops the fermentation. There is no insurrection at this time in the County of Monmouth, to be sure, but, I humbly conceive, there exists among the people a kind of political lethargy and lukewarmness, which, if persisted in, may finally be attended with as fatal consequences as any sudden insurrection could be: Rouse then my friends, and, in order that we may have good men in the Federal Council and Representation, let us exert every nerve, and endeavour to send forward good men to our State Council and Assembly:—But above all, my countrymen, let me warn you to be guarded against the arts and fruits of corruption in our elections and governments. It has been remarked by a very shrewd observer, *(Plutarch)* that he who first introduces treats and presents among a people, to obtain their favor, paves the way for the destruction of that people. Corruption, my countrymen, is of all dangers the greatest a free constitution can be exposed to, and the most to be apprehended; its approach is imperceptible, but its blow, if not prevented, is fatal; its approach is imperceptible, but its blow, if not prevented, is fatal; and you cannot prevent its blow, unless you prevent its approach; it is this (observes a patriotic writer on the danger of mercenary parliaments) that has changed the very natures of Englishmen, and of valiant men, made them cowards; of eloquent, dumb, and of honest men, villains. And have we not some reason to apprehend the same of *Americans?* The only time to guard against corruption, is before it becomes prevalent. If the hands of a majority of those who sit at the helm can be kept clean, they can compel those below them to be honest; and if a few among them should find it their interest to abuse their power, it will be the interest of all the rest to punish them for it, and then our government will act mechanically, and a rogue will as naturally be hanged as a clock strikes twelve when the hour is come. I trust, my countrymen, you will take these things into serious consideration, and act accordingly at the ensuing election;[2] for rely upon it, our greatness, yea, our political salvation, absolutely depends upon keeping our Elective, our Legislative, and by that means our Executive and Judicial Powers, to future ages, untainted, unseduced, vigilant for the public safety, jealous of, and watchful over the rights of the people:—This is the fountain head from whence we are to look for all our political happiness, and the redress of our grievances.

W.E.I.

Monmouth County, Sept. 20, 1788.

1. James Wilson (1742–1798) of Pennsylvania was a prominent Federalist. For a biographical sketch, see DHFFE, 1, 428.
2. State elections for the Assembly and Council to be held on 14 October.

Jonathan Dayton to John Cleves Symmes, New York, 22 October (excerpt)[1]

The federal year is so near its expiration, that we now no longer make a house, altho' a few weeks ago the representation was more compleat than had been known before since 1776—It is to me very doubtful whether we shall have nine States on the floor again between this and the meeting of the new Congress, however much the situation of our affairs in the west or the turn and State of European politics may require it.[2] The people [in] their rage for the new constitution seem to act as if the whole business of the Union, nay every thing besides should give way to or stand still until, its operation, and many of them really think that with a kind of Magic process it will at the instant of its commencement rid us of all our embarrassments and make our circumstances flourishing. Altho' strongly prepossessed and very partial in favor of that system (especially when compared with the present) I cannot nevertheless go all lengths with such enthusiasts. Time and a variety and succession of political indiscretions have brought upon us the calamities we are experiencing, and nothing but time and a series of wise, prudential managements and political economy will extricate us from them. In order to counterballance the evil predictions of its enemies, the favorers of the new government have been [lead?] to utter prophecies with regard to it as extravagant on the other hand, the many have given into the belief and suffered their expectations to be unreasonably raised, expectations not to be gratified, and which in the event of their disappointment will probably furnish the first ground of discontent and give a new opening for antifederalism under more favorable auspices than heretofore to revive it's attacks. Sincerely do I pray, my friend, that my apprehensions may prove to be ill founded. Secondly do I wish that the hopes of the most sanguine may be answered, but well I know that the success of an experiment like this is too apt to depend upon the impressions which it makes at it's outset and neither you nor I can [undertake?] to say that this is not one of the last tryals to be afforded to this or any other country, whether the people have ability to govern themselves or must in all cases submit to receive a master of their own or others chusing.

1. Tr, John Cleves Symmes Papers, 1788–1796, DLC. Printed: Beverley W. Bond, Jr., ed., *The Correspondence of John Cleves Symmes, Founder of the Miami Purchase: Chiefly from the Collection of Peter G. Thomson* (New York, 1926), 204–07. Symmes (1742–1814) held many political and judicial positions in New Jersey before moving to the Northwest Territory in the summer of 1788. Congress appointed him one of the three judges for the territory in early 1788, and he remained a territorial judge until Ohio became a state in 1803.

2. The Articles of Confederation, which in most situations required consent from only a majority of the thirteen states to enact legislation, required the consent of nine states before certain actions could be taken. Treaties and letters of marque and reprisal required the consent of nine states (see DHRC, I, 91–92).

Robert Hoops to Governor William Livingston, Sussex Court, 29 November[1]

The many and particular Acts of Friendship I have received from your Excellency induces me to trouble you on the present subject.

My Friends in this County intend puting me in nomination as one of their Representatives for this State, it is an Honor I by no means aspired to but as it is their wish have assented and must confess it will flatter my vanity not a little should it meet Your Excellencys approbation. Your countenance I am well assured will add much to my prospect of Success—

P.S We have not yet got law appointg the mode of Election—

1. RC, William Livingston Papers, MHi.

John Stevens, Jr., to John Stevens, Sr., Hoboken, 4 December[1]

I wrote you a few days ago by Gilbert, since which I have received yours by Mr. Rutherd.[2] It would be very convenient to me to be a representative to Congress, tho' I am not very sanguine as I am not inclined to take the pains that some will in order to get in; I have a few days ago writen to the speaker,[3] and have mentioned the matter to him; I also sent him a number of my pamphlets to distribute among the members, and a draught of a constitution for this state together with a pretty long letter, which

I desired he might communicate to the House,[4] So you see I have given them a sample of my abilities, by which to judge how well I may be qualified for this Business. If therefore you think there is any chance I have no sort of objection to my name being made use of. Rachel and the Children are all well, Robert runs alone and grows very lively and diverting.

1. RC, Stevens Family Papers, NjHi. John Stevens, Sr. (1716–1792), a merchant, was the Hunterdon County delegate to the Council, 1776–1781, and was a delegate to Congress in 1784. He was president of the state Convention in 1787.

2. Probably John Rutherfurd.

3. Benjamin Van Cleve was Speaker of the Assembly.

4. See [John Stevens, Jr.], to Benjamin Van Cleve, 21 November 1788, Part One.

Richard Cox, Jr., to Jonathan Dayton, Mt. Holly, 8 December[1]

This morning Major Bloomfield breakfasted with me on his way to Gloucester Court, he inform'd me the names of the gentlemen that our Legislature had agreed to run for members of the federal Congress,[2] you may well suppose that we should have been happy to have seen your name amongst the number; but as their determination is not binding on us we determined to use our influence in runing the names mentioned in the inclos'd ticket, which the Major desired me to inclose you.[3]—My father[4] was present at the same time and assured us of his influence in the County of Monmouth, where I doubt not but our Cincinnati brethren will use their utmost endeavors in your favor.—

I trust you'l excuse the liberty I have taken in making use of your name without consulting you on the subject.—

Be Pleas'd to make my best respects to Mrs. Dayton & family Genl. & Mrs. Dayton, Genl. & Mrs. Ogden, My dear friend Capt Ogden & family with all other my intimate acquaintance in your place.—[5]

1. RC, Dayton Miscellany, NjHi. Cox (1755–1816) and Dayton were officers in the same New Jersey Continental Army regiments during the Revolution; at the end of the war Cox was a major. Cox was treasurer of the state chapter of the Society of the Cincinnati for many years. His business interests in Mt. Holly included a general store, a gristmill, a sawmill, and an iron works.

2. Cox is referring to the Junto ticket, which a group of West Jersey assemblymen, supported by a few East Jersey assemblymen, drew up during the Assembly session. The ticket was composed of Elias Boudinot and James Schureman from East Jersey, and Thomas Sinnickson and Lambert Cadwalader from West Jersey.

3. Enclosed with this letter was a small piece of paper on which were written (probably in Joseph Bloomfield's handwriting) the names of Elias Boudinot, Jonathan Dayton, James Schureman, and Thomas Sinnickson.

4. Richard Cox, Sr. (1727–1800), was a prominent citizen of Monmouth County.

5. The references are to Elias Dayton, Matthias Ogden, and Aaron Ogden, respectively.

A Freeholder, New Jersey Journal (Elizabethtown), 10 December

To the INHABITANTS *of* NEW-JERSEY.

Fellow Citizens,

Within a few weeks you will be called upon to give your suffrages for *four men* to represent you in the Congress of the United States. This important privilege ought to be estimated by you at its true value, and your unbiassed judgment should be exercised upon this occasion: And now, my fellow citizens, suffer me to warn you from being misguided by some of those who, for quite another purpose, you have placed great trust in.

I happened lately to be at Princeton, where a number of *great men* were sitting,[1] and I discovered that a junto had formed a ticket for you, which is to be secretly ushered into the several counties as if not coming from them: as I do, from my heart, most cordially abhor and detest all secret cabals and juntos, I think it a duty incumbent upon me, to apprize you of their conduct, that you may avoid the snare that is privately laid for you.

The ticket which they have formed consists of the following names, *Elias Boudinot* and *James Schuurman*, of East-Jersey, and *Lambert Cadwallader* and *Thomas Sinnickson*, of West-Jersey. Some of these gentlemen, if it had not been for the very improper manner in which they are attempted to be passed on you might be well entitled to your votes; but under the present circumstances, as we have many as suitable men, it will be proper to reject them; and particularly at this time, as a lesson to our *great men* not to meddle with matters which does not belong to them.

I shall, in a future paper, present you with some strictures upon the conduct of two of those gentlemen, which will, I trust, satisfy you that they ought not to be the men of your choice; at present I shall close, after using a privilege which every citizen is entitled to, that is, of nominating four candidates, who I intend to vote for—*Jonathan Dayton* and *Thomas Henderson*, of East-Jersey, and *John Cox* (of Trenton)[2] and *Joseph Ellis*, (of Gloucester) of West-Jersey.

These gentlemen have at least one advantage over the others—they are not proposed by a secret junto.

A FREEHOLDER.

Burlington, December 4, 1788.

1. The legislature, which met from 28 October to 1 December 1788.
2. Cox (c. 1731–1793), father-in-law of John Stevens, Jr., was a Philadelphia merchant before the Revolution. He moved to the Trenton area and operated the Batsto Furnace in Burlington County from about 1773 to 1778. Cox represented Burlington County in the Council, 1781–1782, before moving back to Philadelphia in 1790.

Robert L. Hooper to Jonathan Dayton, Trenton, 17 December[1]

I have not received a line from you since we parted at Princeton, and from what has since been disclosed to me I suppose the result of your Conference's with Messrs. Ketchells & Martin[2] have not been so pleaseing as we had reason to expect when we parted. A few days after the Legislature rose the Speaker came to my house to inform me that he had been urged by the Members from Somerset,[3] by Mr. Cook and Mr. Stilwell[4] to suffer them to Nominate him for one of the Representatives—I found him much attatched to Mr. Clark and opposed to Mr. Boudinot, his Ticket therefore (if he is in Nomination) will be Clark, Dayton, Scureman & Vancleave, but I have since been told that his friends have advised him agains[t] the attempt—however it may be with him, from the circumstance it is clear, that I was not the primary object with any of the Gentlemen whose names I have mentioned above.—by this time you must be fully informed of their intentions. The appointment is not an Object with me.—I wish to recede, but will faithfully endeavour to secure your Election so far as my influence can be extended in this County and in Sussex.

I am convinced that the five westermost Counti[e]s, to wit, Burlington (except the three uper Townships) Gloucester, Salem, Capemay & Cumberland will run Boudin[o]t, Scureman, Sinnicson and Cadwalader with great unanimity.—They are warmly opposed to Mr. Clark, you & myself. Many of the Gentlemen of the Law have joined in this Ticket and will oppose your Elect[i]on, *particularly in Somerset.* Mr. Patterson[5] is much in favour of Colo: Cadwalader—but I am much mistaken if he or Sinnicson will run in this County. Colo. Thompson[6] is in league with the western Partizans and will push their Ticket in Sussex—It is my wish to see Mr. Boudinot chosen, but the people are opposed to the Gentlemen of the Law

I have been informed by Major Hoops, that his Friends in Sussex will nominate him—he is active and sincere—perhaps it may be right to get him to join in our Ticket. I expect to see him at Princetown when the Council meets in January—

You will oblige me by forwarding the inclosed to Colo. Cumming[7] by a safe han[d]—

[P.S.] Write to me by post. I have recd. a Letter from Major Lloyd[8] Dated the 10th. He is gone to Sussex in good spirits—at the meeting of the Grand-Lodge he will give us the fullest information he can get—

1. RC, James T. Mitchell Autograph Collection, PHi. The letter was addressed to Dayton in Elizabethtown.

2. Abraham Kitchel (1736–1807), a Morris County farmer and a county judge, represented Morris in the Assembly, 1778–1779, and in the Council, 1786–1788, 1793–1794, and 1796–1800. He and his younger brother, Aaron Kitchel, were candidates for Representative. Ephraim Martin (1733–1806) represented Somerset County (1779 and 1781–1789) and Middlesex County (1795, 1797, and 1799–1805) in the Council.

3. Benjamin Van Cleve was Speaker of the Assembly. Robert Blair, Edward Bunn, and John Hardenbergh represented Somerset County in the Assembly in 1788.

4. Ellis Cook (c. 1731–1797), a Hanover, Morris County, taverner and farmer, was a Morris delegate to the provincial congresses in 1775 and 1776. He represented Morris County in the Assembly, 1776–1777, 1779, and 1781–1790, and in the Council, 1791–1792 and 1795. Joseph Stilwell, a Monmouth County militia captain during the Revolution, represented Monmouth in the Assembly, 1786–1800.

5. William Paterson had been elected Senator on 25 November 1788.

6. Mark Thomson (1739–1803) was born in Montgomery County, Pennsylvania, but by 1760 was living in Sussex County, New Jersey. He represented Sussex in the Assembly in 1779, and in the Council, 1786–1788, and later served in the House of Representatives, 1795–1799.

7. John Noble Cumming (c. 1752–1821) operated an extensive stage line that carried the United States mail between New York and Philadelphia; he also operated a chain of taverns along the route. He was a principal member of the East Jersey Company, which purchased land in John Cleves Symmes's Miami Purchase.

8. Richard Lloyd.

Anti Cabalisticus, New Jersey Journal (Elizabethtown), 17 December

Happening to cast my eye over the New-Jersey Journal for the last week, I was very much edified and entertaned with the *language* and *argument* contained in a paragraph of political ingenuity, subscribed "*A Freeholder.*"[1] As I judged it *purely original* in *stile,* and remarkably singular in the force and manner of *reasoning*, I could not forbear giving this public testimony of the opinion I had conceived of its merit. The author of this *admirable production*, has united, in its composition, the great essentials of perfect writing, to wit, *just conceptions* and *clear expressions*; with a happy mixture of *salt, point*, and *epithet*. In the *last* species of invention, he shines with unrivalled lustre. As for instance:—*Junto, great men, detestation, secret cabals, abhorrence*, and many more that will occur to the reader of this *unparalleled performance*, and no where else to be found, but on the records of the gun-powder plot. Besides, Mr. Printer, there is a peculiar beauty in two or three of these phrases, not observable by common critics. The term *junto* discovers great *historical knowledge*;[(a)] *cabal*, the most *profound erudition*;[(b)] and a delicious *irony* is contained in the epithet, *great men*.—But, Mr. Printer, to come to the *argument* of the writer, no proposition in Euclid was ever made plainer, by the assistance of *axioms, right lines*, and *circles*, than the *impropriety* of acceding to this junto nomination: from the *positions, proofs*, and *syllogistic conclusions* of the *Freeholder*. This appears, 1st; from the *mode* of *nominating*; 2dly; from the *incapacity* of the *nominated*: or more logically, the *first* objection is *ad modum*: the *second, ad hominem*. Last, then, The *Freeholder* argues against the *manner*—that it was carried on *in fraudem reipublicæ, privately*, by a *number* of *great men; clandestinely*, at *Princeton*, during the *session* of the *legislature*; and *wrongfully*, by men in *high trust and credit* in the state of New-Jersey, without *due* notice, or indeed *any* notice at all, to this *worthy Freeholder*, and others of equal *note* and *importance*. From these premises, then, it most plainly follows, that the *manner* of framing this ticket is, in every light, *exceptionable*. But, 2dly, the argument applies *ad hominem*—the *persons* agreed upon are personally *ineligible*: For, 1st, they are rendered *incapable* of holding an office, as they are put in nomination by persons not *duly qualified* to nominate, to wit, a *junto* of *great men*. 2dly, *Because* the *Freeholder* has found out in the state, four *other* men of *equal* abilities, with the *additional* merit of being recommended by *himself*, without the interposition of any *great men*, or *men* in *high trust* and *credit* in New-Jersey.— 3dly, *Because* the *Freeholder*, at some *future time*, is to *stricturize two* of the junto-nomination; of course they *all* die together; the ticket, in *his* opinion, being *indivisible*. "Heu! infelices alienus vulneribus concidunt." 4thly, *Because* the *rejection* of this ticket will teach this *caballing junto* a *lesson "not to meddle in matters not belonging to them,"* (in verbis autoris). 5thly; *Because* it is *presumptuous* for any set *of men* to *run* a ticket upon the public in a *secret* manner, without *first publishing* their intention in the *New-Jersey Journal*. 6thly, *Because* the *right* of nomination is in *individuals*, and not in *collective bodies*; therefore this *junto* acted *contra legem terræ*. 7thly, *Because* the *Freeholder*, being an *individual*, and a *privileged citizen*, will *not* vote for Elias Boudinot, James Schurman, Lambert Cadwallader, and Thomas Sinnickson, being *defecti facultatibus*. And 8thly and lastly, *Because* the said *Freeholder will* vote for Jonathan Dayton, Thomas Henderson, John Cox, and Joseph Ellis, being *approbati facultatibus*.

Thus, Mr. Printer, is this *junto* exposed, their schemes frustrated, and the representation from New-Jersey established, through the keen sagacity, the invincible arguments, the unerring judgment, and inimitable pen of the *patriotic citizen* and *modest Freeholder*.

ANTI CABALISTICUS.

(a) Junto or junta—the association of Spanish provinces under Padilla, which was stiled the Holy Junta. They united in order to resist the oppressions of Charles the Vth. and to obtain a restoration of their ancient constitutions, rights and privileges. Rob. Hist. Ch. V.[2]
(b) Ars-Cabala, from the Hebrew, mystical tradition.

1. 10 December 1788, above.
2. William Robertson, *The History of the Reign of the Emperor Charles V* . . . (3 vols., London, 1769).

William Bradford, Jr., to [Elias Boudinot], Philadelphia, 23 December (excerpt)[1]

By all the information I receive from West Jersey, I find the people there are so determined upon running you for a member of Congress, that I am not surprized at your acquiescence. There are occasions where a person appears to be so particularly called on that it seems like an indifference to public opinion to refuse; & sometimes gives an offence that is long remembered. As I hinted to you in my former letter, I apprehend the house of Representatives will afford a greater field for talents, & usefulness than the Senate.[2] That assembly will undoubtedly be in a great degree a popular one in which eloquence & abilities will have a greater chance for success than in the select body of Senators. The objects of discussion will be so important in the first Congress, that it seems to me, a man's industry, & knowledge cannot in the course of the present Century, have the same oppertunity of being serviceable. At the same time, a seat in that house must be very ineligible unless one can safely abandon all other business.—I hope that your election if it should take place will in the end contribute to bring us nearer together. There are several ways in which this may be effected.—

1. RC, Wallace Papers, PHi. The address page of the letter is missing, but from the letter's content the addressee was undoubtedly Elias Boudinot. Bradford (1755–1795) was married to Boudinot's daughter, Susan Vergereau. He was attorney general of Pennsylvania, 1780–1791; an associate justice of the state Supreme Court, 1791–1794; and United States attorney general from 1794 until his death.
2. Bradford is probably referring to his letter of 14 November 1788 to Boudinot, the relevant portion of which is printed in DHFFE, I, 341.

John Stevens, Jr., to John Stevens, Sr., Hoboken, 23 December (excerpt)[1]

In your two last letters you wish to know whether it would be agreable to me to be put up as a candidate for representative. I wrote you a fortnight ago[2] in answer to your first letter, that it would be very convenient to me. But since that time I hear the assembly have formed a ticket which the members from this county, I understand, have agreed to support:[3] I have also been inform[ed] that Colo. Cox is to be set up—under these circumstances I do not think there is much chance of my succeeding. However we can talk about it when I come up. I have heard nothing from the Chancellor[4] since the date of his last letter to you. Rachel joins me in love to mama. The Children are both well.—

1. RC, Stevens Family Papers, NjHi.
2. 4 December 1788, above.
3. The Bergen County representatives in the Assembly in 1788 were John Benson, Isaac Nicoll, and John Outwater.
4. Robert R. Livingston (1746–1813), chancellor of New York State, 1777–1801, was married to Mary Stevens, sister of John Stevens, Jr.

Jonathan Dayton to Joseph Bloomfield, Elizabethtown, 24 December[1]

Your very friendly letter of the 16th. came to my hands this morning and I assure you sir I feel myself flattered by the favorable sentiments which it expresses towards me still more from a wish which I have to preserve your good opinion than from any earnestness or anxiety with regard to the approaching election. I thank you for the trouble you have already taken & the exertions you are continuing to make with respect to me in your quarter, of which I had already had intimations by letters from Major Cox[2] & from another friend in the west.—I am sorry that the zeal of the three gentlemen whose names you mention & of others in Salem in favor of their ticket should carry them such lengths as the attempting to prejudice the people within the circle of their influence against me—On occasions like the present I can make great allowances for a more than common earnestness in men in favor of the candidates whom they patronize; but zeal has it's proper bounds & limits & these may surely be said to be transg[r]essed, where an attempt is made to recommend favourites at the expence & to the undeserved injury of the reputation of their competitors—I challenge them to point out any dishonest or dishonorable action in my private station or any act or measure of my public life derogatory to the interest of the people whom I served & of the country in which I lived—This being the case you will doubtless agree with me that I have nothing to apprehend from the malevolence of any wherever I am known or wherever I can be heard—I shall however be not the less indebted to you to contradict reports & counteract their effects so far as you feel at liberty & can think yourself justified in doing it. In Burlington I know, your influence is weighty—In Gloucester, I have more friends, I trust, than my opponents count upon & even lower there are a few who have voluntarily & unasked for, given me friendly assurances.

The young gentleman who was the bearer of your letter acquaints me that you propose to visit this part of the state in the course of next week—I shall expect then to see you & shall talk on these subjects more confidentially & more at large than can readily be done on paper or within the compass of a letter.

1. FC, Jonathan Dayton Papers, MiU-C.
2. Probably Richard Cox, Jr.

Jedidiah Morse to Samuel Breese, Elizabethtown, 27 December (excerpt)[1]

I have conversed with Mr Boudinot respecting the ensuing Election—He has consented to have his name put up—& I hope there is no doubt of his carrying the Election in opposition to Mr Clark, who, though a good man in other respects, is, I conceive wrong in his politics.

1. RC, Morse Family Papers, CtY. The letter was addressed to Breese in Shrewsbury. Morse (1761–1826), a native of Woodstock, Connecticut, married Elizabeth Ann Breese, daughter of Samuel Breese, in May 1789. In April 1789, Morse became pastor of the First Congregational Church in Charlestown, Massachusetts, where he remained for over thirty years. He is probably best known for his works on geography, notably *The American Geography* . . . (Elizabethtown, N.J., 1789) and *The American Gazetteer* . . . (Boston, 1797). Breese (1737–1800), born in New York City,

was an early Shrewsbury settler and became a wealthy landowner there. He was a Monmouth County judge, a colonel in the New Jersey militia in 1776, and a delegate to the state Convention in 1787.

Jonathan Dayton to the Reverend Andrew Hunter, Elizabethtown, 29 December[1]

A few days ago I received a letter from Majr. Bloomfield acquainting me that you had concurred with him in the resolution to run my name with your respective interests in the approaching election for Representatives in Congress. I never in the least doubted your good will & friendship toward me, but I am aware that that resolution affords a more than common proof of it, since in promoting my name you will have to oppose the current of opinion in your quarter in favor of another ticket which I hear is forwarded and supported by certain influential characters among you and even in your very town. A regard to character rather than any anxiety with respect to my success in the election prompts me to inform you that I have been told undue means are adopted to prejudice the minds of your people against me and to request that you would oppose your knowledge of me, so far as it will go, to every ill founded assertion & malicious insinuation tending to make unfavorable impressions toward me. I defy the charges of any man whether they relate to my public or my private character, & so soon as I shall have ascertained who are the persons that are dealing out their calumny so liberally against me, I shall not scruple to call them to a strict account.

Be so good as to inform me whether the lower counties will be united in any one ticket or like ours will be divided & whether Doctr. Dick[2] is spoken of as a candidate among you. Acquaint Doctr. Henry[3] if you please that I thank him for his good intentions expressed towards me but I am at a loss to know to whom I am indebted in Cumberland for their interest there as mentd. in the Major's letter but without a name. I shall be much obliged by your giving me in your answer a circumstantial detail of the interest that is making & of the plans likeliest to succeed in the west—The ticket which has been given out in your quarter as one formed by the legislature was not formed by a majority of that body nor has it been assented to by any county east of Burlington, but will meet with pointed & powerful opposition this way, as a ticket—

When you write, direct to me at Elizth. Town in N. Jers: where any letters put into the post office at Philadelphia will find me the most of the winter—

1. FC, Dayton Miscellany, NjHi. Hunter (1751–1823) was pastor of the Presbyterian churches in Woodbury and Blackwood, Gloucester County, 1786–1797; a Gloucester County delegate to the state Convention in 1787; a professor of mathematics and astronomy at the College of New Jersey (Princeton), 1804–1808; and a United States Navy chaplain, 1810–1823.

2. Samuel Dick (1740–1812), a Salem County physician, represented his county in the provincial congress, 1776; was a militia colonel the same year; and was a member of the Assembly, 1776–1777. He attended Congress, 1784–1785, and was Salem County surrogate, 1785–1804.

3. Robert R. Henry (c. 1755–1805) graduated with Dayton from the College of New Jersey (Princeton) in 1776, served as a surgeon in the New Hampshire Line of the Continental Army from 1777 to the end of the war, and practiced medicine in Somerset County, New Jersey, thereafter.

New Jersey Journal (Elizabethtown), 31 December

TICKET.—As the time for the nomination and indeed for the election of members of Congress is near at hand, a citizen of New-Jersey begs leave to propose to his fellow citizens the four following persons as fit objects of their choice, VIZ. Abraham Clark, Jonathan Dayton, James Schureman, and Dr. Witherspoon; these are men whose attachment to their state and country, and whose abilities in its service, are too strongly impressed on the minds of the people at large, to make a repetition of them on this occasion in any degree necessary.[1]

1. This item was reprinted in the *Brunswick Gazette*, Philadelphia *Federal Gazette*, Philadelphia *Independent Gazetteer*, and Philadelphia *Pennsylvania Packet*, all 6 January 1789.

John Stevens, Jr., to John Stevens, Sr., Hoboken, 1 January 1789 (excerpts)[1]

I received yours by Charles last evening, and return you my most grateful acknowledgements for the pains you have taken in my behalf—As you inform me the candidates will be numerous, there may possibly be some chance of success, having been in Office so long I am pretty generally known throughout the State— . . . Perhaps it would not be amiss for you to write to a number of the Principle people in the lower Counties, having served so long [in?] the Legislature you are acquainted [with several?], I think applications will come [better?] from you than from me on this occasion—The Smiths of Bur[lington?][2] perhaps might be brought to give their [influence?]. There will probably be so great a div[isi?]on of the votes that there is really no forming any probable conjecture who will get in.—

1. RC, Stevens Family Papers, NjHi.
2. There were several politically prominent Smiths in Burlington County at this time. Two of them, Joseph and Richard S. Smith, were brothers and Quakers. Joseph (1742–1798), a wealthy Burlington township landowner and officeholder, represented Burlington County in the Council, 1787–1788. Richard S. (1752–1796), a Moorestown merchant and landowner and a Chester township officeholder, represented Burlington County in the Assembly, 1784–1785 and 1787.

John Lawrence to William Livingston, Burlington, 5 January (excerpt)[1]

As to Politicks we have little stiring here; The Federal Ticket[2] will run generally to the Westward of Trenton except in this County where there is an Opposition but I believe feeble.

The People have set their faces against the C-l-k-t-s and D-t-n-t-s—[3]

I hope your Electors will act with prudence and Caution so as to secure that great and good Man G: W—

1. RC, William Livingston Papers, MHi. There were several prominent men named John Lawrence in New Jersey at this time, but the writer of this letter was probably the Burlington lawyer and loyalist often called John Brown Lawrence. Before the Revolution he was mayor of Burlington;

represented the city in the colonial assembly, 1760–1768; was a member of the colonial council, 1771–1775; and was appointed a Burlington judge of oyer and terminer, 1772.

2. The Junto ticket.

3. Clarkites and Daytonites.

John Cox to William Richards, Bloomsbury, 7 January (excerpt)[1]

I have long wanted to pay you a visit, but cou'd not make it convenient, either want of health or unavoidable business has heretofore constantly prevented, But I now flatter myself with the pleasure of seeing you in the course of this or the next month, possibly at our Election for Representatives in Congress which by a late Law is to be holden at 8 different places as under mentioned, which will afford the good People of Egharbour an opportunity of giving in their Votes without the trouble of Riding fifty or sixty Miles for that purpose[2]—as it is a matter of the highest importance that we shou'd have *good* Men to serve us, I hope those entitled to vote will *generally* turn out on the occasion, which is a sufficient reason for a removal of the Poll on future Elections. heretofore the Election has been confined to *one* spot, by which the Inhabitants of the lower parts of the County[3] have been deprived of the privilege of Voting—The Poll is to open at Burlington on the 2d Wednesday in February next, which may, & I take for granted will be adjourned from thence to the following places, viz—Crosswicks, [at?] the sign of the X' Keys[4] in Evesham; to Penny Hill; New Mills; Moore's Town; Lumberton & Clam Town—The Poll will be adjourned in like manner in the County of Gloucester from the usual place of opening to Haddonfield; Swedesborough; Mays Landing, Wrangleborough Mill, & Absciom—

By the fœderal Constitution the Legislature have a right of Electing both Senators & Electors—Our House of Assembly not satisfyed with the privileges given them by Constitution, thought proper previous to their breaking up to name four men for Representatives Viz Elias Boudinot of Essex; Mr. Scureman of Brunswick; Colonel Lambert Cadwaleder of Trenton, & Mr. Sinnicson of Salem which four Gentlemen we are told the Western Members have engaged to Run—Many of the first Characters in this part of the State are not a little displeased with the conduct of the House, & seem determined to oppose the Ticket, or at least two or three of the Members named therein, & flatter themselves that every person who entertains just notions of liberty will join them [in opposition?] by giving their Voices for a different Ticket. [The?] Gentlemen proposed to be Run by Us are the following Viz

Elias Boudinot of Essex;

John Stevens Junr. of Bergen

Robert Hoops of Sussex—&

Robert L. Hooper of Hunterdon or Doctor John Weatherspoon of Somerset as the Voters may choose—If you should accord in Opinion with Me, which I flatter myself you will, that the above named Gentlemen are suitable Characters to Represent Us, I am induced to [hope?], that you will not *only* give them your Vote, but what will be of infinite consequence to them your *Interest*, which, I have not a doubt is very considerable, & that you will exert it on the approaching occasion. If my Health will permit I shall most certainly be with you on the Day of Election, as I have the interest of the Candidates that I have mentioned much at Heart—

1. RC, New Jersey Manuscripts, 1663–1853, PHi. The letter was apparently written at "Bloomsbury Farm," Cox's estate near Trenton. The letter is badly mutilated; some missing words have been supplied from a printed version in PMHB, XI (1887), 501–02, where the letter is misdated 1 January 1789. Richards (1738–1823) worked at Batsto Furnace in Burlington County, 1768–1774; rose in rank to militia colonel during the Revolution; and became resident manager at Batsto in 1781. Between 1786 and 1790 Richards obtained principal interest in the furnace and title to much surrounding land.

2. See New Jersey Election Law, 21 November 1788, n. 3, Part One.

3. Burlington County.

4. Cross Keys.

A Free Elector, New Jersey Journal (Elizabethtown), 7 January

To the ELECTORS OF NEW-JERSEY.

Friends and Countrymen,

Behold the important moment is drawing near, when your country will call upon you to give your suffrages for representatives of the Congress of the United States.

This grand, this invaluable privilege ought to partake of your most serious attention and command your most free and unbiassed judgments; and let it be remembered, that this is the intended hour of our political salvation. And further my dear friends, permit me for a moment to warn you against all party affairs, as it seldom fails of being productive of much mischief, and too often affords a secure shelter for the lurking and subtil assassin. Suffer not yourselves to be misguided by the artful misrepresentations of such wretches, but abhor and detest the unprincipled being, who for the sake of party or some sinister views takes the opportunity at a time of election, as generally best suiting his wicked purpose, of calumniating; and sorry am I to add, often stabbing with too much success, a character whom probably he has not the most distant knowledge of.—I should have concluded without attempting to hold up any characters to your view for nomination, was it not from a forcible conviction that my friends and fellow citizens in general, cannot in all probability have that personal knowledge which would in some measure be requisite on so important an occasion;—therefore I shall beg the indulgence of bringing to their view the following characters, VIZ. Josiah Hornblower, of Essex; James Schureman, of Middlesex; Dr. Thomas Henderson, of Monmouth; and James Ewing,[1] of Cumberland—men whose abilities and integrity we have experienced.

Middlesex, December 15.

Mr. Kollock,[2] at the time of my writing the above I fully intended it for your useful paper, but upon a second reflection I could not decide whether it was justifiable or no, to recommend, or hold up to the public view any person or persons for their nomination, except in the mode prescribed by law; therefore this will account for its not appearing at an earlier period as might be expected from the date. But as I since see it is a liberty taken by many, I shall without further hesitation reassume the subject with a few observations. In the first place then I will propose to my fellow citizens, a view of the proceedings of New-York and Virginia, and what conclusion must we necessarily draw from their proceedings? A most disagreeable one. Virginia has already chosen senators, men of antifederal characters.[3] Now let us turn to New-York, and if they have not chosen men of the same stamp, unhappily we see it was not for want of a majority in that legislature. What my friends can we conclude from this, but that the infatuated anti-constitutionalists so far from throwing aside all opposition, are determined to throw still greater obstacles in the way if possible? I need not admonish you to beware of the mischief that must ensue, should they, unfortunately for America, have a majority in that respectable body the congress of the United States. I would moreover observe to you, that the men I have mentioned are sincere advocates, and firmly attached to the federal constitution.

A Free Elector.

1. Ewing (1744–1823), a member of the Assembly from Cumberland County, 1778–1779, moved to Trenton shortly after 1780. He was state commissioner of loans, auditor of public accounts, a pension agent for the Confederation Congress, and a commissioner of loans for the first federal Congress. He was mayor of Trenton, 1797–1803.
2. Shepard Kollock was publisher of the *New Jersey Journal* from 1786 to 1818.
3. William Grayson and Richard Henry Lee were elected in November 1788.

Samuel Dick to Governor William Livingston, Salem, 7 January[1]

The Measures of the Legislature to unite the Voice of the several Parts of the State in one Ticket and my own Nomination as A Candidate were equally unknown to me untill a few days before Mr. Mayhews[2] going to Council; The time was too short for deliberate Consideration as to the Step most proper to be taken on the Occasion, But having now made up my Mind in a Wish *to decline the Competition* Request your Excellency as you Cannot withdraw my name from the List to make *the most explicit Declaration thereof* in my behalf to the Gentlemen of the Council now Convend as the Means of its being generally known thro' the State—

Whilst this Honorable Appointment is Justly an Object with some of the first Characters in the State, my Declaration may be by some deemd a *Nolo Episcopari*, But with your Excellency I hope for full faith, when I aver, that Impressed with a sense of the Value of the Esteem of my Country Sufficient to keep me awake to honorable pursuits I have made a deliberate Estimate of my own powers and find them best adapted to the limited but pleasing Duties of Superintending my domestic Affairs and Educating my Infant Family And Experience has Indelebly Impressd me with the Opinion that National Care does not Include that of a Family As the Major includes the Minor proposition—Most Cordially therefore Concurring in the Nomination by the Legislature I give all fears of Antifœderalism to the Winds and view it only as an Electioneering Phantom which will Vanish at the Approaching Dawn of an Energetic Government—Indeed it can scarcely be thought there is in the Union a Rational Creature, who would with Malice prepense attempt the Subversion of a Government founded on Principles of such equal Liberty and was *Antifœdus* himself to Appear intrenchd to the Chin in all the proposed Alterations He might be routed by the Assertion of this Truth, Our Government is an Experiment, Susceptible of Amendments when Time shall have shewn them Necessary And those Amendments to be Effected by that same Spirit of Union and Accomodation which first gave birth to its Constitution—This last Expression had nearly sufferd Expunction as it gave encouragement to many others of the like Stamp to be very importunate for admission But as on A Subject so trite where the Pro's and

Con's must have frequently Appeard in their best Array, My Sentiments may prove only Second-handed and must be paid for in the post-office by the Penny weight[.] I will be frugal of your Excellencys Purse and time and give them the Apostles Dismission—Go thy way at this time & I will hear thee at A More Convenient Season. But Neither the Frugal Consideration Nor Any other shall deprive me of the real Satisfaction of Assuring you of that perfect Esteem and Regard with which I have the Honor to be your Excellencys most Obedient Humble Servt.

1. RC, William Livingston Papers, MHi.

2. John Mayhew (d. 1797), a Pittsgrove, Salem County, landowner and county judge, represented Salem in the Assembly, 1778–1780, and in the Council, 1785 and 1787–1793.

John Beatty to Governor William Livingston, Princeton, 9 January[1]

My uniform declaration, since my resignation of a Seat in Congress, of accepting no appointment under Government, which would lead me from home; would I trusted have prevented my name, from being returned to your Excelly, as a Candidate, for the Representation, to be sent from this State under the new Constitution: but finding this not to be the Case, & that my name is made use of: I have to request your Excelly either wholly to Suppress it, in your proclamation to the public; or if this is not practicable, that a Note may be added to the End of it; purporting my desire, that no Votes may in this Manner be thrown away; as I decline the Honour intended me, by those friends, who have placed my name, on the list of nomination

1. RC, William Livingston Papers, MHi. Beatty (1749–1826), a Princeton physician, represented Middlesex County in the Council, 1781–1782; was a delegate to Congress, 1783–1785; and was a member of the state Convention in 1787. He was a member and Speaker of the Assembly in 1789; served in the House of Representatives, 1793–1795; and was New Jersey secretary of state, 1795–1805.

Joseph Bloomfield to Governor William Livingston, Woodbridge, 12 January[1]

Being informed that I have been put in nomination, as a Candidate, at the ensuing Election, for a Representative in Congress, I take the earliest opportunity to inform Your Excellency; that I decline standing a Candidate, and beg the favour of Your Excellency to notice the same, when the nomination shall be published agreably to Law.

1. RC, Lloyd W. Smith Collection, NjMoW.

Franklin Davenport to Elisha Boudinot, Woodbury, 12 January[1]

The time draws near, when we shall begin our Choice of the four Gentlemen who are to represent us in the lower House—A free communication from the Eastward is what we want—The Opposition to the federal or Western Ticket is scarsely visible here—a few of Capt Dayton friends mean to run him & Dr Witherspoon in the room of Mess Cadwallader & Sinnickson, but so few indeed are they, that comparatively speaking they are nought—If I should say 20—Col Ellis says I mention too many—we can muster here from 12. to 1800 & all for one set of men—Do for goodness sake join us as much as possible—dont leave *one* of the four formed at Princeton out—you want us to be united—be so yourselves & success will attend us—let not the best men tempt you to change—but if a thought should strike any of you to run a favourite alone, or with others, in order to get him in—think of our Exertions here, think how determinedly & unitedly we are pushing all, & you will join us I am sure—we must sacrifice some of our Friends to keep out bad men—we might have heretofore formed a better set, but if we divide now, we shall have a Worse—

Again Success attend you & may the Western ticket be your Choice

1. RC, Boudinot Correspondence on Deposit from the American Bible Society, NjP. The letter was signed "Fra Davenport" and was endorsed by Boudinot as being from "Francis Devenport Esq." However, the handwriting is that of Franklin Davenport (1755–1832), a Woodbury lawyer and a nephew of Benjamin Franklin. Davenport was the first Gloucester County surrogate in 1785; a member of the Assembly, 1786–1789; a presidential Elector in 1792 and 1812; a United States Senator, 1798–1799; and a member of the House of Representatives, 1799–1801.

John Rutherfurd to Robert Morris, New Brunswick, 13 January (excerpt)[1]

With respect to politics the whole state is busied in making nominations for Representatives in Congress[.] thirty or forty are said to be in nomination and near half that number are very busy in making interest either in person or by their friends[.] each county is anxious to send one or two members and the people unfortunately consider themselves as inhabitants of their particular counties instead of the state at large, those most likely to succeed are Schureman and Sinnickson the other two will probably be chosen from among the following viz. Cadwallader Hooper Dayton Clark and Boudinot[.] On considering our conversation at your house I declined being nominated in the county I live and elsewhere where I was asked there would have been not the least probability of my succeeding and it would only have been adding another name to a list already too large. I return many thanks to those friends who were kind enough to think of me

1. RC, Robert Morris Papers, NjR. The letter was addressed to Morris in New York City. Rutherfurd incorrectly dated the letter "Jany. 13th 1788," which Morris corrected to 1789 in his endorsement. Morris (c. 1745–1815), a New Brunswick lawyer, was the son of Chief Justice Robert Hunter Morris of the New Jersey colonial supreme court. Morris became the first Chief Justice of the state Supreme Court in 1777, serving until 1779, when he returned to private law practice. From 1790 until his death he was a United States district judge, district of New Jersey.

Lists of Nominees for Representatives Received by the Governor, 13–17 January

According to the election law, passed 21 November 1788, each qualified voter could nominate four persons for Representatives. The nominations had to be presented to the county clerks of the Court of Common Pleas by 12 January 1789 (thirty days prior to the election on 11 February). The clerks were required to send a copy of the nominations to the governor twenty-four days before the election, and the governor had to publish a list of the nominees at least eighteen days before the election.

The county clerks reported the names of the nominees to the governor in a variety of forms. The Gloucester County return, below, illustrates the most common form. The returns for Burlington, Cumberland, Middlesex, Somerset, and Sussex counties have been summarized. No returns to the governor have been found for Bergen, Cape May, Essex, Hunterdon, Monmouth, Morris, and Salem counties.

All returns printed or summarized below are from the manuscript returns in the William Livingston Papers, MHi.

Nominations from Gloucester County[1]

A Copy of the Nominations of Representatives in
Congress, for the County of Gloucester—
vizt

No 1

"Nomination for Representatives in Congress

Elias Boudinot
Lambert Cadwalader
Thomas Sinickson
James Schureman

Esqrs.

Decemr. 2d. 1788.

Joseph Cooper."

filed 4th. December 1788

No. 2

"Members for the House of Representatives in the
Congress of the United States—

Elias Boudinot
Lambert Cadwallader
James Schureman
Thomas Sinnickson

Jany. 10th. 1789.

Jos: Hugg.
Jno: Blackwood
Benjn. Whitall
Jno. Wilkins
Jno S: Whitall
Joseph Low
William Ellis
Aaron Hewes
Joel Wescoat
Jonathan Hacker
Mark Brown"

Filed 10th Jany. 1789

Woodbury Jany. 9th. 1789

No. 3

"The following Gentlemen are Nominated as Candidates for the Representatives of the State of New Jersey in the House of Representatives in the Congress of the United States, and are to be Voted for on the Second Wednesday in February next & According to a Law for that purpose provided Viz:

Dr. John Witherspoon
Elias Boudinot Esqr
Jonathan Dayton Esqr
James Schureman Esqr

Signed, Andw: Hunter
John Sparks."
filed 10th. Jany 1788—

I do hereby Certify that the foregoing are true Copies from the Originals in my Possession

[signed] E: Clark Clk.

Summary of Nominations from Burlington, Cumberland, Middlesex, Somerset, and Sussex Counties

Persons Nominated	Number of Nominations
Burlington County[2]	
Elias Boudinot	26
Thomas Sinnickson	26
James Schureman	21
Lambert Cadwallader	21
Jonathan Dayton	4
John Cox	3
Thomas Fenimore	1
Robert Hoops	1
Benjamin Van Cleve	1
Cumberland County[3]	
James Schureman	2
Thomas Sinnickson	2
Joseph Smith	2
Samuel Dick	1
Jonathan Dayton	1
Lambert Cadwallader	1
Elias Boudinot	1
John Sheppard	1
Jeremiah Eldredge	1
Middlesex County[4]	
James Schureman	31
John Witherspoon	18
Thomas Sinnickson	17

Persons Nominated	Number of Nominations
Middlesex County (cont.)	
Elias Boudinot	16
Abraham Clark	13
Jonathan Dayton	12
Lambert Cadwallader	10
Robert L. Hooper	6
John Stevens, Jr.	6
Robert Hoops	4
Josiah Hornblower	4
Joseph Smith	4
Benjamin Van Cleve	4
Samuel W. Stockton	2
Thomas Henderson	1
Somerset County[5]	
John Witherspoon	9
James Schureman	7
Abraham Clark	6
Elias Boudinot	5
Thomas Sinnickson	5
Jacob R. Hardenbergh	3
Josiah Hornblower	3
Jonathan Dayton	2
Robert Hoops	1
Aaron Kitchel	1
Jeams Levi	1
Benjamin Van Cleve	1
Sussex County[6]	
Robert Hoops	58
Jonathan Dayton	46
James Schureman	31
Abraham Kitchel	27
Lambert Cadwallader	25
Robert L. Hooper	12
Charles Stewart	12
Elias Boudinot	10
Thomas Sinnickson	8
John Stevens, Jr.	5
John Cox	2
James Linn	2
Abraham Clark	1
Hugh Hughes	1
Robert Ogden	1
James L. Somerset	1
Mark Thomson	1
Benjamin Van Cleve	1

1. Governor Livingston endorsed the document as being received on 14 January 1789.

2. Only Burlington nomination tickets numbered 2–3, 9–10, 14, and 16–36 have been located; each of the 26 known voters who made nominations, submitted a separate ticket. The individual tickets were filed with the county clerk, John Phillips, from 16 December 1788 to 7 January 1789. Phillips forwarded the tickets to Governor Livingston on 12 January 1789; they were endorsed as received the next day.

3. The Cumberland return, with nominations by John Burgin, Burgiss Allison, and Providence Ludlam, was certified as "A true Copy of the Tickets received & filed in my Office pursuant to Law" by the county clerk, Jonathan Elmer. It is dated 12 January 1789 and was endorsed as received by the governor on 17 January. The three tickets are dated 23 and 24 December 1788 and 7 January 1789, respectively.

4. The Middlesex return of 14 tickets (from 37 voters) was certified by the county clerk, Jonathan Deare, as "True Copies of the Original Tickets filed in my Office." It is dated 13 January 1789 and was endorsed as received by the governor on 14 January. The individual tickets are dated from 18 December 1788 to 7 January 1789.

5. The Somerset return of 9 tickets (from 11 voters) was certified by the county clerk, Frederick Frelinghuysen, as "A true Copy of all the Nominations filed in my Office." It is dated 12 January 1789 and was endorsed as received by the governor on 14 January. The individual tickets were filed with the clerk's office from 16 December 1788 to 8 January 1789.

6. The Sussex return of 25 tickets (from 61 voters) was certified by the county clerk, Charles Rhodes: "The above is a true Copy of the Nomination filed in my Office this 12th January AD 1789." It was endorsed as received by the governor on 13 January. The individual tickets were filed with the clerk's office from 18 December 1788 to 2 January 1789.

Proclamation by Governor William Livingston, 19 January[1]

By the Governor of the State of
New-Jersey.

The following is a true list of the names of every Candidate nominated to the choice of the people of this State as Representatives in the Congress of the United States and returned to me by the respective Clerks of the Courts of Common Pleas in the several Counties of this State and which according to the directions of a certain act of the Legislature in that behalf lately made and provided, I am to cause to be published in certain Newspapers therein mentioned, viz.

Elias Boudinot,
James Schureman,
Lambert Cadwallader,
Joseph Sheppard,[2]
Henry Stites,[3]
J. Bloomfield, { *declines to serve.*
Thomas Sinnickson,
Joseph Ellis,
Philemon Dickinson,
Samuel Dick { *declines to serve.*
Jonathan Dayton,
Thomas Henderson,
John Witherspoon,
Robert Hoops,
S. W. Stockton { *declines to serve*
Robert L. Hooper,
William Winds,
James Parker,
Benjamin Thompson,[4]
J. Kinsey, { *declines to serve.*
John Neilson,
Frederick Frelinghuysen,[5]
Abraham Ogden,
Samuel Tuthill,[6]
William Woodhull,[7]
Josiah Hornblower,

Joseph Smith, *declines to serve*
Abraham Clark,
Benjamin Van Cleve.
Charles Stewart,[10]
Abraham Ketchel,
Aaron Ketchel,
Col. J. Cox, *declines to serve.*
Mark Thompson,
James Linn, *Somerset,*
Robert Ogden,[15]
John Stevens, jun.
Hugh Hughs,[16]
Robert S. Jones,[17]
Thomas Fenimore,

Jacob R. Hardenburgh,[8]
Rev. John Armstrong,[9]
J Beatty, Esq. *declines to serve.*
Whitten Cripps,
Dr. McWhorter,[11]
John Mehelm,[12]
Dr. Samuel Smith,[13]
J. Chetwood *declines to serve.*
Patrick Dennis,[14] *ditto.*
Silas Condict,
John Rutherfard,
John Fell,
John Stevens,
Jeremiah Eldridge,

Given under my hand the nineteenth day of January 1789.

WIL. LIVINGSTON.

1. *New Jersey Journal*, 21 January 1789. The proclamation was also printed in the *Brunswick Gazette* and *Federal Post*, both 27 January. In neighboring states the proclamation was published in the Philadelphia *Federal Gazette*, 22 January; Philadelphia *Pennsylvania Mercury*, 24 and 29 January; New York *Daily Advertiser*, 24, 26, and 28 January; and *New York Daily Gazette*, 26, 27, and 28 January.

2. Jonathan Elmer, clerk of Cumberland County, informed Governor Livingston on 3 March 1789 that the correct name was "John," not "Joseph" Sheppard. Elmer said that "Joseph" was incorrectly inserted in the copy he had sent to the county sheriff (Bridgeton, RC, William Livingston Papers, MHi).

3. Stites, a Cape May County landowner, was county sheriff, 1788–1790.

4. There were apparently two men named Benjamin Thompson who were prominent in New Jersey at this time. One Benjamin Thompson, a migrant to New Jersey, served from 1783 to 1785 as a congressional commissioner to settle currency accounts with New Jersey residents. The other Benjamin Thompson, an extensive landowner of Upper Alloways Creek Township, Salem County, was superintendent of a glass factory before the Revolution. In 1788 he purchased five thousand acres of land around the Hibernia Furnace in Morris County.

5. Frelinghuysen (1753–1804), a lawyer, was clerk of the Somerset County Court of Common Pleas, 1781–1789, and represented Somerset in the Assembly, 1784 and 1800–1803, and in the Council, 1790–1792. He was a delegate to the state Convention in 1787 and was a United States Senator, 1793–1796.

6. Tuthill (1725–1814) was practicing medicine in Morristown by 1751. He was appointed a Morris County judge in 1760 and reappointed in 1768, 1776, 1788, 1793, and 1798; he was the county clerk from 1766 to 1776.

7. Woodhull (1741–1824), a Morris County Presbyterian clergyman, was a Morris County member of the Assembly, 1776–1777; a county justice of the peace, 1780–1811; a county judge, 1782–1823; a delegate to the state Convention in 1787; and a member of the Council, 1789–1790. He was a New Jersey circuit court judge from 1808 until his death.

8. Hardenbergh (1737–1790) was president of Queens College (Rutgers) and minister of the Dutch Reformed Church in New Brunswick. He was a Somerset County delegate to the state Convention in 1787 and an assemblyman, 1788–1789.

9. This is probably the Reverend James Francis Armstrong (1750–1816), pastor of the Presbyterian Church in Trenton. He was a chaplain during the Revolutionary War, and in 1782 and

1783 he was minister of the Presbyterian Church in Elizabethtown. From 1786 until his death Armstrong was pastor of the Trenton church. In 1787 he was chaplain of the state Convention.

10. Stewart (1729–1800), of Hunterdon County, was a lieutenant colonel in the Hunterdon militia and commissary general of issues in the Continental Army during the Revolution. He was a member of Congress, 1784–1785.

11. Alexander MacWhorter (1734–1807) was minister of the First Presbyterian Church in Newark from 1759 to 1776. After serving as a chaplain during the Revolution and after brief preaching assignments in North Carolina and Pennsylvania, 1779–1781, he returned to his Newark church, where he ministered until his death.

12. Mehelm (1735–1809) represented Hunterdon County in the provincial congress in 1775 and in the Assembly in 1776 and 1781. He served as county surrogate, 1776–1787, and he became a judge of the county Court of Common Pleas in 1779 and was reappointed in 1786 and 1791.

13. Samuel Stanhope Smith (1750–1819), a Presbyterian clergyman, taught at the College of New Jersey (Princeton), 1770–1773 and 1779–1812. He was president of the college, 1795–1812.

14. Dennis was naval officer of the port of Elizabethtown from 1787 to about 1790.

15. Ogden (1746–1826), a Sussex County lawyer, landowner, and officeholder, was the older brother of Matthias and Aaron Ogden. Either he or his father represented Sussex County in the Council, 1778–1779, and in 1787 he represented Sussex County in the state Convention. Ogden was a member of the Assembly in 1790.

16. Hughes (1742–1790), a Sussex County landowner, iron-forge operator, and officeholder, was a nephew of Colonel Hugh Hughes of New York. He served as county sheriff, 1769–1772; was a member of the provincial congress in 1775; and served in the Assembly in 1780 and in the Council from 1781 to 1783. In 1788 he was appointed a justice of the peace.

17. Jones (1745–1792) was secretary of the American Philosophical Society, 1771–1779. He represented Burlington County in the Assembly, 1787–1789, and served on the Burlington Common Council, 1788–1790.

Governor William Livingston to Samuel Dick, Elizabethtown, 25 January[1]

Be persuaded that it is not through willful neglect that I have not until now acknowledged the receipt of your letter of the 7th inst.[2] I make it a rule to answer every letter, from the meanest creature in human shape, as soon as I have leisure to do it; and I cannot therefore be supposed inattentive to those gentlemen of distinction and gentlemen who are endeared to me by old acquaintance and the amiableness of their characters. But the conjunction of bodily indisposition, and the greater variety of public indispensible business that I have for a considerable time past met with, made it impossible for me to do myself the pleasure of discharging so agreeable an office as that of answering sooner than I now do. But, my dear sir, I wish you had given me a more agreeable commission to execute, than I find I must, according to the tenor of your letter, carry into execution. Your requests, it is true, shall always with me carry with them the nature of a command; but I am sorry that your present one—"*aut volens aut nolens*" be considered mandatory, for it seems you have left me no other choice than the alternative of erasing your name from the "List of Nominations," or to write against it, "Dr. Dick declines to serve." I had a particular reason to wish you to stand as a candidate, and finally appear to be one of the four *elected*, because (without compliment I say it), though we have had many in Congress, who in other respects were possessed of such qualifications as men in that station ought to be endowed with, a great part of them have been totally destitute of that knowledge of mankind, and that certain politeness, which Lord Chesterfield calls *attention*, without which the greatest talents in other things will never make a man influential in such assemblies. But if it must be so that either you cannot or will not go, I must submit.

1. Stephen Wickes, *History of Medicine in New Jersey, and of Its Medical Men . . . to A.D. 1800* (Newark, N.J., 1879), 233. The letter was addressed to Dick in Salem.
2. Printed above.

Public Declinations by Nominees, 27 January-10 February[1]

Brunswick Gazette, 27 January

To the Citizens of New-Jersey.

Seeing my name on the list of nomination for Congress, transmitted by the Governor to the printer for publication, I desire that I may not be considered as a candidate.

PHILEMON DICKINSON.

Hermitage, 20th Jan. 1789.[2]

MR. PRINTER,

Hearing that my name is on the list of candidates for representatives in Congress, received from the Governor for publication, and wishing that not a single vote may be lost at the ensuing important election, I take this method to inform the public that I desire not to be considered as a candidate on that occasion.

FREDERICK FRELINGHUYSEN.

January 22, 1789.

MR. PRINTER,

Having seen my name on the list of candidates for representatives in congress, transmitted by his Excellency the Governor to the different printers, I do hereby inform the public, that I desire not to be considered as a candidate on that occasion.

JACOB R. HARDENBERGH.

January 26, 1789.

MR. ARNETT,

Having seen my name inserted in the list of Candidates proposed to the Citizens of this State for their choice of representatives in the Congress of the United States, transmitted by his Excellency the Governor to the printers for publication, I hereby return my thanks to the Gentlemen who have thus distinguished me by their favorable opinion, and inform the public that it is my desire I may not be considered as a candidate.

JOHN NEILSON.

New-Brunswick, 21 January, 1789.[3]

Mr. ARNETT,

Observing my name among the candidates for representatives to Congress, sent by the Governor for publication, I beg the public not to consider me as a candidate.

SAMUEL SMITH.

Princeton, January 24, 1789.

Brunswick Gazette, 3 February

Mr. PRINTER,

Observing that the name of John *Stephens* is inserted in the list of candidates for representatives in Congress (as it may be conceived that I was intended by the above name) it is necessary to inform the public that I desire not to be considered as a candidate.

JOHN STEVENS, Senior.

Hunterdon county, Lebanon Valley, January 29, 1789.[4]

Brunswick Gazette, 10 February[5]

As my name is inserted in the list of no[minati?]on for representatives *contrary* to my [stated?] intentions, the public are thus informed, and [the se?]veral Sheriffs are requested to make known [that I?] shall not consider myself a candidate at the [ensuing?] election.

JOS. E[LLIS?]

Pennsylvania Packet (Philadelphia), 10 February

We are requested to inform the Public, that the Honorable Jeremiah Eldredge, esq; declines being elected a Representative for the state of New-Jersey in Congress.[6]

1. For private declinations that occurred previous to Governor William Livingston's proclamation, see Samuel Dick to Livingston, 7 January 1789; John Beatty to Livingston, 9 January 1789; and Joseph Bloomfield to Livingston, 12 January 1789, all above.

2. This notice was also printed in the *Federal Post*, 27 January 1789, and *New Jersey Journal*, 28 January and 4 February. Brief notices that Dickinson declined candidacy also appeared in the Philadelphia *Pennsylvania Packet*, 7 February; Philadelphia *Independent Gazetteer*, 9 February; and *New York Morning Post*, 12 February.

3. This item was also printed in the *New Jersey Journal*, 28 January 1789.

4. John Stevens, Sr., also asked Governor Livingston, in letters of 25 and 28 February 1789, to identify the Stevens on the nomination list as his son, "Junior," and he reminded Livingston that he had publicly declined to run for Congress (Lebanon Valley, RC, William Livingston Papers, MHi).

5. The newspaper from which this item is taken is badly mutilated.

6. This notice was also printed in the Philadelphia *Pennsylvania Gazette*, 11 February 1789.

PART FIVE

THE ELECTION OF REPRESENTATIVES

I.
Election Campaign

The election law for Representatives specified that the polls were to open on 11 February 1789 and to continue open—by adjournment—until "legally closed." The legislature's failure to specify a termination date for the elections allowed local officials to manipulate the elections, and the resulting disputes over the election returns ultimately had to be resolved by the United States House of Representatives.

Seven counties completed their elections by late February and soon after reported their results to Governor William Livingston. Six of the seven were East Jersey counties: Bergen, Middlesex, Monmouth, Morris, Somerset, and Sussex; the only West Jersey county reporting was Hunterdon (Hunterdon was occasionally classed as an eastern, rather than a western, county). The returns from these counties were thus available to the governor and Privy Council when they met to count the votes on 3 March. No winners were certified, however, as the returns from six counties were still not available.

The elections in the West Jersey counties of Burlington, Cape May, Cumberland, Gloucester, and Salem were completed by early March. When the governor and Privy Council met again on 18–19 March, they had returns from twelve of the state's thirteen counties (Essex County had still not made a return). The election was decided on the basis of the twelve returns, and the governor proclaimed the winners on 19 March. The election in Essex County (East Jersey) continued until 27 April, and the governor received the Essex results on 3 May.

The principal commentary on the election campaign is in the documents printed below. Election vote totals are printed in Part Five:II, below. Abraham Clark's central role in the election is reflected in the documents printed in Part Five:III, below. Additional post-election commentary is printed in Part Six.

R, Federal Post (Trenton), 18 November 1788

The ELECTION.
Zealous Patriots heading rabbles,
Orators promoting squabbles;
Free Electors always swilling,
Candidates not worth a shilling!
Butchers, Farmers, and Carmen,
Half-pay Officers, and Chairmen;
Many Zealots, not worth nothing,
Many perjured Persons voting;
Candidates, with Tradesmen pissing,
Cleavers, Bagpipes, Clapping, Hissing;
Warmest Friends in Opposition,
Hottest Foes in Coalition!

Open Houses, paid to tempt the
Rotten Votes, with Bellies empty;
Boxing, Drinking Rhyming Swearing,
Some Fools laughing, some despairing;
Fevers, Fractures, Inflammations,
Bonfires, Squibs, Illuminations;
Murd'rers, daring all detection,
Pray, Gentlemen, how do you like the Election,

R.

William Bradford, Jr., to Elias Boudinot, Philadelphia, 15 January 1789[1]

Your determination to accept a Seat in the house of Representatives, if chosen, gives great pleasure to the fœderal Gentlemen here to whom I have mentioned it. The want of law characters from this state could in a great measure be supplied by your knowledge of our laws and circumstances, and we trust that the new Congress will (in their first acts at least) feel themselves legislating for the Nation & Superior to the local prejudices which have too often distracted and dishonored that body under the old Constitution.

1. *Henkels Catalog*, No. 1280 (27 May 1921), p. 4, item 37.

Impartial, Brunswick Gazette, 20 January

Friends and Countrymen,

At this important æra, when the fate of this extensive territory is balancing between two vast extremes of blissful harmony or direful anarchy; what mind is there capable of the least reflection which feels not the most anxious solicitude for the event? and how greatly may the event be affected by the choice we are now about to make of men to represent us in the grand congress of these again United States.—Is there not reason to fear that the terms of our union are not as yet so firmly rivited as that we might not be soon divided by the wickedness of a party, if backed by the weakness or the prejudices of honest well wishing men, should a majority of such as are opposed to the Constitution be sent from the several states to Congress?—From my retired situation, and the nature of my business, I have not had, I confess, an opportunity of satisfying myself how far it would be in the power of such a Congress to affect the existence of the present Constitution—But such delays as certainly will be in their power to practice, and out of our's to prevent for a time, might in our present critical situation effectually work its destruction. The distresses that would follow such a sad catastrophe will be too numerous and too horrible to be related at present. Let us therefore my countrymen improve the noble privilege wisely afforded us by our legislature, in impartially choosing the best from the many good men we have among us who are sincere constitutionalists, and as the injuries that would be in the power of such as are opposed to it are so great, let us therefore have the same precaution in our choice which Cæsar had respecting the choice of his wife, that she should be not only chaste but not even suspected. Let mens former services be never so numerous and important, or their present professions ever so fair, if they are only suspected of being opposed to the constitution, let us not send them while we can find others nearly as good who are known to be staunch friends to it.

To me it appears a much smaller risque to send one of the court party who is friendly to it than a commoner who is suspected of being unfriendly, as it would be much easier to remove such a man should he not promote the interests of the body of the people than to unite the states again, if they are once more severed apart for want of unanimity in the present constitution and for the purpose of making the dangerous experiment of making a better. As I hope never to be one of those who wish and aim at the aggrandizement of a few, and at the depressing of the multitude, so I hope none such will ever bear rule among us. From the examples furnished us by history and the plainest dictates of reason we have just ground to conclude that the happiest governments are such as derive[1] all authority from the collective body of the people, where property and influence are pretty equally divided which equality appears essential to the existence of a republican form of government. Unless we could have the monstrous supposition that the Almighty had been so partial as to make the most of us merely to minister to the happiness of a few.

If my anxiety for the election of such as will warmly support and vigorously inforce the present constitution until it is amended (if needful) in a constitutional way, is illy-founded, I shall be glad to be relieved of it, as I would choose at all times, but more especially on such important occasions to be IMPARTIAL.

Somerset, January 12, 1789.

1. The *Brunswick Gazette* printed "divide." The *New Jersey Journal*, which reprinted the entire article on 28 January 1789, corrected it to "derive."

New Jersey Journal (Elizabethtown), 21 January

A correspondent reminds us that the important time is now drawing near, when we must determine on the security of our freedom, by a prudent choice of *Representatives* for the Congress of the United States.—It therefore requires the independant and unremitted exertions of every honest member of the community; not only in guarding against the deceptions of the artful and ambitious, (whose motive are ever concealed under the delusive wiles of plausibility,) but also to gain a representation that not only *knows*, but *feels*, the wants and wishes of their constituents:—Those who know where the burthen lies and whose shoulders are already placed to its support; whose property is not accumulated from public employment, and whose minds are free from Local Views.—If such characters can be elected, (and such we have among us) we may expect a favorable alteration in government, but a bad administration of the best government, in the universe, will prove oppressive to its community.—Our correspondent further begs leave to offer a nomination which he thinks coincides with the above sentiments, VIZ.—Abraham Clark, Jonathan Dayton, James Schuurman and Robert Hooper. The first of which characters has borne with applause his full proportion of the burthen of politicks since the first dawn of liberty in this country;—he has supported a firmness through the most gloomy times, and ever guarded with integrity the interest that has been entrusted to his care—he therefore stands beyond the reach of calumny; a suitable person to repose our greatest confidence in.

The other characters tho' not so long experienced in public business—are men of approved abilities and integrity—and promise therefore a proportionable advantage.

From The Reverend Andrew Hunter, Woodbury, 22 January[1]

As the time is at hand when we are to Elect Men to Represent the State of New Jersey in Congress, I think it my duty to write to some of my friends, among whom I take the liberty of Ranking you, to request them to Use their Influence that persons may be Appointed to that verry Important duty who will be most likely to Answer the Views and purposes of the State. For my own part I have no personal Interest to serve, nor any favorite party to Assist; but as a Citizen whose life has been for some Years past grafted on the safety of the State—I Consider myself bound in Conscience to promote to Important Offices Men of the most Approved Abilities and Integrity. I have no personal Enmity or Resentment at any Character that may be proposed to the public Choice, but wish to Use any Influence that I may have in favor of the most deserving. Were I to give my Voice for Men whom I judge to be Unacquainted with the Science of Government when I have others in my Choice I should think myself guilty of a Crime against my Country, and against posterity.

The most Important business that ever was transacted by any body of Men in this Country will Come before the New Congress, and doubtless the most shining Characters will be sent up to it by the different States. I might say With Confidence that the fate of thousands yet Unborn will depend upon their deliberations. This being the Case, it appears to me, that the part a Member of the Commonwealth shall take in this business, the Vote he shall give, the support he shall Afford or the Opposition he shall make is as much a Question of personal duty, and as much Concerns his Conscience as the determination of any thing which relates to his Conduct in private life.

The Men that Appear to me to be most Eligible are, Doctor Witherspoon, Elias Boudinot, Jonathan Dayton and James Schureman or Doctor Dick—If these Gentlemen, whose Abilities you are well Acquainted with, should meet your Approbation, I would beg your Influence and exertions in their favor. If you should think of any others who may be of more approved Integrity and Abilities I would be glad to be Informed of them before the Election.

1. RC, Gratz Collection, PHi. The letter's address page is missing.

Tench Coxe to James Madison, New York, 27 January (excerpt)[1]

The election of New Jersey for Electors is federal. This with the choice of their Senators augurs well with regard to the reps. I do not find any doubt that there will be two fedts. among them, most probably three and I think very probably four. The federalism of Jersey, and its obligations and inducements to adhere to the union & a vigorous system of federal politics will be a pretty strong Security for the good Conduct of her Representatives.

1. RC, Madison Papers, DLC. Printed: Rutland, *Madison*, XI, 429–33. For other excerpts from this letter, see DHFFE, II, 397; Chapter XIII, Part Two; and Chapter XIV. Coxe (1755–1824), an ardent Federalist, was representing Pennsylvania in the Confederation Congress at this time.

Candidus, Federal Gazette (Philadelphia), 27 January

To the INHABITANTS *of* NEW-JERSEY.

The time now approaches when each of you will have a right to vote for four representatives for this state in the great federal legislature. As the interest of each individual, when combined, makes the joint interest of the society or government at large, so it becomes the duty of every member of the community to speak freely on a subject so interesting to all. By a candid communication with one another, the channels of information will be opened, and thereby persons properly qualified may be more generally agreed upon.—Such men as will be best calculated to answer the great purposes for which they will be elected.

I utterly disclaim, as I believe I ever shall, all party views and designs, and I hope my fellow-citizens, especially on such great national points, will not suffer them to enter their minds.—Let us away with them—They are generally intended more to serve and promote the interest of individuals, than the public weal. Let us with candour and seriousness enquire, what are the principal and most necessary qualifications for our representatives, and then with equal candour and freedom from prejudice, let us fix upon four men out of those in nomination, who are generally allowed to possess those qualifications in the greatest perfection.

First then, I look upon *integrity and virtue* to be the best foundation for a good character:—built upon the rock, storms and tempests may assail; but they can never destroy it. These principles are always the same, invariable and consistent, and will shew their good effects in public, as well as private life. Under their influence, men cannot consent to act contrary to what they sincerely believe to be right:—They cannot, for the sake of *popularity*, go into measures, which they *know* to be injurious to the true interests of society:—They will always act agreeably to their judgments, and the dictates of a good conscience, let the consequence be what it may. Our representatives should not only be professors of religion and virtue, but persons of exemplary lives and conduct.—These men will not seek popularity, but wait till popularity seeks them.

Secondly, our representatives should have *sufficient abilities* to carry them through so important and difficult a task with honour and advantage to the state; and let me tell you, my countrymen, common abilities will not be found sufficient. The work of the new government is but begun:—the plan[1] given to us by the late convention at Philadelphia, is but the outline of what we have to fill up:—a number of intermediate supports are absolutely necessary to be placed with great skill and judgment, in order to keep firm, the general frame of this extensive building, or it will totter over our heads, and may possibly crush us by its fall.

Our representatives, in order to be useful, should have extensive information, and be well acquainted with the different interests of the different states, and should have a general knowledge of the laws of the land; for this reason, one of the counties of Pennsylvania (Northumberland) acted very wisely, when in their instructions to their deputies, who were to recommend proper persons to represent that state in the lower house of the new Congress, they required them to endeavour to get an eminent law-character as one, knowing that more laws would originate in the House of Representatives than in Senate, and that in framing laws legal knowledge is necessary;[2] otherwise the interest of the state might be lost for want of knowledge in drafting those laws, and being fully apprised of the extent and import of legal phrases. Our legislature has put one of this class into the senate,[3] I trust the People will shew themselves equally prudent by putting one into the House of Representatives, where they will be most wanted. Our representatives should also be well versed in the laws of nations, in the history and progress of society and government; otherwise they will be liable to be deceived and decoyed by artful, unprincipled men, or antifederal states, with false quotations from history; and examples and precedents may be palmed upon them, for particular purposes, without detection, although those facts were never recorded in history.

In the third place, I believe there are very few *good citizens of this state* who will deny, that our representatives ought to be *federal men*; that is to say, favourers of the new government. It is to be feared, that there are some among us so perverse, that, from an affectation of cunning, and seeing farther than other people, become blind to the real interest of New-Jersey; and that have, from the beginning, and will continue, either openly or secretly, to oppose the carrying into effect the plan offered to us by the patriots of America. The limits of a newspaper essay will not suffer me to go into the numerous advantages of it to this state; it will, for the present, be sufficient for us, who have, in some degree, felt the burden of taxes, to recollect, that we have long been tributary to the great commercial cities of New-York and Philadelphia, by paying to their merchants at the rate of 40,000£ a year, duties on merchandize brought from thence into this state. We shall now equally partake, with those cities, of the benefit of all duties or imposts on merchandize imported; for those duties being paid forward into the continental treasury, New-Jersey will be entitled to its proportionate part, which will very much lessen the taxes of the good people of this state; after having our breath almost squeezed out of our body, by two such great weights, pressing hard against our sides, we shall be enabled by this timely relief, to draw up our elbows, and once more to breathe with ease. Besides it appears to me one of the most absurd things in the world, that in order to try the strength and goodness of the wheels of government, we should *hire* men to clog those wheels, and throw such obstacles in their way as would prevent their moving at all. What should we think of a neighbour, who having ordered a new pair of shoes, would, when finished, say to the maker of them, "here take these shoes again, alter them and I will pay you for the alteration." "What sir! before you have tried them on? how is it possible you should know whether they will pinch you?" ["]Never mind that, I choose it should be done." Should we suppose that this man had any just pretensions either to reason or common sense, certainly not. We, at great expence, sent our first characters, to frame this governmental machine, we ought to be satisfied with their work, and not tear it to pieces again before trial—this would be childrens play indeed. The people at large are always the best judges of the operation of a government, for they judge by their *feelings*; while we know ourselves freemen, we can never be such ideots, as to feel without speaking—when a majority of the community speak, our legislatures have never, nor will they ever, think it prudent not to listen to the general voice—when two thirds of our legislatures, or Congress think proper to recommend another general convention for the purpose of altering the constitution, that very constitution says, it must and will be done:[4] therefore at any rate there is no necessity of urging this business; and it is cruel at the present time, that the peace of the United States should be endangered by restless spirits, some of whom would best answer their ends, by introducing anarchy and confusion among us.

In the last place, our representatives should be men of such *property* as to put them above making their daily wages in Congress an object of interest and profit. They should also be men of considerable landed property. Agriculture ought to be the first, as it is the most useful object of these United States. While we have hands to till our farms, they will with the blessing of Providence, produce us the staple articles of our own consumption as well as of exportation. The cultivation of our grounds ought therefore to be encouraged, and the land not too much burdened with taxes. If therefore we send men of landed property to Congress, whether they should be tradesmen, merchants, lawyers or divines, as interest binds more or less all men, the general farming interest cannot be forgotten; for when a land tax is laid, it must be a general one, so that when they tax your farm or mine, they must tax their own in an equal proportion.

I will conclude with a few general remarks. It must appear to all who will read the new constitution that there is more real necessity for sending men of great abilities to the house of representatives than to the senate: because in senate, the states stand on level ground, each state has an equal voice; but it is far otherwise in the house of representatives. Observe the difference—Delaware state is entitled to *one* only, the state of New-Hampshire to three, and New-Jersey to four; but Pennsylvania has a right to eight votes in that house, Massachusetts to eight, and Virginia to ten. Here the large states will have great advantage over the smaller ones. The small states should therefore be wise enough to pick out men of great abilities to guard their interest, and of such property as will be a safe-guard against bribery and corruption, should any be attempted. For the honor and interest of society, in such important concerns, let us reflect seriously, and act with openness and candour—let us not suffer our passions or resentments, private or hostile, or narrow and illiberal prejudices against any particular trade, calling or profession to run away with our judgments, or draw a cloud over men of real integrity and abilities, in whatever part of the state they may be found. Their interest is ours, and one cannot be affected without the other: if we cannot trust such men, we are in a desperate condition indeed: for there is nothing in this world besides, worth trusting.

I am a native, and have long been an inhabitant of this state, and confess I have, as well as the most of my family and connections preferred the life of the independent and industrious farmers, and I believe, they have as much honesty and integrity as any class of people whatever; but God forbid that I should possess a temper of mind so unchristian-like and wanting in toleration, as to suppose, that we farmers alone are blessed with such qualities, and that any other classes of men in society are excluded from them! I have a great veneration for honesty and honest men, but if I wish or expect to be well served in great and difficult affairs, I must employ men of ability as well as honesty; otherwise my business will inevitably suffer: not for want of honest intentions, but for want of knowledge and information. It is very well to have men of judgment for our representatives, but it is better to have men of judgement with *speaking* abilities too, otherwise we shall not hear much of their judgment, except on taking a vote, we shall find AY or NO tacked to their names. If the men we should send, should not be able to take part in the important and frequent debates of the nation, but sit in *awful silence for the question*, I do not see how they can with propriety be called our representatives, unless we acknowledge ourselves to be a *dumb* people. No! no! as we must send representatives to Congress and support them there, let us have *real services for our money*, none of your *nothings* for *somethings*.

Let us send some men however out of the four, who, when the expected antifederal motion for another expensive general convention to alter the constitution, is made:—when the interest of the great states is strongly opposed to the small, or when the interest of New-Jersey is particularly in danger, can rise, and from their extensive information and general knowledge, oppose with success the torrent of antifederal eloquence, which will be poured from several quarters of the house.

Now, my friends, if you join with me in thinking the qualifications mentioned, necessary; read over and over the list of nomination for this state lately published, and see which men, out of those, who will consent to serve, will best answer the foregoing description.—As it cannot be supposed that all the electors are personally acquainted with the four men, who ought to be chosen, we must in such cases take the information and opinion of men of known veracity and good character, who are better acquainted with them.

Thus I solemnly and sincerely think; and having now communicated my thoughts to my fellow-citizens, which right I enjoy in common with all, I shall hope my freedom of expression will not offend any man, as I can with a good conscience say, that if any thing is illy expressed, *it is well meant.*

CANDIDUS.

State of New-Jersey, January 20th, 1789.[5]

1. The *Federal Gazette* printed "place"; the *New Jersey Journal,* which reprinted the entire article on 28 January 1789, corrected it to "plan."

2. See Instructions to the Northumberland County Delegates, 16 October 1788, DHFFE, I, 314–15.

3. William Paterson.

4. Article V of the Constitution gives Congress the right to propose amendments to the states for ratification, but Congress cannot call a convention on its own initiative. If two-thirds of the states apply to Congress, it must call a convention.

5. This article was also printed in the *Brunswick Gazette* on 27 January 1789, but the only extant copy of the *Gazette* for that date is badly mutilated. The article was reprinted in the *New Jersey Journal,* 28 January. For a reply and a suggestion that "Candidus" might be Elias Boudinot, see "A Candid Enquirer," *New Jersey Journal,* 11 February, below.

Index, New Jersey Journal (Elizabethtown), 28 January

Mr. Kollock,

In my travels thro' the Jerseys, I have met with many persons who censure the conduct of *one* of their late delegates to congress for attempting to surrender (as they say) to the Spaniards the claim which the United States have to the navigation of the Mississippi river.[1] As I happen to be some what acquainted with that transaction, I beg leave, thro' the medium of your paper, to state the outlines of it, in order to do justice to that gentleman.

The Spanish Monarch, by his minister Mr. Gaurdoque, proposed to congress a treaty of amity and commerce on certain terms of great advantage to the United States, particularly to the northern and eastern parts of it; such as opening their ports in Spain for the reception of all the produce of the United States, (tobacco indigo, and rice excepted) under such duties and regulations as congress should think proper to name; but at the same time claimed the sole and exclusive right to the navigation of the Mississippi, and also an extension of territorial boundaries differing from those contained in the definitive treaty with Great Britain: To which congress, as I am informed, proposed to forbear navigating the Mississippi from latitude 31° to the ocean, for 15 or 20 years, on the following conditions, viz. That new Orleans should be made a free port for all vessels belonging to the United States, to export from thence, to any part of the world, the produce of their western territories; that the vessels navigating the Ohio and Mississippi to new Orleans, should return with such articles only as far as latitude 31°, as the Spanish government should permit; but from thence upwards the right to a free navigation should remain with the United States. These Sir, are the out lines of that business; which, in my opinion, are very far from a relinquishment of any rights belonging to the United States, or such as deserve censure; nothing surely could be intended by Congress, but a forbearance to exercise a certain right for a short period of time, for very valuable considerations, and thereby, at the same time, strengthening the claim of the United States to that right by implication: How this business came to be so much misrepresented in New-Jersey, or why the vote of one of their late delegates should be so highly censured, appears misterious, when it is well known that every gentleman then in Congress, from New-Hampshire to Maryland, (except one) voted repeatedly for the measure; and many of them men who are held in the highest estimation for their virtue, and political knowledge; men whose abilities do honor to their country.—Here would I stop, did not duty urge me to proceed; and I sincerely wish I could without wounding the feelings of any person, by interpreting the defamation of so respectable a character, to have originated from misinformation; but when I reflect upon his being personally singled out, and the odious colours in which this affair has been represented, I cannot account for it on any other principle than that of attempting to injure his reputation amongst his fellow citizens, at a time when he is in nomination as a candidate for the ensuing election.

Had this affair been represented in its proper light, which is too lengthy for my pen at present, so far would it have been from defaming his character, that it would have heightened the esteem of his fellow citizens, and operated powerfully in his favor with the wise and thinking part of the people.

INDEX.

January 26, 1789.[2]

1. "Index" is probably referring to Lambert Cadwalader, who was on the Junto ticket. Cadwalader and Josiah Hornblower represented New Jersey in Congress in late August 1786 when Congress voted on the Jay-Gardoqui treaty negotiations. Both voted consistently with the northern (or "eastern") states to alter Jay's instructions, i.e., they voted to accept commercial advantages offered by Spain in exchange for Spain's control over the lower Mississippi River for a specified number of years. Abraham Clark and Jonathan Dayton led the movement in New Jersey to overturn Hornblower's and Cadwalader's votes (JCC, XXXI, 565–70, 574–607, 610–13; McCormick, *Experiment*, 227–29, 292).

2. This article was reprinted in the Philadelphia *Independent Gazetteer*, 17 February 1789.

A Friend to New Jersey, c. 1 February[1]

TAKE CARE!!!

BY an Act of the Legislature, passed at Princeton, intituled, "An Act for carrying into effect on the part of the State of New-Jersey the constitution of the United States, assented to, ratified and confirmed by this State, on the eighteenth day of December, in the year of our Lord one thousand seven hundred and eighty-seven,"

The power of choosing Senators to represent this State in general Congress, is given to the Legislature of this State in joint-meeting assembled;—

The power of choosing Electors, to choose a President and Vice-President, is given to the Governor and Legislative Council;—

And the nomination and election of Representatives is given to the Inhabitants at large;—

From which it appears to have been the intent of the Legislature, that there should be three distinct powers, to complete the important trust delegated to the whole.

The two first have been executed, I conclude, to the satisfaction of the people—but I am sorry to say, some undue means seem to have been contrived, and prepared to be carried into execution, that are likely to defeat the intention of the Legislature as to the last.

It is not denied that the members of the General Assembly, or most of them, had frequent meetings to agree on a Ticket to be recommended to their constituents, the most proper for their choice, which was at length done, and *Elias Boudinot, Lambert Cadwallader, Thomas Sinnickson and James Schureman, Esqrs.* were the men,—which ticket the greatest pains have been taken in the western counties, to establish immediately after the adjournment of the Legislature; and I am told many of the most respectable citizens of Trenton, having entered into the combination have signed a writing, in which they pledge themselves each to the other to support the ticket with all the interest they can make, fearing that some of the electors who were disposed to do it, might be induced to give their votes to some person more eligible, that might appear in nomination agreeably to the law of the State, if not thus bound to prevent it.

There is no doubt but every elector in the State had a right to nominate four candidates as representatives, but the importance of this election requires, that the public should be informed who were the candidates, in the mode directed by the law, that every citizen entitled to a vote might be prepared to give it with candor and uninfluenced. But when a number of the Assembly that had given to the different branches of the Legislature distinct powers, enter into a cabal purposely to defeat the only priviledge left to the people at large, endeavouring to enforce by a premature publication, a ticket of their own framing, by printing and distributing it before the publication of the general nomination—and when the inhabitants of one town in the State, who have for several years past assumed to themselves a kind of superiority over all other places, and as is well known have frequently intruded in the direction of publick matters, have pledged themselves as above related, to support that ticket, which must appear to every person of candor to be quite out of rule, however eligible the worthy gentlemen in nomination may be, or however ignorant either of them were of the measure; I must confess it appears to me the contrivers and prosecutors of it have something more in view than the public good; and it is from this sentiment that I think proper to communicate it to the citizens at large that they may guard against its effects.

As a proof that this measure has prevented many electors from giving their suffrages to candidates they would have preferred, I insert a paragraph of a letter from a gentleman in Burlington of the first consequence there, to his friend in East-Jersey, dated Jan. 22, 1789, before the general nomination was published;—

"*I KNOW nobody in Jersey that I would give my vote for as a representative in Congress with more pleasure than yourself; and I believe that others as well as myself would have done any thing you could have asked to support the ticket, but you are certainly too late for any thing at present, for at the conclusion of the late assembly a ticket was fixed in a private way by the members of both Council and Assembly, to support which we have made use of all the means in our power in all the counties in the western division.* —— —— —— —— —— *all have endeavoured to instill the principle of unanimity, and I really believe the matter to be fixed beyond recall.*"

With a jealousy becoming a freeman of the State, and tenacious of the inestimable priviledges I share in common with my fellow-citizens, I have pointed out what appears to me to have a tendency to destroy the freedom of election, which every citizen ought to hold sacred, more particularly at a time when we have before us the most important one to the state as well as the nation, that ever was held in New-Jersey, and on which our consequence, and perhaps existence as a nation greatly depend. How far it ought to operate on the minds of the electors is submitted to their own consideration by

A FRIEND *to* NEW-JERSEY.

1. Broadside Collection, Rare Book Room, DLC. James Parker apparently wrote this broadside (see Richard Stockton to Elias Boudinot, 20 February 1789, below). The broadside is undated; from internal evidence it probably circulated about 1 February.

Joseph Bloomfield to Jonathan Dayton, Burlington, 7 February[1]

I returned last evening from Monmouth Court of Oyer & Terminer &c. where I had been near a fortnight—I found in my office Your Letter of 22d. last—Your favour of 24 Decr.[2] I received on 8. Jan.—on the 10th Janry, I told Capt. Ogden,[3] that if You had any thing to communicate with respect to the ensuing election, I should be glad to see You on 12 (Monday) at my Fathers, where I should not continue, *but two days*, as I left Mrs. Bloomfield confined to her room and nothing but my Fathers low state of health induced me to visit Woodbridge—after this, You may well suppose, I was much surprized, to find by Your last letter, that You had "waited three days in ElizTown expecting to see me".—

As to the subject of Your Letters—I have just had a consultation with our Friend Norcross,[4] who has been more in the county lately, & had opportunity of better information than myself—He says, the Junto-Ticket (Boudinot, Schuurman, Cadwallader & Sinnicksen) is universally adopted, from what He can learn throughout all West-Jersey, some few Army-Friends, and over whom they have influence, excepted, & who are determined to run Cap. Dayton instead of Cadwalader. We find also, *upon due consideration*, that the least opposition & stir we make the better, as it may throw the Zealous Advocates of the Junto-Ticket, off their guard; and if so, there will not be so much pains taken, as there otherwise will be, to turn out the Quaquers, to oppose the Presbyterian plan (as they term it) to run in Clark, Dayton, Witherspoon & Henderson—But, *we shall act as matters appear, at the time of Election.*

Norcross is proposed for an Inspector, and we mean, if possible, to prevent the Poll being moved from this City—if we succeed in this, we shall gain a great point—You will have many Votes in Monmouth, but I find the Western-Ticket has travelled among the Knotty Quaquers settled in Shrewsbury, & who, as a Society, I am afraid will adopt it too generally—

Every Voter must be turned out to the Eastward, or else, the Western-Ticket will succeed—I have great hope of the success of Your Election, in the cleverness (if I may use the expression) the Eastern Yeomenry have always shewn in their general attendance at Elections, & in the Stiff-necked-backwardness (if allowed the expression) in turning out of our Quaquers in W. Jersey, & who are ⅞th. of the Body of the People Cumberland & Cape May excepted—

I some times wish, I had let my name run as it would have taken votes from Cadwallader—You have a long scroll thrown together in haste, & which, I shall send over to the Post-office in Bristol, & hope Bessenet will take more care of it than He did Your last to me.

1. RC, Ely Collection, NjHi. The letter was addressed to Dayton in Elizabethtown.

2. Dayton to Bloomfield, 24 December 1788, Part Four. Dayton's letter of 22 January 1789 has not been located.

3. Probably Aaron Ogden (1756–1839), an Elizabethtown lawyer, younger brother of Robert and Matthias Ogden, and son-in-law of John Chetwood. He was clerk of Essex County, 1785–1803.

4. William Norcross (d. c. 1804), a Burlington merchant, had served with Bloomfield and Dayton in the Third New Jersey Regiment of the Continental Army.

Franklin Davenport to Ebenezer Elmer, 9 February[1]

Our Mutual friend Mr Laurence[2] sent me a Letter of which the inclosed is a Copy—It is provoking to think, that the friend[s] of Cap Dayton, will take in any Character, however Obnoxious or however illy qualified, to answer their purposes—their cry I suppose is, Any body *with* Dayton—ours is any body *but* Clark—the best means must be made use of to keep out the last man—these are, an Union in one set of men & indefatigable Exertions, to make the people turn out—our Ticket is the Princeton one, as it is called; altho' we do not altogether approve of it, yet it has got such a head now, & no one of the Characters bad—we unite, to keep out a worse Representation—we must give up a Little—three out of the four are clever, & if by uniting & voting for the whole we get our choice as to three we do well indeed—Do my dear sir, stir up, let no stone be unturned to answer the good federal Western purpose—they boast to the East we shall have no Western Representation—for we are a *little* divided, & *very* lukewarm—too true as yet—but let us disappoint them—let us by one more glorious Effort, place it in our power, to boast to future Ages, that West Jersey the Virtuous few of the West, have fixed the whole State upon a footing with the most federal in the Union—

1. RC, Gratz Collection, PHi. Elmer (1752–1843), a Bridgeton physician and younger brother of Jonathan Elmer, held many Cumberland County offices after the Revolution, including judge of the Court of Common Pleas, justice of the peace, county clerk, county collector, and surrogate. He also served in the Assembly, 1789–1791, 1793–1795, 1817, and 1819; in the Council, 1807; and in the House of Representatives, 1801–1807.

2. Probably John Lawrence.

A Citizen of New Jersey, Brunswick Gazette, 10 February

To the respectable INHABITANTS
of NEW-JERSEY.
No. 1.

A wise man, it is said, was asked what was the easiest and what was the hardest thing in the world; to which he replied, that it was the easiest thing in the world to give advice, and the hardest to take it. As our election for choosing representatives to serve under the new federal constitution is at hand, and advice is so easily given, I shall point out a few of those qualifications which I think we ought to look for in those gentlemen who are nominated before we give them our votes on this occasion. But I am afraid many people act in the choice of representatives as a great part of mankind do in choosing wives, that is, either to be entirely governed by interested motives, or first fix their fancy upon the object, and then, in their imaginations, clothe them with every necessary qualification, though they may be possessed of but very few of them. Yet, although the bulk of mankind are governed by indirect motives in almost all they do, there are still a few who wish to act uprightly, for the sake of which, I shall mark down the few following qualifications, some of which are more, and some less essentially necessary, in order to their being useful members of that branch of the federal legislature.

1st. Every wise and good man will allow, that integrity, with a fair and unexceptionable moral character, are absolutely necessary qualifications in the men we make choice of. Enquire also whether the men for whom your votes are solicited are good members of society at home—whether they do, by paying a decent regard to the duties of religion, shew to the world that they believe the divine authority of the scriptures and the truth of revealed religion—whether they attend any place of public worship, or give any of their property to support or propagate religion.

It would be absurd to trust our interests in this world with men who do not believe in the next.—Human laws are often found slender ties even upon the makers of them when they have no conscientious principles to restrain them from injuring us. What a baleful influence must it have upon the morals of the people, should their rulers, instead of attending divine worship on the sabbath, make it their day of amusements—of dining out with their friends and spend the afternoon of it over the bottle, perhaps, in ridiculing that religion of which they ought to be the ornaments and support.

2d. Let the men we choose be such as have shewn by their conduct in the late war that they are firmly attached to the revolution.—With all due deference to the superior judgment of our worthy Governor respecting the sermon at York-Town converting the tories: I rather think that the introduction at Trenton but alarmed them.—The opening up of the doctrinal part at Saratoga threw them into terrors of conscience, and the powerful application at York-Town, laid them under deep convictions, which produced only an external reformation, for I much doubt their being yet true converts, and therefore would not trust them.

3d. The men we choose ought also to be federalists—every person must see the impropriety, especially in a state that adopted the constitution unanimously, of choosing those to direct the execution of a government, the erection of which they were in principle opposed to.

4th. By all means choose men of education to represent you, at least be assured that they are good English scholars: What a miserable figure must *even* a man of good natural sense make in that house who can neither write nor speak the English language with any degree of propriety.

5th. They ought also to be men of some reading—men acquainted with history both ancient and modern—men who have some knowledge of the sciences, and sensible of the necessity and advantage of trade and commerce to a nation, in order to [stimulate] its growth in power and opulence.

6th. They ought to be men of clear estates, not involved in debt or embarassed in their circumstances; creditors often operate on the fears of their debtors, and lead them into their undue measures; besides it would be the height of injustice to a creditor to give his debtor a protection against him for the term those men are chosen for.

7th. Men of great fortunes, unless they have given evident proofs of their patriotism, are improper to be chosen. There are certain degrees of wealth that sets men in their own esteem so far above the commonality that they can hardly consider themselves of the same species, and renders them insensible to the feelings of the poor.

8th. Endeavor to get men who have had some acquaintance with legislative business. Men generally serve a number of years in order to acquaint themselves with trade, or some branch of mechanical business, and we have no reason to suppose they are born legislators.

9th. Unless necessity obliges us we should not choose men, who, to serve us, must sacrifice the incomes of a lucrative profession at home; such, of course will expect a reward adequate to the sacrifice they make; and men of œconomy, in easy circumstances, who have but little business on their hands, and of middling abilities, will be likely to serve us as well and at a more moderate rate than the other class, though their abilities be more shining. And I am very much mistaken if we do not find the new government sufficiently expensive without giving high wages to the legislators.

10th. I am not very fond of choosing young men for legislators, although I know that wisdom is not tied to grey hairs, and that "In hoary youth Mathusalems may die," yet I believe every judicious man will grant that age crowned with wisdom and experience is safer to confide in than giddy inexperienced youth. The constitution has wisely provided against those under twenty-five serving, and I should have no objection to their being twice that age.

11th. By all means choose men of resolution and firmness—men who will be proof against the droppings of the bottle, treats and entertainments; those things are often found useful engines in carrying points with legislators, and they are more peculiarly exposed to those temptations when they sit in large cities.

12th. We should make it a point to vote for men whose estates lay principally within this state, and not to vote for those who to appearance are very busy making interest for themselves.

I am, Gentlemen of this State,
Your sincere Friend, and
A CITIZEN *of* NEW-JERSEY.

A Citizen of New Jersey, Brunswick Gazette, 10 February

No. 2.

When I undertook to point out to my fellow-citizens the qualifications that should entitle men to our votes in the ensuing election, I did not know that my name would be in the nomination; but finding that to be the case, it is but a piece of justice, due, both to myself and the public, though it may cost me some mortification to review what I have written, and endeavor to judge impartially from the marks I have laid down, whether I have any right to suffer my name to continue in that list or not; and

1st. As to my integrity and moral character, delicacy forbids that I should say any thing about them. I have lived twenty-seven years in the county in which I now reside, and of course my neighbours will be the best judges of those. But I acknowledge I am one of those unfashionable people who believe in divine revelation, and in a future state of rewards and punishments.

2d & 3d. As to my being a whig and a federalist, I believe there is little reason to doubt of either.—I served in every convention that was held in the state before the government was organized, and some years in the assembly after, and went very fully into the most spirited measures that were taken in opposition to Britain. I generally accepted offices to serve both in the field and cabinet when they were likely to lead to the gibbet and the halter, but have been less anxious about them since than many who were scarcely known in the war, but whom the sunshine of peace have since warmed into political existence.

4th. In the next place comes education, and I am afraid I shall not stand the test on that head. I am what people call a good English scholar, and when I was a lad I attempted the languages, but through a derangement in my finances, and a bodily indisposition that I was taken with at that time, I was obliged to give over the pursuit.

5th. As to reading and an acquaintance with the sciences, trade, &c. I have read but little law and less on physick; I have read the Grecian, Roman, and English histories; some authors upon Geography, natural and moral Philosophy, but as to Astronomy I know nothing about it. I have often seen what they call the north star, or pole, and they tell me there is one they call the south pole, but I have never seen it. As to the planets, whether they are inhabited or not I cannot tell. If they are, they are not within the jurisdiction of the federal government, and as to treaties of commerce with them, since the balloon business is laid aside, they are entirely out of the question; but should that business be revived, our credit is at so low an ebb that I doubt whether our bills would pass better there than they have of late in some other places, *even tho' they were indorsed by the Pennsylvania Senator.*[1] With respect to trade and commerce, I have never had any other knowledge of them than by keeping a little store in the country, by which I obtained a comfortable subsistence for some years; but I have read in the story books, as 'Squire Western would call them, how that old and new Tyre, Alexandria, Carthage, Britain and Holland, have rose to power and greatness through that means, and I believe the gold and silver would not have been so plenty in Jerusalem in Solomon's time, nor would he have had so many pretty things to shew the Queen of Sheba when she came to see him, had it not been for the profitable traffic that he carried on with Ezion Gober, Tharsis, and other places in the East-Indies; and I make no doubt but North-America has as many valuable materials for trade as any country, upon the globe, but how to improve them best for that purpose R----t M----s[2] will be much better able to tell Congress than I am.

As to the remaining qualifications, I think I have a pretty just claim to each of them, but unfortunately they happen to be of the less important kind, so that upon the whole I believe I had better decline standing as a candidate in the ensuing election, but I hate to be alone, and as there are a goodly number of gentlemen in nomination with me, who may with great propriety join in declining, I should be very glad of their company.

I am, gentlemen, your very
Humble servant,
A CITIZEN *of* NEW-JERSEY.

1. Robert Morris, elected United States Senator on 30 September 1788, had been the Confederation Congress' superintendent of finance from 1781 to 1784.

2. Robert Morris.

An Elector, Brunswick Gazette, 10 February

To the Electors of New-Jersey.

Friends and Countrymen,

You are in a short time to make choice of four persons to represent you in the fœderal legislature. I have therefore ventured to lay before you the few following hints for your impartial consideration.—A few years has only elapsed, since you were engaged in a revolution of government that excited the admiration and gained the applause of a whole world; by your virtuous exertions you have made a rapid progress towards founding a great empire as the basis of civil and religious liberty, and acquired that fame which in the annals of mankind will ever belong to a people who so nobly encountered all difficulties and compleated the arduous task in spite of every opposition.— You are now just entering on the stage of another revolution no less important than the one that established your independence—having for several years past experienced the want of a more energetic government than the articles of confederation could afford, in order to secure your rights, you have agreed to a plan recommended to each of the states by the federal convention—a plan which the wisdom of these rising states had led them to adopt, and grown out of that experience which we had of the weakness and inefficacy of the old; blessed with such a constitution as this, you may have it in your power to render your country one of the happiest spots on the surface of the globe—of being one of the most opulent and affluent, and of acquiring a name, the most durable and ennobling to man;—but that these advantages may be long felt and enjoyed, consider that a constitution, however favorable it may be to the liberties of the people, is nothing without it is wisely and honestly administered. The time is fast approaching when this system must begin to operate, I trust, therefore, that at the ensuing election, you will be fully convinced of the great necessity of sending such persons to the new congress as are well qualified to assist in its first operation; throw aside all party and faction; being born for liberty, unite in one common cause—*the public good.* What at any time can be more important? What can a nation be more concerned about than the choice of persons to represent them in their public councils, who are to be the makers of their laws and the guardians of their liberties? You are fully sensible that this new form of government meets with the most violent opposition in some of the states, and that the opposers are of conspicuous characters, and some of them already elected members in the new congress; no doubts therefore can remain, but that they will use their utmost exertions in postponing proceedings under the constitution, in order that a general convention may be called for the purpose of proposing amendments; they are determined not to give it a fair and impartial trial, in order that its defects may be more particularly ascertained; these efforts, if proving successful in its first operation, must inevitably terminate in anarchy and confusion. If there are such characters now offered to your choice, avoid giving them your suffrages, examine carefully and impartially, acquaint yourselves with the merits or demerits of every candidate, and obtain the best information you possibly can, who are possessed of the necessary qualifications to represent you in that august body. You must be sensible that at the present unsettled state of the country it requires men who are firm friends to this new system, and men possessed of the strictest integrity and the greatest abilities, but of the two last requisites consider the first of them as the most important, for although an honest heart may make amends for a weak understanding, yet abilities cannot supply the want of strict integrity. Let them be men who are well acquainted with the grievances of your country, the causes of them, and the means of redressing them; who possess courage and inclination to make use of their natural freedom and act for themselves, not having a slavish dependance on any particular sett of men, so as to vote contrary to their own inclination for fear of disobliging them; men who are possessed of affluence above corruption, and understanding above imposition, who, although surrounded by the inviting calls of ambition, and the fair prospect of affluence, will not countenance one single act of oppression; who can immediately discern the subtilty of an argument, although enforced with the powers of oratory, and countenanced by a servile majority, whose actions are not for the aggrandizing of individuals, but whose every effort of their abilities will be exercised to convince you that they have an anxious desire of promoting the general good of mankind, and whose voices alone are to establish the standard of justice.

You are now, my fellow-citizens, enjoying, under the smiles of indulgent heaven, many singul[ar?] advantages above the rest of mankind—you have [at?] this time formed to yourselves a government [in?] peace, while other nations found their empires [in?] blood—you enjoy more indulgence, more ease, mo[re?] security, with respect to your religion, liberty a[nd?] property, than any subjects in any country wh[ate?]ver. These are but a few of the many privil[eges?] you enjoy, flowing from a state of independe[nce;?] therefore improve them to the best advantage, [as?] in the language of an eminent poet, "*Deter*[*mined*?] *hold your Independence*, for that once destroyed, [- - -] founded, freedom is a morning dream, that [- - -] aerial from the spreading eye."[1]

An ELECTOR

February 9, 1789.

1. The right-hand margin of the newspaper is mutilated at the last paragraph of this item.

A Candid Enquirer, New Jersey Journal (Elizabethtown), 11 February

Mr. KOLLOCK,

I lately observed in your paper of January 28th, a publication signed Candidus.[1] From many circumstances not necessary to mention, this same Candidus is both the writer and person intended to be recommended for the suffrages of the people at the Election for representatives. He mentions the qualifications necessary for filling that station, such as wealth, integrity, oratory, law knowledge, &c. all these he wishes to have believed are united in himself; and in order to take in the farmers, he uses the expression, *we farmers*; but let me ask Candidus how long he has been a farmer, and considered by them as one of their number? And as to his great wealth, let me enquire where it is, and by what means he acquired it? Whether, if he has it, it was not out of the hard earnings of *we farmers?*—This wealth he supposes necessary to keep down the wages of the members, as such can be under no inducement to wish any but a very small reward for their attendance; this bait has not covered the hook. Do the wealthy usually render their services the cheapest? not in common. Has this usually been the case with Candidus? Has he rendered any services at a cheap rate? Perhaps he will say no, not while he was in low circumstances, but now he is got above a desire for wealth; no no, none will believe this. Was this the governing principle of a certain gentleman in Philadelphia, who, in a short space, before it was suspected, to the displeasure of many, drew so many thousand dollars out of the public treasury to decorate his palace, profusely furnish his table, and clatter through the streets in a chariot?[2] Let me ask this same gentleman, this WE FARMERS, who it was declared that *the common people have no business to know what their rulers do, but should submit to them in silence, and that one meal in a week of meat was sufficient for them?*—Let Candidus answer these questions truly, and he will greatly oblige,

A CANDID ENQUIRER.

1. See "Candidus," Philadelphia *Federal Gazette*, 27 January 1789, above. The article was also printed in the *New Jersey Journal*, 28 January.

2. Apparently a reference to Elias Boudinot.

New Jersey Journal (Elizabethtown), 11 February

This day commences the Election for the members to represent this state in the Federal House of Representatives, to be convened in March next.

New Jersey Journal (Elizabethtown), 11 February

O yes! O yes! O yes!

All certificate mongers! affidavit men! affirmers, &c. &c. are informed that, during the temporary reign of calumny and torturing of characters, they will meet with encouragement proportionate to their abilities and conscience. If they have the sophistical knack of misrepresentation, *and can affirm roundly, it will be an additional recommendation. Apply to the confederated junto, in the purlieus of the hustings.*[1]

1. This article was reprinted in the *Brunswick Gazette*, 17 February 1789.

Joseph Lewis Diary, 11–20 February[1]

Wednesday 11th. do. [cool] and some clouds. This day I served as one of the Clerks at our Election for representatives in the New Congress which are to meet next month.

Thursday 12th. Cold & some snow. Continued at election in Morristown.

Friday 13th. Very cold. Went to Troy to attend the election & at night lodged at Mr. Bogart's, Boonton.

Saturday 14th. Clear & cold. Continued at election at Troy then returned home at night.

Sunday 15th. Clear & cold.

Mond. 16. Cloudy and snow from 4 to 11 in morning. I rode to Roxbury to attend election; at night lodged at Mr. Fearclos's with Saml Tuthill Esqr.

Tuesday 17th. Clear & cold. Continued at election and at night returned home.

Wednesday 18th. Clear in part. Election continued at MorrisTown.

Thursday 19th. Cold. Election ended last night & we counted votes this day.

Friday 20th. do. Finished counting votes this day.

1. Tr, Joseph Lewis Diary, 1783–1795, NjHi. Printed: New Jersey Historical Society *Proceedings*, LXII (1944), 108–09. Lewis (1748–1814), of Morristown, was Morris County clerk, 1782–1787, and a judge of the county Court of Common Pleas, 1800–1805.

David Brearley to Jonathan Dayton, Trenton, 12 February[1]

I received your favor of the 9th this morning. The Election for this County commenced yesterday at Ringo's,[2] and as far as I can learn from those who were there, it appears that there is no settled plan of voting in the County.—there were vast numbers there, but without any leaders in whom they had confidence, and that the votes ran very much at random.—for Hooper and Vancleve they were nearly equal, for Cadwallader less than the others, and for Candidates out of the County—nothing fixed or certain—many voting for Mr. Clark, yourself, Doct. Witherspoon &c. To day the election is at Pennington, and to morrow it will be at this place, by which time I expect they will obtain more system. Col. Hooper has not returned from Ringo's, and from him I expect more certain information. The Old Major has not been here since I had the pleasure of seeing you.—I am surprized at his silence, nevertheless I have heard from several persons that he is very active and industrious,—Joseph Biddle[3] is likewise doing a good deal. I have seen Mr. Sam. Hugg[4] of Gloucester and find that the jarring interests of that County are very much United in favor of what they call the Assembly Ticket. Not so in Salem County, there they will divide, but how they will run in Cumberland I have not been able to learn.

I have heard that Mr. Combs[5] has behaved, respecting you, very improperly, but I was never in his company and therefore it is only hearsay, and I am inclined to believe that two or three people here, are endeavoring to make the most of it, in order to serve electioneering purposes.[6]

1. RC, Fogg Autograph Collection, MeHi.

2. Ringo's, a tavern located northeast of Lambertville, Hunterdon County, was an important political meeting place during the Revolutionary War era (Charles S. Boyer, *Old Inns and Taverns in West Jersey* [Camden, N.J., 1962], 205–07).

3. Biddle (1739-c. 1792) represented Burlington County in the Assembly, 1779 and 1785–1790. He also was town clerk and assessor for Springfield Township in the 1780s.

4. Samuel Hugg represented Gloucester County in the Assembly, 1778, 1781–1783, and 1790.

5. Probably John Combs of Perth Amboy, who represented Middlesex County in the Assembly, 1776, 1782–1788, 1791, 1799, and 1802; he was appointed a justice of the peace in 1788.

6. Dayton was accused of illegal trading during the Revolution (see John Lawrence to Elias Boudinot, 16 February 1789, and Joseph Bloomfield to Dayton, 25 February 1789, both below).

James Kinsey to Elias Boudinot, 16 February[1]

All that Can be either done or said to induce our people to turn out does not so fully Answer the purpose as I wish So that In Burlington County I do not Expect above 1500 Votes—In the Whole of the five lower Countys I think there will Not be More than 4500 Votes or 5000 at the Most—There are few people who Vote for Dayton, in lieu of Either Cadwallader, & Schuurman[.] But I fancy You May depend on All the Votes Almost to a Man in Your faver[.] I have Not heard One person here Object to You so that I hope there's Not the least Danger of Your being one of those Returned

I do not Wonder at What You Write respecting our great Man, and I think You will not do Yourself Justice, If You do not show a proper resentment of Such Usage, I always thought it better, to have an Open yn a Secret Enemy, If All Used so woud follow this same Mode he woud Know better than to Interfere in the Elections which he ought not to do in any Case[2]

I have putt the Numbers in My first paragraph lower than in My Own Apprehension they will Turn out the Season of the Year the present Snow & Cold operate against the Increase and Yet I believe they Will Not be less[.] Surely in All the other Countys You May Reckon 1500—Supine[ne]ss Seems to have seized our people that I am Sorry to see so that I believe there is More Bustle in the Choice of a Constable than Among us on the present Occasion.

[P.S.] I have not Recd the Letter by post to this day

1. RC, Boudinot Papers, NjR. Kinsey did not note from where he was writing, but he lived in Burlington. The letter was addressed to Boudinot in Elizabethtown.

2. The "great Man" referred to here is probably Governor William Livingston. In a letter from Elias Boudinot to Livingston, c. 5 February 1789, Boudinot wrote: "After I left your Excellency yesterday, I sketched off, in a hurry, the substance of the Conversation that passed at your House the last time I dined there, and sent it to New Ark to Mr. [William Peartree] Smith, who this Morning returned it to me with his Certificate at foot.—I enclose a Copy to your Excellency, before I make it public, in hopes that you will be convinced that you wholly misapprehended me in that Conversation; and as Mr [John] Blanchard has sent me word that he will propagate the Story wherever he can, my friends have insisted on this Measure to countervail his Measures—to which I hope your Excellency will have no Objection; and if you think proper, will mention your misapprehension of the Conversation, if asked on the Subject—" (Elizabethtown, RC, William Livingston Papers, MHi).

John Lawrence to Elias Boudinot, Burlington, 16 February[1]

I last Evening reced your's by Mr: Reed and have the Pleasure to Inform you that Matters will turn Out Agreably to our most Sanguine Expectations—

Wednesday 334 Votes was taken in here. Thursday on a few hours Notice 117 was taken at Moores Town Friday 118 at the Cross Keys Saturday above 200 at Lumberton. This day they Open the Pole at Clam Town where we Count on near if not 300—Wednesday at the New Mills where we Expect the like Numbers Thursday at Penny Hill 200 Friday at Croswick's 250 Saturday at Burlington 150 at least from the remains of Chester Evesham and Burlington wch. did not come in on the first Notice—[2]

I have Attended four places and shall meet them at the New Mills Wednesday and go the Rounds—

I reced a Letter from Trenton Informing of a Combination form'd by Col. Ogden Hooper[3] and others in wch. it was Resolv'd to run Clark Dayton Hooper and Sinickson in One Ticket and give up every other Candidate in the State

I Imediately sounded the Alarm and sent off Letters to Gloucester Salem and Cumberland which with the Affair between Clark and Shotwell,[4] Dayton and Combs[5] will I Expect have their Desir'd Effect[.] my Son is One of the Clerks has also Duplicates

There is no Opposition in this County except The Attny. Genl. Doctr. Ross and a few others who are Endeavoring to serve Capt. Dayton here[6] they did not throw in above 10 Votes at Moorestown Doctr. Bloomfield and one more at the Cross keys 4 or 5—at Lumberton where they rallied the chief of their force not 20—

It will not Injure but reather Strengthen the Western Ticket as I have seen several in which no other Alteration is made but Dayton in the place of Schureman—You may Depend on the greatest Exertions and Unanimity in the Counties of Gloucester Salem, Cumberland and Cape May. As to the two other Western Counties are not so well Inform'd—

I think the Conduct of the C—k—t—s[7] in pushing the Test agst. the Quakers[8] will bring forward many here who perhaps otherwise wod have staid at home—

In all my Letters have Endeavor'd to Impress this Idea United we Stand Devided we fall—

I Wish you Success

1. RC, Emmet Collection, NN. The letter was addressed to Boudinot in Elizabethtown.

2. In the margin opposite this paragraph someone—probably Lawrence—added up the votes taken through Saturday (769) and those estimated to be taken the following week (1,200).

3. Probably Abraham Ogden and Robert L. Hooper.

4. See "A Freeholder," *Brunswick Gazette*, 10 February 1789, Part Five:III, below.

5. See David Brearley to Jonathan Dayton, 12 February, above.

6. Joseph Bloomfield was attorney general. John Ross (1752–1796), a Mount Holly physician, had served in the army with Dayton during the Revolutionary War. In August 1789 President George Washington appointed him collector of the Port of Burlington.

7. Clarkites.

8. A 1783 law required voters to take the prescribed loyalty oath to the state if they were challenged by the election officials. Many Quakers refused to take this oath. These requirements were repealed in 1788.

Walter Rutherfurd to John Stevens, Sr., New York, 16 February (excerpt)[1]

We hear from Jersey that they are very busy with the Elections which they expect will continue most of this Week. We sincerely hope your Son may succeed.

1. RC, Stevens Family Papers, NjHi.

William Bradford, Jr., to Elias Boudinot, Philadelphia, 17 February (excerpt)[1]

Last Saturday I broke away from the Court & made a forced march to Burlington where Susan & I spent two very agreeable days without stiring out of Mr. W's[2] parlour. From those who dropped in as well as from the master of the house I had an opportunity of being initiated in the politics of your state. Every body seemed to be *positively* charged with the Electioneering Spirit, & ready to communicate it on the slightest approach. I began to feel the effects of this political Electricity and to wish myself at liberty to exert it: but I *hurried* off this morning—and find the atmosphere of this city a powerful conductor of this imported Zeal.

I find that you are not exempt from the vexations which croud round the best Citizen when he first starts in the political race. From all I can learn these will only serve at a future day to encrease your reward. I was mistaken when I wrote last both as to the beginning & duration of your Elections. That in Burlington County I am informed will not be closed untill next Monday night.

The Election of General Washington and Dr. Adams seems to be ascertained. This is a great point in the circle of Events that must conspire to establish the fœderal Government.

1. RC, Wallace Papers, PHi. The letter was addressed to Boudinot in Elizabethtown.

2. Joshua Maddox Wallace. Wallace (1752–1819), Bradford's brother-in-law, was a Burlington merchant, land speculator, and lawyer. He was appointed a judge of the county Court of Common Pleas in 1784; was a member of the Burlington Common Council, 1785, 1788–1789, and 1797–1798; was a delegate to the state Convention in 1787; and was a Burlington County member of the Assembly in 1791.

New Jersey Journal (Elizabethtown), 18 February

A correspondent observes, that the Americans seem to be very jealous, even of each other; that they have an independent spirit too aspiring for their own interests, and seem to be afraid of giving up the least right of *freemen*; every man wants to have all power in his own hands, but we must learn to *unite* as of *old*; when with one hand and heart we determined to die or be *free*; let us now then unite to establish a firm basis of our political and future happiness; to establish a constitution, wherein our just rights will be secured; wherein we shall find one continued scene of uninterrupted tranquility; and let us place those men in office, who have been *tried*, as the soldier and the statesman, whose disposition and circumstances will put them above the base bribes of evil-doers.—We have already tried a constitution, in which no person has power—let us under the new constitution, resume the more pleasing themes of humanity and peace; let those who have been building castles in the air, now employ their time in disseminating all the blessings of agriculture, manufactures and commerce; let us now more nobly emulate each other, in the enlightning researches of genius, the investigation of philosophy, and the culture and perfection of the useful and elegant arts.

John Mehelm to Governor William Livingston, Readingtown, 20 February[1]

Your Excellency's favour came to hand on the first day of the Election. I was satisfied that the persons I mentioned as proper to be in the appointment for Electors would fully meet your wishes or I should not have taken that liberty. I had also some hopes that they would be agreeable to a Majority of the Council, as they had both been old Counsellors Uniform whigs, and verry respectable Characters who had suffer'd in their Country's cause. But what shall we say to these things! Mankind are the same capricious beings, we find, that they have been in every age And we may think ourselves verry happy that we are not banished from the land we had a hand in saving from Slavery as many of the good old Roman and Grecian Patriots were.

I am much oblidged to your Excellency for the Satisfaction you express in seeing my name in Nomination. It went in in a Verry late hour. A Number of the Neighbours who had frequently mentioned the Matter to me depended upon a Tavernkeeper in the Neighbourhood who appeared Verry Zealous about having me up to take in a Ticket with my name as he told them he had business at Trenton. He went down and lodged with Col. Hooper whether the Colonel's bottle had any influence in the Matter or not is altogether uncertain but he came back a thorough convert to his Interest and said nothing about me on his return and they did not find out for some time that he had Neglected sending in my Name. Docr: Scott[2] and some of my friends in Somerset had prepared a Ticket, they told me, in which my name was Included but upon frequent inquiries finding my name was not up in hunterdon concluded that I had prevented it being sent myself and did not send in theirs. Hearing those different stories put me in mind of Tom dreadnought when the Parish Officers disputed so long about the place of his birth Tom said he thought in his Soul at last that they would not let him be born any where at all. However a Gentleman in the Next Township finding how matters Stood sent his Servant on purpose, I'm informed with a Ticket in which my Name was inserted a day or two before the time for Nomination was expired. but finding so many up in our County I had thoughts of declining Immediately but was advised to omit it for some time on the probability of a Compromise taking place among the People and a Ticket being Settled for the uper Counties or at least for this County[3] but that measure failing of Success Col. Stewart and myself have both declined. but as some Counties may not have had timely Notice of our declining perhaps there may be a few Votes for us which we would wish if it be consistant with your Excellencys duty on this occassion you would omit publishing.

It is said your Excellency had the Votes of this State for the Vice presidency and I do not know whether to be pleas'd or displeas'd with it—If you were not Governor of Jersy I should heartily Acquiese in your having the Votes of the Thirteen States for that Appointment. However whether in or out of Office I believe I shall Ever be

Dr sir your Excellencys Sincere &
most obedt hbl Servt

1. RC, William Livingston Papers, MHi.
2. Moses Scott (1738–1821), a New Brunswick physician, served as a Continental Army hospital physician and surgeon, 1777–1780.
3. Hunterdon.

Richard Stockton to Elias Boudinot, 20 February[1]

I have but a moment to inform you the State of politicks as far as I can learn in this part of the State—the Western people not only adhere to their general plan but put it in Execution with spirit—In Gloster it is said they will at least make good their calculation of 1,500 votes—in Burlington they will exceed that number—they turn out well and do not expect to close till Saturday night—In Hunterdon the votes are much split—Dr Witherspoon & your self run almost unanimously the lower part of the County—It is said that Clark runs pretty strong in the upper part—In Somerset they[2] have carried all before them—I went up on Monday but found I could not even mention your name—Ludlows letter was in every body's hand and they pretended to believe it[3]—I therefore pushed as many tickets as I could with Sinnicksons name who before had been left out by all parties—Parker published a letter from west Jersey in which a friend tells him that he could not assist him because he had *engaged* to run the general ticket—he published it to raise the resentment of the people agt that plan which he was pleased to say abridged the right of voting & kept out men better qualified for the Station[4]—It had an effect in this neighbourhood—they were bent upon running Dr Witherspoon—they were to a man oposed to Clark—but there being no person to shew them the danger of the proceeding they run Witherspoon singly in a Ticket—they would not take yourself & the rest in on whom they had agreed lest you should hurt him—this was on Saturday—when I returned & pointed out how much such conduct helped Clark without rendering any essential service to the Dr they were sorry they had pursued this plan—The pole closed on tuesday night and stands as follows—Schurrman 992 Clark 899 Dayton 774—Cripps 489—Linn 244—Witherspoon 189 Sinnickson 72 Hoops 110—Parker 26—Boudinot 30—Van Cleave 19—Cadwallader 23—Mehelm 3—Stevens—19—Kitchel 2,[5]—Hornblower 3—McWorter 1—Henderson 1—Winds 1—Hooper 5—Uncle Sam[6] writes me that in Sussex Hoops had refuted the Coalition scheme—but that Thomson had agreed to run Cadwallader Hoops Clark & Dayton—In Monmouth you run very generally—Clark runs with one party—but they are not very strong—from this State it appears to be a matter of great doubt who will be the third & fourth Man—

I look upon your Election as secure—the controversy lies between Western & Eastern candidates—pray send me a State of the poles to the Eastward as I am anxious to see how it ended—I will send the accounts from the lower Counties if I can get them before they are published—Let me know how the Injunction business ended—if you did not succeed pray enter the necessary rules for bringing it to the most speedy hearing—delay is all they want—we are all *stirring* at both houses and desire to be kindly remembered to all friends

1. RC, Boudinot Correspondence on Deposit from the American Bible Society, NjP. Stockton did not note from where he was writing, but he lived near Princeton. The letter, written in the morning, was addressed to Boudinot in Elizabethtown. Stockton (1764–1828), a nephew of Elias and Elisha Boudinot and Samuel W. Stockton, was at this time selling land warrants as an agent for John Cleves Symmes's Miami Purchase. He was a graduate of the College of New Jersey (Princeton) and studied law in Newark with Elisha Boudinot. He was admitted to the state bar in 1784 and practiced law in Princeton.

2. Supporters of Abraham Clark and Jonathan Dayton.

3. This is possibly a reference to Israel Ludlow (c. 1766–1804), a Morris County resident before 1789 and a friend of Jonathan Dayton. Ludlow was appointed a surveyor in Symmes's Miami Purchase in 1787 and moved to the site of Cincinnati, Ohio, in September 1788. No "letter" of Ludlow's has been located.

4. See "A Friend to New Jersey," c. 1 February 1789, above.

5. Both Aaron and Abraham Kitchel received votes for Representative.

6. Probably Stockton's uncle, Samuel W. Stockton.

Joseph Bloomfield to Jonathan Dayton, Bristol, Pennsylvania, 25 February[1]

I have been confined some days to this place, and like to continue here attending Dr. McIlvaine,[2] who has been, & now is, dangerously ill with the [Gout?], in his head—which has prevented my taking that active part I wished to have done in the election.

I was over last Evening in Burlington, & found enclosed from our Friend Ross,[3] and to my surprize the election still open & adjourned to Crosswicks the second time, where it is to be holden this day,—Tomorrow, it is to be opened the second time, at Moores-Town—on Friday, return again to Burlington and be closed on Saturday.—It was the first resolution of the Inspectors to have closed, as of Saturday last but an express (as I am informed) from Eliz. Town, brought by Wm. Griffith,[4] accompanied by Rd. Stockton, Esqr. of Princeton, occasioned the last maneuvre—Griffith & Stockton went on to Woodbury in Gloucester, where they intended to close the Poll on Monday, but I hear, it is again to travel over that County. the advocates for the Assembly Ticket (as they call it) say, they now have an accurate state of the Polls in all the Counties, Eastward of ~~Trenton~~ Burlington, except Essex, where they count upon 2500 for Clarke & same number for your self, & are determined to regulate their conduct, so as to exceed Your numbers.—the Bell-Weathers of Cadwallader & Boudinot are riding night & Day for this purpose—

Every thing they can possibly invent is detailed out against Mr. Clark & Yrself—besides what is mentioned in Ross's Letter—the old story of Combs[5] is brought up and told with aggravated circumstances, particularly that a Bill in Chancery, is filed agt. You to disclose the illicit-fraudulent London trade in this business &c. I waited on Mr. Kinsey,[6] early in the election & inquired whether He had filed a Bill—He said He had not, but that application was made to him by Combes for this purpose, and He intended to draw same, soon as his business will admit—that Comb's state of facts if supported, would without doubt procure the desired relief &c &c &c.

Notwithstanding the exertions intended to be made, I believe the rigid Quaquers will not turn out—those that usually Vote, & are called ranting-Quaquers, have generally given their suffrages—there was 1802 Votes in the Burlington Box last Evening—there will not be above 200 or 250 Votes more obtained, and tis supposed that Gloucester will take in about as many; Salem Cumberland & Cape May are calculated at 2000 more so as to make about 6,000 in these 5 Counties, of which (the Junto say,) 5000 at least will be for the *Federal* Ticket & give all four a majority—Thus I have given You the Politicks in this section of the state—I wish the Account could be more favorable—If Your Essex-Election is not closed You must turn out 3000 Votes, or I fear we shall not succeed in our wishes—Had the Polls in this County[7] & Gloucester closed as first intended, there would not have remained a doubt of Mr. Clarks & Your Election, as there would not have been more than 3,000 Votes taken in this & Gloucester County. You should have written Your Friends in this quarter every intelligence in Your power, & that daily—Boudinot has kept a daily correspondence with Wallace, Lawrence, Ellis Davenport &c.[8] it would have given Life & Spirits to those who were sailing against Wind & Tide & a violent fresh bearing all before it.

Ross, Coxe's Major & Col.[9] Norcross & Myself are the only Persons who advocated Your Election in this County—I am afraid less has been done by Hunter in Gloucester—& altho' Cripps divided Sinnickson's Interest in Salem, Yet Cadwallader & Boudinot have generally run in that County, as I have heard—If You have more Votes to the Eastward of Burlington than Clark, I have still good hopes of Your Election as Sinnickson, polls far short of Boudinot & Cadwallader—Boudinots Friends see this, and are now running Boudinot instead of Cadwallader & Sinnickson, in hopes of bringing in Boudinot—and Cadwalladers Friends do the same to the exclusion of Boudinot—this also gives Your Friends fresh hopes of Success, I wish we may not be disappointed.

[Endorsements][10]

We have Red the above Letter and it appears to be a true state of what has happen'd[.] keep open your Pole

Arnold for himself & Marsh[11]

by all means keep open the poll in Essex Until we Return.

Danl Marsh[12]

1. RC, Gratz Collection, PHi. The letter appears to be dated 23 February, and the endorsement dates it 23 February. Yet Bloomfield wrote in the dateline, "Wednesday" (i.e., 25 February), and in his letter of 27 February to Dayton he refers to his letter of 25 February. The letter has consequently been dated 25 February.

2. William McIlvaine (1750–1806), Bloomfield's brother-in-law, practiced medicine in Philadelphia and Bucks County, Pennsylvania, and in Burlington County.

3. Dr. John Ross, of Mount Holly.

4. William Griffith (1766–1826), a lawyer, was Burlington County surrogate, 1790–1799; a member of the Assembly in 1818 and 1823; and mayor of Burlington, 1824–1826.

5. Probably John Combs, of Perth Amboy.

6. Probably James Kinsey.

7. Presumably Burlington.

8. Joshua M. Wallace, John Lawrence, Joseph Ellis, and Franklin Davenport.

9. Probably "Major" Richard Cox, Jr., and "Colonel" John Cox.

10. The two endorsements, both in handwritings different from the text of the letter, follow immediately after Bloomfield's complimentary closing.

11. Probably Jacob Arnold (1749–1827), Morris County sheriff, 1780–1783 and 1786–1789, and a member of the Assembly, 1784–1785 and 1789–1790.

12. Daniel Marsh (d. 1803), of Raway, was an Essex County justice of the peace and a Court of Common Pleas judge. He represented Essex in the Assembly, 1780, 1783, 1785–1786, 1789, and 1793, and in the Council, 1798–1800.

Robert Morris to Timothy Ford, New York, 26 February (excerpt)[1]

Election for the members of the lower house in Jersey not finished. Schureman supposed certain. Dayton & Clark probable. Boudinot, Sinexon, Cadwallader & Crips doubtful, all the rest little chance. A squabble in this State between Federals & Antis

1. FC, Robert Morris Papers, NjR. Ford (1762–1830), a native of Morristown, graduated from the College of New Jersey (Princeton) in 1782, studied law with Morris, moved to South Carolina in 1785, and was admitted to the state bar the following year.

Joseph Bloomfield to Jonathan Dayton, Burlington, 27 February[1]

Since my last of 25: currt.[2] about 230 Votes have been taken in this county—there is about 2050 Votes in our Burlington Box.—Hollinshead,[3] Norcross Ross Cox & myself were all at Moores Town Yesterday I did not return home till after one this morning[.] Col Cummings & Jona Rhea[4] & Majr. Howell[5] have had a meeting at Moores-Town—after which they all Went on to Haddonfield where the Glout. Election was opened & where it is said they expect to bring up their Poll to 2500 Ellis is indefatigable—Cummins & Rhea returned last night late & intended to reach Crosswicks—Boudinot is their object but the Hue & Cry made by them is "turn out Clarke"—"it is in the power of West Jersey & they *must do it*["]—the consequence is, I am afraid, as Mr. Clarke has more Votes to the Eastward than yourself that they will throw You both out—Sinnickson is the Man the junto are most afraid of—Can You not procure a majority of Mr. Clark?—My calculation including Salem & all the Counties to the Eastward except Essex is as follows—Clarke 4518—Dayton 3756—Cadwallader 1717—Boudinot 1614—Sinnickson 1196—In Cape May the Poll closed only 85 Votes taken—that is in your favour. Cumberland Election still open as the County Court is sitting that Week—they expect 1000 or 1200 Votes—Salem Election closed—Poll as follows, Schuureman 228—Clarke 35 Dayton 42. Boud. 631—Cad. 731—Sinnicksen 868—Cripps 741.—Glout. will strain hard to settle the Election for the junto Ticket—their Votes are unanimous for this Ticket—I hope Burln. Election will be closed this day, You shall here from me soon as the Votes are counted off—

I wish You would let me here from you after yr. Essex Election—I wish You could by some means outnumber Clarke—if You can do this I should suppose Your Election safe as Sinnicksen cannot have Clark's amount—

Please excuse haste—I have to send this scroll over the River to Bristol for this mornings Stage &c.

[P.S.] There was a plan formed on Wed. to accuse Arnold & Marsh *as Spies*—but altho *Cummings & Rhea* came into the County & passed on to Glous. & Very bussy in the Election; there was nothing said, but esteemed *as on the right Side.*[6]

1. RC, Dayton Miscellany, NjHi. The letter, written in the morning, was addressed to Dayton in Elizabethtown and was marked to be sent "By Post."

2. Printed above.

3. Probably John Hollinshead (d. 1789), who was Burlington County sheriff, 1788–1789 and possibly earlier years. However, it could also be Thomas Hollinshead, Burlington County member of the Assembly, 1792–1793.

4. Jonathan Rhea (1754–1815), a Monmouth County and Trenton lawyer, was admitted to the bar in 1784 and twice elected clerk of the Monmouth County Court of Common Pleas before moving to Trenton.

5. Richard Howell (1754–1803) represented Gloucester County in the state Convention in 1787. He moved to Trenton shortly thereafter. He was clerk of the state Supreme Court, 1788–1793, and governor, 1793–1801.

6. On a separate sheet Dayton made some calculations; among them are these tables:

Cape May	85	Cape May	60
Salem	731	Salem	731
Burlington	2100	Burlington	1800
Cumberland	1000	Gloucester	1800
Gloucester	2100	Cumberland	600
	6016		4991
7 Eastern	983	7 Eastern	990
	6999		5981
Deduct lost	999		
	6000		

Joseph Bloomfield to Jonathan Dayton, Burlington, 28 February and 1 March[1]

[28 February[2]]

In my letter of last Evening[3] (wh I sent by Stage, under cover to Saml Smith) I give a state of the Burlington-Poll & measures pursued to carry the junto-Ticket—I will mention the substance of that Letter.—

Norcross, Hollinshead and myself went to the election at Moores-Town, on our way through Mount-Holly, we sollicited the company of Ross & Cox, and who followed on, but we could do little or nothing in that quarter, Rd. S. Smith who keeps a Store in Moores-Town & of great influence having taken unweried pains to support the junto Ticket & prejudice the People against Mr. Clark & Yourself—There was a meeting of Col. Ellis, and two other leading characters from Gloucester at R. S. Smith's and the Burlington-Gentry Danl. Ellis,[4] Joshua M Wallace Danl. Newbold,[5] &c: &c. in consequence of Cummings & Jona. Rheas visit on that day into the Western-Counties—Maj. Howell of Trenton was with them—after this, we could get no intelligence of the number of Votes taken—It was given out that the Poll probably would be closed at Burlington, when at same time there was a fixed determination to travel the second time to Kellum's (called cross-Keys in Evesham) and to the New-Mills—By what I can learn their Generalissimo Col Ellis, prescribed 2500 at least, and if possible more, could they be obtained in Burlington—then returned with his chosen-Friends to Haddonfield (only 8 miles off) where the Gloucester Election was then Polling to co-operate with the Burlington-

Election at Moores-Town. Thus their measures have been concerted to support their junto-favorite-Ticket, originally the Embryo of Col. Ellis and which He is determined shall be brought forth into Life—

There was about 2295 Votes in the Box when the Poll adjourned last Evening from Burlington to Kellum's Cross-Keys.

Soon as Austin[6] arrived I had a meeting with Norcross & Hollinshead, both unwell with colds taken in their late return from Moore's-Town Thursday night—after consultation—I dispatched one of my Clerks[7] to Woodbury—and Hollinshead (though very unwell) set out for Mt. Holly to wait Ross's return from Kellums (Cross-Keys)—

It is now after eleven at night—Hollinshead has returned, and says, Ross informed him that about 100 or 120 votes He supposed was taken—that the Clerks pretend they have not lately numbered the votes & therefore cannot take the trouble to count them—(The Clerks are Rd. R. Smith, cozen of Rd. S. Smith a Son of John Lawrence & a Son of Dl. Ellis) the Inspectors all of the same Class, one of them Tom Hewlings,[8] who returned but very lately from Nova-Scotia.—

Ross finding that the Tickets He give out, were generally changed by those who watched for this purpose—and no Confidence to be placed in any man—He sent up for volunteers among the Workmen of Taunton-Iron-Works, and in Martial parrade led up 25 with the Proprietor Hastings[9] and who voted immediately from Ross's hand, to the no small vexation & mortification of the Inspectors & Junto-solid-compact—But all this I fear has a tendency to rouse and excite our opponents to greater opposition and industry in turning out every one without exception—and indeed, the Blind, lame, sick & even decrepid-old-age, is not suffered to be at their desired ease, at home.—In order, to induce the rigid Quaquers to turn out, who heretofore said—"They did not feel a Freedom to vote" the advocates for the junto-ticket, have raised another story, truly ridiculous indeed—Yet, serves the purpose for which it is propagated, among the uninformed weak part of this Society—"Come Friend—go to the Election and vote for the Ticket recommended by the Assembly—vote for the Fœderal Ticket—the West-Jersey Ticket—the Quaquer Ticket, recommended by Friends,—Come, turn out, oppose the Presbyterian Ticket—the Presbyterians want another War—they want another opportunity to distrain Your goods for pretended Militia-duty"—

The Peaceable Quaquer, says,—

"No, I don't feel a Freedom, Thee must excuse me, I never intend to interfere in Government-matters, it is against my Principles"—

"You don't feel a Freedom,—You will loose Your freedom, Your Liberty and Your Property,—nay more, Your Religion, if you do not;—we Church People see very clearly these Presbyters. want to rule—and, then—there will be no other Religion suffered in this Country, but Presbyterianism, the most arbitrary and tyrannic of all Religions—But, Dayton & Clarke are bloody men—are men for War—they want another War that they may make their fortunes—By distress from the Quaquers—and, if they get into Congress, they will join with the New-England-Congress-Men and we shall have War & Blood-shed immediately—the Gentlemen in our West-Jersey-Ticket, are good peaceable Men,—they will oppose all War-measures—Congress will be brought to Philada., maybe to Burlington, and the Markets will then be good, we shall have no Paper-money—Clarke & Dayton was the means of making the present Paper trash—they had it made to pay their Debts, particularly Clarke, I can shew You this in Print & Certified by Your Friends the Shottwells of Rhaway, who have been cheated by this Clarke[10]—But War is their present scheme, particularly Dayton, who with his Father and all his Presbyterian-Family of the Ogdens, have shed a great deal of Blood,—they all thirst for Blood again—nay, Dayton & Clarke, after having War awhile, will, if they can, hang all the Quaquers, as they formerly did in New-England—and as poor Carlile[11] was during the late War in Philada. in 1778—Elias Boudinot, altho' then a Congress-Man, Pleaded for Carlile and wanted to save his Life, but Presbyterian Joe Reed, then Governor had him hanged because He was a Quaquer,—and pardoned all the Presbyterians, who were condemned to be hanged also, for the same charge as against Your Friend Carlile—who was a member of Your meeting & often visited at Burlington at your quarterly-meetings—Lambert Cadwalladers Brother[12] wrote a peice against Joe Reed for this conduct—now Your Friends Elias Boudinot & Lambert Cadwallader are in this Ticket—and also, James Schureman, who last Fall got the Law passed to free the Poor Negroes, who have all voted for him—as to Sinnicksen the last name in this printed ticket, You know He lives in Salem & that all his Family-connections are Friends—these are the honest, good men you ought to Vote for—But, if you want War and to be persecuted by the Presbyterians,—Stay at home, & see who will pity You when Your goods are distrained and Your Meeting-Houses are made barracks, as here to fore, for Soldiers & men of war" Much more such stuff is dealt out to the poor Quaquer, particularly, that two Scotch-Presbyterian-*Hirelings* are joined in the Ticket of Clarke & Dayton—meaning Witherspoon & McWhorter.—upon this,—the wife, Mother, and all the Family, cry out—"go, go, go to the Election and vote for the Printed-Ticket" &c: &c.—The Poor Friend being alarmed at the situation of his Society, finds "Freedom" takes the Printed-junto-Ticket, & away He goes, with such of his Neighbours as He can influence by telling them the same melancholy tale—to keep out the blood-thirsty-Presbyterians, and to prevent War, Blood & Slaughter.

[1 March[13]]

My Clerk John White is this moment returned—Enclosed is Mr. Hunters Letter which contains no more than what I have already written to You—

I suppose from the best information I can procure that there will be from 25, to 26,00 votes taken in Burlington—

My Clerk tells me that the Gloucester Election was held yesterday at the Tavern near Pensaukin Bridge, within 200 Yards of this County & about 6 miles from Coopers Ferry a Place not mentioned in the Election-Law & which I take to be illegal—

Let me hear from You by Post—send me Your last Eliz. Town Papers for a month back—Remember me to Mrs. Dayton & all Friends

in haste

1. RC, Jonathan Dayton Papers, NjR.

2. This portion of the letter was datelined "Late Saturday Evening."

3. No Bloomfield letter dated Friday evening, 27 February 1789, has been located. Bloomfield's letter of Friday morning, marked to be sent "By Post," is printed immediately above.

4. Daniel Ellis (1728–1794) was Burlington Township clerk, 1763–1779 and 1782–1791, and assessor, 1761–1776 and 1784.

5. Daniel Newbold (1757–1815), who lived near Mount Holly, was a member of the Assembly, 1788–1790, and a Burlington County justice of the peace.

6. Possibly Caleb Austin, who owned much land and a sawmill around the old Ætna Furnace (now Medford Lakes) in Burlington County.

7. John White.

8. Thomas P. Hewlings (d. 1793), a loyalist during the Revolution, represented the city of Burlington in the colonial assembly, 1772–1775.

9. George Hastings operated the Taunton Furnace in Burlington County from 1785 until Sheriff John Hollinshead sold it to pay Hastings's debts sometime in 1789.
10. See "A Freeholder," *Brunswick Gazette*, 10 February 1789, Part Five:III, below.
11. Abraham Carlisle.
12. John Cadwalader.
13. This portion of the letter was datelined "Sunday ½ After Eleven A.M."

Tench Coxe to John Adams, New York, 1 March (excerpt)[1]

The Jersey Election is not yet closed. There seems no doubt of their being well disposed as all the candidates are known to be friendly to the constitution, except one whom I know pretty well & from whom I have no fears—[2]

1. RC, Adams Papers, MHi. For other excerpts from this letter, see Chapter XIII, Part Three, Representatives Election Commentary; and Chapter XIV.
2. This is undoubtedly a reference to Abraham Clark.

Privy Council Meeting, Tuesday, 3 March

On 27 February, Governor William Livingston, assuming that the polls had closed, asked four members of the Legislative Council to meet with him, as a Privy Council, to count the votes. The governor, anticipating the meeting, had earlier drafted minutes for the Privy Council proceedings, with blank spaces left for the meeting date (in February) and for the names of the four winners (MS, William Livingston Papers, MHi).

According to a personal calendar of election dates kept by the governor, he expected county election officials to deliver election results to the county sheriffs on about 16 February, with the sheriffs forwarding the results to the governor by 26 February. He expected to submit the results to the Privy Council on about 1 March (MS, William Livingston Papers, MHi). The meeting was eventually scheduled for 2–3 March, so that the elected Representatives could appear in Congress at its opening on 4 March.

However, when the Privy Council met in Elizabethtown on 3 March, election returns from only seven counties (six from East Jersey) were available. Councillors Abraham Kitchel and Ephraim Martin, both from East Jersey and sympathetic to Abraham Clark and Jonathan Dayton, argued that the election should be decided on the basis of the returns then available. To support their case they persuaded a fifth councillor, Peter Haring of Bergen, to attend the meeting. But Governor Livingston refused to call the question and adjourned the meeting to 18 March. If the returned votes had been counted on 3 March, James Schureman, Abraham Clark, Jonathan Dayton, and Robert Hoops would have been the first four finishers. Lambert Cadwalader would have finished in ninth place, Elias Boudinot in tenth, and Thomas Sinnickson in fifteenth.

There is no official record of the Privy Council meeting on 3 March. The principal accounts of it are in evidence presented to the committee of the House of Representatives which investigated the contested New Jersey election (Certificate of Governor William Livingston to the Congressional Committee of Elections, 20 June 1789, and Evidence Presented to the Congressional Committee of Elections, 13 August 1789) and in newspaper commentary about the dispute, all printed in Part Six. These documents also discuss the Privy Council meeting of 18–19 March.

Brunswick Gazette, 3 March

From the votes given in, and the accounts from the different counties where the polls are not closed, we may venture to say the die is cast, and that James Schurman, Abraham Clark, Jonathan Dayton, and Elias Boudinot, Esqrs. are the representatives,—however there is a chance for Lambert Cadwallader, Esq.

William Norcross to Jonathan Dayton, Burlington, 4 March[1]

I received a Letter from Col Ogden[2] ye. 27th Ult, which was Answerd. by the Express as fully as in my Power, I promisd to give the Earliest Information of the Close of the poll in this County, which was Don as mentiond. only in Supposition in my Letter at Penny Hill Last Night[.] it fell out Exactly as was Expected they Closd. and Counted out a part of the Tickets, (about 20,) and Adjourned to this City to finish; they have been busy till Eight O Clock this Evening and have not gone through but abt the Half, the whole that are yet Turnd out for you are 62 and as mentiond in my Letter I dont believe that it will amount to 200, the Number taken in the County is 2826 so that from what has been said you may be able to form a Judgment, Gloucester is not Closd that we have heard but suppose it was last Evening. but from Doctor Hunters Letter you will see that not much is to be lookd for there and very few indeed not Exceeding 250 or 300 in All the Western Counties, the Leading Bellweathers of the Junto Ticket wish to influence the Judge and Inspectors to take up Two or three more days in Counting off the Votes though the Inspectors are so Heartily tired of the Election that I believe their Inclination is to Close tomorrow Evening[.] Notwithstanding they have done and will do all they can to Serve the Junto Ticket, we suppose this Last Maneuvre to be in Consequence of a Letter Received by a Certain County Court Judge from an Elizabeth Town Candidate[3] I wish you all Happiness

1. RC, Dayton Miscellany, NjHi. The letter was apparently read by Joseph Bloomfield and forwarded to Dayton, along with Bloomfield's letter to Dayton, 5 March 1789, immediately below.
2. Abraham Ogden was often referred to as "Colonel"; Matthias Ogden, as "General."
3. Probably Elias Boudinot.

Joseph Bloomfield to Jonathan Dayton, Burlington, 5 March[1]

I extremely regret that our Friend Norcross, cannot give a more favorable acct of the Burlington-Election, than what He has within written[2]—nor, is it in my power to give any additional information.

Col. Ross & Lt. Clark[3] came to this place late Monday Evening—Ross with a view to go on to Eliz. Town—& give a full Acct. of the Election but the danger of crossing the Delaware prevented—Ross, Clarke Norcross & four other Friends, supped & staid with me till near Day-light; we comforted ourselves & resolved to be happy, notwithstanding the Chagrin & Mortification we experienced during the late Election.

If the Delaware should be passable at the final enumeration of the Votes & I can give any intelligence whatever I will write You accordingly—

I beg the favour of You to forward enclosed soon as possible to Woodbridge

1. RC, Dayton Miscellany, NjHi. The letter was written in the morning.

2. Bloomfield is probably referring to Norcross' letter to Dayton, 4 March 1789, immediately above.

3. Probably William Clark (1756–1853), a farmer in that portion of Elizabethtown Borough which became Westfield Township, Essex County, in 1794. Clark and Dayton had served together in the army during the Revolution.

William Norcross and Joseph Bloomfield to Jonathan Dayton, Burlington, 5 March[1]

[Norcross to Dayton]

Agreeable to my Promise of Yesterday, have now to inform you that the Election of this County is Closd. this Evening, the Exact return is sent Inclosd—so that you will find from the Beginning I have not been much amiss in my Judgment—Cumberland Gloucester nor do I believe Salem has yet Closd—, from every account as before in my last the Number You will get there will be Small[.] Your Letter to Mr Bloomfield of ye. 2d Inst. I have seen. the whole of which respecting us I am well Pleasd with, but all that we can say is if we have not had Success we have Deservd it when we have the Satisfaction of seeing each Other more can be said

NB This County has and I Expect Gloucester will Exceed our Expectation

[Bloomfield to Dayton[2]]

The Burlington Election is at last declared in great triumph—to the mortification of Your Friends—Sinnickson leads in this County as He was almost in every Ticket—Boudinots & Cadwalladers several Friends omitted their names for a few hours in the morning of the Day of the meeting of Cummings & Ellis &c. at Moores Town, after which they joined for the Junto Ticket[.] Your name was run by Your Friends, instead of Schuureman most generally, which Acc'ts for Schuureman having less Votes than the other three—

Your favour of 2d. Currt. my Servant brought from Bristol this morning—one from Norcross & myself was put in the Post-office for You under cover to Saml Smith[3]—after Norcross & Hollinshead had the perusal of Your Letter I forward[ed] same to Ross, for perusal of Ross, Coxe[4] & Clarke, being the only Persons, with Col Cox of Trenton[5] who mentioned Your name for the Federal Congress, & for which, we have received more or less insult & abuse—East-Jersey has gained one advantage in the hasty close of their Polls,—they now know the strength of the Western Counties, and can at any future time, dictate to them as they please—if another contest should ever arise, I hope to triumph in my turn, and remind some of the Western-Zealots of their present sneering conduct.—

Soon as the Gov. & Council declare the Gentlemen Elected, I shall be glad of a Line by Post or Stage—

1. RC, Dayton Miscellany, NjHi. The two letters (Bloomfield's following immediately after Norcross' on the same sheet of paper) were addressed to Dayton in Elizabethtown. Bloomfield marked the letters "duplicate," and Dayton endorsed them as "Duplicate."

2. Bloomfield datelined his part of the letter "Late Thursday Evening."

3. See Norcross' and Bloomfield's letters of 4 and 5 March 1789, respectively, immediately above.

4. Probably Richard Cox.
5. Probably John Cox.

Joshua M. Wallace to Elias Boudinot, Burlington, 5 March[1]

Our Inspectors have just now finish'd counting the Numbers of our Poll which are as follows—

Sinnickson	2800	Hooper	24
Boudinot	2763	Hoops	20
Cadwallader	2728	Henderson	11
Schureman	2689	Vancleve	7
Dayton	118	Clark	7
Witherspoon	61	Fenimore	3
Stephens	30	Parker	1
		Thompson	1

The whole Number of Votes taken was 2826 of which you want but 63—Had you not been *a Lawyer* I am persuaded you would have been the highest on the List—The Idea that you had lost many Votes in your own County, from the Supposition that you were a Western Member, engaged you many here.

Our Intelligence from Gloucester County, is that the Poll still continues open, and that 2400 Tickets have been received—From Cumberland we have no Information that can be depended upon, but I believe the Poll is not closed—The Fear of injuring a Cause which they were anxiously engaged to support induced our Inspectors to close the Poll—Unless more Votes than you expected are taken in Essex, the Western Ticket will be safe—

You will oblige me much by any Information concerning your Election—tho we cannot now assist you by our Exertions our Anxiety is not lessned—Should we now be successful, it will probably on a future day be to your Advantage that we have done no more at present—

1. RC, Wallace Papers, PHi. The letter, datelined "7 OClock P.M.," was addressed to Boudinot in Elizabethtown.

James Parker to [Cortlandt Skinner], c. 5 March[1]

We are all very anxious in this quarter of the world, and looking forward to our new Constitution. Many are doubtful whether it will take place as it is, or be subjected to be amended by another convention; if the latter, we shall have no Constitution without bloody noses. Eleven States have agreed, some of them conditionally, and the dominion (Virginia) is ready to join those who have made the conditions. There are many anti-federalists amongst those who are to go to Congress, who have many behind them of the same political sentiments. General Washington will undoubtedly be President, by a great majority, if not unanimously. John Adams, Vice-President. The fourth instant was appointed for the day of meeting, but they will not get together until at least a month after, if so soon.

Our election for Representatives began the 11th Feb'y (which day, 63 years ago, I was born), and it is not yet ended. The five western counties below Asanpink [Creek],[2] determined to put in their men, it is said don't intend to close the poll till Wednesday next. All the other counties, except Essex, closed ten days ago;[3] this will keep up that jealousy that has ever been between the two divisions.

The great struggle is whether the temporary seat of Congress shall be New York, or Philadelphia.[4] The Governor and Privy Council, who are to declare the elected, say they will not receive the returns from the different counties after the time mentioned in the law; if so, West Jersey will be disappointed, and the State in an uproar, however consistent this resolution may be.

I was long solicited, and as long refused my consent to a nomination; but at length declared, but so late that it answered no other purpose than to show what I might have done, had I declared in time. I lost every chance in West Jersey, where the suffrages would have been much in my favor, and plans early formed shut me out where my interest was very considerable.[5]

1. William A. Whitehead, *Contributions to the Early History of Perth Amboy . . .* (New York, 1856), 134–35. For a longer excerpt from this letter, see Charles W. Parker, "Shipley: The Country Seat of a Jersey Loyalist," New Jersey Historical Society *Proceedings*, n.s., XVI (1931), 136–38. The printed letter, probably from a file copy or draft, was undated, but from internal evidence it appears to have been written about 5 March.

Whitehead identifies the recipient as Parker's brother-in-law, who was living in England. This was undoubtedly Cortlandt Skinner (1727–1799). Skinner, a lawyer, represented the town of Perth Amboy in the colonial assembly, 1763–1775 (Speaker, 1765–1770 and 1772–1775); was attorney general of the colony, 1754–1775; and served as a brigadier general of the New Jersey loyalist troops, 1776–1782. After the war Skinner settled in Bristol, England.

2. Burlington, Gloucester, Salem, Cumberland, and Cape May counties.

3. Of the seven counties in East Jersey, only Essex County had not closed its poll by 23 February.

4. For further comments about the relationship between the Representatives election and the seat of Congress, see William Bradford, Jr., to Elias Boudinot, 25 March 1789; Parker to Skinner, March 1789; Thomas Hartley to Jasper Yeates, 31 August 1789; Hartley to Tench Coxe, 2 September 1789; and Elias Boudinot to Elisha Boudinot, 2 September 1789, all Part Six.

5. See Parker's broadside, "A Friend to New Jersey," c. 1 February 1789, and Richard Stockton to Elias Boudinot, 20 February 1789, both above.

Federal Gazette (Philadelphia), 6 March

In the counties of Summerset, Bergen, Sussex, Monmouth, Hunterdon, Middlesex and Morris, in the state of New-Jersey, at the late election for representatives in the New Congress, it appears that Messrs Schureman, Dayton, Boudinot and Van Cleve are highest on the returns. Returns from the other counties in that state are not yet come to hand.[1]

1. All but the last sentence of this article was reprinted in the Philadelphia *Pennsylvania Mercury*, 7 March.

Joshua M. Wallace to Elias Boudinot, Burlington, 6 and 8 March[1]

[6 March]

This Morning I dispatch'd a Messenger to Mr. Stockton at Princeton with an Accot. of the State of the Votes in our County, and inclosed a Letter for you containing the same Information which I requested Mr. Stockton to forward.[2]

While I am made happy with the Prospect that the Efforts of this County will be subservient to the Purpose of introducing Men of Integrity & Abilities to the House of Fœderal Representatives, it gives me additional Satisfaction that they will be introduced by those who act upon Principles of Honor & Good faith. The Unanimity of the People of this County shews the Regard they have to their Promises—

Capt. Dayton's Friends here have generally been in your Interest, and had it not been consider'd as a Point of Honor to support the Western Ticket just as it was agreed upon, he would have had several hundred Votes which Mr. Schurman now has—A considerable Jealousy has prevail'd with Respect to the Principles of the latter from his voting for Mr. Clark as Senator—[3]

Mr. Cadwallader's Friends have behaved with the greatest Honor—I wish if you think it proper that you would write to Mr. William Newbold,[4] who exerted himself in a distinguished Manner to promote our Cause—Mr. Caleb Newbold[5] has also been an industrious and useful Friend—as our Views are extended beyond the present Election, I wish that an Interest of such Consequence may be secured—

Our Worthy Friend Mr. Kinsey has been earnestly engaged in the Business—I have never known him so anxious on any other Occasion—Our Counsellor Mr. Joseph Smith has been your steady and serviceable Advocate—A Mr. John Lee who lives near Mountholly, and who has been a Client of yours, brought forward two hundred Votes—Your Attention to him, if but in a Paragraph of a Letter to some of your friends in this Quarter will be a lasting Bond—

[8 March[6]]

The above I had written to have been dispatch'd by our Sheriff who proposed to have set off for Essex yesterday Morning with the returns[7]—This Day Mr. Kinsey shewed me a Letter from you,[8] in Consequence of which we went out to Mr. Joseph Smith's this Afternoon in Order to induce him to be at Elisabeth Town in proper Season[.] He thinks if it were necessary or expedient that he should attend, Mr. Chetwood would have given him Information.[9] A Letter from Mr Chetwood to him by the Return of the Sheriff, mentioning the probable Advantages of his Presence, would prevail upon him to go on—Should Mr. Chetwood not write, a Letter from yourself would be of Service[10]—Early to Morrow Morning we shall dispatch a Messenger to Gloucester with the Purport of whose Dispatches I shall inform you hereafter[.] Let us be inform'd particularly of the State of Affairs by the Return of the Bearer Mr. Hewlings our Sheriff—but let the Information be by Letter.

1. RC, Wallace Papers, PHi. The letter was addressed to Boudinot in Elizabethtown.

2. See Wallace to Boudinot, 5 March 1789, above.

3. For Schureman's Senate vote, see *New Jersey Journal*, 3 December 1788, Part Two.

4. William Newbold (1736–1793), a Quaker landowner in Springfield and Chesterfield townships, Burlington County, and an uncle of Caleb and Daniel Newbold, was a member of the Council, 1784–1786 and 1789–1790.

5. Cabel Newbold (1763–1853), younger brother of Daniel Newbold, was a landowner in Springfield Township, Burlington County. He held many local offices and was elected to the Assembly in 1791 and to the Council in 1792.

6. Wallace datelined this part of the letter "Sunday 8th. March—7 OClock P.M."

7. Sheriff Abraham Hewlings did not leave until Monday morning, 9 March. See Wallace to Boudinot, 11 March 1789, below.

8. Probably Boudinot to James Kinsey, 6 March 1789. That letter, which is mentioned in Wallace

to Boudinot, 11 March 1789, below, has not been located. See also Kinsey to Boudinot, c. 9 March 1789, below.

9. Smith and John Chetwood were Council members, representing Burlington and Essex counties, respectively.

10. See Wallace to Boudinot, 11 March 1789, and Smith to Governor William Livingston, 12 March 1789, both below.

James Madison to George Washington, Philadelphia, 8 March (excerpt)[1]

The N. Jersey Reps. are not yet announced. Mr. Clarke it is supposed will be one, Mr. Cadwallader, Mr. Boudinot, and Mr. Shureman, are talked of as the others.

1. RC, Washington Papers, DLC. Printed: Rutland, *Madison*, XII, 5–6.

James Kinsey to Elias Boudinot, c. 9 March[1]

The Attempt mentioned in Your last has frightned Us[.][2] I have had a Consultation with Mr Wallace and We agree there is No Method so proper to Guard against future Steps of the Kind As to prevail on All the Western Councillers to Attend—We have Waited on Mr Smith who you know will not willingly be Carried from home[.] We have Written to Ellis and with a little of Your Assistance Showing Your Sentiments as to the Necessity I think We shall prevail on all but Cape May & Probably him too to Go[3]—If this Shall be Kept a perfect Secret till the Time the Surprise It Occasions will do Much

I have Already told them in answer to the Objection We are not Summoned:—So much the better You will Shew a Spirited Attempt not to be imposed on & will Convince all that You deem the Matter of so Much Importance that You Come so far to Inspect the propriety of the proceedings[.] Are We Right or Wrong for On Your Letter We shall either press it or putt a Stop to the Measure but I repeat Keep the Whole a Secret even from Your Most Confidential Frd—In haste I am Yr frd

[P.S.]—pray do all the Business of getting me Absolution for thus employing the Most part of the Day

1. RC, Boudinot Family Papers, NjR. The letter was addressed to Boudinot in Elizabethtown. The letter has no dateline, but from internal evidence it is apparent that it was written about 9 March.

2. Boudinot's letter of 6 March (mentioned in Joshua M. Wallace to Boudinot, 11 March 1789, below) has not been located. Kinsey is certainly referring to the attempt of Dayton and Clark sympathizers on the Privy Council to force a vote on accepting the election returns which had been received up to the time of the Council meeting, 3 March 1789. Six of the seven counties reporting by that date were East Jersey counties.

3. Joseph Smith and Joseph Ellis were Council members from Burlington and Gloucester counties, respectively. Cape May County was represented in the Council by Jeremiah Eldredge.

Benjamin Huntington to Samuel Huntington, New York, 11 March (excerpt)[1]

No members from Maryland Delaware nor Jersey have yet appeared. New Jersey have been in Strift between Eastern & Western Counties in Polling for Representatives. The Object of the Western Counties is to gain Strength to Remove Congress to Philadelphia & for that Purpose kept open the Poll untill a Day or two Since in order to bring every body in to Vote and by that Means Carry the Choice.

1. RC, Samuel Huntington Papers, CtHi. Benjamin Huntington was representing Connecticut in the House of Rperesentatives. Samuel Huntington was governor of Connecticut. For biographical sketches of both men, see DHFFE, II, 53–54.

Joshua M. Wallace to Elias Boudinot, Burlington, 11 March[1]

We are exceedingly anxious to hear from all Friends in Essex—the last Accots. from thence are contained in your Letter of the 6th. Inst. to Mr. Kinsey—[2]

I wrote to you by our Sheriff Abraham Hewlings Esqr., who left Burlington on Monday Morning with the Return of Votes from this County—The Poll of Gloucester I believe is not yet closed, the Number of Votes taken in you will be made acquainted with by Mr. Griffith—

It is probable that the Members of Council from Gloucester, Salem, & Cumberland, will be in Essex on the 18th. Instant, if the most pressing Solicitation can induce them. I mentioned to you in my Letter by Mr. Hewlings,[3] that Mr. Smith of this County, had told Mr. Kinsey & myself upon our urging him to go, that he was persuaded Mr. Chetwood would write to him, if it were necessary for him to be there—if you think it necessary, do not fail to urge Mr. Chetwood—a Letter by express (if one is not already on the Way here,) may arrive in Season—Should Mr. Chetwood decline writing, a Letter from yourself to Mr. Smith assigning the Reasons why you wish him to be there, might answer the Purpose.

The Dispatches Mr. Kinsey recd. were forwarded to our Friends in the Southern Counties on Monday Morning, and with our Letters delivered to Colo. Ellis at Gloucester at 11 OClock in the forenoon—Colo. Ellis purposes to be here on Sunday on his Way to Essex, & will call on Mr. Smith to accompany him.—

I find notwithstanding the Election you can attend to your Chancery Business, by which it is evident, you are not so much concern'd in the Event, as your Friends are—For my Part—my thoughts are fix'd on but one Subject, and that is *the Election*—

1. RC, Wallace Papers, PHi. The letter was addressed to Boudinot in Elizabethtown.
2. See Wallace to Boudinot, 6 and 8 March 1789, and James Kinsey to Boudinot, c. 9 March 1789, both above.
3. 6 and 8 March, above.

New Jersey Journal (Elizabethtown), 11 March

The poll of this county[1] is adjourned until Wednesday the 18th inst. at Elizabeth-Town.—It may safely be conjectured, that this measure is adopted in consequence of the manauvres of the five western counties in delaying their returns beyond the time prescribed by law, in order to profit by a knowledge of the returns from the eight counties in the east—It is however to be hoped that no tricks or evasions will serve to prevent a pure representation or cheat the people out of the men of their choice.[2]

1. Essex County.
2. This article was reprinted in the Philadelphia *Pennsylvania Packet,* 16 March 1789.

Joseph Smith to Governor William Livingston, Burlington, 12 March[1]

I have just recd the Govrs. letter of the 10th. Inst and am very sorry such doubts and difficulties should in the Govrs. opinion be likely to arise in determining who ought to be returned as our Representatives as to make it necessary to summon a full Council at this very difficult time of getting together—I should not choose to be remiss in the discharge of a Duty, but really so many difficulties seem to be in my way at present that it appears to me very doubtful whether I shall be able to meet Council, however if I should not I have the fullest confidence those of the Council who may meet will with the Govr. do what shall appear to them to be right

1. RC, William Livingston Papers, MHi. Smith represented Burlington County in the Council.

Walter Rutherfurd to John Stevens, Sr., New York, 13 March (excerpt)[1]

Every Body cry out Shame against Jersey for keepg open some of their County Polls, they suspect there is no Order or Government in the State, it is now reported that the Polls are not to close this 3 Months[.] poor Jersey is made a laughing stock of—[2]

1. RC, Stevens Family Papers, NjHi. The letter was addressed to Stevens in Lebanon, Hunterdon County.
2. In a letter written the same day, 13 March, John Rutherfurd told his father, Walter, that ". . . your intelligence of the Jersey election was new to us as we had not heard the event, I am curious to hear further particulars, and the notions of the New Congress" (Tranquility, FC?, Rutherfurd Papers, NHi). John was replying to Walter's letter of 10 March.

Jonathan Dayton to [John] Ross and [Richard] Cox, Elizabethtown, 15 March[1]

As I am convinced you must have some anxiety to know what is likely to be the issue of the late election for Representatives in Congress, I cannot suffer the opportunity (which Mr. Spragg's visit to this place affords me) to pass, without writing to you on the subject. The poll in Essex is still open & from what I can collect since my return from New York on yesterday, will very probably continue so for some time.—The people in this quarter feel a degree of warmth, bordering almost upon resentment, at the advantage they think has been taken of these counties in the unreasonable continuance of the western polling—Applications have been made from several of the neighbouring counties to the Judge & Inspectors of Essex by no means to close their poll until justice shall be done to them either by permitting them to reopen their polls and take the votes which have not already been given in or by setting aside the present & ordering a new election. For my own part, I am so exceedingly apprehensive lest the present temper & spirit of the people should be increased into a flame not easily to be extinguished & likewise fearful lest the whole transaction may resolve itself into a violent contention & dispute between Eastern & Western Jersey, thence producing animosities & divisions which never can be healed, that I am resolved to discourage any further resistance or opposition to a final & immediate determination of the matter, altho' that determination is sure to be unfavorable to me. I am the more cheerfully induced to make this resolution from another consideration perhaps no less important than the former—It is of most essential consequence that the new government should commence it's operation under the most favorable auspices & as mildly & harmoniously as possible, therefore altho' the harsh & unfair methods practised in the west to carry election points, might in some situations & on principles of retaliation justify on our parts measures otherwise extravagant & unwarrantable, I cannot nevertheless (circumstanced as this country is) think it would be either politic or wise to have recourse to them.

The low artifices that have been practised, the vile reports that have been propagated by the partizans of opposition to prejudice & inflame the *friends* or *Quakers* against me & others are wicked in the extreme—happy is it for them that I am not the man they represent me viz. "a thirster after blood" for they have surely said & done enough to have provoked a man of that description to glut his appetite upon them—When they traduced me the worst they presumed the most upon the mildness of my temper, for they could not but know that falshoods like theirs deserved severe chastisement.—Amid all my reflections on this subject I have among others this consolation that the time may, & probably will, come when the Quakers, a people whom for many reasons I respect, will be convinced that they have been grossly imposed upon by artful & designing men & will thereafter divert their resentment from me against their deceivers.

The Governor has summoned every Member of the Council to a privy Council on Wednesday to enter into some decision with regard to the election; what the result will be I know not, but I apprehend that it will avail but little, since the law appears to preclude them from entering into any decisive measure before the returns of all the counties are given in, the duty of the privy council in this case being merely ministerial & not in the least degree judicial.

Remember me affectionately to my other friends Bloomfield Hollinshead, Norcross, Clark &c.

I am told that Mr. Reckless of Reckless town has acted as a friend on this occasion, if it be so, do not fail to make my acknowledgments to him for the part he has acted

1. FC, Jonathan Dayton Papers, MiU-C. A notation on the letter says it was sent to "Majors Ross & Cox," i.e., John Ross and Richard Cox.

John Pintard to Elisha Boudinot, New York, 17 March (excerpt)[1]

I flatter myself that yr. brother will be elected at last & that he will moreover be the speaker of the Ho. of Representatives towards which I am exerting my feeble efforts & doubt not if he is returned in time but that he will succeed—[2]

1. RC, Boudinot-Pintard Papers, NHi. The letter was addressed to Boudinot in Newark. Pintard was a wealthy New York merchant.

2. Frederick A. Muhlenberg of Pennsylvania was elected Speaker of the House of Representatives on 1 April. Elias Boudinot took his seat in the House on 23 March.

Brunswick Gazette, 17 March

The electioneering scene is changed—and Elias Boudinot, James Schurman, Lambert Cadwallader, and Thomas Sinnickson, appear to be highest in nomination, and the strife (if any) will be betweeen Clark and Sinnickson—the poll of Essex, which is adjourned till to-morrow, it is said will not be opened again—the Governor has, or is about to call his council, and our correspondent informs us, it is more than probable the electioneering business, which has been carried on in the eastern and western counties with a great deal of finessing, will be argued before congress, who are to determine whether it has been conducted in a legal manner, if not, we cannot tell what will be the result.[1]

1. This article was reprinted in the *New York Daily Gazette*, 19 March 1789; Philadelphia *Pennsylvania Packet*, 23 March; Philadelphia *Pennsylvania Mercury*, 24 March; Philadelphia *Pennsylvania Gazette*, 25 March; and Philadelphia *Pennsylvania Journal*, 28 March.

Triumph, New Jersey Journal (Elizabethtown), 18 March

THE LEGISLATIVE COUNCIL OF THE STATE IS SUMMONED—*They are to sit in privy council on Wednesday—to decide on what?—Whether eleven counties are thirteen—and whether the votes from a part are the votes from the whole of the state.*

Come forward thou MAN of might—come forward thou BELLWETHER of the junto flock, thou COUNSELLOR of Gloucester.[1]—No wisdom is required of thee on this occasion, nothing impossible to thee is asked.—Bring with thee but thy cunning, but bring all thou hast.—Prove the affirmative of those two propositions—thy party will then be successful—thyself triumphant. Be advised however, mighty and kingly as is thy craft, not altogether to depend on it alone. Thy weight, and the muddiness of the roads, will make it prudent for thee to move on slowly. Take counsel on the way; the best that thou canst find to fortify and arm thee at all points against the approaching warfare. Thou wilt naturally consult first and most especially thy good natured neighbour, that *oracle* of the law whose professional and marvellous wisdom might almost change the town of *Woodbury* into a modern *Delphos*.[2]—He will expound to thee the laws, not of ancient Rome or less ancient England, but of later Jersey, nay of thy own and his formation. Regard the explanations he shall give thee, for if *any* laws have ever been his study, *these* are *they*. He scorns to mingle knowledge, and therefore thou needest not to fear that thou wilt be burthened with quotations either from the pandects of Justinian or the statutes of Britain. As thou passest thro' Burlington, neglect not to visit that *wiseacre* of the bench,[3] that *judicial constellation*—to *thee* I recommend him, to aid thee in the acquirement of a needful supply of *that* article by some called *common sense*. I would not deceive, by making thee suppose that he has a fund within himself, from which he can supply thee; on the contrary, like *thee* he wants, like *thee* has long been in quest of it, but by this time, perhaps, he may have discovered where it is to be had, and will accompany or direct thee in its pursuit. Every *other* sense, or at least so much as thou wilt need on this occasion, can be spared thee by his lady—*She* has long been in possession of a more than common portion, and willing to retain the superiority which nature gave her, has taken care to deal out of her abundant store very sparingly to the Judge. Thou must not fail to see and take one lesson at least from the little *Newbold* lawgiver of Burlington.[4] He will teach thee that, however prudent it might have been in the days of yore for the ancestors of you both to confine their communications to Yea and Nay, it is necessary now for *thee*, in imitation of *him*, to leave off that plainness of style and branch out in all the copiousness of language—a little *swearing* may possibly profit thee on this occasion; if I mistake not, thou already knowest the rudiments of *this* science, and but a few hours under Dan's tuition will make the alphabet as familiar to thee, as to thy tutor. If, like Daniel of old, he prophesyeth to thee of things to come, for his name's sake believe him, but most especially if he foretelleth that thou wilt return home no wiser than thou comest out. Thy confidential SECRETARY at Trenton[5] must not be left unnoticed—*He* will convince thee that, as in political arithmetic, two and two have been often found to make but one, so in political addition *eleven* and *one* may signify *thirteen*. His scholastic knowledge will enable him to possess thee of that figure in rhetoric called *Synecdoche*, by virtue of which the whole is not only taken for the part, but very frequently likewise the *part* is taken for the *whole*. This latter application of it will suit thy purpose to a hair, but as in lessons of *rhetoric* thou has never been so apt a learner, nor thy memory so retentive as in those which *Dan* administers, I would advise thee, if thou wishest to have this figure at command, to bring the *scholar* too.—As thou approachest nearer to the scene of deliberation, remember that there lives at Princeton *one* who often deigned to visit thee in the heat of your elections, and in the west to mingle in thy counsels—Askest thou what thou mayest expect from him?[6] I answer—not a further knowledge of the law—true it is, he has it, but it is equally true he has acquired it at the expence of too intense and laborious application to share it even with thee—If thou shouldest need additional store of assurance, thou mayest replenish at this fountain—He may be prevailed upon to lend it thee, but not without a promise to return it as thou repassest Princeton on they way homeward—thinking as he does that the pride of family is best displayed through so dazzling a medium, thou must not expect to receive it free from such conditions.

As thou comest to Brunswick I would recommend it to thee to pass on and turn not either to the right hand or to the left; neither to see the *Senator* in Middlesex,[7] nor the Lawyer or *would be* Counsellor of Somerset.[8] *They* are on thy side, and doubtless wish thee well, but unfortunately for thee they have been too little conversant with the *legerdemain* of words to aid thee in the business. Hasten next to Elizabeth, and tarry not on the way. On thy arrival there thou wilt be received and welcomed, not only by the counsellor, but by the two brothers[9] of the law of that place and of Newark, by their limbs, their students and their clerks. Thou shouldest regard them all, however different in degree, however distinguished in rank. Each one has been serviceable to thee in turn, from *him* who wrote the billets, to *him* whose nimble heels galled with spurs the nags that bore them. The Newark *Colonel*[10] too, and even the *Divine*,[11] will greet thee, and join thee in thy consultation with the brotherhood, of which, by adoption they are members. Judge, justice and physician, cryer, constable and bully will all come down to view thee, and welcome to the EAST their *western Cooperator*. Their hands and hats uplifted will proclaim their joy—their words and voice united, will sound forth thy name, and huzzas thrice repeated, gladden all the air. Majestic in their march, and slow, but proud in gait, they will escort thee to the palace house of government—place of solemn counsel, there immured within the walls of secret conclave, they must leave thee to thy own imaginations and devices, they *must* retire, and anxiously expect the time, when thou shalt once again come forth, and there proclaim to open mouths and ears,—"OUR PARTY IS SUCCESSFUL—IT IS OURS TO

TRIUMPH."[12]

1. Joseph Ellis.
2. Franklin Davenport.
3. Probably Joshua M. Wallace, who had been a judge of the Court of Common Pleas in Burlington County since 1784.
4. Daniel Newbold.
5. Possibly Samuel W. Stockton.
6. Richard Stockton.
7. Possibly Benjamin Manning, who represented Middlesex County in the Council in 1788.
8. Possibly John Hardenbergh, who represented Somerset County in the Assembly in 1788.
9. John Chetwood and Elias and Elisha Boudinot.
10. John Noble Cumming.
11. Probably the Reverend Alexander MacWhorter, minister of the First Presbyterian Church in Newark and Cumming's brother-in-law.
12. This article was reprinted in the *Brunswick Gazette*, 24 March 1789.

Essex, New Jersey Journal (Elizabethtown), 18 March

MR. KOLLOCK,

As the law for the election of our Representatives for Congress, is not in the possession of every man, I have thought proper to request you to publish the seventh section thereof, which respects the duty of the Governor and privy Council, in order that the people may better understand the strictures which any departure from the letter or spirit of it may probably give rise to.

Sect. 7. "Be it enacted, &c. That the Governor of the state for the time being, shall within four days after receiving the lists from the several counties in this state, lay the same before the privy Council of this state to be summoned for that purpose, and after casting up the whole number of votes from the several counties for each candidate the said Governor and Council shall determine the four persons who shall have the greatest number of votes from the whole state, to be the persons duly chosen to represent this state in the said Congress of the United States, and the said governor, shall commission each, and every of them under the great seal of this state, &c."

Quere. Was the summoning of the privy Council on Tuesday[1] for this purpose, when seven counties only had returned their votes, in any wise warranted by this law?

If *that* act was warrantable on *that* ground, how will the Council justify themselves in not deciding on that day upon the returns already given in?

Is the summoning of the privy council to meet to-morrow on the same occasion, when eleven counties only have returned, more legal than the former?

Will not the same sense of duty, the same want of power, which prevented their deciding in the former case, forbid also a decision in the latter?

If it was necessary *then* (as the governor and two certain counsellors expressed their opinion) that all the returns should be before them before they could cast up and declare who were duly elected. Is not the same thing equally necessary and proper *now?*

Is not the power that is vested in the privy council by this law, of a nature altogether ministerial, and not judicial?

Are they (the council) any thing more than the tellers of the votes of the state? And do they do their duty if they leave a part untold?

Can that sacred seal of office, the great seal of the state, be with propriety, or consistency affixed to commissions for men in whose favour the voice of the state has neither been declared nor indeed been known?

These are questions of a serious import, and perhaps after to-morrow's deliberations will be brought home and applied to every member of that body. The people's privileges are dear to them, and they should know who it is that dares to sport away their rights. Names shall not be spared, for on occasions solemn as the present, any delicacy in that particular would be highly criminal.

ESSEX.

March 17, 1789.[2]

1. 3 March.
2. This article was reprinted in the *Brunswick Gazette*, 31 March 1789.

Privy Council Proceedings, Wednesday-Thursday, 18–19 March[1]

On 3 March 1789, after the Privy Council reached no decision on the election returns, Governor William Livingston adjourned the Council meeting to 18 March. By the time the Council reconvened on that date, twelve of the thirteen counties had filed election returns (Essex was still missing), and the Council, by a vote of 9 to 3, announced the winners of the election based on those returns. The three dissenting councillors, all from East Jersey, explained their position in a formal protest, which was entered in the Council proceedings.

Details of the Privy Council meeting of 18–19 March are in two principal sources: the Council's proceedings (below) and the evidence presented to the committee of the House of Representatives which investigated the contested election (Part Six).

At a Meeting of the Privy Council at Elizabeth Town the 18th. day of March 1789

Present

His Excellency the Governor

The Honourable

John Chetwood	Joseph Ellis
Benjamin Manning	John Mayhew
Asher Holmes	Robt. Lettice Hooper
Ephraim Martin	Abraham Kitchel
Joseph Smith	Samuel Ogden
	Mark Thomson Esquires

The Governor and Privy Council being met in consequence of a certain Act of The Legislature of this State passed the twenty first day of November last intitled An Act for carrying into effect on the part of New Jersey the Constitution of the United States, assented to, ratified and confirmed by this State on the eighteenth day of December in the Year of our Lord One thousand seven hundred and eighty seven, in expectation that before this day every County in this State would have returned to the Governor a list of the Candidates voted for in such County to represent this State in the Congress of the United States, But so it is that one of the thirteen Counties into which this State is divided hath not yet made such return, and as this State may suffer detriment by remaining unrepresented in the Congress of the United States, The Governor and Privy Council think it for the publick Good and agreeable to the true intent and meaning of the said Act at this day to cast up the whole number of Votes from the twelve Counties of this State that have made such return leaving the decision of the legality of the election of the four persons who have the Majority of Voices from the twelve Counties that have made such return as aforesaid upon the special matter, and above representation thereof, to those to whom it appertains, And upon casting up the whole number of Votes from the said twelve Counties which have made return for all the Candidates voted for to represent this State in the Congress of the United States by the said twelve Counties

The Governor and Privy Council do determine that the four persons who have the greatest number of Votes from the said twelve Counties for such representation as aforesaid, are James Scureman Lambert Cadwallader, Elias Boudinot and Thomas Sen-ickson Esquires, And the said Privy Council do advise His Excellency the Governor to frame his Proclamation agreeably to this determination

March 19th. 1789. The honorable Jeremiah Eldridge Esquire joined the Privy Council as a Member thereof and agreed to the foregoing determination[2]

The following Gentlemen protested against the foregoing proceedings in the words following

We think it a duty which we owe as well to the State as to our imediate Constituents to dissent from and enter our protest against the Vote carried in the Privy Council (of which we are Members) this day, & against their determination and proceedings relative to their declaration of the persons chosen to represent this State in Congress for the following reasons Vizt.—

1. Because the returns from seven Counties only were made at the time evidently intended and by plain construction of the Law appointed for the whole thirteen Counties to have sent in their returns to the Governor Vizt. the day immediately preceeding that on which the Congress were to proceed to business[3]

2dly. Because all the returns have not yet been delivered in nor been laid before the Council, one County not having sent in theirs

3dly. Because the time appointed by Law to commission the Members is either altogether passed or has not yet arrived: It must be considered as past if it be admitted that the law expressly or constructively prescribes any limitation, and as not yet arrived if without limitation, the returns of all the Counties within the State are necessary—

Abrm. Kitchel
March 18th. 1789 Asher Holmes
Ephr. Martin[4]

1. MS, Minutes of Governor's Privy Council of New Jersey, I (1777–1796), Nj. Governor Livingston prepared two drafts of these minutes, apparently anticipating the Council's meeting. The shorter of the two was prepared for either a February or March meeting and had blank spaces where the names of the four winners were to be inserted. The second draft was endorsed by Livingston as "Rough Minutes of Privy Council 18 & 19 March 1789," and it included the names of the four winners. Neither draft contained the protest of the three councillors. Both drafts are in the William Livingston Papers, MHi.

2. Although the complete document, including the "protest," is dated 18 March 1789, this action on the nineteenth was apparently inserted here to record Eldridge's concurrence with the vote taken on the eighteenth.

3. Congress was scheduled to convene on 4 March 1789.

4. For further elaboration of Martin and Kitchel's objections to the Privy Council's proceedings on 3 March, see "A.B.," New York *Daily Advertiser*, 31 August 1789, Part Six.

Proclamation by Governor William Livingston, 19 March[1]

BY HIS EXCELLENCY
WILLIAM LIVINGSTON, Esq.
Governor, Captain General and Commander in Chief in and over the State of New-Jersey and the Territories thereunto belonging, Chancellor and Ordinary in the same.
PROCLAMATION.

Whereas by a certain act of the legislature of this state, passed the twenty first day of November last, entitled, "An Act for carrying into effect, on the part of New-Jersey, the constitution of the United States, assented to, ratified and confirmed by this state on the eighteenth day of December in the year of our Lord one thousand seven hundred and eighty seven;" It is among other things enacted, that the Governor of this state for the time being, shall within four days after receiving the lists of the candidates voted for to represent this state in the Congress of the United States, lay the same before the Privy Council of this state, to be summoned for that purpose, and after casting up the whole number of votes from the several counties for each candidate, the said Governor and Privy Council shall determine the four persons who shall have the greatest number of votes from the whole state, to be the persons duly chosen to represent this state in the Congress of the United States, and that the said Governor shall also make known their names to the Public by Proclamation without delay; as by the said act reference being thereunto had will appear.

And whereas the Governor and Privy Council did meet the eighteenth day of this present month of March, in consequence of the said act of Legislature in expectation that before that day every county in this state would have returned to the Governor a list of the candidates voted for in such county to represent this state in the Congress of the United States;—but so it is, that one of the thirteen counties into which the state is divided, hath not yet made such return, and as this state may suffer detriment by remaining unrepresented in the Congress of the United States, the Governor and Privy Council thought it for the public good, and agreeable to the true intent and meaning of the said act, to cast up at that day the whole number of the votes from the twelve counties of this state that had made such return, leaving the decision of the legality of the election of the four persons who have the majority of voices from the twelve counties that have made such return as aforesaid, in this and every other respect upon the special matter and the above representation thereof to whom it appertains:—And upon casting up the whole number of votes from the said twelve counties that have made such return for all the candidates voted for to represent this state in the Congress of the United States by the said twelve counties, the Governor and Privy Council did determine that the four persons who have the greatest number of votes from the said twelve counties for such representatives as aforesaid, viz., James Schurman, Lambert Cadwallader, Elias Boudinot and Thomas Sinnickson, Esqs. and the said Privy Council did advise the Governor to frame his Proclamation agreeably to this determination.

I do therefore hereby make known, publish and declare, that the four persons who have the greatest number of votes from the twelve counties who have made such return for such representatives as aforesaid, are the said James Schurman, Lambert Cadwallader, Elias Boudinot and Thomas Sinnickson, of which all those whom it may concern are to take notice and govern themselves accordingly.

Given under my hand and seal at arms, in Elizabeth-Town the nineteenth day of March, in the year of our Lord one thousand seven hundred and eighty nine.

WILLIAM LIVINGSTON.

1. *Brunswick Gazette*, 24 March 1789. The proclamation was reprinted in the Philadelphia *Pennsylvania Packet*, 30 March; Philadelphia *Independent Gazetteer*, 1 April; *Carlisle Gazette*, 8 April; and Baltimore *Maryland Gazette*, 10 April. Governor Livingston had drafted a proclamation to be issued sometime in February, leaving blanks for the names of the four winners (MS, William Livingston Papers, MHi). However, for this printed version an additional paragraph (the second) was added to explain some of the election irregularities.

James Madison to George Washington, New York, 19 March (excerpt)[1]

In New Jersey, the election has been conducted in a very singular manner. The law having fixed no time expressly for closing the polls, they have been kept open three or four weeks in some of the Counties by a rival jealousy between the Eastern & Western divisions of the State, and it seems uncertain when they would have been closed, if the Governour had not interposed by fixing on a day for receiving the returns, and proclaiming the successful candidates. The day is past, but I have not heard the result. The Western Ticket in favor of Skureman, Budinot, Cadwallader, & Sennickson if this be the name, is supposed to have prevailed, but an impeachment of the election by the unsuccessful competitors has been talked of—

1. RC, Washington Papers, DLC. Printed: Rutland, *Madison*, XII, 22–23. For another excerpt from this letter, see Chapter XIII, Part Three, Representatives Election Commentary.

Commissions of the New Jersey Representatives, 21–28 March

Governor Livingston drafted a commission for the four elected Representatives on 21 March, but no copies of the formal commissions have been located. Elias Boudinot and James Schureman both noted a delay in receiving their commissions. For more speculation on the subject, see Abraham Clark to Jonathan Dayton, c. 31 March 1789; "Essex," *New Jersey Journal*, 1 April 1789; and "One of Seven Thousand," New York *Daily Advertiser*, 31 July 1789; all Part Six.

Governor William Livingston's Draft of a Commission for Representatives, 21 March[1]

The State of New Jersey
To the honourable
Esquire Greeting

Whereas it appears to his Excellency William Livingston Esquire Governor and Commander in Chief of this State and to the Privy Council that you have been elected by the People of this State a Representative to Represent the same in the House of Representatives of the United States agreeably to the true intent & meaning of a certain Act of the legislature in that behalf lately made & provided You the said are therefore by these presents commissioned to represent & vote in behalf of this State in the House of Representatives of the United States for & during the time limited in the Constitution of the said United States.

In Testimony whereof the Great Seal of the State is hereunto affixed Witness William Livingstin Esquire Governor Captain General & Commander in Chief in and over the State of New Jersey and Territories thereunto belonging Chancellor & Ordinary in the same at Elizabeth Town the twenty first day of March in the year of our Lord one thousand seven hundred & eighty nine & of our Sovereignty & Independence the thirteenth

Elias Boudinot Diary, 23 March[2]

I arrived at N York on Monday the 23d March & took my Seat in Congress the Governor to send my Commission thro Mr Chetwood

John Chetwood to Governor William Livingston, Elizabethtown, 26 March[3]

In the last evening received a Mes[sage?] from Mr. Boudinot in New York wherein [he?] mentions it was expected, there [– – –] be a sufficient number of [Representatives?] from the different St[ates? – – –] and requests me to call on [– – –] for his Commission and forward the [same?] immediately by some safe conveyance—. I sh[ould?] have done myself the pleasure to wait on your Excellency this Morning, but for a bad cold I took a day or two past which has rendred me very unwell. I have therefore sent my Son and if your Excellency thinks proper to send the Commission by him I will forward the same to Mr. Boudinot agreeably to his request—

James Schureman to Governor William Livingston, New Brunswick, 28 March[4]

My embarassment how to conduct myself in the present conjuncture will be a sufficient apology for troubling your Excellency with this address—I wish to avoid giving any reasonable pretext for censure by not going on to New York, and should be pained to impede the operations of Government by unnecessary delay,

The house of Representatives have nearly a Quorum, should a deputation from Jersey be wanting to complete it the attending Members will be clamorous against the state— The proclamation without a commission cannot be authoritative. Does your Excellency consider it as the province of the Gentlemen named in the former to apply for the latter; have official communications on the subject miscarried, or is the confused situation of the election an obstruction to making out the Commission? in either case I should be sorry to embarass by precipitation or incur blame for neglect.

1. MS, William Livingston Papers, MHi. The endorsement on the draft reads: "Dr of Commission for the Jersey Delegates in the House of Representatives of the United States—1789 21 March 1789."

2. MS, Boudinot Papers, PHi.

3. RC, William Livingston Papers, MHi. The upper part of the letter is badly mutilated.

4. RC, William Livingston Papers, MHi.

II.
Election Returns Printed in the Newspapers

No official county vote totals received by Governor William Livingston prior to the Privy Council meeting on 18–19 March 1789 have been located. However, newspapers began reporting election results, often fragmentary, shortly after the polls opened on

11 February 1789; election results were also cited in personal correspondence. Cape May and Cumberland were the only counties for which no results were reported in the newspapers; however, a number of newspapers reported the official vote totals for the four winning candidates, which included the results from these two counties. These reported totals did not include the Essex County return, as the Privy Council's determination was based on all returns except that of Essex County. The official Essex County return (Part Six), dated 30 April 1789, was received by Governor Livingston on 3 May. From these sources the statewide vote totals for the leading candidates can be estimated.

	Statewide Vote Totals Exclusive of Essex County	*Essex County*	*Statewide Vote Totals*
James Schureman	12,597[a]	1,274	13,871
Elias Boudinot	8,603	448	9,051
Lambert Cadwalader	8,685	17	8,702
Thomas Sinnickson	8,240	124	8,364

a. As reported in the Philadelphia *Pennsylvania Gazette*, 25 March, and Philadelphia *Pennsylvania Mercury*, 26 March. The Philadelphia *Pennsylvania Packet*, 24 March, and Philadelphia *Freeman's Journal*, 25 March, reported Schureman's total as 12,537.

	Statewide Vote Totals Exclusive of Cape May, Cumberland, and Essex Counties[b]	*Essex County*	*Vote Totals Exclusive of Cape May and Cumberland Counties*
Abraham Clark	4,525	2,762	7,287
Jonathan Dayton	3,875	2,984	6,859

b. The county vote totals for Clark and Dayton vary by up to ten votes in the newspaper printings.

An anonymous correspondent in the *Brunswick Gazette*, 15 September 1789 (Part Six), reported that Cape May County had voted unanimously for the western ticket. Therefore, since the only other unreported county, Cumberland, was a lightly populated, western county, it is virtually certain that Clark and Dayton did not receive enough votes to place them among the top four finishers even when the Essex County vote is included.

However, had the election been decided on the basis of the returns available to the governor and Privy Council on 3 March, the winners would have been Schureman, Clark, Dayton, and Robert Hoops. The returns were from seven counties: the East Jersey counties of Bergen, Middlesex, Monmouth, Morris, Somerset, and Sussex; and Hunterdon in West Jersey. The election returns were printed in the newspapers beginning on 24 February.

Brunswick Gazette, 24 February 1789

The following is a list of candidates for representatives from this state to the Congress of the United States, lately held in this state, with the number of votes taken for them in the counties from which returns are received, viz.

SOMERSET.

James Schureman,	992	Thomas Sinnickson,	72
Abraham Clark,	899	Elias Boudinot,	30
Jonathan Dayton,	774	James Parker,	26
Whitten Cripps,	489	Lambt. Cadwallader	23
James Linn,	244	Benj. Van-Cleve,	19
John Witherspoon,	189	John Stevens, jun.	19
Robert Hoops,	110		

MIDDLESEX.

James Schureman,	898	Tho. Sinnickson,	104
Abraham Clark,	682	John Stevens, jun.	81
John Witherspoon,	503	Elias Boudinot,	57
James Parker,	446	Lambt. Cadwallader,	38
Jonathan Dayton,	403	Robert Hoops.	17
Thomas Henderson,	170	Josiah Hornblower,	16
Benj. Van-Cleve,	160	Aaron Kitchel,	15

HUNTERDON.

James Schureman,	946	Elias Boudinot,	185
Benj. Van-Cleve,	754	John Stevens, jun.	158
Abraham Clark,	710	Jonathan Dayton,	135
John Witherspoon,	635	Thos. Sinnickson,	131
Robert L. Hooper,	586	Thos. Henderson,	94
Robert Hoops,	468	Whitten Cripps,	32
Lambt. Cadwallader	455	—— Kitchel,[1]	23
James Parker,	247		

MONMOUTH.

Thos. Henderson,	445	James Parker,	142
James Schureman,	434	Robert L. Hooper,	131
Jonathan Dayton,	406	Aaron Kitchel,	99
Elias Boudinot,	352	Lambt. Cadwallader	66
Abraham Clark,	213	John Witherspoon,	47
Benj. Van-Cleve,	159	Thos. Sinnickson,	21

There were several other candidates in nomination, but from the smallness of the number of votes they had, we have not inserted them.

1. Both Aaron and Abraham Kitchel were candidates.

Daily Advertiser (New York), 24 February

A correspondent in New-Jersey has sent us the following statement of the votes given for representatives to Congress in the counties to which the names are annexed, and where the poll is already closed:[1]

	Morris	Somerset	Bergen	Middlesex	Monmouth	Totl.
Schureman	1160	992	366	915	434	3867
Dayton	1241	784	358	403	406	3192
Clark	1180	899	125	679	213	3096

	Morris	Somerset	Bergen	Middlesex	Monmouth	Totl.
Parker	529			446	142	1117
Cripps	532	470		6	5	1013
Van Cleve	475			160	159	794
Boudinot	16	30	286	57	352	741
Hoops	416					416
Henderson			155	170	445	770
Hooper	19				131	150
Witherspoon				503	47	550
Sinickson				105	21	126
Cadwallader				35	66	101

1. The *New York Journal*, 26 February 1789, reported only the total vote each of the thirteen candidates received in the five counties. The totals were the same as those printed here, with the following exceptions: Schureman, 3,897; Dayton, 3,162; Cripps, 1,613; Van Cleve, 764; Hoops, 716; Hooper, 750; and Sinnickson, 129. The *Journal* noted that it had excluded "several others who had but few votes."

New Jersey Journal (Elizabethtown), 25 February

The following is a list of the votes taken in the several counties below-mentioned, for members to the federal house of representatives for this state.

BERGEN.

Boudinot	286	Clark	125
Schuurman	366	Fell	124
Dayton	358	Henderson	155

MORRIS.

Clark	1180	Witherspoon	10
Dayton	1241	Abrm. Ketchel	2
Schuurman	1160	Fennemore	6
Parker	529	Hughs	1
Vancleve	475	M. Thompson	1
Cripps	532	Jno. Stevens	6
Hoops	416	Silas Condict	1
B. Thompson	42	Woodhull	9
Boudinot	16	Winds	4
Linn	23	Frelinghuysen	1
Hooper	19	Sinnickson	5
Hornblower	13	Cadwallader	8
Tuthill	3	Henderson	1
A. Ketchel	12		

SOMERSET.

Clark	899	Linn	274
Schuurman	992	Witherspoon	189
Dayton	784	Hoops	110
Cripps	470	Sinnickson	72
Boudinot	30		

MIDDLESEX.

Schuurman	915	Cripps	6
Clark	679	Henderson	170
Dayton	403	Vancleve	160
Witherspoon	503	Sinnickson	105
Parker	446	Cadwallader	35
Boudinot	57		

MONMOUTH.

Henderson	445	Ketchel[1]	99
Schuurman	434	Cadwallader	66
Dayton	406	Witherspoon	47
Boudinot	352	Sinnickson	21
Clark	213	Cripps	5
Vancleve	159	Hardenburgh	5
Parker	142	Rutherford	4
Hooper	131	Smith	1

HUNTERDON.

Schuurman	946	Boudinot	185
Vancleve	754	J. Stevens, jun.	158
Clark	710	Dayton	135
Witherspoon	635	Sinnickson	131
Hooper	586	Henderson	94
Hoops	468	Cripps	32
Cadwallader	455	Ketchel	23
Parker	247		

1. Both Aaron and Abraham Kitchel were candidates.

New Jersey Journal (Elizabethtown), 25 February

Extract of a letter from Sussex, dated Feb. 23.

At the close of the poll in this county, the votes stood as follows. Not more than one third of the electors voted.

Robert Hoops	1026	Elias Boudinot	48
Abraham Clark	674	Robert L. Hooper	40
James Schuurman	664	Thomas Sinnickson	21
L. Cadwallader	404	William Winds	3
Jonathan Dayton	397	John Rutherford	2
James Linn	235	_____ Ketchel[1]	2
John Witherspoon	219	Fred. Frelinghuysen	2
Benj. Van Cleve	203	John Neilson	1
John Stevens	177	Robert Ogden	1
Whitten Cripps	141	John Armstrong	1
James Parker	86	John Mehelm	1
Charles Stewart	63		

1. Both Aaron and Abraham Kitchel were candidates.

Daily Advertiser (New York), 26 February

In our paper of Tuesday we published the returns of the votes given in several of the counties of New-Jersey for Representatives to Congress; the following has since come to hand:

HUNTERDON County.

James Schureman	946	Elias Boudinot,	185
Benj. Van Cleve,	754	John Stevens, jun.	158
Abraham Clark,	710	Jonathan Dayton,	135
John Witherspoon,	635	Thos. Sinnickson,	131
Robert L. Hooper,	586	Thos. Henderson,	94
Robert Hoops,	468	Whitten Cripps,	32
Lambt. Cadwallader,	455	________ Kitchel,[1]	23
James Parker,	247		

1. Both Aaron and Abraham Kitchel were candidates.

Brunswick Gazette, 3 March

Returns received since our last.

	SUSSEX.		
Robert Hoops,	1026	Benj. Vancleve.	203
Abraham Clark,	674	John Stevens,	177[1]
James Schureman,	644	Whitten Cripps,	141
Lambt. Cadwallader	404	James Parker,	86
Jonathan Dayton,	397	Elias Boudinot,	48
James Linn,	235	Thomas Sinnickson,	21
John Witherspoon,	219		
	MORRIS.		
Jonathan Dayton,	1241	Benj. Vancleve,	475
Abraham Clark,	1180	Robert Hoops,	416
James Schureman,	1160	Robert L. Hooper,	19
Whitten Cripps,	532	Elias Boudinot,	16
James Parker,	529	John Witherspoon,	10
	BERGEN.		
James Schureman,	366	Thos. Henderson,	155
Jonathan Dayton,	358	Abraham Clark,	125
Elias Boudinot,	286		
	BURLINGTON[2]		
Jas. Schureman,	1885	Robt. L. Hooper,	173
Tho. Sinnickson,	1417	John Stevens,	164
Lmbt. Cadwallader	1397	Abraham Clark,	148
Elias Boudinot,	1371	Tho. Fenimore,	117
Jonathan Dayton,	597	Benj. V. Cleve,	97
John Witherspoon,	411	Thos. Henderson,	29
Whitten Cripps.	323	Benj. Thomson,	21
Robert Hoops,	189		

1. The *Brunswick Gazette* initially gave these 177 votes to Charles Stewart; a correction giving the votes to Stevens was made in an "Errata" on 10 March 1789.

2. On 10 March, the *Brunswick Gazette* reported that this list for Burlington was not "a just one" (see immediately below).

Brunswick Gazette, 10 March

The list of votes from Burlington published last week was not a just one, but the following is exact.

Tho. Sinnickson	2800	Jonathan Dayton	118
Elias Boudinot	2763	Robert Hoops	20
L. Cadwallader	2728	Abraham Clark	7
Jas. Schureman	2686	Benj. Van-Cleve	7
	S A L E M.		
Sinnickson	886	Boudinot	672
Cadwallader	731	Dayton	41
Cripps	700	Clark	35

The six highest in nomination, at this stage of the election is James Schureman, 8346—Abraham Clark, 4526—Lambert Cadwallader, 4445—Elias Boudinot, 4342—Thomas Sinnickson, 4040—Jonathan Dayton, 3873.—It will make a very material odds when we add 3000 from Essex to the lists of Dayton and Clark; we apprehend that this number will settle the matter beyond a doubt.

Federal Gazette (Philadelphia), 11 March

We are informed, by good authority, that on Tuesday last the poll was closed for the election of Federal Representatives in the county of Burlington, in our sister state of New-Jersey. Upon counting off the tickets, (in all 2826) the following gentlemen had the highest number of votes, viz.

Thomas Sinnickson, of Salem county,	2800,
Elias Boudenot, of Essex county,	2763,
Lambert Cadwallader, of Hunterdon county,	2628,
James Shureman, of Middlesex county,	2689.[1]

1. This report appeared in the Philadelphia *Pennsylvania Gazette* on the same day and was reprinted in the Philadelphia *Pennsylvania Mercury*, 12 March 1789; Philadelphia *Pennsylvania Packet*, 13 March; Philadelphia *Independent Gazetteer*, 14 March; and Hartford *American Mercury*, 23 March.

Daily Advertiser (New York), 21 March

Extract of a letter from Elizabethtown,
dated yesterday morning, March 20.

Our election for Representatives has been carried on with great warmth—12 of the counties have closed their polls, and brought in a list of votes to the Governor. In this county (Essex) the poll is still open—Yesterday the Council which had been assembled by his Excellency, advised him to make a return from the votes then brought in.—In consequence of this decision, Mr. Schureman, Mr. Cadwallader, Mr. Boudinot, and Mr. Sinickson, will be elected.

Federal Gazette (Philadelphia), 21 March

The following gentlemen appear, by a proclamation of the governor of New-Jersey, to be duly elected the representatives for that state, in the congress of the United States.

Hon. James Schurman,	
L. Cadwalader,	*Esquires.*[1]
E. Boudinot,	
T. Sinnickson,	

1. Similar reports of the winners of the New Jersey election were widely reprinted in newspapers from New York City northward.

Pennsylvania Packet (Philadelphia), 24 March

The following gentlemen are elected to represent the state of New-Jersey in the House of Representatives of the United States:—

James Schureman,	12537 votes
L. Cadwalader,	8685
E. Boudinot,	8603
T. Sinnickson.	8240[1]

1. The same vote totals were printed in the Philadelphia *Freeman's Journal*, 25 March 1789.

New Jersey Journal (Elizabethtown), 25 March

After investigating the returns of the votes given in from twelve counties of this state, for members to the General Congress, last Wednesday, by the Governor and Council, they declared Elias Boudinot, James Schuurman, Lambert Cadwallader, and Thomas Sinnickson, Esq'rs. duly elected.[1]

1. This item was reprinted in the Philadelphia *Independent Gazetteer*, 30 March 1789.

Pennsylvania Gazette (Philadelphia), 25 March

On Saturday, the 14th instant, the election for fœderal representatives in the Congress of the United States, for the state of New-Jersey, closed at Woodbury, for the county of Gloucester; upon counting off the tickets (3274 in the whole) there appeared for the following candidates the numbers as follow, viz.

Thomas Sinnickson,	3271	John Witherspoon,	3
Elias Boudinot,	3270	Jonathan Dayton,	2
Lambert Cadwallader,	3269	Thomas Henderson,	1
James Schurman,	3267	Whitten Cripps.	1

It is pleasing, says a correspondent, to find so much union and perseverence in the western counties of New-Jersey. From their elections alone has, what is called, the western ticket been carried by a large majority. Burlington and Gloucester gave better than 6000 votes for one ticket. That ticket has lately, to wit, the 19th instant, been declared by the Governor and Privy Council of New-Jersey to have been successful. Upon counting off the whole number of votes from the State, exclusive of Essex county, there appeared, as follows, viz.

James Schurman,	12597	Elias Boudinot,	8603
Lambert Cadwallader,	8685	Thomas Sinnickson,	8240

Our correspondent has further to remark, that, although Essex has not closed, the Governor and Council have counted off the whole votes, and proclamation has issued in favor of the last mentioned gentlemen.[1]

1. This article was reprinted in the Philadelphia *Pennsylvania Mercury*, 26 March 1789.

III.
Abraham Clark and the Election

Abraham Clark, an East Jerseyite, was a particular target of proponents of the Junto ticket. During a long and distinguished career in colonial and state affairs, Clark had taken controversial positions on many issues. As a leader of the "radical" forces in state politics in the 1780s, Clark angered many with his advocacy of paper money, reform of the state's legal system to drastically reduce the influence of lawyers, and debtor relief measures. Junto supporters often included Jonathan Dayton, another "radical" leader and a Clark protégé, in their attacks on Clark.

The Federal Constitution was very popular in New Jersey (the state Convention had ratified it unanimously), and thus Clark's suggestion that the Constitution should be amended was interpreted by some as opposition to the Constitution. He explained his position most clearly in a letter to Thomas Sinnickson, 23 July 1788, and, publicly, in the *New Jersey Journal*, 4 February 1789, but his opponents nevertheless persisted in accusing him of Antifederalism.

Some of the sharpest public attacks on Clark were made by "Martin B. Bunn," in seven letters published in the *Brunswick Gazette*, 24 February-7 April 1789. Generally satiric in nature, the letters, published after most of the counties had closed their polls, contain great detail about the elections, particularly in Somerset County. The pseudonym "Martin B. Bunn" was probably derived from the names of three Somerset legislators who supported Clark: Ephraim Martin, Robert Blair, and Edward Bunn (see Richard P. McCormick, "New Jersey's First Congressional Election, 1789 . . .," WMQ, 3d ser., VI [1949], 240n).

The documents referred to above are printed in this part. Additional commentary about Clark's role in the election is contained in documents printed in Part Five:I, above, and Part Six.

Abraham Clark to Thomas Sinnickson, New York, 23 July 1788[1]

I am favoured with yours of the 12th. instant by Major Story which I recd.—yesterday,—his Journey I find has been unsuccessful.[2]

As to my sentiments respecting the New System of Government, altho' you do not ask, yet, as I find by your Letter it will be Acceptable, I think it not amiss to give them.—They have at no time been concealed.—I never liked the System in all its parts. I considered it from the first, more a Consolidated government than a federal, a government too expensive, and unnecessarily Oppressive in its Opperation; Creating a Judiciary undefined and unbounded.—with all these imperfections about it, I nevertheless wished it to go to the States from Congress just as it did, without any Censure or Commendation, hoping that in Case of a general Adoption, the Wisdom of the States would soon amend it in the exceptionable parts;[3] Strong fears however remained upon my mind untill I found the Custom of Recommending amendments with the Adoptions began to prevail.—This set my mind at ease. It became clear in my opinion from the Oppositions, and the general concurrence in proposing amendmts that the present plan must undergo some alterations to make it more agreable to the minds of the great Numbers who dislike it in its present form. The Amendments I wish are not numerous;—many proposed by the different Conventions appear of but little Consequence, yet some are important and must be Acceded to if ever the Government sits easy. From this State of the matter, wishing amendmts. as I do, you will readily conclude I anxiously wish every State may come into the adoption in order to effect a measure with me so desireable; in which case, from the general current of amendments proposed, we shall retain all the important parts in which New Jersey is interested.

To your quere about our paper money, I dare not venture a Conjecture what effect the new Government will have upon it. I suppose, however, no interference will be had in that or any Law now in force so far as respects Citizens of the same State. In Continental affairs, and between Citizens of different States I suppose the case will be otherwise, our paper probably will not then be received in the Treasury of the United States, or in our State by Citizens of another State, in which Cases it will cease to be a legal tender.

As to the Arrears of Taxes payable to the Continental Receiver, I believe our paper will readily be received: The difficulty of obtaining money from the exhausted State of our finances makes our money, notwithstanding the loss sustained upon it, eagerly sought after; I know public Creditors are anxious to Obtain orders on our Loan officer when they can hear he hath any of our paper on hand; large orders have been given upon him which the holders Accepted in expectation of receiving paper only: As to Specie they know at present none is expected.

If any remedy is applied to our paper money it must come through our Legislature: I believe it would have a good effect if the Interest and such of the principle as may be paid in was destroyed, and the amount of the Interest raised by taxes.

It is said the Speaker is about calling our Legislature on account of the Adoption of the New Constitution; this is altogether unnecessary as the New Congress will not be convened before February, the Situation of several States require such a distant time; the Usual time of meeting in October will be soon enough to make the necessary provision for Appointing officers &c.[4]

We have been some time in Suspense about the event of the New Constitution in this State; The Accounts of last evening were that the Convention had Adjourned to a future day; if that is the Case they mean at next meeting to adopt it. before I seal this I may likely hear whether the above report is true or not.

P.S. I cannot find that the Acct. of the Conventions Adjourning is Supported by any good Authority.

1. RC, Conarroe Autograph Collection, PHi. The letter was addressed to Sinnickson in Salem, New Jersey.

2. John Story (1754–1791), of Philadelphia, served in several Continental Army quartermaster units during the Revolutionary War, and was the Pennsylvania commissioner to settle accounts of individuals with the United States in 1786. He was in New York trying to obtain satisfactory compensation from Congress for his wartime military services.

3. Congress adopted Clark's suggestion of sending the Constitution to the states without passing judgment on it (DHRC, I, 330–31).

4. A special session of the New Jersey legislature met 27 August-9 September 1788, but it made no provisions for the first federal elections. Its major action was a bill ceding land to Congress for a federal district.

Brunswick Gazette, 3 February 1789

We are authorised to inform the public that notwithstanding it is published in the Trenton paper that the hon. Abraham Clark had declined to serve as a delegate in Congress for this state, that gentleman is to be considered as a candidate at the ensuing election.[1]

1. No Trenton announcement has been located.

Joseph Riggs's Deposition, New Jersey Journal (Elizabethtown), 4 February[1]

Be it remembered, that on the 31st day of January, Anno Domini 1789, personally appeared before Matthias Ward, Esq. one of the Judges of the Inferior Court of Commonpleas for the county of Essex—Joseph Riggs, Esq. who being duly sworn, saith, that he is an inhabitant of the city of New-York, and that Abraham Clark, Esq. a member of congress from New-Jersey, was frequently at his house after the new constitution had been published; and the said Abraham Clark, Esq. frequently expressed his disapprobation of it—declaring that he did not like a consolidated government—but wanted each state to retain its independent sovereignty—And said he only wanted the present congress to have a little more authority; and that he would oppose the new constitution [with] all in his power.—These sentiments he not only expressed once, but frequently in the hearing of this deponent, and that of a number of other persons who were from time to time in his house.

JOSEPH RIGGS.

Sworn before me the day
and year above written.
Matt. Ward.[2]

1. Riggs (1720–1798), who operated a boarding house in New York City at this time, had been a resident of Newark and Essex County, New Jersey, before 1783. He had been a businessman, Newark officeholder, and county magistrate.

2. This item was reprinted in the *Brunswick Gazette*, 10 February 1789.

Abraham Clark, New Jersey Journal (Elizabethtown), 4 February

Mr. Kollock,

The following it is desired may find admission into your paper.

To a person desirous of passing quietly through life with as little show and parade as possible, wishing rather to deserve esteem, than to obtain applause, any address to the public respecting himself, must be disagreeable, and, in some cases improper; yet in others, not only excusable but a duty. A charge, however false, which remains uncontradicted is readily believed. Every man in public life must expect to pass through ill, as well as good report, and though his calumniators are often too insignificant to merit a reply, or even occasion any resentment, yet it may sometimes happen otherwise. At present I am attacked, not openly in the public prints that I have heard of, but in a secret manner by letters, certificates, &c. sent privately into every part of the state, containing gross misrepresentations, and the most palpable falshoods, in order to prejudice the minds of the citizens against me at the coming election, and prevent my being appointed to a confidential trust: A trust of so much importance to the citizens of New-Jersey, that a diffidence of my abilities to execute it in a proper manner to their advantage, forbids any attempt of mine to push myself into it. It is however my duty, as well in private as in public life, to remove every unjust and illiberal charge against me, more especially, as in the present case, when coming from persons who, if they had a disposition for it, might render useful services to the community; I need not name them, they are characters well known in Jersey, as is also the cause of their clamours which may be considered as very remote from their regard to the interest of the citizens of the state. Those letters and certificates I have mentioned though intended as private stabs, from their number and circulation are become public and very notorious. One of their insinuations is that I am antifœderal, and an enemy to the new government. The charge of antifœderalism is of so general and undefined a nature, that had it not been followed by that of an enemy to the government, I should not have thought it worthy of notice, as that epithet is frequently given to all those who dare venture to suspect the least defect in the Constitution, in which is included by far the greatest part of the inhabitants of the United States: How far this charge is applicable to me, I leave the impartial public to judge. That I used every means in my power in the different stations I filled, to obtain an efficient government, is well known and cannot be denied. When the plan of the new government appeared, I found it not such as I had wished and expected; I perceived, as I supposed, some parts of it bearing too hard upon the liberties of the people, and giving some unnecessary powers to those who were to administer it: This I never scrupled to mention when my opinion was desired. Notwithstanding my dislike to some parts, considering the situation the United States was in, and the provision made in the Constitution for amendments, I cheerfully gave my assistance to send it to the states for their consideration, judging that New-Jersey, from its local situation and circumstances, could not with propriety reject it, notwithstanding its imperfections; presuming at the same time, that the new Congress would endeavor to amend it as soon as other important business for putting the government into operation would admit. This I yet hope and expect will, in a proper time, be effected in Congress, but not by a future general convention, which would be inexpedient and dangerous to the union by leaving us without government for years to come. The story so industriously propogated, that I made offers to, and used endeavors with the Convention of Jersey to prevent their ratifying the Constitution, is so far from being true, that I never exchanged one word to my remembrance or belief, with any one member of our Convention on the subject of the Constitution, until long after its ratification, or ever wrote to one of them upon that subject; nor did I use any means whatever tending to a rejection of it, which I had a right to do if I thought proper, when the Constitution was under consideration; a right which I trust I shall at all times, if necessary, exercise without fear or scruple, when our liberties are the subject of deliberation. This in brief, as near as I can state it, is the sum total of my antifœderalism and enmity to the new government, if any are pleased to call it such.

One of my opposers, in concurrence as I am told with others, has gone so far as to obtain, or fabricate certificate[1] which has been circulated through the state, certifying, that I had tendered state securities in discharge of a debt, there being a law for that purpose in certain cases;[2] a silly charge if true, too trifling to be noticed, were it not that great things are expected from it by its publishers. The truth after all is, that I never was possessed of such a kind of certificate as the law authorized a tender of, and that I never by myself or by any other person, either tendered or offered a certificate of any kind in payment of a debt, or for sale, except for the purchase of land over the Ohio.

Another insinuation of those civil gentlemen, my opposers (from which they draw an inference that I shall promote dessentions in the government) is, that I am opposed to a certain gentleman which it is expected will be the highest officer in the government: A gentleman high in my estimation, and who in preference to all others, I wish may have the appointment to that important station. This insinuation, I am told, is founded upon a supposed transaction in Congress many years ago, which I have good reason to believe never happened, and which I never heard any intimation of till a few months past.

In addition to the above, my letters are taken up and secreted, or the direction altered, and sent a contrary way to what was intended; in order to prevent a seasonable discovery of the nefarious practices of my enemies.

From this short statement of facts, which duty obliges me to make, the public will judge what kind of gentlemen I have to contend with; I shall not however, at this time, make any remarks upon their illiberal and indecent conduct, but leave them to such farther measures as they may think proper to pursue; they will no doubt continue very busy, and should they confine themselves to truth, or alledge that I have not abilities equal to the important trust of a representative, I shall not contend with them. It is strange they should attempt to propogate falshoods about me, when, from the errors I have probably committed in a long course of public service, one would imagine they might have mustered up truths sufficient to publish to my disadvantage.

I must not conclude without observing, that the present is an important crisis; a new untried[3] government is to be put into operation, every thing under providence, depends upon the persons who are to conduct it; for unless wisdom and cool deliberation direct our councils, dissentions will probably arise that may end in our final ruin; which may Heaven prevent, is the sincere prayer of the public's

Most obedient and humble servant,

ABRA. CLARK.

* * * * * * *

Mr. KOLLOCK,

Since I delivered you a piece for publication,[4] respecting certain matters propogated about me, in New-Jersey, I have been informed from such authority that I cannot doubt the truth of it, that it is announced in a public paper printed in Trenton, that I had declined serving as a representative to the new Congress. As I have not seen the paper, I am ignorant in what manner it is published, whether by a letter forged in my name, or information given by way of intelligence; be it in either way, it is wholly unauthorised, and void of truth, and is a new piece of villainy proceeding from the same source as the former, which I have taken notice of. Is this the way a certain gentleman,[5] once filling a high station, is to be brought forward in the election? And is he, (as may be expected from the connection) of the same principles with the chief author of the false reports against me? If so, and our representatives in general should be of the same cast, the commonality may indeed be brought to the state he supposes they ought to be. This I request you will insert in your paper, in contradiction to the report of my declining; in doing which you will oblige, Sir,

Your humble servant,
ABRA. CLARK.

New-York, February 1, 1789.[6]

1. The word "certificate" was added in an "Errata," *New Jersey Journal,* 11 February 1789.
2. See Jacob Winans's Certificate and Aaron Clark's Affidavit, *New Jersey Journal,* 11 February 1789, below.
3. The word "untried" was substituted for "united" in an "Errata," *New Jersey Journal,* 11 February 1789.
4. The "piece" was printed directly above, separated by asterisks, as it is here.
5. Presumably Elias Boudinot.
6. Both letters were reprinted in the *Brunswick Gazette* and New York *Daily Advertiser,* 10 February 1789.

A Freeholder, Brunswick Gazette, 10 February

To the Electors of New-Jersey.

In a late Publication by one of the Candidates for a seat in Congress, he declares,[1]

1. *That New-Jersey, from its local situation and circumstances, could not, with propriety, reject the Constitution.*
2. *That he did not use any means whatever tending to a rejection of it.*
3. *That he had used every means in his power to obtain an efficient government.*
4. *That he had never tendered Certificates in payment of debts.*

What confidence is to be put in these solemn declarations of his, let the following affidavits and certificates of gentlemen of established character determine.

[Joseph Riggs's Deposition reprinted here.[2]]

To whom it may Concern.

Being called upon to certify what Mr. Abraham Clark said to me on the subject of the Federal Constitution, when serving in quality of a member of the general assembly for the county of Bergen, in the fall of 1787, *at Trenton; and conceiving it to be proper, in order to prevent mistakes, I beg leave to give a fair state of the matter as far as I can recollect. On the evening of the day on which the assembly adjourned, Mr. Clark came to my lodging and enquired if the assembly was like to break up, and being answered that they had already adjourned, he expressed a regret that he had missed the opportunity of conversing with the members previous to their adjournment—said he thought it necessary that a convention should be appointed to alter the state constitution, as its powers were almost destroyed or swallowed up by the new government; that he thought New-Jersey had been too precipitate in adopting the new plan of government, since he was well informed that New-York would have made large concessions to this state in consideration of their declining that measure; and that they would not only have given up the impost, but would be willing to refund the amount of the duties by them collected in a state capacity—that people talked of taring and feathering him, but that if they would provide him with a good coat, which would last five or six years, he would be satisfied; for that within that time, they would build a temple for it. He said farther, that the new government would be very respectable abroad, but oppressive at home, if it was exercised as it then stood—declared himself an enemy to the appellate jurisdiction by the new constitution allowed to congress—that he was opposed to the power of altering the times and places of election therein given—to direct taxation without controul—and that he thought the executive and legislative branches were too much blended, &c. &c.*

Hackensack, Feb. 6, 1789. *ADAM BOYD.*[3]

Whereas Abraham Clark, Esq. in a late publication, endeavouring to obviate a charge brought against him, of tendering certificates in payment of a debt—amongst other things has the following words. "The truth after all is, that I never was possessed of such a kind of certificate as the law authorized a tender of; and that I never, by myself or by any other person, *either tendered, or offered a certificate of any kind in payment of a debt, or for sale, except for the purchase of land over the Ohio."*[4]

I JACOB SHOTWELL,[5] *being one of the people called Quakers, do solemnly declare, and certify, that the said Abraham Clark was indebted to me in one bond, conditioned for the payment of eighty eight pounds seven shillings and ninepence, bearing date* 7*th month,* 28*th,* 1772.—*Also, in one other bond, conditioned for the payment of thirty pounds, dated* 12*th month,* 31*st,* 1773.—*Also, his son, Aaron Clark,*[6] *in one other bond, conditioned for the payment of twenty pounds, dated* 17*th of the* 9*th month,* 1774, *which the said Abraham became security for.—And on the* 29*th of the* 10*th month,* 1784, *the above named Aaron Clark (son of the said Abraham Clark) came to my house with two other men, and tendered in state notes (as he said) the sum of* £120 *for payment of all the above sums, and a debt due from Jacob Winants; and told me at the same time, that his father had a hand in it.—The certificates I refused—and the said Abraham Clark hath never called upon me, or taken one step towards settling the said debts since, although I went to his house (and he not being at home) I left a message, requesting that he would come and see me on the subject.*

Given under my hand at Rahway, the 6*th day of the* 2*d month,* 1789.

JACOB SHOTWELL.

Signed in the presence of JOSEPH SHOTWELL.

Now my Fellow Citizens, judge for yourselves—Can the interests of the state of New-Jersey be safely intrusted to such a person?

A FREEHOLDER.[7]

1. See Abraham Clark, *New Jersey Journal*, 4 February 1789, immediately above.
2. See Joseph Riggs's Deposition, *New Jersey Journal*, 4 February 1789, above.
3. Boyd (1746–1835), a Hackensack businessman, was a member of the Assembly, 1782–1783, 1787, and 1794–1795; Bergen County sheriff, 1778–1781 and 1789–1791; and a member of the House of Representatives, 1803–1805 and 1808–1813.
4. See Abraham Clark, *New Jersey Journal*, 4 February 1789, immediately above.

5. Shotwell, a Quaker leader, was a Rahway merchant.

6. Aaron Clark (c. 1750-c. 1811), the oldest son of Abraham Clark, was a resident of Elizabethtown. He had served as an artillery officer during the Revolution, and by the end of 1790 was living in Washington County, Pennsylvania.

7. This article was preceded in the newspaper by reprints of Abraham Clark's two letters, first printed in the *New Jersey Journal*, 4 February 1789 (see immediately above).

Jacob Winans's Certificate and Aaron Clark's Affidavit, New Jersey Journal (Elizabethtown), 11 February

A publication, in a hand-bill, having been circulated, respecting tenders of Certificates, the following Certificate and Affidavit is inserted to place that transaction in its true light.

THESE ARE TO CERTIFY, that in or about the year 1784, agreeably to a law of this state, I caused a tender of state certificates to be made to Jacob Shotwell, in payment of a bond, in which Abraham Clark, Esq; was bound as surety for David Ross unto said Shotwell; which bond I had engaged to discharge in part of a payment for land I purchased of said Ross: That a tender of this debt, in Continental Money, had before been made at my request, in the year 1777. That this tender of certificates was made at my request, and in my behalf, by Aaron Clark, son of said Abraham: That I always conceived that said Abraham Clark had no right to interfere in my payment of said bond, as I had a right to pay it in any legal manner most convenient to me: That this tender was made at my special request, in which said Abraham Clark had no hand or concern; nor did he, to my knowledge or belief, know any thing of the transaction. Witness my hand this 10th day of February, 1789.

JACOB WINANS.

AARON CLARK, of Elizabeth-Town, being duly sworn, deposeth, That in the year 1777, he, in the presence of two witnesses, made a tender in Continental Money to Jacob Shotwell, for the payment of two bonds, one from his father Abraham Clark, Esq; for about thirty pounds, and the other from himself for twenty pounds, which money the said Jacob Shotwell refused to receive: Since which time does not know of any transaction having taken place between the said parties respecting the said bonds: That in or about the year 1784, this deponent, at the special instance and request of Jacob Winans, made a tender of State Securities unto said Jacob Shotwell for payment of a bond, in which the said Abraham Clark was security for David Ross unto said Shotwell, which bond the said Jacob Winans had (as he understood) become paymaster for: That this deponent never knew of any securities or certificates being tendered for the two bonds first above mentioned: And that the said Abraham Clark never had, to his knowledge or belief, any concern or agency in tendering certificates to said Shotwell or any other person, for any debt whatever; and that he is fully of opinion, he never mentioned his father's having any hand in this tender, as such an assertion would have been false.

AARON CLARK.

Sworn this tenth day of February, 1789, before me,
ISAAC WOODRUFF.[1]

1. Both documents were reprinted in the *Brunswick Gazette*, 17 February 1789. Winans, of Elizabethtown, was Aaron Clark's brother-in-law. He was a captain of an Essex County light horse unit during the Revolution.

Martin B. Bunn, Brunswick Gazette, 24 February

To the Hon. ABRAHAM CLARK, *Esq.*

My dear and respected Friend,

The election for the county of Somerset is closed—and it is with the most inexpressible satisfaction that I inform you of our success, beyond our most sanguine expectations. Our ticket was every thing to almost every body, and the sanctifying power of your dear name, placed even Col Crips,[1] *though unknown among us, the fourth on the glorious list. I inclose a statement of the votes, as I received them from the sheriff, and the more you look at it the more you must be convinced of our complete victory in this county, over the enemies of our excellent plan of government. Let not, my dear friend, an uneasy thought take possession of your mind, because the Brunswick lad*[2] *has a few more votes than yourself in our county; it is a circumstance which I shall so explain as to redound to your honour—but this in proper time.*[3]

At present I will confine myself to such general information on the subject as I conceive immediately material, both to raise your mind to that pitch of rational pride, which ought to be the result of having your past disinterested and noble services so emphatically acknowledged by a respectable county of this state; and also to increase your attachment to those chosen friends, who have so nobly stept forth in your behalf.—You know, sir, that after the first plan of operation[4] *was given up, in consequence of the* affectionate *union of interest with your worthy neighbour (an event, which,* for the honour of human nature, *ought never to be forgotten) our next plan, terms having been made with the western Colonel,*[5] *to promote the new ticket with all our power, and especially to trumpet forth your most shining virtues to the public ear, in this and the adjacent counties, and to be prepared at all points on the days of election, with tickets, speeches, runners and bullies for the important occasion. Every part, my dear friend, of this most excellent plan has been executed to admiration;—the state of the votes in this county, in part, evinces this; and when we hear from the other counties, it will, we trust, be more fully demonstrated.—Your great abilities—your shining piety—your fœderal principles—your inviolable attachment to the rights of the people—and your noble atchievements as a stateman, for the advancement of the interest of this state, have all, in their turn, received from our lips their merited applause. That great and good man, whose services for his* bleeding country, *I hope you will now soon be able most amply to reward, performed wonders in our glorious cause.—Before the election he spared no pains nor expence in your service—he rode abroad with all his wisdom about him—he assembled your friends from every quarter—he harangued to men, to women, to children, to the very trees of the wood;—your praises he resounded in stately domes, in cottages and in barns;—the rich, the poor, the grave, the gay; the fopling and the dunce heard him and wondered.—Nor was he alone—many other worthies, who have either aided you in the glorious administration of the government of New-Jersey, or who have felt its happy effects on their fortunes or political importance, were equally zealous;—in short, sir, when the election commenced, we, your friends, appeared like disciplined troops in the field of war—our chieftain having assigned each his part, every thing was effected according to our wishes. Some toiled at framing the glorious ticket, others distributed;—some reasoned, some harangued in different quarters; nor were there wanting others, whose brawny arms would have forced conviction if our eloquence had failed—when opposition reared its head we formed around our orator, in concentric circles, more irresistable than the Macedonian phalanx, and bore down all before us. It afforded, sir, the most refined pleasure to hear our leader expatiate to the listning croud on your various and amiable qualifications:—he at last compared you to the goodly tree, which beareth goodly fruit, and to prove his allegory, he shewed the clubs the boys had thrown. The multitude convinced, almost overran the clerks and inspecters, rushing forward to testify their approbation of your meritorious services, and to save their country from destruction, by placing its most important concerns under the shadow of your all-preserving wings.—But, sir, when the election closed, and our success appeared, then every bosom throbbed with joy, which was increased by the pleasing expectation that our sister counties had concurred in so happy a choice, and of shortly seeing your name enrolled among the rulers of this western empire—an event in which the rich will rejoice, and the poor will leap for gladness—these will expect, without the toils of labour, thrice a day to plunge their knives into the fatted calf or stalled ox; whilst those with joy presage the happy hour when property shall have a mark, and when* contracts shall be sacred.—*Accept, therefore,* THOU MAN OF THE PEOPLE, *my warmest congratulations on this happy occasion, and may that spirit who taught you so affectionately to pray for the good of this country, teach you to rule it in mercy, and to remember the poor.*

I have thus, my dear friend, given you a short account of our success in this county, merely to prepare your mind for a more particular detail of our atchievements in the defence of your reputation from the calumny of the wicked. This task still remains, and shall be the subject of future epistles. I will fairly state every interesting incident, and not refer you to the chronicles of others.—The insidious hints thrown out against you by many ill-disposed persons—the reasonings of some ignorant creatures, or the famous handbill published by your enemies—the violent, though vain attempts of the lawyers, to prejudice the minds of the people against you, and the manner in which they ridiculed your blessed address to the freemen of this state, together with the means we employed to silence the whole opposition, shall all be recounted with the faithfulness of an historian bent on truth.—I will conclude the whole by placing before you an account of our prospects as to the future government of our dear country. And that you may also have some foretaste of our future happiness, permit me to tell you, that, by your exertions we expect the new constitution will, without the expence of consulting us again on the subject, be amended to our wishes on the floor of Congress; and, having now fully gotten into our hands the power of managing elections, that we shall soon, in this state, have the several departments of government filled with men of probity, who will walk humbly and disdain to oppress the poor; nay, we doubt not but we shall shortly rejoice in the total extermination of the lawyers, those pests to society: in hearing of the destruction of their pernicious books, their writs of hebeas corpus, of error and of certiorari; and that we shall have in this state a little *magna charta, and a small pocket volume of wholsome laws, which will amply supply all the farrago of learned nonsense, with which we have been so long teazed and oppressed.*[6] *This good work, my dear friend, you have long since nobly begun, and may he who, after your departure from the school of the geometrician, so graciously inspired you with universal knowledge, so guide and direct you and us, that we may complete the glorious undertaking.*

I am, Sir,

With profound respect,

Your humble servant,

MARTIN B. BUNN.

February 23, 1789.

1. Whitten Cripps.

2. James Schureman.

3. Also appearing in the *Brunswick Gazette*, 24 February 1789, were vote totals for Hunterdon, Middlesex, Monmouth, and Somerset counties. They are printed in Part Five:II, above.

4. For more on this "plan," see "Martin B. Bunn," *Brunswick Gazette*, 3 March 1789, immediately below.

5. Probably Joseph Bloomfield.

6. In 1784 the New Jersey legislature passed "An Act for Regulating and Shortening the Proceedings of the Courts of Law," which reduced the influence and privilege of lawyers in New Jersey courts. Abraham Clark was the principal proponent of this law.

Martin B. Bunn, Brunswick Gazette, 3 March

To ABRAHAM CLARK, Esq.

Electioneering is not like legislation, acquired by the mere addition of *esquire* to our names.—It requires much knowledge of men and manners; a thorough acquaintance with the different turns and dispositions of the people; and, above all, a great presence and readiness of mind, when unexpected events turn up, tending to thwart our designs. The best pursued plan frequently proves abortive, by the incapacity of its managers, to take the necessary measures, "or the spur of the occasion," to counteract the various arts and manœuvres of an enemy. Preparation indeed is very necessary, and this alone in common cases will ensure success; but, in contested elections, unless the patrons of a ticket have ingenuity and address so as to turn the arrows of opposition with redoubled force against opposition itself, and at all times to be ready, on every quarter, effectually to resist, preparation may be overcome by unexpected strokes of policy. The manner in which we, your friends, conducted ourselves in these respects, I mean now to relate according to promise.

And first, as to preparation.—I observed to you in my last, that we spared no pains in recommending you to the people, from the day that our members returned from the legislature, to the day of election; but, sir, we had also as warmly recommended Mr. Sinnickson, and, as you know, meant to run him in our ticket—fortunately we received timely information that you had taken your neighbour by the hand, and that this plan might prove fatal both to yourself and him;—this caused us at once to change our *sentiments*, and notwithstanding that we had so generally recommended the first to the leading men, we succeeded in making them adopt the new one, without the least difficulty—such and so strong is the attachment of this people to your interest!—Having fixed upon our ticket, our next step was to secure voters, and for this purpose we made great exertions. You must know, sir, that a considerable part of this county[1] is inhabited by Low Dutch people, a very respectable, industrious, and by far the wealthiest part of the community; these, sir, or at least a great part of them, have, for years past, been much displeased with the *system* of government we have been pursuing in this state—enemies to paper money, and of all those gracious acts of our legislature, by which *unfortunate* debtors have been so generally favored and relieved;—these, therefore, have generally, when they have come out to elections, rather sided with our opponents, who, by their means, have sometimes met with partial success. But, sir, we took such effectual steps to secure the Dutch interest, in our favor, by gaining over to our side two of their *leading* characters, and by getting you recommended to them by one of their society, whom, among this religious people, it would be thought next to blasphemy to contradict, that we were well assured before the election, that the danger from this quarter had nearly vanished. Too much praise cannot be bestowed on the two persons above alluded to;—they exerted the most unwearied diligence and activity in your behalf, refusing even rest and the common comforts of life, whilst your interest required their attention—the one refused to hear any thing said against you; the other nobly hinted that he would risque more than tongue in your defence—their zeal increased by the hour, and the more they were opposed the more they were determined in your favor. I trust our state legislature will do something for them, but, as your's is likely to be the largest treasury, I will transmit you their names; for, surely, "for all this they ought to be remembered for good." But, sir, the most beneficial thing we did before the election was, the information we gave throughout the county of your having, by your zeal in the service of your country, drawn upon you the enmity of the lawyers, who would therefore most probably oppose your election, and the directing of all our friends to brand them and their adherents with the name of the *Court-Party*, who in all countries have ever aimed at abridging the *liberties* of the people. With these preparations, added to others formerly made to help our friends into the state legislature, we took the field; and, sir, no sooner was the election opened, but forward came the *court-party* and their adherents, and represented you as inimical to the new constitution, and in plain language called you an Antifederalist.—We denied your antifederalism in the very strongest terms, and our *leader* read the journals of congress to the people, which, he observed never lied, and by which it appeared that you was the first in that august body who moved to put the new constitution in motion. To this they replied, that you had done this merely to deceive the people, and when you knew that any farther opposition to this constitution would shortly send you back to your farm and compass;—that before nine states had adopted it, you had used all possible means to prejudice the people against it;—that you had called it a *chesnut-bur*, a dreadful cathartic, which would purge New-Jersey to death;—that in all your conversations you had discovered a desire that the old congress might have been continued with some additional powers; which opinion they represented as dangerous to the rights of the people, declaring that the old congress vested with the necessary powers to govern the nation would of course have become a dreadful body of tyrants; that your whole line of conduct, whilst in the legislature of New-Jersey, had been such, as must convince every rational man of your being possessed with principles diametrically opposed to a constitution, which expressly guards against the iniquity of *tender* and *ex post facto* laws, and against laws impairing the obligation of contracts; and then for further proof of your opposition to the constitution, they produced the handbill, containing the declarations of Riggs and Boyd on the subject. In short, they made such a clatter about your antifederal principles, that some good men began to waver, and some indeed returned home to consider. In the midst however of the contest, an honest belgic, it is said, exclaimed in your favor to the following purport—"Ik heb de bruy van al dew mallighkeydt; ik kan de helft neit verstaan—de Domine en Abram seggen dat Clarick is een braav keeril, en ik hoor hy is een baas van een lant-meeter.—Jullie weeten dat Congress hebben duysende ackers te koop, & zy zullen zo een man mankeeren, en of hy dan *fetterel* is of *antifetterel*, dat mag myn niet scheelen; ik zal voor Clarrick stemmen, & zoo moeten jully allegaar, jongers."[2]—My neighbour who understands the language, tells me that the substance of this declaration is, that Congress would want a surveyor among them, and as such, it was no matter what your principles were. There certainly was weight in the observation, and many voted for you immediately after. But, sir, your friends deigned them a more serious reply, and convinced the bulk of the people that you was highly worthy of their confidence. The subtance of this reply, with an account of the continued opposition, I now meant to relate, but one of my friends having just come in with an account of the votes from six other counties, I feel so rejoiced at our great success, that I must necessarily devote the remainder of the day to chearful festivity. I am, your's, &c.

MARTIN B. BUNN.

February 26, 1789.

1. Somerset.
2. "I am concerned about all the difficulties; I cannot understand half of it—Domine and Abram say that Clark is a good man, and I hear that he is a master surveyor.—You know that Congress has thousands of acres to sell, and they would miss such a man, be he Federalist or Antifederalist, I do not care about that. I shall vote for Clark, and so must all of you young men."

Martin B. Bunn, Brunswick Gazette, 10 March

To the Hon. Abraham Clark Esq.

My dear and respected Friend,

I have just heard from Burlington;—what in the name of wonder can have bewitched that people?—I wish there was not a Quaker in North America. They have corrupted our language; they have refused to fight for their country in the day of her danger—by their filthy lust for gold and silver, they have, for years past, endeavoured to render our commerce as difficult as that of antient Sparta—and, though experience ought to have flashed conviction into their sober faces, they have remained inveterate enemies of our blessed paper currency, by which our state has been preserved from threatned destruction; they have charged us with the sins of our children, and now, to fill up the measure of their iniquity, they have publickly preferred men to you, whose names ought not to be written on the same page, considering either their integrity or abilities.—Sir, I fear a plot!—I strongly suspect these tremulous gentry, convinced of the impossibility of keeping you at home, mean to provide you with a "*thorn in your flesh, and a messenger of Satan to buffet you.*"—I shudder at the idea!—a LAWYER[1] to be the representative of a free people!—farewell beef and cabbage to the commonalty of this extensive empire!—farewell the wished-for amendments to the new constitution!—farewell liberty and bread and butter forever!—But hold, sir, I resume my spirits; the other western counties will not act so base a part, and in Salem, our friend the Colonel[2] knows what he is about.—I proceed to the history of our electioneering. We said so much, my dear friend, in your favor, in opposition to the *court-party* that I scarce know where to begin, and I believe I will have as great difficulty to know where to end. We made no bones of it, sir, to tell the people that Riggs was a worthless fellow, and that Boyd either never signed the piece published, or, if he had, there was nothing in it, which made against you.[3] That as a politician in the pay of New-Jersey, you had a right to make a bargain with New-York; that getting back the many thousands from that state, which it had iniquitously taken from us in duties, would greatly enrich our treasury—much more so than the new constitution, after all the boasting about it; that as you appeared to have gained the confidence of the government of New-York, it certainly would be highly politic to send you to Congress, for, that though the new constitution has been adopted by New-Jersey, you might perhaps still, for a simple *ay* or a *no*, make a good bargain with New-York for your constituents as well as for yourself;[4] that as to building a temple for your new coat, if the *gentry* would wait and see the issue of the present election, they would not think it so improbable an event, that a temple would shortly be raised to a *much meaner garment* of so great a man; that your opinion as to the respectability of the new government *abroad*, and its oppression at *home*, was clearly right; for, that abroad, with our ambassadors, consuls, Plenipotentiaries and envoys extraordinary, *with hard money in their pockets*, we should look like a rich and potent people:—But, that at home, high duties on RUM to pay their gentlemen abroad and no power left in the assembly to make paper-money or certificates a tender for debts, or, to dissolve hard bargains, or, to shut up the court of justice, must and would, unless the constitution was amended, oppress the poor;—That your disapprobation of the appellate jurisdiction of congress in certain cases, was a mark of the highest political wisdom, for that this would, in a great measure prevent courts and juries from favouring their own citizens as they ought to do; and, that all appellate jurisdiction in general, must be odious and detestable to a free and enlightened people; that there was not a single justice of the peace, in the state of New-Jersey, unless one of the court-party, but, in his very soul, loathed and abhorred them; and, that at the very last sitting of the legislature, the abolition of certioraries had been gloriously begun;—that you approved with great propriety, the power of altering the times and places of election; for, that this would check the chance of intrigueing so necessary to the very life of a republican government; that it would prevent a state from withholding its representation in the federal legislature, however necessary such withholding might be for the public good, and that no legislative body ought to have any thing to say about the election of its members—it being no part of sovereignty;—that with equal propriety you opposed the uncontroulable power of taxation given to the new government, the former method, by *requisitions* being much less oppressive to the people, and calculated in time to have induced the Dons, the Mynheers and the Monsieurs to have taken certificates for payment of their demands—nay, that we might shortly have made our paper money a lawful tender for those debts and defied their resentment; for that they, knowing those who were active during the late brilliant war, have had much rest from public business, we having in mercy employed mostly *new* hands since the peace, would not have dared to rouze our sleeping lions;—That your thinking the legislative and executive branches too much blended in the new constitution was a proof of your consistency of sentiment, and happily accounted for your remaining attachment to the old congress government, in which the legislative, the executive, and the judiciary powers were so *wisely* seperated, and which with ["]*a little more power*" might hence have been so *sweetly* administered. That as to your line of conduct in the legislature of New-Jersey, it had been such, as had deservedly gained you the confidence and respect of the people; that you had checked the griping cruelty of avarice, and by a wise system of jurisprudence promoted that equality among the citizens, which is so necessary in every republic;—That after we had, by our folly, parted with all our hard cash for British and French gewgaws, and when our unfeeling creditors expected shortly to confine OUR free born limbs in loathsome prisons, you had *proclaimed liberty to the captives*, and generously supplied us with an abundance of money;—that by this conduct you had greatly promoted industry, revived drooping commerce, and excited a spirit of improvement throughout the land;—that this money having been five times at least, in the hands of the merchants of New-York and Philadelphia, &c. it being no currency in their states, our citizens had purchased it from them at a discount of thirty per cent. whereby the state gained the enormous sum of one hundred and forty-five thousand pounds clear money;—a circumstance which those wrongheads have never considered, who are now with the most barbarous cruelty and contrary to the express bargain of the state with its citizens, rapidly depriving us of this great and glorious advantage;—that to crown all your labours of love to your country, you had effected what the wisest politicians have often essayed, and as often been baffled in the attempt, that is, that you had by one single act of Assembly effectually crushed the Lawyers, in such a manner, as must render you to the latest times the object of your country's highest esteem, and our state the envy of all her neighbours;—that by this one glorious law you had so simplified the proceedings in the court of justice that persons of common capacity could now manage their own causes, the consequence of which had been and would continue to be a valuable increase of eloquent speakers among the farmers and mechanics, whose natural abilities formerly were buried, by their being obliged to employ attorneys to transact their business;—that having relieved the unhappy debtors from the enormous costs with which they were formerly saddled by the wicked Lawyers, you had, with incomparable sagacity, foreseen that these vultures would probably get their ravenous claws in the pockets of the creditors, and therefore, by the same law so lengthened the settings of the courts, as to oblige them to spend such their illgotten pelf for the good of the community.—In short, that had not the shallow politicians now in power, begun to change the system of government you had so gloriously founded, *New-Jersey* and *Rhode-Island* would soon have been the ATHENS and LACEDEMON of this western world. Thus, my dear sir, did your friends nobly overcome your enemies, and great was their consternation on the occasion. But I wish not to fatigue you; in my next I will give you a farther account of their other wicked attempts to deprive their country of your services—wishing you a good night's rest.

I remain
with great respect,
your most humble servant,
MARTIN B. BUNN.

The Printer will thank Martin B. Bunn *if he could favor him with his pieces that are intended for publication earlier in the week.*

1. Elias Boudinot.
2. Whitten Cripps.
3. See Joseph Riggs's Deposition, *New Jersey Journal*, 4 February 1789, and "A Freeholder," *Brunswick Gazette*, 10 February 1789, both above.
4. This appears to be a reference to Clark's support for New York City as the site for the federal capital; see McCormick, *Experiment in Independence*, 247–250.

Martin B. Bunn, Brunswick Gazette, 17 March

To the Hon. Abraham Clark, Esq.

My dear Friend,

I have all this week been so vexed at the treatment we have met with from our supposed friend in Salem,[1] that until this moment I had determined not to write to you by the present opportunity; I can therefore now, as the carrier waits, only address a few lines to you, lest you should think that I had forgotten you.

You have indeed, sir, no conception of the consternation into which we threw the court-party, by the argument which I mentioned in my last. I never before so plainly saw the truth of the observation which I once heard you make, that lawyers taken *from* the bar, where they come prepared to quibble and split hairs, are no match for farmers and surveyors of moderate capacities, discussing the great affairs of a nation.—They first attempted to get clear of the name of *court-party*, which they said was very improperly applied to them; but, sir, they had been too well *christened* before the election, and that by hands *too holy*, to succeed in the business. They talked much of the services rendered to America, by the gentlemen of the law, during the late glorious war;—that their pens, their tongues and their swords had all been engaged in the cause of freedom;—that if they had as a body opposed the revolution, this country would have found them a formidable foe, and that it well behoved [them] now to consider the tendency of their conduct;—that it was the interest of their profession to promote the cause of liberty, because in free countries alone they could thrive;—that where tyranny swayed her iron sceptre, and where the will of a despot was the rule of conduct, there could not be, nor was there any employment for lawyers, but there only, where the life, liberty and property of the subject were secured by the equal, permanent and universal rules of law;—in short, that we were all one large family, embarked in the same vessel, and all equally interested in the public good. But, my dear sir, all they said, or could have said, was like "pouring water on a drowned mouse"—The people had been forewarned of the noise that would be made by these gentry, and the event convinced them that your *merit* was the cause of their enmity.—Your particular friends had no occasion to interfere, the bulk of the voters expressed their belief, that your having "*clipped the wings*" of the lawyers, and your being able to "*out-write*" and to "*out-talk*" them, were the real sources of their opposition to your election.—In the next place, my dear friend, they attempted to injure you by recommending Doctor WITHERSPOON to the people; they called him a great *Scivillion* (if our leader remembers the word right) and talked of wondrous great things he had done in the old Congress, for the Jerseys, and of a mighty fine book he had written about *money* and *a barrel of oil*;[2] nay, they went so far as to declare that you was no more to be compared to him in point of knowledge and abilities than a calf to an old fox.—I confess, sir, your friends were at first a little staggered;—nothing could safely be said against the old gentleman's abilities, and his public services were notorious in our county—but, my good sir, though a little alarmed at seeing them carrying off a number of good men, we soon found that this was furnishing us with another glorious opportunity to manifest our abilities at electioneering, and to convince you more fully of our inviolable attachment to your interest;—and, sir, by a well concerted plan which was as well executed, we did in a few minutes check their career, and finally were crowned the victors in the contest.—But on this subject I shall write to you more fully hereafter; at present I shall conclude, with returning you our most humble and hearty thanks for sending us, at this very critical period, two experienced electioneering bullies from your place; for the pretty *O yes* handbills[3] they brought with them, and, above all, for that very *sensible* and *modest* letter which you wrote by them to one of our inspectors, (God bless him too, I hope he will be sheriff next year) which I assure you caused many to *return* whose hearts had been *turned* away from us; and the conduct of your messengers also worked together for good; they had just seen your dear face, they brought good tidings, and they spoke handsomely concerning you. There was a time, sir, when these two honorable gentlemen would have been sent home from our election with a hearty drubbing, and loaded with insults, and this sir, the court-party would have called spirit, but, sir, we have done with those Pagan tricks, and excepting the liberating of the negroes of our Dutch friends, you and your friends may do in this county what seemeth good in your eyes, ONLY my dear friend, "*when it shall be well with you, then remember*" our leader, the son of Joseph, "*for good.*"

I am Sir, in great haste,

Your most humble servant,

MARTIN B. BUNN.

March 14, 1789,

1. Whitten Cripps.
2. Possibly John Witherspoon ["A Citizen of the United States"], *Essay on Money, As a Medium*

of Commerce; With Remarks, on the Advantages and Disadvantages of Paper admitted into general Circulation (Philadelphia, 1786).

3. See *New Jersey Journal*, 11 February 1789, Part Five:I, above.

Martin B. Bunn, Brunswick Gazette, 24 March

To the Hon. Abraham Clark, Esq.

My dear Friend,

I wish in my soul that we had known as much at the time of our election,[1] as you did in your county;[2]—we could at least have doubled the votes in your favour by observing your generous plan. It afforded me the most pleasing satisfaction to receive authentic information, that, among many hundreds of other virtuous citizens, who could not think that they had sufficiently testified their unbounded regard for your person, by a single vote, a worthy Dutchman from our county, who had given in his ticket at Somerset Court-house, voted for you again at Elizabeth-Town, and again at Newark;—good honest soul! I will send you his name, and I pray that he may be remembered in the day of *distribution.*—But I was to tell you how we got clear of Doctor Witherspoon—we held a council sir, determined on our plan of operation, and executed it in the following manner.—Our leader opened the business, and with a nobleness of soul, which would have done honour to an antient Roman, he observed, that he would not endeavour to raise one man's house upon the ruins of another man's house—"Doctor Witherspoon," said he, "*is a sensible very sensible man, but*" he paused "*But he is a foreigner,*" cried one of his aids—the word flew through the multitude like fire through a vanity-grass field—our leader sat down. "*But he is a priest*" exclaimed another, and a very grave and worshipful justice of the peace quoted Paul's epistles to Timothy to prove the impropriety of sending priests to Congress—"*But he is a Scotchman*" was sounded forth from a pair of lungs more noisy than the former. The word and every letter of it alarmed the *Dutch* people. The Duke D. Alva, the Pope or Lord North would now have had a better chance among the good folks, than the old Doctor—one of them, it is said, in a rage exclaimed, "Ik weet de scotse natie heelt voan enwig vyandig geweest teegens hit Vaderlant; zy benydense selss de maagere Herrinkjes die de braave Hollanders, in de wede and vreye oceaan van once lieve Heer, met veel ongemak, bekoomen; en ik weetook dat zy benster een zeer morsig volk, enlien teegen ien, als wy Scotsmanner naa de Congress senden zoo zee doar schielyk een wet weesen tagens het lakerdag's serobben van onse huyzen, endan, myn lieve wrienden, weeten Jullie, zelder geen leeven weesen met onse wyven."[3] The meaning of this speech I have not yet been told, but the effect was, that the court-party after mumblingly repeating the three all-powerful words *Foreigner, Priest, Scotchman,* retired in disgust, and we shouted for joy.

They next attempted to injure your interest by warmly recommending Colonel *Hoops,* who, they gravely observed was *no Priest,* and of whose spirit and upright principles, they said many fine things. But, sir, here again they failed, for we had nearly *done the business* for this gentleman before the election, by informing the people that some time ago he had *refused to dine with a barber,* at Morris-Town—you must know sir, barbers, among us, from their great knowledge in politics, and from their being best acquainted with what is going on in the world, and also from their communicative disposition, are persons of no small rank, but generally, are esteemed at least *second-rates* in the scale of precedency. This conduct of Colonel Hoops, therefore deservedly gave umbrage to the bulk of our people; and injured him as much, *nearly,* as if he had treated an *assembly-*

man with the same indignity—besides, sir, his refusing to let Mr. Tonsor partake with him of a leg of mutton, savoured a little too much of the *lawyer-candidate*, who wished to reduce the virtuous commonalty to buckwheat-cakes, and to have all our oxen, all our calves, all our sheep, and all our pigs devoured among the wicked court-party;—and I can assure you sir, the people had sense enough to see their danger, and I believe would have bewared of the man, without farther argument.—However, to make sure work, the first aid-de-camp of our glorious leader hinted to the people that Colonel Hoops was a Deist and Atheist—there need not another syllable—the court-party again retired, and we again triumphed over our enemies.—By this time, my dear friend, we expected no farther opposition from the court-party, but we were much disappointed, and we had still to encounter their dying and most furious efforts; for being reinforced on one of the days of election, when a very reputable part of the county were to give in their suffrages, they made a most violent and barbarous attack on your address to the people, published in the news-papers[4]—this they called "*The humble petition of Abraham Clark to the citizens of New-Jersey to continue him in public service.*" But, sir, I should trespass on your patience, should I at present relate the particulars of this day's encounter, I shall therefore now only say that it was such as had almost induced a number of us to apply to our leader and to request him to *stretch forth his arm and let loose our bullies upon the foe.* Yourself, Colonel Crips, your friends throughout the state, who have had the honour to join you in those salutary measures which have so much promoted the happiness and glory of New-Jersey, all, *all* of us were abused—and, though our leader at once silenced their rage against Colonel Crips, by observing that he looked upon the Colonel to be a man of *as great* abilities as himself, which at once satisfied all our people, yet sir, the malice of their tongues against you, your publications and your friends was not so easily curbed.—Happy for us however, we did by a strategem which I know will do us honour, when told, render it perfectly ineffectual.

I am, sir,

with respect

your most humble servant,

MARTIN B. BUNN.

March 16, 1789.

1. In Somerset County.
2. Essex.
3. "I know that the Scottish nation has been hostile toward the fatherland for centuries; they even envied the thin little herrings that the good Dutch took with great difficulty from our good Lord's wide and free ocean; also, I know that they are a dirty people, every one of them, if we send a Scot to the Congress, they will quickly enact a law against the washday scrubbing of our houses, and then, my dear friends, you know, there is no point in life for our wives."
4. See Clark's public letters printed in the *New Jersey Journal*, 4 February 1789, above.

Martin B. Bunn, Brunswick Gazette, 31 March

To the hon. Abraham Clark, Esq.

My dear and respected Friend,

These few lines come to acquaint you that I AM SICK.

Your's, &c.

MARTIN B. BUNN.

Martin B. Bunn, Brunswick Gazette, 7 April

To the Hon. Abraham Clark, Esq.

My dear and respected Friend,

Is it so, or is it all a dream?—Can it be that the Governor and Council have had the *effrontery* to pronounce the junto-ticket duly elected, before they received the votes from your county,[1] which at the same time declared to them that they did not choose to have the state represented by *such fellows*?—Oh for a lodge in the wilderness!—for some secret retreat, where ear could not hear me, where eye could not see me!—O liberty! what a stab didst thou receive when thy *guardian angel* was thus dismissed from the helm of public offices! well might our friend in the Essex Journal,[2] who foresaw our ruin, abuse the court-party from Woodbury to Newark, and back again to Princeton—had I his pen, I would pour out my curses not only upon them and their *wives*, but on their very children, born and unborn.—Let *them* call this elegant production the *snarling of disappointment*, all our friends say, they never before saw a lady so *handsomely* introduced, or so *delicately* praised.—O my friend, what is now to become of our dear country? how is this "new united government to be put in operation without thy wisdom and thy cool deliberation to direct our councils."[3]—The face of our country, sir, is wholly altered—the voice of mirth is banished from our tents—our songsters are changed into mourners—our fidles have broken their strings—the wicked court-party with exulting language tell us to weep for our idol, and already begin to cast their *wishful* looks upon our herds, our flocks and our farms, and with their eyes to parcel them out among themselves and their friends—one of them has had the insolence to write me a letter on the subject of our disappointment, and deridingly pretending to condole with me on the mournful occasion.—What, my dear sir, is to be done? our leader, you know, has given a fresh proof of his inviolable attachment to your interest, and clearly shewn that he builds *all* his hopes of the future glory of our country, on your being our pilot at this important crisis—believe me, sir, the people at large, are deeply impressed with the same sentiment and only wait for your directions to co-operate with the good folks of your county, in every measure which shall be deemed necessary to frustrate and nullify this wicked election—let us, therefore, receive your instructions, without delay, and the only strife shall be, who shall be foremost in promoting your glorious cause.—It would be of infinite service, my dear friend, for you, at this time, to publish another piece about the new constitution, and to warn the people, in the most pathetic terms, of their danger: the single *hint*, which you have given, has had an amazing effect, so that the very people who at first, with uplifted hands declared their highest approbation of the new plan of government, and that they would support it with their lives and fortunes, now speak a very different language, and, I am told, it has had the same good effect throughout East-Jersey—another warm piece, informing the people that the new constitution contains the seeds of slavery; that it will reduce them to the most abject state of vassalage, and in fifteen years make them all tenants to the *great* folks, would therefore, I am clear, answer the most beneficial purposes to our cause, and procure you a seat in the federal legislature, in spite of West-Jersey, the governor, and all the lawyers in Christendom. There is no occasion to assign any reasons for your opinion, only assert in *round* terms, I pledge my honour, the people will believe—think of it, my dear friend and adopt this plan, or such other, as to your superior wisdom shall seem better, only, for your dear country's sake, be not inactive on this very interesting occasion.—And, if after all that can be said, written, and done, we *must* lose you in our federal councils, it is *sweet* consolation, that we shall then have you in our state-legislature, where you may repair the *breaches* which in your absence have been made in the walls of our political Jerusalem, and where you may repay the inhabitants of West-Jersey and the wicked lawyers, for all the evil they have said and done against you.—For this reason I proceed to tell you how the court-party went on, in our county—they vehemently asserted, sir, that no man of sense could require better proof than your own publication, either of your antifederal principles, or, of your ignorance in the science of politics—they observed, that you had plainly distinguished yourself from that class of citizens who wished for amendments to the constitution, and shewn that its total destruction was the object of your wishes; for that nothing could so effectually destroy it, as for congress to usurp the power of altering one iota or tittle of its contents. That had you ever opened a book on legislation, or had you by any other means gained the knowledge necessary for the important station you were now aspiring after, you would have known, that "*Legislators who derive their power from the constitution, can never change it, without destroying the foundation of their authority.*" That the very idea of forming a constitution, presented to the mind of every man of common sense, the fixing upon some fundamental laws, for the government of a nation, which cannot be changed, without their express consent—that if your idea of legislation was adopted by our future rulers there would indeed be no "*hard bearing upon the liberties of the people,*" for that, literally speaking, they would have no liberty at all—that nothing could be more absurd than your idea that all government would be dissolved whilst a new convention were considering of amendments to the constitution, and that both this and your *modest presumption,* that congress would undertake the business of amending, as soon as they had leisure, were clear proofs to every considerate man, that you either had not knowledge enough for a legislator, or, that you had a disposition to tyrannise over the liberties of the people, by usurping a power, the most dangerous that could be conceived—that your telling the people that some parts of the constitution did bear hard upon their liberties, was merely to *catch the ears* of the ignorant, and to induce them to believe, that you had, with eagle's eyes, discovered foibles in it, which had escaped the federal convention, that by alarming their fears, they might be prevailed upon to apply to the author of the *wise* discovery to save them from the lurking danger—that if you was at that individual moment called upon to point out the parts which you aimed at by the vague expressions which you so wisely called "the sum total of your antifederalism," you would be at a loss for an answer—that the people at large were as capable naturally, and as well informed as yourself to determine on the subject, and ought to judge of the constitution for themselves—that if they would read it, they would find all power still lodged in their own hands, and the persons necessary to fill up the different departments of government, immediately, or mediately of their own creation—that if on experiment, or in the present opinion of the people, amendments were necessary, the method of obtaining them was clearly pointed out by the constitution itself, and no doubt would be pursued; but that the general plan of the government had been opposed by none, who were not warped by interest, or swayed by pure malevolence of heart—that as to the story which you said had been propagated respecting your tampering with the Jersey convention, they declared, it must have been raised by your own minions; for that, considering the character of the gentlemen who composed that convention, the worst of your enemies could never have suspected you of such *consummate impudence,* and that you would never have contradicted the report, had not the constitution against your wishes, been adopted by the necessary number of states—that your whole conduct respecting this constitution had been full of inconsistencies, and was the clearest proof of your superlative vanity—that with one breath you declared that parts of it bore hard upon the *liberties of the people*, and in the next sentence, you proclaimed the cheerfulness with which you sent it to be adopted—that whilst the states had it under consideration, and before nine of them had adopted it, you had in no single instance spoken or acted in its favour, but had been *notoriously* antifederal in all your conduct and conversation—that when, by the benign interposition of providence, contrary to your expectations, and to the great joy of all good men, the constitution was adopted, convinced by the argument of THIRTY SHILLINGS per day, you had changed your coat and your company and sent word from New-York that you was opposed to a new convention, that the constitution was *every thing* to New-Jersey, and that you would support it with all your might—that though you so *modestly* spoke of your want of abilities, and so *elegantly* declared that you would not "push yourself into the important trust," you had left no stone unturned to promote your election, and that, though you did not understand even the term *constitution*, you had presumed to set up your opinion on the important subject of the new government, against the united opinions of the most shining characters for wisdom, integrity and patriotism in this western world.—Thus, my dear friend, and still more did these wicked wretches abuse you, but it puts me in such a passion, since our mishap, to repeat their vile speeches, that I cannot proceed.—Pray send me by the post, one of the petitions for setting aside the election.[4]

I am sir,

with respect

your humble servant,

MARTIN B. BUNN.

1. Essex.
2. See "Triumph," *New Jersey Journal*, 18 March 1789, Part 5:I, above.
3. This is a paraphrase from Abraham Clark, *New Jersey Journal*, 4 February 1789 (see above).
4. See Joseph Bloomfield to Matthias Ogden, 1 April 1789, Part Six.

Brunswick Gazette, 15 September

A correspondent informs us that the life of MARTIN B. BUNN is despaired of;—He has long been in a lingering condition; sometimes better and sometimes worse; until the news of a late event quite deprived him of his senses.[1]—He has, however, had some lucid intervals, occasioned by the assurances of his friends, that the gentleman, to whom he lately addressed so many affectionate letters, will certainly, in a few weeks, be the chief Magistrate of New-Jersey; which assurances, accompanied with lively descriptions of the felicity of his native state, under such a leader, have at times, almost raised him from the dead, and enabled him to sing for joy.—During his possession of his intellectuals, his attendants have prevailed upon him to make his testament and last will, in which we are told, he has most generously provided for the new *Governor* and his secretary, *Fonty Triumph.*

1. Presumably news that the House of Representatives had decided, on 2 September 1789, to seat the "sitting" Representatives from New Jersey.

PART SIX

AFTERMATH OF THE ELECTIONS

Speculation about the election of Representatives continued throughout the spring and summer of 1789. Governor William Livingston's proclamation of 19 March (Part Five:I) announcing the winners of the election, reflected the controversy. The governor noted that James Schureman, Lambert Cadwalader, Elias Boudinot, and Thomas Sinnickson had received the most votes in the twelve counties which reported their returns prior to the Privy Council meeting on 18 March, and that one county (Essex) had not yet reported. The responsibility for judging the legality of the Privy Council's determination was left "to whom it appertains," i.e., the House of Representatives.

East Jersey supporters of Abraham Clark and Jonathan Dayton, led by Matthias Ogden, appealed to the House of Representatives to invalidate the election. They complained of irregularities in the election and in the governor's actions in declaring the winners. The House—aware that it was setting a precedent—proceeded cautiously in its investigation. On 25 May it gave its committee of elections the authority to hear "proofs and allegations" from both sides in the dispute, and in June the committee received written testimony on the case. On 15 July the full House refused to grant the committee the authority to send a commission to New Jersey to take testimony about the election. Denied this authority, the committee heard oral testimony in New York during August, and issued its final report to the House on 18 August. The report, in six articles, merely summarized the principal facts in the dispute and made no recommendations. The House considered the report on 1 September and after some debate, voted on 2 September that the sitting members "were duly elected, and returned."

Many of the documents detailing the dispute in the House of Representatives over the New Jersey election are unofficial. The only surviving official record is the House journal, which outlines the actions taken by the whole House. There are no extant records of the meetings of the committee of elections, and all petitions and written evidence submitted to the House or House committee have been destroyed. Fortunately, copies or rough drafts of several of these items have been preserved in personal papers and local records. Newspapers and the *Congressional Register* also supply further evidence of the actions taken by the House of Representatives, as they often printed more detailed accounts of the debates in the full House than did the House journal.

Except where another location is indicated, the documents referred to above are printed in this part.

Tench Coxe to James Madison, Philadelphia, 24 March 1789 (excerpt)[1]

The Jersey Election by the difference of Mr. Clarke, has proved more favorable than I expected.

1. RC, Madison Papers, DLC. Printed: Rutland, *Madison*, XII, 27.

Alexander White to Adam Stephen, New York, 24 March (excerpt)[1]

The Assembly of New Jersey fixed no precise definite time for closing the Polls or making returns of their Elections—in consequence a kind of rivalship between the Eastern and Western Divisions occasioned the keeping the Polls open an unreasonable time—one county I believe has not yet closed—however the Governour on Wednesday last proceeded on the Returns which had been made and certified the Members chosen one of whom is come on and we expect the other three this Evening or tomorrow—It is somewhat remarkable that Circumstances should so early occur to prove the necessity of vesting Congress with the Power of regulating Elections—[2]

1. RC, Adam Stephen Papers, DLC. For another excerpt from this letter, see Chapter XIII, Part Three, Representatives Election Commentary. The letter was addressed to Stephen in Berkeley County, Virginia. For a biographical sketch of White, a Representative from Virginia, see DHFFE, II, 422–23. Stephen (1730–1791), a military veteran of the French and Indian War and a major general in the Continental Army during the Revolution, represented Berkeley County, Virginia, in the Virginia House of Delegates, 1780–1784. He voted to ratify the Constitution in the Virginia Convention in 1788.

2. For an elaboration of White's views, see *Virginia Gazette*, 1 April 1789, Chapter XIII, Part Two.

Brunswick Gazette, 24 March

From Essex county we learn, that petitions are handing about, praying the honorable Congress to set aside the election—that one of the candidates who has been up in that part of the state seems to favor the design—should this be the case we can easily judge whether he really would wish to act that friendly part to the state that many of his advocates supposed.—We cannot hesitate to say, if we speak with candor, that the present representation is as equitable as could have been expected, and composed of as worthy characters as the state affords, though there is many who may make objections to each of them, and had others been chosen the murmurs of the people would not have been less. It has been remarked that out of the fifty four candidates whose names were published by the Governor, scarcely one has escaped the lash of some slanderous tongue.[1]

1. This article was reprinted in the Philadelphia *Pennsylvania Packet*, 30 March 1789; Philadelphia *Pennsylvania Mercury*, 31 March; Philadelphia *Pennsylvania Journal*, 1 April; Philadelphia *Pennsylvania Gazette*, 1 April; and *Carlisle Gazette*, 8 April. A brief paraphrase of the article was printed in the *New York Journal*, 2 April, and reprinted in the *Hudson Weekly Gazette*, 7 April.

Brunswick Gazette, 24 March

To the JUDGES *and* INSPECTORS *of the Election in Essex, for Representatives to Congress.*

GENTLEMEN,

Whereas we the Subscribers, FREEMEN and CITIZENS of the County of Essex, are fully convinced that the liberties of every free People, depends on the freedom of Elections for their Representatives; and that the present Election involves in it, matters of the greatest importance; and whereas it is notorious that designs are formed by the minority, to disappoint a large unsuspecting majority of the men of their choice; which designs are founded in the hopes of evading the true intent and meaning of our Election law, and availing themselves of its defects; and whereas in order, the better to effect their purposes, means are useing to have the Poll of Essex closed, from various specious pretences.—We therefore thus publicly request and pray; that you will not on any account, close the Poll of Essex, so long as it is probable, that the keeping it open will serve to counteract, and frustrate the combinations against us; as we wish to remain unrepresented, until we can have a FAIR Election; rather than submit to a representation, in which we have no choice nor confidence.

Elizabeth-Town, March 12, 1789.

Versification of the above petition, by a customer.

Oh hear us, ye judges—we're baffled—we're crost
And vex'd, that we scarce can support the reflection!
Horse and foot we are routed—our ticket is lost
Unless you can help us to damn the election.

2

But ye are the judges!—*and sure ye surpass*
A Daniel in judgment, in spirit young Fotham!
Not juster of old was the famous judge Midas
Nor wiser, believe us, the wise men of Gotham.

3

This election we're certain can ne'er stand the test,
That we *are the* people, *we clearly can shew;*
Those vile western counties are heathen at best,
But we are the children of Abram *you know.*

4

Deliver us, good judges! *from men of high station,*
From rich men who clatter about in their coaches,
From lawyers—those vermin—*the pests of the nation,*
From the payment of debts *and our hearts reproaches.*

5

From him who can leave all our lies in the lurch;
From the man who good beef *to the* idle *begrudges,*
Who impiously sits with his hat on in church—
From him—we beseech you deliver us good judges.

6

May it please you to give us one free from controul,
Who to bless us with plenty of paper *is willing;*
Who hates the new-roof *and its friends in his soul,*
And who nobly can live for a week on a shilling.

7

May it please you to give us the man of our choice,
Who to free us from debt *a most faithful drudge is—*
That we in his tenders *may ever rejoice;*
In this, we beseech you to hear us good judges!

8

In our own pit we fell, and we are vex'd to the soul,
We are caught in the snare our wise ones proposed—
Yet in you is our help—if ye close not the poll,
Why then, do you see, the poll will not be closed.

9

To assist us, dear judges, you must strive day & night,
Nor must ye on Sundays in idleness sit,
For sure on the sabbath 'tis lawful and right
To help the poor ass, that falls into the pit.

10

Tho' we by our tricks have destroyed our ticket,
Yet still by those tricks *we'll that ticket restore—*
Like the wise man we read of, who jump'd in a thicket
To scratch in his eyes, it had scratch'd out before.

11

Then huzza, dear judges, keep open the poll,
While there's life there is hope—and the trick is so clever,
Since no time is fixed—you are free from controul,
And the poll may be open for ever and ever.

Chorus by *all* the Judges.

Then keep the poll open—keep open the poll—
It ne'er *shall be clos'd—nor in foul nor in fair weather,*
Huzza! we will judge without rule or controul,
And we'll keep the poll open for ever and ever.[1]

1. The petition and poem were reprinted in the Philadelphia *Pennsylvania Gazette*, 25 March 1789, and *Providence Gazette*, 11 April.

William Bradford, Jr., to Elias Boudinot, Philadelphia, 25 March (excerpts)[1]

I have just received your letter of the 21st. and by one from our Mamma to Susan, I find that you had set out for N York. The determination of your Election gives great pleasure to every body here, and many seem to have taken great interest in the contest. The fœderalists think they have become stronger by the event, and those who look for a removal of Congress gather new hopes from it.[2] I cannot think that the folly and chagrin of the disappointed candidates will carry them so far as to bring their objections before Congress. If it should be the case, I believe there is nothing to be apprehended from it. The case you speak of in our state was one not much analagous to yours. The act of Assembly required the citizens to chuse ten electors on a certain day & the returns were to be made to the Council; but several of those returns not being made on the day when the Electors were to meet the Council were obliged or necessitate[d] to proceed on those which had come to hand.—[3]

I must beg frequent communications of such things as are proper to be known. Should the debates be taken in short hand & published much Curiosity will be gratified at an easy rate. . . .

Mrs Wallace is with us, and we have had much amusement with Mr Triumph's performance.[4]—Why can not these people hide their mortification a little better.—I am just told that the versified Petition has appeared in Hall's paper of this day.[5] How it got there I cannot conceive & it must be algebra to every body here who neither know the allusions nor can comprehend the meaning of it.

1. RC, Wallace Papers, PHi.

2. Many observers believed that the Junto Representatives would favor moving Congress from New York to Philadelphia, while the Clark-Dayton faction would try to keep Congress in New York. See also James Parker to Cortlandt Skinner, March 1789; Thomas Hartley to Jasper Yeates, 31 August; Hartley to Tench Coxe, 2 September; and Elias Boudinot to Elisha Boudinot, 2 September, all below.

3. No election for presidential Electors was held in Fayette County, Pennsylvania, as not enough people appeared to vote on election day. The state Supreme Executive Council declared the winners in the election based on the returns received from the other counties and the city of Philadelphia. See DHFFE, I, 384, 388–389.

4. See "Triumph," *New Jersey Journal*, 18 March 1789, Part Five:I.

5. See the *Brunswick Gazette*, 24 March 1789, immediately above. The article was reprinted in Hall and Sellers's Philadelphia *Pennsylvania Gazette*, 25 March 1789.

A Lover of Order, New Jersey Journal (Elizabethtown), 25 March

Friends and fellow countrymen of the county of Essex, to you is the following address, directed by a person who feels for your reputation. You have for a long time deservedly enjoyed the character of being staunch and resolute friends to your country. You stood firm from the beginning to the end of the late war; although your persons and property were immediately exposed to the insult and depredation of the enemy, through almost the whole of it. You nobly scorned to sacrifice your liberty to your present ease and safety. And since the peace, you have conducted yourselves as good citizens, as friends to order and good government. You saw and lamented the imperfection of the late confederation, and heartily and eagerly joined in adopting the new constitution. Thus far your character as a county, is good, and stands among the foremost in this, or any of the thirteen states. Now let me ask you, my fellow countrymen, are you not sullying this fair character in the eyes of all good men, by your conduct in this election? Do you not disturb the peace of the community by violating the spirit of a late law of the state? And do you not in this instance, by fair construction, rebel not only against this, but against the United States? Because you declare by your conduct, that this state should not have a representation in Congress. Let the warmest of you, who were for keeping the poll open, answer the following questions. Did not the law direct you in positive terms to close it, and make a return of the Candidates voted for? And is it not the spirit of the law, that the return should be made as soon as the votes could conveniently be taken in? Did not the Judge and Inspectors therefore act contrary to the sense and meaning of the law, by adjourning the poll for a week in the first instance, and for a longer time in the second? But admitting that the law is really as lame as you represent it, and that your present conduct does not fall under its censure, let me ask you where is your patriotism, where is the love of your country fled? Has it entirely forsaken you now at this critical period, when it is most wanted? Or are your eyes shut to the dangers that surround you? If the latter is the case, let me intreat you to open them before it is too late. Allow me to present you with a picture of your country, as lately drawn by the feeling pen of one of the ablest of our American patriots.

"We may indeed with propriety be said to have reached almost the last stage of national humiliation. There is scarcely anything that can wound the pride, or degrade the character of an independent nation, which we do not experience. Are these engagements to the performance of which we are held by every tie, respectable among men? These are the subjects of constant and unblushing violation. Do we owe debts to foreigners and to our own citizens, contracted in a time of imminent peril, for the preservation of our political existence? These remain without any proper or satisfactory provision for their discharge. Have we valuable territories and important posts in the possession of a foreign power, which, by express stipulations ought long since to have been surrendered? These are still retained, to the prejudice of our interests not less than of our rights. Are we in a condition to resent, or repel the aggression? We have neither troops, nor treasury, nor government, (meaning for the Union)[.] Are we even in a condition to remonstrate with dignity? The just imputations on our own faith, with respect to the same treaty, ought first to be removed. Are we entitled by nature and compact to a free participation in the navigation of the Missisippi? Spain excludes us from it. Is public credit an indispensible resource in time of public danger? We seem to have abandoned its cause as desperate and irretrievable. Is commerce of importance to national wealth? Ours is at the lowest point of declension. Is respectability in the eyes of foreign powers a safe-guard against foreign encroachments? The imbecillity of our government even forbids them to treat with us; our ambassadors abroad, are the mere pagents of mimic sovereignty. Is a violent and unnatural decrease in the value of land a symptom of national distress? The price of improved land in most parts of the country, is much lower than can be accounted for by the quantity of waste land at market, and can only be fully explained by that want of private and public confidence, which are so alarmingly prevalent among all ranks, and which have a direct tendency to depreciate property of every kind. Is private credit the friend and patron of industry? That most useful kind which relates to borrowing and lending, is reduced within the narrowest limits, and this still more from an opinion of insecurity than from a scarcity of money. To shorten an enumeration of particulars which can afford neither pleasure nor instruction, it may in general be demanded, what indication is there of national disorder, poverty and insignificance, that could befal a community so peculiarly blessed with natural advantages as we are, which does not form a part of the dark catalogue of our public misfortunes." The FEDERALIST, No. 15.

Candor must own this picture is not too highly coloured. What friend to his country therefore, can view it without shuddering for fear of the consequences. And in addition to the above it ought to be observed, that our situation as a state, is more peculiarly distressing, as being tributary to the states of New-York and Pennsylvania. Do we not pay a greater tax annually into their treasuries, than to our own, by the duties they have imposed on foreign goods? I verily believe we do. But what the amount is, I cannot say with certainty. Let it be more or less, it is something which we pay for nothing. Whereas the same duties when levied by the government of the Union, will be applied for the payment of our debts foreign and domestic; and as we are creditors of that Union, a proportionable part of the money will return into our own pockets. You see therefore, the great and peculiar interest we have in this government. You also may see into the policy of the state of New-York, who under the idea of proposing amendments to the new constitution, is endeavoring to delay the opperation of it as long as possible. But if the state of New-York, by her local situation, continues thus to take advantage of us, and opposes the new constitution, which would abridge this privilege, we ought, unitedly to imbrace it as our only relief. If therefore, a majority of us in this county have been disappointed in our ticket, a regard for the interest of our state and country, and for our own reputation as a county, should induce us without murmuring to fall in with the ticket which has succeeded, and thereby give our assistance to strengthen the new government. By this conduct we shall prove, that a sense of the perilous situation our country is in, and a regard for her future welfare, have weight enough with us to suppress our selfish views, passions and prejudices.

A LOVER of ORDER.[1]

1. This article was reprinted in the *Brunswick Gazette*, 31 March 1789.

Alexander Hamilton to Jonathan Dayton, 26 March[1]

Circumstances prevented my seeing a certain Gentleman. But I have reflected more fully on the subject of our conversation.

I continue strongly inclined to the opinion that the Council ought to have canvassed prior to the day appointed for the Meeting of Congress upon the returns then before them, and that the subsequent canvass has been irregular and is void.

But as to the second point—the prudence of an appeal to Congress, in this commencement of the Government, my doubts have been rather strengthened than diminished by reflection.[2]

1. RC, Hamilton Papers, DLC.

2. The Clark-Dayton forces considered hiring Hamilton to present their case to the House of Representatives, but he either was not offered the case or, if offered it, declined it (see Elias Boudinot to Elisha Boudinot, 14 April 1789, below).

Erkuries Beatty to Josiah Harmar, Philadelphia, 31 March (excerpt)[1]

The State of New Jersey is all in an uproar too, about their election for Representatives to Congress & it is supposed that old Clark who is not in, will endeavour to oversett the whole business—This proceeded I believe from a defect in the Constitution of the State & continued in the Law, Stating or fixing no time for the closing of the Polls. One County of the State is yet open & suppose will continue so this long time, altho' the Governor has issued his proclamation of the returns he had in his possession the persons appointed, which I am afraid will cause an unhappy debate in Congress.—

1. RC, Harmar Collection, MiU-C. Beatty (1759–1823), brother of John Beatty, served under General Harmar as paymaster to the United States Army on the Ohio frontier and as commandant at Vincennes. Harmar (1753–1813), of Pennsylvania, was the commanding officer of the United States Army on the Ohio frontier from 1784 to 1791.

Abraham Clark to Jonathan Dayton March[1]

If you can have it ascertained Govr. will not issue commissions as the law directs,[2] I think it advisable that you send Colo. Wadsworth[3] the Law with some remarks such as you think proper, and this as soon as possible.

I feel myself out of all patience with Col. Hamilton. He really appears to be, what I have some times thought him, a shim sham politician. He must needs soon run himself aground. His politics are such as will not stand the test. He will soon refine them to nothing. . . .

He is clear that by the Law the Govr. & Council ought to have declared the number on the third of March, but thinks prudence requires our acquiescance in the last advise of Council for fear of making a Noise that will disturb this young infant child of his; which if it is to be so nursed and raised by our giving up all our liberties most dear & valuable—a fair representation—we had better let the Creature die; I am for nursing it properly with wholesome food and raising up to a proper state of manhood to support us in those privileges we are contending for—Give up our most valuable privileges for fear of giving uneasiness! What a strange idea! . . . .

Give up those privileges, which government is designed to secure to us! give us our Rights to secure what he means, which is nothing.

Besides, is it giving quiet to the General Government to raise a State into a ferment which might prove extremely detrimental to the Government, and perhaps fatal, to it; for a silence in a business where so many thousands are concerned is not to be expected. The United States cannot but become acquainted with this business; and unless Justice is sought for by us and granted by Congress, a much greater injury will arise to the Government than can happen by a manly opposition in a Constitutional way. The more I think of this business, the more I am out with this great little trifling genius.

And will say no more about him at present; only I wish you to answer his Letter & show him his absurdities; by giving his brains a little shock, it may in some measure settle them; not with the view of any assistance from him, which I do not wish; however carefully preserve his letter.[4]

1. *The Magazine of History, With Notes and Queries*, V (January-June 1907), 108–09. The ellipses are in the original printing, which dated the letter March 1789.

2. For further discussion about the sending of the commissions, see Commissions of the New Jersey Representatives, 21–28 March 1789, Part Five:I.

3. Jeremiah Wadsworth, Representative from Connecticut.

4. See Alexander Hamilton to Dayton, 26 March 1789, above, and Elias Boudinot to Elisha Boudinot, 14 April 1789, below.

James Parker to Cortlandt Skinner, March[1]

"Should they appoint another convention to amend the exceptionable parts [of the Constitution] it is thought dissension and bloodshed will ensue. Should it be carried into execution with all its energy, the citizens at large will feel what they have ever been strangers to, and it is more than probable that the Horse hitherto rode with a slack rein, when he comes to be held up and spurred, will kick. In short, our situation is such that we require an energetic government at the same time that we cannot submit to it; and I fear there are too many amongst us that have other views than the good of the public at heart." Alluding to the question of the removal of Congress from New

York to Philadelphia, he says:[2]—"this has already had such an effect upon the citizens of the two places that they seem to bear the greatest enmity to each other, and it has raised such an opposition in the election of representatives for this State, that East and West Jersey were never more opposed than at the present moment.[3] . . . It is amazing to think what numbers go back to the western world, and now to Genesee and Niagara, and still we are overstocked with people for our mode of farming. I think the year 1789 the most alarming, both to America and Great Britain."

1. William A. Whitehead, *Contributions to the Early History of Perth Amboy* . . . (New York, 1856), 135. The ellipses and brackets are in the original printing. Whitehead does not date the letter, and only notes that it was sent to Parker's brother-in-law in England. The letter has been dated March 1789 because of the reference to the first federal elections.

2. This phrase was interjected by Whitehead.

3. For more discussion about the division of East and West Jersey and the location of the federal capital, see William Bradford, Jr., to Elias Boudinot, 25 March 1789, above; and Thomas Hartley to Jasper Yeates, 31 August 1789; Hartley to Tench Coxe, 2 September 1789; and Elias Boudinot to Elisha Boudinot, 2 September 1789; all below.

Joseph Bloomfield to [Matthias] Ogden, Burlington, 1 April[1]

Your Letter of 29 last with the printed Petition enclosed came to hand Yesterday—I have conversed with our Friend Norcross and propose to visit Ross & Coxe in order to collect the desired information; and will communicate whatever can be obtained to Capt. Ogden[2] & Mr. Williamson[3] at Trenton next Week.

If a day should be assigned to hear the Petitioners, it will be best for some Gentleman to visit the Western Countys to consult with confidential Persons the Wittnesses to be subpoened to prove the irregularities which can be collected & pointed out—among others in the County of Gloucester, the Election was held at Persoukin or Hepburn's Tavern—Votes were brought in and received towards the close of the Poll, when the Electers did not attend, but sent their names & Votes, (*as I have been told,*) particularly, that a Person valued himself upon bringing in ten or a dozen at a time—our old Chaplain[4] can most probably give the names of the Persons to be subpoened, though He has injured himself exceedingly by being opposed to the junto Ticket—Indeed I almost wish, that we could reconcile ourselves to the Persons declared, in order that our State may not be deprived some time of a Representation—

I have received two Letters from Capt Dayton & sent them on to Ross, of which please acquaint Cap Dayton.

My best wishes are for the success of the Petition, but I much fear an additional mortification in the "Triumph" of the "Bellwether of the Junto Flock."—

1. RC, Alphabetical Series, NjHi. The letter was addressed to "Genl. Ogden."

2. Aaron Ogden.

3. Probably Matthias Williamson (c. 1752–1836), an Elizabethtown lawyer. He was admitted to the bar in 1774, and during the Revolution he was successively a colonel, a brigadier general, and a quartermaster general in the state militia, 1775–1780.

4. The Reverend Andrew Hunter.

Essex, New Jersey Journal (Elizabethtown), 1 April

Mr. Kollock,

The author of the queries in your paper of the 18th,[1] forbears, for the present, to make any strictures or remarks upon the votes or determinations of the privy council, or of particular members at their late meeting, relative to the election of our representatives. He has no dispute with *men* but with *measures*, and he should think it criminal to drag the former into view, and expose their names to the public, except when it is absolutely necessary, in order to reform, or prevent the pernicious effects of the latter. Whatever may have been the views, the wishes or the advice of a majority of that body, it must frankly be confessed, that the proclamation issued by his Excellency, is remarkable for that ingenuousness which has characterized him in his administration. The fair and candid statement contained therein, places the business on its true and proper ground. From the whole tenour of the proclamation, three conclusions may fairly be inferred, and drawn, viz. That the Governor entertains, in his own breast, strong doubts of the legality of the election and return—That he has thought proper to refer the decision thereupon to the house of representatives, "to whom it appertains;" and *this* in such terms as carry with them a strong recommendation to that branch of Congress to take it under their consideration—And lastly, that commissions, under the great seal, will not be issued to the four gentlemen mentioned therein, but bearly certificates of like purport, and agreeing, in substance, with the proclamation. As those gentlemen cannot be said (in the words of the law) to "have the greatest number of votes from the *whole state*," or "to be the persons duly chosen to represent this state in the Congress of the United States;" and as the proclamation refuses to recognize them as such, commissions will probably be denied them by the Governor; and without these, by what authority, or right, they will be admitted to their seats, is at least questionable.

ESSEX.

March 30, 1789.

1. See "Essex," *New Jersey Journal*, 18 March 1789, Part Five:I.

Samuel A. Otis to Jonathan Dayton, New York, 9 April (excerpt)[1]

When do you come forward? I mean the Jersy petitioners: Will it not be a better time now than in the hurry of business?

1. RC, Lloyd W. Smith Collection, NjMoW. The letter was addressed to Dayton in Elizabethtown. Otis (1740–1814), a Boston merchant, was elected secretary of the Senate on 8 April. He held the post until his death. For a biographical sketch, see DHFFE, I, 755.

Elias Boudinot to Elisha Boudinot, New York, 14 April (excerpt)[1]

I recd yours of yesterday, and am glad to hear that you have safely got back from Trenton, thro' such bad Roads—I recd the Letter from Trenton, but really think there is no great need of taking much trouble about the Business, as notwithstanding all their Pother, I suspect it is only designed to keep the People's Passions up for another Election next fall[2]—Cap D----[3] was here a few day[s] since and assured Mr Paterson that he had relinquished all attempts in the Business and had advised others to do the same—Mr Hamilton authorized me to say that he was not feed at all—Mr Livingston has not been applied to in the Business—He heard him give his Opinion in point agt them—and indeed I believe they never have applied to any body but Mr Hamilton.[4]

I think however to be prepared for the worst, you had better get Mr Grummonds affidavit & say no more about it—I will advise you of the first step they take—I think your Petitions should only be signed by the best People of known good Character—I wish you could get one headed by the Governor—Mr Chetwood &—

1. RC, Gratz Collection, PHi. The letter was addressed to Elisha in Newark.

2. Shortly after he took his seat in the House of Representatives, Elias Boudinot informed his wife, Hannah, that from all he could "discover," there was "no probability" that his opponents would be able to unseat him (New York, 2 April 1789, RC, Stimson-Boudinot Collection, NjP).

3. Jonathan Dayton.

4. The East Jerseyites who supported Abraham Clark and Jonathan Dayton considered hiring Alexander Hamilton to present their case to the House of Representatives. Hamilton, by stating that he was not "feed," indicates that he either was not offered the case, or if offered it, did not accept. See also Hamilton to Dayton, 26 March 1789, above.

Brunswick Gazette, 14 April

A TRIP *to the* WEST.

When partizans were in great strife
As ever man and scolding wife—
Then says to Abra'm, Daniel Marsh,
The news from Morris is not harsh,
For here's our *Mercury* just arrived
With box as high as a spring tide;
Our friends he says have done their duty
And changed tickets for your booty.
So you at home may safely stay
And we'll to Burlington strait-way,
Where we shall let those *Quakers* know
Their opposition moveth slow;
The sleigh prepared we'll quick set off
Lest we should be too late to *scoff*,
The keggs of yore not half so stout,
As we'll convince them in this rout,
For when they see such men of might
They'll leave all *Friends* their nails to bite;
With spirits bold they forthwith flew
But when arriv'd found something new;
Says *Wether* what does all this mean?
My *Bell* shall sound with echo keen,
I'll let them know by my commands
Those *Goats* shall sep'rate from the Lambs:
When Daniel hear'd this declaration
His heart it set in palpitation,

So to friend Mercury turn'd his pate,
A parly yet may save our fate;
To this the god but only smil'd
Dear sir—what makes you look so wild?
For by such conduct Abra'm looseth,
The *spirit* as yet scarcely moveth;
But Daniels heart being so perplext
He strict adhear'd to his old text:
Then fifteen minutes were allow'd,
Tho' Mercury scorned—Daniel *bow'd*;
Then said my friend, lets leave this place,
Nor mind if they should us *disgrace*;
We'll to old Abra'm and consider
Some method to subdue this *Wether*:
When Mercury whispering gave consent,
The time expir'd away they went;
So horses at New-Market start,
They sallied forth as quick as dart;
Whilst all this time lay Abra'm snug
As thief in mill or louse in rugg,
Not dreaming what had yet befel
Before his friends return'd to tell,
Which news unto him being told,
The blood thro' every vein ran cold;
Then call'd his friends and made his will
Resign'd his breath—so now lay's still:
His fun'ral o'er and all things ended
The mourners stood a while suspended,
The will being read he left his heirs,
Certficates, Goats, Bulls and *Steers*,
In hopes they might some effort make
The Constitution yet *to break.*—

Joseph Bloomfield to Jonathan Dayton, Burlington, 17 April[1]

Mr. H. from Gloucester[2] informed me this morning, that Dr. George Wm. Campbell[3] with one Cheesman one of the Inspecters received Votes by *themselves* in a particular part of the C[ounty] of Glout. Dr Campbell acted as Clerk to Cheesman the Inspt. & those Votes so received Passed into the Box—that Col. Joseph Hugg,[4] being confined to his Bed, through sickness, sent his vote by the same Dr. Campbell & which also passed into the Election-Box—

Mr. H. says, that Dr. Ebenezer Elmer of Cumberland, was in Your Interest, & will be the proper Person to obtain information about the Cumberland-Election—

Apply to Saml, Sharp[5] about the Salem Election.

As to ye Burlington-Election I cannot yet fix any thing of consequence—the Inspecters were cautious, as they knew one of the Inspectors communicated their proceedings to me—

Capt. Dennis[6] has promised to deliver this with his own hand & assured me of *his being one of us.*

1. RC, Dayton Miscellany, NjHi.
2. Probably the Reverend Andrew Hunter of Woodbury, Gloucester County.
3. Campbell (c. 1747–1798) was a Woodbury physician.
4. Hugg (c. 1741–1796), a wealthy Gloucester landowner and a brother of Samuel, was a justice of the peace and a judge of the county Court of Common Pleas.
5. Samuel Sharp (1756–1805), a Salem County Quaker, was a member of the Assembly, 1786 and 1790–1791.
6. Probably Patrick Dennis.

Samuel A. Otis to Jonathan Dayton, New York, 27 April (excerpts)[1]

I am in daily expectation of the Jersey contest and my constant wish is that one of them & I care not which may be ousted to make room for your Honour—I confess however I wonder at the delay— . . .

[P.S.] I never saw Neighbour B—t[2] until this session[.] His manners are pleasing & his abilities far from contemptible—But the Sailors say "many a fine ship has a *lee lurch.*["] Burn this by Contract—

1. RC, Gratz Collection, PHi. The letter was addressed to Dayton in Elizabethtown.
2. Presumably Dayton's "neighbor" in Elizabethtown, Elias Boudinot.

House of Representatives Proceedings, Tuesday, 28 April[1]

The Speaker laid before the House a letter from Matthias Ogden, referring to sundry petitions annexed thereto from a number of citizens of New-Jersey, complaining of illegality in the late election of Representatives for that State to this House.

The said letter was read, and, together with the petitions accompanying it, ordered to lie on the table.[2]

1. *Journal of the House of Representatives of the United States* (New York, 1789). Hereafter, the House proceedings are cited by date only. For a modern edition of the House journal and a history of its evolution, see Linda Grant DePauw et al., eds., *Documentary History of the First Federal Congress of the United States of America*, III (Baltimore and London, 1977).
2. No petitions opposed to the conduct of the elections in New Jersey have been located.

House of Representatives Proceedings, Wednesday, 29 April

The petitions of the citizens of New-Jersey, whose names are thereunto subscribed, complaining of the illegality of the election of Representatives to Congress for that state, as referred to in Mr. Ogden's letter of yesterday, were read: Whereupon,

Ordered, That the said petitions be referred to the committee of elections, and that it be an instruction to the said committee, to report a proper mode of investigation and decision thereupon.[1]

1. The members of the standing committee of elections were Fisher Ames (Massachusetts), Egbert Benson (New York), Daniel Carroll (Maryland), George Clymer (Pennsylvania), Nicholas Gilman (New Hampshire), Benjamin Huntington (Connecticut), and Alexander White (Virginia).

Newspaper Account of the House of Representatives Proceedings, Wednesday, 29 April[1]

PROCEEDINGS OF CONGRESS.
HOUSE OF REPRESENTATIVES OF THE
UNITED STATES. . . .

A letter from Matthias Ogden, Esq; of New-Jersey, addressed to the Speaker, inclosing a petition and remonstrance of a number of citizens of New-Jersey, alledging that certain irregularities had prevailed at their late election, and that undue means had been used to bias the voters; also complaining of the return made by the Governor; was read, together with the petition, and committed to the committee of elections.

1. New York *Daily Advertiser*, 30 April 1789. Several New York newspapers regularly printed the proceedings or accounts of the proceedings of the House of Representatives. The *Daily Advertiser* accounts were usually the earliest and most complete, and they have therefore been used in this volume unless a better account was located in another newspaper. Francis Childs, publisher of the *Daily Advertiser*, collaborated with John Swaine to publish the *Journal of the House of Representatives of the United States*.

Essex County Certificate of Election for Representatives, 30 April[1]

Abraham Clark	2762
Jonathan Dayton	2984
James Scureman	1274
Elias Boudinot	448
Robert Hoops	505
Robert L Hooper	188
Josiah Hornblower	679
Whitten Cripps	469
Benjamin Van Cleve	206
Thomas Henderson	290
John Witherspoon	105
Thomas Sinickson	124
James Parker	248
Lambert Cadwallader	17
William Winds	223
Robert Ogden	64
Abraham Ogden	14
John Rutherford	12
Alexander McWhorter	52
Silas Condict	106
William Woodhull	6
John Fell	13

Joseph Sheppard	20
Henry Stites	69
Samuel Tuthill	6
Aaron Kitchel	268
Abraham Kitchel	30
Patrick Dennis	1
Hugh Hughes	2
John Stevens	1
Charles Stewart	1
Frederick Frelinghuysen	6
Jacob Hardenburgh	2
James Linn	13

We do hereby Certify to whom it may concern, that at an Election for representatives in the Congress of the United States held in the County of Essex begun on the eleventh day of february last and ended on the twenty seventh day of this instant, the above is a true list of all the persons voted for, and of the number of Votes taken for each, As Witness our hands and seals this thirtieth day of April in the year of our Lord 1789—

[signed] Jereh: Ballard Inspector
William Halsted Judge &c Caleb Camp, Inspector
Manning Force Inspector

1. MS, William Livingston Papers, MHi. An endorsement on the document, apparently in Governor Livingston's handwriting, reads: "Return of the Election in Essex received the 3d of May 1789." For other election returns, see Part Five:II.

House of Representatives Proceedings, Tuesday, 12 May

The Speaker laid before the House . . . a petition of a number of the citizens of the state of New-Jersey, whose names are thereunto subscribed, in opposition to a petition of sundry other citizens of the said state, complaining of the illegality of the election of Representatives from that State, returned to serve in this House.

Burlington County Petition to the House of Representatives, 13 May[1]

Resolved that the following Petition be fairly copied and signed by the President of this Board & attested by the Clerk

To the Honorable the Representatives of the United States in Congress assembled.—

The Humble Petition of the Board of Justices and chosen Freeholders of the County of Burlington, in the State of New Jersey

Sheweth

That a Petition hath been circulated through the said State of New-Jersey, and signed by a Number of its Citizens, in order to induce your Honorable House to supersede the Election of the Representatives who have been Commissioned by his Excellency the Governor of the said State.—That the Facts set forth in the said Petition are either unfounded or misrepresented—That the said Petition has a Tendency to deprive the said State of a Representation in Congress for a considerable length of Time, and thereby to embarras the Government of the United States in its very Organization—That in this County the suffrages of the People, have been fairly taken and the Members returned and Commissioned by his Excellency the Governor, are the free and approved Choice of the Electors of said County—That the late Election hath been attended, with a very heavy Expence to the County, and we wish not to see it repeated unnecessarily.—That the Conduct of the Members now returned to represent this State in Congress, is satisfactory to your Petitioners, and to the Inhabitants of the County in general.—

We therefore humbly pray that the same Election may be held Valid; and confirmed by your Honorable House, without further trouble & Expence.—

And your Petitioners shall ever pray

Signed by the unanimous Order and in behalf of the Board

May 13th. 1789. John Lacey President

Attest

Thomas M Gardiner Secretary.

1. MS, Burlington County Board of Justices and Chosen Freeholders Minutebook, 1722–1790, NjR. This is the only petition located regarding the contested New Jersey election. Although it is not definitely known that this petition was submitted to the House of Representatives, it is likely that it is one of the petitions referred to in the House on 15 May (see House of Representatives Proceedings, 15 May, below).

House of Representatives Proceedings, Thursday, 14 May

Ordered, That the petition of the citizens of New-Jersey, which lay on the table, be referred to the committee of elections, that they do examine the matter thereof, and report the same with their opinion thereupon, to the House.

House of Representatives Proceedings, Friday, 15 May

Several other petitions of the citizens of New-Jersey, praying that the election of Representatives from that State may be declared valid, were presented to the House, and ordered to be referred to the committee of elections.[1]

1. See Burlington County Petition to the House of Representatives, 13 May 1789, above.

House of Representatives Proceedings, Thursday, 21 May

Mr. Clymer, from the committee of elections, to whom it was referred to report a proper mode of investigation and decision on the petitions of a number of the citizens of New-Jersey, complaining of the illegality of the election of the members holding seats in this House, as elected within that State, made a report which was read, and ordered to lie on the table.

Newspaper Account of the House of Representatives Proceedings, Thursday, 21 May[1]

Congressional Intelligence.
HOUSE OF REPRESENTATIVES. . . .

The committee of elections, to whom were referred the several petitions from the citizens of New-Jersey, respecting the election in that state for representatives in Congress, reported a resolution, that a committee should be appointed with authority to receive and hear evidence on the subject of those petitions; that a day should be appointed on which this committee should sit for the above purpose, and that the Speaker should be requested to transmit a copy of that resolution to the Governor of New-Jersey, with a request that he would cause the same to be published in the several newspapers within that state.

1. New York *Daily Advertiser*, 22 May 1789.

House of Representatives Proceedings, Monday, 25 May

The House proceeded to consider the report from the committee of elections, to whom it was referred to report a proper mode of investigation and decision, on the petition of a number of the citizens of New-Jersey, complaining of the illegality of the election of the members holding seats in this House, as elected within that State; and the said report being amended, to read as followeth:

That it will be proper to appoint a committee, before whom the petitioners are to appear, and who shall receive such proofs and allegations, as the petitioners shall judge proper to offer, in support of their said petition, and who shall, in like manner, receive all proofs and allegations from persons who may be desirous to appear and be heard in opposition to said petition, and to report to the House all such facts as shall arise from the proofs and allegations of the respective parties.

RESOLVED, That this House doth agree with the committee in the said report, and that it be an instruction to the said committee of elections to proceed accordingly.[1]

1. The New York *Daily Advertiser*, 26 May 1789, briefly summarized the House action of 25 May, noting that Egbert Benson of New York presented the committee recommendations to the House.

[Matthias Ogden] to Governor William Livingston, Elizabethtown, 6 June[1]

I herewith enclose a copy of the report of the Committee of elections upon the subject of the petitions from this state, complaining of an undue election &c. a copy of the resolution of the house of Representatives of the United States thereupon & also of the letter from the Chairman of the Committee which accompanied them. Your Excellency will perceive from the perusal of those papers that an hearing has been granted to the complaints of the petitioners & that a day is assigned for the receiving of such proofs & allegations as they may judge proper to offer. Believing that your Excellency is willing to give every possible information respecting a transaction of so great importance to those over whom you preside, I take the liberty of asking in behalf of the petitioning electors amounting to upwards of six thousand, that your Excellency would be pleased to favor us with a copy of the returns from the different counties of the votes for Representatives as above mentioned, particularly specifying on each, the day on which they were given in. If any facts which may tend to throw light on the subject in dispute and which can neither be collected from those returns or from the proclamation, have at any time arisen within your Excellency's knowledge & official observation, I trust that your Excellency will not be unwilling or refuse to communicate them to me, in order that I may lay them before the Committee & that, by that mean, the house of Representatives may be possessed of as clear a statement of the facts & of the whole transaction, as the nature of the case will admit of.

I enclose likewise one of the petitions & have the honor to be &c.

1. FC, Jonathan Dayton Papers, MiU-C. The file copy of the letter, signed "M.O.," is in Jonathan Dayton's handwriting.

Governor William Livingston to Matthias Ogden, Elizabethtown, 8 June[1]

I have received your letter of the 6th instant[2] by which "you ask me in behalf of the petitioning electors amounting to upwards of six thousand, that I would be pleased to favour you with a copy of the returns from the different counties, of the votes for representatives as above mentioned, particularly specifying on each, the day they were given in." my answer to which is that I do not at present see the propriety of complying with your request, as I cannot think it official to make copies of those returns for individuals though they apply in behalf of the Petitioners, which may be with or without any authority from the Petitioners; nor were those papers returned to me as into an office obliged to give copies to every applicant; and tho' every citizen of New Jersey may be finally intitled to see them, yet certain it is that not every individual can be entitled to a copy of them from me, because of the impossibility which such a supposition must necessarily involve: But what I conceive, will equally serve the purpose of the Petitioners (whom I consider in a more respectable light than an Individual) & appears to me much more official, I am willing on the request of the Committee of Congress, to furnish them with such copies (the parties paying the copies under my inspection) for the mutual benefit of the contending parties; or to produce the original returns to the Committee on the hearing, or both.

I know of no such facts Sir as you allude to that could possibly be of any use to *communicate you*, as the only two which I officially know & which can have any influence in the matter in controversy will prove that two certain facts set forth in the Petition respecting myself are greatly misrepresented & therefore I presume would not answer your purpose—

As I am informed that the hearing in this case is postponed to the 16th of this month, & therefore will not come on, (as is specified in the papers you transmitted to me) on the 10th, those will be [tim'd?] for a farther consideration of this matter, & if I can be convinced by any person upon whose judgment & impartiality I can depend, that I am now mistaking, I shall chearfully change my present opinion, as I can assure you that I am not influenced by the least bias or predilection in favour of either the contending parties; but heartily wish that strict justice may be done, & as far as it is my duty officially to promote so desireable an object, no partialities, if any I had would, I think, divert me from the path of public rectitude—

1. RC, Manuscript Group 25, Miscellaneous Manuscripts, NjHi. The letter was addressed to Ogden in Elizabethtown.
2. Printed immediately above.

Certificate of Governor William Livingston to the Congressional Committee of Elections, 20 June[1]

The Certificate of the Governor of the State of New Jersey as to the first, second, third, fourth—seventh eighth, & ninth facts insisted upon by those of the Citizens of New Jersey who have complained of the illegality of the election of the Members who hold seats, as delegates from the said State in the house of representatives of the Congress of the United States—.[2]

First—As to the first fact the Governor certifies that he did on the said twenty seventh day of February last past write such Letter as is set forth in the schedule A. (except that by the original draft of the said letter it appears that the time fixed for the meeting of the Privy Council of the said State was on the Monday next ensuing the date of the said Letter, & not on Tuesday as is mentiond in the Schedule aforesaid) to four of the Privy Council of the said State, which is the number he [issued?] summons to to prevent disappointment altho three would have constituted a quorum for the business then to be transacted—And the said Letter was directed to the four Members of the Council who resided nearest to the Governor which is also his usual practice to prevent unnecessary expenses to the State,

Second—The Governor certifies that the elections in the several Counties mentioned in the second fact were closed & the returns thereof made as is expressed in the Schedule B—

Third—With respect to the third fact he certifies that this four Members of this Council as summoned as aforesaid did accordingly meet at the time & place for that purpose mentioned in his said letter—and he, being informed after having sometime deliberated upon the subject matter of their meeting that another Gentleman of the Council[3] was in town (whom he then thought was accidentally there but has since been informed & verily believes was solicited to come by private persons in order to be present at the said meeting in hopes of his voting if the returns should be there [examined?], & that the elections declared) he accordingly sent for him, by which means five Members of the Council were assembled—

Fourthly—He does not recollect that three of the Council gave such advice & opinions as are stated in the fourth fact, but verily believes that only two concurred therein which nevertheless may be ascertained by haveing recourse to the Members of the Council then present—No minute being made of the said Meeting because there was not a majority for declaring the elections from the returns then received—Nor would there have been a majority had three of the Council actually been of the opinion herein beforementioned as the Governor conceived himself entitled by the law to a vote on that occasion, and would have been against the measure—And further that a majority of the Members then present did agree to meet again on the same business on the 18th. day of the same month without a new summons from the Governor—

7th. That four of the said Members did accordingly meet on the said 18th. day of March with the addition of seven others who had been summoned in the mean time—and continuing to sit on the 19th was then joined by another of the Council[4] who had also been summoned since the last meeting—That nine of the said Members did advise the Governor as in his Proclamation declaring the Candidates elected as set forth—

8th—That three of the said Members did enter a protest against those proceedings—

9th—That the returns of the elections for the County of Essex was received on the said third of May—

1. MS, William Livingston Papers, MHi. Livingston labeled this "Certificate delivered to a Committee of Congress respectg the New Jersey Election." Although it is not definitely known that this document was submitted to the House committee, Elias Boudinot referred in a House debate on 15 July to "what has been certified by the executive magistrate" of New Jersey (see House of Representatives Debates, 15 July, below).

2. No petition or document listing specific "facts" about the dispute has been located.

3. Peter Haring.

4. Jeremiah Eldredge.

House of Representatives Proceedings, Tuesday, 14 July

Mr. Ames, from the committee of elections, to whom was referred the petition of a number of the citizens of New-Jersey, complaining of the illegality of the election of the members holding seats in this House, as elected within that State, made a report, which was received and ordered to lie on the table.

House of Representatives Proceedings, Wednesday, 15 July

The House proceeded to consider the report made yesterday by the committee of elections on the petition of a number of the citizens of New-Jersey, complaining of the illegality of the election of the members holding seats in this House, as elected within that state; and the said report being twice read at the clerk's table, was debated,[1] and ordered to lie on the table.

1. See immediately below.

House of Representatives Debates, Wednesday, 15 July[1]

The house proceeded to consider the report made yesterday by the committee of elections on the petition of a number of the citizens of New-Jersey, complaining of the illegality of the election of the members holding seats in this House, as elected within that state.

This report stated that certain allegations in the petition required the testimony of some witnesses, which the committee did not think themselves authorised to collect: they, therefore, requested the direction of the house in the manner of proceeding with respect to such testimony; also with respect to the request of the petitioners in favour of the sitting members, that they might be heard by counsel.

Mr. Boudinot

Observed that he could answer for himself, and he believed for the other Jersey members, that the suffrages of their constituents had not been solicited by them, nor had they been any ways concerned in any of the transactions at the election complained of. In consequence of the commissions received from the governor and council of New-Jersey, who had declared the election legal; he and his colleagues appeared in the house; the governor's conduct had been censured upon the occasion; however, their proceedings have been published and laid before the house, and the petitioners have agreed that they shall be admitted as evidences in this case. He thought it unnecessary that the petitioners in favour of the election, should be heard by counsel. He said the sentiments of the other sitting members coincided with his: They gave up every advantage that might arise from this, rather than occasion the great delay that must attend it.

The committee, said he, have applied to the house for power to send a commission into New-Jersey, to take testimony, in contradiction of what has been certified by the executive magistrate;[2] now I submit to the house, whether this certificate, admitted to be true on all hands, is not the best evidence the nature of this case requires, and whether it will be necessary to send through that state, a commission to examine every person, who chuses to offer evidence on the subject. I think such a measure will produce great evils, as a precedent, and many others in its operation; in the first place, such evidence will be taken *ex parte*, because it will be next to impossible for the opposite party to attend, in order to cross-examine the witnesses. It will put the petitioners to great expence and inconvenience, and after all, the uncertainty will be as great, as it is at this moment.

But the precedent, I conceive, will be extremely dangerous; if a contested election should take place in New-Hampshire or Georgia, we shall be obliged to send a commission into those states, for the purpose of obtaining testimony, which after all can never be so satisfactory as *viva voce* evidence—and more time may be spent in executing this commission, where the judges have to travel from district to district, through a state of 5 or 600 miles extent, and examine every judge, inspector and elector, than the representation is chosen to sit.

We thought it proper to lay these reasons before the house, and there leave the matter to their decision, to which we shall submit with chearfulness: We came here with an ardent desire to carry the constitution into effect, actuated by this motive, we mention to the house, the great attention, which ought to be paid to secure the freedom of election, upon which alone the whole fabric depends.—It is not that we dread the fullest investigation, that we submit these sentiments, it is our anxiety to have the question of our election speedily determined, and not delayed by what we conceive a useless measure.

The question before the house appears to be, whether it is necessary to obtain a few additional witnesses, at great uncertainty and expence, or whether the evidence already before them, and what may further be advanced by the petitioners, *viva voce*, is not sufficient to decide upon.

Mr. Ames

Brought forward several resolutions, which he thought would bring the question, alluded to by the honorable gentleman from Jersey (mr. Boudinot) fairly before them; the first prescribed the mode of taking depositions by commission.

This being read, together with the papers containing the charges, &c. and the certificate of the governor,

Mr. Benson

Observed, that the house had referred this business to the committee of elections, to report facts arising from the proofs, that it appeared to the committee, that certain facts respecting the manner in which the election was conducted, might be material, but the testimony could not be procured by them, without the aid of the house, they had therefore made a report of this nature. He thought the house had better consider whether the facts alluded to by the committee, were material or not, if they were not material, the house would not adopt the resolutions proposed by mr. Ames, but if they were, then those resolutions will come properly before them.

Mr. Vining

Opposed mr. Ames's proposition, for empowering the judges of New-Jersey to take this evidence: He was in favor of receiving the testimony *viva voce* before the house: the vicinity of that state would render this mode not inconvenient, and if it should be found necessary to form commissions for this purpose in distant states, provision might be made accordingly.

Mr. Lawrence

Remarked that it had been questioned how far the house had a right to interfere in the election of particular states, but that congress has received a discretionary power, from the constitution to regulate the time, manner, and place of holding elections;—and it is stated in another clause, that the election and qualification of its own members shall be judged by the house; by this means all transactions relative to such elections are included; consequently they may determine in what manner the investigation of such a subject shall be prosecuted, if any doubts arise on that point, the sense of the house must be taken thereon.

Mr. Benson.

Proposed a day to be assigned on which the parties should have a hearing before the house on the question, either by themselves or by counsel, whether, by the constitution, an enquiry can take place before the house relative to the facts alledged.

Mr. White objected to counsel being introduced in the present instance, he judged the house as competent to decide this business as they had already been to determine many other constitutional questions.

Mr. Jackson

Was of opinion that no such question could be admitted with propriety: One election has been determined without the aid of counsel or *ex parte* evidence, and he saw no reason in the present case why a different mode should be substituted. The authority of this house is not to be called in question by an individual; there cannot be a doubt of its jurisdiction in the case: One gentleman has been tried by the house upon the evidence that was brought before us: It will not be pretended that the delicacy and feelings of that gentleman could be less than those of the gentlemen concerned in the present question; it would be inconsistent and unjust to subject one member to a particular mode of trial, and then deliberate whether that same mode shall be adopted with respect to another.[3]

Mr. Seney

Said he did not doubt the jurisdiction of the house, but as some objections had been made by the petitioners, and they had prayed to have the point settled, he thought they ought to be indulged; that every citizen had a right to be heard in his own defence, where he considered his right concerned.

It was then moved, that the report of the committee should lie on the table, in order to take up the proposition of mr. Benson.

Mr. Ames

Objected to this proposition as the greatest inconveniencies might arise from it; it would discourage a number of people from applying for justice, especially those who lived remote from the seat of government, provided they were obliged to attend in person, and give their testimony. The eligibility of taking depositions in many instances, particularly the present, in preference to the delays, uncertainty, and enormous expences that would inevitably attend, the mode proposed by the motion was clear to his mind.

After some desultory conversation, mr. Benson withdrew his proposition.

Mr. Lee

Proposed that the report should be recommitted, and the committee authorised to send for evidence, papers, and records, and report a special state of facts: He said that it was the custom of the British house of commons upon similar occasions, to leave the whole business to a committee, and observed that the example of so old, and so experienced a legislative body, could be followed with safety and propriety.

This motion was withdrawn, after some desultory conversation had taken place upon it.

The question on the report of the committee then recurred; on the question, whether the judges of the supreme court in New-Jersey should be authorised to take depositions on the subject of facts, alledged by the parties? When,

Mr. Seney

Moved that Wednesday next be assigned for the parties to appear, and be heard by their counsel before the house, of which notice should be given—and that the committee be discharged.

Mr. Livermore

Observed that the house was much embarrassed; but sir, said he, I foresaw it from the first appointment of the committee; I object to counsel being introduced into this house, to discuss a previous question. This house is the judge in its own elections. We have appointed a committee to examine; but have not vested them with power to determine. They have not so much as a power to hear. If we have pursued a wrong step, why should we proceed any further. Let the committee be discharged, and a day appointed to hear the parties. It is my determination to hear before I judge. The committee should be discharged if they cannot proceed further without our aid. The subject now before the house is material, and of the greatest importance, and although we have been heretofore wrong, we may now set ourselves right.

I have no objection, that counsel should be heard upon the merits of the principal question. Though after an investigation of facts, we have determined in one instance, and why we cannot do the same now, I cannot conceive.

Each house is to judge of the elections, returns and qualifications of its own members. What means the word judge? Why it corresponds with the ancient maxim to hear, and determine. Now how can the house determine without hearing? If the house is to judge, we must bring all the evidence before us, although the committee may have heard it twenty times over.

Mr. Madison

Thought if the jurisdiction of the house was called in question, it would be proper to hear counsel on that point, because it must be indelicate to determine a question respecting their own jurisdiction, without hearing what could be advanced against it.

Mr. Page

Was in favor of recommitting the report, and letting the committee proceed upon the duty to which they were originally appointed;—he said if the jurisdiction of the house was questioned, the parties had an indubitable right to be heard by counsel, and he hoped no gentleman would refuse the people of the United States a privilege of this important nature, which had been always enjoyed by the subjects of Great-Britain.

Mr. Stone

Thought the authority of the house, to determine any question respecting the election of any of its members, was so clearly expressed, and understood from the 5th sect. of the 1st article of the constitution, that no doubt could be entertained by the petitioners, or any one else; consequently it would be a waste of time, to spend any in hearing counsel on that point: He had no objection to admitting a limited number on the merits of the main question, if it was required.

Mr. Boudinot

Informed the house, that the petitioners meant to withdraw, then request to be heard by counsel.

Whereupon mr. Seney withdrew his motion for making it the order of the day.

The question again recurred, for inserting a commission to go into Jersey to take evidence,

But it growing late, the house adjourned.

1. Thomas Lloyd, ed., *The Congressional Register; or, History of the Proceedings and Debates of the First House of Representatives of the United States of America* . . . (3 vols., New York, 1789), I, 77–82.

2. See Certificate of Governor William Livingston to the Congressional Committee of Elections, 20 June 1789, above.

3. William Smith's victory over David Ramsay in South Carolina had been challenged by Ramsay on the grounds that Smith had not been a citizen of the United States for seven years at the time of his election—as required by the Constitution. The House voted in favor of Smith, 36 to 1, on 22 May 1789. See DHFFC, III, 22, 28, 38–39, 57–58, 69, 70; DHFFE, I, 195–96.

Newspaper Account of the House of Representatives Proceedings, Wednesday, 15 July[1]

Congressional Intelligence.

HOUSE of REPRESENTATIVES. . . .

Mr. Ames moved to take up for a second reading the partial report of the committee appointed on the subject of the Jersey election. This report stated, that certain allegations in the petition referred to them, must be supported by the testimony of witnesses, which the house had not given them authority to collect, requesting the aid and direction of the house in what manner they should proceed to collect that testimony. And further moved a resolution prescribing a mode of ascertaining evidence in New-Jersey by depositions taken before a judge of the supreme court of that state.

Mr. Boudinot was opposed to this. He said the dispute lay between the two parties who by their petitions contended for and against the legality of the election. He himself with his colleagues had come forward under the sanction of a full and unequivocal commission from the executive of New-Jersey, who had declared the election legal. The petitioners on behalf of the election had a wish to be heard by counsel on the facts to be brought before this house; but he was willing to relinquish any advantages which could arise from this on account of the great delay that must attend it, and its establishing a precedent which in future might be found extremely inconvenient. Similar cases, he said, might occur in the extreme parts of the continent. As to the irregularities which, it had been said, had taken place in the conduct of the election, he observed that the laws of the state were competent to punish any misdemeanor which had been committed—The true point was whether the house would make the enquiry on the evidence already before them, or at most from a few additional witnesses which might conveniently be adduced.

The clerk then read the charges and the papers submitted to the special committee, which pointed out the irregularities in the conduct of the governor of New-Jersey; and of the officers who managed the election; the certificate of the governor as far as those charges concerned himself, and the resolve proposed by Mr. Ames relative to the procuring testimony in Jersey.

Mr. Benson said the point first to be determined by the house was, whether the facts respecting the manner in which the election was conducted, was cognizable by this house.

Mr. Vining was opposed to the sending a commission into Jersey. There was no mode in which the facts could come up fairly in evidence, but before this house. The Judges in Jersey might be interested and biassed. They were possibly in a question which agitated the whole state, themselves parties concerned. The facts to be evidenced were few, and a few witnesses might support or overthrow them.

The clerk then read the counter petition of several inhabitants of New-Jersey in behalf of the election, praying that the house would permit them to be heard by counsel on the question, whether the proceedings in Jersey under the election law of that state were cognizable by this house.

Mr. Lawrence was convinced for his own part that the house had a compleat constitutional power to judge of the elections and qualifications of its own members, and of all proceedings respecting these elections. If there were doubts, he wished to take the sense of the house upon that point.

Mr. Benson then moved, that the petitioners should be heard by their counsel, on this question, whether an enquiry could constitutionally take place before the house, relative to the facts alledged.

Mr. Jackson, thought that no such question could be admitted. It was improper that any individual should be allowed to call in question the powers of this house. There was no doubt of the jurisdiction. It had been declared in the case of Mr. Smith, of South-Carolina, it would be inconsistent and very unjust to subject a member to a trial before the house in one instance, and immediately deliberate whether they should do it in another.

Mr. Seney said, he had no doubt as to the jurisdiction of the house. Still, as the petitioners had objected to the jurisdiction, and prayed the point to be settled, he thought they ought to be regarded; and that every citizen, where his rights were concerned, had a right to be heard in his defence.

A motion was then made that the report of the committee should lie on the table in order to take up the proposition of Mr. Benson, which was carried.

On this question Mr. AMES made a number of observations to prove the impropriety of bringing this great question before the house—He repeated the arguments which had been advanced relative to the unimpeachable jurisdiction of the house.

Mr. BENSON withdrew his proposition.

Mr. LEE after some remarks to prove the great delays and difficulties which would take place if the general subject of the election with all the proofs came before the house, proposed that the report be recommitted and the committee be authorised to send for evidence, papers and records and report a special state of facts. He enforced the propriety of this measure by the examples of Great Britain and almost all the American States.

Mr. SENEY thought the committee could not be invested with this power of sending for papers, &c. The power was in the house: but it could not be assigned to any other body.

This motion was also withdrawn.

This question then remained on the original report and request of the committee, that the house would determine whether they should have authority to apply for depositions to be taken by the judges of Jersey.

Mr. AMES moved that the deposition of witnesses should be taken only in West-Jersey.

Mr. BOUDINOT again contended that this mode of procuring evidence was improper, and a precedent big with inconveniencies.

The question was then taken on the first clause of the original propositions submitted with the report of the committee, to wit, that the judges of the supreme court of New-Jersey, be authorised to take depositions on the subject of the facts alledged in the petition. This was negatived.

Mr. SENEY then moved, that Wednesday next be assigned for the parties to appear and be heard by their council before the house, of which they should have notice, and that the committee be discharged.

Many other objections were made to this. It was said the committee could not be discharged. Their report was still before the house, which was only a request to the house for an explanation of their powers.—That they had not yet discharged the business which was committed to them.

The motion was negatived; and after some further conversation in which no question was taken—a motion was made to adjourn which, was carried.

1. New York *Daily Advertiser*, 16 July 1789. The New York *Gazette of the United States*, 18 July, also printed a detailed account of the House debates of 15 July.

One of Seven Thousand, Daily Advertiser (New York), 31 July

Messrs. CHILDS and SWAINE,

As the petitioners against the sitting members from New-Jersey have not an opportunity of being heard in the house of representatives on certain points respecting the contested election which have lately been discussed there, you will be pleased to give place to a few strictures on the speech of Mr. B—t, mentioned in your paper of the 16th as delivered the day preceding, in consequence of a motion prescribing the manner in which evidence should be procured.[1]

In the first sentence Mr. B. tells the house that "the dispute lay between the two parties, who by their petitions contended for and against the legality of the election."

Intimating, it is presumed, by this, that he and his colleagues cannot be considered as parties, and thereby making an apology for their entering into the debate, and perhaps paving the way for the impropriety which possibly might follow of their attempting to vote upon the subject. In the next sentence he says that "he himself with his colleagues had come forward under the sanction of a FULL and UNEQUIVOCAL commission from the executive of New-Jersey, WHO HAD DECLARED THE ELECTION LEGAL." Is the commission "full?" Let it be examined—Let it be compared with and tried by the law.[2] The governor and privy council, says the law, shall determine the four persons who shall have the greatest number of votes from the whole state to be the persons DULY CHOSEN to represent this state in the Congress of the United States. Do the governor and privy council declare it in the case of the sitting members? The proclamation[3] which is their act, or advice, and contains their determination, says no such thing. The commissions themselves, when brought to the fair and proper test (the law) are not "full." In two of them the word DULY has been erased, but not so entirely but that it may be seen that such word was once inserted; in the other two it has been altogether omitted. The law considered the word as of importance and prescribed it. The governor and privy council, who are the executive, and the referees not only avoid saying that the sitting members were DULY CHOSEN, but avoid even to say that they were CHOSEN. The governor who had prepared his commissions for the first meeting of the council on the third of March, makes them answer for the second meeting on the eighteenth after the word "DULY" was struck out.[4] Is the commission unequivocal? Compare it with the law in the instance abovementioned—Compare it with the proclamation throughout—The persons who are mentioned therein (are not duly chosen to represent the state but) have the greatest number of votes from the twelve counties, says the proclamation, are elected to represent the state, says the commission.

Have the Executive declared the election legal? Review the proclamation—The executive far from asserting in that instrument that the election was legal, do on the other hand very clearly manifest that they themselves are doubtful of it, and expressly "refer the decision of the legality of the election of the present sitting members, to whom it appertains," meaning the house of representatives.

Mr. B—— next goes on to say, "that the petitioners on behalf of the election had a wish to be heard by counsel on the facts to be brought before this house, but he was willing to relinquish any advantages that could arise from this on account of the great delay." It is difficult to ascertain what advantages Mr. B——, putting himself, as he professedly does, in the place of his party, relinquishes in this case—The house in taking up the matter, and referring it in the manner they did to their committee, had already decided against him and his side of the question, so far as respected the jurisdiction of the house, and sufficiency of the facts.

Mr. B—— further observed, that "as to the irregularities which it had been said, had taken place in the conduct of the election, the laws of the state were competent to punish any misdemeanor which had been committed." The law of the state is indeed competent to the infliction of a trifling fine upon the judges of the election, but it is not competent to administer the remedy asked for by the people from the house of representatives; it cannot remove the sitting members, whose seats are the fruit of the illegality complained of.—The petitioners call for redress, and not for punishment—Little will it avail to fine a few individuals for misdemeanors, while the evil occasioned thereby is continued. How ingeniously does he try to shift the penalty from himself upon the judges, by endeavouring to have the matter referred to the state tribunal!

He well knows that however THEY may there be punished, he and his colleagues are without its reach, and may in defiance of it hold their seats securely.

But Mr. B—— and his brethren shall not so escape; there is a spirit of justice and of independency in the house of representatives on which the several thousand of electors who have remonstrated against the late election and return for New-Jersey confidently rely for a redress. The members of that house will dare do right, even if in doing it, should be involved the unpleasant task and the disagreeable necessity of depriving of their seats certain persons who have been associated with them as members—They will remember that this instance of a contested election must stand as precedent on their records, and that if they depart in their decision upon it from the path of rectitude, they may not only lead astray a future house of representatives, but will encourage illegal and irregular elections, contaminate the purity of representation, give up the independency of the house, and sacrifice the dearest interests of the union.

One of Seven Thousand.

New-Jersey, July 20, 1789.[5]

1. For Elias Boudinot's House speech of 15 July 1789, see Newspaper Account of the House of Representatives Proceedings, 15 July, immediately above.

2. The New Jersey Election Law, 21 November 1788, Part One.

3. Proclamation by Governor William Livingston, 19 March 1789, Part Five:I.

4. No formal commissions have been located. Govenor Livingston's draft commission of 21 March 1789 (Part Five:I) does not use the terms "duly" or "chosen"; instead it states that the Representatives have been "elected . . . agreeably to the true intent & meaning of a certain Act of the legislature" and were therefore "commissioned to represent & vote in behalf" of New Jersey in the House of Representatives.

5. This article was reprinted in the *New Jersey Journal*, 12 August 1789.

Evidence Presented to the Congressional Committee of Elections, 13 August[1]

Aaron Kitchel Esqr[2]—He is one of the Council for New Jersey—He was summoned to attend a privy Council on the 3d. March—The Govr. informed him that returns were not all come in, but he hoped they would by that day. He met accordingly—The Govr. laid before them (being 4 Counsellors met) returns from 7 Counties, all which had been opened, and were drawn out in alphabetical order—

The Council were not agreed about the Matter when propositions were made for adjourning. Some were for concluding the Business, others not; after some Time, they were informed that Judge Harring[3] (another of the Counsel) was in Eliz Town whom they sent for—They had reason to know how the Votes of the 4 Members were, and that they were equally divided as appeared by their reasoning, except the Govr—after Herring came in, they asked the Govr. to put the Question—He refused it, as the Returns were not all in—Herring from his reasoning appeared to be for finishing the Business—When the Govr refused, some of the Counsel said then they had nothing to do further—Govr then requested Counsel to meet on the 18th—

Witness does not know whether he then agreed to it or not, but he did afterwards—There was no Question taken for adjournment—but does not know but that a Majority might have agreed to meet on the 18'—but rather thinks they did not from the Governor's after Conduct[.] The objections to an Adjournment was, that the Law did not authorise them to Meet at a farther day—Govr did not take any advice of the Council relative to calling on a greater Number—

He attended again on the 18th—Judge Herring did not come—12 Council met—The Govr then shew Returns from 12 Counties arranged in alphebetical order—Three Council objected to proceeding or doing any thing in the Business on the same Principle that the Govr objected before, as one County had not sent in any Return—If there was any limitation the Time was past, if there was none, the Time was not come.—Question was put & Carried, with three negatives—The Govr. then asked the Council to assist in drafting a Procln. The Question was then put if 4 Members were duly elected This put the Matter on new Ground, especially as they had recd some Information of improper Conduct on Judges & Inspectors of some Counties[.] The 3 Members delivered in a Protest in writing—[4]

The Govr said that he would not declare them duly elected, but would leave it to those to whom it did belong—The Council would not determine on the 4 duly elected—There is no limitation as to time of closing the Election in the Act of Assembly, but it is the general opinion & practice, that the Representatives in the State Legislature, must receive their Certificates the Day before the Session or they cannot take their Seats—Remembers one Instance when it was the recieved Opinion of Govr & Members of Legislature, that unless Certificate was given previous to Session, it was void—

Peter Harring Esqr.—lives abt 30 Miles from Eliz Town—Was at Eliz. Town. Mr Arnold brought him a Billet from Govr. & went with him to his House—They were just done Dinner—Mr Kitchel moved that Election should be determined that day. Then Colo Martin rose & made a pretty smart motion to take the Question[.] Govr said he would not.—Witness then said that they had nothing to do further— *Mr Blanchard & Marsh came to his House just before day the same Morning as he understood they had rode in the night—they said some of his Friends wanted him at Eliz Town but did not tell him on what Business—he has never yet given his opinion about the Election—They brought no Message from the Govr but said some of the Council was to be at Eliz Town that day—when he arrived at Eliz Town he went to Genl Daytons & staid till he went to the Govrs.—Arnold soon came in and went to the Govr. but soon returned with a Billet from the Govr.—Witness would not have attended, had not Marsh & Blanchard come for him—They told him there was like to be some dispute in Council about the Election & his Friends wanted him to come—

Mr. Winson said to shew the Reason of sending for Mr Harring he would prove that Mr Blanchard a close Friend of the Govr., knowing there would be a division in the Council was anxious to keep the Govr. from Censure & therefore went for Mr Harring—

Mr Kitchel again—After Council had met & some reasoning by the Members—Mr Arnold came into the Govrs. and wanted to see him—Arnold said I wont interrupt Business—The Govr. asked him to take a Glass of Wine—Mr Arnold said Mr Herring another Counsellor is in Town—Colo Martin wished he was present—Govr said he had no Servt at hand who would send for him—Martin then said Mr Arnold would go, who agreed if the Govr would write a Billet which he did—Arnold went & brought Mr Harring—On the 18th. March, the Govr blamed Mr Arnold for imposing Mr Harring on him—Witness was chagrined and told Mr Blanchard of it, who informed him that he had told the Govr. that he had done it himself to oblige the Govr., as he knew there would be a tye in the Council—He knows not whether Blanchard & Arnold were partizans in the Election or not till since the determination—& since no farther than being Petitioners—Arnold behaved as a Judge of Morris Election in an unexceptionable Manner—

Jacob Arnold Esqr.—The Monday after the first Meeting on 3d March, he went to the Govr. to inquire abt the Returns from West Jersey—The Govr told him that he did not like him—that he understood he (Arnold) had contrived to introduce Herring in the Council but if all the Council had been for declaring the Election on the first day, he would not have done it—Witness answered that 9/10th of the People & 3/4th. of the Lawyers would give it as their Opinion [that?] it should have been declared on that Day—On which the Govr said it was his opinion too—Witness said he would never leave nor forsake the Election till it was settled—. Witness asked the Govr. what Commission he could give & how it would read if dated the 18th March.—Govr said he did not know that he should give any, but would state the Facts & send them to Congress—*The Evening before the meeting of Council on 3d of March it was talked of among a few Friends, that as there were but 4 Counsellors, if they could get another, it would prevent the matter being cast on the Govr in case of a division—He first saw Mr Harring at Genl Daytons from thence Witness went to the Govrs. for the express purpose of introducing him there—When Witness went in, Coll Martin asked him what News—he answered none—Martin said is there none? he answered none but that Mr Harring is in Town—Martin said Your Excly had better send for him.—Govr said he had no Servt. but wanted all the Council he could get—Martin or Kitchel said, Arnold will take a Billet and had better bring Harring up—Arnold said he would take the Billet but wanted to go to New Ark & could not return—but at last he consented & brought him there—Mr Blanchard was pretty warm in the Election—

1. MS, William Livingston Papers, MHi. The document is in Elias Boudinot's handwriting and is titled: "Evidence given before the Committee on the Jersey Election Augt. 13, 1789." The notes are in rough, almost shorthand, form and were evidently made by Boudinot at the committee hearing. Two large crosses were made in the margin of the document (they are indicated here at the appropriate places in the text by asterisks), apparently to relate Peter Haring's version of the events preceding his arrival at the Privy Council meeting with the version given by Jacob Arnold. For more information about this hearing of the committee of elections, see Elias Boudinot to Elisha Boudinot, 15 August 1789, immediately below.

2. Abraham, not Aaron, Kitchel represented Morris County in the Council; Aaron represented Morris in the Assembly at this time.

3. Peter Haring.

4. Asher Holmes, Abraham Kitchel, and Ephraim Martin signed the protest. See Privy Council Proceedings, 18–19 March 1789, Part Five:I.

Elias Boudinot to Elisha Boudinot, New York, 15 August[1]

I have not been able to write you since the hearing on the Petition—The Petitioners appeared by Mess. Winson & Aaron Ogden with Colo Ogden—The[y] examined Mess. Kitchel, Harring & Arnold—The two last to my Surprize, who on a Cross Examination brought out the who[le] business of sending for Harring & runing him on the Govr—Their Testimony amounted to nothing more than to shew their Combination in a Party & determination to carry their Point at all Events—I moved for a farther day merely to shew that the Essex Election had been carried on with violent designs to prevent a Representation—

I am called to congress and can only say farther, that by the Committee's Refusal to give a longer day, I suppose they think it not worth while—

1. RC, Boudinot Papers, PHi. The letter was addressed to Elisha in Newark.

House of Representatives Proceedings, Tuesday, 18 August

Mr. Clymer, from the committee of elections, reported, that the committee pursuant to the instruction to them contained in the resolution of the twenty-fifth of May, relative to the petition of a number of citizens of the state of New-Jersey, complaining of the illegality of the election of the members of this House, as elected within that state, do ascertain the following facts, as arising from the proofs, to wit:

1st. That the elections for members of this House held within that state, in consequence of an act of the legislature thereof, entitled, "An act for carrying into effect on the part of the state of New-Jersey, the Constitution of the United States, assented to, ratified and confirmed by this state, on the eighteenth day of December, one thousand seven hundred and eighty-seven," passed the twenty-first of November, one thousand seven hundred and eighty-eight, were closed in the several counties of Bergen, Morris, Monmouth, Hunterdon, Somerset, Middlesex, Sussex, Salem, Cape-May, Cumberland, Burlington and Gloucester; and the lists of the several persons voted for, and the number of votes taken for each, were received by the Governor at the respective times appearing from the said lists, and the indorsements thereon, which lists accompany this report.[1]

2d. That the election in the county of Essex, the remaining county in the state, closed on the twenty-seventh of April, and the list was received by the Governor on the third of May.

3d. That in consequence of a summons from the Governor, (a copy whereof accompanies this report) dated the twenty-seventh of February, to four of the members of the council, a privy council, consisting of the Governor, and the four members so summoned, did assemble at Elizabethtown on the third of March, and being so assembled, Mr. Haring, another member of the council, received a note from the Governor, (a copy whereof accompanies this report) in consequence whereof Mr. Haring did then also attend the privy council as a member thereof.

4th. That the Governor then appointed another meeting of the privy council, to be held on the eighteenth of March, at which day the Governor and eleven members of the council did assemble, and did then determine from the lists of the twelve counties specified in the first fact above stated, the four members now holding seats in this House, the four persons elected members of this House within that state; against which determination of the council three of the members then present did protest; and a protest, (a copy whereof accompanies this report) was with the consent of the council delivered into the council in form on the subsequent day.

5th. That there was no determination of the Governor and privy council in the premises until the eighteenth of March.

6th. That the Governor did on the nineteenth of March issue a proclamation, (a copy whereof accompanies this report.)

ORDERED, That the said report do lie on the table.[2]

1. None of the supporting documents referred to in the report were printed with the report in the House journal.

2. This report was printed in the New York *Daily Advertiser*, 20 August 1789, and *New Jersey Journal*, 26 August, among other places. A copy of the report is in the William Livingston Papers, MHi.

The *Daily Advertiser*, 26 August 1789, reported as "Business of Yesterday," the item: "On motion of Mr. GOODHUE the house agreed to take up on Monday next the report of the committee relative to the Jersey election." There is no mention of such House action on 25 August in the House journal or *Congressional Register*, nor is there any action reported for 31 August ("Monday next") in the same sources or newspaper accounts of House activity. According to the House journal, the House considered the report on 1 September.

Thomas Hartley to Jasper Yeates, New York, 31 August (excerpt)[1]

This City is greatly agitated about the Business of fixing the permanent Seat of Residence—

Even a Temporary Adjournment to Philada. is also spoken of—but all is uncertainty—By way of Manœuvre the New Yorkers are attempting to set aside the Jersey Election.[2]—I am attending to that Business—which makes this Letter so short—

1. RC, Yeates Papers, PHi. The letter was addressed to Yeates in Lancaster, Pennsylvania. Hartley (1748–1800) represented Pennsylvania in the House of Representatives; for a biographical sketch, see DHFFE, I, 417. Yeates (1745–1817), a wealthy lawyer and jurist, voted to ratify the Constitution in the Pennsylvania Convention in 1787.

2. On 27 August 1789 the House of Representatives agreed to take up, on Thursday, 3 September, a motion "for establishing the permanent residence of Congress." The motion was taken up and debated at great length on 3 September. There were rumors that some New York and New England Representatives would try to unseat the sitting New Jersey Representatives because they were believed to favor Philadelphia over New York as the site for the federal capital. For other references to this controversy, see Hartley to Tench Coxe, and Elias Boudinot to Elisha Boudinot, both 2 September 1789, below.

A.B., Daily Advertiser (New York), 31 August

Messrs. Childs and Swaine,

As it has been asserted by some, with a view to affect improperly the decision upon the question now in agitation in the honorable the House of Representatives respecting the contested election in New Jersey, that a majority of the privy council convened on the 3d of March, were not for casting up the returns and commissioning on that day, you will be pleased to publish a copy of the enclosed certificate, and to hold the original for the inspection and perusal of such as may apply for the purpose. It is signed by three of the five members of the privy council, who were summoned to meet on the before mentioned day, to determine upon the business of the election.

Your's, A.B.

New-Jersey, Aug. 29, 1789.

This may certify to whom it may concern, that we the subscribers being members of the privy council consisting of five, convened on the third of March, which was the day immediately preceding that on which the new Congress were to commence their proceedings, did then in council declare it as our opinion, that the returns at that time in the hands of the governor should be cast up, and that the four highest of the candidates on the lists of such returns, should be considered and proclaimed to be the persons duly elected to represent the state of New Jersey in the House of Representatives of the United States, and should be commissioned accordingly. We also certify that the governor did decline and refuse to take any vote of his council upon the subject, giving as a reason for such his refusal, that the return from all the counties in the state not being yet transmitted to, and lodged with him, the matter did not properly come before them for their decision and declaration. That we did ask for the question to be put, and the vote be taken, alledging as an argument in favor of our request, that agreeably to the tenor and spirit of the law for the election of our representatives in Congress, and likewise agreeably to that of the law for the election of state legislators upon which the former is founded, as well as consistently with the uniform custom and practice in the conduct of our state elections, the returns ought immediately to be examined, inspected, and cast up, in order that the commissions might bear date a day at least precedent to that prescribed for the commencement of the proceedings under the new constitution.

EPH. MARTIN,
ABRM. KITCHELL,
PETRUS HARING.

State of New-Jersey, June 1789[1]

1. For questions about the authenticity of this certificate, see *Brunswick Gazette*, 15 September 1789, below. For Kitchel and Martin's official protest to the Privy Council's proceedings on the election returns, see Privy Council Proceedings, 18–19 March 1789, Part Five:I.

House of Representatives Proceedings, Tuesday, 1 September

The House proceeded to consider the report from the committee of elections, of the eighteenth of August last, relative to the petition of a number of the citizens of the state of New-Jersey, complaining of the illegality of the election of the members holding seats in this House, as elected within that state, which lay on the table, and having made some progress therein,

ORDERED, That the farther consideration of the said report be put off until to-morrow.

Newspaper Account of the House of Representatives Proceedings, Tuesday, 1 September[1]

Congressional Intelligence.
HOUSE OF REPRESENTATIVES. . . .

Mr. VINING moved the house to take up the Jersey election, the consideration of which had been postponed.

Mr. SENEY objected—he thought it most proper for the house to proceed in the judiciary bill. This objection being over ruled, the house resolved to take up the report of the committee on the election.

The Clerk then read the report of the committee, stating the facts arising from the proofs.

Mr. STONE moved to postpone the business and to assign a day, when the parties should be heard by themselves and their counsel. This motion was objected to by Mr. VINING, as the subject was reduced to a small compass by the committee, who had examined the whole matter thoroughly, and as each member was perfectly competent to judge on it with ease. It was also observed that the petitioners had abandoned the ground which Mr. STONE contended for.

The Clerk then, as the Speaker read the articles of the report singly, proceeded in reading the documents which accompanied that report.

After some conversation respecting the form in which the subject should be brought to an issue, Mr. Benson moved a resolve that all the votes taken in at the election subsequent to the third of March are void and of no effect.

Mr. Goodhue seconded this motion.

Mr. Vining moved, that it should be ascertained how the votes stood on the 4th of March, the day on which the Congress were to assemble; he tho't it necessary to determine this fact before the house proceeded any further. The house ought to have all the facts before them, which could possibly be of any use in the final decision.

Mr. Lawrance Mr. Goodhue, Mr. Ames and Mr. Sedgwick opposed going into this enquiry, as it would probably give an improper bias. To know the state of the votes might affect the determination of the principles from personal considerations.

The Speaker declared that the motion of Mr. Vining was not in order, as it was proper that the committee alone should ascertain the facts.

Some various conversation took place on Mr. Benson's motion, and it was withdrawn.

Mr. Smith (S.C.) then moved a resolution comprehending a general statement of facts, on which he wished the house to decide.

Mr. Vining moved, that the house should come to a resolution, that the facts reported by the committee are not sufficient to set aside the election.

Mr. Sinnickson suggested to the house as a fact, that in the county of Cumberland, the votes were all received on the 3d of March, but as the judges of election sat till 4 o'clock the next morning in counting them, they thought proper to date the return on the 4th of March, though all the votes were received previous to that day.

A debate on the general subject then took place between Mr. Scott and Mr. Hartley for, and Mr. Lawrance and Mr. Stone against the validity of the election of the sitting members. The house adjourned without coming to a decision.

Substance of Mr. Lawrence's speech on Tuesday, on the Jersey Election.

I must confess the subject is of a nature not altogether agreeable; because if members for whom we have a personal esteem, should be excluded from a seat, the event would be attended with feelings of regret on our part. But I think it necessary that we should express freely our real sentiments. The constitution has given this body a right to judge of the elections, qualifications and returns of its members, tho' the mode of their election in the first instance has been referred to the laws of the several states. It is the business of this house therefore to determine whether the election of the sitting members has been conformable to the law which was enacted for that purpose. I presume this will be the question. If it has been agreeable to the law; it will be the duty of this house to make the declaration. If it has not, the house must declare the election invalid.

The law of New-Jersey declares that the election of the members shall be in the same manner and under the same regulations as the election of representatives for the legislature of the state. It is necessary therefore to enquire what was that mode from which we are to conclude respecting this election.—The law relative to the election of representatives in the State Assembly fixes no time of limitation for giving in the votes and declaring the election; but the practice under that law has ever been to declare the returns of the elected, previous to the meeting of the legislature. The late law had evident respect to the time at which Congress were to meet. By reasonable construction, therefore, we must conclude that the intention of the law was, that the election should be declared before the day appointed for the assembling of the Congress. This is plain when we consider the uniform practice of the state.

It may be asked further, what was the sense of the people of New-Jersey on the subject. It appears that a majority of the counties in Jersey did actually close their poles and make the returns previous to the 4th of March. If we are to reason therefore from the conduct of a majority of the state, we may conclude that their opinion was agreeable to this construction. It appears also the governor gave this construction. This appears from his letter to the members of the council, requesting their attendance on the third of March, as he expected on that day the whole election returns. He knew what reason he had to expect it. If he had not supposed it material, he was not obliged to summon them on that day—it is clear to me from these circumstances that the election ought to have been declared on the third of March, and that the authority of the governor expired with that day. If we admit a contrary supposition, that he had a continuing authority, it would lead to abuses. If he might extend it a day, he might protract it a month, or to an unlimited time. It might defeat the election, or it might put it in the power of the governor to determine who should be the sitting members; in short it would put the law in the power of the governor. But it never can be rationally contended that the law should have an operation which may defeat the design of it, or be committed to a discretion, which may produce the same effect.

But admitting that the Governor's authority was not expended, and that he had a right to delay, it becomes a question, to what time he should extend this delay. It appears from the clause in the law which confers the power on the Governor, that he is obliged to determine from *the greatest number of votes of the whole state.* The inference from this will be, that the Governor and council were to wait till they had received all the votes from all the counties. But it may be said that this would put it in the power of a single county to defeat the law. Admitted—Whose fault is it? If the state would pass a law putting it in the power of a county to defeat the law, the state must suffer the consequences. The time fixed by the Governor for the second meeting of the council was arbitrary.

From these considerations, I think it must result, that the election of the present members from New-Jersey was not conformable to the law, and therefore not valid.[2]

1. The "Congressional Intelligence" is from the New York *Daily Advertiser,* 2 September 1789; John Laurance's speech is from the *Daily Advertiser,* 3 September 1789.

2. This account of Laurance's speech was also printed in the *New Jersey Journal,* 16 September 1789.

New Jersey Journal (Elizabethtown), 2 September

We hear from New-York, that the contested election of this State, which is now pending before Congress, and was made the order of day for Monday last, was postponed until yesterday, when it was brought on; and, in the course of the debates, many specious arguments were made use of both for and against it—but their ultimate decision we have not heard.

Thomas Hartley to Tench Coxe, New York, 2 September (excerpt)[1]

The New-Yorkers made a push at the Jersey Election yesterday—it will be determined to Day[2]—On to Morrow the Motion for a permanent Residence comes on—I wish we may be able to give a good account of it—

1. RC, Tench Coxe Papers, PHi.
2. For other references to the attempts of New Yorkers to unseat the New Jersey Representatives, see Hartley to Jasper Yeates, 31 August 1789, above, and Elias Boudinot to Elisha Boudinot, 2 September 1789, below.

House of Representatives Proceedings, Wednesday, 2 September

The House resumed the consideration of the report from the committee of elections, touching the petition of a number of the citizens of the state of New-Jersey, complaining of the illegality of the election of the members holding seats in this House, as elected within that state: Whereupon,

A motion being made and seconded that the House do agree to the following resolution:

RESOLVED, That it appears to this House, upon full and mature consideration, that James Schureman, Lambert Cadwalader, Elias Boudinot, and Thomas Sinnickson, were duly elected and returned to serve in this House, as representatives for the state of New-Jersey, in the present Congress of the United States.

It was resolved in the affirmative.

Newspaper Account of the House of Representatives Proceedings, Wednesday, 2 September[1]

Congressional Intelligence.
HOUSE OF REPRESENTATIVES. . . .

Mr. VINING then brought forward his motion respecting the validity of the Jersey election in a new form, viz. "Resolved, that James Schureman, Lambert Cadwallader, Elias Boudinot, and Thomas Sinickson, were duly elected and properly returned members of this house."

Mr. SHERMAN made a number of observations in support of the validity of the election.

Mr. SMITH (S.C.) spoke on the same side. The following is the substance of his argument:

This is a subject which requires considerable attention. I confess I had doubts yesterday. I have since made up my opinion. It appears to me the matter turns on the construction of the law of New-Jersey. In the first place the law admits of a construction that the returns ought to be made, and the election announced on the third of March.

It admits of another construction, that the election ought not to be declared, till all the returns from all the counties in the state were made. We must give the law a reasonable construction. It appears from the preamble, that the election should be declared the third of March, because it mentions that the constitution should begin to operate on the 4th of March, and the preamble implies that the election should be made known at that time. There is no particular time prescribed when the returns should be made; but it appears that there is a reference to the practice and usage of the state. Now by the law regulating the election of the representatives in the state legislature, there appears to be no time limited for the returns of the election. It appears also that this construction was given by the seven counties who made their returns previous to the 4th of March. It appears also that the governor had this in idea by summoning the council. These observations were made yesterday, and they had weight on my mind. In answer to this construction it may be said that it is done away by the act which declares that the Governor and council shall cast up the votes from [the] *whole* of the returns of *all* the counties, and therefore the 4th of March was not the proper time, unless the returns were all then made, which it is probable was contemplated at the time of the passing of the law. It will appear that absurdities will follow from either of the constructions. If you take the first, it might so have happened that no county may have made the returns. Would it then have been required that the Governor should declare the election? or that the Governor should decide on the votes of one county, if only one had returned? On the other hand to wait till all the returns had been made would be equally absurd, because it would be in the power of one county to defeat the election.

The question then is, whether the executive power has not a discretion—and whether he ought not to exercise that discretion to carry the law into execution—If this is admitted, another question arises whether the executive exercised that discretion in a justifiable manner. It appears that the Governor, previous to the 3d of March, summoned the council and laid before them the returns on that day. But it seems also that the Governor thought it probable that all the returns would not then be made—As on the 3d of March, there were only the returns of seven counties made; as it was merely matter of construction, it appears to me that the Governor and Council had a right to exercise their discretion, in postponing the determination for such a reasonable time as would allow the returns to be sent in; and that this is one of those cases where the executive may properly interpose its authority where the law is dubious, and yet must be carried into operation. Some latitude must be given to the executive in similar cases—were it denied the executive authority would be almost useless.—The Governor when he summoned the Council, observed that the returns would probably be all made by the 3d of March, and upon that presumption did he summon them. The next question is, whether the Governor should not have protracted the determination till all the returns were made? I think not, for the reasons before stated; it is sufficient if he waited a reasonable time, so that the returns might have all been made. twelve out of the thirteen were actually made, Congress were assembling, and a very reasonable time had been allowed: the Governor was then justified in announcing the election.

It may be said that this discretionary power might be abused, because the governor might watch the opportunity when his friends were highest on the list, and then close the election. True, such abuse was possible, and were it proved, would be a good ground of setting it aside; but all power is liable to abuse; the returning officers have it in their power to commit abuses at all elections, yet they must be trusted; it does not appear that the governor acted unfairly, on the contrary, he seems to have consulted the interests of his state, by sending its representatives in proper time to Congress, and at the same time receiving the suffrages of his fellow citizens, as long as was consistent with the public good.

The question being taken on Mr. Vining's motion, was carried in the AFFIRMATIVE.

1. New York *Daily Advertiser*, 3 September 1789.

Elias Boudinot to Governor William Livingston, New York, 2 September[1]

I have the pleasure of informing your Excellency that our long Contested Election was finally determined about 12 oClock this day in favour of the sitting Members by a unanimous Vote (except one) after an investigation of several Hours—

The principle which lead the House was, that the Governor & Council would have been inexcusable if they had not delayed the Matter, when they found but 7 Counties had returned their Lists—

1. RC, William Livingston Papers, MHi. The letter was addressed to Livingston in Elizabethtown.

Elias Boudinot to Elisha Boudinot, New York, 2 September[1]

I catch a Moment during an Argument, to let you know that the Vote on the Election is past this Moment—It came on yesterday Morning—We had previously discovered a violent maneuvering among the N York Members & a few Eastern Members, in order to oust us, to prevent our appearing on Thursday[2]—Their Opposition became so bare faced on the Argument as to strike every bye stander with surprize—After many Maneuvers & cross Motions, a tolerable one took place—I was dissuaded from starting the Business, by which the Facts were by no means understood especially as a contra publication, I now enclose was handed to every Member just before the Business coming on; supposed to have been written by Mr Burr, but not known—The Argument was adjourned till this Morning when it was again taken up & this Moment determined by a unanimous Vote in favour of the Election, except one Vote Mr John Lawrence of N York—I write while attending to an Argument & therefore you must excuse the Scrawl—

Remember me to the Gentn of the Bar with the Judges &c

1. RC, Manuscripts and Historical Section, Rare Books, Law Library, N. The letter was addressed to Elisha in Trenton.

2. Thursday, 3 September 1789, was the date set for the House of Representatives to consider the location of the federal capital. For the opposition of New Yorkers to the sitting New Jersey Representatives vis-à-vis the location of the federal capital, see also Thomas Hartley to Jasper Yeates, 31 August 1789, and Hartley to Tench Coxe, 2 September 1789, both above.

Fisher Ames to George Richards Minot, New York, 3 September (excerpt)[1]

The Jersey election is decided in favor of the sitting member[s], by a large majority. The case, though confined to the construction of their State law, was very complex. I have seldom kept my mind in suspense till the vote was called. In this case, I remain still in suspense, inclining sometimes *pro*, sometimes *con.*

1. Seth Ames, ed., *Works of Fisher Ames: With a Selection from His Speeches and Correspondence* (2 vols., Boston, 1854), I, 70. Ames was a Representative from Massachusetts; for a biographical sketch, see DHFFE, I, 743. Minot was clerk of the Massachusetts House of Representatives.

William Bradford, Jr., to Elias Boudinot, [Philadelphia], 6 September (excerpt)[1]

I am much obliged to you for your late communications, and am rejoiced that the Election business terminated without a division. I could not doubt of the final issue of the question, but there is a mode which some people have of starting difficulties that might have rendered the determination less satisfactory. In your case to make the triumph complete, the decision should have been (as it turned out to be) nearly unanimous.—

1. RC, Wallace Papers, PHi. Bradford did not indicate from where he was writing, but from the contents of the letter it is clear it was written at Philadelphia.

Brunswick Gazette, 8 September

Congress have at length finished the business of the Jersey election by confirming the members from this state who have been returned.

Q, New Jersey Journal (Elizabethtown), 9 September

NE DOLEAS PLUS NIMIO.

Last Wednesday, about 4 o'clock P.M. at Federal Hall, in the city of New-York, died of debility *and a* broken heart, *the unfortunate Madamoiselle PETITION, aged six months.*

She was a native of New-Jersey, of conspicuous *parentage, and much beloved by all her* relations; *and although of so tender an age, she appeared to possess many of the virtues of her progenitors—But, alas! neither youth, nor beauty, nor innocence could prevail against the stern decree of fate. A* hereditary *disease accompanied her into the world; and notwithstanding all the assistance that* art *or* money *could procure, soon consigned her to that oblivion which had swallowed up ten thousand of her predecessors.*

And now ye friends, who mourn sincere,
This gentle maid, with many a tear,
Tho' her example teach ye all,
That death pervades e'n Fed'ral Hall:
Let me soft friendship's aid extend,
And mark the point where grief shall end:
When pain and sorrow all shall cease,
And in their turn come joy and peace;
Full four weeks hence—by Jove decreed,
Th' election comes;—and then take heed;
That day shall all your grief subside,
And joy flow in a mighty tide:
Good C.[1] *shall grasp the helm of state,*
Five hundred pounds will make him great:
Young D—,[2] *born to shining fame,*
Shall in the council *loud declaim;*
Whilst M.[3] *and O—,*[4] *statesmen born,*
In lower house *shalt make reform.*

Thus right once more the land shall sway,
And sov'reign compact *all obey.*

Q.[5]

1. Probably Abraham Clark.
2. Probably Jonathan Dayton, who was elected to the Council (from Essex County) in October.
3. Probably Daniel Marsh, a Clark-Dayton ally, who was elected to the Assembly (from Essex County) in October.
4. Possibly Aaron or Matthias Ogden.
5. This item was reprinted in the New York *Daily Gazette*, 11 September 1789.

Brunswick Gazette, 15 September

Copy of a letter from a gentleman in Elizabeth-Town, to his friend in this city.

Dear Sir,

Enclosed you have the New-York paper of the 3d inst.[1] *containing an account of the debates in Congress on the subject of our late election, which is at length determined (with only one negative) in favor of the sitting members, as I always expected. You have also an hand-bill, said to have been sent to each member of the house just before their going in to a discussion of this question. You will no doubt take notice of an extraordinary speech of Mr. L——*[2] *which surprised us much here, as from his general character we supposed him to be a sensible, prudent man. It is evident that he has not only spoken but voted on this important question without ever looking into the facts. The law of this state to which he refers* did *express a time for closing the election,* viz. *"when the votes or tickets of all the electors present are delivered in or a reasonable time for that purpose shall have been allowed." The design of the law evidently was to give a* sufficient *time to take in the votes of every elector within the several counties of the state. But Mr. L—— says the practice of this state has been to declare the members elected, previous to the meeting of the legislature, and from thence draws his conclusion against the late election. As no evidence of such a practice was reported by the committee, it is pretty clear that the* hand-bill *was his only source of information.—The truth is, that the practice here has been to* close the Poll *by* 12 *o'clock of the night preceding the day of meeting of our legislature. But Mr. L—— did not reflect on the consequences of his doctrine: If the returns were to have been declared on the 3d of March, the day previous to the meeting of congress; then he should have deducted therefrom the four days allowed by the law, to judges and inspectors, for counting the votes, ten days allowed for the sheriff to return, and four days to the Governor to summon the council, and this would have brought him to the* 13*th February, on which day every poll should have been closed.—The election began on the* 11*th of the same Month—so that Mr. L—— allows but three days for holding the election, tho' eight places were assigned by the law for opening the poll at, in the county of Burlington, some of them fifty miles apart. Mr. L—— says this seemed to be the sense of a majority of the counties, and also of the Governor—This is curious kind of Logic—those counties who had but few electors attending, and closed their polls at an early day, and from their vicinity to the Governor,*[3] *could immediately send their lists within the time limited, from the closing of the poll, are made to give a construction to the law from their local situation and smallness of numbers.—The county of Essex could have made her returns in an hour, as the Governor does not live six miles from the place of closing the poll, but the county of Cape-May might reasonably require eight or ten days. How then can any argument be drawn from the conduct of the seven counties, in making their returns before the rest; their doing so was owing entirely to their situation; and* *not from any idea that a return was absolutely necessary by the* 3*d of March:—the Governor says in his letter or summons to the council, it is* probable *the returns may all come in by the* 3*d of March—but when the council met he tells them at once, they were not all come in, and that the law required them to wait 'till the* 18*th of March, to which day he adjourned them—by which it is evident the Governor gave a reasonable construction to the law and concluded, that the* 3*d of March was the time for closing the polls in every county, and allowing fourteen days for counting the votes and transmitting the lists as allowed by the law; the* 18*th March was the day for the meeting of council to take the same under their consideration,—and this is Mr. L—s evidence that the Governor was of opinion the returns should have been declared on the* 3*d of March. Mr. L—— asserts that this construction would put it in the power of the Governor to prefer the candidates he liked best, by declaring on some day when they had a majority of votes:—but it appears that no latitude is given—the number of days being fixed and determinate in the law—but Mr. L—— further says if his construction is wrong—and the Governor and council were to declare from the votes of the whole state, then they should have waited 'till the third of May, many weeks after the sitting members had taken their seats;—this was urged notwithstanding the apparent impropriety of putting it in the power of any one county however small to defeat the state of any representation whatever in congress. The county of Essex attempted this—and would have thrown the state into the greatest confusion if such a construction had prevailed. From the state of facts as represented by Mr. L—— four periods were formed to which the attention of the house was called—I mean the* 13*th of February, the* 3*d of March, the* 18*th of March and the* 3*d of May; he could never have given himself the trouble of examining the state of the election at each of these periods. On the* 13*th of February, Cape-May only had closed and was unanimous in favor of the present members—on the* 3*d of March, eleven counties had closed, leaving the majority for the same gentlemen, from several hundred to about* 5000*—on the* 18*th of March,* 12 *counties had made returns which added to the majority about* 3000*—and on the* 3*d of May, the returns from the whole state had come in, when the majority for the same members was from a thousand to* 6000*.—From what premisses then Mr. L—— drew his conclusions, it is hard to say—surely not from the state of facts, from the similarity of language; I suspect his argument was nothing more than a repetition of the* hand-bill, *without further reflection. The propagating that hand-bill was considered by the members individually as a very indecent and unbecoming attempt to influence their minds with reasons and arguments not arising out of the facts before them, and could they have discovered the officious person, would have no doubt inflicted upon him an exemplary punishment.*[4]

I observed about the same time the publication of Messrs. Kitchel and Harring's certificate dated in June,[5] *altho' it had been refused as evidence by the committee and afterwards contradicted under oath by both those gentlemen, as I have been well informed from the minutes of their testimony in the hands of Mr. L——. This was another extraordinary step to prejudice the minds of the members.*

Enclosed you have a return of the votes of all the counties with the dates of their closing, as also a petition signed by a number of inhabitants of Essex, delivered in to the inspectors during the election which will justify many of the observations I have made.—In short, sir, this whole business has discovered a degree of obstinate perseverance in blunders that can scarcely be accounted for; it is happily finished at last to the great satisfaction, I verily believe, of much of the greatest and most respectable part of our fellow citizens.

I am Sir,
Your's &c.

Elizabeth-Town, Sept. 9, 1789.

1. See Newspaper Account of the House of Representatives Proceedings, 2 September 1789, above.

2. For John Laurance's speech in the House of Representatives, see Newspaper Account of the House of Representatives Proceedings, 1 September 1789, above.

3. The returns were sent to the governor in Elizabethtown, Essex County.

4. See Elias Boudinot to Elisha Boudinot, 2 September 1789, above.

5. See "A.B.," New York *Daily Advertiser*, 31 August 1789, above.

Elector, New Jersey Journal (Elizabethtown), 30 September

To the ELECTORS of EAST JERSEY.

Having read a paragraph in Mr. Kollock's paper, upon the death of Madamoiselle Petition,[1] to which is annexed an elegy for the purpose of comforting the friends and mourners of the deceased; yet I find it has not given direction how to obtain the desired object that will cause—

Joy to flow in a mighty tide,
And grief, and sorrow, lay aside.

Without a doubt the author had reference to the ensuing election. But I have often seen the fairest prospects disappointed, for want of proper care and industry, when the means to obtain the same were very easy, if the persons concerned had but known what to have done, and how to have done it. What to do is already pointed out, and how to do it I shall endeavor to show. And, if those melancholy mourners are not so drowned in grief as to stupify and bereave them of reason, to raise their spirits and give them courage, more difficult things, of the like nature, have been obtained by persons making use of such means as they had in their power; and let them take courage when there is example and precedent to direct them.

1st. Let them have a number of persons present, at opening the election, for judges and inspectors, properly instructed how to obtain the office, and how to conduct when appointed, who, if they are sworn to conduct the election fairly, will not be so timerous as to pay any regard to their oaths, but manage the election in such a manner that you may be certain to obtain what you desire: Let them get into some private room, that your opposers may not know who votes, or what they are doing. If such persons for judges and inspectors are not to be found among you, I am informed that there are plenty in West Jersey, where you may send for them—Burlington and Glocester being the capitals.

2dly. Be sure to have some impudent, hardy fellow to attend the judges and inspectors with a good club, D—— N—bold[2] if you can get him, that if any person offers any dirty blotted ticket, which is not printed by your direction, he may drive him away, or compel him to take such an one as you approve of, and give it in to the inspectors at the window—Let no person attend near the place unless he is in your interest; and if any persons, that you suspect are unfriendly, should attend from the neighbouring counties, let them be drove away.

3dly. You should be very generous—have rum in great plenty provided by a man of the first character (a councellor if you can get one) with instruments of music; and let the same be made known, that people may attend that otherwise would not: Then take a tour through your county, and take in votes at the peoples' houses, not refusing infants nor blacks, by this means you may obtain some hundreds of votes more than there is persons entitled to vote in your county; and if the time limited by law should not be long enough, keep on till you go through with your business, if it should take two or three weeks longer for the purpose; for if the Governor and Council, after solemn deliberation, declared a like measure legal, and affixed the Great Seal of the state to the same, will not the Legislature of New-Jersey follow the example and give your friends their right?

But, perhaps, you may say, that all will not avail; that the House of Assembly will not receive your friends—and will send them back without giving them a seat.

I answer, Will they not have other business on hand to attend to? will they not be engaged in procuring emoluments for themselves and friends—and either think they cannot or will not send for witnesses to prove facts concerning their election? Perhaps they may appoint a committee to make some enquiry into the circumstances, but your friends will be present to counteract any measure that may be taken to vacate their election; and if they are any way artful they will influence the other members to let them keep their seats.

If you should still object, and say, That you may get into difficulties, be indicted or fined, or some way hurt in your reputation.

I answer, You need not be afraid in that case—it must be your own county men that must indict,—your own sheriff that must call them—therefore be sure to have the sheriff your friend, and you need not fear; and as for your reputation, that will not be hurt if you are not punished; but, if you succeed, such conduct will redound to your glory.

And now, my friends, will not advice, example nor precedent keep you from mourning? As those that mourn without hope, will you sink into despondency? Will you not rather exert yourselves—be resolute and industrious? Persevere with firmness to obtain your much desired object; for if in the end, such measures should prove ruinous, there is still consolation, it will involve your opposers in the same ruin with yourselves. But if you sink into despondency, give way to melancholy, and persist in those notions you have hitherto practised, of observing the laws respecting the election, which of late, by the practice of the Great Men in our land, have been reprobated, the Lord may have mercy upon you, but believe me you will find no favor from government.

ELECTOR.

1. See "Q," *New Jersey Journal*, 9 September 1789, above.
2. Daniel Newbold.

NEW JERSEY CANDIDATES

Boudinot, Elias (1740–1821), Elected Representative and Candidate for Senator

Born in Philadelphia, the son of a merchant and silversmith, Boudinot received a classical education in Philadelphia. In about 1753 the Boudinots moved from Philadelphia to Princeton, where Boudinot's father became postmaster. Elias studied law with his brother-in-law, Richard Stockton, Sr., and was admitted to the bar in 1760. Shortly thereafter he opened a law office in Elizabethtown. He was named a trustee of the College of New Jersey (Princeton) in 1772 and held the position until his death. Boudinot was a member of the Essex County committee of correspondence, 1774; a delegate to the provincial congress, 1775; and a commissary general of prisoners (with the rank of colonel) for the Continental Army, 1777–1778. He attended Congress, 1778 and 1781–1783, and was President of Congress, 1782–1783. He was also acting Secretary for Foreign Affairs in 1783. After the Revolution, Boudinot returned to Elizabethtown and resumed his law practice; in 1790 he became the first lawyer to practice before the United States Supreme Court. He served in the House of Representatives until 1795, when he was appointed director of the United States Mint, at which time he moved to Philadelphia. He held the Mint directorship until his retirement from public office in 1805, when he moved to Burlington. In 1816 he was elected the first president of the American Bible Society.

Brearley, David (1745–1790), Presidential Elector

Born at "Spring Grove," near Trenton, Brearley attended the College of New Jersey (Princeton), but did not graduate (he was awarded an honorary master's degree in 1781). He studied law in Princeton, was admitted to the bar in 1767, and established a practice in Allentown, Monmouth County. He was a lieutenant colonel and then a colonel in the Monmouth County militia, 1776, and a captain and then a colonel in the New Jersey Line of the Continental Army, 1775–1779. From 1779 to 1789 Brearley was Chief Justice of the state Supreme Court. In 1782 he was appointed a congressional commissioner to arbitrate the Wyoming Valley dispute between Connecticut and Pennsylvania. He was vice president of the state Society of the Cincinnati, 1783–1790, and grand master of the New Jersey Masons, 1786–1789. In 1787 Brearley attended the Constitutional Convention and signed the Constitution; later that year he was a Hunterdon County delegate to the state Convention. In 1789 he was appointed a United States district judge, district of New Jersey, a position he held until his death.

Cadwalader, Lambert (1743–1823), Elected Representative

Born near Trenton, Cadwalader was the son of a prominent physician and Pennsylvania provincial councillor. In 1750 the Cadwalader family moved to Philadelphia, where Lambert was educated. In 1757 he entered the College of Philadelphia (University of Pennsylvania), but left before graduating. He and his brother, John, were

Philadelphia merchants prior to the Revolution. In 1765 he signed the Pennsylvania non-importation agreement. He was a delegate to the Pennsylvania provincial conference in 1775 and to that state's constitutional convention in 1776. In early 1775 Cadwalader became captain of a Philadelphia militia company. In 1776 he was a lieutenant colonel and then a colonel in the Pennsylvania Line of the Continental Army, and he served until he was captured by the British at Fort Washington, New York, in November 1776. Released on parole, Cadwalader returned to his estate, "Greenwood," near Trenton, and remained there until his resignation from the army in early 1779. He was a New Jersey delegate to Congress, 1785–1787. He served in the House of Representatives, 1789–1791 and 1793–1795. He was a cousin of John and Philemon Dickinson and was the latter's brother-in-law.

Clark, Abraham (1726–1794), Candidate for Senator and for Representative

Born on a farm between Rahway and Elizabethtown, Clark was the son of a farmer and county magistrate. He received little formal education, but developed legal skills in his work as a surveyor and as an agent for real estate transactions. In 1767 Clark was Essex County sheriff and clerk of the New Jersey colonial assembly. In 1774 and 1775 he was a member of the county committee of correspondence. In 1775 and 1776 Clark attended the provincial congresses, and in 1776 and 1777 he represented Essex County in the General Assembly. He attended Congress, 1776–1778, and signed the Declaration of Independence. After serving in the Legislative Council in 1778, Clark returned to Congress, 1780–1783. He served in the Assembly again, 1783–1785; attended the Annapolis Convention in 1786; and served in Congress again, 1786–1788. Clark refused an appointment to the Constitutional Convention in 1787, and gave only lukewarm support to the proposed Constitution. He was New Jersey commissioner to settle accounts with the United States, 1789–1790, and served in the House of Representatives from 1791 until his death.

Condict, Silas (1738–1801), Candidate for Representative

Born probably in Morristown, Condict was a member of the Morris County committee of correspondence in 1775, and in 1776 he served on the committee of the provincial congress that drafted New Jersey's constitution. He was county clerk from 1776 to 1782. He represented Morris County in the Legislative Council, 1776–1780, and New Jersey in Congress, 1781–1783. Condict was appointed to five-year terms as a county judge in 1785, 1790, and 1799. A member of the General Assembly, 1791–1794, 1796–1798, and 1800, he was that body's Speaker from 1792 to 1794 and in 1797.

Cripps, Whitten (1740–1796), Candidate for Representative

A resident of Lower Penns Neck and Mannington, Salem County, Cripps was a lieutenant colonel and then a colonel in the Salem militia between 1776 and 1779. He served in the General Assembly in 1777 and 1778. In 1780, 1782, and 1786 he was a member of the Legislative Council. Cripps was county sheriff, 1783–1786 and 1789–1792. In 1787 he represented Salem in the state Convention.

Dayton, Jonathan (1760–1824), Candidate for Representative

Born in Elizabethtown, Dayton was the son of Elias Dayton, a wealthy merchant. He graduated from the College of New Jersey (Princeton) in 1776 and received a master's degree in 1783 and an honorary LL.D. in 1798. Dayton served in the Continental Army throughout the Revolution, mostly with the New Jersey Line and often in regiments commanded by his father. He was briefly a prisoner of war in 1780, and he retired from service, with the rank of captain, in 1783. Following the war, Dayton studied law and was admitted to the bar. During the late 1780s and early 1790s, he was an agent for John Cleves Symmes's Miami Purchase; in 1795 Dayton, Ohio, was named in his honor. He represented Essex County in the General Assembly, 1786–1787. In the Constitutional Convention in 1787, Dayton actively promoted the interests of the small states as delineated in the "New Jersey Plan." Despite some reservations, Dayton signed the Constitution. Following the Convention, he sat in Congress, 1787–1788; served in the Legislative Council, 1789; and returned to the Assembly in 1790, serving as Speaker. Dayton served in the House of Representatives, 1791–1799 (Speaker, 1795–1799), and was elected to one term in the Senate, 1799–1805. Implicated in the Aaron Burr conspiracy, Dayton was arrested in 1807 and charged with high treason; he was, however, never brought to trial. He served Essex County in the Assembly again, 1814–1815. Dayton was Matthias Ogden's brother-in-law.

Elmer, Jonathan (1745–1817), Elected Senator

Born in Cedarville, Cumberland County, Elmer received a classical education and graduated from the College of Philadelphia (University of Pennsylvania) in 1768 with a bachelor of medicine degree. He began to practice medicine in Bridgeton (where he resided the remainder of his life), and earned a doctor of medicine degree from the College of Philadelphia in 1771. In 1772 Governor William Franklin appointed Elmer sheriff of Cumberland County, but he was replaced shortly thereafter because of his defense of colonial rights. In 1775 Elmer attended the provincial congress. During the Revolution, Elmer served as a surgeon in the New Jersey regiments. Soon after the Revolution he gave up his medical practice in favor of legislative and judicial service. He was Cumberland County clerk, 1776–1789; attended Congress, 1777–1778, 1781–1783, and 1787–1788; was a member of the Legislative Council in 1780 and 1784; and was a county surrogate, 1784–1804 and 1812–1813. He drew a two-year Senate term, serving from 1789 to 1791; he failed to win reelection. In 1791 he was appointed a county justice of the peace and a judge (later presiding judge) of the county Court of Common Pleas. He was reappointed to these posts in 1797, 1802, and 1812.

Fell, John (1721–1798), Candidate for Representative

Born and educated in New York City, Fell, a wealthy merchant, was senior partner in John Fell & Company, which by 1759 owned several sea-going, armed, merchant vessels. He later moved to Bergen County, where he bought 220 acres of land. In 1766 he was appointed a judge of the Court of Common Pleas, a position he held until 1774. In 1775 Fell was a member of the Bergen County committee of correspondence and of the provincial congress. In 1776 and 1777 he was a member of the Legislative Council. From 1776 to 1786 he was again a judge of the Court of Common Pleas and was known for harsh judgments against loyalists. He was captured by loyalists in 1777 and jailed in New York City. He was paroled and then released in 1778 after a year in captivity. In the same year he was elected to Congress, where he served until 1780. In 1782 and 1783 he was again a member of the Council. Fell was a Bergen County delegate to the state Convention in 1787. He sold his Bergen County estate in 1793 and moved to New York City and then to Dutchess County, New York, where he died.

Fenimore, Thomas, Candidate for Representative

Fenimore operated a tavern in Jacksonville, Burlington County, from 1770 to 1775. In 1776 he represented Burlington in the provincial congress. During the early years of the Revolution he was a major in the New Jersey militia. Fenimore was a member of the General Assembly, 1777–1782. In 1778 and 1779 he was on the township committee for Springfield, and from 1778 to 1782 he was an assessor for Springfield.

Henderson, Thomas (1743–1824), Candidate for Representative

Born in Freehold, Monmouth County, Henderson was the son of a prominent farmer. He graduated from the College of New Jersey (Princeton) in 1761 and then studied medicine with Nathaniel Scudder, setting up a practice in Freehold in 1765. Although he had a long public career and owned a large mill and a farm, Henderson always continued to practice medicine. In 1774 he was a member of the Monmouth County committee of safety. In 1775 he was commissioned a lieutenant in the New Jersey militia and in 1776 was promoted to major and then to lieutenant colonel. In 1776 he was a surrogate of Monmouth County and in 1777 a member of the Legislative Council. He was elected to Congress in 1779, but declined to serve. In 1780 he was a member of the Monmouth County committee of retaliation—a quasi-vigilante group that watched over suspected loyalists. That same year he was elected to the General Assembly, where he served until 1784. In 1783, and again in 1799, he was appointed a justice of the Court of Common Pleas. He was a presidential Elector in 1792. In 1793 and 1794 he was a member and vice president of the Council. In 1795 Henderson was elected to the House of Representatives, where he served one term. He was a member of the Council again in 1812 and 1813.

Hooper, Robert Lettis (c. 1730–1797), Candidate for Representative

Born probably in Perth Amboy, Hooper was descended from a wealthy family with large landholdings in New Jersey and Pennsylvania. His grandfather had been Chief Justice of New Jersey. In 1762 Hooper owned a store in Philadelphia, but soon after that was speculating in land, principally in western Pennsylvania. During the Revolution he served as a deputy quartermaster general in the Continental Army and then returned to New Jersey, making Trenton his home. In 1781 he inherited, through his marriage to Elizabeth Erskine, the Ringwood Iron Works. He was appointed to five-year terms as a judge of the Hunterdon County Court of Common Pleas in 1782, 1787, and 1792, and from 1785 to 1788 he was a member and vice president of the Legislative Council. He was an honorary member of the Society of the Cincinnati and was the first deputy grand master of the New Jersey Masons.

Hoops, Robert (c. 1750–c. 1800), Candidate for Representative

In 1769 Hoops came to Sussex County, where he purchased 500 acres of land in what became the town of Belvidere. There he built and operated a saw mill and a grist mill. Shortly thereafter he also built and operated a slaughterhouse, which supplied the Continental Army during the Revolution. In 1776 he was a captain and then a major in the Hunterdon County militia; for a short time before resigning from military service in 1777, Hoops was deputy commissary-general of issues for the Continental Army. He was Sussex County's representative in the Legislative Council, 1777–1778. He was appointed to five-year terms as a judge for Sussex County in 1779, 1784, and 1789. He was again in the Council, 1784–1785 and 1789–1790. He represented Sussex in the state Convention in 1787. Sometime before 1800 Hoops sold his New Jersey property to Robert Morris and moved to Virginia.

Hornblower, Josiah (1729–1809), Candidate for Representative

Born in Staffordshire, England, Hornblower studied civil engineering. He was hired by John Schuyler of Belleville, New Jersey, to come to the United States to erect a steam engine for a copper mine on the Passaic River. In 1753 he smuggled out of England plans for the first steam engine to be built in America. Hornblower remained in New Jersey and managed Schuyler's copper mine. In 1756, during the French and Indian War, he was commissioned a captain, but was not in active service. During the Revolution, Hornblower was a commissioner for tax appeals and a member of a committee to present Newark's grievances to the legislature. He was elected from Essex County to the General Assembly in 1779 and 1780, serving as Speaker in the latter session. He was elected to the Legislative Council, 1781–1784, and he served in Congress, 1785–1786. In 1790 Hornblower was appointed a judge of the Essex County Court of Common Pleas, a position he held until his death.

Kinsey, James (c. 1731–1803), Presidential Elector and Candidate for Representative

Born in Philadelphia, Kinsey was the son of a prominent lawyer who was Speaker of the Pennsylvania and the New Jersey colonial assemblies and Chief Justice of the Pennsylvania provincial supreme court. Kinsey studied law and was admitted to the New Jersey and Pennsylvania bars in 1753. He practiced law in both colonies, but resided in Burlington, New Jersey, from about 1750 until his death. He represented the city in the colonial assembly, 1772–1775. He was a member of the Burlington County committee of correspondence, 1774–1775, and was a delegate to Congress, 1774–1775. As a Quaker, Kinsey withdrew from active politics and discontinued his law practice during the Revolution. After the war he represented Burlington County in the General Assembly in 1784 and in the Legislative Council in 1791. In 1789 Kinsey was appointed Chief Justice of the state Supreme Court, serving on the bench until his death.

Kitchel, Aaron (1744–1820), Candidate for Representative

Born in Hanover, Morris County, Kitchel was a farmer's son and the younger brother of Abraham Kitchel. He attended common schools and was apprenticed to a blacksmith—a trade he practiced when not in public office. He was probably an army volunteer during the Revolutionary War. From 1777 to 1787 Kitchel served as a justice of the peace. He represented Morris County in the General Assembly, 1781–1782, 1784, 1786–1790, 1793–1794, 1797, 1801–1804, and 1809. He served as a county judge, 1785–1790. Kitchel was a member of the House of Representatives, 1791–1793, 1794–1797, and 1799–1801, and of the Senate, 1805–1809. He was a presidential Elector in 1816.

Linn, James (1749–c. 1820), Candidate for Representative

Born in Bedminster, Somerset County, Linn graduated from the College of New Jersey (Princeton) in 1769. He then studied law and was admitted to the New Jersey bar in 1772. He married William Livingston's daughter Mary in 1771. Linn began his law practice in Trenton, but soon returned to Somerset County, where he became a judge of the Court of Common Pleas in 1776. The same year he was a member of the provincial congress. During the Revolution, Linn served as a captain and later as a major in the Somerset County militia. He was a member of the Legislative Council in 1777 and 1793–1797; he also served in the General Assembly, 1790–1791. He served in the House of Representatives, 1799–1801. In the latter year President Thomas Jefferson appointed him supervisor of the revenue for New Jersey, a post he filled during Jefferson's two terms. In 1805 he became New Jersey's secretary of state; he held this position until his death.

Moore, David (1747–1803), Presidential Elector

Born in Cumberland County, Moore was a Deerfield Township farmer. In 1776 he was appointed a lieutenant in the western company of the state artillery (attached to the Continental Army), and he subsequently saw action at Brandywine, Paoli, Germantown, and Monmouth. Moore resigned his commission in late 1778, but served again as a militia captain near the end of the war. Shortly thereafter, the state legislature appointed Moore a colonel in the militia. He was a member of the board of freeholders for Deerfield, 1785–1788, 1790–1791, 1793–1799, and 1801–1803. He represented Cumberland County in the General Assembly, 1793 and 1796–1797, and in the Legislative Council from 1801 until his death.

Neilson, John (1745–1833), Presidential Elector and Candidate for Representative

Born at Raritan Landing, Middlesex County, Neilson was the son of an Irish-born physician and merchant who died eight days after Neilson's birth. Neilson was adopted by his uncle, who was also a merchant. He entered the College of Philadelphia (University of Pennsylvania) in 1758, but left before graduating. He settled in New Brunswick, where he worked in his uncle's shipping business until the Revolution. Neilson served in the state militia, 1775–1780, reaching the rank of brigadier general. He was appointed to Congress in 1778, but declined to serve. He represented Middlesex County in the General Assembly in 1779 and served as a state deputy quartermaster general, 1780–1783. Following the war, Neilson returned to his New Brunswick mercantile business. In 1787 he was appointed to the Constitutional Convention, but he resigned before the Convention met. He represented Middlesex County in the state Convention in 1787. From 1795 to 1798 he was a judge of the county Court of Common Pleas. From 1796 to 1821 he was successively register and recorder of New Brunswick. In 1796 he was again a presidential Elector. He served again in the Assembly, 1800–1801, and in the Legislative Council in 1813. He was a trustee of Queens College (Rutgers) from 1782 until his death.

Ogden, Matthias (1754–1791), Presidential Elector

Born in Elizabethtown, Ogden was the son of a tanner, local officeholder, and Speaker of the colonial assembly, and was the brother of Robert and Aaron Ogden. He attended the Elizabethtown Classical School, conducted by Tapping Reeve. Ogden joined the Continental Army in 1775 as a volunteer and was promoted to lieutenant colonel in early 1776. He saw considerable action during the war, and Congress promoted him to brevet brigadier general in 1783. After the war, Ogden returned to Elizabethtown, studied law, and was admitted to the bar. Among his business interests was land speculation, especially as a shareholder in the East Jersey Company, which bought and sold land in John Cleves Symmes's Miami Purchase. His only legislative service was as an Essex County member of the Legislative Council in 1785.

Parker, James (1726–1797), Candidate for Representative

Born in Perth Amboy, New Jersey, Parker became a New York City merchant involved in the West Indies trade by 1750. His primary interest then turned to landed property, and he moved back to Perth Amboy. There he became a member of the East Jersey Board of Proprietors and was the board's surveyor general for several years. In 1764 he was appointed to the colonial council; he was mayor of Perth Amboy in 1771. In 1775 Parker resigned from the council, moved to Hunterdon County, and attempted to remain neutral in the developing revolutionary controversy. In 1777, after refusing to take an oath of allegiance to the state of New Jersey, he was confined in Morristown as a political prisoner. After several months he was released from jail and then from restrictions in exchange for the release of John Fell.

Paterson, William (1745–1806), Elected Senator

Born in County Antrim, Ireland, Paterson was the son of a tinplate maker and peddler. Paterson and his family came to America in 1747 and first located in New Castle, Delaware. During the next three years the Paterson family moved from place to place, including Trenton, New Jersey, and several Connecticut towns. In 1750 the family settled in Princeton, where Paterson's father operated a general store and speculated in land. Paterson completed preparatory studies in the Latin grammar school at the College of New Jersey (Princeton) around 1759. He graduated from the college in 1763, received a master's degree in 1766, studied law in Princeton with Richard Stockton, Sr., and was admitted to the bar in 1769. In the latter year, Paterson opened a law practice and a general store in New Bromley, Hunterdon County. In 1772 he returned to Princeton for a short time and then moved to South Branch, Somerset County, where he operated another store and taught law.

In 1775 and 1776 Paterson represented Somerset County in the provincial congresses. He represented the county in the Legislative Council in 1776 and was New Jersey's attorney general, 1776–1783. In 1777 he was a Somerset County militia officer and also a member of the state council of safety. In 1779 he moved from South Branch to a confiscated loyalist estate on the north bank of the Raritan River, near Raritan, in Somerset County. In 1780 he was elected to Congress, but he declined to serve. After his resignation as attorney general in 1783, Paterson moved to New Brunswick to practice law. In 1787 Paterson attended the Constitutional Convention, where he championed the cause of the small states. Paterson signed the Constitution and supported ratification in New Jersey. He drew a four-year Senate term in 1789, but resigned his Senate seat in November 1790, shortly after his election as governor of New Jersey. As governor, Paterson supported the development of an industrial city on the falls of the Passaic River, which was named Paterson in his honor. He was governor until 1793, when he was appointed an associate justice of the United States Supreme Court.

Rutherfurd, John (1760–1840), Presidential Elector and Candidate for Representative

Born in New York City, Rutherfurd was the only son of Walter Rutherfurd, a prosperous merchant and landowner. Rutherfurd graduated from the College of New Jersey (Princeton) in 1776, studied law with Richard Stockton, Sr., and William Paterson, was admitted to the bar in 1782, and began to practice law in New York City in 1784. In 1787 Rutherfurd gave up his law practice and moved to "Tranquillity," a large estate in Allamuchy, Sussex County (now Warren County), New Jersey, that was given to him by his father. He represented Sussex County in the General Assembly, 1789–1790; was elected to the United States Senate in 1790; was reelected in 1796; and served until his resignation in December 1798. After his Senate resignation, Rutherfurd moved from "Tranquillity" to "Belleville," an estate near Trenton. From 1804 until his death Rutherfurd was president of the East Jersey Board of Proprietors. From 1807 to 1811 he served as a commissioner to lay out new streets in New York City. In 1808 he moved to "Edgerston" on the Passaic River, in what is now Rutherford, Bergen County. He was on the New York-New Jersey boundary commission, 1826, and on the New York-New Jersey-Pennsylvania boundary commission, 1829–1833. Rutherfurd was a delegate to the Anti-Masonic Convention in Baltimore in 1831.

Schureman, James (1756–1824), Elected Representative

Born in New Brunswick, Schureman was the son of a wealthy merchant. In 1775 he graduated from Queens College (Rutgers) and during the next several years was an officer in the Middlesex County militia. Schureman represented Middlesex County in the General Assembly, 1783–1785; attended the Annapolis Convention, 1786; attended Congress, 1786–1787; and served again in the Assembly in 1788. He served in the House of Representatives, 1789–1791 and 1797–1799, and in 1799 was elected to complete the unexpired Senate term of John Rutherfurd. Schureman served in the Senate until February 1801, when he resigned to protest the impending inauguration of Thomas Jefferson as President. Schureman was mayor of New Brunswick, 1801–1813; was a member of the Legislative Council in 1808, 1810, and 1812; and served in the House of Representatives again, 1813–1815. He was again mayor of New Brunswick from 1821 until his death.

Sinnickson, Thomas (1744–1817), Elected Representative

Born near Salem, Sinnickson was the son of a wealthy landowner and county officeholder. He was educated in common schools and became a successful merchant while still a young man. Sinnickson was a captain in the Salem County militia during the early years of the Revolution. In 1778 he was appointed naval officer of the Western District of New Jersey. Sinnickson represented Salem County in the General Assembly in 1777. He was appointed to five-year terms as a county justice of the peace in 1780, 1785, 1790, 1795, and 1799. Sinnickson was a member of the Assembly again, 1782, 1784–1785, and 1787–1788, and he served in the House of Representatives, 1789–1791 and 1797–1799. He was a judge of the county Court of Common Pleas, 1790–1804. Sinnickson served in the Legislative Council, 1794–1796, and was a presidential Elector in 1800.

Stevens, John, Jr. (1749–1838), Candidate for Representative

Born in New York City and raised in Perth Amboy, Stevens was the son of John Stevens, a prominent New Jersey politician and landowner. He graduated from Kings College (Columbia) in 1768, and in 1771 was admitted to the bar, although he never practiced law. Early in the Revolution he was commissioned a captain and appointed Hunterdon County loan officer to collect money for the Continental Army; he advanced to the rank of colonel by the end of the Revolution. Stevens was treasurer of New Jersey from 1777 to 1783. In 1784 Stevens bought a large tract of land on the west side of the Hudson River (which incorporated most of modern-day Hoboken), and he devoted the remainder of his life to mechanical inventions and managing his estate. His primary accomplishments were the development of steamboats and steam locomotives for railroads.

Van Cleve, Benjamin (c. 1740–1817), Candidate for Representative

Born probably in Maidenhead (now Lawrenceville), Hunterdon County, where he was raised, Van Cleve served in the New Jersey militia during the Revolution. In 1776 he was commissioned a captain and was promoted to major in 1777. He resigned from the militia in late 1777 to serve in the General Assembly, to which Hunterdon County voters reelected him almost every year through 1802. He served as Speaker, 1785–1786 and 1788. In 1789 he served in the Legislative Council. Van Cleve was appointed to five-year terms as a justice of the peace for Hunterdon County in 1776, 1781, 1786, 1791, and 1796. In 1782 he was appointed a judge of the Court of Common Pleas. He was county clerk in 1791.

Winds, William (1727–1789), Candidate for Representative

Born in Southold, Long Island, Winds moved to Morris County, New Jersey, when still a young man. There he purchased a large tract of land near Dover, which he farmed until his death. In 1757 he served as a captain of a New Jersey company during the French and Indian War; he may have been present at the battle of Ticonderoga. Shortly after this campaign he was appointed a justice of the peace for Morris County. From 1772 until 1775 he served in the colonial assembly. During the Revolution he served in the First New Jersey Battalion and the New Jersey militia, rising in rank from lieutenant colonel to brigadier general. He resigned from the army in 1779. In 1780 Winds was a Morris County representative to the General Assembly, and he was a member of the state Convention in 1787. He was a long-standing member of the Presbyterian church and willed much of his estate to the church in Rockaway, New Jersey. He died in October 1789.

Witherspoon, John (1723–1794), Candidate for Representative

Born near Edinburgh, Scotland, Witherspoon was the son of a Presbyterian minister. He graduated from the University of Edinburgh with a master's degree in 1739 and a divinity degree in 1743. Following his ordination in 1745, Witherspoon became an outspoken leader of the popular, or orthodox, party in the Scottish Presbyterian Church. In 1766 he was elected president of the College of New Jersey (Princeton), but he declined the election. He was offered the post again in 1767, and this time he accepted and moved to America. Witherspoon was inaugurated president in 1768; during his tenure he expanded the college curriculum, professorships, and library. Witherspoon's active opposition to British policies toward the American colonies was spelled out in his essay, "Thoughts on American Liberty," written in 1774. While expressing loyalty to the king, he condemned British measures and suggested ways of opposing them. Witherspoon was active during the Revolution as a member of the Somerset County committee of correspondence, 1774–1775, and a county delegate in the provincial congresses, 1775–1776. He served in Congress from 1776 to 1782. While in Congress, Witherspoon signed the Declaration of Independence and the Articles of Confederation. He also represented Somerset County in the Legislative Council in 1780. Following the Revolutionary War, Witherspoon returned to his full-time duties at Princeton, and began to rebuild the university, which had been occupied by both the British and American forces during the war. He represented Somerset County in the General Assembly in 1783 and 1789. In 1786, as "A Citizen of the United States," Witherspoon published a pamphlet entitled *Essay on Money, As a Medium of Commerce . . .*, in which he criticized paper money policies. In 1787 he was a Somerset County delegate to the state Convention. Witherspoon died at "Tusculum," his country home near Princeton.

CHAPTER XIII

The Elections in New York

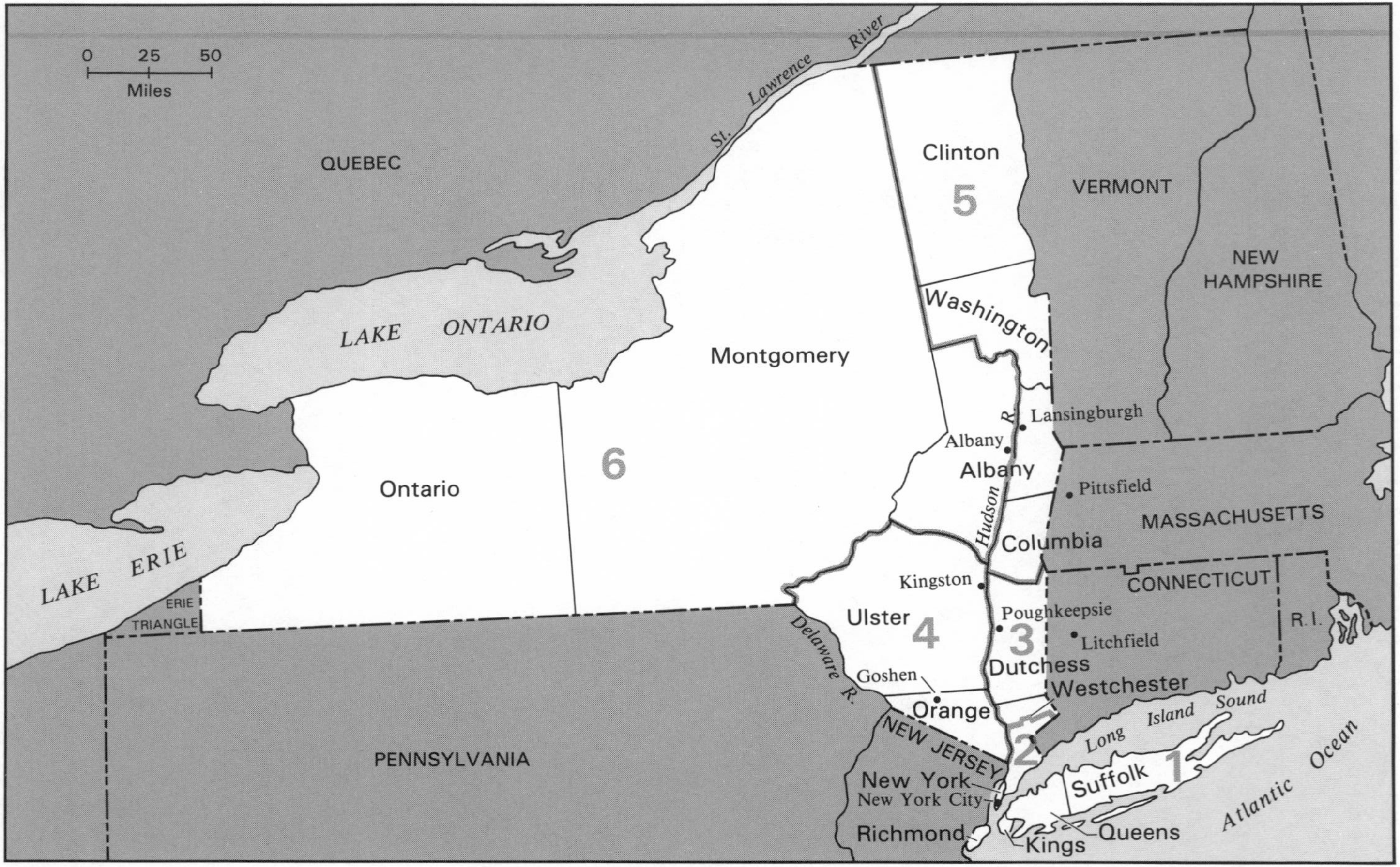

Cartographic Laboratory UW–Madison

New York Congressional Districts, 1789

(Based on Lester J. Cappon et al., eds., *The Atlas of Early American History* [Princeton, N.J., 1976], 72–73.)

INTRODUCTION

Few states felt the impact of the Revolution more than New York. New York City was occupied by British troops from the summer of 1776 until the late autumn of 1783; northern and western areas of the state were constantly threatened by British troops and their Indian allies. The occupation seriously threatened the authority of the newly formed state government and deprived the state of the import and tonnage duties which had underpinned colonial finances. The state had, moreover, a large and influential loyalist population. Not only did the loyalists hamper the patriot war effort, but the confiscation and disposition of loyalist property by the state provoked one of the most bitter controversies of the war years. Also, the devotion to the patriot cause of the numerous tenants who farmed on the Hudson River manors was doubtful, especially after state authorities ruthlessly suppressed major tenant revolts in 1776 and 1777.

The Revolution also severely fractured the political party structure. Since about mid-century a faction headed by the Delancey family had sparred with the Livingston clan and its allies for control of the colonial government. However, the Delanceys, as the "court party," were swept aside when British civil authority collapsed in 1775–1776, and they were replaced by patriot leaders who rose rapidly in power and influence during the war. These leaders, most notably George Clinton, Melancton Smith, and Abraham Yates, Jr., represented and articulated the interests of the upriver Hudson valley counties of Albany, Dutchess, Orange, and Ulster. Clinton's election as the state's first governor in 1777 symbolized their rapid rise to power. Although the patriot leaders frequently disagreed sharply with their more conservative allies (many of whom were holdovers from the prewar Livingston faction) on war policy, the contending parties were able to form effective governing coalitions during the war to counter the powerful British and loyalist threat to the state's independence.

The state constitution of 1777 reflected this wartime cooperation in its generally moderate tone and provisions. The constitution was drafted by the fourth provincial congress, which transformed itself into a convention in July 1776 and finished drafting the constitution in April 1777. It was put into effect without being submitted to the people for ratification.

The constitution provided for a bicameral legislature consisting of an Assembly and Senate. The Assembly was to have at least seventy members, elected annually and apportioned on the basis of voting population. All males age twenty-one and older were eligible to vote for assemblymen, provided they were county residents for at least six months, owned freeholds worth at least £20 or rented tenements worth at least 40 shillings annually, and had been rated and paid taxes to the state. The Senate consisted of twenty-four freeholders from four districts: the Eastern District had three; the Middle, six; the Southern, nine; and the Western, six. The senators were elected to four-year terms by men owning freeholds worth at least £100. The senatorial districts were apportioned on the basis of freeholders.

Asserting that "an opinion hath long prevailed among divers of the good people of this State that voting at elections by ballot would tend more to preserve the liberty and equal freedom of the people than voting *viva voce*," the constitution directed that "a fair experiment be made, which of those two methods of voting is to be preferred" (Thorpe, V, 2630). The legislature was given the authority, as soon as the war ended, to provide for voting by ballots. (The governor and lieutenant governor were elected by ballot beginning in 1778; the first assemblymen and state senators chosen by ballot were elected in 1787.)

The governor and lieutenant governor were elected for three-year terms by freeholders qualified to vote for state senators. The governor wielded considerable power, most notably as head of the Council of Appointment (which consisted of four senators, one from each district, elected by the Assembly). The governor, with the approval of the Council, appointed all officeholders not otherwise provided for in the constitution. A veto power over legislation was exercised through the Council of Revision, which was comprised of the governor, the chancellor, and the judges of the Supreme Court (or any two of them acting with the governor). All bills passed by the legislature had to be submitted to the Council for "revisal and consideration"; Council objections to bills could be overridden by a two-thirds vote in each house of the legislature.

The cooperation between the contending political factions which produced the state constitution was also apparent in the state's relations with Congress during the Revolutionary War. New York desperately needed military and financial support from Congress and the other states; state authorities consequently recognized the need for a strong central government. The New York legislature promptly ratified the Articles of Confederation in February 1778, and in February 1780 it ceded to Congress the state's claims to lands west of its present-day boundaries, which Congress ultimately accepted in 1782. The legislature's most dramatic expression of support for Congress was made in July 1782 when it approved resolutions drafted by Alexander Hamilton asserting that the powers of the central government should be expanded and that Congress should be authorized to provide an independent revenue for itself. To effect this fundamental change, the legislature recommended that Congress take steps to assemble a convention to amend the Articles of Confederation.

The legislature's resolution of July 1782 was consistent with Congress' own initiative in 1781 to gain additional revenue. The congressional Impost of 1781, approved by Congress in February 1781, was an amendment to the Articles of Confederation which imposed a duty of 5 percent on imported goods, to pay war debts. In March, New York was one of the first states to ratify the impost amendment, but with the condition that it not take effect until all the states had ratified. By late 1782 all of the states except Rhode Island had approved the impost, but that state's continuing opposition—coupled with Virginia's repeal in December 1782 of its earlier approval—doomed the initiative. The New York legislature, noting that the Impost of 1781 stood no chance of winning approval, repealed its law approving the impost in early 1783. In its act of repeal, however, the state offered Congress the proceeds of a state-imposed impost of 5 percent—at such time as the other states made similar provisions.

Following defeat of the Impost of 1781, Congress renewed its quest for an independent income in April 1783 by proposing a revenue plan to the states that had as its cornerstone an impost of 5 percent on imported goods. However, to appease critics of its plan of 1781, Congress proposed that the impost be limited to twenty-five years and that the impost collectors be appointed in each state by the governor (although subject to congressional control and removal). By the time the New York legislature considered the Impost of 1783 in early 1784, the war had ended and enthusiasm for granting Congress important new sources of income had waned somewhat. The new realities were reflected in passage of a state impost in March 1784, which imposed specific duties on certain enumerated articles and a general 2½ percent duty on all remaining imported goods. New York no longer needed financial aid from Congress. Supporters of the congressional Impost of 1783 nevertheless continued to push for its approval in 1785 and 1786, and the legislature finally approved an amended version in the latter year. However, a provision that the governor—rather than Congress—control the impost collectors, induced Congress to reject New York's approval. Congress appealed to New York to reconsider its amendments, but the legislature in February 1787 refused to alter its stance, and thus the Impost of 1783 died.

New York's reluctance to approve the congressional imposts on Congress' terms reflected the fact that import duties were the cornerstone of the state's revenue system. These duties and the income from sales of forfeited loyalist estates greatly lessened the need for internal taxes (especially taxes on land) in the immediate postwar years. This reality was not lost on Governor Clinton's supporters, who predominated in the upper Hudson River counties where farming was paramount and where land taxes would consequently hit the hardest. While reluctant after the war to surrender the impost to Congress, New York had one of the best records of payments on congressional requisitions for funds among the states. The state also approved Congress' request, made in 1784, that it be given broader authority, for a fifteen-year term, to regulate trade with foreign nations. New York gave its approval in 1785, with the condition that all of the states agree to the measure and that no duties could be raised by Congress in New York without the approval of the legislature.

Although New York's support for measures to strengthen Congress vis-à-vis the state governments waned somewhat after 1783, prominent nationalists like James Duane, Alexander Hamilton, John Jay, and Philip Schuyler continued to champion Congress' cause. Their efforts in 1782 to have a convention convened to amend the Articles of Confederation had failed when Congress refused to act on the New York legislature's resolution calling for a convention; not until 1786–1787 were conditions again favorable for such initiatives. This time Virginia made the first move: in early 1786 its legislature appointed commissioners to meet with delegates from the other states to consider measures to increase Congress' control over commerce. The convention met at Annapolis, Maryland, in September 1786.

Egbert Benson and Hamilton represented New York at the Annapolis Convention, and Hamilton drafted the convention's report to the states calling for a convention, with broad authority, to meet in Philadelphia in May 1787. The report recommended that the proposed convention be empowered "to take into consideration the situation of the United States, to devise such further provisions as shall appear to them necessary to render the Constitution of the Foederal Government adequate to the exigencies of the Union . . ." (DHRC, I, 184). During the course of Congress' consideration of the Annapolis report, the New York delegates—acting on instructions from their legislature—proposed that Congress in effect ignore the report and specifically limit the scope of a convention, under congressional auspices, to a revision of the Articles of Confederation. The New York motion was defeated, although the limitation on the proposed convention's scope was ultimately reflected in Congress' call on 21 February 1787 for the Philadelphia Convention. On 6 March the New York legislature appointed Hamilton, John Lansing, Jr., and Robert Yates as delegates to the Constitutional Convention and reiterated Congress' instructions that the convention was being convened for "the sole and express purpose of revising the Articles of Confederation."

In the Constitutional Convention, Lansing and Yates sided with those who wished to retain a federal form of government (as embodied in the Articles of Confederation), while Hamilton was one of the most outspoken nationalists. The New Yorkers were frequently absent from the Convention, however, and after 10 July (when Lansing and Yates left the Convention permanently) the state was not officially represented by the required two delegates. Hamilton signed the Constitution at the official signing ceremony on 17 September 1787, although he was signing only for himself (not for New

York State) and despite his feeling that the central government created by the Constitution was not strong enough.

The Constitution was generally well received in the state during the fall and winter of 1787–1788. Most of the newspaper commentary was favorable, although Antifederalist writings were numerous. Hamilton tried to capitalize on the Constitution's public popularity by forcing Governor Clinton to publicly commit himself on the Constitution, but Clinton refused to respond to Hamilton's pressure. New York Federalists were aided by the pace of ratification in the other states; by the time the legislature met in early January 1788 to consider the resolutions of the Constitutional Convention (forwarded by Congress to the states on 28 September 1787), Delaware, Pennsylvania, New Jersey, Georgia, and Connecticut had already ratified the Constitution.

Among the documents Governor Clinton forwarded to the legislature at its opening was a public letter from John Lansing, Jr., and Robert Yates to the governor, dated 21 December 1787, explaining their actions in the Constitutional Convention and outlining their objections to the Constitution. The two delegates asserted that the legislature had explicitly limited their powers to a revision of the Articles of Confederation, and that they were, in any case, opposed to the creation of the "consolidated government" provided by the new Constitution. They were committed, they said, to "the preservation of the individual states, in their uncontrouled constitutional rights," and they outlined the various ways in which the proposed "consolidated" government would ultimately destroy the civil liberties of the people (*New York Journal*, 14 January 1788).

Antifederalists in both the Assembly and Senate attempted to attach some statement of disapproval of the Constitution and the proceedings of the Constitutional Convention to the legislature's call for a ratifying convention. They failed, however, and the approved resolution provided for a convention to meet at Poughkeepsie on the third Thursday in June, with the election of delegates to be held in late April and early May. Apportionment of delegates was the same as for the Assembly. All free male citizens at least twenty-one years old could vote for delegates. The elections, which began on 29 April, featured printed slates of party candidates and widespread campaigning; the Antifederalists won a solid victory. More than two-thirds of the sixty-five delegates elected were Antifederalists; only the delegates from New York, Kings, Richmond, and Westchester counties were Federalists.

In the state Convention, which opened at Poughkeepsie on 17 June 1788, the Federalists were led by Hamilton and Jay. James Duane, Robert R. Livingston, and Richard Morris also lent prestige to the Federalist cause. Melancton Smith led the Antifederalists, assisted by Governor George Clinton (president of the Convention), John Lansing, Jr., Gilbert Livingston, and Robert Yates. The Antifederalists were determined to amend the Constitution before ratifying it, or, failing that, to ratify while reserving New York's right to secede from the Union if amendments were not considered by the new government within a specified time. The Federalists were opposed to any conditional ratification, arguing that Congress would not accept New York into the Union on such terms. Formal debate on the Constitution lasted until 2 July, by which time news of the ratification by the ninth and tenth states, New Hampshire and Virginia, respectively, had reached the Convention. That news effectively ended any chance that the Convention would adjourn without ratifying, and it forced the Antifederalists to seek an acceptable compromise on amendments.

For several weeks following the end of the formal debate, the two parties maneuvered to reach compromises on amendments that would allow a majority of the delegates to vote for ratification. The final votes, on 25 July, provided for a circular letter to the other states, asking them to join New York in applying to Congress to call a convention to amend the Constitution, and for a form of ratification that did not make amendments a condition of approval. The instrument of ratification included a list of "impressions" and "Explanations" about rights which were consistent with the Constitution and which could not be abridged or violated, and it provided that the state Convention was ratifying "in confidence" that a list of proposed amendments—attached to the instrument of ratification—would "receive an early and mature Consideration." Furthermore, until a constitutional convention could be called to consider amendments, New York was ratifying "in full Confidence" that certain enumerated powers of Congress would not be exercised (DS, Ratifications of the Constitution, DNA). The Convention formally voted to ratify, 30 to 27, on 26 July.

The state Convention had two important legacies for the first federal elections. First, the Antifederalists had been forced to make concessions—under the pressure of events—which left some of them bitter and resentful. Melancton Smith, a principal architect of the Convention compromises, became a special target of disgruntled Antifederalists; his Convention activities severely damaged his chances for a Senate seat. Although the Antifederalists had failed to achieve their primary objective, i.e., previous amendments, they nevertheless had put on the record their objections to the Constitution and their proposed amendments, and they had secured the state's commitment to a second constitutional convention. All of these issues would be paramount in the first federal elections.

Second, the Convention sharpened party lines between Antifederalists and Federalists. The Clintonians, who rose to power rapidly during the Revolution and had solidified their position during the Confederation as defenders of the state's interests and as the champions of the "middling" classes, were with few exceptions, the Antifederalists of the late 1780s. The Federalists, on the other hand, had evolved from the conservative patriots of the war years to the nationalists of the 1780s. They were the party of the great landed families (although that distinction had weakened somewhat by the end of the Confederation) and New York City commercial interests.

These two well-defined political parties were poised to resume the fight over ratification when Governor Clinton called the state legislature into session in early December 1788 to respond to Congress' Election Ordinance of 13 September. The legislature's response and the accounts of the resulting first federal elections are contained in the documents printed in this chapter. New York did not choose any presidential Electors, due to the prolonged feuding over the method of selecting them by the Antifederalist-controlled Assembly and the Federalist-controlled Senate. That same feuding delayed the election of Senators Rufus King and Philip Schuyler, both Federalists, until mid-July—four months after the first Congress convened in New York City. The state's Representatives were also tardy in attending the first Congress; the elections for Representatives were held from 3 to 6 March, with the results announced by the official canvass on 11 April. The winners were Antifederalists John Hathorn and Jeremiah Van Rensselaer, and Federalists Egbert Benson, William Floyd, John Laurance, and Peter Silvester.

NOTE ON SOURCES

The proceedings of the New York legislature for 1788 and 1789 are taken from contemporary printings: *Journal of the Assembly of the State of New-York* . . . (Albany, 1788 and 1789), and *Journal of the Senate of the State of New-York* . . . (Albany, 1788 and 1789).

The manuscript journals of the Assembly and Senate for those years are not extant. Proceedings of the Council of Revision are from the manuscript minutes of the Council in the New-York Historical Society, New York City. Few manuscripts of official documents are extant; exceptions are the election law for Representatives (New York State Library, Albany), the official canvass of the votes for Representatives (James Duane Papers, New-York Historical Society), and the credentials of the New York Senators (National Archives, Washington, D.C.). Newspapers are the sources for most official documents, e.g., proclamations, notices of elections, and drafts and texts of election laws, and they are virtually the only source for debates of the Assembly, Senate, and joint conference committees of the legislature.

Thirteen newspapers were published regularly in New York State at the time of the first federal elections. Six were published in New York City, although only four of them printed a significant number of original articles about the elections: *The Daily Advertiser* (daily), published by Francis Childs; *The New-York Daily Gazette* (daily), published by Archibald and John McLean; *The New-York Packet* (semi-weekly), published by John and Samuel Loudon; and *The New-York Journal, and Weekly Register* (weekly), published by Thomas Greenleaf. The other New York City newspapers were *The Morning Post, and Daily Advertiser* (daily), published by William Morton, and *The New-York Weekly Museum* (weekly), published by John Harrisson and Stephen Purdy, Jr. The latter two newspapers largely limited their coverage of the elections to routine and factual accounts, and to reprints of articles first printed elsewhere.

Three weekly newspapers, which printed few original articles about the elections, were published in Albany: *The Albany Gazette*, published by Charles R. Webster; *The Albany Journal: or, the Montgomery, Washington and Columbia Intelligencer*, published by Charles R. and George Webster in conjunction with *The Albany Gazette*; and *The Albany Register*, published by Robert Barber.

In Poughkeepsie, *The Country Journal, and Dutchess and Ulster County Farmer's Register* (*The Poughkeepsie Journal*, after 7 July 1789) was published weekly by Nicholas Power. *The Hudson Weekly Gazette* was published weekly by Ashbel Stoddard. Two other upstate newspapers printed very little about the elections: *The Federal Herald*, published weekly by John Babcock and Ezra Hickok at Lansingburgh, and the *Goshen Repository, and Weekly Intelligencer*, founded in January 1789 by David Mandeville and David M. Westcott and published weekly. Two Boston newspapers, *The Massachusetts Centinel* and *The Herald of Freedom, and the Federal Advertiser*, published significant articles about the New York elections, while several Philadelphia newspapers reprinted many articles which appeared first in New York newspapers.

Broadsides contain important information about the elections in New York, especially the election of Representatives. Broadside collections are located at the Albany Institute of History and Art, the New-York Historical Society, the Library of Congress' Rare Book Room, and the University of Michigan's Clements Library. The notes to the documents indicate the wide range of sources from which personal correspondence has been taken. The most useful collections are the Bancker Family Papers, King Papers, Lamb Papers, and John Smith of Mastic Papers, all at the New-York Historical Society; the Tench Coxe Papers, Historical Society of Pennsylvania; and the Rush Papers, Library Company of Philadelphia.

For background about the elections and the period, see Thomas C. Cochran, *New York in the Confederation: An Economic Study* (Philadelphia, 1932; reprint, Clifton, N.J., 1972); Linda Grant DePauw, *The Eleventh Pillar: New York State and the Federal Constitution* (Ithaca, N.Y., 1966); John P. Kaminski, "New York: The Reluctant Pillar," in

Stephen L. Schechter, ed., *The Reluctant Pillar: New York and the Adoption of the Federal Constitution* (Troy, N.Y., 1985); Staughton Lynd, *Anti-Federalism in Dutchess County, New York* (Chicago, 1962); E. Wilder Spaulding, *New York in the Critical Period, 1783–1789* (New York, 1932); and Alfred F. Young, *The Democratic Republicans of New York: The Origins, 1763–1797* (Chapel Hill, N.C., 1967).

CHRONOLOGY, 1788–1789

1788

13 September	Confederation Congress adopts Election Ordinance for first federal elections.
8 December	Special session of the state legislature convenes in Albany.
11 December	Governor George Clinton presents Congress' Election Ordinance to joint session of legislature.
13 December	Comprehensive bill for electing presidential Electors, Representatives, and Senators introduced in Assembly. Bill for appointing presidential Electors introduced in Senate.
15 December	Bill for appointing Senators introduced in Senate.
18 December	Senate passes bill for appointing presidential Electors and sends it to Assembly.
20 December	Senate passes bill for appointing Senators and sends it to Assembly.
22 December	Assembly passes comprehensive bill for first federal elections and sends it to Senate. Assembly rejects Senate bill for appointing presidential Electors. Assembly appoints committee to draft application to Congress to call a second constitutional convention.
23 December	Assembly rejects Senate bill for appointing Senators.
31 December	Senate amends Assembly comprehensive bill for first federal elections and returns it to Assembly.

1789

2 January	Assembly rejects Senate amendments to Assembly comprehensive bill for first federal elections and returns it to Senate.
3 January	Senate adheres to its amendments to Assembly comprehensive bill for first federal elections and returns bill to Assembly.
5 January	Joint conference committee of Assembly and Senate debates Assembly comprehensive bill for first federal elections; Assembly and Senate refuse to compromise—bill dies.
7 January	Date specified by Congress for choosing presidential Electors in all the states.
9 January	Bill for electing Representatives introduced in Senate.

15 January	Senate passes bill for electing Representatives and sends it to Assembly.
19 January	Bill for electing Senators introduced in Assembly.
21 January	Assembly amends Senate bill for electing Representatives and returns it to Senate.
22 January	Assembly passes bill for electing Senators and sends it to Senate.
23 January	Senate accepts Assembly amendments to bill for electing Representatives.
24 January	Bill for electing Representatives sent to Council of Revision for approval. Bill for appointing presidential Electors introduced in Assembly.
27 January	Bill for electing Representatives approved by Council of Revision; bill becomes law. Senate amends Assembly bill for electing Senators and returns it to Assembly.
29 January	Assembly passes bill for appointing presidential Electors and sends it to Senate. Assembly committee reports on application to Congress to call a second constitutional convention.
2 February	Senate amends Assembly bill for appointing presidential Electors and returns it to Assembly.
3 February	Assembly rejects Senate amendment to bill for appointing presidential Electors and returns it to Senate; Senate adheres to its amendment; joint conference committee of Assembly and Senate debates bill; Assembly refuses to compromise. Assembly rejects Senate amendments to bill for electing Senators and returns it to Senate.
4 February	Date specified by Congress for presidential Electors to vote for President. Senate refuses to compromise on bill for appointing presidential Electors—bill dies. Assembly and Senate exchange resolutions for appointing Electors; none approved and thus no Electors appointed. Senate adheres to its amendments to bill for electing Senators and returns it to Assembly.
5 February	Assembly passes resolution calling on Congress to convene a second constitutional convention.
7 February	Senate concurs with Assembly second convention resolution.
9 February	Joint conference committee of Assembly and Senate debates bill for electing Senators; Assembly and Senate refuse to compromise—bill dies.
3 March	State legislature adjourns.
3–6 March	Elections for Representatives held in each of the 6 congressional districts.
4 March	First federal Congress convenes in New York City.
11 April	Legislative committee appointed to canvass votes for United States Representatives declares Egbert Benson, William Floyd, John Hathorn, John Laurance, Jeremiah Van Rensselaer, and Peter Silvester duly elected.

6 July	Special session of the state legislature convenes in Albany.
8 July	Bill for electing Senators introduced in Assembly.
10 July	Assembly passes bill for electing Senators and sends it to Senate.
11 July	Senate amends Assembly bill for electing Senators and returns it to Assembly.
13 July	Assembly rejects several Senate amendments to bill for electing Senators and returns it to Senate; Senate withdraws amendments; bill sent to Council of Revision for approval.
15 July	Bill for electing Senators vetoed by Council of Revision; Assembly fails to override; bill dies. Philip Schuyler chosen United States Senator by concurrent resolution of Assembly and Senate.
16 July	Rufus King chosen United States Senator by concurrent resolution of Assembly and Senate.

THE DOCUMENTS

PART ONE

BACKGROUND OF THE ELECTIONS

Abraham G. Lansing to Abraham Yates, Jr., Albany, 3 August 1788 (excerpt)[1]

I received your Letter of the 30 Ulto. by last evening's Stage—the News of the adoption had been in Town some days past, and our Friends are much better pleased with it then we had reason to expect[2]—The Bill of Rights which is interwoven with the adoption is considered by the Majority of those to whom I have shewn it as a security against the Encroachments of the Genl. Government—I do not suppose the Idea altogether futile but the adoption is notwithstanding unconditional in every acceptation of the words—upon the whole I believe or *endeavour* to believe that it is best to both in a political and private light—for had the Constitution been so adopted as that Congress would not accept it—yourself and our Friends would have incurred blame & Censure if any serious commotions had ensued—as we stand our Friends in this quarter are firmly united—and I trust we shall be able to send such Members as will assist in bringing about the reformation we wish—Hints have been given that you will be proposed for a Senator—I wish you to favor me with your Confidential Sentiments & wishes on this Subject that I may Conduct myself accordingly.—

The Federalists have published an Invitation to all the Inhabitants (one of which I enclose)—They are preparing to rejoice on Friday next—and every Exertion is made by them to draw as many of our Friends into the Measures as they can—but I believe they will not bring many into the field.[3]—Numbers of our Friends have applied to me and others on the Subject—they say they were given to understand that we were all to rejoice together and that all animosity would then subside—such as have applied to me I have reffered to the publication—and asked whether they could suppose that we would wish to insult our Friends in the Country by joining in a Rejoicing—proposed by a Body of Men who Stile themselves the Federal Committee—while we have a Committee and Chairman of our own[4]—this observation convinced them of the propriety of our determination.—

My Brother[5] arrived here yesterday afternoon and we have had a meeting last night—when it was determined that we should remain quiet at home on the rejoicing day, and if no insult is offered to either of us, not to molest them in the least—this Line of Conduct was judged most prudent—circumstanced as we are, the aid we should require to oppose the Federalists would be our Friends from the Country—and if they should be introduced the Consequences would no doubt be very serious to us all[6]

For some time past we have began arrangments to procure another Printer in this City and we have fallen upon a plan to engage young Barber for the purpose—he has formerly been an apprentice to Webster and of late has been at Journey Work with Mr. Greenleaf.[7]—I wish you to inform yourself from Mr Greenleaf whether he judges him addequate to the undertaking—I enclose you proposals for the paper—which we wish you to shew our Friends cause as many subscribers to be procured as possible—

1. RC, Abraham Yates Papers, NHi. The letter was addressed to Yates in New York City. Lansing (1756–1834), a lawyer, was surrogate of Albany County, 1787–1808, and treasurer of New York, 1803–1808 and 1810–1812. Yates (1724–1796), a prominent patriot during the Revolution, represented the Western District in the state Senate, 1777–1790; served in Congress, 1787–1788; and was mayor of Albany, 1790–1796. He opposed ratification of the Federal Constitution.

2. The New York Convention ratified the Federal Constitution on 26 July 1788 by a vote of 30 to 27.

3. An elaborate civic procession to celebrate New York's ratification of the Constitution held in Albany on 8 August is recorded in Joel Munsell, ed., *The Annals of Albany* (10 vols., Albany, 1850–1859), I, 330–35. Munsell took his account of the procession and celebration from the *Albany Gazette*, 28 August 1788, which is no longer extant.

4. Lansing is undoubtedly referring to the Antifederalists' Albany Republican Committee, directed by Jeremiah Van Rensselaer.

5. John Lansing, Jr. (1754–1829), who voted against ratification of the Constitution in the state Convention as a delegate from the city and county of Albany. He represented New York in the Constitutional Convention in 1787 (although he withdrew before the Constitution was completed); was mayor of Albany, 1786–1790; was a justice of the state supreme court, 1790–1801 (Chief Justice, 1798–1801); and was chancellor of New York, 1801–1814.

6. On 4 July 1788 Federalists and Antifederalists in Albany had had a violent confrontation when Federalists turned an Independence Day celebration into a celebration of the Virginia ratification (see *New York Journal*, 14 July). The *Hudson Weekly Gazette*, 12 August, reported a peaceful 8 August celebration: "We have the pleasure to assure our readers, that the greatest harmony and good order prevailed during the procession in Albany, on Friday last."

7. Robert Barber published the *Albany Register*, beginning in October 1788. "Webster" was probably Charles R. Webster, publisher of the *Albany Gazette* (founded in 1784) and the *Albany Journal* (founded in January 1788, with George Webster). Thomas Greenleaf published the *New York Journal* in New York City; it was one of the leading Antifederalist newspapers in the country.

Abraham Yates, Jr., to William Smith, New York, 22 September[1]

I have your favour of the 19th before me—In Respect to the New government we exactly Agree in Opinion—The case now is simple All agree that Amendmt are Indispensibly necessary—And where we had it in our own power before the Convention have transferred it to the union at Large and we now cant get the amendments unless ⅔ of the states first agree to a Convention and as many to agree to the Amendments—And then ¾ of the several Legislatures to Confirm them: That this will be an uphill Affair—You may see when you call to mind that Congress lately had ten weeks before they could agree w[h]ere the New government was to meet—But so it is And we must make the best of it. our only safety now is in geting the Amendments Confirmed—I mean to try for it and I believe the first thing Necessary will be to pass a Law to Inhibit the state officers (the Legislature Executive And Judicial) from takeing the Oath to support the New government untill our amendments have been Confirmed in due form—my Next will contain more upon this subject[2] I have no time (Your son[3] goes of[f] to manor) than to add that I Remain Your sincere friend And Humble sert

1. RC, NCmM. The letter was addressed to Smith at the Manor of St. George on Long Island. Smith (1720–1799) was a Suffolk County judge, 1771–1775; a member of the provincial congresses, 1775–1777; and a state senator (representing the Southern District), 1777–1783.

2. Yates, writing as "Sidney" in the *New York Journal*, 4 December 1788, addressed his opinions to the members of the New York legislature. A draft of the newspaper article, in Yates's handwriting, is in the Abraham Yates Papers, NN.

3. John Smith (1752–1816), who represented Suffolk County in the Assembly, 1784–1785, 1787–1794, and 1798–1800; served in the state Convention in 1788 (where, although an Antifederalist, he voted to ratify the Constitution); served in the House of Representatives, 1799–1804, and United States Senate, 1804–1813; and was a major general in the state militia at the time of his death.

Native American, Daily Advertiser (New York), 6 October

An Address to the FREEMEN *of* UNITED AMERICA.

The Constitution agreed upon in Philadelphia, having received the approbation of a sufficient number of states to give it efficacy, and Congress having determined that the legislature shall meet in the city of New-York, in March next.—The time cannot be far distant when you, my fellow-citizens, will be called upon to exercise a right which hitherto has laid dormant—a right the most dear to freemen—upon the just use of which, your present happiness and future welfare depends.—I mean the right of delegating your powers to representatives, for the administering of the federal government, so far as it depends upon legislation.—Much good is expected to result from this new organization of the powers of government.—It depends upon you, whether the good shall be realized. I hope therefore, that I shall not be deemed presumptuous, in endeavoring to direct your views to that class of mankind, who alone are able to make you a prosperous and a happy people. To every man of observation, it must clearly appear, that the author of nature has thought proper to mingle with the rest of mankind a few, on whom he has been graciously pleased to bestow a larger portion of the divine spirit of knowledge, than is given in the ordinary course of his providence to the sons of men. These are they, whose wisdom so far transcends the common run of mankind, that they appear to be born to instruct, to guide, to preserve human kind; they are limited to no class or order of men, but pervade the whole system. Happy would it be for mankind, that their hearts partook of the divine spirit in an equal degree with their heads, then would there be no occasion for my troubling you with this address, but alas! men of talents are not always men of virtue. Men of talents divide themselves into three classes. The first of which, are those who make a proper use of their talents, when they do so, they exhibit to us examples of the highest virtue and truest piety. The second class, are those who misapply their talents; instead of being the protectors of mankind, they are their worst enemies: then, they commit a most sacrilegious breach of trust, and, as far as in them lies, defeat the designs of providence. This is the greatest of all crimes, and is attended with the worst consequences. The third class, are those who make no use of their talents; these are not so highly culpable as those who misapply their talents:—but, as talents are the gift of the Almighty, for the benefit of mankind, he, who makes no use of them is guilty of a crime. It would be an invidious task to sketch the outlines of the two latter characters. Suffice it, that I throw together a few of the most striking traits in the character of a good man of talents, from which class I presume to hope your choice will be made.—General consent points out men of talents in every community; the good man may be known by his modesty. He courts not praise nor a great name—his desire is to be useful to mankind—he exerts himself for their benefit—his acts are dictated by virtue—they are steady and uniform—the applause of his own conscience, is his best reward—he believes the first duty of men, next to that of worshipping the deity, is ministering to the wants of his fellow-creatures.—Disinterestedness, benevolence, probity, charity, fortitude, and perseverance, are exhibited on all proper occasions—industry and application, carries him to the summit of attainable knowledge—bring him forward into public life—his good qualities do not forsake him—he becomes the guardian angel of his country.—Watchful to avert the most distant evil, and to maintain, or procure good order, due obedience to the laws—peace, plenty—he believes that the true end of government is not to deprive mankind of their natural liberty, but to regulate their conduct, so as to attain the supreme good of the whole—for which purpose, he is ever anxious so to balance the government, that neither tyranny nor licentiousness shall prevail.—Such are the men, on whom your choice should fall.—I have said, men of talents pervade the whole system of nature; and good men, I believe, are to be found among the landed, the commercial, the monied, the manufacturing part of the community, nor do I presume to affirm that the learned professions have not their full proportion; but there is one branch of the latter class, who, altho' they do not presume to think they have all the virtue of the community centered in them—too generally think that the abilities necessary for conducting public business, as their exclusive birth-right;—the habit of public speaking, so necessary in legislative business, places them in a more conspicuous point of view than others. But experience has taught me to believe, that abilities equal to the management of your business, is to be found in other classes—not that I wish by any means to see this class of men excluded, provided they have the necessary qualities, which I have already pointed out.—But always remember, that landed men are the true owners of the political vessel, they cannot quit you in a storm, therefore are more materially interested to keep you at peace, and promote your welfare, than any other class in the community. Remember, that on the proper use of this power of delegating your authority, which returns to you every two years, depends the prosperity of your country and your posterity—be not deceived—it is a business that cannot be indifferent to your welfare—perhaps to your peace—select out then, men of the greatest talents, which have been improved by education, study, and reflection—let the good qualities of their hearts equal those of their head—let them possess a proper knowledge of the principles of agriculture, commerce, politics, finance—let them be able to disclose their knowledge in a manly, nervous, accurate stile—do this and you will act wisely, and becoming the dignity of freemen and Americans.—Reverence yourselves and act honestly, and your new form of government cannot fail to benefit you.—That it may long continue to do so, is the most ardent prayer of a

NATIVE AMERICAN.

New-York, October 4, 1788.[1]

1. This article was reprinted in the Philadelphia *Federal Gazette*, 13 October 1788.

Daily Advertiser (New York), 7 October

Mr. CHILDS,

A Correspondent wishes that a writer in your paper of yesterday, under the signature of "A Native American,"[1] would direct his piece to be re-published, with a proper acknowledgement (by marks of quotation, or otherwise) to a celebrated author, for furnishing him with certain elegant expressions, which the writer has palmed upon the public as his own. Men of talents, it is granted, sometimes involuntarily transfer into their own writings, the impressions which the sentiments of eminent authors make upon their minds; and even now and then, inadvertently make use of a phrase which may appear to be borrowed:—But, when writers copy whole sentences and paragraphs, without even a verbal alteration, and without giving the original author credit for them; it is a sure mark of little genius and a dishonest mind.

Your Correspondent would not have taken notice of this Plagiary, or presented the detection to the public, had not the "Native American" seemed to deserve it by the illiberal spirit which dictated his address. Did the writer imagine that the people needed to be informed what were the characteristics of a good man; and that it was their duty to chuse men of abilities and virtue to govern them? Was it not rather his object to excite a jealous spirit in the people; and to influence them against a profession, which has been too often the subject of party invective, and vulgar declamation?

All moderate and reasonable men wish that popular elections in the United States, may ever be conducted in a manner entirely free from that spirit of cabal and intrigue, which have disgraced those of the European republics. All reasonable men, therefore, will unite to censure and condemn any attempts to influence the people against particular classes of citizens.

1. See "Native American," *Daily Advertiser*, 6 October 1788, immediately above.

Proclamation by Governor George Clinton, 13 October[1]

By His Excellency GEORGE CLINTON, Esquire, Governor of the State of New-York, General and Commander in Chief of all the Militia, and Admiral of the Navy thereof.

A PROCLAMATION.

Whereas events have taken place since the rising of the Legislature, which render it necessary that they should be convened at an earlier day than that fixed by law for their annual meeting[2]—I DO THEREFORE by these presents require the *Senate* and *Assembly* to meet at the *City Hall*, of the City of *Albany*, on *Monday*, the Eighth Day of *December* next: Whereof all concerned are to take notice, and govern themselves accordingly.

GIVEN under my Hand and the Privy Seal at the city of New-York, *this thirteenth day of* October, *in the thirteenth year of the* Independence *of the said* State.

GEO. CLINTON.

1. *New York Packet*, 14 October 1788. This proclamation was also printed in the *Daily Advertiser*, 15 October; *New York Journal*, 16 October; *Federal Herald*, 20 October; and *Country Journal*, 21 October.

2. The first session of the legislature usually began in mid-January.

John Jay to Edward Rutledge, New York, 15 October (excerpt)[1]

I thank you for your friendly letter. . . .[2]

You have seen from the public papers that the new Constitution was with difficulty adopted in this State. The opposition which was violent has daily become more moderate, and the minds of the people will gradually be reconciled to it in proportion as they see the government administered in the manner you mention. The measure of a new convention to consider and decide on the proposed amendments will, I think, be expedient to terminate all questions on the subject. If immediately carried, its friends will be satisfied, and if convened three years hence, little danger, perhaps some good, will attend it.

1. Johnston, III, 362. The ellipses in the document are in the printed copy. Jay (1745–1829) held many diplomatic, judicial, and legislative posts in a long public career, among which were service in Congress, 1774–1776, 1778–1779, and 1784; secretary for foreign affairs for the Confederation Congress, 1784–1789; and Chief Justice of the United States, 1789–1795. In 1788 (as a delegate from New York City and County) he voted to ratify the Constitution in the state Convention. For a biographical sketch of Edward Rutledge, of South Carolina, see DHFFE, I, 224.

2. Probably Rutledge's letter of 20 June 1788 to Jay. Rutledge, writing from Charleston, South Carolina, expressed the hope that the Federalists would be as successful in New York as they had been in South Carolina; sacrifices were, he noted, "worth making for the good old cause" (Johnston, III, 339).

Federal Republican Committee to County Committees of New York, New York, 4 November[1]

Gentlemen,

The circumstances and Situation of Things both before, and some time after, our Convention had met, warranted an universal Opinion among all Federal Republicans, that it was proper to adopt the new Constitution, only on Condition that those important Alterations, which were considered Necessary to the Protection of political and civil Liberty, should be made; and this was founded not only on the defects of the Constitution, but on the Anticipation that there would have been a Majority in several of the State Conventions of the same Sentiment with our own, from whom we should have derived Support; but in pursuing our Opposition in this Form, the Sentiments and Opinions of many in our Convention were changed, not, as we have reason to believe, as to the Principles of Opposition, but as to the expediency of adopting it under an Alteration of Circumstances, so that this State should continue in the Union; at the same time giving such Constructions to some of its Articles, and relying on the Sentiments of a Majority in the United States with Respect to an Opinion of its Defects, that the Government would be restrained in the exercise of its most offensive and dangerous Powers until a new Convention should have an Opportunity of reconsidering and revising it before it should have its full operation—This Alteration of Sentiment with respect to a conditional Adoption, and the Mode of adopting it in its present Manner, it is to be presumed was caused by the Reception of it by nine States successively, by which the Government was capable to be put in Operation, and likewise the immediate and subsequent Adoption of it by Virginia, perhaps one of the most influential and important States in the Union—The Confidence of those who were of these Sentiments, was excited because many of the most important States had acknowledged it by small Majorities, and almost all in such a Way as was expressive of its Defects, and hence they considered Amendments as certain, subsequent as precedent—Thus, unsupported by any of the States in the Prospect of a conditional Adoption, and for these Reasons, it became a political Calculation with them, whether it was not most for the Interest of this State, under all Circumstances, to continue in the Union, and trust, for the Reasons aforesaid, for amendments: Unhappily this occasioned a Diversity of Opinion among our Friends in the Convention, who were for a conditional Adoption only—however, the Question, as you well know, was at last carried in the way it now Stands.

Altho' a Division took place, both within, and without the Convention, on this Point, and for these Reasons, yet we hope that a Confidence remains on the Minds of all, that each was governed by the Principles of Rectitude, and that the Efforts and Exertions of each other collectively, as well as individually, will be considered as a Duty in future, and made use of to obtain the great Objects we have all had, and still have in View, to wit, the requisite amendments, by having a general Convention called immediately, or as soon as possible after the Organization of the New Government.

With this design we conceive it will be very necessary to advert to the ensuing Election of Members to represent this State in the Assembly of the General Government, and to endeavour to elect such Characters who are in Sentiment with us on the Subject of Amendments; nor is the Mode of Election a Matter of small Importance, when it is considered that one Mode may throw the Balance in the Hands of the Advocates of an arbitrary Government, while another may be favourable to equal Liberty.

The Activity and Duplicity of the principal of those who have contended for unequivocal Adoption, and an uncontrouled Exercise of the New Constitution, notwithstanding their Promises to assist in procuring a Convention for the Purposes already mentioned, have given us just Causes of Suspicion, that those Promises were made with a View to deceive.

To facilitate a Communication of Sentiment and free Discussion on this Subject with you and our Friends in the other Counties, and thereby further the great Objects of our Pursuit, and oppose with success the subtle Practices of the Adversaries of constitutional Liberty, have induced us to form ourselves into a Society for the purpose of procuring a general Convention agreeable to the circular Letter of the late Convention of this State,[2] and we beg leave to recommend to your Considerations the propriety of your joining together, without Delay, for the like Design.

We have only to add, that whatever diversity of sentiment may have taken place among the friends of equal Liberty in our late Convention, we are fully persuaded, that they will unite their utmost Exertions in the only mode that is now left, and should the present Opportunity which is now offered at the organization of the Government not be properly improved, it is highly probable such a favourable one will not be again presented, and the liberties of the People will then depend on the arbitrary Decrees of their Rulers.[3]

1. MS, Lamb Papers, NHi. The Federal Republican Committee was formally organized at Fraunces's Tavern, New York City, on 30 October 1788. At that meeting the committee resolved to send circular letters to the Antifederalist county committees throughout New York and to Antifederalist leaders in other states (see n. 3, below). The letters were approved at the committee's next meeting on 4 November and ordered to be sent out. The Federal Republican Committee was composed of leading Antifederalists and was organized "for the purpose of procuring a general Convention, agreeable to the circular Letter of the late Convention of this State. . . ." The members were Marinus Willett (chairman), Melancton Smith, David Gelston, John Lamb, Ezekiel Robins, Solomon Townsend, Nathaniel Lawrence, James M. Hughes, Samuel Jones, and Charles Tillinghast (MS, Lamb Papers, NHi).

Many of the committee members had been active in a Federal Republican Committee organized earlier in the year to force amendment of the Constitution prior to ratification. John Lamb had led that earlier effort.

2. For the Circular Letter of the New York Convention, 26 July 1788, see DHFFE, I, 44–45.

3. The circular letters to Antifederalists in the other states urged them to join the New Yorkers in demanding a convention to amend the Constitution. The letters asserted that such a convention was "the only mode that is now left," and that it might be the Antifederalists' last chance to effectively amend the Constitution (MS, Lamb Papers, NHi).

New York Packet, 7 November

At no period since the establishment of our liberty, were the affairs of our country more seriously interesting than now. Congress having fixed on a time for commencing proceedings under the new Constitution, it behooves every citizen to pay some attention to the important subject. The invaluable privileges of representation, the enjoyment of the rights of free men, and the advantages of political liberty, have been already sufficiently impressed on our minds—they are blessings the most exalted and important which society can boast of, and ought to pervade and animate the citizens of every free government; for if the sacred rights are treated with indifference and inattention, we may have to lament that we ever became free and independent. It is from a just and upright legislature that this country can expect to be relieved from her present embarrassments, and establish her future prosperity; and it is from that truly patriotic spirit which dignifies and adorns every friend of liberty, that we can preserve the blessings of peace and happiness. Let us then with a becoming firmness investigate the characters of those candidates for power and preeminence, that may offer to represent us under the new Constitution. To scrutinize those who may exhibit themselves to the public as the political guides of a whole community, is a duty we owe to mankind and our country:—And if we should be so happy as to place our confidence in men of liberality, integrity and virtue, we may expect to transmit our independence to future generations; but if wicked men should step into authority, they will encourage animosities in every department of society, impede the progress of government, obstruct all moral improvement, retard the operation of the most salutary laws, and promote the establishment of a government that may deprive us of all the privileges of freemen.

Daily Advertiser (New York), 7 November

Mr. Childs,

It is a question with some people, whether the *new constitution* will admit of electing representatives in the federal government *by districts*. It is my opinion, it will not, on any fair construction whatever. But if it would, policy would forbid it.

1st. By dividing a state into districts and electing one representative for each, the freemen are limited to *one vote each*; whereas in choosing from the state at large, every freeman has as many votes as the state may have delegates.

2d. The division into districts supposes what is not true, that genius, abilities, honesty and other qualifications for legislators, are *equally diffused in a state*; or else debars the freemen the privilege of choosing from among the *best qualified*.

3d. District elections will create and perpetuate those local prejudices and errors, which embarrass all our state proceedings. The delegates will more or less think they represent *their districts only*, and not the whole state: Just as the deputies of a town or county in the state legislatures, think their business is to act only for *their particular towns or counties.* This is a very stupid opinion indeed, but it is often discoverable—and should, if possible, be guarded against in regulating the federal representatives.

Objection. The people should be acquainted with the men they choose—and their representatives should be acquainted with the interests *and feelings* of every part of the state: Therefore the people should be *obliged* to choose men from different parts of the state.

Answer. All the people are not and never can be personally acquainted with their delegates. They know their reputation or public character; and this is generally sufficient to direct them to a judicious choice.

As to the delegates' knowledge of the interest and feelings of people in every part of the state, it must be observed, that representatives in Congress act for the *state*, and not *for districts*. Their knowledge therefore and their direction, in cases, where their authority is subject to state control, must be derived through the legislature of that state, where all the interests, *feelings*, partialities and errors of all corners of the state are collected into a point.

The practice of electing from the state at large, has existed long in a neighboring state, where the members of the Upper House of Assembly are chosen in that manner. Those who are acquainted with its operation, suppose it the *best* mode. But its excellence depends much on a peculiarity in that state; which is, a *double election*. There are two annual elections; one in April, the other in September. In September, the freemen vote for *twenty men*, as senators—The votes are returned to the General Assembly in October, and numbered. The twenty persons, who have the most votes are said to be in *nomination*; their names are published, and the freemen are confined to *these* at their election in April; and from these twenty, *twelve* persons are chosen for senators. A similar mode is ordained for choosing representatives in Congress; except that they first choose for the *nomination*, DOUBLE the number of representatives.[1]

This mode has a singular advantage—the men of most information generally unite upon the best characters, and give a lead to the public mind; at the same time, the men who are candidates are held up to public view, *always* six months, and *some times* three or four years, that their character may be universally ascertained. It is for this reason that men are seldom thrust in or out of office suddenly by the violence of party. They generally come into office gradually as their characters are known; and they usually go out of office in the same manner.

1. Connecticut elected its assistants, i.e., members of the upper house, the Council, as outlined. Beginning in 1779 the state chose its delegates to Congress in a similar manner: the voters nominated not more than twelve delegates each September, and the following April the voters elected seven of the twelve—of whom not less than two nor more than four were to attend Congress. This process was continued in the first federal elections; see Connecticut Election Resolution, DHFFE, II, 24–26.

Publius Secundus Americanus, Daily Advertiser (New York), 10 November

Mr. Childs,

It is doubted by a correspondent in your paper of Friday,[1] whether the new constitution will admit of electing representatives in the federal government by districts.—In my opinion it will on a construction even tolerably fair—but if it did not, still good policy and our future welfare declare strongly in its favour.

1*st.* By dividing a state into districts and electing one representative for each, the freeman's vote is of some consequence to the man of honesty and worth, with whose character he is acquainted, whereas in choosing from the state at large, he has to vote for men of uncertain principles, yet who in fame might far surpass his worthy friend.

It is very true, according to your correspondent's plan, greater men would probably be chosen than after the manner of election by districts.

Were all great men good, I should approve this plan. As to the bribe which he holds out in his first clause of a greater share of votes to freemen, it is such an insult to the understanding as they will easily perceive and resent.

2*d*. The second objection of your correspondent is best grounded; but still I think there are men of genius, abilities, and more particularly, honesty enough in any one district, to act as representatives when chosen.

3*d*. District elections may be of advantage to the new government, by preventing the states from falling into parties, which they would more probably do, if the election for every representative was general through each state.

Here your correspondent, after reprobating the idea of locality, says, "The delegates will more or less think they represent their districts only and not the *whole state*;" which last expression ought evidently, according to his own argument, to have been the *United States*.

4*th*. The people should be acquainted with the men they choose.

This proposition however your correspondent finds fault with, and conceives that we can be as well acquainted with mens' characters at the distance of 6 or 700 miles, as in our own district. O Wisdom, where art thou fled!

Your correspondent, who just before writes so strongly against the local ideas of districts, now proves his own mind as strongly infected with the same partiality, not indeed towards a single district, but what in this instance is much worse, towards a single state: For the general government has nothing to fear from district prejudice, but from the more *enlarged prejudice* towards individual states.

Upon the whole, I should conceive that the method of general election would only tend to keep those in office who are already so, and be for the advantage of all those whose fame is more extended than their honesty is perfect. In the mean time, men of real merit would be concealed, and probably live and die in oblivion.

All these consequences I conceive would follow, exclusive of the still more dangerous one of forming state parties.

PUBLIUS SECONDUS AMERICANUS.

1. *Daily Advertiser*, 7 November 1788, immediately above.

New York Journal, 20 November

It is conjectured, says a correspondent, that the mode, about to be adopted by the several legislatures, of dividing the states into districts, for the appointment of the federal representatives, will create disturbances, for, say many, if each district elects its member, he will not be the choice of the people, but of a partial district only, &c. Privilege at elections, continues our correspondent, was ever guarded with jealousy by Americans.[1]

1. This article was reprinted in the *Country Journal* and *Hudson Weekly Gazette*, both 25 November 1788.

Alexander Hamilton to James Madison, New York, 23 November (excerpt)[1]

In this state it is difficult to form any certain calculation. A large majority of the Assembly was doubtless of an Antifœderal complexion; but the scism in the party which has been occasioned by the falling off of some [of] its leaders in the Convention leaves me not without hope, that if matters are well managed we may procure a majority for some pretty equal compromise. In the Senate we have the superiority by one.

1. RC, Madison Papers, DLC. Printed: Syrett, V, 235–37. For another excerpt from this letter, see Chapter XIV.

DeWitt Clinton to Charles Clinton, New York, 25 November (excerpt)[1]

I expect that our Legislature will elect antifed. Senators—this will unquestionably be the case if the adopting & non adopting Antis do not divide which calamity I hope God in his goodness will avert—Mr. A. Yates or Mr. Lansing from the Northern parts of the state & Mr. Tredwell or Mr. M. Smith[2] from the Southern are spoken of as Senators[3] I expect that the session of our Legislature will be longer than is generally imagined—Next thing the elections for Governor Lieut. Govr. &c. come on—I expect Party will then run high—I believe the feds. are at a loss whom to set up for Governor in opposition to the present one—Perhaps Mr. Chief Justice Morris or Mr. Benson will be held up—neither from present appearance stand any chance of success—

1. RC, Personal Papers Miscellany, DLC. The letter was addressed to Charles Clinton in Montgomery, Ulster County. For another excerpt from this letter, see Chapter XIV. DeWitt Clinton (1769–1828), Charles's nephew, strongly opposed ratification of the Constitution. He later was a United States Senator, 1802–1803; mayor of New York City, 1803–1807, 1808–1810, 1811–1815; and governor, 1817–1823 and 1825–1828. Charles Clinton (1734–1791), a brother of Governor George Clinton, was a practicing physician in Ulster County.

2. Thomas Treadwell (1743–1831) was a judge of the court of probate, 1778–1787, and he represented Suffolk County in the Assembly, 1777–1783, and the Southern District in the state Senate, 1786–1789. In 1788 he voted against ratification of the Constitution in the state Convention. He also served in the House of Representatives, 1791–1795. Melancton Smith (1744–1798), a prominent patriot during the Revolution, served in Congress, 1785–1787, and represented New York City and County in the Assembly in 1792. Smith, an Antifederalist, was largely responsible for the compromises that led to New York's ratification in the state Convention in 1788, where he represented Dutchess County.

3. The Federalist expectations for senatorial appointments were slightly different. On 5 February 1789, Thomas Lee Shippen, a Pennsylvanian traveling in Europe, wrote to Thomas Jefferson that he had heard from Staats Morris, son of Lewis Morris, "that Duane or his father will probably be Senator for the lower Country interest in N.Y. & some Albany man for ye upper" (London, RC, Jefferson Papers, DLC).

A Federal Republican, New York Journal, 27 November[1]

NUMBER I.

The present is a most important crisis in our public affairs—It calls for the utmost attention of every patriot, and loudly admonishes the people to be active and vigilant in the exercise of their constitutional privileges.—A compleat revolution will soon take place in our government.—The new constitution being adopted by eleven of the thirteen states, and an ordinance of Congress passed for carrying it into operation;[2] nothing is now wanting but to elect the executive and legislative officers, to give it capacity to go into exercise. The period is at hand when the choice of these is to be made, it has commenced in several of the states, and in a short time the citizens of this state will be called upon to give their suffrages for men to exercise, great, extensive, and important powers in the legislature of the United States.

It is of the highest moment that they use this right with prudence and discretion—The change which this new system of government will effect upon the policy and condition of the United States, will be very material—The powers with which it vests the rulers, are very extensive and multiform—And it will require great integrity, patriotism, and prudence to direct those who administer the government, to keep within those bounds of moderation and wisdom, which will render it acceptable and a blessing to the people. It is at all times, and under all circumstances, highly proper and necessary for the people in a free government to be careful in the choice of their rulers. In an elective republic it is the most essential mean of preserving liberty and of having an administration promotive of the public good. But there are a variety of reasons to urge a more than ordinary degree of care and circumspection in the choice of persons to commence proceedings under the new system. It is not my intention to enter into an investigation of the merits of the new constitution, or to enquire whether this state pursued its true interest, and acted agreeably to sound policy in adopting it or not. The merits of the constitution has been canvassed by able men on both sides, both in print and in public debate—The system is adopted, and it is the duty of every true friend to his country to acquiesce, and to use their influence to procure such an exercise of the powers granted by it, as will promote the public good and secure public liberty—But I am persuaded the plan is imperfect, capable of great improvements, and that it needs them; and of this opinion is undoubtedly a great majority of the people of this state, and I believe of the United States—This being the case, it is especially the duty of the people to be active, vigilant, and united in the choice of such persons as they can confide in to use their endeavors to procure amendments. Besides the constitution is complicated it reaches to a variety of cases, in which it may interfere with the exercise of the powers left to the state governments—Men of prudence should therefore be chosen to exercise the powers granted by this constitution, who will act with circumspection and caution. It is my intention, if leisure will permit, in some future papers to make some farther observations on this subject, and to endeavor to shew the propriety and necessity of revising and amending the system, and to point out the duplicity of conduct and disregard to the public good of some, who now oppose any alterations in it, though previous to its adoption they declared themselves in favor of amendments.[3]

A FEDERAL REPUBLICAN.

1. For the suggestion that "A Federal Republican" is probably Melancton Smith, see Young, *Democratic Republicans*, 123. Young bases his supposition on the similarity of ideas expressed in "A Federal Republican," *New York Journal*, 1 January 1789, and Melancton Smith to John Smith, 10 January 1789, both printed in Part Two.

2. For Congress' Election Ordinance, 13 September 1788, see DHFFE, I, 132–33.

3. See "A Federal Republican," *New York Journal*, 11 December 1788 and 1 January 1789, below and Part Two, respectively.

Massachusetts Centinel (Boston), 10 December

NEW-YORK, Dec. 2[1]

Our Legislature meets at Albany the 8th inst. Their complexion is antifederal; but it is said, from the moderation and candour exhibited by his Excellency the Governour, and several of the leading characters, that the organization of the new Government will be carried through without the least interruption. The persons for Senators have not yet been agreed upon—some suppose they will be taken from both parties.

1. No printing of the article in a New York newspaper has been located.

A Federal Republican, New York Journal, 11 December (excerpt)[1]

The FEDERAL REPUBLICAN, *No.* 2. . . .

No revolution ever took place, that could more truly be said to be for the people, than the one which we have seen in this country—Power was in great measure opposed to it through the whole union.—It originated in the purest whig principles—was supported on the broad basis of the equal rights of mankind—and the form of government which were agreed to, recognized these principles, and the administration has moved upon them. In the progress of the general government, it has appeared to the conviction of almost every man, that the powers under the confederation were not adequate to the management of the general concerns of the union. A very general concurrence of sentiment therefore took place to revise the system—For this purpose a convention of the states by their delegates assembled, and the result of their deliberations was not merely an extension of the powers, but a change of the form of government, this has been submitted to all the states, and acceded to by eleven of them. The officers are now choosing, and the system will soon be in operation. An entire revolution is about taking place without war or bloodshed. In the discussion of this great question there has been a great division of sentiments with regard to the merits of the plan proposed—It has been urged by those who were opposed to it, that the great principles of the revolution has been too little attended to in its formation—that it embraces objects not necessary to be committed to the care of a general government—that sufficient checks are not placed in it to restrain the rulers from an abuse of power—that it will annihilate the state governments on whom we must depend for the preservation of our liberties; and, that it will operate to deprive the people of those rights, which they have so dearly earned—On the other side, it has been said, that these apprehensions are imaginary—that although there are imperfections in the plan, yet, on the whole, it is a well ballanced government, and that sufficient security is afforded against every abuse by committing the power of electing their rulers to the people. To this it is replied, that very little safety will be derived from the right of the people to elect—For that this power will be rather nominal than real—that the number of representatives will be so small, and so great a number concerned in chusing them, that the influence of a few will always predominate.—It is not my design to investigate this subject, as to repeat all that has been said upon it—It is not necessary for my purpose—It has been the general opinion in this state, of both parties, if we may judge from their professions that there are defects in the plan—the same sentiment has prevailed throughout the union. And hence it is, that the most prevailing arguments that the advocates for the system have used, have been drawn, not from its merits, but from the expediency of adopting it, considering the [critical][2] situation in which the country was. The language has been, if we must have a government adopt this, and we will cordially unite in making amendments. No inducement whatever would have prevailed upon the convention of this state to have ratified the constitution, had they not had confidence that a general union would have prevailed to submit it to the revision of another general convention. It is manifest from the proceedings of the conventions of many of the other states, that the same motives influenced them. In our own state, almost every sober thinking man declared, without reserve, their wishes to have the system revised—But what is the present language of many of the leading men who advocated the adoption of the constitution. Do they now urge the necessity and propriety of another convention? Nothing is further from their present persuit. They now say, it is wise and proper to give the government a trial. The goodness or badness of the scheme will be proved from experiment—If it should prove defective on a trial of ten or twenty years, then we shall be better able to amend it—But if it be true that the liberties of the people are not well secured under it, in twenty years it may, and probably will be too late to secure them. What are we to think of men who hold this language after they have pledged themselves to unite in procuring another convention? Can we refrain from suspecting that they are unfriendly to equal liberty,—that they have in view a system of government which they dare not avow, and which they mean to fix over the people of this country by insensible degrees, and without their perceiving it until it is accomplished? It is time for every disinterested man and real friend to his country to open his eyes, and act with decision.

All who were sincere in declaring that they wished for a re-consideration and amendments to the system will do so, and will give their voices decidedly in favor of such men to represent them as will firmly pursue the plan recommended by the convention of this state. A variety of unanswerable arguments, beside the defects in the constitution itself, point this out as the wise, prudent, and patriotic line of conduct which ought to be pursued.

A FEDERAL REPUBLICAN.

1. For speculation that "A Federal Republican" is Melancton Smith, see "A Federal Republican," *New York Journal*, 27 November 1788, n. 1, above.

2. The *New York Journal* printed "ivitual" here.

Herald of Freedom (Boston), 22 December

NEW-YORK, December 13. . . .[1]

The anti-federal party in this state, are very busy in striving to gain the suffrages of the freemen of this state, for Governour Clinton to represent New-York in the Senate of the United States; for they are fearful that he will be ousted the next election for Governour, and a more consistent and federal character elected in his room. In this, however, as in most of their plans, it is more than probable they will be thwarted. Since the adoption of the Constitution, the federal cause in this state, as well as the others, has gained ground rapidly.[2] There is but one Printer who will be the echo of the abuse the antifederal party are industriously levelling at the most exalted and respectable of the federalists; and his dependence on the celebrated antifederal Printer of Philadelphia is perhaps the greatest stimulus he has for devoting his press to the republication of Judge B——n's abuse of the Hon. Robert Morris, G. Clymer, and other venerated characters in Pennsylvania.[3]

Should Gov. C——n miss getting into any federal office, and likewise be unsuccessful at the next state election, it is more than probable he will find himself necessitated to retire to the humble vale of obscurity—to the no small chagrin of his party and dependents, and the real joy and satisfaction of every staunch federalist, and well wisher to the happiness and prosperity of these American States.

1. No printing of the article in a New York newspaper has been located.

2. Up to this point the article was reprinted in the Portland, Maine, *Cumberland Gazette*, 8 January 1789.

3. The writer is probably referring to two of the most ardent Antifederalist newspapers in the country: Thomas Greenleaf's *New York Journal* and Eleazer Oswald's Philadelphia *Independent Gazetteer*. Between 16 October and 11 December 1788 the *Journal* reprinted the second series of "Centinel" essays (nos. 19–24) from the *Independent Gazetteer*. "Centinel," believed by many contemporaries to be George Bryan (but later proved to be his son, Samuel), carried on a running political attack on leading Pennsylvania Federalists, including Robert Morris and George Clymer. Morris's and Clymer's responses in the *Gazetteer* were also reprinted in the *Journal*. For details about the "Centinel" essays, see DHFFE, I, 308–09. Greenleaf, who had bought the *New York Journal* from Oswald in 1787, was also financially indebted to Oswald (see Ebenezer Hazard to Jeremy Belknap, New York, 10 May 1788, MS, Belknap Papers, MHi).

Herald of Freedom (Boston), 9 January 1789

NEW-YORK, December 30.[1]

It has frequently been asserted, that the *Antifederalists* acted from principle, in their recent violent opposition to the adoption of the new Constitution; nay, more—it has even been asserted by some, that they acted from an honest principle.—But, says a correspondent, it has proved quite the reverse; the event has proved that assertions are not always facts, and that words are sometimes used without meaning, at least, without meaning to convey the real idea they apparently hold forth.

For example, continues our correspondent, look through our towns and counties—there will you see the visage which once was distorted with grimaces direful at the bare mention of the Federal Constitution, now quite calm and composed, when conversation is introduced respecting the officers who are to administer the new government. Even the *Lamb*[2] which, so recently appeared like the wolfe, has resumed a gentleness more suitable to its nature; and but few say ought to the prejudice of federalism. The reasons are obvious—they begin to be sensible that some peculiar state offices will not, as under the old Confederation, in future, "*drop fatness*;"—and they think it high time to prepare for gaining a *bite* at the federal "*loaves* and *fishes*."—Would men, who really acted from pure and honest principles, so soon veer about, and change their sentiments from the pitiful consideration of self interest?—Surely not—There are some, however, who still pretend to clinch on upon their former hold; but even they, hold on as if it pained their very heart-strings; and doubtless they will *Clint*[(a)] so hard as to get themselves squeezed out of all offices very soon—which the Lord of his infinite mercy grant, as a just punishment for their obstinate opposition to the light of their own eyes.

(a) *We suppose our correspondent means* Clinch.[3]

1. No printing of the article in a New York newspaper has been located.

2. John Lamb (1735–1800), a patriot leader during the Revolution, was a prominent Antifederalist who corresponded with Antifederalists in other states and who coordinated the opposition to the Constitution. He was elected to the Assembly in 1784, and the same year was appointed collector of customs for the port of New York. In 1789 he was reappointed collector under the federal government and continued in office until his resignation in 1797.

3. The article was reprinted in the Portsmouth *New Hampshire Spy*, 13 January 1789.

PART TWO

PASSAGE OF THE ELECTION LAW AND LEGISLATIVE ATTEMPTS TO APPOINT PRESIDENTIAL ELECTORS AND SENATORS

Party dissensions in New York climaxed in the legislative session that began in December 1788. With the Federalists controlling the Senate and the Antifederalists dominating the Assembly, efforts to appoint federal officers developed into bitter partisan quarreling. A law directing the election of Representatives was enacted, but numerous bills, resolutions, and joint conference meetings on the procedure for electing presidential Electors and Senators failed to establish a compromise between the Assembly and Senate. The result was that no Electors or Senators were elected in the 1788–1789 legislative session. For an outline of the numerous bills' progress through the legislature, see "Chronology" in the frontmatter to this chapter.

Assembly and Senate Proceedings, Thursday, A.M., 11 December 1788[1]

The Senate

A message from His Excellency the Governor was received, requiring the attendance of the Senate in the Assembly-Chamber.

The President accordingly left the chair, and with the Senate, attended His Excellency, and being returned, reassumed the chair and informed the Senate, that His Excellency the Governor had made a Speech to the Legislature, of which he had obtained a copy, which being read, is in the words following. viz.,

Gentlemen of the Senate and Assembly,

I WAS induced to convene you at this time, that I might have a seasonable opportunity of laying before you the proceedings of the Convention of this State, lately held at Poughkeepsie, and the ordinance of Congress for putting into operation the Constitution for the United States,[2] which was adopted by that Convention.

While I submit this important subject to the Legislature, it is my duty to call your particular attention to the amendments proposed by our Convention, to this new system of general Government. It will appear from the instrument of ratification, that a declaration of rights with certain explanations are inserted, in order to remove doubtful constructions, and to guard against an undue and improper administration; and that it was assented to on the express confidence, that the exercise of different powers would be suspended, until it should undergo a revision by a General Convention of the States. You will also perceive by the Circular Letter addressed to our Sister States,[3] that several articles of it appeared so exceptionable to a majority of the Convention, that nothing short of the fullest confidence of obtaining such a revision, could have prevailed upon a sufficient number to have ratified it, without stipulating for previous amendments; and that all united in opinion, that a speedy revisal of the system would be necessary to recommend it to the approbation and support of a numerous body of our Constituents, and to allay the apprehensions and discontents which the exceptionable articles of it had occasioned. These considerations, and a conviction of the truth of the observation, "that no Government, however constructed, can operate well, unless it possesses the confidence and good will of the great body of the people," will, I am persuaded, be sufficient to engage your best endeavors for effecting a measure so earnestly recommended by the Convention, and anxiously desired by your Constituents. . . .[4]

Ordered, That His Excellency's Speech, with the several papers accompanying the same, be committed to a committee of the whole. . . .

The Senate resolved itself into a committee of the whole, on His Excellency's Speech and the papers accompanying the same; after some time spent thereon, Mr. President reassumed the chair, and Mr. Williams from the committee reported, that it was the opinion of the committee, that a respectful answer be given to His Excellency's Speech, and that he was directed to move for leave to sit again; which report he read in his place, and delivered the same in at the table, where it was again read and agreed to by the Senate: Thereupon,

Ordered, That Mr. Yates, Mr. Lawrance and Mr. Philip Schuyler, be a committee to prepare and report a respectful answer to His Excellency's Speech.

Ordered, That the committee have leave to sit again.

The Assembly

A message from his Excellency, the Governor was delivered by his private Secretary, that His Excellency requires the immediate attendance of this House in the Assembly Chamber.

Mr. Speaker left the chair, and with the House attended accordingly, and His Excellency the Governor, and the Honorable the Senate, who had also attended, having respectively retired, *Mr. Speaker* reassumed the chair, and reported to the House, that His Excellency had been pleased to make a speech to both Houses of the Legislature, and to deliver him a copy thereof. The same being read is in the words following, viz. . . .[5]

Resolved, That His Excellency the Governor's Speech be taken into consideration immediately, and the House proceeded to the consideration thereof accordingly.

Ordered, That His Excellency's Speech be forthwith printed.[6]

Resolved, That a respectful address be presented to His Excellency the Governor in answer to his Speech.

Ordered, That a committee be appointed to prepare a draft of the said address, and that Mr. Jones, Mr. Harison and Mr. Yates, be a committee for that purpose.

1. *Journal of the Senate of the State of New-York*, . . . (Albany, 1788 and 1789), and *Journal of the Assembly of the State of New-York*, . . . (Albany, 1788 and 1789). Hereafter Senate and Assembly proceedings are cited by date only. Both the Senate and Assembly journals record that each house began its daily session at 10:00 A.M.; some days the journals record the Senate or Assembly reconvening for an afternoon session. Consequently, the proceedings printed in this chapter are marked "A.M." or "P.M.," depending on when the session they are taken from began.

2. For Congress' Election Ordinance, 13 September 1788, see DHFFE, I, 132–33.

3. For the Circular Letter of the New York Convention, 26 July 1788, see DHFFE, I, 44–45.

4. In the remainder of the speech the governor discussed recent dealings with the state's Indian tribes, the congressional requisition for funds for the current year, and several state matters.

5. For Governor Clinton's speech, see Senate Proceedings.

6. The governor's speech was widely printed in the state's newspapers, beginning with the *Daily Advertiser*, 15 December 1788.

Senate Proceedings, Friday, A.M., 12 December

Mr. Williams from the committee of the whole, to whom was referred His Excellency's Speech, and the papers accompanying the same, reported, that it was the opinion of the committee, that the ordinance of Congress for putting into operation the Constitution for the United States . . . be [committed to a special committee]. . . .

Ordered, That Mr. Lawrance, Mr. Tredwell and Mr. Peter Schuyler, be a committee to consider and report on the ordinance of Congress for putting into operation the Constitution for the United States.

Assembly and Senate Proceedings, Saturday, A.M., 13 December

The Senate

Mr. Lawrance from the Committee to whom was referred the ordinance of Congress, for putting into operation the Constitution for the United States, reported, that it was the opinion of the committee, that a bill should be ordered to be brought in, for regulating the manner of appointing electors, who are to elect the President and Vice President of the United States of America, under the Constitution, mentioned in the act of Congress of the 13th of September last; which report he read in his place, and delivered the same in at the table, where it was again read and agreed to by the Senate: Thereupon,

Ordered, That the same committee do prepare and bring in a bill accordingly. . . .

Mr. Lawrence from the committee appointed for that purpose, according to order, brought in a bill *for regulating the manner of appointing electors, who are to elect the President and Vice-President of the United States of America*, which was read the first time and ordered a second reading.

The Assembly

Mr. Jones moved for leave to bring in a bill, for carrying into effect, on the part of this State, the Constitution of the United States, assented to, and ratified by the Convention of this State.

Ordered, That leave be given accordingly.

Mr. Jones according to leave, brought in the said bill entitled, *An act for carrying into effect on the part of this State, the Constitution of the United States, assented to and ratified by the Convention of this State, on the twenty-sixth day of July last*, which was read the first time, and ordered a second reading.[1]

1. On 19 December 1788 the *Daily Advertiser* printed some details of the bill presented on the 13th: "In this bill it is proposed to choose the electors and senators in the same mode as the members of the present Congress are now chosen—and that the representatives be chosen by districts—*Long-Island* and *Staten-Island* to be one district; *New-York* and *Westchester* one district; *Orange* and *Ulster* one district; *Dutchess* one district; and the remainder of the state to have the other two members." The same summary was reprinted in the *Independent Journal*, 20 December, and *New York Journal*, 25 December. A similar account was printed in the *Country Journal*, 23 December. For a further refinement of the districts, see Assembly Debates, 20 December, below.

Assembly and Senate Proceedings, Monday, 15 December

The Assembly, A.M.

The bill entitled . . . *An act for carrying into effect on the part of this State, the Constitution of the United States, assented to and ratified by the Convention of this State, on the twenty-sixth day of July last,* [was] read a second time, and committed to a committee of the whole House.

The Senate, P.M.

The bill entitled, *An act for regulating the manner of appointing electors, who are to elect the President and Vice-President of the United States of America*; was read a second time and committed to a committee of the whole.

Mr. Lawrance moved for leave to bring in a bill *for the appointment of Senators, to represent this State, in the Senate of the United States of America.*

Ordered, That leave be given accordingly.

Mr. Lawrance according to leave brought in the said bill, which was read the first time and ordered a second reading.

Senate Proceedings, Tuesday, A.M., 16 December

The bill entitled *An act for the appointment of Senators to represent this State in the Senate of the United States of America*, was read a second time, and committed to a committee of the whole.

Mr. Duane from the committee of the whole, to whom was referred the bill entitled *An act for regulating the manner of appointing electors, who are to elect the President and Vice President of the United States of America*, reported, that they had made some progress in the bill, and had directed him to move for leave to sit again.

Ordered, That the committee have leave to sit again.

Assembly and Senate Proceedings, Wednesday, A.M., 17 December

The Senate

Mr. Duane, from the committee of the whole, to whom was referred the bill entitled, *An act for regulating the manner of appointing electors who are to elect the President, and Vice-President of the United States of America*, reported, that in proceeding in the enacting clause of the bill, Mr. Tredwell made a motion to expunge that part of the clause which directs the mode of appointing the electors, which is in the words following, viz. "That the Assembly of this State shall nominate and appoint on the first Wednesday in January next four persons as electors; that immediately after the said appointment and before the adjournment of the House, the said Assembly, shall give notice thereof, and the names of the persons so appointed to the Senate of the said State; that the said Senate upon receiving such notice shall nominate and appoint on the said first Wednesday in January, four other persons as electors," and to substitute the following in its stead, viz. "That the Assembly and Senate shall on the first Wednesday of January next appoint eight persons for electors, in the mode established by the Constitution of this State for the appointment of Delegates to represent this State in the General Congress of the United States of America."[1] Debates arose upon the said proposed amendment, and the question being put thereon, it passed in the negative, in manner following, viz.

FOR THE NEGATIVE.

Mr. Philip Schuyler,	Mr. Vanderbilt,
Mr. Douw,	Mr. Lawrance,
Mr. Micheau,	Mr. Morris,
Mr. Peter Schuyler,	Mr. Roosevelt,
Mr. Fonda,	Mr. L'Hommedieu.

FOR THE AFFIRMATIVE.

Mr. Yates,	Mr. Swartwout,
Mr. Hopkins,	Mr. Townsend,
Mr. Williams,	Mr. Tredwell.
Mr. Van Ness,	

That having proceeded in the bill, and made several amendments thereto, Mr. Tredwell moved that the same be rejected, and the question being put on the said motion, it passed in the negative in the same manner as on the first question.

Mr. Duane, further reported that the committee had gone through the bill and agreed to the same, which report he read in his place and delivered the bill in at the table where it was again read and agreed to by the Senate. Thereupon,

Ordered, That the bill as amended be engrossed.

Mr. Peter Schuyler from the committee of the whole to whom was referred, the bill entitled *An act for the appointment of Senators to represent this State in the Senate of the United States of America*, reported, that the committee had made some progress in the bill, and directed him to move for leave to sit again.

Ordered, That the committee have leave to sit again.

The Assembly

Mr. Havens, from the committee of the whole House, on the bill entitled, *An act for carrying into effect on the part of this State, the Constitution of the United States, assented to and ratified by the Convention of this State, on the twenty-sixth day of July last*, reported, that after the said bill had been read in the committee, the first enacting clause was again read, in the words following, viz.

"Be it enacted by the People of the State of New-York, represented in Senate and Assembly, and it is hereby enacted by the authority of the same, that the Senators to be chosen in this State for the United States, shall be chosen as follows, that is to say, the Senate and Assembly of this State shall each, openly nominate as many persons as shall be equal to the whole number of Senators to be chosen by this State, after which nomination the Senate and Assembly shall meet together, and compare the lists of the persons by them respectively nominated, and those persons named in both lists shall be Senators for the United States, and out of those persons whose names are not in both lists, one half shall be chosen by the joint ballot of the Senators and Members of Assembly so met together as aforesaid."[2]

That the said paragraph having been read, Mr. Harison made a motion that the latter part of the paragraph, viz. the words "And those persons named in both lists, shall be Senators for the United States, and out of those persons whose names are not in both lists, one half shall be chosen by the joint ballot of the Senators and Members of Assembly, so met together as aforesaid," should be obliterated, and that the following should be substituted in stead thereof, viz.

"And if the same person or persons, is or are named in both lists, he or they shall be a Senator or Senators, for the United States; but if the said lists shall agree only as to one of the persons therein named, and in all other cases where only one person is to be chosen and the two nominations disagree, then one half of the persons named in such lists, and not included in both, shall be chosen by the joint ballot of the Senators, and Members of Assembly, so met together as aforesaid; but if more than one person is to be chosen, and the lists shall not agree as to either of the persons named therein, then the Members of the Senate shall at such meeting choose by ballot one of the persons nominated as aforesaid by the Assembly, and the Members of the Assembly shall in like manner choose one of the persons nominated as aforesaid by the Senate, and the two persons so chosen shall be Senators for the United States."

That the Question having been put on the motion of Mr. Harison, it passed in the negative in the manner following, viz.

FOR THE NEGATIVE.

Mr. Jones,
Mr. Carman,
Mr. G. Livingston,
Mr. Kortz,
Mr. Yates,
Mr. Frey,
Mr. Stauring,
Mr. SPEAKER,
Mr. Van Dyck,
Mr. J. Van Rensselaer,
Mr. Hardenbergh,
Mr. Veeder,
Mr. Winn,
Mr. Duncan,
Mr. Tearse,
Mr. Savage,
Mr. Webster,
Mr. M'Cracken,
Mr. Thompson,
Mr. Bay,
Mr. Schoonmaker,
Mr. Tappen,
Mr. Griffen,
Mr. Carpenter,
Mr. J. Smith,
Mr. D'Witt,
Mr. Wisner,
Mr. Adgate,
Mr. Harper,
Mr. Schenck,
Mr. Akins.

FOR THE AFFIRMATIVE.

Mr. B. Livingston,
Mr. Gilbert,
Mr. Van Cortlandt,
Mr. Seaman,
Mr. Barker,
Mr. Harison,
Mr. Hoffman,
Mr. H. Van Rensselaer,
Mr. Younglove,
Mr. Watts,
Mr. Livingston,
Mr. Horton,
Mr. Low,
Mr. Bancker,
Mr. Vandervoort,
Mr. Rockwell,
Mr. Verplanck,
Mr. Cornwell,
Mr. Giles,
Mr. Dongan.

That the question having been then put on the said original paragraph of the bill, it was carried in the affirmative.

That the committee had made further progress in the bill, and had directed him to move for leave to sit again.

Ordered, That the said committee have leave to sit again.

1. Article XXX of the state constitution stipulated: "That Delegates to represent this State in the general Congress of the United States of America be annually appointed as follows, to wit: The senate and assembly shall each openly nominate as many persons as shall be equal to the whole number of Delegates to be appointed; after which nomination they shall meet together, and those persons named in both lists shall be Delegates; and out of those persons whose names are not on both lists, one-half shall be chosen by the joint ballot of the senators and members of assembly so met together as aforesaid" (Thorpe, V, 2634–35).

2. This was the method New York used to choose delegates to the Confederation Congress. See n. 1, immediately above.

Assembly Debates, Wednesday, 17 December[1]

In a committee of the whole on the bill for putting the new government into operation;

Mr. Havens in the chair.

On reading the clause which declares that the senators for the United States shall be chosen by the joint ballot of both houses,—

Mr. Harrison rose and addressed the chairman as follows:—

It is my intention, sir, to propose an amendment to the clause now under consideration—I am persuaded that the gentlemen of this committee will, in all their deliberations, be governed by a sincere regard for the interest of their country, and that they will not suffer party views to interfere with that great and important object:— These, sir, are the sentiments of my mind with respect to other gentlemen, and whilst I entertain such an opinion of the motive by which they are actuated, I may surely hope from their candor, that they will attribute the same principle to me.

The committee, sir, I flatter myself, will indulge me if, before I go more particularly into the subject matter of the clause, I remind them of the great importance of the object which is meant to be attained by it; it cannot escape the observation of gentlemen, if they will turn for a moment to the new constitution lately adopted by this state— they must then be convinced that it is of the utmost moment to the welfare and happiness of our country that we should be duly represented in the senate of the United States.

Sir, The important powers of making peace and war, of forming treaties and of appointing public officers, are the peculiar powers of that body in conjunction with the president; it must therefore be considered by every gentleman who hears me, as of the utmost consequence that we should have representatives *there*, to watch over and defend the interests of the state upon every occasion. This surely is an important consideration, and must strike every one who reflects upon it in the most forcible manner.

But there are other considerations which more *particularly* affect this state, and which should make us anxious to secure a representation in the senate of the United States. It is well known that the residence of Congress is an object of magnitude, and the money introduced by it into our state of great and general advantage to our citizens. The effects, indeed, of their residence may be more immediately felt at the capital; but nevertheless they diffuse themselves throughout all parts of the state, and I am persuaded that even the inhabitants in the distant counties of Montgomery and Washington partake of them, though in a less degree. The real importance of this object will appear, sir, in a more striking light if we consider the unremited efforts which have been made by the state of Pennsylvania to draw Congress from us. Sir, there can scarcely be a doubt that if we should fail of a representation in the general senate, she will succeed in her attempt, and in such an event we should be deprived of a great and fruitful source of wealth and prosperity.

It may perhaps be urged, and it cannot reasonably be doubted that the representatives of this state in the house of representatives, will be attentive to the preservation of our interests, but our relative weight in that body appears inconsiderable to what we possess in the senate. The combination of a few of the great states to the southward would be sufficient to deprive us of Congress, if it depended wholly on the lower house. But if we are represented in the senate, we shall have a greater chance of security against any such combination, because *there* the larger and the smaller states, being on an equal footing with respect to numbers, we have a higher probability of success, in our efforts to retain Congress, perhaps for a series of years. And I trust that this important consideration, in addition to those which are furnished by the letter of the constitution, must have no little influence on our present deliberations. Sir, there is another consideration which, from the known sentiments of many among us, I am confident must particularly affect the committee—I mean, Sir, the subject of amendments to the new system of government, which many are looking forward to with an anxious eye. It would be well to remember that the success of any measures which may be adopted upon this subject, must depend in a great degree on our having representatives in the senate of the United States, and therefore I cannot suppose that we shall persist in any plan which may prevent such a representation.

Having availed myself of the indulgence of the committee, in representing the reasons which induce me to think that the object of the present clause is of such high importance, I now proceed to state the motive I had for insisting upon that topic, and the conclusion which I think is deducible from it, with regard to the clause now under consideration. In the first place then, it must result as a necessary consequence, that if the object of the present clause is of the highest importance, we ought to embrace such measures, and such measures only as produce a moral certainty of securing the end which we have in view.

The committee must be sensible that we can take no effectual measures upon this subject without the concurrence of the senate. If therefore, we pursue a measure in which it is not probable that the senate will concur, we must lose our representation in the senate of the United States. In this view of the subject it becomes the duty of the committee to consider attentively what effect the measure proposed must have upon the other branch of our legislature: According to the form of our state constitution, the two houses possess a negative upon each other; and as the new order of things which has arisen, was not in contemplation when our state constitution was framed, we are left free to exercise our discretion upon the present occasion;—all that can be required is, that the regulations which we now adopt shall be such as are consistent with the ideas and wishes of the other house.

The committee will remember that if the clause under consideration is adopted in its present form, the senate must divest themselves of the constitutional negative upon our proceedings which they now possess. How far they could be justified in giving up *that* negative may deserve our serious consideration. The powers which either house has derived from the constitution, I regard as a *sacred trust*, which they are not at liberty to resign, but on the contrary are bound to exercise for the benefit of their constituents.

But whatever may be our opinions upon this subject, I am fully satisfied that as the senate are in the actual possession of this negative, and as they have it in their option to assert their claim to equality with us in the nomination of senators for the United States, they will never be induced to surrender this constitutional right, or to adopt a mode of appointment, which will subject them to be controlled by a majority of this house.

Contemplating the subject in the light I have placed it; pursuaded that the senate, as a collective body, can never be induced to resign the power which they have exercised in the appointment of commissioners and other officers not provided for by the constitution; and convinced that they must object to the bill in its present form, because the appointment of senators for the United States is thereby placed wholly in the power of this house, I am firmly of opinion that if the committee adhere to the bill, as it now stands, we shall have no representation in the senate of the United States.—Should this be the case, then follows a train of evils which I have before adverted to—we shall be bound by treaties which we had no share in forming; involved in wars which we had no opportunity of opposing, and governed by officers whom we had no choice in appointing: We shall lose Congress—and shall lose what is the favorite object of the present day, The probability of obtaining a revision of the new system of government.

In point of prudence, therefore, as well as of right, we ought to adopt such a mode of appointment as the senate can acquiesce in. I do not wish sir, that the house should part with any of its rights; but I do not consider it as possessing a right superior to that of the senate, upon the present occasion.

In all probability, however, it will be objected that our state constitution has designated a mode for the appointment of delegates to the general government, similar to the one contained in the bill, and that it ought to prevail in the present instance. I confess that I view the subject in another light. I consider the state constitution as having a reference only to such an appointment as might arise under the old government, where Congress was differently constructed and had different powers. A new order of things (as I before mentioned) has now arisen. The constitution of the United States has directed that the continental senate shall be chosen by the legislature of each state. The mode is not particularly prescribed; but whatever mode of election the legislature shall appoint, will be constitutional. The senators are to be chosen by the legislature; and it cannot, I think, be disputed that the senate of this state are a branch of the legislature, and in all the powers of legislation, equal with this house.

I do not suppose it necessary, sir, to dwell longer upon this subject. My proposition is such as I imagine may meet the approbation of the senate and ensure the end which at present we have in view. From the prudence of the committee, I am led to hope that they will concur in such measures as may secure our representation in the senate of the United States, and afford a prospect of obtaining the great objects which depend upon it.[2]

Mr. *Lansing*—Fully impressed, sir, with the same ideas of the importance of the subject, as the hon. gentleman who has brought forward the motion, I shall be equally assiduous to attain the great objects we have in view. But, sir, however important and interesting may be the determination of this house, we ought to pursue that line of conduct which is warranted by the constitution, and which we can justify to our constituents. It is often the case that we contemplate objects in different points of light, and draw different conclusions from the same premises. This at present is the case with the hon. gentleman and myself. I consider this as a great constitutional question, which concerns the privileges of this house. In the distribution of power, by the constitution of the state, the senate have a very great share; they have a right to determine what is the law of the state by being a court of appeals—they have an equal vote in all bills—they have also a right to appoint all the officers of the state; for though only four exercises this right, yet it is incumbent on the assembly to select four persons out of the senate to compose the council of appointment;—to counterbalance all this, what has been provided for the exercise of the assembly—they have a right to prefer impeachments exclusively, and of originating money bills; (though this, it is known, is a matter of contest yet between the two houses)—another power is, that if the two houses differ in choosing members of Congress, a joint ballot must determine; this is the provision made by the constitution of the state; and though a new order of things has arisen, yet it cannot alter the constitution. The committee can recollect that this provision was made prior to the existing confederation; it must therefore be considered as a general one, and it was intended to give an advantage to the assembly from their numbers. This I consider as the proper distribution of constitutional powers. Let us then adhere to what the constitution says; it declares that the two houses shall nominate, and if they differ, a joint ballot must determine; we have therefore no discretion on the subject. What has been the practice in other states? on a recent occasion the state of Virginia has elected, by a joint ballot of both houses, as their constitution is like our own, of consequence this precedent must have weight with us.[3] But I believe it will be difficult to shew that the constitution of the state will not apply to the new constitution; indeed it is true, that by the new constitution the legislature of the state has lost part of its privileges—for it is only to choose the members of one branch of the new government. After making a few more observations, he concluded by saying, unless I hear better reasons given, I must be of opinion that the two houses must determine their differences by a joint ballot.—I hold that the amendment will be an unnecessary, nay, wanton departure from the constitution. In Massachusetts, it is true, they adopted a provision like this; and what was the consequence of it—the two houses differed in their choice, and much embarrassment ensued.[4] This will be our situation unless some mode can be devised to bring our differences to an issue. I will confess, however, that if there was any rule to be adopted, different from the constitution, the mode proposed would be the least exceptionable to my mind.

Mr. *B. Livingston.*

I rise, Mr *Chairman*, to support the amendment.—It is admitted on all hands, that the business before us is of great moment. We are now, Sir, to execute an important trust delegated to us by the new federal constitution. In discharging this duty, we shall, I am persuaded, be actuated by no other motive than a regard to the public weal. Under this conviction I shall take the liberty to offer my sentiments to this committee.

When we consider the large but necessary powers delegated to the senate of the United States—when we reflect that they have the sole power of trying impeachments—and that in conjunction with the president they are to make treaties, and to appoint ambassadors, and other public ministers, the importance of a representation in that branch of the national legislature will readily be perceived. Let it also be recollected that our metropolis is fixed on for the place of their residence, but how long this may be the case without due attention on our part, is extremely precarious: certain it is that the measure was not entered into without great opposition; and that a neighboring state is so little intimidated by the victory we have obtained, as publicly to declare her intention of renewing the contest on the first convenient opportunity. Her friends are not so few or inconsiderable as not to require the most strenuous efforts on our part to prevent her success. The numerous advantages resulting from having our capital the seat of government, have been too ably delineated by the honorable gentleman who moved the amendment, to require a further enumeration of them. If then, Sir, a representation in the senate be of such consequence, does it not behove us so to frame the bill before us as to afford a reasonable hope that the other branches of the legislature will give their assent to it? Can we, Sir, reasonably expect the concurrence of the senate as it now stands? Can we expect they will commit an act of suicide, and voluntarily deprive themselves of every effectual agency in the appointment of senators?—Have they not had a recent instance of their insignificance when obliged to join in a ballot with us for delegates?—Of five respectable characters nominated by them, we had not the complaisance to choose one[5]—They must feel too sore under this disappointment readily to consent to being a second time reduced to the same humiliating situation. Is it not then, Sir, risquing too much, pressed as we are for time, so to form our bill as to subject it to objections which are too obvious to escape notice?

The honorable gentleman who was last on the floor, was pleased to call this a great constitutional question. If he had reference to the constitution of the United States, I accord in sentiment with him—but if he had in view the constitution of our own state, I see no danger of its suffering violence on this occasion. Let us first consider the question with a view to the constitution of the United States—We there find it declared that the senate shall be composed of two senators from each state, *chosen by the legislature thereof*. Who, Sir, compose the legislature of this state?—the senate and assembly at least, if not the council of revision—How do these two houses exercise legislative powers?—Do they meet, debate, and vote together—or separately? If on other occasions they invariably pursue the latter mode, why on this are we to expect them to act differently? Were they even to yield to our wishes, would there not be danger (the choice not being made in a legislative mode) of having the senators returned upon our hands? Indeed, I am so fully persuaded that the senators should be appointed by an act of the legislature, that I am only induced to advocate the amendment as the least exceptionable of the two modes under consideration.

Let us now, Sir, see whether our own constitution be in danger—for it has been asked with some degree of animation, whether the new constitution has annulled that of our own state? I answer in the negative, but that if the two in any degree interfere, the former (being the supreme law of the land) must prevail. In the present case, however, it is not easy to discover any interference. The new constitution knows of no such delegates to Congress as are mentioned in that of our own state. The legislature of the United States is to consist of two branches—If the senators are to be chosen in the mode prescribed by our constitution, why not the representatives also? Are not the latter as much delegates to Congress as the former?—and yet no one doubts they are to be chose by the people. If then it be admitted that the state may be controlled by the general constitution in one particular, why not grant it this control in another of an exactly similar nature? But we are told that at the time of passing our state constitution, there was no general confederation in existence, and that therefore it had in eye every possible general constitution that might take place. True it is, Sir, that at the time our constitution was agreed on, the confederation was not compleated: Equally true it is, that a Congress then existed; and that our constitution contemplated only the choice of the delegates who were to represent us in that body, while under its then government. Had the confederation, which was afterwards ratified by this state, provided that the delegates should be chosen by the people at large, does any gentleman doubt that that mode would have obtained in our state, our own constitution notwithstanding.

Some arguments, sir, against the amendment, have been drawn from the examples of other states, and the embarrassments which Massachusetts met with in her late choice of senators; but those embarrassments, if they deserve the name, terminated in a very respectable delegation, and cannot, if the amendments be attended to, occur in our choice, the different houses not having a negative upon each other. I would wish, indeed that the amendment had gone that length at least, and had proposed the Massachusetts mode of choosing by concurrent resolutions.

It is not necessary, sir, to enlarge on this subject. It is not probable that the senate will agree to the clause in question. If they do, it is not clear that the election by a joint meeting, will be a constitutional choice. Rather, then, than risque any thing in a matter of so much magnitude, I flatter myself we shall think it prudent to agree to the amendment proposed.

Mr. *Jones* then rose to oppose the amendment. [But his voice was so low, and there being so much noise in the gallery, that our notes of his speech are rather imperfect.] This bill, said he, is to be a lasting one, not one for the moment, and to answer the present occasion, it is drafted on the plain principles dictated by the constitution of our state, and the constitution of the United States. I am sorry that in considering this question we should go into a discussion of the rights and privileges of the two houses;—this is not our province, we ought only to consider one question, which is, whether the ground we have taken is constitutional or not? and if we have taken the true constitutional ground, we are never to consider what the other house probably may do. We are to consider whether the mode is right and proper, independent of any other consideration, and whether the mode comes nearest the constitution of this, and the constitution of the United States. But if difficulties arise, which I trust will not, and the senate conceive that our bill infringes on their privileges, let us then have a conference, and endeavor for an accommodation; but it is time enough to consider their privileges when they state them to us. I produced that bill now before the committee, from a conviction of the necessity of it; as the new constitution declares that the states shall pass acts to prescribe the times, places, &c. of holding elections, there became a necessity to produce such a bill, and I trust every member will think I was right, and that it ought to be formed as near the constitution of our own state as that of the United States would admit. We have always had a representation in the Congress of the United States, and our constitution pointed out the mode by which the legislature should appoint them. It has been mentioned, and it is true, that at the time the constitution of this state was formed, there was no confederation. The constitution therefore contemplates representatives of the United States, under a general constitution, whether framed as the confederation afterwards was, or however it might be modified.

There is no alteration in our circumstances we are still to be represented in the same manner as we were before, tho' it is true there is to be another branch: why then should we not choose our representatives in the mode pointed out by our constitution; shall we throw it all away—shall we say that our constitution is annihilated, if this is the case let us then begin by forming a new constitution. But gentlemen say this election ought to be by an act of the legislature; in reply to this, I think nothing more is necessary than to read the new constitution itself. It is not to be supposed that the convention at Philadelphia ever contemplated a former[6] act of legislation for the appointment of senators:—With respect to the amendment now proposed, if we think proper to depart from the constitution, it appears to be the nearest to it of any that can be offered, but it is defective in one instance—it seems to suppose that we are always to choose two senators. They are to be divided into classes, it is hardly possible that they will both go out at one time, but if that should happen, the time will come when there is but one senator to be chosen—the amendment has no provision against such an event—it is therefore an improper one. We ought to form our act so that it cannot be defeated by any possible event. There will be some inconveniencies, frame the bill as you will, and this will happen in all popular governments—if therefore the majority of the assembly should overbalance the whole weight of the senate, we must suppose it right, as it will be the more likely to agree with the wishes of the people. The gentleman seems to think it is wrong, that this house, if it is unanimous, can appoint all the delegates to Congress; but is this a reason why we should make a law in violation of our constitution to gratify a party? For my part I have no views but to serve my country; I have no ambition for myself—no personal hopes nor expectations from the measure. I am only anxious that we do not depart from our constitution and give up the dearest rights of the people. If, however, necessity should drive us into an accommodation, we can then do it; but I trust that in this stage of the business we will not adopt the amendment. I trust the senate will concur with us. These are my sentiments, and I hope no man will take exceptions to them. I have no wish but to frame the bill in such a manner as to ensure an election.

Mr. Harrison. I concur in sentiment with the gentleman who spoke last, that we ought not to change the constitutional mode of doing business merely to gratify a party. I also concur with the idea, that if the constitution of our state had a reference to this subject, it would be binding upon us; but, sir, we do not agree as to that point, and altho' the gentlemen on the other side have dilated largely on the situation in which the country was at the time our constitution was formed, yet the conclusion from that argument is wholly against them; for tho' it is true, that at the time of making the constitution of this state, the articles of confederation had not been agreed to, yet it is also true that the framers of the constitution contemplated the then subsisting Congress, and that they had only in view the appointment of delegates to that body as it was then constructed, and with the powers which it then possessed. It has been observed, and must strike the mind of every man, that had the articles of confederation prescribed any rule of election different from our constitution, it must have been adopted; but as the confederation declared that the appointments should be conformable to the constitutions of the different states, or as their legislatures should direct. No difficulty has hitherto arisen. Now, sir, we have adopted a new system of general government, totally varying from the former, which declares that the choice of senators in the general government shall be by the legislature of the state; not that they shall be chosen in the old mode prescribed by the constitution. Our constitution therefore has no reference to the present subject; and as it does not apply, it becomes us to exercise our authority by the rules of prudence, and a regard for the interests of our constituents. The necessity of designating a mode of election, results from the new constitution itself, which abrogates that part of our state constitution, relative to the appointment of delegates, and makes it necessary for us to bring in the present bill.

Sir, a gentleman who has been lately on the floor, has argued strangely on this subject from the new constitution itself, he seems to confine his ideas only to one clause of the constitution, the regulation of time, place, &c. I wish he would take up the constitution in all its views, and pay some attention to a preceding clause, where it is declared that the senators shall be chosen by the legislature; it is not one branch then that can make this choice. Whenever therefore this house alone shall make a choice, it will be insufficient to satisfy even the words of the new constitution. I conceive that the gentleman is also mistaken, when he says that we ought not to consider the opinions of the other house. Sir, I trust I am as fully attached to, and ever shall be as ready to support the constitution of my country as any man among us; but, sir, when the constitution is silent, when we are about framing a system that is to give efficacy to the new government, in which we are so deeply interested, I shall consider it prudent to do what it is probable will be agreeable to both houses. Why shall we pursue a measure which we have every reason to believe they will negative. It is reasonable to consider not only our own inclinations and wishes, but those also of the persons who are to concur with us. We shall commit an improper waste both of time and public money if we employ ourselves to devise plans which we know will be ineffectual. Being left free to act discretionally upon the present occasion, I trust we shall be guided only by a regard to the prosperity of our country. It has been said that the law now under consideration is not for the present moment, and that we should legislate for posterity. The maxim is true to a certain extent, but if we should legislate only with a view to posterity, we shall commit as great a folly as the man who heaps up riches and starves himself, with the idea of possessing an affluent fortune at a future period. It is our duty, sir, to calculate our laws in such a manner as to produce immediate good, for future legislatures can always new model them, and thus they may at all times be agreeable to the circumstances and wishes of the people. With respect to the gentleman's observations on the incorrectness of my motion, I readily acknowledge it, and I trust the candor and indulgence of the committee, who know the hasty manner in which it was drawn, will permit me to correct it. Sir, Virginia has been cited as a precedent, and the mode adopted in several other states with regard to this subject have also been mentioned; but these can have no weight with us—we are to judge from our own circumstances, and the frame of our own government. On this occasion, I trust, that I am as free from personal motives as any man in this house; and I hope they will all think with me, that it is most prudent to adopt such measures as are likely to succeed.

Sir, one of the gentlemen who has been on the floor has given a delineation of the constitution, and supposes that the advantage of a joint ballot was intended to give this house a check on the other; I believe, sir, that the framers of the constitution had no such idea—they only pointed it out as what they supposed the most proper way to choose delegates to the then Congress. Had the present government been under consideration, their ideas might have been different. I might add much to the arguments already urged; but I trust what has been said will sufficiently evince the propriety and necessity of the proposed amendment.

Mr. *Lansing*—With respect to appointing the senators by an act of the legislature, it is well known that our constitution points out three branches—at least that the council of revision have so far a negative as to make it necessary to pass a bill by two thirds of both houses—the council will therefore control the two houses; this I believe neither the senate nor assembly will be fond of. I believe it is unnecessary to trouble the committee any longer on the subject; as for myself, I have fully delivered my sentiments, and have no doubt but that the senators must be appointed in the mode prescribed by our constitution; as it always had in view the appointment of representatives, to the national government, however modified. The adoption of the new system does not therefore in the least alter our situation;—except that the old constitution partook of a federal feature—the new one, of a consolidation.

The more I reflect on the subject, sir, the more I am convinced that the state constitution must be adhered to, and that we have no right to exercise our discretion on the occasion. But it is said why go to the trouble of passing a bill if the constitution points out the mode, the reason is obvious, the new constitution requires that the time, place and manner of holding elections should be pointed out by the legislature.

The motion having been amended, is as follows.

[Here insert the motion.][7]

The yeas and nays being called for, it passed in the negative.

[Here insert the names.]

The committee then rose, and the house adjourned.

1. *Daily Advertiser*, 26 and 27 December 1788. The newspaper reports of legislative debates and proceedings printed in this chapter are generally from the *Daily Advertiser* because they were usually the earliest and most complete public accounts. The *Daily Gazette* occasionally printed extensive accounts of the debates and proceedings, while the *Country Journal*, *Morning Post*, and *New York Journal* generally printed less complete, albeit frequent, reports. In the documents that follow, routine and purely factual newspaper accounts of legislative debates and proceedings that offer no new information, as well as reprints of earlier reports, have not been printed or noted.

2. For Harrison's motives in presenting his amendment, see Assembly Debates, 2 January 1789, below.

3. For Virginia's election of United States Senators by joint ballot, see DHFFE, II, 280–82.

4. For Massachusetts' election of United States Senators, see DHFFE, I, 511–28.

5. On 16 December 1788 the Assembly and Senate, in joint session, elected David Gelston, John Hathorn, Samuel Jones, Philip Pell, and Abraham Yates, Jr., to serve in the last Confederation Congress. Following the procedure outlined in Article XXX of the state constitution, the Federalist-dominated Senate had separately nominated Egbert Benson, Leonard Gansevoort, Alexander Hamilton, Ezra L'Hommedieu, and John Laurance, while the Antifederalist-dominated Assembly had nominated the five eventual winners. An attempt to nominate Hamilton was defeated in the Assembly. The victory of the Assembly's slate of candidates reinforced Federalist fears of the perils of electing Senators by joint ballot.

6. Although the newspaper printed "former," the word "formal" was undoubtedly intended.

7. This account of the debates printed the Harison amendment and the roll call on the amendment above these debates. These brackets and those just below are in the original newspaper printing. For the amendment and roll call, see Assembly and Senate Proceedings, 17 December 1788, immediately above.

Assembly and Senate Proceedings, Thursday, A.M., 18 December

The Senate

The engrossed bill entitled, *An act for regulating the manner of appointing electors, who are to elect the President and Vice President of the United States of America*, was read a third time, and Mr. President having put the question, whether the said bill shall pass, it was carried in the affirmative, in the manner following, viz.

FOR THE AFFIRMATIVE.

Mr. Philip Schuyler,	Mr. Lawrance,
Mr. Douw,	Mr. Morris,
Mr. Micheau,	Mr. Roosevelt,
Mr. Peter Schuyler,	Mr. Duane.
Mr. Vanderbilt,	

FOR THE NEGATIVE.

Mr. Yates,	Mr. Swartwout,
Mr. Hopkins,	Mr. Townsend,
Mr. Williams,	Mr. Tredwell.
Mr. Van Ness,	

Thereupon, *Resolved*, That the bill do pass.

Ordered, That Mr. Vanderbilt and Mr. Hopkins, deliver the bill to the Hon. the Assembly, and request their concurrence. . . .

Mr. Peter Schuyler from the committee of the whole, to whom was referred the bill entitled *An act for the appointment of Senators to represent this State in the Senate of the United States of America*, reported, that the committee had made some further progress in the bill, and directed him to move for leave to sit again.

Ordered, That the committee have leave to sit again.

The Assembly

Mr. Jones from the committee appointed to prepare a draft of a respectful address to His Excellency the Governor, in answer to his Speech, reported that the committee had prepared a draft accordingly; and he read the said draft in his place, and delivered the same in at the table, where it was again read.

Ordered, That the said draft of an address, be committed to a committee of the whole House.

Mr. Havens from the committee of the whole House, on the bill entitled, *An act for carrying into effect on the part of this State, the Constitution of the United States, assented to and ratified by the Convention of this State, on the twenty-sixth day of July last*, reported, that the committee had made further progress in the bill, and had directed him to move for leave to sit again.

Ordered, That the said committee have leave to sit again.

[The Assembly received the bill for appointing Electors from the Senate.]

The said bill was read the first time, and ordered a second reading.

Assembly Debates, Thursday, 18 December[1]

Went into a committee on the bill for putting the new constitution into operation; Mr. Havens in the chair.

After having passed by the clause which divides the state into districts,

Mr. Adgate moved, that the person to be chosen should be an inhabitant of the district.

This motion produced some conversation,—Mr. Jones, who was opposed to it, said, that he did not conceive that the constitution of this state, nor of the United States, would admit of such a clause; for as the constitution of the United States prescribed no other qualification than that the representative should be of a certain age, and an inhabitant of the state, to add any other qualification would be unconstitutional.

Mr. Adgate replied to this, that if the argument of Mr. Jones had any weight, it was as forcible against the dividing the state into districts, as against his proposition; but he thought it did not apply.

Mr. Gilbert thought the only way to make the law agreeable to the people, would be to let the election be general, throughout the state. Indeed he did not suppose the constitution would admit of an election in any other mode.

Mr. Harrison was also opposed to the amendment; he thought it would be an infringement of the constitutional rights of the people, as it might fetter them in their choice, which ought to be perfectly free and unrestrained.

Mr. Harpur and Mr. Lansing also opposed the amendment on the ground that it was unconstitutional.

The question being put, the amendment was lost.

Mr. B. Livingston then moved for an amendment, to strike out the word "*one*" and to insert the word "*six*". To support this motion, he said that the constitution gave every man a right to vote for six men, and that it would be an arbitrary stride of power to restrain him to vote only for one. He also contended that men chosen by districts could not be considered as representatives of the state—they were only representatives of districts. He said that there was a manifest analogy between state and county representatives; the city and county of New-York, for instance, sent nine members to the assembly—supposing that the county was parcelled out into nine districts, each member that was chosen would not be the representative of the county, but of the particular district he came from, and would of consequence be only attached to their local views and interests. He cited the examples of Connecticut, New-Jersey, and Pennsylvania, where the elections were general. And as a further proof of the necessity of the amendment, he stated the difficulty of dividing the state so as to give general satisfaction—besides the continual increase of the state would render it necessary to pass a new bill every year or two, our election law therefore, could only be a temporary one.

Mr. Jones opposed the motion—he said it went to the total destruction of district elections. If six men were to be voted for throughout the state, the people would be obliged to vote for men that they could not know—it was to give the people a chance for a fair representation, that the state should be divided into districts, and that each district should choose only one. With respect to local attachments, I am said he, elected for the county of Queens, shall I, therefore, consider myself as representing only Queens County—no, I consider myself, and hope we all do, as representatives of the state. We may as well say that we ought not to vote by counties, but that every man throughout the state should vote for sixty-five representatives. But, he insisted that by the form of ratification of the constitution of this state, a right was reserved to the legislature to divide the state into convenient districts, and to apportion the representatives. As therefore, in his opinion, it was for the good of the state to divide it into districts—he hoped the amendment would not be adopted.

Mr. *Lansing* observed, that with respect to the two arguments on which the amendment was founded, that the constitution did not admit of district elections, and that if it did, it would not be expedient to adopt that mode, that as to the constitutional objection, the ratification of the constitution gave full power to the legislature, from the reservation contained in it; there could therefore be no doubt of the authority of the house to divide the state into districts. As [to] the propriety of electing by districts, he thought it must be obvious to every man, that that was the most likely way to obtain a representation of the people, for it was not to be supposed that a man who gave in his vote for six men, throughout the state, could be so well acquainted with them, as with one man in the particular district where he lived. And as the people did not like to be represented by men they did not know, an election throughout the state might disaffect them to the government.

These observations were replied to by Mr. Livingston, who was again answered by Mr. Lansing. When the question being called for, it was determined in the negative.

The committee then rose, and reported that they had made some further progress in the bill.

A message from the senate was then read, that they had passed a bill for the appointment of the electors;—the bill was then read a first time, and ordered a second reading.

The principle on which this bill is formed is, that the assembly shall choose four, and the senate the other four electors.

1. *Daily Advertiser*, 29 December 1788.

Assembly and Senate Proceedings, Friday, A.M., 19 December

The Senate

Mr. Peter Schuyler from the committee of the whole, to whom was referred the bill entitled *An act for the appointment of Senators to represent this State in the Senate of the United States of America*, reported, that in proceeding to the first enacting clause of the bill, Mr. Tredwell moved, "That the mode of appointing Senators to represent this State in the Senate of the United States of America, be the same as the mode of appointing Delegates to the Congress of the United States of America, as prescribed by the Constitution of this State." Debates arose upon the said motion, and the question being put thereon, it passed in the negative, in manner following, viz.

FOR THE NEGATIVE.

Mr. Philip Schuyler,	Mr. Lawrance,
Mr. Douw,	Mr. Morris,
Mr. Micheau,	Mr. Roosevelt,
Mr. Fonda,	Mr. L'Hommedieu,
Mr. Vanderbilt,	Mr. Duane.

FOR THE AFFIRMATIVE.

Mr. Yates,	Mr. Swartwout,
Mr. Hopkins,	Mr. Townsend,
Mr. Williams,	Mr. Tredwell.
Mr. Van Ness,	

Mr. Peter Schuyler further reported, that the committee had gone through the bill, made amendments thereto, and altered the title in the words following, viz. *An act respecting the appointment of Senators to represent this State in the Senate of the United States of America*, which report he read in his place, and delivered the bill in at the table, where it was again read; Mr. Yates, thereupon moved, that the same be rejected, and Mr. President having put the question on the said motion, it passed in the negative, in manner following, viz.

FOR THE NEGATIVE.

Mr. Philip Schuyler,	Mr. Lawrance,
Mr. Douw,	Mr. Morris,
Mr. Micheau,	Mr. Roosevelt,
Mr. Peter Schuyler,	Mr. L'Hommedieu,
Mr. Fonda,	Mr. Duane.
Mr. Vanderbilt,	

FOR THE AFFIRMATIVE.

Mr. Yates,	Mr. Swartwout,
Mr. Hopkins,	Mr. Townsend,
Mr. Williams,	Mr. Tredwell,
Mr. Van Ness,	Mr. Humfrey.

Thereupon, *Ordered*, That the bill as amended be engrossed.

The Assembly

The bill entitled, *An act for regulating the manner of appointing electors who are to elect the President and Vice-President of the United States of America*, was read a second time, and committed to a committee of the whole House. . . .

Mr. Havens, from the committee of the whole House, on the bill entitled *An act for carrying into effect on the part of this State, the Constitution of the United States, assented to and ratified by the Convention of this State, on the twenty-sixth day of July last*, reported, that in proceeding on the bill, *Mr. Speaker* made a motion, that a recital preceding one of the enacting clauses, should be obliterated, which recital was in the words following, viz.

"And whereas, the time fixed for appointing electors for choosing the President[1] and Vice-President of the United States, will not admit of their being chosen by the People of this State."

That debates arose on the said motion, and that the question having been put thereon, it was carried in the affirmative, in the manner following, viz.

FOR THE AFFIRMATIVE.

Mr. Gilbert,	Mr. Savage,
Mr. G. Livingston,	Mr. Webster,
Mr. Barker,	Mr. M'Cracken,
Mr. Kortz,	Mr. Bay,
Mr. Yates,	Mr. Schoonmaker,
Mr. Frey,	Mr. Tappen,
Mr. Stauring,	Mr. Griffen,
Mr. SPEAKER,	Mr. J. Smith,
Mr. Van Dyck,	Mr. D'Witt,
Mr. J. Van Rensselaer,	Mr. Wisner,
Mr. Hoffman,	Mr. Adgate,
Mr. Veeder,	Mr. Harper,
Mr. Winn,	Mr. Schenck,
Mr. Duncan,	Mr. E. Clark.
Mr. Tearse,	

FOR THE NEGATIVE.

Mr. Jones,	Mr. Horton,
Mr. Carman,	Mr. Carpenter,
Mr. B. Livingston,	Mr. Low,
Mr. Van Cortlandt,	Mr. Bancker,
Mr. Seaman,	Mr. Vandervoort,
Mr. Hardenbergh,	Mr. Rockwell,
Mr. Harison,	Mr. Verplanck,
Mr. H. Van Rensselaer.	Mr. Cornwell,
Mr. Younglove,	Mr. Akins,
Mr. Thompson,	Mr. Giles,
Mr. Watts,	Mr. Dongan.
Mr. Livingston,	

That the said recital was accordingly obliterated.

That in proceeding further in the bill, a paragraph was read in the words following, viz.

"After which nomination the Senate and Assembly shall meet together and compare the lists of the persons by them respectively nominated, and those persons named in both lists shall be electors—And out of those persons whose names are not in both lists, one half shall be chosen by the joint ballot of the Senators, and Members of Assembly so met together as aforesaid."

That the said paragraph having been read, Mr. Harison made a motion that the latter part of the paragraph viz. "And out of those persons whose names are not in both lists one half shall be chosen by the joint ballot of the Senators and Members of Assembly, so met together as aforesaid," should be obliterated, and the following paragraph inserted instead thereof viz.

"And the persons named in both lists shall be electors; and if the said lists shall disagree only as to one of the persons named in each of the said lists, then one of the two persons not named in both lists shall be chosen by the joint ballot of the Senators and Members of Assembly, so met together as aforesaid; but if the said lists shall disagree as to more than one of the persons named in each of them, then the number of persons to be appointed as electors, (after deducting those in whose nomination both lists agree) shall be divided as equally as possible; and if it will admit of division into two equal numbers, the Senators then met as aforesaid shall chuse by ballot one half of the number still remaining to be chosen out of the persons nominated as aforesaid by the Assembly, and not included in the list of persons nominated by the Senate; and the Members of the Assembly shall, in like manner choose the other half the number still remaining to be chosen, out of the persons nominated by the Senate, and not included in the list of persons nominated by the Assembly as aforesaid; but in case an equal division cannot take place as aforesaid, then the Senators shall choose one more of the electors than the Members of Assembly are to chuse, but the choice shall in all other respects be in the manner herein before prescribed."

That debates arose on the amendments proposed by the motion of Mr. Harison; and that the question having been put whether the committee did agree to the same, it passed in negative, in the manner following, viz.

FOR THE NEGATIVE.

Mr. Jones,	Mr. Webster,
Mr. Carman,	Mr. M'Cracken,
Mr. G. Livingston,	Mr. Thompson,
Mr. Kortz,	Mr. Bay,
Mr. Yates,	Mr. Schoonmaker,
Mr. Frey,	Mr. Tappen,
Mr. Stauring,	Mr. Griffen,
Mr. SPEAKER,	Mr. Carpenter,
Mr. Van Dyck,	Mr. J. Smith,
Mr. J. Van Rensselaer,	Mr. D'Witt,
Mr. Hardenbergh,	Mr. Wisner,
Mr. Veeder,	Mr. Adgate,
Mr. Winn,	Mr. Harper,
Mr. Duncan,	Mr. Schenck,
Mr. Tearse,	Mr. Akins,
Mr. Savage,	Mr. Clark.

FOR THE AFFIRMATIVE.

Mr. B. Livingston,	Mr. Livingston,
Mr. Gilbert,	Mr. Horton,
Mr. Van Cortlandt,	Mr. Low,
Mr. Seaman,	Mr. Bancker,
Mr. Barker,	Mr. Vandervoort,
Mr. Harison,	Mr. Rockwell,
Mr. Hoffman,	Mr. Verplanck,
Mr. H. Van Rensselaer,	Mr. Cornwell,
Mr. Younglove,	Mr. Giles,
Mr. Watts,	Mr. Dongan.

That the said amendment proposed by the last mentioned motion, was thereupon rejected.

That the committee had made further progress in the bill, and had directed him to move for leave to sit again.

Ordered, That the said committee have leave to sit again. . . .

The House then resolved itself into a committee of the whole House, on the draft of a respectful address, in answer to the speech of His Excellency the Governor at the opening of the session; and after some time spent thereon, Mr. Low from the said committee reported, that the committee had made some progress therein, and had directed him to move for leave to sit again.[2]

Ordered, That the said committee have leave to sit again.

1. The *Journal of the Assembly* mistakenly printed "Representatives" instead of "President," here.

2. The *Daily Advertiser*, 29 December 1788, reported the nature of the discussion: "Went into committee on the draft of an answer to the Governor's speech. Mr. Low in the chair. The same being read, and a motion made by Mr. B. Livingston to amend it; a desultory debate arose on the propriety of reading the circular letter, and the proceedings of the late convention. After a short time spent thereon, the committee rose and reported the progress they had made."

David Gelston to John Smith, New York, 19 December[1]

I catch the present minute to scratch you one line by our Mutual Friend Doctor Gardiner[2]—we are well—hold on *upon* your *right* as a Member of the Assembly—choose your Senators to the great Court of the Nation—as you have hitherto Choosen Delegates to Congress—or in some mode equally Republican—as to Fœderal principles—as by whatever name it may [be] called—I know nothing of—in a word let all your deliberations and all your Votes—be truly Republican—advantageous & beneficale to your Country—I have not time to give you particular directions—let me know what you are about—be minute—be particular—precise in your information, I don't like your Broad Hints—it may be—& perhaps—& possibly &c &c—&c. it is so courtly—so like apeing the *great Man*—I have not time to add another word—only that I am your assured Friend

1. RC, John Smith of Mastic Papers, NHi. The letter was addressed to Smith in Albany. Gelston (1744–1828) represented Suffolk County in the provincial congresses, 1775–1777, and in the Assembly, 1777–1785. He represented the Southern District in the state Senate, 1791–1794 and 1798–1802; was surrogate of New York County, 1787–1801; and collector of the port of New York, 1801–1820.

2. Probably Nathaniel Gardiner, who represented Suffolk County in the Assembly, 1786 and 1788–1790.

Assembly and Senate Proceedings, Saturday, A.M., 20 December

The Senate

The engrossed bill entitled, *An act respecting the appointment of Senators, to represent this State in the Senate of the United States of America*, was read a third time.

Resolved, That the bill do pass.[1]

Ordered, That Mr. Hopkins and Mr. Williams, deliver the bill to the Honorable the Assembly and request their concurrence.

The Assembly

Mr. Havens from the committee of the whole House, on the bill entitled, *An act for carrying into effect on the part [of] this State the Constitution of the United States, assented to, and ratified by the Convention of this State, on the twenty-sixth day of July last*, reported, that on coming to the blank in the bill, where the allowance per day to the electors to nominate the President and Vice-President was to be inserted, *Mr. Speaker* made a motion, that the words twenty shillings should be inserted in the said blank. That debates arose on the said motion, and that the question having been put thereon, it was carried in the affirmative, in manner following, viz.

FOR THE AFFIRMATIVE.

Mr. B. Livingston,	Mr. Watts,
Mr. Gilbert,	Mr. Livingston,
Mr. Seaman,	Mr. Horton,
Mr. Barker,	Mr. Bay,
Mr. Kortz,	Mr. Tappen,
Mr. Yates,	Mr. Low,
Mr. Stauring,	Mr. Bancker,
Mr. SPEAKER,	Mr. Vandervoort,
Mr. Van Dyck,	Mr. Harper,
Mr. J. Van Rensselaer,	Mr. Verplanck,
Mr. Harison,	Mr. Cornwell,
Mr. Hoffman,	Mr. Akins,
Mr. Winn,	Mr. Dongan,
Mr. Webster,	Mr. Sands.

FOR THE NEGATIVE.

Mr. Jones,	Mr. M'Cracken,
Mr. Carman,	Mr. Thompson,
Mr. Van Cortlandt,	Mr. Schoonmaker,
Mr. G. Livingston,	Mr. Griffen,
Mr. Frey,	Mr. Carpenter,
Mr. Hardenbergh,	Mr. J. Smith,
Mr. Veeder,	Mr. D'Witt,
Mr. H. Van Rensselaer,	Mr. Wisner,
Mr. Younglove,	Mr. Adgate,
Mr. Savage,	Mr. Rockwell,

Mr. Schenck,	Mr. E. Clark,
Mr. Giles,	Mr. Patterson.

That the committee had gone through the bill and made amendments, which he was directed to report to the House; and he read the report in his place, and delivered the bill and amendments in at the table, where the same were again read, and agreed to by the House.

Ordered, That the bill and amendments be engrossed.[2]

[The Assembly received the bill for the appointment of Senators from the Senate.]

The said bill was read the first time, and ordered a second reading.

1. The *Daily Advertiser*, 29 December 1788, in its report of the Assembly proceedings for 20 December, noted parenthetically that the Senate had "inserted" the names of Philip Schuyler and Robert Yates as Senators in the bill. The *Albany Journal*, 22 December, reported that the Senate had nominated Schuyler and Yates for Senators, and that news was repeated in the *Federal Herald*, 29 December; *Country Journal*, 30 December; *New York Packet*, 30 December; *New York Journal*, 1 January 1789; and in many out-of-state newspapers, as well as [John Smith to Melancton Smith], c. 31 January, below. Several other out-of-state newspapers reported that the two men had been elected (see Boston *Massachusetts Centinel*, 24 December, below). The official Senate proceedings make no mention of any nominations.

2. For the election districts for Representatives established by committee, see Assembly Debates, 20 December 1788, immediately below.

Assembly Debates, Saturday, 20 December[1]

. . . the house went again into a committee on the bill for putting the new constitution into operation.

The following is the division of the state as agreed to by the committee.

Suffolk, Queens, Kings, and Richmond counties, to be one district.

New-York and Westchester, (excepting the towns of Cortlandt, York-town, Steven-town, Salem and North-Salem,) to be one district.

Dutchess, and that part of Westchester excepted in the foregoing district, to form another district.

Ulster and Orange to be one district.

Columbia, Washington and Clinton counties, with the remainder of the state on the east side of Hudson river, to form another district.

That part of Albany county on the West of Hudson river, and the county of Montgomery, to form another district.[2]

The bill having been gone through, the committee rose and reported the same, when it was ordered to be engrossed for a third reading.

1. *Daily Advertiser*, 29 December 1788.

2. In the final version of the New York Election Law, 27 January 1789, below, this district included Ontario County, which was formed from Montgomery County in January 1789.

Abraham Bancker to [Evert Bancker], Albany, 20 December (excerpt)[1]

We are driving away at legislation Business. A Majority of Federalists in Senate; a Minority in Assembly. Consequently we must expect many of our Acts to be Negatived by each other in the course of the Sessions, which, by the bye, is likely to be a very long one. You have an Antifederal Representation in Congress for the current Year. Mr. Jones, Mr. Pell, Mr. Hathorn, Mr. Abm. Yates Junr: & Mr Gelston.[2] This will not be all; prepare yourself to hear more News of a similar Nature, very Shortly.

1. RC, Bancker Family Papers, NHi. Although the address page of the letter is missing, the addressee is undoubtedly Evert Bancker. Abraham signed the letter as "Your Affectionate Nephew," and in his letter of 28 December 1788 to Evert, Abraham refers to his earlier letter written from Albany. Also, in a letter to Evert Bancker, 29 December, Adrian Bancker refers to a letter Abraham wrote to Evert on 20 December (Castleton, Staten Island, RC, Bancker Family Papers, NHi). Abraham Bancker (1760–1832), son of Adrian and nephew of Evert, was Richmond County clerk, 1781–1784, county sheriff, 1784–1788; a member of the Assembly, 1788–1790; and a delegate to the state Convention in 1788, where he voted to ratify the Constitution. He was also surrogate of Richmond County, 1792–1809, and a presidential Elector in 1804. Evert Bancker (1721–1803), a merchant, represented New York City and County in the provincial congresses, 1775–1777, and in the Assembly, 1777–1783 and 1786–1788 (Speaker, 1779–1783).

2. For the election of delegates to the Confederation Congress, see Assembly Debates, 17 December 1788, n. 5, above.

James Duane to John Jay, Albany, 20 December[1]

I set off in a hurry which alone prevented my calling upon you for which I had a variety of Motives. One was to explain the reasons which induced me to transmit to you a State of facts on a subject which I thought somewhat interesting, and the more so as it had produced a Visit from three reverend Doctors the evning before I commencd my Journey—Their object was to prevent a flame which they saw rising & which might affect a Harmony they had much at heart. I did not know but you might think it of importance enough to merit a pacific paragraph to keep the federal Interest out of the reach of Animosity. Time alone prevented my attempting it for I was interrupted by my Fellow traveller who was impatient to proceed. I know your goodness will excuse the Liberty I took, and your prudence will decide for the best.

I shoud not have enter'd into this little detail, but from a wish to give you a Sketch of our legislative Situation. In the respective houses there is a small majority opposed to each other: five in the Senate to about double the number in the Assembly. The latter have taken the first opportunity of throwing the Gauntlet by turning out on the Joint ballot all the four federal Delegates whom we supported in vain. A strong proof of their Enmity as that office is a mere feather at present![2] S. Jones[3] whom they have substituted for one takes the lead on their side and apparently with great boldness and decision. The next Step is the appointment of Electers & Senaters. we insist it shall be done by Law to secure a negative both with respect to the men & the manner: they on a Joint ballot of both houses which woud put every thing in their power. Each have proposed bills on their respective principles and both seem tenacious—If the assembly perserfere neither Electers nor Senetors will be appointed tho' I am not without hopes of an accommodation by consenting to an equality of weight in the proposed Appointments. Mr Townshend we find decidedly against us; Mr Fonda for us;[4] The rest of the Senaters on each side as we conjecturd before we left New York. You will from hence form a Judgement of the Events of this Session

1. RC, Jay-Iselin Collection, NNC. The letter was addressed to Jay in New York City.

2. For the election of delegates to the Confederation Congress, see Assembly Debates, 17 December 1788, n. 5, above.

3. Samuel Jones (1734–1819), one of the state's most prominent lawyers, represented Queens County in the Assembly, 1786–1790, and the Southern District in the state Senate, 1791–1799. He was an Antifederalist leader in the state Convention in 1788, where he voted to ratify the Constitution. Jones was recorder of New York City, 1789–1796, and state comptroller, 1797–1800.

4. Samuel Townsend (d. 1790), of Queens County, represented the Southern District in the state Senate, 1784–1790. Jellis Fonda (1727–1791), of Montgomery County, represented the Western District in the state Senate, 1777–1781 and 1788–1791.

Assembly and Senate Proceedings, Monday, 22 December

The Assembly, A.M.

The engrossed bill entitled, *An act for carrying into effect on the part of this State, the Constitution of the United States, assented to and ratified by the Convention of this State, on the twenty-sixth day of July last,* was read a third time.

Resolved, That the bill do pass.

Ordered, That Mr. Younglove and Mr. Duncan, deliver the bill to the Honorable the Senate, and request their concurrence.

The bill entitled, *An act respecting the appointment of Senators to represent this State in the Senate of the United States of America,* was read a second time and committed to a committee of the whole House.

Mr. Low from the committee of the whole House, on the draft of a respectful address to his Excellency the Governor at the opening of the session, reported that the said committee had gone through the said draft without amendment, which he was directed to report to the House; and he read the report in his place, and delivered the said draft in at the table, where it was again read and agreed to by the House

Ordered, That the said draft of a respectful address be engrossed.

Mr. J. Smith from the committee of the whole House, on the bill entitled, *An act for regulating the manner of appointing electors, who are to elect the President and Vice President of the United States of America,* reported, that after the said bill had been read in the committee, Mr. Adgate made a motion that the bill should be rejected; and that the question having been put on the said motion it was carried [in] the affirmative, in the manner following, viz.

FOR THE AFFIRMATIVE.

Mr. Jones,	Mr. Tearse,
Mr. Carman,	Mr. Savage,
Mr. G. Livingston,	Mr. Webster,
Mr. Kortz,	Mr. M'Cracken,
Mr. Yates,	Mr. Thompson,
Mr. Frey,	Mr. Bay,
Mr. Stauring,	Mr. Tappen,
Mr. SPEAKER,	Mr. Griffen,
Mr. Van Dyck,	Mr. Carpenter,
Mr. J. Van Rensselaer,	Mr. D'Witt,
Mr. Hardenbergh,	Mr. Winser,
Mr. Veeder,	Mr. Adgate,
Mr. Winn,	Mr. Harper,
Mr. Duncan,	Mr. Havens,

Mr. Schenck,	Mr. Patterson,
Mr. Akins,	Mr. Scudder.
Mr. E. Clark,	

FOR THE NEGATIVE.

Mr. B. Livingston,	Mr. Horton,
Mr. Gilbert,	Mr. Low,
Mr. Van Cortlandt,	Mr. Bancker,
Mr. Seaman,	Mr. Vandervoort,
Mr. Barker,	Mr. Rockwell,
Mr. Harison,	Mr. Verplanck,
Mr. Hoffman,	Mr. Cornwell,
Mr. H. Van Rensselaer,	Mr. Giles,
Mr. Younglove,	Mr. Dongan,
Mr. Watts,	Mr. Sands.
Mr. Livingston,	

That it was thereupon *resolved*, as the opinion of the said committee, that the said bill should be rejected, which he was directed to report to the House. Thereupon,

Resolved, That the said bill be rejected.

Mr. Low from the committee of the whole House, on the speech of His Excellency the Governor, and the papers which accompanied the same, at the opening of the session, reported, that the committee had agreed to a resolution, which he was directed to report to the House, in the words following, viz.

"*Resolved*, As the opinion of this committee, that a committee be appointed to prepare a draft of an application of the Legislature of this State to Congress, requesting them as early as possible, to call a Convention for proposing amendments to the Constitution of the United States."

And that he was directed by the said committee to move for leave to sit again.

Mr. Low read the report in his place, and delivered the same in at the table, where it was again read and agreed to by the House.

Thereupon, *resolved*, That Mr. Jones, Mr. Harison, Mr. B. Livingston, Mr. Havens and Mr. Bay, be a committee to prepare a draft of an application of the Legislature of this State to Congress, requesting them as early as possible, to call a Convention for proposing amendments to the Constitution of the United States.[1]

Ordered, That the said committee of the whole House have leave to sit again.

The Senate, P.M.

A message from the Hon. the Assembly by Mr. Younglove and Mr. Duncan, was received with a bill for concurrence entitled, *An act for carrying into effect on the part of this State, the Constitution of the United States, assented to and ratified by the Convention of this State on the twenty-sixth day of July last*, which was read the first time, and ordered a second reading.

1. For the committee's report, see Assembly Proceedings, 29 January 1789, below.

Assembly and Senate Proceedings, Tuesday, A.M., 23 December

The Senate

The bill entitled, . . . *An act for carrying into effect on the part of this State, the Constitution of the United States assented to and ratified by the Convention of this State, on the twenty-sixth day of July last*; [was] read a second time and committed to a committee of the whole.

The Assembly

The engrossed address to His Excellency the Governor, in answer to his speech at the opening of the session, was read, and is in the words following, viz.

To His Excellency GEORGE CLINTON, Esquire, Governor of the State of New-York, General and Commander in Chief of all the Militia, and Admiral of the Navy of the same.

The Respectful Address of the Assembly, in answer to His Excellency's Speech.

WE, the Representatives of the People of the State of New-York, in Assembly convened, are deeply impressed with the importance of the change which is soon to take place in the General Government, in consequence of the Constitution, ratified by the Convention of this State, lately held at Poughkeepsie; and we are fully convinced, that the necessity of adopting measures, in conformity to the ordinance of Congress, for putting that Constitution into operation, rendered it peculiarly requisite that the Legislature should be assembled at a seasonable and early period:

United with your Excellency and the late Convention of this State, in the sentiment "that no government can operate well unless it possesses the confidence and good will of the People;"[1] and impressed with the highest respect for the opinion of a large proportion of our constitutents, as well as for the unanimous sense of the Convention, expressed in their circular letter, we shall pursue, with an ardor and perseverance adequate to the importance of the object, every measure which will tend to induce a speedy revision of the general system of government, by a new Convention. And we are convinced, that such a revision only, can allay the apprehensions excited by those parts of that system which are considered as exceptionable. . . .[2]

Assembly-Chamber, December 23d, 1788.

Ordered, That Mr. *Speaker* subscribe the said address on behalf of the House.

Ordered, That the said address be presented to His Excellency by the whole House.

Ordered, That Mr. Tearse and Mr. Savage wait on His Excellency the Governor, and request to be informed when he will be pleased to be attended by this House, with their respectful address. . . .

Mr. Tearse reported that pursuant to the order of the House, Mr. Savage and himself had waited on His Excellency the Governor, to know when he would be pleased to be attended by this House with their respectful address, and that His Excellency had been pleased to appoint to-morrow, at twelve of the clock, for that purpose.

Mr. Patterson, from the committee of the whole House, on the bill entitled *An act respecting the appointment of Senators to represent this State in the Senate of the United States of America*, reported, that after the said bill had been read in the committee, Mr. G. Livingston made a motion, that the bill should be rejected.[3] That the question having been put on the said motion, it was carried in the affirmative.—That it was thereupon resolved as the opinion of the committee, that the said bill should be rejected; which he was directed to report to the House.

Mr. Patterson read the report in his place, and delivered the same in at the table, where it was again read, and agreed to by the House. Thereupon,

Resolved, That the said bill be rejected.

1. Circular Letter of the New York Convention (see DHFFE, I, 44–45).

2. The remainder of the Assembly's address discussed recent dealings with the state's Indian tribes, the congressional requisition for funds for the current year, and several state matters.

3. The *Daily Advertiser*, 30 December 1788, after noting that Livingston had moved to reject the bill, reported that "Mr. Jones, after expressing his disapprobation of the bill, seconded the motion."

Assembly and Senate Proceedings, Wednesday, A.M., 24 December

The Assembly

Mr. Speaker then left the chair, and with the House attended his Excellency the Governor, with their Respectful Address, according to his appointment, and being returned, he reassumed the chair, and reported that the House had attended his Excellency the Governor with their address, and that his Excellency had been pleased to return an answer thereto, and to deliver him a copy of the answer, which was read, and is in the words following, viz.

Gentlemen,

Permit me to tender you my warmest acknowlegments for this polite and obliging address, and to assure you I derive the highest satisfaction from the sentiments which you are pleased to express on the different subjects submitted to your consideration.

GEO. CLINTON.

Albany, 24th, December 1788.

Ordered, That the Respectful Address of this House to his Excellency the Governor, and his Excellency's answer be forthwith printed.[1]

The Senate

Mr. Yates from the committee appointed for the purpose, reported, the draft of an answer to His Excellency's speech, which he read in his place, and delivered the same in at the table, where it was again read, and thereupon, the Senate proceeded to consider the same by paragraphs, when the five first paragraphs were read in the words following, viz. "Sir, When we reflect on the embarrassments of our National Government, destitute of support or energy, exposed to insult from abroad, and submitting to it within our acknowledged limits, languishing under a disadvantageous foreign commerce, and totally deprived of a fur trade, formerly so valuable, we cannot but contemplate the approaching change, as a great and most desireable blessing.

Under such an impression, we must think your Excellency fully justified in the exercise of your prerogative, in convening the Legislature at an earlier day, than that prescribed by law, for the usual annual meeting.

If, in your Excellency's opinion, the public business had admitted thereof, we trust, you would have called us together at an earlier period, as we consider the appointment of electors, to supply the high confidential trust of President and Vice-President of the

United States, the manner of which is not expressly defined, but left to the direction of the respective Legislatures, to be of such magnitude, that if sufficient time had intervened for a general election, we should on our part, have referred it to the suffrages of the People at large, with the utmost satisfaction.

We receive with pleasure your Excellency's communications, of the proceedings of the State Convention, and consider their ratification of the Fœderal Constitution, as a happy means of cementing the Union, and of relieving the United States from the many evils they experienced, from the weakness and defects of their former confederation.

Convinced Sir, of the truth of the observation, "That no government, however constructed, can operate well, unless it possesses the confidence and good will of the great body of the People,"[2] we cannot but contemplate the adoption of the present system, by so large a majority of the States, with the utmost satisfaction, as it affords a happy presage, that it will experience that "Confidence and good will" but since it is susceptible of salutary improvement, and as it is our inclination as well as duty, to pursue every constitutional measure, to ensure to the government, the greatest possible degree of such "confidence and good will" and as respect for the late Convention, is an additional motive, we shall without hesitation, recommend a submission of the system, to a general Convention."

Mr. Yates, thereupon moved, that the same be expunged, and the following substituted in its stead, viz. Sir, We the Senate in Legislature convened, return your Excellency our cordial thanks for your speech.

The important and interesting subject, which it became your duty to submit to the consideration of the Legislature, rendered it necessary to convene them at this time, and we chearfully acquiesce in the measure.

The Constitution for the government of the United States, being ratified by the Convention of this State, it shall be our first business to make the necessary arrangements for carrying it into effect, while at the same time, we cannot refrain expressing our perfect concurrence with the sentiments contained in their circular letter, and your Excellency's speech, respecting the amendments proposed.

We are sensible that a revision of the system, by a Convention of the States, will be necessary, not only to correct its defects, and recommend it to the approbation and support of a numerous body of our constituents, but to allay the apprehensions which the exceptionable parts of it have so justly and generally occasioned, and under these impressions, and a conviction of the truth founded on the experience of ages, "that no government can operate well, unless it possesses the confidence and good will of the great body of the People," your Excellency may rest assured, that our best endeavors will be used, to bring about an early revision of the system, a measure so earnestly recommended by the Convention, and anxiously desired by our constituents.

Debates arose upon the said proposed amendment, and Mr. President having put the question thereon, it passed in the negative, in manner following, viz.

FOR THE NEGATIVE.

Mr. Philip Schuyler,	Mr. Vanderbilt,
Mr. Douw,	Mr. Morris,
Mr. Micheau,	Mr. Roosevelt,
Mr. Peter Schuyler,	Mr. L'Hommedieu,
Mr. Fonda,	Mr. Duane.

FOR THE AFFIRMATIVE.

Mr. Yates,	Mr. Swartwout,
Mr. Hopkins,	Mr. Townsend,
Mr. Williams,	Mr. Tredwell,
Mr. Van Ness,	Mr. Humfrey.

Mr. Tredwell then moved to expunge the third paragraph, which was again read, viz. "If, in your Excellency's opinion, the public business could have admitted thereof, we trust, you would have called us together at an earlier period, as we consider the appointment of Electors to supply the high confidential trust of President and Vice-President of the United States, the manner of which is not expressly defined, but left to the discretion of the respective Legislatures, to be of such magnitude, that if sufficient time had intervened for a general election, we should on our part have referred it to the suffrages of the People at large, with the utmost satisfaction."

Debates arose on the said motion, and Mr. President having put the question thereon, it passed in the negative, in manner following, viz.

FOR THE NEGATIVE.

Mr. Philip Schuyler,	Mr. Morris,
Mr. Douw,	Mr. Roosevelt,
Mr. Micheau,	Mr. Townsend,
Mr. Peter Schuyler,	Mr. L'Hommedieu,
Mr. Vanderbilt,	Mr. Duane,
Mr. Hopkins,	Mr. Hoffman.

FOR THE AFFIRMATIVE.

Mr. Yates,	Mr. Swartwout,
Mr. Williams,	Mr. Tredwell,
Mr. Van Ness,	Mr. Humfrey.

Mr. Tredwell, then moved to expunge the fourth paragraph which was again read, viz.

"We received with pleasure your Excellency's communications of the proceedings of the State Convention, and consider their ratification of the Fœderal Constitution as the happy means of cementing the Union, and of relieving the United States from the many evils they experienced from the weakness and defects of their former confederation;" and to substitute the following in its stead, viz. "We learn with pleasure from your Excellency's communications of the proceedings of the State Convention, that their ratification of the Fœderal Constitution was not unconditional and without reserve, and we cannot but hope that their mode of ratification, and their circular letter, may be the happy means of bringing about the amendments proposed, and thereby of compleating and cementing the Union of these States, and of relieving the minds of a great part of the community from the anxious apprehensions of evils from the undefined powers of the new Government, much greater than they have ever experienced, or can be apprehended from the weakness and defects of the old one." Debates arose upon the said proposed amendment, and Mr. President having put the question thereon, it passed in the negative in manner following, viz.

FOR THE NEGATIVE.

Mr. Philip Schuyler,	Mr. Micheau,
Mr. Douw,	Mr. Peter Schuyler,

Mr. Fonda,	Mr. L'Hommedieu,
Mr. Vanderbilt,	Mr. Duane,
Mr. Morris,	Mr. Hoffman.
Mr. Roosevelt,	

FOR THE AFFIRMATIVE.

Mr. Yates,	Mr. Swartwout,
Mr. Hopkins,	Mr. Townsend,
Mr. Williams,	Mr. Tredwell,
Mr. Van Ness,	Mr. Humfrey.

Mr. Tredwell, then moved to expunge the fifth paragraph, which was again read in the words following, viz. "Convinced Sir of the truth of the observation, "that no Government however constructed, can operate well, unless it possesses the confidence and good will of the great body of the People," we cannot but contemplate the adoption of the present system by so large a majority of the States, with the utmost satisfaction, as it affords a happy presage that it will experience "that confidence and good will," but since it is susceptible of salutary improvement, and as it is our inclination as well as duty to pursue every constitutional measure to ensure to the Government the greatest possible degree of such "confidence and good will," and as respect for the late Convention is an additional motive, we shall without hesitation recommend a submission of the system to a general Convention," and to substitute the following in its stead, viz. "Convinced Sir of the truth of the observation, "that no Government however constructed can operate well, unless it possesses the confidence and good will of the body of the People," and considering the adoption of the present system by so large a proportion of the States with such earnest recommendations of amendments, and the total rejection of it by two, until amendments take place, as a demonstration, that it cannot experience that "confidence and good will" unless it undergoes many essential alterations and improvements; and esteeming ourselves bound to promote a measure so earnestly recommended by the Convention, and so anxiously desired by our constituents, your Excellency may rest assured, that we shall use our utmost endeavors to bring about an early revision of the system." Debates arose upon the said proposed amendment, and Mr. President having put the question thereon, it passed in the negative in manner following, viz.

FOR THE NEGATIVE.

Mr. Philip Schuyler,	Mr. Morris,
Mr. Douw,	Mr. Roosevelt,
Mr. Micheau,	Mr. L'Hommedieu,
Mr. Peter Schuyler,	Mr. Duane,
Mr. Fonda,	Mr. Hoffman.
Mr. Vanderbilt,	

FOR THE AFFIRMATIVE.

Mr. Yates,	Mr. Swartwout,
Mr. Hopkins,	Mr. Townsend,
Mr. Williams,	Mr. Tredwell,
Mr. Van Ness,	Mr. Humfrey.

The four last paragraphs being then read, Mr. President put the question? Whether the Senate do agree to the said report, and it was carried in the affirmative in manner following, viz.

FOR THE AFFIRMATIVE.

Mr. Philip Schuyler,	Mr. Morris,
Mr. Douw,	Mr. Roosevelt,
Mr. Micheau,	Mr. L'Hommedieu,
Mr. Peter Schuyler,	Mr. Duane,
Mr. Fonda,	Mr. Hoffman.
Mr. Vanderbilt,	

FOR THE NEGATIVE.

Mr. Yates,	Mr. Swartwout,
Mr. Hopkins,	Mr. Townsends,
Mr. Williams,	Mr. Tredwell,
Mr. Van Ness,	Mr. Humfrey.

Thereupon, *Ordered*, That the said draft be engrossed.

1. The Assembly's address and Governor Clinton's reply were widely printed in New York newspapers, beginning with the *Daily Advertiser*, 31 December 1788.
2. Circular Letter of the New York Convention (see DHFFE, I, 44–45).

Massachusetts Centinel (Boston), 24 December

In New-York, we hear, a compromise between the parties is agreed upon, in the election of Senators—Gen. SCHUYLER to be elected from the Federalists—and Mr. YATES, or LANSING,[1] from the *formerly* opposers to the Constitution.[2]

1. Probably John Lansing, Jr.
2. This false report was reprinted in at least nine New England newspapers. In early January 1789 five of the same newspapers reported that Philip Schuyler and Robert Yates had been elected Senators. The Worcester *Massachusetts Spy*, 1 January, reported that Schuyler and Yates had been elected, but noted on 8 January that they had only been nominated by the state Senate—not elected. Another story originated in the *Massachusetts Centinel*, 3 January (with a New York dateline of 23 December 1788): "The utmost harmony prevails in our Legislature, and has shewn itself in a liberal compromise in the choice of Senators." No printings of these false reports have been located in New York newspapers (for circulation of similar news in New York newspapers, see Assembly and Senate Proceedings, 20 December 1788, n. 1, above). This expectation of a compromise between Federalists and Antifederalists in the election of Senators had been voiced earlier when James Madison wrote Thomas Jefferson: "As one branch of the Legislature of N. York is attached to the Constitution, it is not improbable that one of the Senators from that State also will be added to the majority" (Philadelphia, 8 December 1788, RC, Madison Papers, DLC). See also Alexander Hamilton to James Madison, 23 November 1788, Part One.

The Baltimore *Maryland Journal*, 16 January 1789, reported that the Assembly had rejected the Senate's nomination of Schuyler and Yates; this report was repeated in the Edenton *State Gazette of North Carolina*, 5 February.

Comte de Moustier Journal, 25 December[1]

The Legislature of New York now assembled at Albany is divided by two parties of Federalists and Antifederalists. The latter having managed to appoint delegates from their party to the present Congress, the Senate, the majority of which is attached to the new Constitution, proposes that each house on its own choose one Senator to the new Congress. In the case where the two houses are not able to agree on an election, the Constitution of New York prescribes that it be done by *joint ballots*, that is to say the Senate and the Assembly would ballot together, but the Assembly being much larger, the Senate knows that they would dominate.

1. MS (translated from French), Extraits du Journal de M. de Moustier, in Extraits des papiers de la Légation de France aux Etats-Unis, I, Part II (Cahier 3), 41–42, Benjamin Franklin Collection, CtY. Moustier served as France's minister plenipotentiary to the United States from 1787 to 1789.

D. Van Schaack to Theodore Sedgwick, 25 December (excerpt)[1]

We are anxious to hear the event of the political Struggles in your State. I hope the choice of Federal Representatives will bear a federal complexion, & earnestly wish your name May grace the list—Our Legislature are now engaged in Nominating Senators. The Senate have Nominated Messrs. Schuyler & Yates the assembly, Lansing & the Governors Brother.[2] What the event will be is uncertain—our federal Representatives will be chose by Districts—When you return from Boston I would wish to hear from you as I want to put a number of my affairs into your hands—I wish you an agreeable Jaunt.

1. RC, Sedgwick Papers, MHi. Sedgwick was elected to the House of Representatives from the Hampshire-Berkshire District of Massachusetts; for a biographical sketch, see DHFFE, I, 757.
2. Neither the Assembly nor Senate had formally nominated Senators. Philip Schuyler and Robert Yates were frequently mentioned as candidates; the other references are probably to John Lansing, Jr., and James Clinton. Robert Yates (1738–1801), a justice of the state supreme court, 1777–1798 (Chief Justice, 1790–1798), was an active patriot during the Revolution; a member of the provincial congresses, 1775–1777; a delegate to the Constitutional Convention in 1787; and an Albany County member of the state Convention in 1788, where he voted against ratification of the Constitution. James Clinton (1736–1812) was a brigadier general in the Continental Army during the Revolution; in 1788 he represented Ulster County in the state Convention, where he voted against ratification of the Constitution. He represented Ulster and then Orange County in the Assembly, 1788 and 1800–1801, and the Middle District in the Senate, 1788–1792.

Senate Proceedings, Friday, A.M., 26 December

The engrossed answer to His Excellency's speech was read and agreed to.

Ordered, That the same be signed by Mr. President, in behalf of the Senate.

Ordered, That Mr. Swartwout and Mr. Morris, wait on His Excellency the Governor, to know when and where, he will be pleased to receive the Senate with their answer to his Speech.

The Answer of the Senate to His Excellency's Speech is in the words following, viz.

The Answer of the Senate of the State of New-York, to the Speech of His Excellency *George Clinton*, Esq. Governor of the said State, General and Commander in Chief of all the Militia, and Admiral of the Navy of the same.

SIR,

WHEN we reflect on the embarrassments of our National Government, destitute of support or energy, exposed to insult from abroad, and submitting to it within our acknowledged limits, languishing under a disadvantageous foreign commerce, and totally deprived of a furr trade formerly so valuable, we cannot but contemplate the approaching change, as a great and most desireable blessing.

Under such an impression, we must think your Excellency fully justified in the exercise of your prerogative, in convening the Legislature at an earlier day, than that prescribed by law, for the usual annual meeting.

If, in your Excellency's opinion, the public business had admitted thereof, we trust, you would have called us together at an earlier period, as we consider the appointment of electors, to supply the high confidential trust of President and Vice-President of the United States, the manner of which is not expressly defined, but left to the discretion of the respective Legislatures, to be of such magnitude, that if sufficient time had intervened for a general election, we should on our part, have referred it to the suffrages of the People at large, with the utmost satisfaction.

We receive with pleasure your Excellency's communications, of the proceedings of the State Convention, and consider their ratification of the Fœderal Constitution, as a happy means of cementing the Union, and of relieving the United States from the many evils they experienced, from the weakness and defects of their former confederation.

Convinced Sir, of the truth of the observation, "That no government, however constructed, can operate well, unless it possesses the confidence and good will of the great body of the People,"[1] we cannot but contemplate the adoption of the present system, by so large a majority of the States, with the utmost satisfaction, as it affords a happy presage, that it will experience that "confidence and good will," but since it is susceptible of salutary improvement, and as it is our inclination as well as duty, to pursue every constitutional measure, to ensure to the government, the greatest possible degree of such "confidence and good will," and as respect for the late Convention is an additional motive, we shall without hesitation, recommend a submission of the system, to a general Convention. . . .[2]

By order of the Senate,
PIERRE VAN CORTLANDT, PRESIDENT.

Senate-Chamber, December 26th, 1788.

Mr. Swartwout reported, that Mr. Morris and himself had, agreeable to the order of the Senate, waited on His Excellency the Governor, when he was pleased to appoint one of the clock this day, at his chamber, to receive the Senate, with their answer to his Speech. . . .

Mr. President then left the chair, and with the members of the Senate, waited on His Excellency the Governor, with their answer to his speech, and being returned, he reassumed the chair, and informed the Senate, that upon his delivering their answer, His Excellency was pleased to make a reply, of which he had obtained a copy, which was read in the words following, viz.

Gentlemen,

ON this occasion it would be improper to make any animadversions, either, on the cause which induced to a change of our present system of Fœderal Government, on the merits of the new Constitution; or on the consequences, which may result from its adoption. Nor is it my province to determine how far the ideas contained in your answer will tend to facilitate the attainment of the objects so earnestly recommended by our Convention.—It is sufficient to observe that, in submitting their proceedings to the Legislature, I have discharged my duty by faithfully communicating the sentiments and wishes of the Convention, which, it is to be presumed, are consonant to the will of our Constituents.

Gentlemen,

I regret that the Legislature could not have been convened at so early a period as to have afforded time to have made and carried into effect the arrangements necessary for appointing electors, in the manner which it seems you would have preferred; but, since this was impracticable, you will, I am persuaded, perceive the propriety of pursuing your principle, as far as circumstances will permit, and of adopting such mode of appointment, as shall appear most nearly to approach an election by the People.

Permit me to assure you, that your expressions of regard for the rights of the People, and of zeal for the public welfare, are highly pleasing to me, and that nothing will give me greater satisfaction than to find this laudable spirit manifested in all your conduct.

GEO. CLINTON.

Albany, 26th December, 1788.[3]

1. Circular Letter of the New York Convention (see DHFFE, I, 44–45).

2. The remainder of the Senate's address discussed recent dealings with the state's Indian tribes, the congressional requisition for funds for the current year, and several state matters.

3. A draft of Governor Clinton's reply is in the George Clinton Papers, NHi. The Senate's address and Governor Clinton's reply were widely printed in New York newspapers, beginning with the *Daily Advertiser* and *Daily Gazette* on 2 January 1789.

Also on 26 December 1788, Governor Clinton forwarded to the Senate copies of the second convention resolutions approved by the Virginia legislature on 20 November (which were a response, in part, to the Circular Letter of the New York Convention, 26 July). The governor forwarded the Virginia resolutions to the Senate "with the greater pleasure, from the persuasion, that it will give you satisfaction to find a State, so respectable for wisdom and patriotism, perfectly concurring in sentiment with our Convention respecting the necessity of amendments to the new system of General Government, and the means of obtaining them." The Virginia resolutions, which called on Congress to immediately convene a constitutional convention to amend the Constitution, were read and committed to the committee of the whole, as was Governor Clinton's reply to the Senate's address. The Assembly received the Virginia documents from the Senate on 27 December; they were read and referred to the committee appointed to draft an application to Congress for a second convention. For the text of the Virginia Second Convention Resolutions, see DHFFE, II, 273–79.

Senate Proceedings, Saturday, A.M., 27 December

Mr. Morris, from the committee of the whole, to whom was referred the bill entitled *An act for carrying into effect on the part of this State, the Constitution of the United States, assented to and ratified by the Convention of this State, on the twenty-sixth day of July last,* reported, that the committee had made some further progress in the bill, and directed him to move for leave to sit again.

Ordered, That the committee have leave to sit again.

Robert R. Livingston to St. John de Crèvecoeur, Clermont, 27 December (excerpt)[1]

I shd be very fearful that your predictions with respect to [our] legislature would be verified if I did not hope [that] the Senate will be able to be prevent [any?] positive mischief[.] Negative evils will undoubtedly [flow?] from the disagreeme[nt?] of the two houses[. We shall] probably appoint no electors this [undoubtedly?] will be of little moment except so far as it will deprive us of the means of uniting our suffrage to that of the rest of America, our withholding it will make no alteration in the general arrangment—Shd. we also be without Senators which I think highly probable temporary evils may result from it to the state [but?] none I hope to the union—The Govr. has as you observe been long [sowered?]—He finds himself [lessened?] in the esteem of the publick & tho' (which I think very probable) the strength of the antifederal party & the want of concert in the opposition may serve to continue him in office yet office with all its emoluments loses many of its charms when it is not attended with the respect & favor of the people—[2]

1. FC?, Robert R. Livingston Collection, NHi. The manuscript is mutilated. Some of the conjectural material (in brackets) is taken from an edited version of the letter which appeared in the Elizabethtown *New Jersey Journal*, 21 January 1789, as "Extract of a letter from Albany, dated December 27, 1787." The year should have been "1788"; the author and recipient of the letter were not identified by the newspaper. The edited letter, with the correct date, was reprinted in the Philadelphia *Federal Gazette*, 23 January 1789; Boston *Massachusetts Centinel*, 28 January; *Federal Herald*, 2 February; and Pittsfield *Berkshire Chronicle*, 6 February. Portions of the letter were also printed in the Boston *Independent Chronicle*, 15 January, and Worcester *Massachusetts Spy*, 22 January.

Livingston (1746–1813) represented Dutchess County in the provincial congresses, 1775–1777; served in Congress, 1775–1776, 1779–1780, and 1784–1785; was chancellor of New York State, 1777–1801; was Secretary for Foreign Affairs, 1781–1783; and served as minister to France, 1801–1804. In 1788, as a delegate from New York City and County, he voted to ratify the Constitution in the state Convention. Michel-Guillaume Jean de Crèvecoeur (1735–1813) was born in France and served in the French army in Canada during the French and Indian War. He came to New York in 1759, traveled widely, and then became a citizen in 1765 and settled on a farm in Orange County. Because of his opposition to certain aspects of the American Revolution, he went to France in 1780. He published *Letters from an American Farmer* in 1782 and returned in 1783 to New York, where he served as French consul until his final return to France in 1790.

2. A different opinion of Clinton was expressed by Samuel Otis on 20 January 1789: "The assembly of this State will I am apprehensive give all possible opposition to the new Goverment. You know the character of Mr Clinton & his influence rather seems to encrease—" (to Paine Wingate, New York, RC, Gratz Collection, PHi).

Abraham Bancker to Evert Bancker, Albany, 28 December (excerpt)[1]

Albany is become a gay Place. Public Diversions and Amusements are here to be met with as in New York. Families strive to outdo each other in Dress, Splendor and Gaiety. I have had great Attention paid me by Genl. Schuyler & Ten Broeck & Gansevoort[2] & by the Patrune.[3] The federal Gentlemen have many Invitations to their Houses and are entertained by them, in a truly Sumptuous & princely Manner.

Business goes on gradually. The Bill for Organizing the New Government has pass'd our House notwithstanding it was opposed in it's several Stages; it has now gone up to the Senate, where I am told, it is not well regarded, by reason that no federal Traits are to be discovered in it's Features or Complexion[.] I have to write to several, must on that account close this Letter without proceeding to enlarge it's Contents—

1. RC, Bancker Family Papers, NHi. The letter was addressed to Evert Bancker in New York City.

2. Philip Schuyler, Abraham Ten Broeck, and Leonard Gansevoort. Gansevoort (1751–1810) represented Albany City and County in the provincial congresses, 1775–1777, and in the Assembly, 1778–1779 and 1788. He also represented the Western District, 1791–1793 and 1798–1799, and the Eastern District, 1796–1798 and 1800–1802, in the state Senate; served in Congress, 1788; was an Albany County judge, 1794–1797; and was a judge of the Court of Probates, 1799–1810.

3. Stephen Van Rensselaer (1764–1839), who inherited a vast family estate in present-day Albany and Rensselaer counties in 1769 and the honorary title "patroon" that accompanied it. He represented Albany City and County in the Assembly, 1789–1790 and 1808–1810, and the Western District in the state Senate, 1791–1795. Van Rensselaer was lieutenant governor, 1795–1801, and a member of the House of Representatives, 1822–1829. He was active in many agricultural, educational, and economic enterprises, and was married to Margaret Schuyler, daughter of Philip Schuyler.

Melancton Smith to John Smith, New York, 28 December[1]

I have seen in the Debates published in Childs paper, that the great question, which it was forseen would be agitated, has come on, viz. whether the Senators should be chosen by joint ballot of both houses, or whether the one house should have a negative on the other.[2]

I consider this question as of very great importance, as it affects the operation of the new government—In the investigation of the system, it appeared evidently to many of us, that it was calculated to vest very great and extensive powers in few hands, for long periods and with a small degree of responsibility—This objection applies with peculiar force against the Constitution of the Senate—They will possess powers in extent and degree not known in a single branch of a Legislature, in any free government, that I recollect—They are in the first instance not elected by ye People, but by their representatives—the period of their service is for six years, and during this term they are not removable or amenable—unless for crimes—These considerations had such weight with the convention that in the amendments proposed, a number of checks are recommended to be placed upon the Senate—I am of opinion that however prudently the respective Legislatures may use their power of choosing Senators, there will be great danger of an Aristocracy or a government substantially the same, being established by means of this Body—But if the mode of election be so established, as to give the Senate a negative in the choice of Senators, It is evident the danger will be greatly increased—I do not remember that an Idea of this kind was ever suggested in our Convention, I can truly say it never entered my mind. If it had, it would more strongly confirmed me in my opposition to this part of the system. For if this mode is adopted, it will be in the power of from seven to 13 Members always to prevent an election against the sence of every other member of the Legislature. We ought to lay it to our account, that we shall always have a considerable number of high minded Gentlemen in the Senate who will use all their influence and address to place in the Senate of the U.S. men of their own views & feelings, and the exercise of a power like this will render the office of a Senator in our Legislature much more an object of ambition than it now is: A few men will by this means have it in their power to raise men to this place in the government, that will suit their purposes, or to prevent any election at all—This last consideration, is in itself sufficient in my mind to determine that the one house ought not to exercise a negative on the other—For it appears to me an absurdity to suppose that a constitution should make such a provision for the choice of a Legislature as in its operation may destroy the body—this may be the effect of the mode contended for—If the two houses disagree, who is to decide? It cannot be done, but by one or the other giving up their choice—If both adhere to their opinion, no choice can be made—As to the mode proposed by Mr. Harrison,[3] It appears to me absurd at first blush—It contradicts his own principles. Surely the choice of one house is not the choice of the Legislature. I know of no argument in any degree plausible, that can be urged against the election in the manner that Delegates have heretofore been chosen as directed by our Constitution, but this that the new Constitution says, the choice shall be by the Legislature—This appears to me, a mere play upon words, in order to make the Constitution say, what I am convinced it never intended. I would ask, who chose Delegates under the Confederation? did not the Legislature? I presume every man would answer yes—It is a mere circumstance, whether they are chosen by the houses in their seperate capacity's, or by joint ballot, and I think our own Constitution determines that Circumstance—The reason of the thing is altogether in favour of the mode hitherto pursued—When the very existence of a government depends upon the exercise of a power, common sense dictates it should be so directed as to be practicable in its execution

I beg your pardon for trespassing so long on your patience with this hasty scrawl—I have put my thoughts down just as they occurred. If I had time I would copy this, and make it more perfect—I mean only to suggest hints—It is a strong circumstance in favor of joint ballotting, that not only Virginia, but Maryland, (whose Legislature are said to be federal), adopted this mode, and in Maryland the proposal originated with ye Senate.

If you once pass a Law, giving the Senate a negative, it is not probable it will ever be altered. It is urged, I know, that if you adhere to your system, no Senators will be chosen. If they are not, let the blame be laid where it ought—alluding to my present Ideas, I would never recede from the plan marked out in the Constitution, were I sure no Senator would not be chosen for a Century. I beg the favour of you to write me as often as you can, and let me know the state of politics. make my best respects to Mr. Havens,[4] and all friends as though named—Havens loves to write, and upon condition he will write to me, he shall be entitled to half this Letter the remaining half, will I presume be as much as you would wish—The Letter should have been a better one, if I had time but it has been written in Company; and as the subject of it lies near my heart, I mean to send it by Post, promising you however, I shall do so no more, without first paying the Postage. I would have done it now but the office is upon the point of closing & ye night is so stormy I cannot attend.

1. RC, John Smith of Mastic Papers, NHi.

2. See Assembly Debates, 17 December 1788, above. The debates were printed in the *Daily Advertiser*, 26 and 27 December.

3. For Richard Harison's speech in the Assembly, see Assembly Debates, 17 December 1788, above. Harison (c. 1747–1829), a leading New York City lawyer, represented New York City and County in the Assembly, 1788–1789, and in the state Convention in 1788, where he voted to ratify the Constitution. He was also a trustee of Columbia College, 1788–1829; United States district attorney for New York, 1789–1801; and recorder of New York City, 1798–1801.

4. Jonathan N. Havens (1757–1799) represented Suffolk County in the Assembly, 1786–1795, and also served in the House of Representatives, 1795–1799. As a Suffolk delegate to the state Convention in 1788, he voted to ratify the Constitution (although he was an Antifederalist).

Senate Proceedings, Monday, P.M., 29 December

Mr. Morris, from the committee of the whole, to whom was referred the bill entitled *An act for carrying into effect on the part of this State, the Constitution of the United States, assented to and ratified by the Convention of this State, on the twenty-sixth day of July last,* reported, that the committee had made some further progress in the bill, and directed him to move for leave to sit again.

Ordered, That the committee have leave to sit again.

Senate Proceedings, Tuesday, A.M., 30 December

Mr. Morris, from the committee of the whole, to whom was referred, the bill entitled, *An act for carrying into effect on the part of this State, the Constitution of the United States, assented to and ratified by the Convention of this State, on the twenty-sixth day of July last,* reported, that the committee had made some further progress in the bill, and directed him to move for leave to sit again.

Ordered, That the committee have leave to sit again.

Senate Proceedings, Wednesday, A.M., 31 December

Mr. Morris, from the committee of the whole to whom was referred, the bill entitled, *An act for carrying into effect on the part of this State, the Constitution of the United States, assented to and ratified by the Convention of this State, on the twenty-sixth day of July last,* reported, that upon reading the first enacting clause of the bill, which is in the following, viz. "Be it enacted by the People of the State of New-York, represented in Senate and Assembly, and it is hereby enacted by the authority of the same, That the Senators to be chosen in this State for the United States shall be chosen as follows, that is to say, the Senate and Assembly of this State, shall each openly nominate as many persons as shall be equal to the whole number of Senators to be chosen by this State, after which nomination the Senate and Assembly shall meet together, and compare the lists of persons by them respectively nominated, and those persons named in both lists shall be Senators for the United States, and out of those persons whose names are not in both lists one half shall be chosen by the joint ballot of the Senators and Members of the Assembly, so met together as aforesaid, and the copies of the resolutions of the Senate and Assembly testifying the said choice shall be thereupon delivered to each of the persons so chosen Senators for the United States as aforesaid." Debates arose upon the said clause, and the question being put thereon, it passed in the negative, in manner following, viz.

FOR THE NEGATIVE.

Mr. Philip Schuyler,	Mr. Peter Schuyler,
Mr. Douw,	Mr. Fonda,
Mr. Micheau,	Mr. Vanderbilt,

Mr. Roosevelt,	Mr. Duane,
Mr. L'Hommedieu,	Mr. Hoffman.

FOR THE AFFIRMATIVE.

Mr. Yates,	Mr. Townsend,
Mr. Hopkins,	Mr. Tredwell,
Mr. Williams,	Mr. Humfrey.
Mr. Swartwout,	

That thereupon Mr. Philip Schuyler, moved to substitute the following in its stead, viz. "Be it enacted by the People of the State of New-York, represented in Senate and Assembly and it is hereby enacted by the authority of the same, that the Senators to be chosen in this State, for the United States, shall be chosen as follows, that is to say, the Senate and Assembly of this State shall, if two Senators are to be appointed, openly nominate two persons, and shall respectively give notice each to the other of such nomination; that if both Houses agree in the nomination of the same person or persons, the person or persons so nominated and agreed to, shall be the Senator or Senators to represent this State in the Senate of the Congress of the United States; that if the nomination of either House does not agree in any of the persons nominated by the other, the Senate shall on the same day openly choose one of the persons nominated by the Assembly, and the Assembly shall on the same day openly choose one of the persons nominated by the Senate, and the two persons so chosen shall be the Senators to represent this State as aforesaid; that in every case when two Senators are to be chosen, and both Houses agree only as to one in such nomination as aforesaid, and in every case when only one Senator is to be chosen, either of the two Houses of the Legislature may propose to the other, a resolution for concurrence, naming therein a person to fill the office of Senator, and if the House receiving such resolution shall concur therein, the person so named in such resolution shall be the Senator, but if such resolution shall not be concurred in, either House may on that or any future day, proceed to offer to the other a resolution for concurrence from time to time until they shall agree upon a Senator. That whenever the choice of a Senator or Senators shall be made, the President of the Senate and Speaker of the Assembly shall certify the names of the person or persons so appointed Senator or Senators to the person administering the Government of this State for the time being, who shall thereupon exemplify such certificate under the great seal of this State, and deliver or cause the same to be delivered to the Senator so chosen, or when two are chosen, to one of them." Debates arose upon the said motion and the question being put thereon, it was carried in the affirmative, in manner following, viz.

FOR THE AFFIRMATIVE.

Mr. Philip Schuyler,	Mr. Vanderbilt,
Mr. Douw,	Mr. Roosevelt,
Mr. Micheau,	Mr. L'Hommedieu,
Mr. Peter Schuyler,	Mr. Duane,
Mr. Fonda,	Mr. Hoffman.

FOR THE NEGATIVE.

Mr. Yates,	Mr. Swartwout,
Mr. Hopkins,	Mr. Townsend,
Mr. Williams,	Mr. Tredwell,
Mr. Van Ness,	Mr. Humfrey.

That Mr. Philip Schuyler, then moved that the following preamble and clause be inserted in the bill, viz. "And whereas there is a necessity of a speedy appointment of Senators, to represent this State in the first Senate of the Congress of the United States. Therefore,

Be it further enacted by the authority aforesaid, That the Senate and Assembly of this State, shall by concurrent resolutions determine on a day certain for choosing such first Senators in the manner aforesaid, and that such day shall be within ten days next after the passing of this act, any thing contained in the preceding section of this act, to the contrary hereof notwithstanding." Debates arose upon the said motion, and the question being put thereon, it was carried in the affirmative, in manner following, viz.

FOR THE AFFIRMATIVE.

Mr. Philip Schuyler,	Mr. Vanderbilt,
Mr. Douw,	Mr. Roosevelt,
Mr. Micheau,	Mr. L'Hommedieu,
Mr. Peter Schuyler,	Mr. Duane,
Mr. Fonda,	Mr. Hoffman.

FOR THE NEGATIVE.

Mr. Yates,	Mr. Swartwout,
Mr. Hopkins,	Mr. Townsend,
Mr. Williams,	Mr. Tredwell,
Mr. Van Ness,	Mr. Humfrey.

That in proceeding to the second enacting clause of the bill for dividing the State into six election Districts, Mr. Philip Schuyler moved, that the towns of Poundridge and Bedford, in the county of Westchester, which by the bill, were annexed to the city and county of New-York, and with the southernmost part of Westchester, erected into a District, should be taken therefrom, and annexed to the county of Dutchess, which with the northernmost part of the said county of Westchester, were by the bill erected into another District. Debates arose, and the question being put on the said motion, it was carried in the affirmative, in manner following, viz.

FOR THE AFFIRMATIVE.

Mr. Philip Schuyler,	Mr. Roosevelt,
Mr. Micheau,	Mr. L'Hommedieu,
Mr. Peter Schuyler,	M. Duane,
Mr. Fonda,	Mr. Hoffman.
Mr. Vanderbilt,	

FOR THE NEGATIVE.

Mr. Yates,	Mr. Swartwout,
Mr. Hopkins,	Mr. Townsend,
Mr. Williams,	Mr. Tredwell,
Mr. Van Ness,	Mr. Humfrey.

That having proceeded through the several clauses of the bill and made several amendments, the last clause respecting the appointment of electors, was read, in the words following, viz. "And be it further enacted by the authority aforesaid, that until the Legislature shall make further provision in the premises, the electors to be appointed in this State, for choosing the President and Vice-President of the United States, shall be appointed in the manner following, that is to say, the Senate and Assembly shall, each openly nominate as many persons as shall be equal to the whole number of electors, to be appointed by this State, after which nomination, the Senate and Assembly shall meet together, and compare the lists of the persons by them respectively nominated, and those persons named in both lists, shall be electors, and out of those persons, whose names are not in both lists, one half shall be chosen by the joint ballot of the Senators and Members of Assembly, so met together as aforesaid, &c."

Mr. Philip Schuyler thereupon, moved that the same be expunged, and the following substituted in its stead, viz. "And whereas the time intervening between the present meeting of the Legislature, and the day on which, by the act of the United States, in Congress assembled, electors were to be appointed, for electing a President and Vice-President for the United States, is too short to refer the appointment of the electors, to the suffrages of the inhabitants of this State. Therefore,

"Be it enacted by the authority aforesaid, That until other Legislative provision can be made for such election, the electors who are to meet on the first Wednesday in February, one thousand seven hundred and eighty-nine, shall be appointed in manner following, that is to say, the Senate and Assembly of this State, shall on the first Wednesday in January, one thousand seven hundred and eighty-nine, respectively openly nominate eight persons, and shall respectively give notice, each to the other, of such nomination; that if both Houses agree in the nomination, of the same person or persons, the person or persons so nominated and agreed to, shall be an elector or electors; that if the nomination of either House does not agree, in any of the persons nominated by the other, the Senate shall on the same day openly choose four of the persons nominated by the Assembly, and the Assembly shall on the same day openly choose four of the persons nominated by the Senate, and the eight persons so chosen shall be the electors, for the purpose aforesaid; and in every case where one or more of the electors less than the whole number shall have been agreed upon by both Houses in manner aforesaid, either of the two Houses of the Legislature may propose to the other a resolution for concurrence, naming therein the person or persons, to fill the office of such deficient elector or electors, and if the House receiving such resolution, shall concur therein, the person or persons so named in such resolution shall be an elector or electors, for the purpose aforesaid, but if such resolution shall not be concurred in either House, shall on that day proceed to offer to the other, a resolution or resolutions, for concurrence, until they shall agree upon and have compleated the whole number of eight electors,["] &c. Debates arose upon the said proposed amendment, and the question being put thereon, it was carried in the affirmative, in manner following, viz.

FOR THE AFFIRMATIVE.

Mr. Philip Schuyler,	Mr. Vanderbilt,
Mr. Douw,	Mr. Roosevelt,
Mr. Micheau,	Mr. L'Hommedieu,
Mr. Peter Schuyler,	Mr. Duane,
Mr. Fonda,	Mr. Hoffman.

FOR THE NEGATIVE.

Mr. Yates,	Mr. Swartwout,
Mr. Hopkins,	Mr. Townsend,
Mr. Williams,	Mr. Tredwell,
Mr. Van Ness,	Mr. Humfrey.

Mr. Morris further reported, that the committee had gone through the bill, and agreed to the same, which report he read in his place, and delivered the bill with the amendments in at the table, where they were again read, and agreed to by the Senate. Thereupon,

Resolved, That the bill with the amendments do pass.

Ordered, That Mr. Townsend and Mr. Tredwell, deliver the bill with the amendments to the Honorable the Assembly, and inform them, that the Senate have passed the bill with the amendments therewith delivered.

Assembly Proceedings, Thursday, A.M., 1 January 1789

A message from the Honorable the Senate, delivered by Mr. Townsend and Mr. Tredwell, with the bill and amendments therein mentioned, was read, that the Senate have passed the bill entitled, *An act for carrying into effect on the part of this State, the Constitution of the United States, assented to and ratified by the Convention of this State, on the twenty-sixth day of July last*, with the amendments therewith delivered.

The bill and amendments were read and considered, and after some time spent thereon; ordered, that the further consideration thereof be postponed until to-morrow.

David Gelston to John Smith, New York, 1 January[1]

Your several favors of 14. 17–22 & 28 Ulto. I have had the pleasure to receive—& am very glad to find that you with so many others stand so firm on *strong Republican Ground* (you may or possibly a Critic might suppose by thus expressing myself that I apprehended danger from you or some other of being shaken off—I say it is not fair to draw any such conclusion from the premises—)—do you want any ones opinion respecting the line of conduct to be pursued by the Assembly in regard to the conduct of the Senate—if you wish mine—it is decide[d]ly this—send your Bills by one Member if you please—let the Senate refuse receiving it and be answerable for the consequences—Mr. Harrison says the Senate won't agree—the Senate won't receive &c &c[2]—pray Mr. Harrison what is all that to the purpose—what says the Constitution?—how shall Delegates be chosen? let the Senate Reject the Mode at their Peril & be answerable—most certainly you ought to be impeached if you give up one inch of Ground or Violate any part of the Constitution—in fact it appears to me you have nothing to do—not in the least possible degree—in any [of] your deliberations—so long as you keep the Constitution & keep on the good Ground—whether the Senate will agree to this that or the other—do your duty as you have done & Risque all consequences—I revere—I respect—& have the highest opinion for the Gentlemen who compose that Honble Body—but I cannot be induced to believe—that one of their Votes ought to be esteemed equal to three of the Assembly—will you—now have my opinion of Fœderal Ground—it is in few words—the People at large don't know how to govern nor take care of them selves and it would be much better for them & much easier & more happy for the whole—to have a few *Well Born sensible & Judicious* (they must be Men of great Estates) to Elect Choose & Legislate—

I wish a Representation in the New Government & now wish it may be carried into opperation. I really wish Mr. M. Sm—h[3] may be one of the Senate & I really wish the Rights of the People—the Rights & Priveleges of the Assembly as well as the Senate may be preserved & secured inviolate & perpetuated to the latest Posterity—I wish to say a great deal more to you. I cannot possibly spare time at Present—when & who will be your Senators?—Electors? when meet? who for Representatives? & when Chosen &c &c &c—give my Complts. to Mr. Havens with part of this Letter—it is not in my Power to write him—it is a very busy time with us just now—

I really forgot to return you my thanks for your congratulatory Compliments upon the late appointment Conferred on me[4]—almost the only comfortable consideration that remains in my mind on the occasion is that I expect very little will be done in the present Congress as the Duties of the Office of Lieut. Govr. may be compleatly attended to & discharged by —— as long as the Govr. lives—I have however feel a proper sense of the obligation I am under to my Countrymen for their good opinion of & the Honor confered on me—in whatever Character or Station I may act—I trust I shall never wantonly betray any Confidence reposed in me—I must however seriously tell you—it was what I did not think of till a few Hours before I recd. the information—in spite of my intentions I shall fill this sheet—I have not time to copy or correct—I am writing to a *Friend*—inaccuracies you must overlook—if any parts require secrecy your discretion will be sufficient to determine which & how much[.] write me often—when shall you finish the sessions?—I just now heard that Miss Betsey Smith Daughter of Daniel is thought to be in decline & past recovery—adieu

1. RC, John Smith of Mastic Papers, NHi.
2. For Richard Harison's speech in the Assembly, see Assembly Debates, 17 December 1788, above.
3. Melancton Smith.
4. On 16 December 1788 the legislature elected Gelston to the last Confederation Congress.

Melancton Smith to Gilbert Livingston, New York, 1 January[1]

All we hear of you is from the papers—We receive no more Letters than if there was not in ye City one person who did not beleive the new Constitution was of divine Original. Yet you may rest assured that a number of us retain the same sentiments respecting it we ever did, and that we are not a little interested in the issue of the business before you especially that which respects the choice of Senators—You know my sentiments on the Constitution has been, that it too strongly inclines to an Aristocracy, do the best with it you can without amendments. The scheme now on foot to give the Senate a negative, will add amazing force to this tendency—A few Men combining in the Senate may forever put their veto upon any choice, until it falls upon such men as would serve their purposes—This they would soon do, and by this means either embarrass the government beyond measure, or harrass the Assembly to comply with their wishes.—I trust the Assembly will never yield the point, be the consequences what they may—Better have no Senators for a Century to come than establish a principle, which when once granted never can be reclaimed. For if you once pass a Law or Resolution to grant the Senate the right, it will never be surrendered—It is unnecessary to urge reasons to support the sentiment—I concur substantially with those offered by the federal Republican in Greenleafs paper[2]—They might be much illustrated and enlarged. How stand our old Friends towards you. Is former confidence revived, and old grudges forgotten—For the sake of the cause I wish they may[3]—Union among ourselves is the corner Stone upon which our hopes of success in obtaining amendments must be built—The fair promises and pretensions of most of the leading men who were in favour of the new System are mere illusions—They intend to urge the execution of the plan in its present form—No reliance can be placed in any of them—We ought therefore to strive to maintain our union firm and immoveable as ye mountains, to pursue the object of amendments with unremitting ardour and diligence—Men may differ and will, but if they unite in the main point, they should agree to differ. Politics has consumed so much of my time and thoughts that I should be glad to lay them aside; but the establishing a good government for a great Country is an object of such moment I cannot give it up—It is a matter of too much magnitude. I view it as affecting the whole system of things to ages far remote. It may have a vast effect not only on the comfort and happiness of Men here, but may carry its influence upon the state & condition of that Kingdom which can never be moved. May we stand in our Lot in that Kingdom. Blessed be the King of it, all things are under his controul, and however great the ambition of frail mortals may be he will conduct every event to produce the best end. For even the wrath of Man shall praise him, and the remainder will he restrain—Make my best respects to DeWitt in particular, to Smith Havens and all friends as though named.

[P.S.] Tell all our friends to stand fast—

1. RC, Melancton Smith Papers, N. The letter was addressed to Livingston in Albany. Livingston (1742–1806), a Dutchess County lawyer, served in the provincial congresses, 1775–1777, and in the Assembly, 1777–1778 and 1788–1789. Although an Antifederalist, he voted to ratify the Constitution in the state Convention in 1788.

2. See "A Federal Republican," *New York Journal,* 1 January 1789, immediately below. For speculation that "A Federal Republican" is Melancton Smith, see "A Federal Republican," *New York Journal,* 27 November 1788, n. 1, Part One.

3. Smith and Livingston, along with ten other Antifederalists, had joined the Federalists at the state Convention in 1788 to pass the compromise ratification of the Constitution, which included ratification without previous amendments and a unanimous endorsement of the New York Circular Letter calling for a second convention.

A Federal Republican, New York Journal, 1 January[1]

The FEDERAL REPUBLICAN No. 3.

The manner in which the legislature shall exercise the power, with which they are vested by the new constitution of choosing senators, has become a matter of general conversation, and has occasioned very considerable debates in the assembly, and probably has or will create a dispute between the two houses.

As it is a question of very considerable moment, I beg to be indulged in making a few observations upon it.

There are three modes proposed; the first is, that the senators be chosen in the manner the delegates to Congress have been elected under the confederation; that is, that each house openly nominate, and in case they disagree that they then elect by ballot of the two houses assembled together.[2] The second mode is, that in case of disagreement in both the candidates, each house elect one by ballot, and if they agree in one but disagree in the other, the two houses determine the election by joint ballots.

The third mode is, to appoint them by law, in which each house reserves a negative upon the other.

With regard to these I shall enquire, 1st. Which of them ought to have the preference upon the true principles of government and the reason of the thing.

2. Which is most consonant to our own constitution.

3. Does the new constitution fix the one mode in preference to the other.

With respect to the first point—There is no principle better established in republican governments, than this; that all power in the rulers should be derived from the people for whose benefit all government is instituted—The power is delegated either by the people immediately, or mediately through the hands of those whom they appoint. In all free republics the legislature who exercises the supreme authority, should be elected by the people and responsible to them—and no government can be secured which does not in a great degree possess this quality. In the new constitution the people choose immediately the house of assembly, which is one branch of the legislature—The senate, the other part, are to be chosen immediately by the representatives of the people in their state legislatures—The reason upon which this article is founded appears to be this: the senate is to be composed of two senators from each state. It would be a thing extremely difficult, I may say utterly impracticable for all the people in a state to unite in choosing two men. It would be impossible for them to associate together for this purpose, and extremely inconvenient to consult with each other, and very improbable that a majority would ever unite in favor of any two men. To remedy this inconveniency which resulted from the nature of the thing, the business was committed to the legislature. But if the principle be applied, that a majority of the people ought to elect, it will follow, that when they transfer the right of election to their representatives, the power ought to be exercised by a majority. Each representative should be considered as having equal power in this business, and all of them together as possessing the whole of it; and, therefore, according to this plain principle that the greater should controul the lesser, the larger number ought to elect. Hence it appears, that the first mode is the proper one. But, again, this is the only consistent and practicable mode—Either of the others are either inconsistent, or may in their operation be found impracticable. With respect to the second, which proposes, that in case of disagreement each house shall choose one. It takes from the legislature the right of choosing entirely. For no one can suppose that by any construction, either the senate or assembly can be called the legislature.

The third mode is liable to this objection, that [it] places the majority under the controul of a small minority. The whole legislature consists of eighty-nine members, when they all attend, thirteen of this number may prevent the election of a person, or persons, in which the whole of the remaining seventy-six are united. Such a provision in a matter in which the very existence of a government is concerned, is absurd and repugnant to every just principle of politics.

It is also liable to this material objection, that if it is adopted, it may and probably will frequently defeat any election at all—By this mode, both houses are to concur. But suppose they do not, how is the difference to be determined? It cannot be done. The one or the other must recede or no election can take place. If both houses maintain their opinions, the state will be without senators, and upon the same principle the United States may be without a senate, and the government of the union may be dissolved. If it be said, that such an event can hardly be apprehended, for it can scarcely be supposed, that such a spirit of obstinancy will prevail in the two houses, as to incline them so pertinaciously to adhere to their own choice, as to defeat any appointment. Supposing this to be true, it does not help the matter. For in this case a power will be placed in the hands of a few ambitious and obstinate men always to choose whom they please. Eight or ten men in the senate firmly united together, in favour of men, who will promote their views and designs, may fatigue a great majority into a compliance with their wishes, and thus instead of having the senators chosen by a free and unbiassed voice of a majority of the representatives of the people, they may be thrust into their seats by a small overbearing faction against the wishes of a great majority, both by the people and their representatives.

Such a principle in government is subversive of freedom. It has a direct tendency to elevate the few, to the depression of the many, and will give a tone to the new system of government, that may accelerate the destruction of republican government. The powers of the senate are vastly great. Besides being one branch of the legislature, they possess very important executive authority, and are the highest court of judicatory in the nation. They hold their places for six years, and are not amendable to it under the controul of the states who send them. Most sensible candid men, admit that there is too great an accumulation of power and too small a degree of responsibility in this body. The convention of this state has recommended that their powers be curtailed, and their responsibility increased. But if the mode contended for, be adopted, to appoint by law, or to give the senate a negative in the choice of senators, they will be placed almost entirely beyond the controul of the people—At any rate, the people choose them at second hand through their representatives. But this will put it out of the power of the representatives of the people to choose them, and enable one third of the senate to dictate the choice or prevent ones taking place. This is so flagrantly wrong, that I can hardly conceive that any thing can be said to shew the propriety of it.

I shall now enquire which of the proposed modes of appointment is most consonant to our own constitution. On this head little doubt can be entertained. The constitution is express on the subject of appointing delegates to Congress, and the first mode is perfectly conformable to it. It is said, I know, that our constitution does not at all apply to the case, because the new system has entirely annulled the old confederation, and stands on its own foot. That no such office exists as the constitution contemplated under the name of delegates, and therefore it can be no rule to direct in this business. On this I remark, that although the new form of government has abrogated the old, that yet the senate under the new are charged with most of the important powers and duties of the Congress under the old, especially of an executive nature—and the reason of the provision for choosing delegates, applies with equal force in the one case as in the other—Under both systems they are the delegates of the state; they are to guard its sovereignty, to watch over its rights and represent its interests. Every reason therefore that could induce a choice of this method of appointing under the confederation, apply with equal force under the new government, and therefore this ought to be the mode pursued, unless the new constitution expressly points out another; this leads to the third enquiry—Does the new Constitution fix the one mode in preference to the other?

The following are the only clauses which respect the matter art. 1. sect. 3. "The senate of the United States shall be composed of two senators from each state chosen by the legislature thereof for six years,["] &c.

Art. 1. Sect, 4. The times, places and manner of holding elections for senators and representatives shall be prescribed in each state by the legislature thereof, &c.

From these two clauses taken together the plain sense of the constitution is this, that the legislature are to elect senators at such time and place and in such manner as they shall prescribe—They are authorised to adopt any mode of election they please. All circumstances respecting the election is under their direction. Nothing in this constitution points out any mode. It only reserves a right to the Congress to alter the regulations after they are made or to make new ones. Every legislature then are left to exercise their discretion on this head subject to such rules and restrictions as their own constitutions provide, if any exists.

The case then with respect to the legislature of New-York, stands thus: The new constitution commits to their discretion the manner in which they shall exercise the right of electing senators, but their own constitution directs how this discretion shall be used, in the article providing for the election of delegates. As the reasons on which that article was founded equally applies to senators as to delegates, who differ rather in name than in thing.

But it is said, the constitution has fixed this matter, because it says that the senators shall be chosen by the legislature—When men get attached to a party, or to a sentiment, trifles light as air will have weight to support them in their opinions—Were it not for this, I can hardly imagine any sensible man would lay much stuff upon this argument. It is said the legislature consists of the senate and assembly, that they have equal rights, and therefore both must concur in the choice. I ask the gentlemen who advance this—Who choose delegates under the confederation? I believe they will answer, as every man will, the legislature. It is true that in the exercise of this power they proceeded in a different mode than that they pursued in passing laws. The nature of the case required they should and therefore the constitution provided for it—It is the same in the case before us—The legislature are to choose—the manner is left to them by the constitution. There is not the most remote evidence from the words of the constitution, that it intended to give one house a negative on the other—the expressions are the legislature shall choose, they are to hold an election for senators—The manner they are to prescribe—The idea of choosing and of electing when applied to a body of men, implies, that the voice of a majority is to decide. Had the constitution meant to give one house a negative upon the other, it would have held a different language, it would have directed that senators should have been appointed by law, and then all the formalities observed between the two houses must have been adhered to—But I shall tire your patience and that of your reader. On the whole, as the mode prescribed in the constitution for choosing delegates, is most consonant to the principles of republicanism, most rational, friendly to liberty and safety for the people—As the other modes are attended with difficulties that may defeat a representation, in the senate at all, or place the power of appointment in a faction—As this mode is directed by the constitution in the case[3] of delegates, and equally applies to the case of senators, as the new constitution rather favours than opposes it, I am clearly of opinion it ought to be adopted, and trust it will be by our legislature.

A FEDERAL REPUBLICAN.

1. For speculation that Melancton Smith is "A Federal Republican," see "A Federal Republican," *New York Journal*, 27 November 1788, n. 1, Part One.

2. For Article XXX of the state constitution, see Assembly and Senate Proceedings, 17 December 1788, n. 1, above.

3. Twice in this sentence the newspaper printed "care" when it undoubtedly meant "case."

Assembly Proceedings, Friday, A.M., 2 January

The House then pursuant to the order of the day, proceeded to the further consideration of the amendments, to the bill entitled, *An act for carying into effect on the part of this State, the Constitution of the United States, assented to and ratified by the Convention of this State, on the twenty-sixth day of July last.*[1]

The first amendment being to the first enacting clause, the said first clause was again read in the words following, viz.

"Be it enacted by the People of the State of New-York, represented in Senate and Assembly, and it is hereby enacted by the authority of the same, that the Senators to be chosen in this State, for the United States, shall be chosen as follows, that is to say, the Senate and Assembly of this State, shall each openly nominate as many persons as shall be equal to the whole number of Senators to be chosen by this State; after which nomination, the Senate and Assembly shall meet together, and compare the lists of the persons by them respectively nominated; and those persons named in both lists shall be Senators for the United States; and out of those persons whose names are not in both lists, one half shall be chosen by the joint ballot of the Senators and Members of the Assembly so met together as aforesaid; and the copies of the resolutions of the Senate and Assembly testifying the said choice, shall be thereupon delivered to each of the persons so chosen Senators for the United States as aforesaid."

The first amendment being again read, is to obliterate from the words, *That the Senators to be chosen in this State, for the United States, shall*, to the end of the clause, and substitute the following, viz.

"If two Senators are to be appointed, openly nominate two persons, and shall respectively give notice each to the other, of such nomination; that if both Houses agree in the nomination of the same person or persons, the person or persons so nominated and agreed to, shall be the Senator or Senators, to represent this State, in the Senate of the Congress of the United States. That if the nomination of either House does not agree in any of the persons nominated by the other, the Senate shall on the same day, openly choose one of the persons nominated by the Assembly, and the Assembly shall on the same day, openly choose one of the persons nominated by the Senate, and the two persons so chosen, shall be the Senators to represent this State as aforesaid. That in every case when two Senators are to be chosen, and both Houses agree only as to one, in such nomination as aforesaid, and in every case when only one Senator is to be chosen, either of the two Houses of the Legislature may propose to the other, a resolution for concurrence, naming therein a person to fill the office of Senator, and if the House receiving such resolution shall concur therein, the person so named in such resolution shall be the Senator; but if such resolution shall not be concurred in, either House may on that or any future day, proceed to offer to the other, a resolution for concurrence from time to time, until they shall agree upon a Senator. That whenever the choice of Senator or Senators shall be made, the President of the Senate and the Speaker of the Assembly, shall certify the names of the person or persons so appointed Senator or Senators, to the person administering the government of this State, for the time being, who shall thereupon exemplify such certificate, under the great seal of this State, and deliver or cause the same to be delivered to the Senator so chosen, or when two are to be chosen, to one of them.

And whereas, there is a necessity of a speedy appointment of Senators, to represent this State, in the first Senate of the Congress of the United States: Therefore,

"Be it further enacted by the authority aforesaid, that the Senate and Assembly of this State, shall by concurrent resolutions determine on a day certain for choosing such first Senators in manner aforesaid, and that such day shall be within ten days next after the passing of this act, any thing contained in the preceeding section of this act to the contrary hereof notwithstanding."

That the said enacting clause and amendment having been read, and considered, *Mr. Speaker* put the question, whether the House did concur in the said amendment, and it passed in the negative, in the manner following, viz.

FOR THE NEGATIVE.

Mr. Jones,	Mr. Bay,
Mr. Carman,	Mr. Tappen,
Mr. G. Livingston,	Mr. Carpenter,
Mr. Kortz,	Mr. J. Smith,
Mr. Yates,	Mr. D'Witt,
Mr. Frey,	Mr. Griffen,
Mr. Stauring,	Mr. Wisner,
Mr. Van Dyck,	Mr. Adgate,
Mr. J. Van Rensselaer,	Mr. Harper,
Mr. Hardenbergh,	Mr. Havens,
Mr. Veeder,	Mr. Schenck,
Mr. Winn,	Mr. Akins,
Mr. Duncan,	Mr. E. Clark,
Mr. Savage,	Mr. Patterson,
Mr. Webster,	Mr. Scudder,
Mr. M'Cracken,	Mr. Cantine.
Mr. Thompson,	

FOR THE AFFIRMATIVE.

Mr. B. Livingston,	Mr. Low,
Mr. Gilbert,	Mr. Bancker,
Mr. Van Cortlandt,	Mr. Vandervoort,
Mr. Seaman,	Mr. Rockwell,
Mr. Barker,	Mr. Verplanck,
Mr. Harison,	Mr. Cornwell,
Mr. Hoffman,	Mr. Giles,
Mr. H. Van Rensselaer,	Mr. Dongan,
Mr. Younglove,	Mr. Sands,
Mr. Watts,	Mr. Gardiner,
Mr. Livingston,	Mr. Macomb,
Mr. Horton,	Mr. Crane.

The next amendments being to the second enacting clause, the said clause was read, and a part thereof is in the words following, viz.

"Be it enacted by the authority aforesaid, that this State shall be, and hereby is divided into six Districts, as follows, that is to say, Suffolk county, Queens county, Kings county, and Richmond county, shall be one District, and the city and county of New-York and Westchester county, except the towns of Salem, North-Salem, Cortlandt, York-Town, and Stephen Town, shall be one District, and the county of Dutchess and the towns of Salem, North Salem, Cortlandt, York Town, and Stephen Town, in Westchester county, shall be one District.["]

Two of the amendments to the said clause, being again read, are after *York Town*, to insert the towns of *Poundridge* and *Bedford*, so that the county of Dutchess, and the towns of Salem, North-Salem, Cortlandt, York-Town, Stephen-Town, Poundridge and Bedford, in the county of Westchester should be one District.

The said clause and amendments having been read, and considered, *Mr. Speaker* put the question whether the House did concur with the Honorable the Senate therein, and it passed in the negative, in the manner following, viz.

FOR THE NEGATIVE.

Mr. Jones,	Mr. Bay,
Mr. Carman,	Mr. Tappen,
Mr. G. Livingston,	Mr. Griffen,
Mr. Kortz,	Mr. Carpenter,
Mr. Yates,	Mr. J. Smith,
Mr. Frey,	Mr. D'Witt,
Mr. Stauring,	Mr. Wisner,
Mr. Van Dyck,	Mr. Adgate,
Mr. J. Van Rensselaer,	Mr. Harper,
Mr. Hardenbergh,	Mr. Havens,
Mr. Veeder,	Mr. Schenck,
Mr. Winn,	Mr. Akins,
Mr. Duncan,	Mr. E. Clark,
Mr. Savage,	Mr. Patterson,
Mr. Webster,	Mr. Scudder,
Mr. M'Cracken,	Mr. Cantine.

FOR THE AFFIRMATIVE.

Mr. B. Livingston,	Mr. Low,
Mr. Gilbert,	Mr. Bancker,
Mr. Van Cortlandt,	Mr. Vandervoort,
Mr. Seaman,	Mr. Rockwell,
Mr. Barker,	Mr. Verplanck,
Mr. Harison,	Mr. Cornwell,
Mr. Hoffman,	Mr. Giles,
Mr. H. Van Rensselaer,	Mr. Dongan,
Mr. Younglove,	Mr. Sands,
Mr. Watts,	Mr. Gardiner,
Mr. Livingston,	Mr. Macomb,
Mr. Horton,	Mr. Crane.

Another of the said amendments being to the last enacting clause of the bill, the said clause was again read in the words following, viz.

"And be it further enacted by the authority aforesaid, that until the Legislature shall make further provision in the premises, the electors to be appointed in this State for choosing the President and Vice-President of the United States, shall be appointed in the manner following, that is to say, the Senate and Assembly shall each openly nominate as many persons as shall be equal to the whole number of the electors to be appointed by this State, after which nomination the Senate and Assembly shall meet together and compare the lists of persons by them respectively nominated, and those persons named in both lists shall be electors; and out of those persons whose names are not in both lists one half shall be chosen by the joint ballot of the Senators and Members of Assembly so met together as aforesaid:—And thereupon copies of the resolutions of the Senate and Assembly, appointing the said electors shall be delivered to each of the said electors; and the said electors shall meet together at the City-Hall of the city of Albany, in the county of Albany, on the first Wednesday in February next, and then and there proceed to vote by ballot for two persons, as mentioned in the first section of the second article of the Constitution of the United States, in the manner, and agreeable to the directions therein contained, and the true intent and meaning of the said Constitution; and further to do and perform all other duties enjoined on them by the said Constitution, for which service each of them shall have the daily pay of twenty shillings."

The amendment to the said last clause of the bill being again read, is to obliterate the first part of the said clause as far as the words *so met together as aforesaid*, included, and to insert therein as follows, so that the whole clause with the amendment would read as follows, viz.

"And whereas the time intervening between the present meeting of the Legislature and the day on which by the act of the United States in Congress assembled, electors were to be appointed for electing a President and Vice-President for the United States, is too short to refer the appointment of the electors to the suffrages of the inhabitants of this State. Therefore,

Be it enacted by the authority aforesaid, that until other Legislative provision can be made for such election, the electors who are to meet on the first Wednesday in February 1789, shall be appointed in the manner following, that is to say, the Senate and Assembly of this State shall on the first Wednesday in January 1789, respectively openly nominate eight electors, and shall respectively give notice each to the other of such nomination; that if both Houses agree in the nomination of the same person or persons, the person or persons so nominated and agreed to shall be an elector or electors; that if the nomination of either House does not agree in any of the persons nominated by the other, the Senate shall on the same day openly choose four of the persons nominated by the Assembly, and the Assembly shall on the same day openly choose four of the persons nominated by the Senate, and the eight persons so chosen shall be the electors for the purpose aforesaid; and in every case where one or more of the electors less than the whole number shall have been agreed upon by both Houses in manner aforesaid, either of the two Houses of the Legislature may propose to the other a resolution for concurrence, naming therein the person or persons, to fill the office of such deficient elector or electors; and if the House receiving such resolution shall concur therein, the person or persons so named in such resolution, shall be an elector or electors, for the purpose aforesaid; but if such resolution shall not be concurred in, either House shall on that day proceed to offer to the other, a resolution or resolutions for concurrence, until they shall agree upon and have compleated the whole number of eight electors: And thereupon copies of the resolutions of the Senate and Assembly appointing the said electors, shall be delivered to each of the said electors, and the said electors shall meet together at the City-Hall of the city of Albany, in the county of Albany, on the first Wednesday in February next, and then and there proceed to vote by ballot for two persons as mentioned in the first section of the second article of the Constitution for the United States, in the manner and agreeable to the directions therein contained, and the true intent and meaning of the said Constitution; and further to do and perform all other duties enjoined on them, by the said Constitution, for which service each of them shall have the daily pay of twenty shillings."

The said clause and amendment having been read and considered, *Mr. Speaker* put the question whether the House did concur with the Honorable the Senate therein, and it passed in the negative in the manner following, viz.

FOR THE NEGATIVE.

Mr. Jones,	Mr. Griffen,
Mr. Carman,	Mr. Carpenter,
Mr. G. Livingston,	Mr. J. Smith,
Mr. Kortz,	Mr. D'Witt,
Mr. Yates,	Mr. Wisner,
Mr. Frey,	Mr. Adgate,
Mr. Stauring,	Mr. Harper,
Mr. J. Van Rensselaer,	Mr. Havens,
Mr. Hardenbergh,	Mr. Schenck,
Mr. Winn,	Mr. Akins,
Mr. Duncan,	Mr. E. Clark,
Mr. Savage,	Mr. Patterson,
Mr. Webster,	Mr. Scudder,
Mr. Thompson,	Mr. Cantine,
Mr. Bay,	Mr. M'Cracken.
Mr. Tappen,	

FOR THE AFFIRMATIVE.

Mr. B. Livingston,	Mr. Vandervoort,
Mr. Gilbert,	Mr. Rockwell,
Mr. Seaman,	Mr. Verplanck,
Mr. Barker,	Mr. Giles,
Mr. Hoffman,	Mr. Dongan,
Mr. Younglove,	Mr. Sands,
Mr. Watts,	Mr. Gardiner,
Mr. Livingston,	Mr. Macomb,
Mr. Horton,	Mr. Crane.
Mr. Bancker,	

The other amendments to the said bill, having been severally read a second time, were respectively concurred in by the House.

Thereupon, *Resolved*, That this House do not concur with the Honorable the Senate, in their amendment to the first clause of the said bill, nor in that amendment to the second clause of the said bill, whereby it is proposed to add the towns of Poundridge and Bedford, in Westchester county, to the election District, which includes the county of Dutchess, nor in the amendment to the last clause of the said bill, and do concur in the other amendments to the bill.

Ordered, That Mr. Adgate and Mr. Harper, deliver the bill and a copy of the last preceding resolution, to the Honorable the Senate.

1. The amendments referred to are the Senate's amendments (approved on 31 December 1788) to the original Assembly bill of 22 December.

Assembly Debates, Friday, 2 January[1]

The amendments of the senate to the bill for putting the new constitution into operation, were then taken into consideration.

The first amendment being read, which was to expunge from the bill the clause which provides for the election of senators by joint ballot, and to substitute a mode giving the senate an equal voice in the said election, as a distinct branch of the legislature.

Mr. *Harrison* rose.—The bill, Mr. Speaker, now under consideration, comprehends objects of the first magnitude. It is not therefore to be wondered at that a diversity of sentiment prevails on this occasion. But to carry into effect the new government, we must adopt such measures as the senate can concur in. I have already delivered my sentiments on the manner in which I thought they might agree.[2]—Unfortunately, sir, the committee of the house thought proper to reject the mode that I then brought forward, and which I presented, not that it should be accepted in all its parts, but with a view that it might be modified and made agreeable to both houses, in such way as to ensure an election. With this view I say, I brought forward the amendment—it was rejected, and the bill agreed to as it now stands. Upon examining the amendment proposed by the senate, I find it approaches nearer to the constitution than the one I proposed. It was urged, sir, in the course of that debate, and forcibly, that this was a great constitutional question; I consider it in that light, and am persuaded that gentlemen will consider it to be such. When however, I consider it in that view, I by no means declare that I think it a question settled by the constitution of the state. The constitution does not in pointed terms settle the mode; had this been the case, there could not have been a necessity for the present deliberation. It would have been unnecessary to pass an act for the purpose. Sir, either the constitution has in plain terms directed the mode, and will prevent any interference, or it has left that matter at large, and we can only rest it on constitutional principles. With respect to the terms of the constitution intending to apply to the present general government, I think there is nothing in that constitution to induce us to adopt an opinion of the kind,—for as at the time of making the state constitution, it is certain the framers of it had in view only the appointment of delegates to a body formed as the Congress then was—they could not have intended it to apply to whatever government might thereafter be adopted; and although the confederation afterwards acceded to by this state, permitted the states to choose their delegates in the mode they had hitherto done, no inference can be drawn from it, that the very framers of our state constitution would not have adopted a different mode, if a different government had been thought of.

Sir, by the constitution of the general government, which we have now adopted, powers of a different nature are given, than those contained in the articles of confederation,—the new constitution has divested the senate and assembly of many essential privileges; and as it particularly requires that the senators be chosen by the *legislature*, without any reference to the mode prescribed in our constitution, it abrogates that part of it—and the legislature being composed of two houses—each have an equal voice in the appointment. They must therefore exercise their discretion on the subject. The senate being therefore a distinct branch of the legislature, have certain constitutional powers which are sacred in their hands, and which they cannot part with. The senate and assembly are checks on each other, and neither can give up its constitutional privileges. Considering that these powers which are now to be exercised are a new grant—and considering further that they are powers vested in our legislature by the constitution, surely we cannot suppose that the senate must not at least be requested to concur in the mode, particularly where their privileges are concerned. Sir, when we consider the numbers of which this house is composed, and the very few that constitute the senate, it must be evident that a joint ballot puts the appointment totally in the power of this house. In this point of light, which will be a serious one, considering the matter constitutionally, we ought not to try to force the senate into measures against the constitution; but sir, convinced as I am, that such is the spirit of the constitution, I am induced to consider what is the actual situation of things; on the present occasion I consider that the determination of this house and the senate may affect the peace of our country for a length of time. It is impossible to say what animosity may arise, if the legislature break up without coming to a happy decision. Gentlemen should reflect, and with attention, on those convulsions into which our country may be thrown by a party spirit. These, sir, are alarming evils—I repeat it, and I wish gentlemen to reflect on it seriously. Perhaps it may be said that we are holding up terrors to mislead those who hear us. Sir, far from me be this idea; I would not wish to excite apprehensions in the minds of gentlemen; but what the state of our country will tell them is well founded.—But, sir, it must be admitted that when we are embracing important public measures, it is right that we should consider them in all their consequences, and what effects they may have on some. When I consider the consequence that may attend a non-concurrence; when I consider the affect it may have; that our dearest and best interests may be sacrificed; when I consider how much depends on it, not only with respect to the residence of Congress, but other important objects, I hope gentlemen will believe me, that I am sincere when I say I view it as an alarming evil. Whatever may be the opinion of this house, it is clear from the amendment, that the senate consider it as a constitutional right—it must therefore follow, that unless we adopt such measures as they can concur in, we shall lose our representation in the senate of the United States. Sir, the minds of our constituents are considerably agitated on the present question—it becomes therefore the wisdom of the legislature rather to allay those heats, than to exasperate them. And as both houses possess an equal right on that subject—both houses ought to be consulted on the measures they will adopt to carry into effect the new system of general government. Sir, the senate have sent an amendment to the bill which does not, in the manner our bill was formed, give one house the total choice, but gives each an equal right of election; this house then will have a right to choose one—the senate the other—so that there will be a perfect equality. Whether therefore I consider the subject as a constitutional question, or on the footing of expedience, in either view I must be for concurring. But whatever may be the determination of the majority, I shall rest satisfied that I have acquitted myself to God and my country—and that I have done my duty to the government under which I live.

Mr. *Jones*. This same question has been before decided on in this house; since which I have heard nothing to convince me of the propriety of the amendment, or the impropriety of the bill. I shall not travel over all the ground that the honorable gentleman has, who was just up. It is sufficient in my opinion, that the constitution of our state points out the mode by which officers of the like description are to be appointed. The only question is whether we ought, where the constitution points out a plain and constitutional mode of doing business, deviate from it; if we do, upon what ground are we to go? Again, the mode proposed by the senate neither comports with the constitution of this state, nor of the United States—it differs from both. I would remark, whether the constitution of our state be obligatory or not; I should suppose prudence would direct us to follow that mode by which elections have hitherto been made, and with which our constituents have been satisfied. The gentleman asks, why this act? the question is easily answered—the constitution of the United States requires it, as we must pass a law directing the time, place, and manner of holding elections; had our constitution contemplated precisely the thing, yet it would be proper to recognize it by a law. But, Sir, how do we comply even with the constitution of the general government if we adopt the amendment.—Besides, it does not even ensure an election; for one house, it says, may propose and another concur; suppose they disagree, they may go on proposing and non-concurring, and if neither house will yield, why then there can be no election—is this right? should we not rather adhere to a mode which ensure an immediate decision? I can not suppose, however, that this house is in that situation, that it must yield a great constitutional point, for fear of the consequences. Are not the senate to have the same considerations?—are we? no—we are only alone answerable for the consequences. To consider the question on that ground which is warranted by our constitution, and approaches nearest to the constitution of the United States, in my opinion, the proposed amendment comports with neither, I must therefore vote against it.

Mr. *Harrison*. The gentleman who was last on the floor, has endeavored to draw this matter into a narrow compass, and he would wish the house to turn their faces from a picture of those consequences which may result from a nonconcurrence. With respect to his objections as to the amendment not being even warranted by the new constitution, I should have no objection to meet him on that ground, or any other. I am persuaded that the new constitution is reconcilable with the mode pointed out by the present amendment; it is true that the constitution of the United States has declared that the senators shall be elected by the legislature, which must apply to the acts of the several bodies of which it is composed; had not this been the intent of the framers of the constitution, it would have been proper to have made use of these terms, that they should be elected by the *members* of the legislature. But, Sir, it refers to them in a different manner; in order therefore to satisfy the words of the constitution on which the gentleman seems to rest the point, the election must be by both houses of the legislature, and therefore whatever mode shall be adopted that may deprive one branch of that election is repugnant to the new constitution, because it is necessary that every branch of the legislature should concur in the act. Supposing then the choice to be made against the will of the senate, it would be an election only by the assembly. The words of the constitution cannot therefore be satisfied, unless the choice is made by the equal voice of both houses. I am equally convinced with the gentleman that the senate will consider the consequences of their conduct, as well as we shall; and I am convinced they will not, unless for great constitutional privileges involve our country in, perhaps, inextricable difficulties. Sir, when I am convinced it is the privilege of that house to have an equal voice with us, and when I consider it unconstitutional in us to insist on a mode that will destroy their rights, I say it is proper to call the attention of gentlemen to the situation we are in, and to warn them of the calamities they may draw on their country.

On the question to concur, it was carried in the negative. . . .[3]

The other amendments to the bill were then taken up, and all, excepting one or two trivial ones, were rejected. [Adjourned.][4]

1. *Daily Advertiser*, 10 January 1789.
2. See Assembly Debates, 17 December 1788, above.
3. For the Assembly roll call, see Assembly Proceedings, 2 January 1789, immediately above.
4. These brackets are in the original newspaper printing.

Assembly and Senate Proceedings, Saturday, A.M., 3 January

The Senate

A message from the Honorable the Assembly, by Mr. Adgate and Mr. Harper, was received, with the bill entitled, *An act for carrying into effect on the part of this State, the Constitution of the United States, assented to and ratified by the Convention of this State, on the twenty-sixth day of July last,* together with the following resolution, which was read, viz.

Resolved, That this House do not concur with the Honorable the Senate, in their amendments to the first clause of the said bill, nor in that amendment to the second clause of the said bill, whereby it is proposed to add the towns of Poundridge and Bedford in Westchester county, to the election District which includes the county of Dutchess, nor in the amendment to the last clause of the said bill, and do concur in the other amendments to the said bill. Thereupon,

The Senate proceeded to reconsider their amendments to the first clause of the said bill, respecting the mode of choosing Senators, to represent this State, in the Senate of the United States, and which were not concurred in by the Honorable the Assembly. And after debates being had, Mr. Van Ness moved, that the Senate do recede from their said amendments, and Mr. President having put the question thereon, it passed in the negative, in manner following, viz.

FOR THE NEGATIVE.

Mr. Philip Schuyler,	Mr. Morris,
Mr. Douw,	Mr. Roosevelt,
Mr. Micheau,	Mr. L'Hommedieu,
Mr. Peter Schuyler,	Mr. Duane,
Mr. Fonda,	Mr. Hoffman.
Mr. Vanderbilt,	

FOR THE AFFIRMATIVE.

Mr. Yates,	Mr. Swartwout,
Mr. Hopkins,	Mr. Townsend,
Mr. Williams,	Mr. Tredwell,
Mr. Van Ness,	Mr. Humfrey.

The Senate having reconsidered their amendment to the second clause of the said bill not concurred in by the Hon. the Assembly, whereby it is proposed to add the towns of Poundridge and Bedford, in Westchester county, to the election District which includes the county of Dutchess, Mr. Yates moved that the Senate do recede from their said amendment, and Mr. President having put the question thereon, it passed in the negative, in manner following, viz.

FOR THE NEGATIVE.

Mr. Philip Schuyler,	Mr. Morris,
Mr. Douw,	Mr. Roosevelt,
Mr. Micheau,	Mr. L'Hommedieu,
Mr. Peter Schuyler,	Mr. Duane,
Mr. Fonda,	Mr. Hoffman.
Mr. Vanderbilt,	

FOR THE AFFIRMATIVE.

Mr. Yates,
Mr. Hopkins,
Mr. Williams,
Mr. Van Ness,
Mr. Swartwout,
Mr. Tredwell,
Mr. Humfrey.

The Senate having reconsidered their amendment to the last clause of the said bill, respecting the mode of choosing electors, and which was not concurred in by the Hon. the Assembly, Mr. Tredwell, moved that the Senate do recede from their said amendment, and Mr. President having put the question thereon it passed in the negative, in manner following, viz.

FOR THE NEGATIVE.

Mr. Philip Schuyler,
Mr. Douw,
Mr. Micheau,
Mr. Peter Schuyler,
Mr. Fonda,
Mr. Vanderbilt,
Mr. Morris,
Mr. Roosevelt,
Mr. L'Hommedieu,
Mr. Duane,
Mr. Hoffman.

FOR THE AFFIRMATIVE.

Mr. Yates,
Hopkins,
Mr. Williams,
Mr. Van Ness,
Mr. Swartwout,
Mr. Tredwell,
Mr. Humfrey.

Thereupon, *Resolved*, That the Senate do adhere to their several amendments to the said bill, not concurred in by the Hon. the Assembly.

Ordered, That Mr. L'Hommedieu and Mr. Humfrey, deliver the bill, with a copy of the preceding resolution, to the Hon. the Assembly.

The Assembly

[The Assembly received the bill and the Senate resolution.]

. . . Thereupon,

Resolved, That a conference be held with the Honorable the Senate on their amendments to the said bill, which were not concurred in by this House; and that such conference be held on Monday next at eleven of the clock in the forenoon, at such place as the Honorable the Senate shall be pleased to appoint for that purpose.

The House then, pursuant to the fifteenth article of the Constitution,[1] proceeded to choose by ballot, a committee to manage the said conference on the part of this House; and on the ballots being taken, it appeared, that Mr. Jones, Mr. Adgate, and Mr. G. Livingston, were duly elected for that purpose: Thereupon,

Resolved, That Mr. Jones, Mr. Adgate, and Mr. G. Livingston, be a committee to manage the said conference on the part of this House.

Ordered, That Mr. Verplanck and Mr. Giles deliver a copy of the two last preceding resolutions to the Honorable the Senate.

The Senate

A message from the Hon. the Assembly by Mr. Verplanck and Mr. Giles, was received with the following resolutions which were read, viz.

Resolved, That a conference be held with the Hon. the Senate on their three amendments to the bill, entitled *An act for carrying into effect on the part of this State, the Constitution of the United States, assented to and ratified by the Convention of this State, on the twenty-sixth day of July last*, which were not agreed to by this House; and that such conference be held on Monday next at eleven of the clock, in the forenoon, at such place as the Hon. the Senate shall be pleased to appoint.

Resolved, That Mr. Jones, Mr. Adgate, and Mr. G. Livingston, be a committee to manage the said conference on the part of this House: Thereupon,

Resolved, That the Senate will meet the Hon. the Assembly on Monday next at eleven of the clock, in the forenoon, at the Assembly-Chamber, to hold the conference proposed by the Hon. House on the three amendments to the said bill, not concurred in by the Hon. the Assembly and adhered to by the Senate.

Resolved, That Mr. Duane, Mr. Philip Schuyler and Mr. L'Hommedieu, be a committee to manage the said conference on the part of the Senate.

Ordered, That Mr. Swartwout and Mr. Williams, deliver a copy of the preceding resolutions to the Hon. the Assembly.

The Assembly

A copy of two resolutions of the Honorable the Senate, delivered by Mr. Swartwout and Mr. Williams, was read, that the Senate will meet this House on Monday next, at eleven of the clock in the forenoon, at the Assembly Chamber, to hold the conference proposed on [the amendments to] the bill above mentioned, which were not concurred in by this House, and were adhered to by the Senate; and that Mr. Duane, Mr. Philip Schuyler, and Mr. L'Hommedieu, be a committee to manage said conference on the part of the Senate.

1. Article XV of the state constitution provided: "That whenever the assembly and senate disagree, a conference shall be held, in the preference of both, and be managed by committees, to be by them respectively chosen by ballot" (Thorpe, V, 2632).

John Jay to William Pierce, New York, 3 January[1]

I had Yesterday ye Pleasure of recg. Yr. favor of the 6th. of last month. It is as yet exceedingly uncertain who will be Senators for this State, and consequently it cannot be even conjectured by what leading motives they will probably be influenced in their appointments. Whoever they may be I shall not omit to apprize them of your Services and Character—this I take to be the precise Extent of your Request, and thus far my Desire of serving you may I think be gratified—you are aware Dr Sr that my official Situation prescribes a Degree of Delicacy & Reserve relative to other Departmts. wh. tho sometimes unpleasant is always proper. It gives me pleasure to be persuaded that on this stead our Sentiments correspond, & that you prefer a uniform adherence to Propriety, to any friendly Effort beyond its Limits

1. FC, John Jay Collection, NNC. The letter was addressed to Pierce in Savannah, Georgia. Pierce (1740–1789), a native of Virginia, had served as a Continental Army officer, 1776–1783. He was a Georgia assemblyman, 1786, and a delegate to Congress, 1786–1787, and to the Constitutional Convention, 1787. He was seeking appointment as collector of customs at Savannah.

Cornelius C. Schoonmaker to Peter Van Gaasbeek, Albany, 3 January (excerpt)[1]

in my last altho I was unwell at the time I Stated to you the proceedings of the two Houses on the Subject of organizing the New Constitution the Assembly have since Rejected the two Bills from the Senate Respecting the Appointment of the Electors and Senators the Senate have this Week passed our Bill for Organizing the Government with Amendments[.] they Agree with the Assembly Respecting the Election of Representatives—but Rejected our Mode prescribed in the Bill for Appointing Senators & Electors—and Substituted in its Stead nearly their former Bills—to which the Assembly have disagreed and will this Morning inform the Senate thereof—what the Result of this disagreement will be is not possible to foresee[.] it is probable that there will be a Conference on the Bill and after the Conference the Bill may be lost unless the Senate do give up their amendments—The Fedrals are as keen at Manuvering as ever. The Council of Appointment[2] have for some days been endeavoring to get his excellency the Governor to meet with them that they might make some Appointments, they have Urged this Matter more since the Assembly came to a Resolution to Appoint a new Council, we have reason to believe that had they been able to get the Governor to join with them in council that some very di[s]agree[a]ble appointments to our common cause would have been made. this Matter is now put out of their Power. the Assembly have Yesterday appointed a new Council Composed of Gentlemen who are all in Sentiment with us[3]—The Senate have not Acquired much applause by their Answer to the Governors Speech[4]—into the particulars of which I shall forbear to enter, being Weak—therefore conclude with Wishing You and all our friends a Happy New Year—

1. RC, Peter Van Gaasbeek Papers, NHpR. The letter was addressed to Van Gaasbeek in Kingston. Schoonmaker was representing Ulster County in the Assembly. Van Gaasbeek (1754–1797), a Kingston merchant and leading Antifederalist in Ulster, was a major in the Ulster County militia during the Revolutionary War and a member of the House of Representatives, 1793–1795.

2. Article XXIII of the state constitution required that a Council of Appointment appoint all officeholders whose appointments were not provided for by the constitution. The Assembly annually elected the four state senators (one from each senatorial district) to the council; the governor was president of the council, but voted only in case of a tie.

3. On 2 January 1789 the Assembly elected John Hathorn, Samuel Townsend, Peter Van Ness, and John Williams to the council.

4. For the Senate's answer to Governor Clinton's speech, see Senate Proceedings, 26 December 1788, above.

St. John de Crèvecoeur to Thomas Jefferson, New York, 5 January (excerpt)[1]

here Every Thing wears the most pleasing aspect; the different legislatures of the adopting States are Enacting Laws to put ye new Govt. in motion; the dispute now Carrying on at Albany between the Senate & assembly about Electing the federal Senators by a Joint ballot of the Two houses, will I believe End in a Compromise (for I must Inform you with ye Lower House being all antis, & the upper one all the Reverse) it is therefore probable that Each party will chuse his man—the choice of the Fed. will be Gl. Schuyler, & that of the Ant. will be a Mr. Yates the only one of that parti who Can be listen'd to with Some patience; all the rest being Illitirate & Ignorant; our Govr:

who Sees That nothing can Stop the Federal Tide is very much Chagrined—he Looses dayly Some degree of popularity among his Warmest Partisans who perceiving that, Spite of the Idea, they had of his abilities as well as of the righteousness of their Cause every thing goes agt. them begin to think him less Infallible & the New System less obnoxious. . . .

The State of Massachussets is now busy in making its federal Choice but the Law which prescribes the Mode is so bad, that it is pretended none will be made—fortunately ye Gl. Court being now in Session will promulgate a better one—tis Said that Carolina has Terminated its choice & that there are 4 anti fedralists but we have no particulars as yet—

Notwithstanding all These untoward appearance, I am convinced that ye Nail is clinched; this Country can remain no longer Without a Govt & ye Sticklers for amendments are only Those who are head over heels in debt; our Govr. is not a Man of sufficient abilities To become the head of a Party—Colo. Hamilton is Just set out for Albany, not that he is a Member of the House, but to be on ye Spot & help in directing his Friends.

1. RC, Jefferson Papers, DLC. Printed: Boyd, XIV, 414–17. For another excerpt from this letter, see DHFFE, II, 387. Jefferson was in Paris, 1784–1789, as minister to France and commissioner to negotiate commercial treaties.

Joint Conference Committee Debates, Monday, 5 January[1]

A resolution of the senate was read, concurring in the resolution of the house for holding a conference on the amendments to the bill for putting the new constitution into operation.

Shortly after, the hon. the senate attended, and the president being seated on the right hand of the speaker, the subject of the conference was then read, viz.

The following clause of the bill which the senate wished expunged:

"Be it enacted by the people of the state of New York, represented in senate and assembly, and it is hereby enacted by the authority of the same, that the senators to be chosen in this state for the United States shall be chosen as follows, that is to say, the senate and assembly of this state, shall each openly nominate as many persons as shall be equal to the whole number of senators to be chosen by this state, after which nomination the senate and assembly shall meet together, and compare the lists of persons by them respectively nominated, and those persons named in both lists shall be senators for the United States, and out of those persons whose names are not in both lists one half shall be chosen by the joint ballot of the senators and members of the assembly, so met together as aforesaid, and the copies of the resolutions of the senate and assembly testifying the said choice shall be thereupon delivered to each of the persons so chosen senators for the United States as aforesaid."

The following amendment proposed as a substitute to the same by the senate:

"Be it enacted by the people of the state of New-York, represented in senate and assembly, and it is hereby enacted by the authority of the same, that the senators to be chosen in this state, for the United States, shall be chosen as follows, that is to say, the senate and assembly of this state shall, if two senators are to be appointed, openly nominate two persons, and shall respectively give notice each to the other of such nomination; that if both houses agree in the nomination of the same person or persons, the person or persons so nominated and agreed to, shall be the senator or senators to represent this state in the senate of the Congress of the United States; that if the nomination of either house does not agree in any of the persons nominated by the other, the senate shall on the same day openly choose one of the persons nominated by the assembly, and the assembly shall on the same day openly choose one of the persons nominated by the senate, and the two persons so chosen shall be the senators to represent this state as aforesaid; that in every case where two senators are to be chosen, and both houses agree only as to one in such nomination as aforesaid, and in every case when only one senator is to be chosen, either of the two houses of the legislature may propose to the other, a resolution for concurrence, naming therein a person to fill the office of senator, and if the house receiving such resolution shall concur therein, the person so named in such resolution shall be the senator, but if such resolution shall not be concurred in, either house may on that or any future day, proceed to offer to the other a resolution for concurrence from time to time until they shall agree upon a senator. That whenever the choice of a senator or senators shall be made, the president of the senate, and speaker of the assembly shall certify the names of the person or persons so appointed senator or senators to the person administering the government of this state for the time being, who shall thereupon exemplify such certificate under the great seal of this [state], and deliver or cause the same to be delivered to the senator so chosen, or when two are chosen, to one of them. And whereas there is a necessity of a speedy appointment of senators to represent this state in the first senate of the Congress of the United States:—Therefore,

"Be it further enacted by the authority aforesaid, That the senate and assembly of this state, shall by concurrent resolutions determine on a day certain for choosing such first senators in the manner aforesaid, and that such day shall be within ten days next after the passing of this act, any thing contained in the preceding section of this act to the contrary hereof notwithstanding."

The senate also proposed the following amendment:—

"That the towns of Poundridge and Bedford, in the county of Westchester, which by the bill, were annexed to the city and county of New York, and with the southernmost part of Westchester, erected into a district, should be taken therefrom, and annexed to the county of Dutchess, which with the northernmost part of the said county of Westchester, were by the bill erected into another district."

The last clause in the bill which the senate would also expunge, is in the words following:—

"And be it further enacted by the authority aforesaid, That until the legislature shall make further provision in the premises, the electors to be appointed in this state, for choosing the president and vice-president of the United States, shall be appointed in the manner following, that is to say, the senate and assembly shall, each openly nominate as many persons as shall be equal to the whole number of electors, to be appointed by this state, after which nomination, the senate and assembly shall meet together, and compare the lists of the persons by them respectively nominated, and those persons named in both lists, shall be electors, and out of those persons, whose names are not in both lists, one half shall be chosen by the joint ballot of the senators and members of assembly, so met together as aforesaid, &c."

The amendment they proposed to substitute is as follows:—

"And whereas the time intervening between the present meeting of the legislature, and the day on which, by the act of the United States in Congress assembled, electors were to be appointed for electing a president and vice-president for the United States, is too short to refer the appointment of the electors to the suffrages of the inhabitants of this state:—Therefore,

"Be it enacted by the authority aforesaid, That until other legislative provision can be made for such election, the electors who are to meet on the first Wednesday in February, one thousand seven hundred and eighty-nine, shall be appointed in manner following, that is to say, the senate and assembly of this state, shall on the first Wednesday in January, one thousand seven hundred and eighty-nine, respectively, openly nominate eight persons, and shall respectively give notice, each to the other, of such nomination; that if both houses agree in the nomination of the same person or persons, the person or persons so nominated and agreed to, shall be an elector or electors; that if the nomination of either house does not agree in any of the persons nominated by the other, the senate shall on the same day openly choose four of the persons nominated by the assembly, and the assembly shall on the same day openly choose four of the persons nominated by the senate, and the eight persons so chosen shall be the electors for the purpose aforesaid; and in every case where one or more of the electors, less than the whole number, shall have been agreed upon by both houses, in manner aforesaid, either of the two houses of the legislature may propose to the other a resolution for concurrence, naming therein the person or persons to fill the office of such deficient elector [or] electors, and if the house receiving such resolution shall concur therein, the person or persons so named in such resolution shall be an elector or electors, for the purpose aforesaid; but if such resolution shall not be concurred in, either house shall, on that day, proceed to offer to the other a resolution or resolutions for concurrence, until they shall agree upon and have compleated the whole number of eight electors, &c."

These having been read, the clerk then read the resolutions of both houses, agreeing to the conference; in which it appeared that the senate had appointed Mr. Duane, Mr. Philip Schuyler, and Mr. L'Hommedieu, a committee to manage the conference on the part of that honorable body;—and that the assembly had appointed Mr. Jones, Mr. G. Livingston, and Mr. Adgate, managers on their part.

Mr. Adgate rose. Mr. President, The constitution of the state provides, that when the assembly and senate shall differ concerning a bill they are about to pass into a law, they shall meet together, and have a conference thereon, to be managed by committees to be chosen for that purpose.

The assembly sir, having passed a bill, entitled "an act for carrying into effect, on the part of this state, the constitution of the United States, assented to and ratified by the convention of this state, on the twenty-sixth day of July last."

And the honorable the senate having passed the same, with sundry amendments thereto, some of which not being agreed to by the assembly, has rendered it necessary that a conference be held, for which purpose the two houses are now met.

The evident intention, sir, of holding a conference on such an occasion is, that each house may inform the other of the reasons that they had for passing the bill—and as I am honored with the appointment of a conferee on this occasion, I shall endeavor to state the reasons that appeared to me to have induced the assembly to pass the parts of the bill in difference; and also their objections to the amendments proposed by the honorable the senate.

The reasons, sir, (that now occurs to me) that the assembly had for passing these particular parts of the bill now read, were because that the constitution of the state has directed the manner in which the delegates for the Congress of the United States shall be chosen for this state, and which is the one adopted by the bill as it passed the assembly, and which mode has hitherto been pursued in all the elections made for that august body.

This mode therefore, the legislature have to pursue in the choice of these two representatives of the state in the Congress of the United States, under the new system, as no other is pointed out for the purpose, but the time and manner thereof is expressly left to the respective legislatures by the new constitution, and our constitution having as I before observed, directed the manner, we have no alternative; for without the state constitution we cease to be a legislature, and cannot make the choice required—and if we should presume so to do, it would need (like the general convention at Philadelphia) the approbation of a convention of delegates from the people, to ratify and confirm the same.

Having thus stated the principles on which this part of the bill is founded, I shall only observe that the amendment proposed is without a constitutional right, and contrary to precedency.

To instance, sir, in the late election (but a few days since) both houses proceeded by joint ballot, the mode in the bill, and elected delegates for the general government[2]—and would it not appear extraordinary in us, the same legislature, now to adopt a different mode not warranted by the constitution, by an act like this we shall indeed shew that we have the form of a republican government without the substance. I trust, sir, that the legislature have too great a respect for the constitution of the state, than thus by their own act to abridge and violate it.

Sir, as to the second amendment disagreed to, by which the towns of Poundridge and Bedford are taken from one of the electing districts and added to another; I shall only observe, that by the information obtained by the assembly, the division of the number of inhabitants as they stand in the bill, will not very materially differ in the two, and the line of division would be more natural and plain than the one proposed by the amendment, which would badly shape the said districts, as well as render them more unequal in numbers.

Sir, as to the other amendment for choosing electors, and not agreed to by the assembly, the same reasons will apply to this that applies to the mode of choosing senators.

Yet it may be further observed did time admit, and were it necessary, it would be much more proper to put that part of the business in the power of the people at large, than the mode proposed by the amendment; and as the mode prescribed by the bill brings the choice of the electors nearest to the people at large, therefore the amendment is in a two-fold sense improper.

I know it may be said, that if this bill does not pass, we shall be without a representation in the new Congress.

But, sir, rather than to agree to those amendments which so evidently tend to sacrifice the rights of the people, it would be advisable for this state not to have a representation in it for years and centuries to come.

Thus, sir, I have endeavored in as concise a manner as my abilities would admit, to state some of the reasons for the bill, and objections to the amendments, and shall leave what is further necessary to be observed on the subject to the better abilities of the gentlemen with whom I am honored to be a manager of this conference.

Mr. L'Hommedieu, It is now proper in turn, that the honorable assembly be informed of the reasons why their bill was not agreed to by the senate, and why the same was amended in the manner it now stands: And it may not be improper to observe at this time, that the amendments to the bill, so far as respects the choice and appointment of senators and electors, differing from the mode prescribed in the bills for that purpose, which originated with the senate and without debate, were rejected by the honorable assembly, arose from a disposition in the senate, to accommodate as far as possible, without giving up their rights to the views of the honorable assembly, and to avoid any occasion of offence, by sending back the two bills which had been so recently rejected, in the form of amendments.

The objections of the senate against the bill of the honorable assembly, so far as it respects the choice or appointment of senators and electors, is, that the mode there pointed out, destroys that equality of power which is by the constitution vested in the two branches of the legislature, and puts it in the power of the honorable assembly, they being superior in numbers, to choose or appoint without controul.

The senate are of opinion, which opinion they trust will not be contested, that the only authority which the legislature have for choosing or appointing senators and electors is derived from the constitution of the United States, lately ratified by the convention of this state—This constitution, which being the last act of the people, is paramount to any law or constitution of the state in those points in which their provisions vary, directs, that the choice of senators shall be made by the legislature of the state, which legislature, by the constitution of this state, is formed by the assembly and the senate, which senate and assembly, by the same constitution, altho' unequal in numbers, have equal powers, and a negative on each other in every case, except when it is otherwise directed by the same constitution.

That the clause in the state constitution, directing the appointment of delegates under the confederation, by joint ballot of both houses, and not by act of the legislature is by the constitution lately ratified, and which is now the constitution of this state, become null and void as to the choice and election of senators and electors, and can not be binding on the legislature, or a rule for their proceeding, in the present case, nor be considered in that respect, as any part of the constitution of this state.—Under these impressions the senate could not concur in the mode of choosing or appointing senators and electors prescribed by the bill of the honorable assembly, nor are at liberty so to do, without giving up those rights which are vested in them by the constitution.

The senate have considered the objection made on the part of the honorable assembly, and cannot suppose with them that the mode for the appointment of delegates under the confederation is binding on the legislature in the present instance. At the time of framing the constitution, and for some years before a Congress existed, consisting of a single body composed of delegates from thirteen different states, with equal powers, and annually to be elected; such a Congress and such delegates, in the opinion of the senate, the clause referred to can only be supposed to contemplate, and not senators under the new constitution, whose powers and duration are very different. But whatever may be the sentiments of the honorable the assembly or the senate, respecting the views of the framers of the constitution in this respect, the senate are clearly of opinion, that as the new constitution which is the highest authority, expressly directs that the choice of senators shall be made by the legislature of the state, as was before observed, they are not at liberty to make that choice in the mode proposed in the bill of the honorable assembly by joint ballot, without a violation of the constitution, which gives equal rights and an equal negative to each branch of the legislature, in all their acts which may constitutionally come before them, and which is so essential to the liberties of the people.

The amendments proposed to the bill of the honorable the assembly in the opinion of the senate, are not more liable to objection than any act where the concurrence of both houses is necessary, the mode is a very practicable one—a perfect equality is observed between the senate and assembly in the choice or appointment of the senators and electors. If any delay or embarrassment should take place in this mode of procedure (which ought not to be presumed) it is what all legislative acts are liable to, and ever will be in those states where the legislature consists of two branches, and the same objection may be made to the passing of all laws or any particular law, altho' the same might be essentially necessary for the well being of the state.

The senate have observed, that in the constitution of the United States, directing the choice of senators in the different states by the legislature thereof, the word *choosen* is made use of, and when it respects the appointment of electors in each State, the word *appoint* is used, which words *choosen* and *appoint*, they conceive to be synonymous, and cannot be construed to confine the legislature to the mode prescribed in the bill of the honorable assembly, or in the least to militate against the mode proposed by the amendments of the senate, for the appointment of senators and electors, the senate are confirmed in this opinion, by a clause in the constitution of this state, which declares, "That the *treasurer of this state* shall be *appointed* by act of the legislature, to originate with the assembly: Provided he shall not be *elected* out of either branch of the legislature." Here the words *appointed* and *elected* are both made use of, altho' the appointment and election is to be by act of the legislature, in which the senate have a negative.—This is mentioned only to shew that no such inference can be made against passing the bill as amended by the senate, from the words made use of in the constitution, directing the choice of senators and appointment of electors.

The senate on examining the division of the state into districts, for the election of representatives, by the best information they could obtain, were of opinion, that the towns of Bedford and Poundridge, ought to be added to the county of Dutchess, to make the districts more equal in respect to numbers, and accordingly made that amendment.

Mr. *G. Livingston*. Mr. President, I look upon the business of a conference in a very serious point of view—it is the last provision, which our state constitution has made, in a case like the present, when the two branches of which our legislature is composed, disagree, respecting a bill or any part thereof.

I wish most sincerely, that the present conference, may not consist only in form, but that, such reasoning as may be offered on the occasion, may be attended to with candor, and its due weight given to it—and which I trust will be the case.

I feel myself exceedingly embarrassed on this occasion, especially considering my own insufficiency, the parts and abilities of my opponents, and the importance of the cause I am engaged to defend. Nothing but a consciousness of the rectitude of my intention, a propensity to add my endeavors to preserve the remains of the constitution of this state, and the liberties of the people thereof, and the justice which has been done to a matter of so great consequence by one, and the able manner in which I doubt not, it will be maintained and defended, by the other of my worthy colleagues, could bear me up, in the unequal contest.

The gentleman which preceded me, and who opened the business of this conference, has observed, That there are three of the amendments, of the honorable the senate, to the bill under consideration, in which the house of assembly have not concurred—The first and the last depend nearly on the same principles, and the other, on mere enumeration.

The first is that which respects the election or choice of senators to represent this state in Congress.

The principle which actuated the house, (I have the honor to represent) to withhold their concurrence to this amendment, I conceive to be this, (at least it is that, by which I was influenced, in voting with the majority) I hold, that, in any case, where the new constitution does not *expressly do away*, or *contradict* our state constitution; or where any thing to be done or provided for by us, may be so done or provided for, as that the letter, as well as spirit of our state constitution may be preserved and adhered to, it is, in the last degree binding on us to comply therewith, and to take the same for our guide. And I also hold, That if in transacting any of the matters required of us by the new constitution, we are bound strictly to conform ourselves to the requirements therein mentioned, our own state constitution notwithstanding.

I will now in a concise manner, apply the doctrine above-mentioned, to the matters in controversy, and endeavor to shew—

1st. That the mode of electing senators or members of Congress, in both constitutions, perfectly harmonize and are consistent with each other.

2dly. That the amendment, as proposed by the honorable the senate, is not conformable to either of the constitutions.

3dly. That the clause under consideration, as it stands in the bill, is strictly agreeable to the new constitution.

I am first to shew, that the constitutions perfectly harmonize, in the case before us.

By the 30th section of our state constitution, the mode of electing delegates to Congress, is as follows, each house is to nominate as many persons as shall be equal to the whole number to be appointed, in which, (if both lists agree) this is the mode of appointment: But if the lists do not agree, either in the whole or in part, as many as the lists differ in, are to *be chosen* by a joint ballot of both houses.

By the 3d section of the first article of the new constitution, it is barely directed, that the senators from each state, shall be *chosen* by the legislature thereof.

And the 4th section of the same article directs, that the times, places and manner of holding elections for senators and *representatives*, shall be prescribed in each state, by the legislature thereof.

Now, by comparing the above article from our state constitution, and those before mentioned, from the general constitution, they will be found to be perfectly consistent with each other.—In the first (when there is any disagreement in the nomination) they are to be *chosen* by the joint ballot of senate and assembly. By the 3d section above-mentioned, they are to be *chosen* by the legislature: and by the 4th section before recited, the manner of *electing* (which is tantamount to *choosing*) is to be prescribed by the respective legislatures.—Thus the idea of *choosing*, pervades the whole.

I would here remark, that it was necessary for the convention, in framing the new government, to direct, that the different legislatures, should make the provision, as to the time, manner, &c. of these elections, because the house of representatives to be chosen by the people, were to be included in the election, and were a body not known in the former Congress;—but will any one say, that, because a new provision was necessary, in electing by the people, a branch before unknown, that therefore a new mode must be adopted, in *choosing* members, which were to be elected by the same body they had always been chosen by;—It by no means follows.

There is another reason, why this provision was necessary, which is—that the manner of choosing delegates to the present Congress was not similar in all the states, therefore for the sake of uniformity, as to the bodies by whom the choice was to be made, it was a necessary direction.

I proceed to shew—That the amendment proposed by the honorable the senate, is not conformable to, or consistent with, either of the constitutions;—the language of both, is that of *choosing* and *electing*, the amendment does not comprehend the idea, for it amounts barely to an appointment;—but if it did, I do not think that we are *at liberty* to pursue the *mode* pointed out in it, because it is novel, and not known in our state constitution.—There is a farther objection to this manner of appointment, it is not conclusive, for it may happen, that the different houses do not concur at all, and thus the provision in the amendment, will defeat itself.—If no other objections could be offered, this alone is sufficient to induce a non-concurrence.

The last proposition I undertook to prove was,—That the clause under consideration, as it stands in the bill, is strictly conformable to the new constitution.

To do this, no more is necessary, than to say, that it is, truly taken from the 30th section of our state constitution, and which I trust I have before shewn, is not only not contradictory to, but *the mode of choosing* representatives to Congress, under it, strictly conformable to, and consonant with the new constitution.

Compare the cases.—

Who are to choose?—The legislature.—Who are to be chosen?—Members of Congress, who are to represent the sovereignty of the state, in the same manner as delegates in the present Congress do, being a government over states.

Then why vary the mode?

With great deference to those who differ with us in sentiment, I shall beg leave to state one other argument, which *to me* likewise appears conclusive on this occasion.

Before we took our seats in this legislature, we severally took an oath of allegiance to the state of New-York, as a free and independent state. In this idea, the constitution is unquestionably included under the restrictions, with respect to the new constitution, as before mentioned; in this point of view, all who hear me will perceive, that those who conceive of the matter as I do, cannot possibly in any event, for the sake of accommodation, give up an explicit article, to which we conceive ourselves bound, by a tie so strong, as that of a solemn oath.

Sorry I am, that we are so unfortunate as to differ; but I trust that the honorable the senate will not adhere to their amendment, when they find that we are in a situation, from which I am sure they would not advise us to recede, at the expence of our consciences.

With respect to the last amendment, which goes to the appointing electors, little need be said, as it stands nearly on the same ground with the one I have just considered; and it is objected to on the same principle.

The remaining amendment, in which we have not concurred, is the one which alters two of the districts, for chusing members in the house of representatives of the Congress. We had no certain enumeration of the inhabitants of the several districts in Westchester county, yet the house determined, from the best evidence we could obtain, and we supposed ourselves right, at least we have not yet had any reason to recede.

The question which arises, especially on the first amendment, is a great constitutional one, and of serious concern, I would here beg leave to notice some reasons which I have heard urged in favor of the amendment. It is said that our state constitution, in this case, is void, as it could not contemplate members to the Congress under the new government, as this system was not in existence, when that was formed—I would answer, neither was the confederation,—But it did contemplate representatives of this state to the general government, or Congress of the United States, to be chosen by the legislature; and I think it not easy to shew the essential difference in the members of the senate in the Congress, under the new government, and the manner of their choice—and those mentioned in our constitution, and the mode there mentioned for their election.

It has also been said by some of the advocates for the amendment, that the new constitution divests the senate and assembly of many privileges. Therefore the appointing members to Congress, by the senate and assembly, must and ought to be exercised, in such manner as to them both shall seem best—Gentlemen must be put to a hard shift, to be obliged to use such reasoning as this,—for when the argument is put into plain English, it will speak this language—a part of the privileges, immunities and rights of the states, held under its constitution, are altered, taken away, or abridged; therefore, the whole are gone, and the constitution with them; will not the people be alarmed at this idea?—Was this the language at the late convention, when the new constitution was adopted? So sudden a change of argument is alarming indeed, yet I think it a fortunate circumstance, that the idea has been thrown out, as it will serve as a memento to alarm the vigilance of the good people of this state, the more solicitously to guard against every or any attempt which may be made upon their privileges in this way.

It has been farther said, that a choice by joint ballot, will enable the assembly, as being the most numerous body, to appoint whom they please, the votes of the senate notwithstanding.

The language of this is, that the constitution does not give the senate as much power as they suppose they ought to have. But suppose this should be the case, as the assembly are the most numerous, and are yearly chosen by the people, they will be most likely to make choice of such persons as will be most agreeable to the state at large, and this was undoubtedly the principle on which the mode of election, by joint ballot, in our constitution, was formed.

Expediency has likewise been frequently urged, as an inducement to concur in the amendments; this is a term which has of late become very fashionable, and frequently very convenient.

But I am by no means willing to allow it to be an argument of sufficient force, to break through the bulwark of a compact, so firm and sacred as that of a constitution.

The reason is obvious, for in the case before us, the present legislature are the judges of this expediency;—in some other contingency, a succeeding legislature may determine respecting the *expediency* of some other measure, and thus in time it may possibly become *expedient* to do the whole constitution away; this, I hope, will never be the case:—And I yet would fondly wish, that this honorable legislature (among the members of which are several gentlemen who assisted in framing our state constitution) will hold the same inviolable, on the principles before mentioned, and at every hazard.

Many of the gentlemen present, were likewise members of the late convention of this state, and well know that it was solely a principle of expediency, in *that case* (and which that body had a *right* to judge of) which induced an adoption of the new system, from a conviction that it was the best means to insure the amendments thereto, which were and still are anxiously expected, by a large majority of the people of this state, and who, I trust, will never rest satisfied, till so desirable an end is accomplished.

But the present case is widely different—we think it neither expedient or justifiable on any principle; but that a compliance would amount to betraying the rights of the people, which we consider a deposit too sacred to be bartered for any expediency whatever.

We think the true rule of conduct to be this, to do what we, on mature deliberation, think right and lawful, and leave consequences to him who rules on earth as well as in heaven.

General Schuyler—Conscious, Mr. Speaker, of my inability to do that justice to the purity of the principles which dictated the amendments proposed to the bill, which is the subject of this conference, I regret equally with the gentleman who was last up, in support of the bill, that it has fallen to my lot to be one of the conferees.

The clear and explicit manner, sir, in which the national constitution is worded, on the subject in debate, afforded reason for the senate to conclude, that the only contest would be on the superior eligibility of the one or the other mode, that contained in the bill, or that in the amendments, not doubting but that both houses would have been in sentiment, that the mode of appointing the senators was referred to their discretion; but it is now evident that the honorable the assembly contend that the mode prescribed by the constitution of this state, not only affords an *eligible* rule in the case before us, but is obligatory upon the legislature.

The senate, sir, thinks it cannot be disputed that the new constitution alters the constitution of every state in a variety of important particulars, and being the last *act* of the people, intended to modify and change their former acts—It must undoubtedly prevail wherever there is a clashing—and therefore the only question in *any case* must be whether the new constitution does in the *given case* contain an alteration or not—To ascertain this, the new constitution, not the old, must be consulted, and whenever the sense of the former is intelligible and clear, the inquiry is at an end—Indeed it would be perfectly ridiculous to adhere to the sense of an old compact, where a different meaning appeared in a new one, expressly designed to alter the old one. If this principle is not admitted, then the new constitution is nothing better than blank paper.

The question therefore cannot be what mode has been provided in our old constitution for electing delegates to Congress, but what mode is directed in the new;—refer to this, and we find a manifest departure. The new Congress is to consist of two branches—a senate, and a house of representatives. The representatives are as much *members of Congress* as the *senators*. If our state constitution is to be intended therefore as establishing a perpetual rule for appointing the representatives of this state in the Congress of the United States, and if that rule is not to be considered as done away, or altered by the new constitution then it will follow that the representatives, as well as the senators, must be chosen by joint ballot: this however is not pretended, for the bill in question makes another provision. It must then be acknowledged that the mode prescribed in the state constitution has been essentially altered, and that it does not prescribe a positive rule in the case. It will be to no purpose to contend, that there is an explicit alteration in regard to the representatives, and not in regard to the senators—this still admits that the only enquiry is whether the new national constitution does alter the state constitution in this particular: And to answer this we must consider the natural and fair meaning of the expressions used which relate to the subject, what are these, First, "The senate of the United States shall be composed of two senators from each state, chosen by the *legislature* thereof for six years." Secondly, "The times, places, and manner of holding elections for *senators* and representatives shall be prescribed in each state by the legislature thereof."—Who then are the legislature of this state? our constitution answers, The senate and assembly—How do they usually act together? what are their usual powers? the answer is, they *act* by and *have* a negative upon each other. In the first instance therefore the plain sense of the new constitution in referrence to this state is, that a majority of the senate in senate, co-operating with a majority of the assembly, in assembly, are to appoint the senators: But the other clause cited puts this construction out of doubt—"The legislature of each state is to prescribe the times, places, and *manner* of holding elections for *senators* and representatives." Hence the power of the legislature in respect to the *manner* of choosing senators is equal to that which it has in regard to the *manner* of choosing representatives—The very same *word* in the same *sentence* cannot upon any fair and rational construction be understood in different senses. It cannot in one case mean the senate and assembly acting by joint ballot, in another case in their usual method of law making. The *manner* of choosing the representatives in Congress must be prescribed by law—the *manner* of choosing senators must therefore equally be prescribed by law. The power of directing the mode of choosing senators, we derive from the constitution which the people have established for the government of the United States, not from the constitution of this state, and in the exercise of that power, the senate as an equal branch of the legislature must have an equal vote with the assembly, that is, a negative upon its proceedings.

On the whole it appears evident that the true construction of the new constitution in relation to the point now in question, is this, the legislature must by law prescribe the mode or manner in which the *legislative body* is to elect senators for the Congress—that mode is a matter of pure discretion, independent of any rule in the state constitution, and ought to be so regulated that each branch shall have its due weight, that the will of the people may be respected, who have conferred equal powers on the one and the other. This construction of the senate is countenanced by a similar decision of the legislature of Massachusetts; in which a close attention to the rights of the people, and a regard to their state constitution as inseparably prevails as in this, for their legislature has decided on this question in the same manner as the senate here contend that it should be decided before the adoption of the new national constitution. The delegates to Congress under the old confederation, were chosen by joint ballot of both houses, agreeably to the direction in their state constitution; but, the senators recently appointed there for the new government, have been chosen in such manner as to afford each house that compleat negative for which the senate now contend; but surely their state constitution was equally binding on their legislature, as ours on this; and every individual member there was under the same sacred obligation to maintain, unviolated, their state constitution, as every individual member here is to maintain ours; But the will of the people of that state, signified by their immediate representatives, altered their constitution, and so discharged the members from their oath, so far forth as the alteration in any case extended; and the legislature here are precisely in the same situation in the case before us, as the legislature there. Connecticut has no written constitution, at least none that I know of, and yet since the ratification of the new national government, they have altered the mode of choosing senators, from that which prevailed in the choice of delegates; the latter were elected by the people at large, the former by the concurrent will of both houses, that is, by a legislative act, in which each branch had a negative. The senate is not advised what modes have been adopted by the other legislatures, but if they should have retained the same mode as for appointing delegates to Congress, which was usual in such states, it will only prove, either that their former mode was agreeable to the direction of the new constitution, or that they exercised the legislative discretion which is allowed on the articles which have been cited; and not that the particular state constitution was obligatory in the case.

The senate, sir, have too high a respect for the hon. assembly, not to suppose that the hon. the conferee on their part, who opened the conference, has been mistaken when he asserted that the assembly would deem it preferable that the state should remain many years, even a century, without a representation in the national government, to an appointment in the manner proposed by the amendments. I say, sir, that the hon. the assembly could never intend an assertion, which conveyed so odious an implication on the discretion of the senate, on an occasion in which their great object was the preservation of that constitutional right, without which they would cease to be such efficient guardians of the liberties of the people, as the constitution intended they should be. But if the constitution of the state intended, as it surely does, that in every act to which the concurrence of both houses is requisite, the major will of each house should be signified; and if these coincide, that such coincidence is the legislative will of both. Let us see if the mode intended by the bill, would so operate as to give effect to the will of a majority, The senate when compleat in all its members, consists of 24—the assembly 70.—Hence, a majority of both, when acting jointly, will be 48[.] Let us now suppose, that a person is nominated by the unanimous voice of the senate, but that another person is nominated in the assembly, by a majority of 26, that is 48 for, and 22 against, here upon the ballot, altho' the senate was unanimous, and the assembly divided, yet the assembly would appoint the senators, and whatever the numbers may be in either house, they may be so divided as to have the same effect. Ingenious, sir, must be the mind that can discover in such a mode, an equality of legislative rights—that can discover that negative so essential to each, to check either the intemperance, the folly, or the weakness of the other—that check so wisely established by the constitution as the most effectual check to curb the lust of inordinate power and thirst of domination, which prevails not only in individuals, but too frequently in public bodies.

With respect to the alteration of two of the districts, it is said, that we can not ascertain the exact number of inhabitants in each of the towns of Westchester county. I must confess that the senate could not ascertain this matter precisely. They calculated in this manner—the county of Westchester contains twenty-one towns, and the county contains about 21,000 inhabitants; if then we suppose that all the towns will average, by adding only five towns to Dutchess county, which contains but 32,000 people, that district will then only contain 37,000—while New York, which contains 23,000, having sixteen towns of Westchester added to it, will amount to 39,000. The senate therefore supposed it would be proper to add some other of the towns of Westchester, to the county of Dutchess, in order to make the two districts more equal—besides, sir, tho' property may not be a criterion, yet it ought not to be thrown out of the scale; if therefore there must be an advantage to the one or the other of the said districts—New York they suppose is entitled to the preference. I might add too that the five towns the assembly have annexed to Dutchess, lie in the roughest part of the state, and contain but very few inhabitants.—One of them includes the tremendous mountain of Anthony's Nose; as it is well known therefore, that the most of the inhabitants are in the southern part of that county. The district of New-York, it is to be supposed, will still be too large, even if the amendment of the senate is agreed to.

The same reasoning that applies to the clause respecting the senators, will apply to that respecting the electors—I shall therefore say nothing on that point.

I hope, sir, that the observations that have been made will shew that the senate have insisted upon nothing but their constitutional rights—rights which involve the safety and liberties of their constituents, and which it will be criminal for them to surrender.

Mr. *Jones.*—The subject, Mr. President, which has occasioned the present conference, having been explained by those gentlemen who have gone before me, I proceed to shew the reasons that induced the assembly to frame the bill in the manner they have done; and why they cannot agree to the amendments of the senate.

Sir, the constitution of this state, under which all our powers are derived, was formed before the confederation; in which there is provision made for the appointment of delegates to Congress—our general government had not then assumed a form, and as it was uncertain what the form of it might be, it is to be inferred that the constitution contemplated delegates to a general government, however it might be formed. The assembly therefore say, that as the constitution of the state points out the mode which they have inserted in the bill, there is no discretion left in the legislature. But sir, they do not rest the matter here; they say that the rule laid down in the constitution is a wise and judicious one, in as much as thereby an election is ensured, however the opinions of the two houses might differ. By the amendment proposed, it appears to them that a difference between the two houses might embarrass the public business, and probably leave the state unrepresented. In this view of the matter, they think a joint ballot a happy expedient to ensure an election; that thereby the state may never lose its representation. And I hold it to be a principle not to be departed from; for if we do, we shall have no certainty of being represented in the national government. It must therefore be considered as a wise provision in the constitution of the state. When the confederation was formed, it was therein declared that the delegates to Congress should be appointed in such manner as the legislatures of the several states should think proper. The legislature of this state, therefore, conceiving themselves bound to pursue that plan marked out in the constitution, have conformed their proceedings to it, from that time to the present day. Gentlemen have urged that there was a Congress at the time our constitution was formed; this, sir, is true; but neither the power of that Congress, nor the form of their proceedings were defined. It was undoubtedly intended to form a constitution of some kind; the constitution of the state therefore contemplated a general constitution, not the Congress that was then formed. At the time the election was to be made under the confederation which was acceded to by the legislature of this state as well as of others, they proceeded upon the supposition that the constitution of this state was obligatory upon them; the senate then made no difficulties—no extraordinary privileges were contended for; nor was the public business embarrassed with constitutional questions and delays. True it is that the form of the general government has been altered, by giving to it an additional branch—and by adding an executive; but still the states are to be represented, and the senators to be chosen by them, in a great degree, hold the same place that the delegates to Congress now do: They are to be the representatives of the states. The former only operated on the states, as states, the latter, not only on the states, but the people; hence the necessity of the house of representatives, which are the representatives of the people, and the senate, which is composed of the representatives of the states. The assembly therefore in framing the bill for carrying into effect the constitution of the United States, supposed themselves bound to pursue, so far forth as the constitution of this state pointed out the mode, that plan which is inserted in the bill. Had it been expressly altered by the new constitution, we must have submitted to it. But the constitution of the state not being altered in that particular, the assembly are bound by it, and conceive it their duty to conform to the rule prescribed therein; more especially as upon an investigation they conceive it conformable to the new constitution. These were the reasons that induced the assembly to frame the bill in the manner as it now stands; and I trust that these reasons are solid. Why, sir, should we depart from the mode pointed out by the constitution; is it not to be adhered to? Why deviate from it unnecessarily? Why launch into experiments, the effect of which we can only conjecture?

But, sir, it seems that the objection is founded upon the choice being required to be made by the legislature; I readily agree that the same words in the same sentence, and in the same instrument, unless there is something to control them, must mean alike. And also I am sure that the word legislature in the confederation, meant the same thing as the word legislature in the new constitution. The word legislature undoubtedly must mean the same thing in both cases.

It was mentioned by one of the gentlemen that the senate had sent up two bills which had been rejected. I take it to be foreign to the present subject to go into any consideration of the reasons that induced the assembly to reject those bills; but, sir, I trust they can give good ones. In the course of the business it is asked who are the legislature? It is the senate and assembly, and true it is that they are distinct and independent branches in acts of legislation; but they are not so in electing members of Congress, as appears by the constitution. The bills that were sent to the assembly, proposed modes that did not accord with the idea of an election by the senate and assembly. These bills proposed to appoint the electors and senators by an act of the legislature, a mode not required by the new constitution, and directly repugnant to our own. I mention this in order to ground another important observation; it is said that the terms *appoint* and *elect* are synonymous; that we ought not to conclude from it either the one thing or the other; and as a farther illustration of the principle, an instance is produced of the word *elect* in the constitution of this state, where it speaks of the appointment of a treasurer. I shall readily admit that the words are to receive a reasonable construction in connexion with the other sentences. Upon this ground it is, that the assembly suppose that the words in the new constitution and the words in the confederation, are synonymous. The new constitution says the senate shall be chosen by the legislature; this clearly means an election; but if it could not be connected with other parts of the constitution, I should admit that the word *chosen* might have the meaning which the senate assign to it, but when we come to consider the 4th section of the first article, which declares that "the time, place and manner of holding *elections* shall be prescribed by the legislature; but the Congress may alter such regulations;"—what is the plain idea there? is it not that there shall be an *election*? In passing an act can it be called an election? Will any gentleman say it is possible to prescribe the time, and place, and manner of passing an act?—we can not. Hence it is concluded that the amendment is not conformable to the constitution of this state, or of the United States, which speaks of an election, and supposes an election. To do it by a law, the council of revision must also have a voice in the business, and if three men in that body should be opposed to the bill, it puts it in the power of a minority in either house to prevent an appointment.[3] There is, Mr. President, a great difference between legislative acts, and other acts, that are to be done by the legislature; if one act proposed by either branch of the legislature fails, still the government is not at an end; but if they are to make an election of officers, without which the government cannot operate, then the principle which operated well in the other instance would be destructive in this; it would defeat the very government itself. It is reasonable therefore to suppose that the framers of the new constitution intended that the mode to be prescribed should be such as would secure an election, hence it is that the term must mean an election in the way the word is commonly used. If, sir, the amendment should be acceded to, it forever puts it in the power of any thirteen men in the senate to defeat any election at all;—that a majority should be able to do this in ordinary cases of legislation is nothing; but that a system should be formed to give this power of defeating the government itself, to so small a majority is dangerous, and unconstitutional. It is urged that upon the principle as it stands in the bill, forty eight men could control the senate, but I would ask which is the most safely to be trusted—forty-eight, or thirteen. In the first case the principle is, that the majority make an election, in the latter, the smaller number controls the whole. Would it be wise to form a law on this principle, to put it in the power of so small a number to defeat the election? It is urged that the proposition in the amendment is fair, that the senate and assembly each choose one out of two nominated by the other house. This cannot be called an election; it is confining the election in both instances to a single person. But this is not the strongest objection; it is true, that at this time the legislature are to choose two senators; but the probability is, that for years to come, we are never to choose more than one. This one, then, the senate and assembly are to choose by concurrent resolution—if they disagree, they are to go on non-concurring, till one or the other be tired out. The natural tendency of such a mode is to create and keep a continual spirit of party throughout the state.

Is it reasonable to suppose that if there is a contest that either house will agree to the nomination of the other—nothing in such a case can determine, unless one or the other yield up their opinion; in our mode of each man giving his vote according to his conscience, there must be an election; in the mode proposed by the senate, one or the other must submit, or there can be no election.

But I would again remark, Mr. President, upon the first ground-work of this business, why are we to depart from that rule we find stated in the constitution? But admitting that we were not obliged to adhere to it, and that we were at liberty to exercise a mere discretion, is there any reason why we should so soon leave our constitution and travel into the wide field of conjecture?—In the opinion of the assembly it is not prudent, nor proper, to depart from the state constitution, only where the constitution of the United States has made it necessary. It is said that the constitution of the state is abrogated in this instance, if it is, I can not see any part of it that is good.—But, sir, without dwelling on that point, I say an election can be made conformable to the constitution of this state, and the constitution of the United States. These reasons induced the assembly to pass the bill in the manner they have; and the reasons I have mentioned are some of those which have induced them to non-concur the amendment. I trust that they are sufficient—that they are solid, and such as ought, and I hope will, induce the senate to recede from their amendments; in this case all mischief will be prevented, and an election will be the event. Upon the whole I must conceive that the mode proposed in the bill is not only the most prudent, but is agreeable to our constitution, which we are bound to adhere to. With respect to the arguments of the senate, that the rule laid down in the constitution is not obligatory, that the authority under which we act is a new grant of the people, and that therefore the senate have a right of a negative which they can not give up, is quite new to me—I confess I can not see from whence they are taken; on the contrary, I believe that the constitution of the state is not abrogated, but that it applies to any general government, let it be called by what name it will. That our constitution has been altered no man will deny—but with respect to the part so altered we differ materially;—but even on that ground, supposing the clause in question was altered, is it not reasonable, do not our constituents expect it from us, that we should conform our acts to the constitution we have always lived under?—I would ask, therefore, as the mode proposed by the assembly accords with our own constitution, and does not oppose the spirit of the new constitution, why we should hesitate to adopt it? The amendment of the senate does not accord, but is directly contrary to the constitution of this state, and of the United States. Besides, in its operation, this defect will result, it is impossible to say whether there will, or will not be an election; is this a proper mode? I trust that the senate, upon reflection, will see that the ground on which the bill has been passed by the assembly is proper, and that the reasons which have kept them from agreeing to the amendment are also justifiable.

I have hitherto confined myself to the first article of the amendment, I will just observe that the last article is nearly in the same situation; what therefore applies to the one will apply to the other; for tho' the words are not the same in both cases, the thing itself differs little. It has been remarked, by one of the gentlemen of the senate, that they are alike; sir, there is a difference—the Congress have no control over the state with respect to the electors—the states may exercise their discretion on the mode of choosing them—but in the other instance, the Congress will have a right to alter and control our laws. This, however makes no material difference in the case before us.

I shall say but a few words with respect to that amendment which respects the division of Westchester county—it is of little importance, perhaps, whether the amendment is made or not; but I trust that the reasons that operated in the assembly are solid—and that they stand unimpeached—True it is that we have no way to come at the number of inhabitants in each town; it is impossible to determine with precision. But, sir, the ground upon which a gentleman of the senate has made a calculation is so manifestly wrong, that I will prove that the bill ought to stand as it is; the single ground of calculation is, there are twenty-one towns in the county of Westchester, and then in order to form a ratio, the supposition is made that each town contains an equal number of inhabitants—now it is a fact well known, that the town of Morissinia does not contain freeholders enough to make town officers—it is a fact also well known, that Pelham, Maroneck, Harrison, and I believe some other towns are nearly in the same situation. This shews the uncertainty of any calculations on the subject. The assembly being of opinion that their division is nearest the truth, have therefore the highest reason to suppose that the senate will recede from this amendment.

Mr. *Duane*—Mr. Speaker—The managers on the part of the hon. assembly, as well as the two gentlemen appointed with me by the senate, having performed the task assigned them, it now remains for me to close the present conference.

I need not, sir, repeat at large the clauses of the bill, and the amendments now under consideration. It will be sufficient to premise that the first respects the manner of appointing the senators to represent this state in the senate of the Congress of the United States. The bill proposes that they shall be chosen by the joint ballot of the senators, and members of the assembly collectively, in which case numbers would preponderate. The amendment aims at securing to each house distinctly, an equal right in the appointment, in *their legislative capacity*. A similar provision is made by the bill for choosing the electors of a president and vice-president for the United States, and an amendment is offered by the senate in the same spirit as the first. The other amendment adds the town of Poundridge, and Bedford in Westchester county, to the election district, which includes the county of Dutchess, as described in the bill. The senate trusts, sir, notwithstanding the reasons which have been urged on the part of the hon. assembly against the two amendments first taken notice of, it has appeared, and will be more fully manifested, that they are founded on constitutional principles, which cannot be shaken; and that the last would render the lower districts more equal in the number of voters.

It were to be wished, in the course of these debates, every thing foreign had been laid aside, and the amendments alone examined on their true merits. Our attention would then have been fixed on its proper object. But since a latitude has been taken, before we proceed to the principal points, it may be of use to notice some of the observations which fell from the managers of the hon. assembly, which probably cannot elucidate the subject before us, and might well have been spared. One of those hon gentlemen was pleased to make remarks on two bills which the senate had sent down to the hon. assembly for their concurrence; one respecting the appointment of senators, the other the electors. That they were rejected, one would have thought sufficient to place them out of the reach of any comment at this conference. The senate, however, cannot omit this opportunity, since it is introduced, to suggest the motives which induced them to wish that three separate bills, instead of one, might have been agitated, for carrying the constitution of the United States into effect. They foresaw the embarrassments which would accompany the progress of this business. Under present circumstances the electors for the executive could not be chosen by the people. The constitution then could only be fulfilled by providing three different modes for the appointment of electors, senators and representatives to the Congressional assembly. They therefore conceived it the wisest and safest course to attempt to effect these appointments by distinct bills, that there might be a chance of partial success, if one or more failed. And, sir, may it not yet be regretted, on an occasion of such vast moment, that the sentiments of the senate did not meet with the approbation of the hon. assembly. One of your hon. managers has been pleased expressly to declare that the amendments would be a sacrifice of the rights of the people, and that rather than make that sacrifice, it would be better that the state should go unrepresented in the general government. Sir, if this should be the sense of the hon. the assembly, and it does not become me to question it, by hazarding all in one bill, the whole body of the people may go unrepresented in the assembly of the Congress. The senate, sir, would consider this as a great public calamity; highly dissatisfactory to the state, whether it respects the opinions of those who are desirous of giving the new constitution an experiment in its present frame or of those who wish it may be speedily amended by another convention. This reflection makes the deeper impression, because the clause which concerns the election of representatives by the people seems so capable of accommodation, the dispute turning on an estimate of numbers in two towns, founded in neither house confessedly on conclusive facts.

Sir, an hon. gentleman has been pleased to say that the sacred obligation of an oath binds the hon. assembly to a choice of senators by joint ballot, in the mode prescribed by the constitution, and that therefore they cannot depart from it. But this is begging the question; it is the great object of the conference, as to two of the amendments, to examine whether the state constitution has in this case a binding force, and the affirmative can only be deduced from reason and argument. If it has no force, the oath must be out of the question. The senate, are not insensible of the excellency of the state constitution, nor of their duty to preserve and defend it. Under that constitution it is that they claim an equal share of legislation with the hon. house of assembly, and ground their right to offer the present amendments, as an independent branch of the legislature.

An hon. gentleman has been pleased to offer some reflexions on the manner in which the general constitution was ratified by the state convention. The senate, sir, do not perceive the force or propriety of these reflexions. It is enough for this legislature that the people, by their convention, have assented to and ratified it. On us it is binding. Arguments cannot be necessary to prove it, the very bill now under consideration, is calculated to carry it into effect, recognizes it, and demonstrates its authority.

The hon. gentleman, who immediately preceded me, has amused us some time by a criticism on the different import of the terms elect and appoint. The senate deem this also among the moments that have been mispent; but as it was urged with seriousness, it will be taken up in the course of our remarks on the substantial parts of this conference, to which we shall now proceed.

Mr. Speaker, however dilated, it appears to the senate that the subject of this conference, on the two principal amendments, may be reduced to a very narrow compass; nay to a single enquiry whether the clause of the constitution which directs the manner of appointing delegates to Congress, is obligatory in the present case? If it is not, as the senate contend, then it must necessarily follow, that their right to an equal voice in the appointments under consideration, ought not to be disputed. It is this question which we mean candidly to discuss.

In the course of the debates it has been frequently urged, that the abovementioned clause of the state constitution, must direct the manner of appointing our federal senators, because it was established six months before the articles of confederation had any existence; and therefore that it was intended for any future national government which might be instituted for the United States, and ought now to be applied to the general constitution.

The inconclusiveness of this reasoning will, we presume, be obvious, from a recurrence to well known facts; which preceded the establishment of our state constitution. In September 1774, the first Congress of the United States was held at Philadelphia. In the spring of 1775, it was reassembled.

The battle of Lexington in the summer of that year brought the affairs of these States to a serious and alarming crisis. The Congress proceeded to exercise the highest acts of sovereignty; they declared their independence; absolved the inhabitants from the obligation of allegiance; proclaimed war against Great-Britain; directed the respective states to institute forms of government for their own accommodation; raised armies; emitted money; and appointed ambassadors. In this Congress our state had all along been represented, and took an active part. When we set down to frame our own constitution, many of these acts of Congress were recited as its basis and ground work, as appears by the first printed copies, one of which is now in my hand. To this Congress, members were to be appointed, and to the election of such members the clause of the constitution had a manifest reference. The frame of government, when the unlimited powers of Congress should come to be defined, no man could foresee—no conjecture reach. The constitution in the point of which we are speaking might or might not happen to be applicable to it; controlled by it, there is no doubt it must have been, unless the state should have chosen to withdraw herself from the union. Can it then be said, that the clause respecting the joint ballots had not a full operation and effect, independent of the articles of confederation, or any written frame of government? Certainly it had. It is admitted that when the confederation was ratified, not having essentially altered the administration of the general government; but still entrusting it altogether in the hands of one single body of representatives—the mode which the state constitution had prescribed for the appointment of delegates, was continued; as it was natural to expect. But, sir, in process of time it was found by experience, that the confederation itself was weak and defective, unfit for the government of a great nation; incapable of affording protection from the want of power, and unsafe to be trusted with competent power, for want of those checks and balances which are acknowledged to be essential to the liberty of the people. To these considerations the new constitution owes its existence, and its adoption by so many states. It will afford pertinent conclusions to examine a little into its frame. It does not, like the present confederation, invest all power in the hands of a single body of men. In this respect it bears a great analogy to the constitution of our own state, is built upon the same excellent principles, and guarded by the same checks. The powers are distributed among two independent legislative branches, and an executive, besides the judiciary, constituted for national purposes. The executive has the right of revision and objection, reserving to the two houses, that of adhering to a bill, if two-thirds of each think fit. Such is the inconsiderateness of the human mind, and so prone is it to heat and intemperance, that our happiness in a state of society, greatly depends on the institution and due exercise of such checks. This is a leading feature in our state constitution. Besides the checks already noticed, is added the further precaution of authorising the executive to prorogue the legislature for sixty days, to make room for reflection and composure, when he conceives it necessary.

If, sir, we pursue the general constitution a step further, we find that the assembly of the Congress are to be chosen, not by the joint ballot of both houses or their legislative act, but by the suffrages of the people at large. The senators are to be chosen not by the people, but by the legislature. The executive is to be chosen, neither by the people at large, nor the legislature, but by electors to be appointed by the people or legislature, for the express purpose of making the choice. From the nature of these appointments, it may be fairly inferred, that according to the spirit of the constitution the federal assembly are to be considered as the immediate representatives of the people, and the senators as the immediate representatives of the state legislature. No other reason can be assigned why the members of both houses were not equally rendered eligible by the people, at least with a distinction that the senators should be chosen by the freeholders only.

We have not, we are confident, reasoned from the constitution in terms too strong. In the third section it is declared that the senate of the United States shall be composed of two senators from each state, *chosen by the legislature thereof*; and in the fourth section, that the time, place, and *manner* of holding elections for senators and representatives shall be prescribed in each state by the *legislature* thereof. It need not be proved in this place, that by our own state constitution the supreme legislative authority within this state is vested in a house of assembly and senate; that they can only express their will by a law; or that they have a complete negative on each other in every legislative act. If we examine the source from whence the general constitution derives its existence, and the authority to appoint federal senators, it is not certainly from the citizens or the constitution respected as they are, but the people of eleven of the United States, of which we are but one, expressed by their delegates in the general convention. It is their authority alone, which enables us to debate on the bill and amendments before us. It is the adhering to the true meaning of what they have prescribed, that can give efficacy to any act which may finally be adopted by us on this occasion. But, it is reiterated, that our state constitution has given a rule for the election of delegates under the confederation, which we are bound to observe in the choice of senators under the new constitution. How is this proved? Is the government the same? Is the office of a delegate and senator the same? Is the time for which they are appointed of equal duration? Is the same qualification for each required? No, sir, in all these respects they are essentially different. Whence then proceeds either the obligation or fitness of this rule?

It has been said, that the amendment proposed is without right; but what clearer right can be established than an explicit declaration of the general constitution, that the senators for the Congress of the United States shall be chosen *by the legislature* of each state? and what can be more satisfactorily maintained, than that [for] every act of a legislature, consisting of two independent branches, the consent of both must concur to give it validity. But, sir, it has been further alledged that the amendments proposed by the senate are contrary to precedent. A single instance is assigned that our delegates to the late general convention were elected by ballot agreeably to the mode prescribed by our own constitution. But will gentlemen argue from an event which happened prior to the general constitution against the exercise of a new authority given to the legislature by the constitution itself? Surely it must be of no avail. In its proper place we shall examine the weight of precedent which we trust, instead of discountenancing, will prove a strong argument in favor of the two principal amendments.

It has been urged by the honorable gentleman who opened the conference, that the appointment proposed by the bill is most eligible because it brings the election *nearer to the people*. Another honorable gentleman has expressed himself on the same point in terms still stronger, *the assembly*, says he, *are most numerous, and more likely in their choice to please the people at large*. The last honorable gentleman has gone further, asserting *that there is more safety in the assembly than the senate, because the former are more numerous*. This then appears to be a favorite topic on which the utmost stress is laid, and it calls for particular animadversion. If, sir, the majority of the senators who advocated the amendments, were deducted from the majority who supported the bill in the honorable assembly, the difference would not exceed eight votes in the whole. After finding no greater superiority on a question so interesting, one would have thought an argument of this nature would have been suppressed, instead of being so earnestly reiterated. It is hard to conceive how the safety of the people can be concerned in a circumstance so unimportant.

But if the majority had been much greater, what would it prove? The senate do not contend about a point of expediency, but for a constitutional right. Our constitution has provided that the senate shall consist of 24 members, and the assembly of 70, while it vests equal authority and a complete negative in each. If the disproportion of numbers was a solid objection, it would apply with equal force to every law and to every case, and strike at the constitution itself. Let it be added, that the authority of the senate, in their legislative capacity, equally with that of the honorable assembly, extends over all the dearest rights of the people—their property, their liberty, and their lives. Can it then be in contemplation that there is a distinction between the exercise of such vast power in every general concern, and that of concurring, or refusing to concur in the appointment of an individual to an office, that the first may be trusted to the senate; but in the last, it is necessary *to draw nearer to the people* by yielding to the honorable assembly an uncontrolable exercise of their discretion thro' the superiority of their numbers. There are indeed legislative appointments to offices, in which the public welfare is deeply interested; among the highest of which we rank those now under our consideration. But *here* do the letter or spirit of our own constitution, or the reason or policy on which the checks and balances which it prescribes are founded, justify the doctrine contended for? They do not. To the senate it appears not only that in this instance they have a right to a perfect legislative equality, but that it is as wise and salutary that the effects of heat and intemperance should be guarded against in the appointment of great confidential officers by the legislature, as in the enacting of any law whatever. They discover no room for distinction.

Sir, it has been insisted that the confederation, and the new constitution, on the subject before us, are similar and harmonize, and that the amendment is inconsistent with both. It is true, sir, that the stile of *the Congress* is appropriated to the new government, by the federal constitution; but is its frame in any respect like that described in the confederation? The contrary is undeniable; *there* one body of men were appointed to administer all the powers of government; *here*, as has been shewn before, it is composed of an executive, a senate, and an assembly, and distinct modes are prescribed for their appointment; the first by electors to be chosen for the express purpose—the second *by the legislature*—the last by the suffrages of the people. To two of them clearly the joint ballot can not possibly apply, where then is the harmony?—But it is said that with respect to the senate, the joint ballot is to be preserved;—on what refined distinction can this position be maintained?—Both the spirit and the letter of the new constitution dictate a different language, declaring that the senators shall be chosen, not according to the then existing constitution or laws of the state, but in such manner as the legislature SHALL direct; plainly referring to a future act of provision to be made for the purpose. The amendment then can be no violation of the state constitution in this respect, since a new authority which so far supercedes it as to be admitted supreme and paramount, has evidently vested it in the legislature. Nor is this amendment in any sense repugnant to the new constitution. As a legislature, we can only express our will by a law, in which each branch must have a negative on the other. The exercise of any power, by the members of the two houses collectively deciding by a majority of voices, is not an act of the legislature; nor were it ever practised in any instance but in balloting for delegates, according to a provision in the state constitution, which, as we trust is fully shewn, is now done away.

An hon. gentleman has displayed his talent at criticism by contrasting the import of the terms *electing* and *choosing*, with *appointing*; he insists that the authority of the legislature to *choose*, is the same as if it had been to *elect* senators; and that there can be no election by a law. Our own constitution, sir, conveys a different idea of these terms, and considers them as synonymous. Its authority on the present occasion will hardly be questioned, when it is upon one of its clauses that we are debating. In the 22d act it provides that the treasurer of this state shall be *appointed* by act of the legislature, to originate with the assembly, provided he shall not be *elected* out of either branch of the legislature. The article which institutes a council of appointment, ordains that the assembly shall, once in every year, openly nominate and *appoint* one of the senators from each great district to form a council for the appointment of officers; and declares in the close that the said senators shall not be *eligible* to the said council for two years successively. These the senate presume are sufficient grounds to justify a former observation, that this verbal criticism might on the present occasion have been spared. But, sir, they go much farther; they prove, contrary to the gentleman's opinion, that an election may be made by law—nay, that this is directed and expressly required with respect to one of our highest and most confidential officers—the treasurer of the state. This is a case every way so decidedly applyable, that it can require no elucidation; and it is remarkable, that tho' suggested by one of the managers of the senate who preceded me, no attempt has been made to refute it; as unanswerable, it has been passed over in silence. If we enquire whether an appointment or election, for we shall not contend about the term, is practicable: let experience decide. The fact is that a treasurer has been uniformly elected by law from the establishment of the constitution, without any difficulty or embarrassment. Nor is this the only instance of choosing or electing persons to public trust by law. Many might be adduced, but let two suffice; perhaps there is not an instance in our code of laws where higher confidence was placed in any citizens than in the commissioners for amicably determining the territorial controversy between us and Massachusetts;—her claim extended over a great and most valuable part of our state—it involved even the city in which this conference is held:—nor were they limited in their powers, every thing was submitted to their integrity and discretion:—Were they appointed by a joint ballot of the members of the legislature collectively? No; but by a law in which each branch of the legislature had an equal authority. Again, when commissioners were appointed to hold a treaty for obtaining from the native proprietors of the western country the right of soil; an occasion in which the treasury of the state was laid open to their disposal without reserve: Were they appointed by joint ballot? No;—but by a similar law.—These, sir, were elections and appointments in which each branch had a negative on the other; no difficulty was foreseen—none experienced in carrying them into effect. If we examine why the practice was preferred to a joint ballot, the reason seems obvious—It must have proceeded from a consciousness that the latter would have been an encroachment on the rights of the senate; reducing them from the dignity of an independent branch of the legislature to the humble condition of mere solemn witnesses of the transaction; for the assembly being so numerous, the voice of the senate would be lost on every difference of sentiment between the two houses, which should be brought to that unequal test.

It has been further urged by the same honorable gentleman, that in every election all parties should be obliged to concur, but that if the amendment proposed by the senate was adopted, there would be no certainty of any election; but, sir, this is founded on an apprehension very unfavorable to the legislature. It is to be taken for granted that they will do their duty. Since it is essential to the public welfare that federal senators should be appointed, the presumption ought to be that each house will listen to reason; be governed by a spirit of conciliation; and ultimately unite in the choice of suitable persons. This objection is one of those which proves too much—it extends to every act of legislation, where the two houses may think differently: shall we therefore say it is safer to trust one branch than two, with the legislative authority?

It has been contended that the mode of appointment prescribed by the bill is the most eligible; if I understand the force of this term, it would change the debate to a question of expediency. But, sir, the senate by no means consider the principal point under consideration as one which they may maintain or relinquish at discretion. It is a right of the people secured to them by the constitution of which we cannot dispose. The reasons in vindication of that right have been freely submitted to the candor of the hon. assembly: to us they are conclusive. Constitutionally invested with as great a share in the power of legislation as the hon. assembly, we deem it a sacred deposit, which we are under every obligation to hand down to our successors, and to posterity unimpaired. It is for that equality only we now contend, and it is our opinion that to surrender it would be a breach of trust, and bring upon us deserved reproach.

Mr. *Speaker*.—In the order of debate which I proposed to myself, the next thing to be considered is the amendment respecting the electors of the president and vice-president. Here, sir, the observations already stated on the part of the senate, in general apply in their full force. Indeed some distinctions might be taken, and arguments inferred of no small moment. For instance, these electors can in no sense be regarded as *Delegates to Congress*; to them therefore the balloting clause in the state constitution will on no possible construction refer. But it would be scarcely practicable to enlarge on a question so nearly analagous to the former without repetition and prolixity, and it is time this conference should be brought to a conclusion.

From the last motive, sir, I shall decline a discussion of the amendment, proposing an alteration of the election district which includes the county of Dutchess. It is the more unnecessary, because one of the gentlemen who preceded me has clearly stated the grounds of that amendment. On this solid basis we are contented it should rest.

These, sir, are the observations which we have the honor to submit in the name of the senate, in support of their amendments. In our turn we trust they will be candidly considered, and have their proper weight with the honorable assembly when they come to decide the fate of a bill so essential to the public welfare.

When Mr. Duane had concluded, the senate withdrew.

1. *Daily Advertiser*, 13, 14, 16, 17, and 20 January 1789. The debates were also printed in the *Daily Gazette*, 14, 15, 16, 17, 19, 21, and 23 January, and in the *New York Journal*, 5, 12, 19, and 26 February, and 5 and 12 March.

2. On 16 December 1788 the Assembly and Senate by a joint ballot elected David Gelston, John Hathorn, Samuel Jones, Philip Pell, and Abraham Yates, Jr., to serve in the last Confederation Congress.

3. According to Article III of the state constitution, all bills passed by the legislature had to be approved by a Council of Revision before they became law. If a majority of the council objected to a bill, it was returned to the legislature for reconsideration; the council's objections could be overridden by a two-thirds vote in each house of the legislature. The council consisted of the chancellor, the judges of the Supreme Court (or any two of them), and the governor. See Thorpe, V, 2628–29.

Assembly and Senate Proceedings, Monday, 5 January

The Senate, A.M.

Mr. President, left the chair and with the Members of the Senate proceeded to the Assembly-Chamber, to meet the Hon. the Assembly, for the purpose of holding the conference agreed upon by both Houses, by their respective resolutions of the third of January instant, and after having held the said conference, the Senate returned to the Senate-Chamber, and Mr. President reassumed the chair.

Mr. Vanderbilt, thereupon moved that the Senate do adhere to their said amendments.

Mr. Humfrey, as an amendment to the first motion, moved that the Senate do recede from their said amendments.

Mr. Yates, as a further amendment moved that the question on the last motion be postponed until to-morrow.

Debates arose on Mr. Yates' motion, and the question being put thereon it was carried in the negative, in manner following, viz.

FOR THE NEGATIVE.

Mr. Philip Schuyler,	Mr. Morris,
Mr. Douw,	Mr. Roosevelt,
Mr. Micheau,	Mr. L'Hommedieu,
Mr. Peter Schuyler,	Mr. Duane,
Mr. Fonda,	Mr. Hoffman.
Mr. Vanderbilt,	

FOR THE AFFIRMATIVE.

Mr. Yates,	Mr. Townsend,
Mr. Williams,	Mr. Tredwell,
Mr. Van Ness,	Mr. Humfrey,
Mr. Swartwout,	Mr. Clinton.

Ordered, That the consideration of Mr. Humfrey's motion be postponed until in the afternoon.

Then the Senate adjourned until half past four of the clock in the afternoon.

The Assembly, A.M.

Mr. Speaker, then left the chair and with the House attended the Honorable the Senate in the Assembly-Chamber, pursuant to the resolutions of both Houses for holding a conference on the amendments to the bill, entitled *An act for carrying into effect on the part of this State, the Constitution of the United States, assented to and ratified by the Convention of this State, on the twenty-sixth day of July last*, which were not concurred in by this House; and the said conference being ended *Mr. Speaker* reassumed the chair, and reported to the House, that a conference had been held in the presence of both Houses, on the amendment proposed to the first clause of the said bill, and on the amendments proposed to that part of the second clause of the said bill, which respects the boundaries of the election District, containing the county of Dutchess, and also on the amendment proposed to the last enacting clause of the said bill.

Mr. Harison then made a motion that the House should adjourn until ten of the clock to-morrow morning.

Debates arose on the said motion, and the question being put thereon, it passed in the negative, in the manner following, viz.

FOR THE NEGATIVE.

Mr. Jones,	Mr. Thompson,
Mr. Carman,	Mr. Bay,
Mr. G. Livingston,	Mr. Tappen,
Mr. Kortz,	Mr. Griffen,
Mr. Yates,	Mr. J. Smith,
Mr. Frey,	Mr. Carpenter,
Mr. Stauring,	Mr. D'Witt,
Mr. Van Dyck,	Mr. Wisner,
Mr. J. Van Rensselaer,	Mr. Adgate,
Mr. Hardenbergh,	Mr. Harper,
Mr. Veeder,	Mr. Havens,
Mr. Winn,	Mr. Schenck,
Mr. Duncan,	Mr. Akins,
Mr. Tearse,	Mr. E. Clark,
Mr. Savage,	Mr. Patterson,
Mr. Webster,	Mr. Scudder,
Mr. M'Cracken,	Mr. Cantine.

FOR THE AFFIRMATIVE.

Mr. B. Livingston,	Mr. Watts,
Mr. Gilbert,	Mr. Livingston,
Mr. Van Cortlandt,	Mr. Horton,
Mr. Seaman,	Mr. Low,
Mr. Barker,	Mr. Bancker,
Mr. Harison,	Mr. Vandervoort,
Mr. Hoffman,	Mr. Rockwell,
Mr. H. Van Rensselaer,	Mr. Verplanck,
Mr. Younglove,	Mr. Cornwell,

Mr. Giles,	Mr. Macomb,
Mr. Dongan,	Mr. Crane,
Mr. Sands,	Mr. Bloom.
Mr. Gardiner,	

The House then proceeded to the consideration of the first, second and last clauses of the said bill, entitled *An act for carrying into effect on the part of this State, the Constitution of the United States, assented to and ratified by the Convention of this State, on the twenty-sixth day of July last,* and the amendments proposed to the said clauses respectively.

The first enacting clause and the amendments thereto proposed, as the same are inserted in the Journal of this House, of the second day of January instant,[1] having been read and considered, and debates had thereon, *Mr. Speaker* put the question, whether the House did adhere to the said first enacting clause of the said bill, and it was carried in the affirmative, in the manner following, viz.

FOR THE AFFIRMATIVE.

Mr. Jones,	Mr. Bay,
Mr. Carman,	Mr. Tappen,
Mr. G. Livingston,	Mr. Griffen,
Mr. Kortz,	Mr. Carpenter,
Mr. Yates,	Mr. J. Smith,
Mr. Frey,	Mr. D'Witt,
Mr. Stauring,	Mr. Wisner,
Mr. Van Dyck,	Mr. Adgate,
Mr. J. Van Rensselaer,	Mr. Harper,
Mr. Hardenbergh,	Mr. Havens,
Mr. Veeder,	Mr. Schenck,
Mr. Winn,	Mr. Akins,
Mr. Duncan,	Mr. E. Clark,
Mr. Tearse,	Mr. Patterson,
Mr. Savage,	Mr. Scudder,
Mr. Webster,	Mr. Cantine,
Mr. M'Cracken,	Mr. Bloom.
Mr. Thompson,	

FOR THE NEGATIVE.

Mr. B. Livingston,	Mr. Low,
Mr. Gilbert,	Mr. Bancker,
Mr. Van Cortlandt,	Mr. Vandervoort,
Mr. Seaman,	Mr. Rockwell,
Mr. Barker,	Mr. Verplanck,
Mr. Harison,	Mr. Cornwell,
Mr. Hoffman,	Mr. Giles,
Mr. H. Van Rensselaer,	Mr. Dongan,
Mr. Younglove,	Mr. Sands,
Mr. Livingston,	Mr. Gardiner,
Mr. Horton,	Mr. Macomb,
Mr. Watts,	Mr. Crane.

The second enacting clause of the said bill, and the amendments thereto proposed,[2] which were not concurred in by this House, as they are inserted in the Journal of this

House, of the second instant, were then read and considered; and *Mr. Speaker* put the question, whether the House did adhere to the said second clause of the said bill, and it was carried in the affirmative.

The last enacting clause of the said bill, and the amendment thereto proposed,[3] as the same are inserted in the Journal of this House, of the second instant, having been read and considered; *Mr. Speaker* put the question, whether the House did adhere to the last enacting clause of the said bill, and it was carried in the affirmative, in the manner following, viz.

FOR THE AFFIRMATIVE.

Mr. Jones,	Mr. Bay,
Mr. Carman,	Mr. Tappen,
Mr. G. Livingston,	Mr. Griffen,
Mr. Kortz,	Mr. Carpenter,
Mr. Yates,	Mr. J. Smith,
Mr. Frey,	Mr. D'Witt,
Mr. Stauring,	Mr. Wisner,
Mr. Van Dyck,	Mr. Adgate,
Mr. J. Van Rensselaer,	Mr. Harper,
Mr. Hardenbergh,	Mr. Havens,
Mr. Veeder,	Mr. Schenck,
Mr. Winn,	Mr. Akins,
Mr. Duncan,	Mr. E. Clark,
Mr. Tearse,	Mr. Patterson,
Mr. Savage,	Mr. Scudder,
Mr. Webster,	Mr. Cantine,
Mr. M'Cracken,	Mr. Bloom.
Mr. Thompson,	

FOR THE NEGATIVE.

Mr. B. Livingston,	Mr. Low,
Mr. Gilbert,	Mr. Bancker,
Mr. Van Cortlandt,	Mr. Vandervoort,
Mr. Seaman,	Mr. Rockwell,
Mr. Barker,	Mr. Verplanck,
Mr. Harison,	Mr. Cornwell,
Mr. Hoffman,	Mr. Giles,
Mr. H. Van Rensselaer,	Mr. Dongan,
Mr. Younglove,	Mr. Sands,
Mr. Watts,	Mr. Gardiner,
Mr. Livingston,	Mr. Macomb,
Mr. Horton,	Mr. Crane.

Thereupon *Resolved*, That this House do adhere to their said bill, as to the first, and last clauses thereof, and also to that part of the second clause which respects the boundaries of the election District, that includes the county of Dutchess.

Ordered, That Mr. Dongan and Mr. Havens, deliver a copy of the last preceding resolution to the Honorable the Senate.

The Senate, P.M.

[The Senate received the House resolution.]

The Senate then proceeded to consider the motion made by Mr. Humfrey, viz. "That the Senate do recede from their amendments to the said bill," and after considerable debates being had, Mr. President put the question on the said motion, and it passed in the negative, in manner following, viz.

FOR THE NEGATIVE.

Mr. Philip Schuyler,	Mr. Morris,
Mr. Douw,	Mr. Roosevelt,
Mr. Micheau,	Mr. L'Hommedieu,
Mr. Peter Schuyler,	Mr. Duane,
Mr. Fonda,	Mr. Hoffman.
Mr. Vanderbilt,	

FOR THE AFFIRMATIVE.

Mr. Yates,	Mr. Townsend,
Mr. Williams,	Mr. Tredwell,
Mr. Van Ness,	Mr. Humfrey,
Mr. Swartwout,	Mr. Clinton.

Thereupon, *Resolved,* That the Senate do adhere to their three amendments to the bill, entitled *An act for carrying into effect on the part of this State, the Constitution of the United States, assented to and ratified by the Convention of this State, on the twenty-sixth day of July last,* and not concurred in by the Honorable the Assembly.

Ordered, That Mr. Hoffman and Mr. Duane, deliver a copy of the preceding resolution, to the Honorable the Assembly.

1. This clause directed the mode of choosing Senators.
2. This clause directed the division of the state into districts for the election of Representatives.
3. This clause directed the mode of choosing presidential Electors.

Assembly Debates, Monday, 5 January[1]

Mr. Harrison then moved that the house adjourn, in order to postpone the question till the next day; the arguments of the senate were such, he thought, as required a serious and deliberate investigation; the decision was to be important, and the members ought to take time to weigh the matter well, before they gave their voice on the occasion.

Mr. Jones opposed this motion; the situation of the bill he said, forbid any delay. This matter had been long under the consideration of both houses—the minds of the members he believed were as well prepared as they could be—he therefore thought it best to take the question, and moved for a resolution to adhere to the bill without the amendments.

The question for adjournment was first decided on, and carried in the negative. . . .[2]

Mr. Jones's motion for adhering to the bill without the amendments, was then read, when Mr. Harrison arose.

Mr. Speaker, said he, a conference has at length taken place between the two houses upon the subject of the present bill, which is on all hand[s] acknowledged to be of the utmost importance. I have embraced the opportunity of delivering my sentiments upon this subject on a former occasion,[3] and as I was then of opinion that the senate could not be disposed to give up their right to an equal voice in the choice of senators for the general government, I brought forward a proposition, which I hoped might prove the basis of an accommodation, even if it should not be found perfectly unexceptionable.

Since the conference I am strengthened in the opinion which I before entertained. The senate I am persuaded *will* not, nay I think that they *cannot* resign their pretentions; and when I look forward to the evils which may result from an adherence to our bill, I am anxious that we should examine carefully the ground on which it is framed.—We are still in such a situation as to have time for reflection—We may pause for a few minutes, and weigh with ourselves the consequences which must attend our determination.

I would not be understood, sir, that this house are bound in a greater degree than the senate, to consider the consequences that must result from their conduct—but where those consequences are of so serious a nature, both parties should be cautious, that their conduct is founded upon proper reasons. If the constitution has expressly pointed out the path for us, we are bound to walk in it, let the consequence be what it will—but in order to determine *that question*, it will be necessary for us to examine the pretensions of both parties, and from thence only a proper conclusion can be drawn.

If I have comprehended the arguments in favor of the bill, as framed in this house, they are intended to shew, that we are *bound* to a particular *mode* of election, and that to depart from it would be to deviate from the provisions of our state constitution. Sir, the gentlemen who have brought forward the argument will not (I believe) contend that the senators for the United States fall precisely within the description of delegates to Congress. This ground they themselves have not supposed to be tenable—they have therefore argued not so much from the *letter* as from what they supposed to be the *spirit* of our state constitution. They tell us that this constitution was formed before the articles of confederation, and they infer from thence that our representatives in the general government were intended by the state constitution, whatever might be the frame of that government, or the description of those representatives. Sir, the argument deduced from *that* circumstance alluded to is undoubtedly ill founded; because it is evident that the framers of our state constitution had in contemplation a Congress organized like the present Congress, and that the confederation was supposed to be no more than a confirmation of those powers which Congress had previously exercised—The confederation therefore was considered merely as a continuation of the former system, not like the new constitution as a total revolution in the general government. Hence it is, that when the articles of confederation were adopted by this state, we do not find it to have been considered as a revolution in government—No convention of the people was summoned upon the occasion, but the whole business was completed by an act of the legislature, which proceeded to settle the terms of a government previously instituted, and to which the state constitution had a reference. Upon this construction of the transaction, as our constitution had alluded to a Congress of the United States, consisting of a single body, tho' in many instances exercising indefinite powers, and as the articles of confederation were considered merely as ascertaining the powers of an existing government, it was natural to apply the words of our constitution after the confederation, to the object which it had in view previous to that event; but surely no man will argue from hence that the state constitution would have been binding in this respect, if a new government had been instituted by the consent of the people, differently organized, and with different powers from the one contemplated by that constitution. Sir, I entertain as high a respect for the constitution of my country as any man among us; and I trust that even independent of the obligation of an oath, I should be led by a sense of duty to support it—But, sir, the constitution is liable at all times to the revision of the people; because deriving all its authority from that source, by the same authority it may be altered; and as the new constitution ratified by the late convention is the last act of the people, it must be considered as paramount to all other institutions—Our present Constitution therefore consists of the state constitution so far forth as it has not been altered by the general government, and of the new constitution as the governing system, which must prevail in all cases to which it is applicable. If these positions are right, then it will follow that the old state constitution cannot apply before the present occasion, because the new constitution has interposed certain regulations, by which undoubtedly we are bound to abide.

Sir, Those parts of the new constitution, to which I refer are comprised in the 3d section of the first article of that constitution, where it is said that the senate of the United States shall be composed of two senators from each state, *chosen* by the *legislatures* thereof, for the term of six years; and in the fourth section of the same article, where it is declared that the time and manner of holding *elections*, &c. shall be prescribed by the legislatures.

From these paragraphs of the new constitution, it has indeed been contended that the choice of senators must be in the manner prescribed by the bill in its original state, and in order to establish this doctrine, great stress has been laid upon the word *chosen* and the word *election*, as if they were incompatible with the amendments proposed by the senate.

Sir, upon this subject, the arguments urged by the conferees, on the part of the senate, had considerable weight. I am convinced, not only from their observations, but from my own reflection, that the word *choice* and *appointment* are of the same effect, and to be construed as synonymous. Even in the common occurrences of life, we consider them as of equal import; and hence, when an umpire is appointed by two arbitrators, we use the expression that he has been *elected* or *chosen*—so that whenever the two houses concur in the appointment of senators, they may with propriety be said to elect or choose them. With respect to the time and manner of holding the election, those words may be satisfied by prescribing the time at which the election is to commence, and the manner in which the two houses are to signify their choice, for until they concur, there cannot properly be an election by the legislature.

Sir, the words of the new constitution, which require the senators for the United States, to be chosen by the legislature, can only be satisfied by the choice of the two houses in their legislative capacity. If we attend to the terms of our state constitution, where it prescribes the mode of choosing delegates to Congress, we shall find that it does not speak of a choice by the *legislature*. It mentions the senators and members of assembly, merely as individuals to whom it has referred the election in a particular mode, but does not treat them as the *legislature*, or as being in the exercise of a legislative act. But the new constitution having declared that the choice shall be made by the legislature, and not by the persons who compose the two houses, considered as individuals, the choice in conformity to that constitution must be by the two houses, as distinct and separate branch[es] of the same legislature.

Sir, it has been argued during the course of the late conference, that the provision respecting the choice of delegates in the articles of confederation, and respecting the choice of senators in the new constitution, are similar, and therefore, as a choice by joint ballot was adopted under those articles, should adhere to the same mode of election under the new constitution. The argument, sir, is founded in mistake; for if the two instruments are attended to, we shall discover an important distinction. By the articles of confederation the delegates were permitted to be chosen in such manner as the legislatures of the several states should think proper—*By whom* the choice should be made, was not prescribed; and therefore the legislature of every state was at liberty either to make the appointment or to delegate the election to others. Of course they might even delegate it to the people at large, by the terms of the confederation, and in one of the states (if I am not misinformed) this has actually been done.[4] But how different are the term[s] of the new constitution? The senators of the United States are not only to be chosen in such manner as the legislatures prescribe, but they are to be chosen by the legislatures themselves; but how can our legislature make this choice, except in their legislative capacities, as different branches of the same body? A choice in any other mode, may be a choice by the members of the senate and assembly, but can never be considered as a choice by the legislature.

Sir, one of the gentlemen who argued at the conference, on the part of this house, has observed that either the state constitution has prescribed the mode of election on this occasion, and then it is binding upon us; or if it does not apply, then that the new constitution has left us at liberty to adopt whatever mode we may think eligible, and that in such case, we should prefer the joint ballot, because it has hitherto been used and found to be convenient. If this subject had not already been exhausted, it would be easy to demonstrate that, even upon the supposition of a discretion on this head, the joint ballot is not entitled to our approbation. But, sir, what are the sentiments of the senate upon this occasion? Do they not inform us that they are not at liberty to resign their equal suffrage. As the new constitution has given the right of election to the legislature, they, as one branch of it, are *bound* to preserve that right; and to part with it would be a breach of the confidence reposed in them by their constituents. The power which the constitution has given them, is a sacred trust, which they may not violate. Considering the matter, therefore, in this, which is its proper light, I have no doubt, sir, but that we ought to concur with the amendment proposed by the senate. Our duty, I am fully convinced, requires it from us.

The question was then called for on the said motion to adhere to the bill, in preference to the amendments. . . .[5]

This business being concluded, the house adjourned.

1. *Daily Advertiser*, 20 and 21 January 1789. The debates were also printed in the *Daily Gazette*, 23 and 24 January.

2. For the Assembly roll call, see Assembly and Senate Proceedings, 5 January 1789, immediately above.

3. See Assembly Debates, 17 December 1788 and 2 January 1789, both above.

4. Connecticut and Rhode Island elected their delegates to the Continental and Confederation congresses by popular nomination and election.

5. Although the *Daily Advertiser* records only one roll call here, the Assembly journal records two separate, but identical, roll calls on the first and last clauses of the bill. The journal gives no roll call on the second clause, simply stating that the Assembly adhered to the clause (see Assembly and Senate Proceedings, 5 January, immediately above).

Senate Debates, Monday, 5 January[1]

ALBANY, January 26, 1789.

Extract of a Letter from a Gentleman in this City, to his Friend in New-York.

The legislature having in their present session been for sometime employed in devising laws for carrying the new Constitution into effect, I was induced as far as it was practicable, to pay a particular attention to the debates of both houses on that important and interesting subject; and I now do myself the pleasure to transmit to you a concise state of facts, respecting that business, with the substance of a speech delivered in the senate, which I presume will not appear among the printed debates.

A few days after the session opened, the assembly originated a bill for the appointment of Electors, and the election of Senators and Representatives for the new Government; by which it was provided, that the two first should be elected by the senate and assembly, in the mode prescribed by our Constitution for electing Delegates in Congress. The senate also originated two bills, the one for appointing Electors, which provided that each house should appoint four persons for Electors; the other nominated two persons as senators, and provided, that in future senators should be appointed by law. These bills were passed by the senate in the usual form, and sent to the assembly, and were there twice read and committed to a committee of the whole house, and rejected. The assembly then proceeded to pass their bill, which was sent to the senate and amended by that house, but in a way which did not accord with the principles prescribed in their first bills. Their amendment for chusing Electors provided, that each house should nominate eight persons for Electors; that if they agreed as to one or more, and disagreed as to the others, those which they differed in should be appointed by concurrent resolutions of both houses; that if the two nominations differed in the whole number, the senate should chuse four of the persons nominated by the assembly, and the assembly four of those nominated by the senate, which eight persons should be the Electors. Their amendment for the appointment of senators provided that the senate and assembly should, whenever two senators were to be chosen, separately nominate two persons for that purpose; that if they differed as to both, each house should appoint a person for senator from the other's nomination; that if only one senator was to be chosen, the two houses should appoint by concurrent resolution. This difference produced a conference between the two houses, which did not however, terminate in the conviction of either; for the senate adhered to their amendments by a majority of two,[2] and the assembly to their bill by a majority of eleven.

I shall now proceed to give you the speech alluded to, previously observing, that my situation being such during the debates as not to admit of taking any other than very short notes, I was obliged, in a great measure, to depend upon memory; but as I was most solicitous to preserve the sentiments, I believe that has been effectually done.

Mr. President,

Since the assembly have resolved to adhere to their bill, and have refused to concur with the amendments proposed by this house (for which I think the world must justify them) and it now depends upon this house, whether the bill shall, or shall not pass into a law; the question on the motion before us, for receding from our amendments, becomes so important, that I must beg the indulgence of the house to make a few observations before the question is put.

The dispute between the two houses, Sir, is by no means of a trifling nature, for it affects the fundamental principles of government. Our governments, as all free ones must be, are founded in elections; and it is absolutely necessary, for the security of such governments, that the elections should be as free and unbiassed as possible, that the person chosen may be a true representation of the great body or majority of the electors. Any mode which tends to put it into the power of the minority to control an election, is dangerous to common liberty; as in that case, the persons chosen will not be the representatives of the great body, or majority, but of the *few*, and must inevitably introduce an oligarchy or aristocracy, which the celebrated Blackstone tells us is the most oppressive of all governments. One of the amendments proposed, puts the choice of one senator in the senate and the other in the assembly; neither of these will be chosen by the legislature, which our constitution expressly declares, shall be formed by the assembly and senate together, and consequently such a choice would be inconsistent even with the new Constitution itself, which declares they shall be chosen by the legislature. It also destroys that principle of free elections, by a majority, and tends to throw the government into the hands of *the few*.

The representation in the general government is so extremely feeble and imperfect, as at best to afford but little hopes of its being a true representation of the great body of the people, be the elections ever so free and unbiassed; but if the freedom of those elections are destroyed by any means, the prospect under it will be truly alarming. Our representation in the legislature, is the greatest security we have against arbitrary and oppressive laws being made; and experience teaches, that the trial by jury is the greatest security to prevent violence and oppression in their execution. These are the two principal props of liberty in England, and must be in this country. In the new Constitution we have no security for either of them, for the general Government may in their courts abolish the trial by jury in civil cases, and totally deprive us of the benefit of it in criminal, by leaving an appeal to their supreme court; and the power given them to regulate elections may easily be exercised so as to destroy all that security which arises from a representation in the legislature. To prove this position, I need only instance the different modes which have been proposed during our present meeting for the choice of Senators and Electors. I shall first mention the mode of appointing Senators by a law. This plan would evidently give the council of revision, such a power over the elections, that they would enable about a tenth part of the electors of this state, to control the unanimous voice of the other nine tenths, by putting it in the power of one third of this house, either to prevent an election wholly, or to compel the whole of the other house and two thirds of this, to chuse such men as the one third should name. Is not this, Sir, putting our elections, and consequently our government into the hands of the *few*? Would not this be basely betraying the rights of both houses, and the liberties of our constituents?

I shall next instance the bill sent by this house to the assembly concerning the appointment of Electors; and which, with the one for the appointment of Senators by law, oversets the first principle of elections by the great body or majority of the electors, as has been before shewn; and consequently destroys the grand principle of freedom or republicanism in our governments, to wit, the rule of the majority, and establishes an aristocracy at once. Secondly, because this house being a representation of a minority of the inhabitants of the state, it was not thought proper or safe that we should have an equal right with the assembly in these elections. Thirdly, because the members of this house being chosen for four years, it cannot be supposed that we shall be so likely to chuse proper representatives, or such as will truly express the sentiments and wishes of the people upon every occasion, as the assembly who are chosen annually, not even of that part of the people who are the immediate constituents of this house; for many events may turn up in the course of four years, which were not thought of at the time of our election, and concerning which, therefore, it was impossible our particular sentiments could be known, at the time of our being chosen. This, by the by, shews evidently the use and necessity of annual elections. Fourthly, because the assembly being more amenable to the people, and liable to be turned out at the end of every year, will be more obedient to the known voice of the people than this house, every member of which, let his conduct be what it will, however inconsistent with the public good, or contrary to the will of his constituents, can hold his seat for four years, and the majority of which can never be displaced at any one time, be our conduct and sentiments ever so disagreeable to the wishes and sentiments of the people. Fifthly, because allowing this house to have a negative on these elections, might overturn the Federal Government, by preventing elections entirely, whenever the two houses should disagree in their choice.

Having shewn that we do not derive this right from our own Constitution, I shall next endeavor to shew that we cannot claim it from the new one. This tells us, art. 1st, sect. 3d, "that the Senate of the United States shall be composed of two Senators from each State, chosen by the Legislature thereof for six years:" upon one single word in this clause we found our whole claim; to wit, the word Legislature; this is, in my opinion, a very slender foundation, especially as other words in the same clause militate strongly against us; and the meaning, to which we wrest this word, is inconsistent with another clause in this Constitution, and with several expressions in others. It is said, if this choice must be made by the Legislature, it must be done by the two houses in their separate capacities, in the same manner they do the business of Legislation—that is, by a law. But this appears to me to be a very forced construction, and inconsistent with the next section, which says, "The times, places and manner of holding elections for Senators and Representatives, shall be prescribed in each State by the Legislature thereof; but the Congress may, by law, make or alter such regulations, except as to the place of chusing Senators." Now, if the manner of the election is so fixed by the Constitution, that it must be by law, no room would be left for this latter claim, which leaves the manner to be prescribed by the Legislature or Congress. Besides, what similarity is there between the holding of an election, and the passing of a law? That the Senators must be elected, and not appointed by law or resolution, appears from several passages or expressions in the Constitution. Art. 1st, sect. 3, speaks of "two Senators from each State, chosen by the Legislature,[''] and "of the first election," and of "one third being chosen every second year," and who shall when elected (it does not say when passed into a law) be an inhabitant of the State, for which he shall be chosen. Sec. 4th mentions the manner of holding elections for Senators, and the place of chusing Senators. Sec. 5th says, each house shall be the judge of the elections of its own members. Sect. 6th says, no Senator shall, during the time for which he was elected, &c. Now it is plain from these expressions, that this Constitution had in contemplation an election, a choice, not an appointment by law or resolution, in which one house of the legislature should have a negative upon the other. The language of the Constitution does not hold up such an idea, nor can I suppose that it ever entered into the heads of the framers of it; for this plan reduces the number of votes at the election to two, to wit, the Senate and the Assembly, for each body is to give but one vote; and is it not very strange and unaccountable, if this was to be the case, that they should have made no provision in case of a tie? It cannot be supposed that they would have been guilty of an omission, which not only might, but probably would, prove fatal to the very existence of the government. But it is said, the Legislature cannot act but by law in any case. This position is not true, for our Constitution expressly shews how the Legislature are to act in passing a law, and how they are to proceed in holding an election.

Sir, after having stated the improbability that the framers of a national government could ever have intended a mode of election, which might have been rendered futile and inefficient in case of the disagreement of the two legislative branches; and having demonstrated that all legislative bodies, in the exercise of elective powers, ought to proceed in a mode which will, upon every possible disagreement, carry into effect the powers with which they are entrusted; let us now further examine the dangerous consequences resulting from a contrary position; let us now more fully examine if the mode adopted by this house will not lead to a dangerous infraction of the rights of its citizens, and be productive of checks unknown to all elective bodies.

If, Sir, the election of the members of the national Senate is made by law, this law must be subject, as is before observed to the objections of our revisional council; when those are made, any number above one third of either house approving those objections renders the whole bill abortive, without the possibility of renewing it the same session. This council consists of five members, of whom the Governor is always one. If three members attend, and two of them agree to objections, his Excellency only having a casting vote in case of equality,[3] the will of one house and any number less than two thirds of the other, in an appointment so important as that of the members of the national Senate, is rendered useless as to this State, by the will of two of the Council of Revision. Can this mode, Sir, be supposed to accord with the sacred rights of election, whether exercised by legislative bodies or individuals? Sir, should we obstinately persist in adhering to our amendments, and this bill should be lost, I fear we shall justly incur the censure of our constituents. I fear too that we shall do an irreparable injury to the rights of free election: and I am the more apprehensive of this when I reflect on some other parts of our conduct, which do not hold out, in terms as strong as our constituents had reason to expect, a desire to obtain the amendments which have been recommended by our Convention. I allude, Sir, to the answer of this house to the Governor's speech;[4] but, lest I should be considered as out of order, I shall make no comment upon it, but confine myself to the present question.

We find, from the amendments proposed by our Convention to the new Constitution, that it was their wish to render the Senators more responsible to their constituents. But had our mode of appointment by law taken place, is it not evident that the contrary would have been the case?—I hold, Sir, that we should regard their acts as the voice of our constituents.

For would not the subjecting of the election of the Senators to the negative of this house, and members of which are elected by a part of the people only, and hold their seats for four years, and to the control of the Council of Revision, all of whom (the Governor excepted) hold their offices until they are sixty years old, render the Senators so elected much less dependent on the will of the people, than they were intended to be even by the new Constitution itself. Sir, I appeal then to every gentleman of candor in this house, whether our constituents will have the least reason to believe that we are seriously concerned to obtain the amendments which they earnestly wish, if by one of our first acts we should give a complexion to the government so contrary to their expectations. I believe, Sir, they will hardly consider this as a salutary improvement, and be led to dread the evils which might result from the dangerous impressions it might make, at the moment of putting this government into operation.

Mr. President,

Having shewn that this right to a negative, either by law or resolution, cannot be drawn from our own nor from the new Constitution, I am at a loss from what source the claim in question originates, unless it be from that boundless desire of power which reigns in the human heart, and especially in public bodies, who are seldom contented with the powers with which they are vested, but are continually aiming at their extension. Our pretensions of a right to a negative upon the Assembly in their elections, appears to me to be as unfounded a claim of power as any public body ever made, and as inconsistent with the spirit and letter of both Constitutions, as it is destructive of the common liberties of our country. I shall therefore, Sir, give my hearty voice for receding from a ground which we cannot maintain.[5]

1. Broadside, N. The broadside was printed by Robert Barber & Co., Albany. The complete "Extract" was also printed in the *Country Journal*, 10 February 1789, and *New York Journal*, 12 and 19 February. The *New York Journal*, 19 February, noted that the Senate speech was "on the question to adhere to their amendments in the election bill, after the conference had taken place. . . ."

2. The Senate adhered to its amendments by a vote of 11 to 8.

3. The governor's vote on the Council of Revision was equal to that of every other member. He had neither a casting vote in the case of a tie nor veto power.

4. For the Senate's answer to Governor Clinton's speech, see Senate Proceedings, 26 December 1788, above.

5. The broadside concluded with a paragraph on the passage of the Representatives bill and the text of the Assembly's bill for the election of Senators.

Assembly Proceedings, Tuesday, A.M., 6 January

A copy of a resolution of the Honorable the Senate, of yesterday, delivered by Mr. Hoffman and Mr. Duane, was read, "that the Senate do adhere to their three amendments to the bill, entitled *An act for carrying into effect on the part of this State the Constitution of the United States, assented to and ratified by the Convention of this State, on the twenty-sixth day of July last*,["] which were not concurred in by this House.

Henry Sewall to William Heath, New York, 6 January (excerpt)[1]

The Legislature of this state is now sitting at Albany. The Assembly, it is said, is principally antifederal—but that there is a federal majority in the Senate. It is said also, that such is the opposition of sentiment between those two branches, they cannot concur in any federal measures. Indeed, two important bills—one for the appointment of electors for President & Vice President, and the other for the choice of federal Representatives—have actually been rejected. And from present appearances, it is strongly presumed, that no members for the new Congress will be elected—consequently, that this state will be unrepresented, at least the present year, in the federal Court. The Governor, as appears by his conduct, continues to countenance antifederal measures, under the zealous intent of obtaining a new Convention.

By what I can learn from the Boston papers, I fear we shall not be so happy as to see you possess a seat, this year, in the federal Congress.[2]

1. RC, Heath Papers, MHi. Sewall (1752–1845), in New York City on business, was an Augusta, Maine, merchant. He was a captain and aide-de-camp to General William Heath during the Revolutionary War, and clerk of the United States District Court for Maine from 1789 to 1818. Heath (1737–1814), a Roxbury, Massachusetts, farmer, was a major general in the Continental Army during the Revolutionary War. In 1788 he voted to ratify the Constitution in the Massachusetts Convention, and he served in the state Senate, 1791–1792.

2. Heath received 28 votes of the 1,613 cast for Representative in the Suffolk District of Massachusetts.

John Dawson to James Madison, New York, c. 6 January (excerpt)[1]

In consequence of a dispute which has taken place, & which has continued for three weeks between the two houses of assembly it is expected that there will not be any Senators to the New Government, appointed by this State—The house of delegates, in which there is a large majority unfriendly to the Govert. wish to make the choice by joint ballot, and the Senate insist, that *one* nomination by them shall be elected—how this dispute will end I cannot say, but expect the fear of the seat of Govert. being removed from this place will induce both sides to be less obstinate than otherwise they would be—

1. RC, Madison Papers, DLC. Printed: Rutland, *Madison*, XI, 410–11. The letter has no dateline, but from its content it is clear that Dawson was in New York City, where he was representing Virginia in the last Confederation Congress. The date is conjectural; Burnett dates the letter c. 29 January (*Letters*, VIII, 818), but from internal evidence concerning New York politics, c. 6 January appears to be more appropriate. Dawson (1762–1814) served in Virginia's House of Delegates, 1786–1789; in that state's Convention in 1788, where he voted against ratification of the Constitution; and in Congress in 1788 and 1789. For a biographical sketch of Madison, see DHFFE, II, 417–18.

John Lamb to John Smith, New York, 7 January (excerpt)[1]

I have to acknowledge the receipt of your favor of the 28th. Ultimo inclosing the Albany Paper—for which you will be pleased to accept of my thanks; as it afforded me a very agreable repast.

You will see by Child's Paper, of Yesterday, that the Federalists in Philadelphia, have got the horrors from an apprehension that Governor Clinton, will be elected Vice-President.[2]—This alarm (on their part) I believe must arise from some intelligence which it is probable they have received of the intentions of the Electors in the Southern States.—God grant, that their fears may be well grounded.

I find by the Papers, that, there is a great difference of opinion, between the Senate, and the Assembly, respecting the mode of choosing Senators, and Electors.—I flatter myself, that your House, will not recede, from the mode, which is warranted, not only by the State Constitution,—but, that of the New Government likewise.

1. RC, Lamb Papers, NHi. The letter was addressed to Smith in Albany, where he was attending the Assembly.
2. The *Daily Advertiser*, 6 January 1789, had reprinted an article from the Philadelphia *Pennsylvania Gazette*, 31 December 1788, promoting John Adams for Vice President. The writer reasoned: "As the Southern States will furnish a President, it is reasonable that an Eastern state should furnish the second officer of the new government. Nothing but an union in the choice of Mr. Adams can exclude Governor Clinton from the Vice-President's chair."

Abraham Bancker to [Evert Bancker, Albany], c. 8 January (excerpt)[1]

It gives me pain to inform you that there is no Prospect of our being represented in the Senate of the Untied States for this Year, nor of our having any Agency in the Election of a Presidt and Vice President—Bills have originated for that End both in

Senate and Assembly; both have fallen to the Ground. A Conference between both Houses was held last Monday in the Assembly on the occasion in presence of a crowded Audience. It was managed on the part of the Assembly by Messrs. Jones, G. Livingston & Adgate. On the part of the Senate by Messrs. Duane, Ph. Schuyler & L'Hommedieu, and altho it was managed with becoming firmness and dexterity, their Elocution or arguments did not work powerfully to Conviction for on the votes being taken, after the Conference, it appeared that both Houses remained stedfast to their purpose, vizt. the House of Assembly adhered to the Bill in it's present Form, the Senate would not recede from their Amendments. All this Contest was ostensibly about the Mode, but the Fact is, they contended about the Men, whether they should be federal or Anti-federal—

1. RC, Bancker Family Papers, NHi. The letter has no dateline, although it is endorsed as being received on 10 January. The address page of the letter is also missing, but from the letter's content it is clear that the recipient was Evert Bancker, Abraham's uncle. Abraham signed the letter as "Your Affectionate Nephew." Abraham Bancker was in Albany representing Richmond County in the Assembly.

Senate Proceedings, Friday, A.M., 9 January

Ordered, That Mr. Duane, Mr. Philip Schuyler and Mr. L'Hommedieu, be a committee to prepare and report a bill, *directing the times, places and manner of electing Representatives, in this State, for the House of Representatives of the Congress of the United States.*

Mr. Duane, from the committee appointed for the purpose, according to order brought in the said bill, which was read the first time, and ordered a second reading.

David Gelston to John Smith, New York, 9 January[1]

Your favr. of 4 Current is now before me—in very few words I must answer—I think your only true way would be to Reject all those legislating Bills for Election as I actualy believe it to be a contradiction in terms—if not an affront to common sense & understanding—to Elect—to Choose &c by act or Legislation—why not Choose all your Continental Representatives—in short hold all your Elections by Act of Legislation—it really appears to me so Ridiculous—that I will not say any more about it at present—I think immediately after your rejecting the Bill—you ought to appoint your Senators &c—send the nomination to Senate—& there leave it—if they won't proceed—let them be answerable for all the Consequences—In the next place appoint your Council of Appointment—it ought to have been done before—[2]

Now I must intimate a little about the insuing Election (unless you mean to elect your Governor by Act of the two Houses) as I really believe all this talk about choosing Govr. Clinton Vice President is a mere piece of *finesse* Intrigue design or whatever you please to call it—you must look out—and I believe it is quite time to stir a little—one word more—can any man of sense really suppose that the council of Revision have any thing to do with the appointment of Senators who are or ought to be elected—which must have been the case had you appointed by Act—I have seen your Letter to Mr. M. S.[3]—don't be afraid of the Curses or the P——s of the two or twenty great Characters—as they all come from one Quarter & will not nor ought not to be of any avail—in my opinion on the present subject

I cannot write a long letter this time—my sentiments I have written freely—I have no copy nor time to Copy or Correct—I leave all to your prudence—

it is now late in the Evening—I wish you a good Night—Adieu—

[P.S.] Mesrs. Smith Havens—Gardiner—Tredwell[4]—or any part to either or all at your discretion—or any one you please—

1. RC, John Smith of Mastic Papers, NHi. Smith was representing Suffolk County in the Assembly.

2. On 2 January 1789 the Assembly had appointed John Hathorn, Samuel Townsend, Peter Van Ness, and John Williams as a new Council of Appointment.

3. John Smith's letter of 3 January 1789 to Melancton Smith has not been located. Melancton Smith refers to it in his letter to John Smith, 10 January, below.

4. Probably assemblymen Nathan Smith (Ulster County), Jonathan Havens (Suffolk), and Nathaniel Gardiner (Suffolk), and state senator Thomas Tredwell (Southern District).

Albany Gazette, 9 January

Extract of a letter from a gentleman in New-York,
to his friend in this city, dated Jan. 3.

I observe by the Senate's answer, and the Governor's reply, that that honorable body do not chime with the Assembly.[1] I sincerely wish they may agree as to Senators for Congress, otherwise it may be of bad consequence. Should we prove unrepresented, our New Building for Congress, which is in great forwardness, may be left unoccupied; as nothing is more wanted, with many of the Members of Congress, than a reasonable pretext for their removal: However, I hope wisdom will at last prevail, and suffer matters to go right.[2]

1. For the Senate's answer to the governor's speech to the legislature and the governor's reply thereto, see Senate Proceedings, 26 December 1788, above; the Assembly's answer to the governor's speech is in Assembly and Senate Proceedings, 23 December 1788, above.

2. This article was reprinted in the Philadelphia *Pennsylvania Journal*, 21 January 1789; Philadelphia *Pennsylvania Packet*, 22 January; Philadelphia *Independent Gazetteer*, 23 January; Boston *Massachusetts Centinel*, 24 January; Worcester *American Herald*, 29 January; and Richmond *Virginia Independent Chronicle*, 4 February.

Federal Gazette (Philadelphia), 9 January

It would seem, says a correspondent, from the whole of the proceedings of the governor and assembly of New-York, that they wish to prevent the new Congress sitting in their state. By refusing to appoint senators, they will lose a vote in one branch of the legislature of the United States, upon the question of the future residence of Congress. Surely the grand council of our nation will not honour a government with their presence, where federal principles and characters have been so often insulted. Who will ensure the virtue of our representatives, and senators, in such an anti-federal state?

Strange! that a city, which was, during the war, the sink of British politics, and which is now the *head-quarters* of anti-federalism, should be the seat of the pure republican government of the United States![1]

1. This article was reprinted in the Boston *Independent Chronicle*, 15 and 22 January 1789; Portsmouth *New Hampshire Spy*, 20 January; Portsmouth *New Hampshire Gazette*, 28 January; and Pittsfield *Berkshire Chronicle*, 6 February.

Melancton Smith to John Smith, New York, 10 January[1]

I thank you for your favor of the 3d Instant. Your Letter gave me the first advice of the State of the business between the two Houses. Before now an issue must have been put to the contest. I shall be much disappointed if the Senate ultimately reject your Bill because I have the fullest conviction that the ground they have taken cannot be maintained on any principles. By their amendments, the Legislature are not to choose—, in case two are to be chosen and they disagree. In short in my Idea the mode of choosing Senators admits but of one alternative either they must be appointed by Law, or elected by a majority of the two houses. If the Senate have rejected your Bill, it will require consideration what farther steps the Assembly ought to take. In my opinion they hitherto stand on firm ground. I wish they may maintain it, and take such other measures as will tend to vindicate themselves from blame and fix it on the majority of the Senate, should no appointment take place—It appears to me, that it would be a prudent step, for the Assembly to appoint a day to nominate Senators and to proceed on that day to the nomination, and make ye Senators the offer of going to a choice in the manner directed for choosing Delegates to Congress by our Constitution. This will shew the disposition of the Assembly to elect in the usual mode, & may be the means of releiving the Governor in some measure from an embarressment he may be under, respecting the exercise of the power of filling up the vacancies, if the Legislature should not agree to appoint. I shall be sorry, if Electors should not be chosen to elect the President and vice President, as it is very probable our State and Virginia would agree in the person for vice President—and by their union might very probably determine the choice. I think it would be the means of promoting amendments, if a vice president was chosen who is heartily engaged in the business. If your Bill has fallen through, a question may arise whether electors can be chosen, as the day fixed by Congress for the election is passed. I am of opinion that the Legislature may yet choose. For though the Congress have the power to determine the time of choosing the electors, it does not appear that they have it exclusively. The Words are "The Congress may determine the time of chusing the electors." If the Congress do determine the time under the Constitution, it must be observed, but they may not determine the time, in which case the Legislature have power to do it. The time of holding elections for Senators[2] it is true has been fixed by the Congress under ye. old Confederation in pursuance of a resolution of the general Convention, but I presume this is to be considered as merely advisory, & therefore that it will not invalidate the choice of Electors, though made on a different day. But it appears to me essential, that the Electors should meet on the same day in all the States to give their votes, for so the Constitution declares. At all events, if the two houses should concur in any mode of election, I think it would be best to choose electors and direct them to meet and give their votes on the day appointed for the purpose—If the votes are rejected it will not do any harm.

You seem to apprehend, that because D.— prays and S— swears,[3] they apply for assistance to two opposite powers in the invisible world—You need not be apprehensive of this, for I believe it might be proved that the swearing of the one has as much efficacy in engaging heaven on their side as the praying of the other, and that both are equally acceptable to ye prince of the power of the air. The leaders of the federal party are in my opinion as destitute of prudence, as some of them are of true regard to Republican government. Had this not been the case, they certainly would not have taken so many steps to excite and foment discord and animosity. They ought to have known, that a majority of the Legislature were opposed to them, and therefore that the way to carry points was not by pursuing violent measures, but by manifesting a spirit of conciliation & moderation. The success of their schemes has been answerable to the prudence with which they were laid. I cannot perceive any object they could have in view, in their address to the Governor[4] unless it was to gratify their resentments, and to keep alive & inflame party spirit. The attack on their part was unprovoked, as there was nothing in his speech but what was proper and evidently correspondent to the sentiments of the convention—The consequence was, as they might have foreseen, they got severely drubbed, and now many temperate men of their own party condemn them and justify the Governor—Equally impolitic have they been in urging the appointment of officers, at the eve of the old Councils going out and the new ones being appointed.[5] A person of half common sense, would have seen, if predjudice had not blinded his mind, that such conduct was not only improper in itself but would be considered as calculated to establish a party by the gift of offices. And they might have seen that ye. Assembly would have defeated their design, as they very properly did—

I am surprized that some Gentlemen I could name, go with them such lengths.—If they are Republicans, how is it possible they can avoid seeing the drift of some men and reprobating them?—I have written too much but, you will impute it to my being confined for above a Week with illness. Let me hear the news

P.S. I hear the Bill is rejected.

1. RC, John Smith of Mastic Papers, NHi. John Smith was representing Suffolk County in the Assembly.
2. Although Smith wrote "Senators" here, he undoubtedly meant "Electors."
3. Probably James Duane and Philip Schuyler, Federalist leaders in the state Senate.
4. For the Senate's answer to Governor Clinton's speech, see Senate Proceedings, 26 December 1788, above.
5. See Cornelius C. Schoonmaker to Peter Van Gaasbeek, 3 January 1789, nn. 2 and 3, above.

John Smith to [John Lamb, Albany, 11 January][1]

I have this moment Recd. yours of the 7th Instant[2] By Mr. Cortinius and am happy to find that the Paper I sent gave you a little pleasur[.] The Stage was waiting when I inclosed it or I should have been more particular. You have doubtless heard that after the Conference our Election bill was lost without any persons changing his vote in consequence of the Conference[.] The day being past for chusing electors without any being appointed we shall not be accused of being instrumental in of Geting the chosen Vice President[.] the Senate have got another Bill before them for the Purpose of fixing the manner by which the Representatives are to be elected[.] what the Principles of it is I do not know but if it should be materially different from the one which we had for the Purpose the Assembly will never agree to it[.] we are yet anctious to be represented in the General Government and I am not without hopes of our being able so to ma[na]ge matters that the Bill now before the Senate for the

Election of Representatives may be so altered when it comes to the Assembly as to provide for the choise of Senators[.] the Fedaralists feel not a little uneasy at the thoughts of this States not being represented in the Senate[.] they have made their calcula[tion]s and find that there will be a great chance of congress leaving New York if we should [not] be represented[.] Fonday and Peter Schuler are both gone home[.] it is thought that Fonday will not return[.] Laurence is sick and it is thought will not be able to attend[3] if this should be the case Senate will be equally divided[.] Judge H—[4] is expected in two or three dayes which is yet unknown to the Federalists and will give us a Majority of one if all these matters work as we wish and have reason to expect

1. FC, John Smith of Mastic Papers, NHi. Although the letter has no dateline, it was obviously written from Albany, where Smith was attending the Assembly. From the content of the letter the recipient was undoubtedly John Lamb, who on 17 January 1789 acknowledged receipt of a letter from Smith dated 11 January.

2. Printed above.

3. Jellis Fonda, Peter Schuyler, and John Laurance were Federalist members of the state Senate. Laurance was absent from the Senate from 19 December until 3 February 1789. Fonda and Schuyler were present in the Senate on Saturday, 10 January, and Monday, 12 January. Philip Schuyler was absent from the Senate on Saturday, 10 January.

4. Probably David Hopkins (d. 1813), who was absent from the Senate from 6 until 12 January. Hopkins, a member of the Assembly from Charlotte and then Washington County, 1779–1785, 1792–1793, and 1795–1796, and the state Senate from the Eastern District, 1786–1789 and 1808–1812, had voted against ratification of the Constitution in the state Convention in 1788. He was a judge of the Court of Common Pleas for Washington County.

Senate Proceedings, Monday, P.M., 12 January

The bill entitled *An act directing the times, places and manner of electing Representatives in this State, for the House of Representatives of the Congress of the United States,* . . . [was] read a second time, and committed to a committee of the whole.

[Walter Rutherfurd] to John Rutherfurd, New York, 12 January (excerpt)[1]

[– – –] is our Consternation here on the sad disputes betwixt our [Senate?] and Assembly, which we expect will deprive us of [any?] Representation in the new Congress. our want of Senators will be particularly unfortunate in the Question about the Seat of Government; you would hear how the Govr. jockied the old Council of Appointment, got them turned out, and immediately named none but Anti's to Places.—[2]

1. RC, Rutherfurd Papers, NHi. The letter is unsigned, but it is in the handwriting of Walter Rutherfurd, John's father. The letter was addressed to John at "Tranquillity," his farm in present-day Allamuchy Township, Warren County, New Jersey. Another excerpt from this letter is printed in Chapter XII, Part Three. Walter Rutherfurd (1723–1804), a loyalist sympathizer during the Revolution, was a wealthy import merchant who had moved from New Jersey to New York City after the Revolution. For a biographical sketch of John Rutherfurd, a New Jersey presidential Elector, see Chapter XII.

2. For more about the Council of Appointment, see Cornelius C. Schoonmaker to Peter Van Gaasbeek, 3 January 1789, and Melancton Smith to John Smith, 10 January 1789, both above.

Daily Advertiser (New York), 12 January

On Monday last the 5th inst. a conference was held between the senate and assembly, on the amendments proposed to the bill for putting the new constitution into operation. After debating the matter a whole day, the assembly resolved that they would not agree to the amendments—and the senate resolved that they would not recede. In consequence of which the bill was lost. New-York therefore, will have no agency in the choice of those important officers, the president, and vice-president; nor will she be represented in that body, where her most important interests will be at stake—the senate of the United States.[1]

1. This article was reprinted in the *Daily Gazette*, 13 January 1789; *Morning Post*, 13 January; *New York Packet*, 13 January; *New York Journal*, 15 January; and at least fifteen other newspapers from Boston to Charleston, South Carolina, between 15 January and 11 February.

Tench Coxe to Benjamin Rush, New York, 13 January (excerpts)[1]

New York has again clog'd the federal System by suspending the election of Senators & Electors. Tis thought by many here the Senate will give way. I doubt it much—The Scene of emotion at Albany is almost as great as that at Pougkeepsie was. . . .[2]

I wish our papers were a little milder on the Subject of New York. It does harm here among the foreign people & men in Government. Give this hint to Mr. Brown—and Also our friend Mr. Hall is a charter printer—it may not be amiss to mention it to him—at the same give my respects to him.[3]

1. RC, Rush Papers, PPL. Although Coxe dated the letter "1788," from the context it clearly should be 1789. Other excerpts from this letter are printed in Chapter XIV. Coxe (1755–1824) was one of the most active Federalist writers during the debate over the ratification of the Constitution and during the first federal elections. Rush (1745–1813), a Philadelphia physician, was an active Federalist publicist.

2. The New York Convention that ratified the Constitution was held in Poughkeepsie.

3. Andrew Brown published the *Federal Gazette, and Philadelphia Evening Post*; David Hall, William Hall, and William Sellers published the Philadelphia *Pennsylvania Gazette*. On 25 January 1789, Rush informed Coxe that he had spoken to Brown and Hall: "They will I believe pay some regard to your advice—altho' the feelings of our citizens upon the indignity offered by New York to the new govermt: will render it difficult for them to pursue even their own inclinations with respect to publications in their papers" (Philadelphia, RC, Tench Coxe Papers, PHi).

Country Journal (Poughkeepsie), 13 January

We are informed, that agreeable to resolve, the Honorable the Senate and Assembly had a conference in the Assembly chamber, on the amendments proposed by the Senate to the bill for carrying into effect the new constitution. The conference having ended, and the Assembly not concurring in the amendments, the Senate returned to their chamber—where, after some further consideration, they rejected the bill. From which circumstance, the Assembly having rejected a bill for the like purpose which originated in Senate, agreeable to the State constitution no other can be brought forward the present session.—It is said to be probable, however, (that this State may not go unrepresented in the new Congress), his Excellency the Governor will prorogue the Legislature for a day or two, to call a new meeting.

New York Daily Gazette, 13 January

The fifth of January 1789 (says a correspondent) is likely to form a melancholy epocha in the annals of New-York, and consequently of the United States. In well-constructed republican governments checks are acknowledged to be the result of wisdom, and the bulwarks of freedom. But, like all other human institutions, they are capable of being abused, and may effectuate the ruin of that State, which they were intended to preserve. When the constitution, which was lately planned by the collected wisdom of the Union, was promulgated, it was evident to many enlightened friends of their country, that it was not free from defects. It was equally manifest, that much had been done towards establishing a system of government over thirteen independent States, in which the liberty of the great body of the people was sufficiently guarded on the one side from licentiousness, and on the other, from oppression; in which agriculture received its due weight, and manufactures and commerce experienced such encouragement, as might render them beneficial to the union; and (to be brief) in which the noblest confederation, ever conceived, promised to confer the greatest number of blessings, that could be rationally expected, attended with the fewest possible evils. It would be deemed superfluous to enumerate the objections, which have been made to this system by very respectable bodies of men in every State, since these objections are almost universally acknowledged to have some foundation in reason, and since the constitution points out a safe, easy and honorable method of remedying oversights, and of correcting errors. But it is to be lamented (continues our correspondent) that contention has superseded argument, and that the voice of reason is overpowered by the clamor of discontent. Are we to defeat, untried, a system, which, in many instances, challenges respect, because it is not absolutely free from imperfections? As well might an individual give way to despondency, and even rush willingly on destruction, because, although he ought to exult in the enjoyment of many blessings, he reflects, that some particular good (which however may be procured by moderate exertions) is not immediately within his reach. Time, candor, and a necessary disposition to *bear* and *forbear*, will, it is hoped, prevent the greatest evils, which a nation can dread; and accelerate every degree of happiness which we can reasonably expect.[1]

1. This article was reprinted in the Philadelphia *Pennsylvania Gazette*, 21 January 1789.

Senate Proceedings, Wednesday, A.M., 14 January

Mr. Peter Schuyler, from the committee of the whole to whom was referred, the bill entitled *An act directing the times, places and manner of electing Representatives in this State, for the House of Representatives of the Congress of the United States*, reported, that Mr. Yates moved for the following clause to precede the first enacting clause of the bill, viz. "Be it enacted by the People of the State of New-York, represented in Senate and Assembly, and it is hereby enacted by the authority of the same, That the Senators to be chosen in this State for the United States shall be chosen as follows, that is to say, the Senate and Assembly of this State, shall each openly nominate as many persons as shall be equal to the whole number of Senators to be chosen by this State, after which nomination the Senate and Assembly shall meet together, and compare the lists of the persons by them respectively nominated, and those persons named in both lists shall be Senators for the United States, and out of those persons whose names are not in both lists, one half shall be chosen by the joint ballot of the Senators and Members of the Assembly, so met together as aforesaid, and copies of the resolutions of the Senate and Assembly testifying the said choice shall be, thereupon delivered to each of the persons so chosen Senators for the United States, as aforesaid." Debates arose upon the said motion and the question being put thereon, it passed in the negative, in manner following, viz.

FOR THE NEGATIVE.

Mr. Philip Schuyler,	Mr. Morris,
Mr. Douw,	Mr. Roosevelt,
Mr. Micheau,	Mr. L'Hommedieu,
Mr. Fonda,	Mr. Duane,
Mr. Vanderbilt,	Mr. Hoffman.

FOR THE AFFIRMATIVE.

Mr. Yates,	Mr. Humfrey,
Mr. Hopkins,	Mr. Clinton,
Mr. Swartwout,	Mr. Hathorn.
Mr. Tredwell,	

That in proceeding to the first enacting clause of the bill, which after dividing this State into six election Districts, run as follows, viz. "and that at every election for Representatives of the People of this State, in the House of Representatives of the Congress of the United States, a person who shall have obtained the age of twenty five years, who shall have been seven years a citizen of the United States, and who shall then be an inhabitant of this State, and an actual resident in one of the said Districts shall be chosen by the People of this State, that is to say, by such persons who are or shall be qualified to vote for Members of the Assembly of this State, each of whom shall be entitled to vote for six persons as such Representatives, provided that not more than one of them shall be a resident in any of the said Districts, and that such resident who shall have a greater number of votes than any person within the District shall be the Representative," &c. Mr. Humfrey thereupon moved, that the clause be so amended as that the election for each Representative shall be by the inhabitants of the District only. Debates arose upon the said motion and the question being put thereon, it was carried in the affirmative, in manner following, viz.

FOR THE AFFIRMATIVE.

Mr. Douw,	Mr. Tredwell,
Mr. Yates,	Mr. Humfrey,
Mr. Micheau,	Mr. Hoffman,
Mr. Hopkins,	Mr. Clinton,
Mr. Swartwout,	Mr. Hathorn.
Mr. Townsend,	

FOR THE NEGATIVE.

Mr. Philip Schuyler,	Mr. Roosevelt,
Mr. Fonda,	Mr. L'Hommedieu,
Mr. Vanderbilt,	Mr. Duane.
Mr. Morris,	

Mr. Peter Schuyler further reported, that the committee had gone through the bill, made amendments thereto, and agreed to the same, which report he read in his place, and delivered the bill with the amendments in at the table, where they were again read and agreed to by the Senate. Thereupon,

Ordered, That the bill as amended be engrossed.

Assembly and Senate Proceedings, Thursday, A.M., 15 January

The Senate

The engrossed bill entitled *An act directing the times, places and manner of electing Representatives in this State, for the House of Representatives, of the Congress of the United States*, was read a third time.

Resolved, That the bill do pass,

Ordered, That Mr. Peter Schuyler and Mr. Fonda, deliver the bill to the Honorable the Assembly, and request their concurrence.

The Assembly

[The Assembly received the bill for the election of Representatives from the Senate.]

The said bill was read the first time, and ordered a second reading.

Comte de Moustier Journal, 15 January[1]

The two houses of the New York legislature had a conference on the 5th of this month on the bill proposed by the Antifederalists concerning the election of Senators and Electors of the new President. But they were not able to agree because each party hoped to intimidate the other and force it to yield.

1. MS (translated from French), Extraits du Journal de M. de Moustier, in Extraits des Papiers de la Légation de France aux Etats-Unis, I, Part II (Cahier 4), 3, Benjamin Franklin Collection, CtY.

William Stuart to Griffith Evans, New York, 15 January (excerpt)[1]

Party rage in this State seems to be [– – –] at the Zenith—Our Assembly & Senate which together Compose the Legislature—Have divided on the Choosing of Senators for the New Congress—'tis therefore probable that the State may remain unrepresented for the first year—The possible evil Consequence of this Circumstance to the State of New York are Numerous but the resentment of party can laugh them to scorn.

1. RC, Griffith Evans Collection, PHi. The letter was addressed to Evans in Philadelphia. Stuart (d. 1831) was an officer in the New York militia and Continental Army throughout the Revolutionary War. Evans (1760–1845), a clerk in the Continental Army medical corps during the war, represented the Pennsylvania and federal governments in their efforts to settle western land claims of Indian tribes and settlers in the 1780s and 1790s.

Assembly Proceedings, Friday, A.M., 16 January

The bill entitled . . . *An act directing the times, places and manner of electing Representatives in this State, for the House of Representatives of the Congress of the United States,* [was] read a second time, and committed to a committee of the whole House.

Isaac Moses to Nicholas Low, New York, 16 January (excerpt)[1]

I am Sorry to find you differ so Widly in Polleticks amongst you Above; I hope Still some plan will be Struck Out, to bring on the Question anew, and give us a representation in the new Congress or Else we must expect they will Quit us. Indeed the Philadelphia Gentlemen rejoice, at our Confusion and their hopes are Great—

1. RC, Nicholas Low Papers, DLC. Low (1739–1826), a prominent New York City merchant, banker, and land speculator, represented New York City and County in the Assembly, 1788–1789. He voted to ratify the Constitution in the state Convention in 1788.

Assembly Proceedings, Saturday, A.M., 17 January

Mr. Tappen, from the committee of the whole House, on the bill entitled *An act directing the times, places and manner of electing Representatives in this State, for the House of Representatives of the Congress of the United States,* reported, that the committee had made some progress therein, and had directed him to move for leave to sit again.

Ordered, That the said committee have leave to sit again.

John Lamb to John Smith, New York, 17 January (excerpt)[1]

I have to acknowledge the receipt of your favor of the 11th. Instant;[2]—At the same time, I beg that you will be pleased to accept of my thanks, for your condescension, in communicating to me, the state of Politics, in Albany.—We have nothing new here, but the general Conversation, on the dispute subsisting between the Senate, and Assembly;—And from what I can learn, all the moderate Federalists blame the former.

1. RC, John Smith of Mastic Papers, NHi. The letter was addressed to Smith in Albany.
2. Printed above.

Pennsylvania Mercury (Philadelphia), 17 January

Extract of a letter from New-York, January 12.

Our legislature, by their late proceedings, seem determined to deprive us of the benefits to be derived from the New Congress by their residence in this city. It is the opinion of our politicians, that they (the Congress) will not remain here one week, after the fourth of March.[1]

1. This article was reprinted in the Baltimore *Maryland Journal,* 27 January 1789, and Boston *Herald of Freedom,* 30 January.

DeWitt Clinton to [James Clinton?], New York, 18 January[1]

I wrote you very lately and have not been favored with an answer—which I presume is owing to want of opportunity or hurry of business. The News current in this City originates principally from Albany—We have lately heard that Genl. Lamb is appointed Mayor of this City—Col. Willett Sheriff—Mr. Lansing 4th. Judge of the Sup. Court—Mr. Taylor Mayor of Albany—Mr. P. Yates Recorder—and finally that Mr. Greenleaf is appointed state Printer[2]—I believe that some of the Citizens are fearful that Congress will remove from this City, owing to the non-election of Senators—and instead of laying the blame at the door of your House—they fix it primarily upon the Assembly and ultimately upon the Governor—It is supposed that by a clause in the N Constitution the power of appointing the Senators is lodged in the Govr. if the Legislature do not choose any—As The Executive of each state has a right in case of vacancy to do it—whether vacancy does not suppose a previous filling up or whether the establishment of the office by the Constitution and its not being in the possession of any does not authorize an appointment, I am not able to determine. Probably if any ~~election~~ appointment takes place, it will be prudent and expedient, laying aside every other consideration, to select the senators from the adopting and non-adopting anties—it will perhaps heal every animosity and cement firmly the friends of amendments. This appears most essential at the present period, for we have every reason to believe that the flame which is now burning in the Legislature will spread amongst the People at the next Election—Judge Morris and Mr. I. Roosevelt[3] are here talked of as Candidates for governor—The first it is probable will be held up—he however stands no chance—The feds. will try him or some body else & use every means out as they have hitherto done to bring about their purposes—I am persuaded from what I have heard that the present Governor will have a majority of votes in the Southern District, where his interest is lowest—Long Island stands friendly to his election—& this City cannot muster as many votes as Queens County—& even among Anti members there will be five hundred votes or the [- - -] belies[.] When I mention Queens County it brings into my mind this circumstance which I am sorry to relate—that Mr. Jones has by his late decided & manly conduct lost all the federal popularity he acquired by voting for the adoption of the Constitution[4]

I hope you will excuse this political Letter—My best respects to the governor—I would write to him but I have nothing to mention worthy his perusul—

1. RC, DeWitt Clinton Papers, N. The address page of the letter is missing, but from the letter's content the addressee was probably James Clinton, DeWitt's father. James represented the Middle District in the state Senate, 1788–1792, and in 1788 he had voted against ratification of the Constitution in the state Convention.

At the bottom of the letter, in a handwriting different from Clinton's, is the notation "turn over"; written on the back of the letter, in this same hand, is the comment "I approve of the Contents," followed by—in the handwriting of a third person—"Maria McKesson." McKesson was the sister of John McKesson, business manager for Governor George Clinton and Clerk of the Assembly, 1777–1793.

2. No appointments for mayor of New York City, mayor of Albany, sheriff of New York City and County, or justice of the supreme court were made during the 1788–1789 session of the legislature. Peter W. Yates was appointed recorder of Albany in May 1789. John Lansing, Jr., became a justice of the New York Supreme Court in 1790. Marinus Willett was reappointed sheriff of New York City and County in 1791. John Lamb was never mayor of New York City, and John Tayler was never mayor of Albany. Thomas Greenleaf, publisher of the *New York Journal*, was appointed state printer by a legislative act in January 1789.

3. Lewis Morris and Isaac Roosevelt. Roosevelt (1726–1794), a New York City merchant and president of the Bank of New York, served in the provincial congresses, 1775–1777, and in the state Senate from the Southern District, 1777–1786 and 1788–1792. In 1788 he represented New York City and County in the state Convention, where he voted to ratify the Constitution.

4. Samuel Jones, a Queens County Antifederalist, had voted to ratify the Constitution in the state Convention in 1788. As a member of the Assembly in 1788–1789, Jones voted consistently with the Antifederalists.

Assembly Proceedings, Monday, A.M., 19 January

Mr. Jones moved for leave to bring in a bill, for prescribing the times, places and manner of holding elections, for Senators of the United States of America, to be chosen in this State.

Ordered, That leave be given accordingly.

Mr. Jones, according to leave brought in the said bill, entitled *An act for prescribing the times, places and manner of holding elections, for Senators of the United States of America, to be chosen in this State*, which was read the first time, and ordered a second reading. . . .

Mr. Tappen from the committee, of the whole House, on the bill entitled *An act directing the times, places and manner of electing Representatives in this State, for the House of Representatives of the Congress of the United States*, reported, that in proceeding in the bill, a part of the first enacting clause was read in the words following, viz.

Be it enacted by the People of the State of New-York, represented in Senate and Assembly, and it is hereby enacted by the authority of the same, that this State shall be, and hereby is divided into six Districts, as follows, that is to say, the counties of Suffolk, Queens, Kings and Richmond, shall be one District, and the city and county of New-York, and Westchester county, except the towns of Salem, North-Salem, Cortlandt, York-Town, Stephen-Town and Bedford, shall be one District, and the county of Dutchess, and the towns of Salem, North-Salem, Cortlandt, York-Town, Stephen-Town and Bedford, in Westchester county, shall be one District.[1]

That the same part of the first enacting clause having been read, Mr. Jones made a motion to obliterate the words, *and Bedford*, and to insert *and* before the words Stephen-Town.

That the question having been put on the said motion, it was carried in the affirmative in the manner following, viz.

FOR THE AFFIRMATIVE.

Mr. Jones,	Mr. Thompson,
Mr. Kortz,	Mr. Schoonmaker,
Mr. Frey,	Mr. Griffen,
Mr. Stauring,	Mr. Carpenter,
Mr. SPEAKER,	Mr. J. Smith,
Mr. Van Dyck,	Mr. D'Witt,
Mr. J. Van Rensselaer,	Mr. Wisner,
Mr. Winn,	Mr. Adgate,
Mr. Duncan,	Mr. Harper,
Mr. Tearse,	Mr. Havens,
Mr. Webster,	Mr. Schenck,
Mr. M'Cracken,	Mr. Akins,

Mr. Patterson,	Mr. Cantine,
Mr. Scudder,	Mr. Smith.

FOR THE NEGATIVE.

Mr. B. Livingston,	Mr. Horton,
Mr. Gilbert,	Mr. Bancker,
Mr. Van Cortlandt,	Mr. Vandervoort,
Mr. Seaman,	Mr. Rockwell,
Mr. Barker,	Mr. Verplanck,
Mr. Harison,	Mr. Cornwell,
Mr. Hoffman,	Mr. Giles,
Mr. H. Van Rensselaer,	Mr. Sands,
Mr. Younglove,	Mr. Gardiner,
Mr. Watts,	Mr. Macomb,
Mr. Livingston,	Mr. Crane.

That in proceeding further in the bill, a paragraph was read in the words following, viz.

"And that at every election for Representatives of the People of this State, in the House of Representatives of the Congress of the United States, a person who shall have attained the age of twenty-five years, who shall have been seven years a citizen of the United States, and who shall then be an inhabitant of this State, and an actual resident in one of the said Districts, shall be chosen by the People of each District, that is to say, by such persons, who are or shall be qualified to vote for Members of Assembly of this State, each of whom shall be entitled to vote for one person, as such Representative."

That the same paragraph having been read, Mr. Adgate made a motion, that the words *this State* after the word *inhabitant*, should be obliterated, and the words *such District*, inserted in their stead.

That the question having been put on the said motion, it was carried in the affirmative, in the manner following, viz.

FOR THE AFFIRMATIVE.

Mr. B. Livingston,	Mr. Horton,
Mr. Gilbert,	Mr. Griffen,
Mr. Van Cortlandt,	Mr. Carpenter,
Mr. Seaman,	Mr. Bancker,
Mr. Barker,	Mr. Wisner,
Mr. Kortz,	Mr. Vandervoort,
Mr. J. Van Rensselaer,	Mr. Adgate,
Mr. Hoffman,	Mr. Harper,
Mr. Winn,	Mr. Rockwell,
Mr. H. Van Rensselaer,	Mr. Verplanck,
Mr. Younglove,	Mr. Schenck,
Mr. Duncan,	Mr. Giles,
Mr. Tearse,	Mr. Sands,
Mr. Webster,	Mr. Patterson,
Mr. M'Cracken,	Mr. Scudder,
Mr. Thompson,	Mr. Gardiner,
Mr. Watts,	Mr. Macomb,
Mr. Livingston,	Mr. Crane.

FOR THE NEGATIVE.

Mr. Jones,	Mr. J. Smith,
Mr. Frey,	Mr. D'Witt,
Mr. Stauring,	Mr. Havens,
Mr. SPEAKER,	Mr. Cornwell,
Mr. Harison,	Mr. Akins,
Mr. Schoonmaker,	Mr. Smith.

That the committee have made further progress in the bill, and have directed him to move for leave to sit again.

Ordered, That the said committee have leave to sit again.

1. In its account of the Assembly proceedings, the *Daily Advertiser*, 29 January 1789, printed the remainder of the election districts: "Orange and Ulster, to be one district. Columbia, Washington, Clinton, and the remainder of the state on the east side of the Hudson river, to form one district. That part of Albany county on the west of Hudson river; and the counties of Montgomery and Ontario, to be one district."

George Clymer to Tench Coxe, Philadelphia, [19 January][1]

I have not anything of the least consequence to give in return for your communications—One of which, the difference between the two houses, is in appearance only of importance—for I cannot think it will have any extraordinary result—the Senate probably after a decent show of maintaining privilege will give up the point—especially as you say it is now supported but by a majority of one. It is not for small matters or for great ones, that any party among them will risque the advantage of retaining Congress—to keep them, no means are left unattempted—they freely give their money for a magnificent house and a library forsooth to the new Congress.—And what is more propose for the first time in their history, and in spite of fashion and inclination to become readers themselves. These Acts I fear will prevail for the new Congress may be placed in too delicate a predicament to hazard so invidious and viritable a step as a removal, however unjust or dishonourable it might be to remain. How much ought those to be execrated who have produced this painful and dangerous dilemma?

You seem to think the N Yorkers have a right to a choice of federal electors after the lapse of the appointed day—the recommendation of Congress may not be binding but through what other means could the government have been brought into operation. The doctrine of a creation by a fortuitous concourse of atoms is an improbable one—the stat[es?] separately acting upon chance would never have found a common time for this operation.—If any thing turns up the least material you shall have it from Sir Your most obedt sr

1. RC, Tench Coxe Papers, PHi. Although Clymer dated the letter simply "Monday—January 1789," it is postmarked 20 January (Tuesday). The letter was addressed to Coxe in New York City, where he was representing Pennsylvania in the last Confederation Congress. For a biographical sketch of Clymer, see DHFFE, I, 414.

Richard Platt to Winthrop Sargent, New York, 19 January (excerpt)[1]

Our Legislature are sitting at Albany & have been almost 2 Months, without making any appointment of Senators, or devising any mode for chusing Electors & representatives to the new Congress & from all appearances we shall not be represented in the first Congress—This is thought to be a Plan of Clinton's & his antifœderal friends, in order to get Congress removed from New York, notwithstanding all the Skill, Exertion & address exhibited last Summer by Col Hamilton & our Eastern friends to get them established here; and after which was done, this City subscribed above ten thousand pounds to make a proper Building for their reception—This Building is an addition to our City Hall—and was planned & executed under the immediate Direction of L Enfant[2]—It is elegant & commodious & now nearly fit for use—by March it will be compleat—We have in our Assembly a decided Majority of Antifœderalists, but in our Senate Fœderalism prevails.—

1. RC, Sargent Papers, MHi. Platt (1754–1830), a New York City businessman, served with New York units of the Continental Army throughout the Revolutionary War, rising to the rank of colonel. He was a member of the Society of the Cincinnati. Sargent (1753–1820) served with Massachusetts units of the Continental Army throughout the Revolutionary War, rising to the rank of major; he also was a member of the Society of the Cincinnati. In 1787 Congress appointed Sargent secretary of the Northwest Territory, a post he resigned in 1798 to become the first governor of the Mississippi Territory. He retired as governor in 1801.

2. Pierre Charles L'Enfant (1754–1825) was a French military engineer who served in the American Revolution. He directed the conversion of New York's old city hall into Federal Hall for the new seat of the federal government, and he planned the city of Washington and designed several of its public buildings.

Herald of Freedom (Boston), 20 January

Extract of a letter from a gentleman at New-York to his friend in this town.

The Legislature of this state are now in session; the majority of the Senate are federal, and the other branch anti-federal—they have disagreed in the manner of appointing Senators and Electors, and in consequence thereof, the day on which the Electors should have been appointed, has passed without any choice; this state, therefore, will have no choice in the election of President and Vice-President, and unless an accomodation can take place between the two branches, of which, at present, there is not the smallest indication; they will also be unrepresented in the Senate upon the first meeting of Congress. Whether the Legislature will pass a law, regulating the election of Representatives, is yet uncertain; on this subject they have not perfectly agreed, but the causes of disagreement are so small and unimportant, that it seems impossible they should break up without accomplishing this object.[1]

1. This article was reprinted in the New London *Connecticut Gazette*, 6 February 1789, and Middletown, Connecticut, *Middlesex Gazette*, 7 February.

Assembly Proceedings, Tuesday, A.M., 20 January

The bill entitled *An act for prescribing the times, places and manner of holding elections for Senators of the United States of America, to be chosen in this State*, was read a second time, and committed to a committee of the whole House. . . .

Mr. Tappen, from the committee of the whole House, on the bill entitled *An act directing the times, places and manner of electing Representatives in this State, for the House of Representatives of the Congress of the United States*, reported, that *Mr. Speaker*, pursuant to notice given for that purpose yesterday, made a motion that the committee would reconsider the amendment consisting in obliterating the words *this State*, and inserting the words *such district* in their stead, whereby it was intended that each Representative should be a resident in the district wherein he should be elected, which was concurred in by the committee.

That *Mr. Speaker* then made a motion, that the words *such district*, yesterday inserted as an amendment, should be obliterated, and the words *this State* reinstated in their stead.

That debates ensued on the said motion, and that the question having been put thereon, the committee divided as follows, viz.

FOR THE AFFIRMATIVE.

Mr. Jones,	Mr. Wisner,
Mr. Gilbert,	Mr. Vandervoort,
Mr. Frey,	Mr. Havens,
Mr. SPEAKER,	Mr. Verplanck,
Mr. Van Dyck,	Mr. Schenck,
Mr. Harison,	Mr. Cornwell,
Mr. Hoffman,	Mr. Akins,
Mr. Watts,	Mr. E. Clark,
Mr. Bay,	Mr. Scudder,
Mr. Schoonmaker,	Mr. Gardiner,
Mr. Carpenter,	Mr. Macomb,
Mr. J. Smith,	Mr. Cantine,
Mr. Low,	Mr. Bloom,
Mr. D'Witt,	Mr. Smith.

FOR THE NEGATIVE.

Mr. B. Livingston,	Mr. Savage,
Mr. Van Cortlandt,	Mr. Webster,
Mr. Seaman,	Mr. M'Cracken,
Mr. Barker,	Mr. Livingston,
Mr. Kortz,	Mr. Horton,
Mr. Stauring,	Mr. Griffen,
Mr. J. Van Rensselaer,	Mr. Bancker,
Mr. Hardenbergh,	Mr. Adgate,
Mr. Veeder,	Mr. Harper,
Mr. Winn,	Mr. Rockwell,
Mr. H. Van Rensselaer,	Mr. Giles,
Mr. Younglove,	Mr. Sands,
Mr. Duncan,	Mr. Patterson,
Mr. Tearse,	Mr. Crane.

That the committee having been equally divided, Mr. Tappen the chairman, determined in the affirmative; and it was accordingly carried in the affirmative.

That the committee had gone through the bill, made amendments, and altered the title, by adding thereto the words *of America*, which he was directed to report to the House; and he read the report in his place, and delivered the bill and amendments in at the table, where the same were again read, and agreed to by the House.

Ordered, That the amendments be engrossed.

Assembly Debates, Tuesday, 20 January[1]

Went into committee on the bill to prescribe the times, places and manner of electing representatives of this state in the house of representatives of the Congress of the United States.

Mr. Tappen in the chair.

Mr. *Lansing*—The committee will recollect that they have gone through the bill, and decided on every part of it;—when it was last under consideration, an amendment was submitted to the opinion of the committee, on which a vote was taken and lost. It was to strike out that part of the bill which confined the choice of a representative to be within the district; and to give permission to the electors to seek for a proper person throughout the state. This question was fully discussed on a late occasion when we had a similar bill before this house;[2] a majority of the members were then of opinion that it would be wrong to annex any qualification unknown to the constitution. A majority have since decided that we have that power. I must confess I do not agree with them—and I foresee great embarrassment from the mode as it stands in the bill. It is incumbent upon us to pass the election law conformably to the new constitution. If we in the least deviate from it, Congress, who are to be the judges on this occasion, may determine diametrically opposite to our law. We here declare that the representative shall be an inhabitant of the district for which he is chosen—suppose a contention should arise between two persons, one in the district, the other without; suppose the non-resident to have the majority of votes—what is to be the conduct of the officers at the election; they must return the man qualified in the mode prescribed by this law; the other candidate prefers his pretensions to Congress; what will be their determination when it comes before them; will they not decide agreeable to the constitution, and give the preference to the candidate who has the majority of votes; will they not say that the state had exceeded its authority; and is it not probable that they will annul our act. These considerations, sir, are weighty, and cannot be got over.

The convention of the state have confirmed this principle in the recommendatory amendment, to have a provision made when the system is revised, for the purpose of confining the resident to the district;[3] if this was their opinion, ought it not to have some influence on us. I am the more anxious to have this amended, as I do not wish to create embarrassments on this occasion. For these reasons I move for a reconsideration, though I must confess, from the conversation I have had with members on the subject, I am fearful that this motion will not be successful. I shall not therefore take up much of the time of the committee on the subject. If I thought that a provision of the kind could be made, I should be in favor of it; I think it a good one; but the constitution of the United States will not warrant it. The question for reconsidering was then put, and carried in the affirmative.

Mr. Lansing then moved to strike out the words which made it necessary for the representative to be a resident of the district.

Sir, said he, it may be said, that inconveniencies may arise by the inhabitants of different districts choosing the same man; but in this event, the representative would be at liberty to make his election for which district he would hold his seat—and the other district might again hold an election, so that the inconvenience could not be great. The greatest objection is, that not being a resident of the district, he may be unacquainted with the wishes of the people; but under the constitution of this state, we are in the same situation; however few instances have happened where they have gone out of the district, and we must trust this matter to the good sense of our constituents; they will no doubt choose these men in whom they have the most confidence. I have no wish but to alter the bill so as to make it comport with the new constitution.

Mr. *Adgate*—I can by no means agree with the gentleman who is for amending the bill. I think, Sir, that the clause is proper as it stands; we shall use the very words of the constitution, which says the representative shall be an inhabitant of the state; if then the bill declares that the representative shall be an inhabitant of the district, is he not an inhabitant of the state? Why shall we divide the state into districts, if we do not confine the representative to be an inhabitant of the district, by having the representative from the district, he is more likely to be acquainted with the local matters of the district, and more likely to conform his conduct to the wishes of his constituents. If it is left at large, one character of the state may draw all the attention of the districts, so that instead of six, only one will be chosen:—Tho' this is not probable, still it is possible, and we ought, in framing our laws, to guard against all possible inconveniencies. Besides, we ought to frame our bill on those principles which we wish to operate hereafter. I shall be against the amendment.

Mr. *Jones*. I shall not, on this occasion, enter into any of the arguments respecting the propriety or impropriety of the bill, or the amendment, as they respect convenience; but we are making a law to carry into effect the new constitution; we are therefore to conform it to that constitution—and we have no authority to deviate from it. If then the constitution has pointed out a qualification for the representative, I ask where do we get a power to alter it? If we add one more we may add many others; the constitution then becomes a mere blank paper. It is useless to have any qualification in it if the state legislature can add to them or take from them; if we can say that the man elected shall be a resident of the district; then we can say that he shall be a resident in a particular town—in a particular spot—or on a particular farm;—nay, we may as well say that he shall be a man worth 5000 £. a year. It is a dangerous precedent for the legislature when they are passing a law to carry a constitution into effect to deviate from that constitution in one of its most essential parts. Doubtless if we were to take up our own constitution, we should find various parts of it that we might amend. Has the legislature a power of doing this? If they had, I hope we never should attempt it; there might be parts of it that I might wish to see amended, other gentlemen might differ from me. Again, are we to make the amendments to the new constitution? Surely gentlemen are mistaken. If we can make amendments, we had better set about it; it would be less expensive, and sooner done than by calling a convention of the United States. It strikes my mind in this way, that annexing an additional qualification is an amendment to the constitution, and I do not see how it can be got over. With respect to the merits of it, had the constitution warranted it, I should heartily concur in it; and I shall vote for expunging the clause, not because I think it improper in itself; but because the constitution does not warrant it. To infringe the constitution in the very act for putting it into operation, I think wrong.

Mr. *Duncan*—Notwithstanding what the gentleman has been pleased to say, I think the great body of the people should be consulted on this occasion. I am sure they will think themselves much aggrieved in not having this matter agreeable to their wishes. I should be glad to have that part of the constitution shewn to me, where it says, that the choice of the representatives shall not be confined to an inhabitant of the district. We ought not to oppose the will of the people.

Mr. *Adgate*—Then read that part of the new constitution which speaks of the qualification of representatives: how it can be denied, said he, that a person who is an inhabitant of a district is not an inhabitant of the state, I do not know. Sir, I believe the gentlemen of this house have had this matter long enough under consideration—and it may be unnecessary to repeat arguments. What I have heard now, I have heard before, and it appears to me just the same.

Mr. *Ph. Livingston*—On this question I think it my duty to give my opinion to the committee. I am against dividing the state into districts—and I am against confining the people to vote for one man. I think the constitution entitles every man to vote for six. But if we do divide the state into districts, I see no meaning in it, unless we fix the person to be elected to the district; the argument for this mode seems to be this, that the people should be acquainted with his character, and that the representatives ought to have the feelings and be acquainted with the circumstances of the people, so that six men, from the six districts of the state, will be able to give the information of the whole state—this is the argument for district election. I believe we have several examples for this mode—Massachusetts and Maryland have done so; but in the latter they have given the liberty to the people to choose five others, so that every man has his six votes. I think we are competent to do that; I am for giving the people every thing that the constitution entitles them to;—we have no right to take away five votes from a man, when he ought to have six.—But when you divide the state into districts, if you do not confine the representative to be chosen from among the inhabitants of that district, you expose the state to great inconveniencies. Suppose some highly distinguished character (as has frequently happened in England, instance the late Mr. Pitt) should draw the attention of three or four of the districts, and be elected for all of them, what an embarrassed situation we should be in. I voted yesterday for confining the representative to the district, and I shall do so again to day.

Mr. *Winn*—Unless some of the gentlemen can convince me that an inhabitant of the district is not an inhabitant of the state, I see no cause for altering the bill.

Mr. *Jones*—I wish, in the consideration of this question, that we may confine ourselves to the point in debate; and not travel through the bill and find out other objections. If other parts of the bill is wrong, we will notice them as soon as they come under consideration. The question is simply, shall the representative, of necessity, be a resident of the district?—and our reasoning on other parts of the bill cannot decide that point: If the House have done wrong by dividing the state into districts, the reasoning on that question will not apply to the present. But were we to take up that subject, it can easily be shewn that it is proper, if it is not so, then I hope the committee will put it right. With respect to the observation that I have heard more than once, "is he not an inhabitant of the state, if he is an inhabitant of a district?"—I might answer this question by asking, is not an inhabitant of Albany, an inhabitant of the state—or of any particular spot?—The same answer will apply to both.

If you leave the choice to be made throughout the state, you give the people a better chance to suit themselves;—but whether this is a proper or improper plan is not to be decided by us—the constitution of the national government has not left it in our power; we have no authority to alter it.

Mr. *B. Livingston*. No arguments were necessary to convince me of the unconstitutionality of the election bill before us. On a former occasion I expressed my objections to dividing the state into districts;[4] nor am I yet reconciled to that measure. There is but one safe course to steer in this business: that is to permit every qualified elector to vote for *six* representatives to be chosen from the state at large. In doing this we should stand on firm constitutional ground. But as the senate have not thought proper to pursue that mode, it is not my intention to embarrass the committee with any amendments that may tend to alter the whole frame of the bill. I mean only to shew the impropriety of receding from the determination we came to yesterday, and that the elected should be residents of the district he is to represent. I am aware sir, that it will be difficult to support this position by arguments drawn from the new constitution which is silent as to district elections, but as we have by a former part of the bill divided the state into districts, we should be careful that this mode be attended with as little inconvenience to our constituents as possible. It is from this principle, and not from a conviction that the district mode of election is the best, that I shall give my vote for confining the elected to the district for which he is to be chosen. Unless this is done, we shall not ensure a representation to Congress. If the state be divided into districts, and the electors be at liberty to vote for a person residing elsewhere, we shall run some risque of the state not being fully represented. Suppose any one man to be so popular as to unite the suffrages of the great body of electors, in that case we should have but *one* instead of *six* representatives. It is true this is not a probable, but it is a possible case. Is it then prudent sir, not to provide for a case that is foreseen, and that may possibly happen?

Again—What is the object of dividing the state into districts? Is it not that a man may come from every part of the state, well acquainted with the local wishes and circumstances of the people? If this be the object of the bill, why not render the attainment of it certain, by obliging the representative to be an inhabitant of the district. At present they may all come from one county—All the gentlemen agree that if in our power, it would be the most eligible mode. I say, if we *can* parcel the state into districts, we *can* oblige the people to chuse an inhabitant of the district. And this must be the meaning of our late convention when they declare that it is not inconsistent with the constitution to divide the state into districts, and to *apportion the representatives among the several districts*. Does not this mean that one man is to come from each district? Sir, this question has been so fully discussed that I shall no longer trespass on the patience of the committee. I hope they will not depart from their vote of yesterday.

Mr. *Harrison*—I did not intend to trouble the committee on this subject; however, as the gentleman last on the floor has made use of some arguments that appear extraordinary, I should not acquit myself of the justice I owe my country, if I do not notice them. He says we have *violated* the constitution in one instance, why not in another? Sir, what is the amount of this argument, it is that two political wrongs make one right:—This, Sir, is an argument that I suppose will hardly be adopted by this committee. But I do not think that a division of the state into districts is a breach of the constitution. When the convention at Poughkeepsie had this matter under consideration, they were of opinion that the constitution contained nothing in it to prevent the dividing the state into districts; they adopted the constitution with this explanation—if therefore the

United States thought proper to accept this ratification in that manner, the explanation is as binding as any other part of it; when therefore we divide the state into districts, we do not commit a political wrong—we do not violate the constitution. But when we go farther than the explanation of that convention, and annex a qualification that the constitution does not warrant, we violate it. To say that a man who is an inhabitant of a district is an inhabitant of the state, is no argument at all; we might as well say, that the representatives shall all be citizens of Albany, for a citizen of Albany is an inhabitant of the state; but will any man say that in this case the freedom of choice would not be precluded. The constitution gives permission to choose any man, throughout the state—you here say he shall be an inhabitant of a particular district—is not this a restriction unknown to the constitution. But if we had it in our power, I am not convinced of the propriety of confining the person to the district; it is sufficient, however, for me, that the constitution does not admit of such a limitation.

Mr. *B. Livingston.* The sentiments of the honorable gentleman, who was last on the floor, and my own, differ very widely on the present occasion. I did not, however, expect that he would have had recourse to the explanatory amendments of our convention to support the doctrine he contends for, but that he would have drawn his arguments from the constitution itself. For my own part I consider those explanations in a very different light. I consider that our convention have *unconditionally* adopted the new constitution, and that they have only expressed a *confidence* that certain powers will only be exercised in a certain way.

Sir, the gentleman has said that my arguments tended to prove that because we had violated the constitution in one particular we might in another. I did not mean to be understood in that way—I said that if we had violated the constitution in one instance, we should take care that such violation worked as little mischief as possible. That as the committee had determined on an election by districts, we should endeavor to render that mode as perfect as possible.—That in the present case we were not sure of a representation—I will mention another inconvenience: Congress are ultimately to determine on the qualifications of the elected. A member is returned from Dutchess with 300 votes, which happens to be a majority of the votes in that district. Another candidate in Albany has 3000 votes, but still has not the largest number of votes in that county. They both apply to Congress to take their seats. How will Congress determine? Will they not decide in favor of the latter, and yet according to this law, he will not be the person elected.—Another calculation will exhibit in still more striking colors the absurdity of the plan contended for. Suppose each district to contain 5000 electors; the aggregate number will then be 30,000. In this case a man may have near 15,000 or one half of the whole number of votes in the state, and yet not be entitled to a seat in Congress, while six others who have not more than 2,500 votes each, which is not more than one twelfth of the whole will be our representatives. By what rule of propriety can this be called a representation of the people?

It is well known that the senate intended to have confined the elected to the districts for which they might be chosen, but by some strange inaccuracy or inattention the bill has come down to us in a different shape.

Mr. *Lansing*—If the gentleman has given such sentiments as can be supported, the consequence is that the people of this state have been cajoled; if this sentiment is to prevail, the language is, that the people have ratified one constitution, and are bound by another; but I am induced to believe that on reflection the gentleman will correct that sentiment.

To convince the committee, if they place a confidence in the ratification, I need only refer to it for our authority to divide the state into districts; but if the explanations and reservations therein contained are to be of no effect, then it is clear that the people of this state have been cajoled, and are bound by a contract they did not intend to agree to. But the national government has no power over the people of this state, except what is derived from the ratification by our convention; which, if it is binding on us, is also binding on the general government; if they accept it, it must be with our explanations. I must confess, Sir, that the sentiments I have heard advanced are peculiarly distressing, when we consider our present situation. It is well known that there was a great diversity of sentiment in the state on this subject, and that a great majority of the people were opposed to it; the members of the convention, therefore, were fully impressed with the necessity of a revision of the constitution, and making a proper explanation in the ratification, of these rights which their constituents wished secured to them; at present it is said that these reservations in favor of the people are not binding: Sir, I wish we may hear no more assertions of this kind in this house. I hold that the whole of the compact must be taken together, and that if any part of it is binding, the whole is. Sir, I should not animadvert on this subject, if I did not suppose the sentiment was such as could not be maintained. This is not, however, the matter under consideration; the question is, whether we have a right to annex qualifications unknown to the constitution? If the constitution is to be the line of our conduct, we must amend the bill in the manner I propose.

Mr. *B. Livingston*—The honorable gentleman who has just favored us with his sentiments, has treated the subject in a much more serious light than any thing that dropped from me would justify. Had the gentleman attended to my arguments, he would have spared several observations he has been pleased to make. I did not assert that all our explanatory amendments were to be totally disregarded. This is a sentiment I have heard from no one but the gentleman himself, who has been pleased to put it into my mouth to shew with how much ingenuity he could refute it. I said, Sir, that these explanations were not binding on the national government—that our convention had power only to adopt or reject the constitution, not to explain it; or to make any previous stipulations on the subject. If our convention had this right, that of Delaware had the same, and so had every state in the union—Suppose then these explanations should differ, as they certainly would, who should determine which state had fallen upon the true construction?—I therefore consider nothing as obligatory either upon this state or the national government, but the ratification; at the same time I have so much confidence in the characters who will probably compose the new Congress, as not to doubt that a due regard will be paid to all the explanations of the different states, so far as they can consistently be attended to.

I can hardly think, Sir, that there is any room for the honorable gentleman's suspecting that he has been *cajoled* in this business. Methinks the members who composed that convention were incapable of cajoling each other.

Mr. *Lansing*—Sir, when we ratified that constitution we were freemen, and had a right to make our own stipulations. We declared that we adopted the constitution under certain explanations, and that ratification having been accepted, those explanations are part of the compact.

Mr. *Harrison*—Sir, government is and ought to be considered as a contract between the persons governed, and the governors. When therefore the new constitution was offered to the people, it was as the subject of that compact, of which they might approve or disapprove; they might declare that they would take it in the whole, or in part—it was in the power of the United States, as the governors, to agree to the stipulations made by the people, or to reject them. Sir, if we attend to this idea, I believe gentlemen will be fully convinced that the explanations that are annexed to the ratification must be considered as binding upon the United States; they offered to the consideration of the people of this state, a certain constitution; the people of the state assembled in convention took up that constitution, and say that we understand certain parts of it may admit of doubt, but we are willing to accept, provided that such a sense is affixed to particular articles of it.—If then the United States accept of a ratification containing such an explanation; the explanation is as binding as any part of it. This is the case with all contracts. Sir, when the most common instrument of writing is brought to a man, will it not be in his power to say, I understand a particular article in such a way, and if he signs it under such an explanation, does not his explanation become a part of the contract. This is plain reasoning on the subject. These are my sentiments, and such as I shall always think it my duty to support. I think, however, that we are drawn from the subject. I wish we may have the question.

On the question to agree to Mr. Lansing's motion:—. . .[5]

The committee being equally divided, (Mr. Tappen) the chairman, gave the casting vote in the affirmative.

The committee having amended the bill accordingly, then rose and reported the same; when the amendments were ordered to be engrossed.

1. *Daily Advertiser*, 30 and 31 January 1789. Extensive accounts of the debates were also printed in the *Daily Gazette*, 31 January and 2 February, and *Morning Post*, 2, 3, and 4 February.

2. See Assembly Debates, 18 December 1788, above.

3. In its instrument of ratification of the Federal Constitution, the New York Convention stated its understanding "that nothing contained in the said Constitution is to be construed to prevent the Legislature of any State from passing Laws at its discretion from time to time to divide such State into convenient Districts, and to apportion its Representatives to and amongst such Districts." The Convention also recommended this amendment to the Constitution: "That the Legislatures of the respective States may make Provision by Law, that the Electors of the Election Districts to be by them appointed shall chuse a Citizen of the United States who shall have been an Inhabitant of such District for the Term of one year immediatly preceeding the time of his Election, for one of the Representatives of such State" (DS, RG 11, Certificates of Ratification of the Constitution and the Bill of Rights . . ., 1787–1792, DNA).

4. See Assembly Debates, 18 December 1788, above.

5. For the Assembly roll call, see Assembly Proceedings, 20 January 1789, immediately above.

Assembly Proceedings, Wednesday, A.M., 21 January

The bill entitled an *An act directing the times, places and manner of electing Representatives in this State for the House of Representatives of the Congress of the United States*, with the engrossed amendments, were read a third time.

Resolved, That the bill and amendments do pass.

Ordered, That Mr. Younglove and Mr. Duncan deliver the bill and amendments to the Honorable the Senate, and inform them that this House have passed the bill, with the amendments therewith delivered. . . .

Mr. J. Van Rensselaer, from the committee of the whole House, on the bill entitled *An act for prescribing the times, places and manner of holding elections for Senators of the United States of America, to be chosen in this State*, reported, that after the said bill had been read through in the committee, a paragraph of the first enacting clause was again read, in the words following, viz.

"Be it enacted by the People of the State of New-York, represented in Senate and Assembly, and it is hereby enacted by the authority of the same, that the Senators of the United States, so to be chosen in this State, shall be chosen in the same manner that Delegates to represent this State in the General Congress of the United States of America, are directed to be appointed as aforesaid, by the Constitution of this State."

That the said paragraph having been read, Mr. Harison made a motion, that the said paragraph from the words *by the authority of the same*, should be obliterated, and the following paragraphs inserted instead thereof, viz.

"That the first Senators to represent this State, in the Senate of the Congress of the United States, shall be chosen in the manner following, that is to say; the Senate and Assembly of this State shall each, openly nominate two persons to represent this State in the Senate of the Congress of the United States; after which nomination they shall meet together, and the person or persons named in both lists, shall be a Senator or Senators to represent this State as aforesaid; but if the said lists shall disagree, then and in such case, if they disagree only as to one of the persons named in each, then one of the two persons named in the said lists, and not included in both, shall be chosen by the joint ballot of the Senators and Members of Assembly so met as aforesaid; and the person so chosen shall be a Senator to represent this State in the Senate of the Congress of the United States; and if the said lists shall disagree as to all the persons named therein, then the Senate shall on the day in which the said lists shall be compared, choose by ballot one of the persons nominated as aforesaid by the Assembly, and the Assembly shall on the same day in like manner choose one of the persons nominated by the Senate as aforesaid; and the two persons so chosen, shall be the first Senators to represent this State, in the Senate of the Congress of the United States."

That debates ensued on the paragraphs proposed by the motion of Mr. Harison, and that the question having been put, whether the committee did agree to the same, it passed in the negative in the manner following, viz.

FOR THE NEGATIVE.

Mr. Jones,	Mr. Griffen,
Mr. Kortz,	Mr. Carpenter,
Mr. Frey,	Mr. J. Smith,
Mr. Stauring,	Mr. D'Witt,
Mr. SPEAKER,	Mr. Wisner,
Mr. Van Dyck,	Mr. Adgate,
Mr. Veeder,	Mr. Harper,
Mr. Winn,	Mr. Havens,
Mr. Duncan,	Mr. Schenck,
Mr. Tearse,	Mr. Akins,
Mr. Savage,	Mr. E. Clark,
Mr. Webster,	Mr. Patterson,
Mr. M'Cracken,	Mr. Scudder,
Mr. Thompson,	Mr. Cantine,
Mr. Bay,	Mr. Bloom,
Mr. Schoonmaker,	Mr. Smith,
Mr. Tappen,	Mr. Hardenbergh.

FOR THE AFFIRMATIVE.

Mr. B. Livingston,	Mr. Horton,
Mr. Gilbert,	Mr. Low,
Mr. Van Cortlandt,	Mr. Bancker,
Mr. Seaman,	Mr. Vandervoort,
Mr. Barker,	Mr. Rockwell,
Mr. Harison,	Mr. Verplanck,
Mr. Hoffman,	Mr. Cornwell,
Mr. H. Van Rensselaer,	Mr. Giles,
Mr. Younglove,	Mr. Gardiner,
Mr. Watts,	Mr. Macomb,
Mr. Livingston,	Mr. Crane.

That the committee had gone through the bill and made amendments, which he was directed to report to the House; and he read the report in his place, and delivered the bill and amendments in at the table, where the same were again read, and agreed to by the House.

Ordered, That the bill and amendments be engrossed.

Assembly Debates, Wednesday, 21 January[1]

Went into committee on the bill prescribing the times, places and manner of electing senators for the United States to be chosen in this state;

Mr. J. V. Renssellaer in the chair.

[This bill, which has been brought forward by Mr. Jones, is upon the same principles as the bill lately rejected by the senate, to wit, choosing the senators by *joint ballot.*]

After reading the first enacting clause, Mr. Harrison rose—

Sir, said he, I take it for granted that it was the intention of the gentleman who brought forward this bill, that we should be represented in the senate of the United States; otherwise I am persuaded that he would have thought it unnecessary to offer any proposition upon this subject for the consideration of the house. Assuming this, therefore, as the object of that gentleman, and as the object of the legislature upon the present occasion, it only remains for us to consider whether we are like to attain that object by the bill which is now before us.

We have had sufficient experience, Sir, in the course of this session, to convince us that we are now treading upon *tender ground*; and that unless we take prudence for our guide, we can scarcely hope to arrive in safety at the end of our journey.

It must be unnecessary for me to recapitulate all the proceedings between the two houses of the legislature upon the subject of the present bill—Already have they declared their sentiments in a solemn conference, and there is no reason to suppose that those sentiments have been changed—If, therefore, we expect that the two houses should agree in any proposition, it must be different from those which they have already decided upon.

I have examined the bill, Sir, which is now before us with much attention, and I can find no other distinction between it and the one which lately passed this house, except that the present is in *a new form*. It contains precisely the same proposition in a different dress; and as this is the case, I cannot conceive there is any probability that it will be successful in the other house.

Indeed, Sir, when I consider the manner in which this bill is brought forward, and the circumstances which have already passed between the two houses, I cannot compare it to any thing better than the attempt of an insignificant coxcomb, who has been refused by his mistress, to obtain her favor merely by offering himself in a new suit of clothes. But that I may not appear to treat so important a subject with unbecoming levity, I would *seriously* ask the gentleman who has introduced this bill, I would ask the committee who are to decide upon it, if the mere recital of an article of our state constitution, which the senate has declared not to be applicable to the present subject, can recommend the bill to the suffrages of that house? Can we expect that *this* will be considered as any step towards an accommodation between the different branches of the legislature? I am sure that *we cannot*; and however other gentlemen may think upon this subject, it is my sincere opinion, that if we have no other proposition to offer, we might spare ourselves all the trouble which this will occasion.

As the house have already had the questions connected with the present bill repeatedly discussed upon other occasions, I should perhaps be inexcuseable if I was to take up the time of the committee by the repetition of arguments which have been recently urged, and must be fresh in every mind.—There is one argument, however, which has occurred to me in the course of this transaction, and which I do not remember to have heard—I shall therefore throw it out for the consideration of the committee, who will give it as much weight as it may appear to deserve.

It is said, Sir, that in the choice of senators to represent this state in the general government, we are bound by the terms of our state constitution; but it is at the same time admitted that the national constitution is to be the governing system, and of course, if it can be fairly inferred from the national constitution that the regulation of our state constitution with respect to delegates was not contemplated as the rule to prevail in the choice of senators to the general government, then it will follow that the first proposition, so much insisted upon in this house, must be considered as erroneous.

Sir, the clause of the national constitution respecting the time, place, and manner of choosing senators, appears to me to afford a strong argument that the framers of that government did not contemplate the state constitutions when they made such provision. In the first place they say, "that the times, places and manner of holding elections for senators" shall be directed by the state legislatures. Surely this was an unnecessary declaration if the constitution of the state was to be the directing principle!—Why should they declare that the legislature was in the first instance to prescribe the manner of holding elections, if they were to have no discretion upon that subject, but were bound to adhere rigidly to the state constitution, as it respected delegates?

Pursuing the same clause of the new constitution somewhat farther, we shall find that the Congress of the United States have power to alter such regulations as the state legislatures may have made, except as to the places of choosing senators. Can we suppose that it was the intention of the framers of the clause under consideration, that the state constitution should be the rule upon this occasion, and yet that the Congress should have a power to alter that rule? If this was their idea, why did they not, in the first instance, consider the state constitutions, and propose other rules to be observed, if the rules which they contained appeared to be improper. The very principle upon which the power of altering these regulations appears to be founded, is this, that the regulations which the state legislatures would adopt, could not be known to the convention; and as they might be improper, the general government was invested with a power of altering them, if necessary.

When I consider this argument attentively, I confess, sir, that it has great weight with me, and I cannot conceive that the framers of the national system had any thought of a reference to the state constitutions.

If, sir, I am well founded in my opinion upon this subject, then we are not tied down to the letter of our constitution as it respects the appointment of delegates; and of course the mode of appointment is either to be determined by *the spirit of the constitution,* in which view the legislature consisting of two equal branches, is to make the choice, so as to preserve this equality; or it is left wholly at the discretion of the legislature to adopt such a rule as shall appear to be the best.

If I understand the arguments of some of the gentlemen who are in favor of this bill, I must conclude that they themselves consider the mode as merely discretionary. Why (say they) should we deviate from that mode which has hitherto been practised? Why do they ask the question? It implies that we have the power of deviating, if we think it expedient. I shall not enter into a consideration of the reasons which would induce a deviation, if it is practicable; as this would probably involve us in discussions of too delicate a nature. But, sir, independent of those reasons, we should be governed by prudence upon the present occasion. We have a great and important end which we are endeavoring to attain. Let us adopt a mode that will probably succeed. Let us consider that we *alone* are not *the legislature.* That there is another branch to be consulted, and that if we offer to them measures to which they cannot agree, we are incurring a fruitless waste of our own time and the public money.

Perhaps, sir, it can hardly be expected, considering what has already passed upon this subject, that we should suddenly become cool and dispassionate enough to view it in a proper light. Indeed I suppose it scarcely possible to frame a proposition meant to be lasting, in which both houses will concur; and when I reflect upon the natural operation of the human passions, I can scarce promise myself that they will accord in the one which I shall now offer as a substitute to the bill, and which is meant merely as a temporary expedient; reserving the question between the two houses to be decided by a future legislature. When *they* meet the present heats will in all probability have subsided; and as the people at large will have had time to reflect upon the subject, they will by their choice of representatives in the two houses, manifest their sense of the manner in which it should be decided. The proposition I would make is as follows.

[The amendment proposed was the same as offered to the first bill, except that it was restricted to the choice of the first senators.]

Mr. *Lansing.*—I have already contemplated this business in a variety of lights; and on a former occasion this point has been fully discussed; the same considerations that prevailed then, must have their influence now. It is, however asserted, that unless measures are taken to bring about an accommodation with the senate, the state will be unrepresented; when we were last on this business it was supposed, that if the bill was lost, a question would arise whether we could originate a new one; but this difficulty being removed, we are again called on to give our sentiments. In this situation it is said that this bill has it in contemplation to imitate the example of a silly coxcomb, who puts on a new dress to ingratiate himself with his mistress. If it is the senate that is the mistress, I suppose we have no more occasion to court her, than she has us; and ultimately the people of the state must determine who is to be blamed;—I have not, sir, heard any reason for changing my opinion. The argument that has been drawn from the new constitution, is not so conclusive as the gentleman last on the floor supposes. It is true, by the constitution a power is given to the general government, to make laws to prescribe the times, places and manner of holding elections; but this does not make any alteration with respect to the power to be exercised by the states, and by the constitution of the state under which we derive all our authority, it is declared that the members of Congress shall be appointed in the mode contended for in the clause as it stands in the bill; and it has been shewn, that as the constitution of the state was formed prior to the confederation, when it was impossible to determine in what way the general government would be modified, it must apply to whatever general government should be formed thereafter, whether the members of Congress were to be called senators, delegates, or by any other name. Sir, if this consideration weighed with the committee on a former occasion, and had a tendency to convince them that they ought to adhere to the state constitution, I would ask what can warrant them to agree to any other mode at the present time. Must we, for the purpose of getting a delegation in Congress, depart from principles which we are sure is well founded—must we accommodate to the senate—Sir, are they not responsible for their conduct as well as the assembly. They say that this is a constitutional question which they cannot give up; we hold up the same reasons, and there has been no argument offered to induce me to change my opinion, which is, that the pretensions of the senate are ill founded.

Mr. *Jones* said the question had been so often agitated on this subject, that he would not take up the time of the committee, only to remark, that as a bill had been brought in at the opening of the session, for carrying into effect the new constitution, providing for the election of electors, senators and representatives; and which, on account of a contention between the two houses, had unfortunately been lost—he thought it his duty to bring in another bill to endeavour to get the election of senators; and in framing it, he had gone conformably to the constitution. If, however, the senate should again reject the bill, or add such amendments as would destroy it, it would be an event to be regretted; but the assembly could console themselves with having done their duty.

Mr. *Harrison*.—I am as unwilling to take up the time of the committee, as any of the gentlemen who compose it. But the whole of the arguments in favor of the bill appear to me to be founded upon a mistaken fact. They say that the constitution of the state had in view whatever form of general government might take place, because it was formed a few months prior to the confederation; now if this is not the fact, then all their arguments must fall. The fact is, that the convention that framed our state constitution, had in view only a Congress organised like the present Congress; therefore as they had not in view a general government, like the one lately adopted, we cannot apply the regulations in the state constitution to the subject now before us. The gentlemens' own arguments are against them. But, sir, there is an argument that ought to have weight with the committee, which is, that the amendment will probably meet with the concurrence of the senate. Sir, as they are an independent branch of the legislature, they cannot agree to any proposition which does not hold out an equality. As the one I propose acknowledges their principle, I say it is probable that they will agree to it. I wish we may make the experiment; and though it does not accord wholly with the amendments they lately proposed to a similar bill, yet I think it may succeed. It will at least shew a liberal spirit on the part of the house.

Sir, if we pass the bill in its present form, I conceive it will be only telling the senate you shall have either this mode or none. It is true this house is not bound to make addresses to the senate, but the rights of both houses must be consulted, and if either branch adopts a mode that the other cannot agree to—then I say that this committee will waste their time and the public money fruitlessly.

On the question to agree to Mr. Harrison's motion, it passed in the negative. . . .[2]

The committee then proceeded in the bill, and having agreed to the same, rose and reported, when it was ordered to be engrossed.

1. *Daily Advertiser*, 6 February 1789. The brackets are in the original newspaper printing. The debates were also printed in the *Morning Post*, 7 February.
2. For the Assembly roll call, see Assembly Proceedings, 21 January 1789, immediately above.

John Bogart to Peter Van Gaasbeek, Albany, 21 January (excerpt)[1]

I have great hopes of An Intire Change in our Political Affares, as your Ante members begin to turn out on A more liberal Scale And begin to throw of[f] Self Intrist for the Better establishment of Good order and A well regulated Government

Yeaster Day A Bill Passed the house which was Sent in to them from the Senate for the Chusing Representatives for the Federal Govert—Vz.

the State Being Devided into Six Destricts And Each Destrict to Chuse one Member, But on the motion of Mr. Lansing for the reconsideration of the Above Clause it was Carried in the Affirmative Vz that each Destrict may if they t[h]inck proper take their representative out of any outher Dist Belongin to the State

1. RC, Peter Van Gaasbeek Papers, Senate House Museum, Kingston, N.Y. Bogart and Van Gaasbeek were cousins.

Alexander Hamilton to Samuel Jones, New York, 21 January[1]

As in our conversations on the important subject of a representation in the ensuing Congress I had the pleasure to perceive that you were inclined to pursue a moderate and accommodating line of conduct; and as I have reason to believe that representations will be made of the sense of this city calculated to nourish a spirit of pertinacity in the Majority of the Assembly which may counteract the prudent views you entertain, I have thought it might be useful to possess you of a true state of facts on this head, of which you may make such use as you think proper.

The general sentiments of the citizens are that the Senate are right in the principle for which they contend; but a considerable number are of opinion that it would be better for them to depart from it than to hazard a loss of the seat of government for want of a representation in the Senate. This, however, though an extensive sentiment is far from being universal. I verily believe and I have taken great pains to ascertain the matter that a more considerable number hold that the Senate ought to persevere at every hazard. This I take to be a true account of the state of things here, and you may venture confidently to hold it up in opposition to the exaggerated stories with [which?] the violent partisans will endeavour to preclude the possibility of accommodation.

But if the case were in reality such as it will be represented to be what ought to be the inference from it? Will it therefore be reasonable to sacrifice the interests of the state to a humour utterly averse to all compromise or accommodation? Perhaps it may be supposed that in this situation of affairs the Senate will be induced to yield the point—I sincerely wish that an illusion of this kind may not be productive of mischiefs which we may all have occasion to regret. I flatter myself you will believe me, sir, when I assure you upon my honor that from every thing I know of the disposition of the members of the Senate, I am led to conclude that the majority will *in no event* accede to the unqualified idea of a joint ballot. I am thus emphatical in my assurances on this point because I think it is of the utmost importance that there should be no mistake about it; and that if an adherence to that plan is resolved upon it may be under the full impression that a representation will not take place. And while I make this declaration I cannot but flatter myself that however it may be imagined that I miscalculate the firmness of the Senate it will at least be believed that I am incapable of an attempt to deceive under the sanction I have used.

Truly Sir this is a matter of serious moment. And allow me to hope that you will dispassionately weigh all the consequences of an obstinate adherence to the ground taken in the assembly. I am far from wishing that house to sacrifice its dignity; but I am satisfied this cannot be the case by coming into the compromise we have talked of. The Senate will in this, as far as *principle* is concerned give up more than the Assembly. Permit me to observe that however violence may become certain characters, your situation calls upon you to be an umpire between the zealots of all parties. You Sir as well as myself have assented to the National constitution. Your reputation as well as mine is concerned that the event shall justify the measure and that the people shall have reason from experience to think we have acted well in making them parties to that constitution. And this can only be done by pursuing such measures as will secure to them every advantage they can promise themselves under it. The vanity and the malignity of some men may be gratified by embarrassing the outset of the government; but this line of conduct would be a species of political suicide in every man who has in any shape given his assent to the system. I cannot doubt Sir that this observation will strike you as of great and real force and that you will readily perceive a vast dissimilitude between the situation of those who have concurred in establishing the constitution and those who have uniformly opposed it. An alliance between these two descriptions of men is unnatural and if closely pursued will certainly give cause of repentance to the former.

In taking the liberty to make these remarks I persuade myself you will discover nothing of a disposition unfriendly to you—I therefore make no apology for that liberty—I am much mistaken if we do not now or shall not at a future day agree in the prudence of the suggestions contained in this letter.

1. RC, Hamilton Papers, DLC. The letter was addressed to Jones in Albany, where he was representing Queens County in the Assembly.

Thomas FitzSimons to Tench Coxe, Philadelphia, 22 January (excerpt)[1]

private Letters say that the Citizens of New York have Urged the Senate to wave their Right in the Appointment of Senators. if that is done it will beget a Suspicion that the Residence of Congress is the Motive. & however desireable it is surely not an Honorable one—

1. RC, Tench Coxe Papers, PHi. Coxe was in New York City representing Pennsylvania in the last Confederation Congress. For a biographical sketch of FitzSimons, see DHFFE, I, 415.

Assembly and Senate Proceedings, Thursday, A.M., 22 January

The Assembly

The engrossed bill entitled *An act prescribing the times, places and manner of holding elections for Senators of the United States of America, to be chosen in this State*, was read a third time.

Resolved, That the bill do pass. . . .

Ordered, That Mr. Younglove and Mr. Duncan, deliver the [bill] to the Honorable the Senate, and request their concurrence.

The Senate

A message from the Honorable the Assembly, by Mr. Younglove and Mr. Duncan, was received, with . . . the bill entitled *An act for prescribing the times, places and manner of holding elections for Senators of the United States of America to be chosen in this State*, . . . which [was] read the first time, and ordered a second reading.

With the same message was received, the bill entitled *An act directing the times, places and manner of electing Representatives in this State, for the House of Representatives, of the Congress of the United States*, with amendments thereto, informing that they had passed the bill with the amendments therewith delivered.

Ordered, That the consideration of the said amendments be postponed.

Assembly and Senate Proceedings, Friday, A.M., 23 January

The Senate

The bill entitled *An act for prescribing the times, places and manner of holding elections for Senators of the United States of America, to be chosen in this State*, . . . [was] read a second time, and committed to a committee of the whole.

The Senate proceeded to the consideration of the amendments proposed by the Honorable the Assembly, to the bill entitled *An act directing the times, places and manner of electing Representatives in this State, for the House of Representatives of the Congress of the United States*, one of which amendments being to add to the title, the words *of America*:

Thereupon, *Resolved*, That the Senate do concur with the Honorable the Assembly, in their amendments to the said bill.

Ordered, That Mr. Tredwell and Mr. L'Hommedieu deliver the bill to the Honorable the Assembly, and inform them that the Senate have concurred in the amendments to the bill, and that the bill is amended accordingly.

The Assembly

A message from the Honorable the Senate, delivered by Mr. Tredwell and Mr. L'Hommedieu, with the bill therein mentioned, was read, that the Senate have concurred in the amendments to the bill, entitled *An act directing the times, places and manner of electing Representatives in this State, for the House of Representatives of the Congress of the United States of America*, and that the bill is amended accordingly.

The amended bill having been examined;

Ordered, That Mr. H. Van Rensselaer and Mr. Thompson return the same to the Honorable the Senate.

Assembly and Senate Proceedings, Saturday, A.M., 24 January

The Senate

A message from the Honorable the Assembly, by Mr. H. Van Rensselaer and Mr. Thompson, was received, returning the bill entitled *An [act] directing the times, places and manner of electing Representatives in this State, for the House of Representatives of the Congress of the United States of America.*

Ordered, That Mr. Duane and Mr. Humfrey deliver the bill to the Honorable the Council of Revision. . . .

Ordered, That Tuesday next be assigned, to take into consideration the bill *for prescribing the times, places and manner of holding elections for Senators of the United States of America to be chosen in this State.*

The Assembly

Mr. Jones, moved for leave to bring in a bill, for directing the manner of appointing electors in this State, for choosing the President and Vice President of the United States of America.

Ordered, That leave be given accordingly.

Mr. Jones, according to leave, brought in the said bill, entitled *An act for directing the manner of appointing electors in this State, for choosing the President and Vice-President, of the United States of America*, which was read the first time, and ordered a second reading.

Hugh Williamson to James Iredell, New York, 24 January (excerpt)[1]

The Genl: Assembly of this State after spending near 2 months in pure wrangling, during which Time many of them have had the felicity to make a clear saving of one Dlr per day, have at length agreed to divide the state into six Election Districts for the choice of Representatives in the new Congress. They cannot yet agree about the mode of chusing Senators. The House of commons want to have all Antis & the Senate wish to have at least one of the Congress Senators a federal Man.

1. RC, James Iredell Papers, NcD. The letter was addressed to Iredell in Edenton, North Carolina. Williamson (1735–1819), a North Carolina merchant and physician, served in Congress, 1782–1785 and 1788; in the Constitutional Convention in 1787; in the second North Carolina Convention in 1789 (where he voted to ratify the Constitution); and in the House of Representatives, 1790–1793. Iredell (1751–1799), a prominent North Carolina lawyer and jurist, led the Federalists in the first North Carolina Convention in 1788. From 1790 until his death he was an associate justice of the United States Supreme Court.

Assembly Proceedings, Monday, A.M., 26 January

The bill entitled *An act directing the manner of appointing Electors in this State, for choosing the President and Vice-President of the United States of America*, . . . [was] read a second time, and committed to a committee of the whole House.

Daily Advertiser (New York), 26 January

By Mr. B. Livingston,[1] who arrived in town on Saturday evening from Albany, we are informed, that a bill had passed both houses prescribing the time and manner of choosing Representatives to the Congress of the United States:—By this bill the State is divided into Six Districts, each District is to choose one Representative—but the Electors are not confined in their choice to a person resident within their own District.—That on Wednesday last a bill directing the mode of choosing Senators, which had been brought in by Mr. Jones, passed the house of assembly. Except in the recital there is no difference between this bill, and that clause in the former one which gave rise to the late conference between the two houses, and occasioned the loss of the whole election bill. It was not thought when Mr. Livingston came away, that the senate would give their assent to it. Mr. Harrison moved the same amendment which he had done to the first bill, which was lost by about the same majority.[2]

1. Brockholst Livingston, a lawyer, represented New York City and County in the Assembly, 1788–1789 and 1800–1802. He was the son of William Livingston, governor of New Jersey.

2. This report was reprinted in the *Daily Gazette*, 27 January 1789; *New York Packet*, 27 January; *New York Journal*, 29 January; and at least seventeen out-of-state newspapers from North Carolina to New England.

Jeremiah Mason to John Woodworth, New Haven, 26 January[1]

When I parted with you at Albany I little thought such a length of time would have elapsed before I should again have seen you[.] But on account of my father's unwillingness and some other circumstances I was prevented from returning to Albany as I intended, I am now reading law here in N. Haven with Mr. Baldwin[.] However I have not dropt my intentions of studying in your State[.] In the spring I propose to come up and join you—Our Assembly is now sitting in this place[.] They have the representatives elected and every thing in readiness for the New Government—A few days ago the Assembly passed an act prescribing the form of an oath which is to be taken by all officers in the state government. The purport of the oath is to support the new Constitution. The oath is to be taken before admission into office. Thus you see this state is determined to give the new government every possible assistance. 'Tis reported here that the State of N. York has neglected to choose electors and representatives[.] Our warmest federalists are pleased with the report—Your neglecting to choose electors will make the election of a federal President more certain. As some of your electors would probably have been Antifederal[.] And as to your representatives they are to be elected under the auspices and by the authority of the New Congress—Let them go on as they please—I trouble myself but little about it[.] Tho' from the regard I bear you I cannot help expressing a wish that your heart was more federal—Your friends here are I believe all well Harry in particular—I trust you will write me the first opportunity[.] I believe you will have a chance by Mr. Lyon who will carry this—

1. RC, Betts Autograph Collection, CtY. The letter was addressed to Woodworth in Albany. Mason (1768–1848) graduated from Yale College in 1788 and studied law with Simeon Baldwin. He later became a leading New Hampshire lawyer and jurist (serving as state attorney general,

1802–1805) and a United States Senator, 1813–1817. Woodworth, surrogate of Rensselaer County, 1793–1803, represented Rensselaer in the Assembly, 1803, and the Eastern District in the Senate, 1804–1807. He was a presidential Elector in 1800 and 1812.

Council of Revision Proceedings, Monday, A.M., 26 January[1]

Present His Excellency Governor Clinton
The Honore Mr Justice Yates
The Honore Mr Justice Hobart

Mr Duane and Mr Humfry from the Hone the Senate brought up to the Council a bill about to be passed into a Law By the Legislature entitled An Act directing the Time, Places and Manner of Electing Representatives in this State for the House of Representatives of the Congress of the United States of America which was read the first Time and ordered a second Reading

1. MS, Minutes of the Council of Revision, NHi. Hereafter the Council minutes are cited by date only.

Council of Revision Proceedings, Tuesday, A.M., 27 January

Present His Excellency the Governor
The Honore Mr. Justice Yates
The Honore Mr. Justice Hobart

The Bill entitled An Act directing the Time, Places and Manner of Represen[ta]tives elected in this State for the Congress of the United States of America was read a second time and duly considered whereupon

Resolved that It does not appear improper to the Council that the said bill should become a Law of this State

Ordered that a Copy of the preceeding resolution signed by his Excellency the Governor be delivered to the Honorable the Senate by Mr. Justice Yates

Assembly and Senate Proceedings, Tuesday, A.M., 27 January

The Senate

A message from the Honorable the Council of Revision, delivered by the Honorable Mr. Justice Yates, was read, "that it does not appear improper to the Council that the bill, entitled *An act directing the times, places and manner of electing Representatives in this State, for the House of Representatives of the Congress of the United States of America*, should become a law of this State."

Mr. Hopkins from the committee of the whole, to whom was referred the bill, entitled *An act for prescribing the times, places and manner of holding elections for Senators of the United States of America, to be chosen in this State*, reported, that upon reading the first clause of the bill, in the words following, viz. Be it enacted by the People of the State of New-York, represented in Senate and Assembly, and it is hereby enacted by the authority of the same, That the *Senators* of the United States, to be chosen in this State, shall be chosen in the same manner that Delegates to represent this State in the General Congress of the United States of America, are directed to be appointed as aforesaid, by the Constitution of this State, &c. Mr. L'Hommedieu moved to expunge from the word *Senators* to the end, and to substitute the following in its stead, viz. 'to represent this State in the Senate of the Congress of the United States of America, to be chosen by the Legislature of this State, shall be chosen in the manner following, that is to say, the Senate and Assembly of this State shall, if two Senators are to be chosen, openly nominate two persons, and shall respectively give notice each to the other of such nomination: That if both Houses agree in the nomination of the same person or persons, the person or persons so nominated and agreed to, shall be the Senator or Senators to represent this State in the Senate of the Congress of the United States: That if the nomination of either House does not agree in any of the persons nominated by the other, the Senate shall on the same day openly choose one of the persons nominated by the Assembly, and the Assembly shall on the same day openly choose one of the persons nominated by the Senate, and the two persons so chosen shall be the Senators, to represent this State in the Senate of the Congress of the United States: That in every case when two Senators are to be chosen, and both Houses agree only as to one in such nomination as aforesaid, and in every case when only one Senator is to be chosen, either of the two Houses of the Legislature may propose to the other a resolution for concurrence, naming therein a person to fill the office of Senator, and if the House receiving such resolution shall concur therein, the person so named in such resolution, shall be the Senator, but if such resolution shall not be concurred in, either House may on that or any future day, proceed to offer to the other, a resolution for concurrence, from time to time, until they shall agree upon a Senator.' Debates arose upon the said motion, and the question being put thereon, it was carried in the affirmative, in manner following, viz.

FOR THE AFFIRMATIVE.

Mr. Philip Schuyler,	Mr. Morris,
Mr. Douw,	Mr. Roosevelt,
Mr. Micheau,	Mr. L'Hommedieu,
Mr. Peter Schuyler,	Mr. Duane,
Mr. Fonda,	Mr. Hoffman.
Mr. Vanderbilt,	

FOR THE NEGATIVE.

Mr. Yates,	Mr. Tredwell,
Mr. Williams,	Mr. Humfrey,
Mr. Van Ness,	Mr. Clinton,
Mr. Swartwout,	Mr. Hathorn.
Mr. Townsend,	

That having read the preamble to the bill in the words following, viz. Whereas it is provided by the Constitution of this State, that Delegates to represent this State in the General Congress of the United States of America, be annually appointed as follows, to wit, the Senate and Assembly shall each openly nominate as many persons as shall be equal to the whole number of Delegates to be appointed; after which nomination they shall meet together, and those persons named in both lists shall be Delegates, and out of those persons whose names are not in both lists, one half shall be chosen by the joint ballot of the Senators and Members of Assembly so met together as aforesaid. And whereas by the Constitution of the United States of America, ratified and assented to by the Convention of this State on the twenty sixth day of July last, it is ordained and established, that all Legislative powers therein granted, shall be vested in a Congress of the United States, which shall consist of a Senate and House of Representatives; and that the Senate of the United States shall be composed of two Senators from each State, chosen by the Legislature thereof for six years; and that the times, places and manner of holding elections for Senators and Representatives, shall be prescribed in each State by the Legislature thereof. "Mr. L'Hommedieu, moved that the following be added to the said preamble, viz.—by reason whereof the before recited clause of the Constitution of this State is become of no effect, and it is necessary that the Senators to represent this State in the Congress of the United States of America, be chosen by the Legislature." Debates arose upon the said proposed amendment, and the question being put thereon, it was carried in the affirmative, in manner following, viz.

FOR THE AFFIRMATIVE.

Mr. Philip Schuyler,	Mr. Morris,
Mr. Douw,	Mr. Roosevelt,
Mr. Micheau,	Mr. L'Hommedieu,
Mr. Peter Schuyler,	Mr. Duane,
Mr. Fonda,	Mr. Hoffman.
Mr. Vanderbilt,	

FOR THE NEGATIVE.

Mr. Yates,	Mr. Tredwell,
Mr. Williams,	Mr. Humfrey,
Mr. Van Ness,	Mr. Clinton,
Mr. Swartwout,	Mr. Hathorn.
Mr. Townsend,	

Mr. Hopkins, further reported, that the committee had gone through the bill, made amendments thereto, and agreed to the same, which report he read in his place, and delivered the bill and amendments in at the table, where they were again read, and Mr. President, having put the question, whether the bill as amended shall pass, it was carried in the affirmative, in manner following, viz.

FOR THE AFFIRMATIVE.

Mr. Philip Schuyler,	Mr. Morris,
Mr. Douw,	Mr. Roosevelt,
Mr. Micheau,	Mr. L'Hommedieu,
Mr. Peter Schuyler,	Mr. Duane,
Mr. Fonda,	Mr. Hoffman.
Mr. Vanderbilt,	

FOR THE NEGATIVE.

Mr. Yates,	Mr. Townsend,
Mr. Hopkins,	Mr. Tredwell,
Mr. Williams,	Mr. Humfrey,
Mr. Van Ness,	Mr. Clinton,
Mr. Swartwout,	Mr. Hathorn.

Thereupon, *Resolved*, That the bill with the amendments do pass.

Ordered, That Mr. Hathorn and Mr. Philip Schuyler deliver the bill, with the amendments, to the Honorable the Assembly, and inform them that the Senate have passed the bill, with the amendments therewith delivered.

The Assembly

A message from the Honorable the Council of Revision, transmitted to this House by the Honorable the Senate, was read, "that it does not appear improper to the Council, that the bill entitled *An act directing the times, places and manner of electing Representatives in this State, for the House of Representatives of the Congress of the United States of America*, should become a law of this State." . . .

Mr. Vandervoort, from the committee of the whole House, on the bill entitled *An act for directing the manner of appointing electors in this State, for choosing the President and Vice-President, of the United States of America*, reported, that after the bill had been read in the committee, a part of the first enacting clause was again read, in the words following, viz.

"Be it enacted by the People of the State of New-York, represented in Senate and Assembly, and it is hereby enacted by the authority of the same, that the electors to be appointed in this State for choosing the President and Vice President of the United States of America, shall be appointed in the manner following, that is to say, the Senate and Assembly shall each openly nominate as many persons, as shall be equal to the whole number of the Electors so to be appointed by this State, after which nomination, the Senate and Assembly shall meet together, and compare the lists of the persons by them respectively nominated; and those persons named in both lists shall be Electors; and out of those persons whose names are not in both lists, one half shall be chosen by the joint ballot of the Senators and Members of Assembly, so met together as aforesaid."

That the said paragraph having been read, Mr. Harison made a motion, that the latter part thereof, viz. the words, *and out of those persons whose names are not in both lists, one half shall be chosen by the joint ballot of the Senators and Members of Assembly, so met together as aforesaid*, should be obliterated, and the following inserted instead thereof, viz.

"And if there are any persons whose names are not in both lists, the names of all the Senators so met as aforesaid, shall be written on separate papers, rolled up and put into a box; and from the same box seven names shall be drawn by the President of the Senate, at the said meeting; and in the like manner the names of all the Members of the Assembly so met, shall be written upon separate papers, rolled up and put into a box; and from the same box seven names shall in like manner be drawn by the Speaker of the Assembly, and the fourteen persons whose names shall be so drawn, shall at the same meeting, by joint ballot, choose the one half of the said persons, whose names are not included in both the said lists, to be Electors as aforesaid."

That the question having been put on the amendment proposed by the motion of Mr. Harison, it passed in the negative, in the manner following, viz.

FOR THE NEGATIVE.

Mr. Jones,	Mr. Duncan,
Mr. Kortz,	Mr. Savage,
Mr. Stauring,	Mr. Webster,
Mr. SPEAKER,	Mr. M'Cracken,
Mr. Van Dyck,	Mr. Thompson,
Mr. J. Van Rensselaer,	Mr. Bay,
Mr. Hardenbergh,	Mr. Schoonmaker,
Mr. Veeder,	Mr. Tappen,
Mr. Winn,	Mr. Griffen,

Mr. Carpenter,
Mr. J. Smith,
Mr. D'Witt,
Mr. Wisner,
Mr. Adgate,
Mr. Harper,
Mr. Havens,
Mr. Schenck,
Mr. Akins,
Mr. E. Clark,
Mr. Scudder,
Mr. Bloom,
Mr. Smith.

FOR THE AFFIRMATIVE.

Mr. Gilbert,
Mr. Van Cortlandt,
Mr. Seaman,
Mr. Barker,
Mr. Harison,
Mr. Hoffman,
Mr. H. Van Rensselaer,
Mr. Younglove,
Mr. Watts,
Mr. Livingston,
Mr. Horton,
Mr. Low,
Mr. Bancker,
Mr. Verplanck,
Mr. Cornwell,
Mr. Giles,
Mr. Sands,
Mr. Gardiner,
Mr. Macomb,
Mr. Crane.

That Mr. Harison as a further amendment, made a motion, that all that part of the said first paragraph of the bill, which is herein before inserted, be obliterated, and that a paragraph be inserted instead thereof, in the words following, viz.

"Be it enacted by the People of the State of New-York, represented in Senate and Assembly, and it is hereby enacted by the authority of the same, That —— shall be, and they are hereby nominated and appointed Electors on the part of this State, for choosing the first President and Vice-President of the United States of America."

That the question having been put on the amendment proposed by the last mentioned motion of Mr. Harison, it passed in the negative, in the manner following, viz.

FOR THE NEGATIVE.

Mr. Jones,
Mr. Kortz,
Mr. Stauring,
Mr. SPEAKER,
Mr. Van Dyck,
Mr. J. Van Rensselaer,
Mr. Hardenbergh,
Mr. Veeder,
Mr. Winn,
Mr. Duncan,
Mr. Savage,
Mr. Webster,
Mr. M'Cracken,
Mr. Thomson,
Mr. Bay,
Mr. Schoonmaker,
Mr. Tappen,
Mr. Griffen,
Mr. Carpenter,
Mr. D'Witt,
Mr. Wisner,
Mr. Adgate,
Mr. Harper,
Mr. Schenck,
Mr. Akins,
Mr. E. Clark,
Mr. Patterson,
Mr. Scudder,
Mr. Bloom,
Mr. Smith.

FOR THE AFFIRMATIVE.

Mr. Gilbert,
Mr. Van Cortlandt,
Mr. Seaman,
Mr. Barker,
Mr. Harison,
Mr. Hoffman,
Mr. H. Van Rensselaer,
Mr. Younglove,

Mr. Watts,	Mr. Cornwell,
Mr. Livingston,	Mr. Giles,
Mr. Horton,	Mr. Sands,
Mr. Low,	Mr. Gardiner,
Mr. Bancker,	Mr. Macomb,
Mr. Verplanck,	Mr. Crane.

That Mr. Watts as an amendment, made a motion, that the said first paragraph of the bill as herein before inserted, be obliterated, and that a paragraph be inserted instead thereof, in the words following, viz.

"Be it enacted by the People of the State of New-York, represented in Senate and Assembly, and it is hereby enacted by the authority of the same, That the Senate shall openly nominate eight persons as Electors; after which nomination a list containing the names of such persons, signed by the President of the Senate, shall be sent to the Assembly; *whereupon*, the Assembly shall openly nominate other eight persons, Electors as aforesaid, and shall send a list of such last nomination, signed by the Speaker of the Assembly, to the Senate; and out of the eight persons so nominated by the Senate, the Assembly shall choose four persons by ballot, and out of the eight persons nominated by the Assembly, the Senate shall choose four persons by ballot, which eight persons in such manner chosen shall be Electors."

That the question having been put on the amendment proposed by the motion of Mr. Watts, it also passed in the negative, in the manner following, viz.

FOR THE NEGATIVE.

Mr. Kortz,	Mr. Tappen,
Mr. Stauring,	Mr. Griffen,
Mr. Speaker,	Mr. Carpenter,
Mr. Van Dyck,	Mr. D'Witt,
Mr. J. Van Rensselaer,	Mr. Wisner,
Mr. Hardenbergh,	Mr. Adgate,
Mr. Veeder,	Mr. Harper,
Mr. Winn,	Mr. Schenck,
Mr. Duncan,	Mr. Akins,
Mr. Savage,	Mr. E. Clark,
Mr. Webster,	Mr. Patterson,
Mr. M'Cracken,	Mr. Scudder,
Mr. Thompson,	Mr. Bloom,
Mr. Bay,	Mr. Smith.
Mr. Schoonmaker,	

FOR THE AFFIRMATIVE.

Mr. Gilbert,	Mr. Horton,
Mr. Van Cortlandt,	Mr. Low,
Mr. Seaman,	Mr. Bancker,
Mr. Barker,	Mr. Verplanck,
Mr. Harison,	Mr. Cornwell,
Mr. Hoffman,	Mr. Giles,
Mr. H. Van Rensselaer,	Mr. Sands,
Mr. Younglove,	Mr. Gardiner,
Mr. Watts,	Mr. Macomb,
Mr. Livingston,	Mr. Crane.

That the first paragraph of the bill having been again read, the question was put whether the committee did agree to the same, and that it was carried in the affirmative, in the manner following, viz.

FOR THE AFFIRMATIVE.

Mr. Stauring,	Mr. D'Witt,
Mr. SPEAKER,	Mr. Wisner,
Mr. Van Dyck,	Mr. Adgate,
Mr. J. Van Rensselaer,	Mr. Harper,
Mr. Hardenbergh,	Mr. Schenck,
Mr. Veeder,	Mr. Akins,
Mr. Winn,	Mr. E. Clark,
Mr. Savage,	Mr. Patterson,
Mr. Webster,	Mr. Scudder,
Mr. M'Cracken,	Mr. Bloom,
Mr. Bay,	Mr. Smith,
Mr. Schoonmaker,	Mr. Kortz,
Mr. Tappen,	Mr. Duncan.
Mr. Carpenter,	

FOR THE NEGATIVE.

Mr. Gilbert,	Mr. Low,
Mr. Seaman,	Mr. Bancker,
Mr. Barker,	Mr. Verplanck,
Mr. Harison,	Mr. Cornwell,
Mr. Hoffman,	Mr. Giles,
Mr. H. Van Rensselaer,	Mr. Sands,
Mr. Younglove,	Mr. Gardiner,
Mr. Thompson,	Mr. Macomb,
Mr. Livingston,	Mr. Crane.
Mr. Horton,	

That the committee had gone through the bill, and made amendments, which he was directed to report to the House; and he read the report in his place, and delivered the bill and amendments in at the table, where the same were again read, and agreed to by the House.

Ordered, That the bill and amendments be engrossed. . . .

Resolved, (if the Honorable the Senate concur herein,) That the Printer for the State be, and he is hereby directed, forthwith to print seven hundred copies of the act entitled *An act for directing the times, places and manner of electing Representatives in this State, for the House of Representatives of the Congress of the United States, of America*, and to deliver the same to His Excellency the Governor; and that His Excellency be requested to transmit so many of the copies of the same act, to the Clerks of the respective counties in this State, by special messengers, at the expence of the State, as he shall judge to be requisite, with directions to such Clerks respectively, to forward the said copies immediately to the Supervisor or Inspectors of elections in each town or district within his county, in proportion to the number of inhabitants, and extent of the towns respectively; and that the same Printer be further directed to publish the same act, in one of the news papers to be published in his office.

Ordered, That Mr. Low and Mr. D'Witt deliver a copy of the preceding resolution to the Honorable the Senate.

Assembly Debates, Tuesday, 27 January[1]

Went into a committee on the bill for prescribing the times, places, and manners of choosing Electors who are to Elect the President, and vice President, of the United States.

Mr. Vandervoort in the Chair.

Mr. Harrison.—I am by no means convinced of the propriety of bringing forward any bill for the appointment of electors during the present session. Sir, my doubts arise from a consideration of that article in the new constitution, by which it is ordained that Congress may determine the time of chusing electors, and that the day for *that* purpose shall be the same throughout the United States. It may however be objected, and must unquestionably be admitted, that this article was intended to regulate such appointments as might take place after the first election; but upon examining the subject a little farther, we shall find that the general convention have not been inattentive to the *first* appointment of electors. In their resolutions for organizing the government, they have expressly given power to the existing Congress to fix a day on which the appointment of the first electors shall be made. The Congress have executed this power, and (I am sorry to say) the day which they appointed, has already elapsed.

But although a sufficient reason might perhaps have been deduced from these premises, to arrest the progress of the bill now before us; yet when we consider of how much consequence it is to the state that we should participate in the election of the important officers who are soon to be chosen, when we consider that the voice of the state upon this occasion may possibly be received, if the day of appointing electors should not be regarded as essential, I am induced to try the experiment, even if the success is merely doubtful.

But, Sir, when I contemplate the bill now before us, and reflect upon the various transactions of the present session, I must conclude that the attempt to procure electors in the mode proposed to us is *an attempt* truly *vain.* We have already, in a bill which has been lost, proposed the precise plan for appointing electors, which is contained in the present bill. The senate, Sir, have declared not only by the amendments which they then offered to us, but by the voice of their conferrees, and by their adherence to those amendments, that they could not possibly agree to the plan which we had recommended for adoption.

What then is the language of this bill? Does it amount to any thing more than this, "you have declared in the most solemn and decisive manner that our proposition is one to which you cannot agree, but nevertheless we offer it to you again, and we offer it without the smallest variation." I do not know that any thing in human life can be regarded as trifling with others if such a measure at the present does not answer the description. If any conduct can be considered as an insult to a public body, I must consider this bill as an insult offered to the senate. Sir, this bill in every point of view, is totally improper: What must be the effect of our proceedings if we should send it to the senate in the form in which it now stands? If the senate, Sir, have any firmness; if they have any consistency; if they have any regard to their reputations either as men or as legislators, they must reject the bill or amend it, and send us back the same propositions[2] which they had before sent us,

Should they pursue the milder course, and send us amendments similar to those which they have already offered, what must be the consequence? Either we must agree to them, or there must be a conference between the two houses precisely upon the same subject which they have already conferred on. Can this, sir, be right? Is it a circumstance that our constitution ever had in view? Was it ever intended that twice in the same session the two houses should meet together and confer upon the same subject—to know whether they have changed their sentiments, when there has been no change of men or circumstances to impel them to it?

Under these impressions, and from a conviction that the bill as it now stands must be considered as an insult upon the senate (in which light it strikes me) I am solicitous that the committee should reflect *seriously* upon this subject, and agree to an amendment. I am persuaded, sir, that we cannot suppose the clause of our state constitution which has been so often repeated, applies to electors. It is certain that the powers vested in the president of the United States are *new powers*, which were not contemplated when our state constitution was framed. The office of president is a *new office*, which the framers of our constitution could not have had in view. If this, sir, is the case; if we are forming regulations as to the choice of electors for a new office, unknown to our state constitution it must follow, as a necessary consequence, that the state constitution does not apply on the present occasion, and it is discretionary with the two houses to adopt such a mode as they may suppose to be the best.

If, sir, we are not bound by positive directions of our state constitution to adopt any precise mode as to the appointment of electors; why should we adopt one in which the two houses cannot agree? Why send to the senate the very proposition which they thought themselves obliged to reject but a few days ago?

Sir, it is not necessary even that the choice of electors should be made by the legislature; they may do it if they think proper, or they may refer it to any other persons whom they think proper. Such has been the construction of the new constitution in the different states of the union, and accordingly in one state the appointment of electors has been left to the governor and council; in another it has been referred to the people; and in another again the choice has been made by concurrent resolutions of the two branches of the legislature.[3] From this variety of practice, sir, it must be evident that the different states consider the mode of appointing electors wholly discretionary.

I trust that our conclusion will be similar, and therefore I shall suggest the principles of an amendment to the bill now before us. I would propose, as a regulation for this time only (leaving it to a future legislature to submit the choice to the people, if they think proper) that the two houses should each nominate eight electors; that after the nomination the lists be compared, and the persons named by both houses, shall be electors; that if the nominations disagree, either in the whole or in part, that then the names of all the senators shall be written on separate papers, and put into one box, from which the president of the senate shall draw out the names of seven senators, who with seven members of the assembly to be balloted for in like manner, shall by joint ballot, choose either the whole, or such part of the electors as the two houses may not agree in, from the persons nominated by the two houses.

I am not, sir, tenacious as to this particular mode of appointment. I conceive, however, that in this or some other like it, the object we have in view may be obtained. But if the bill should go to the senate in its present form, we can hope for nothing but a rejection, or perhaps a fruitless conference, and at all events a *waste* of our *time*, and of the *public money*,

Mr. *Jones*,—Far be it from me to bring forward propositions to insult the senate; nor do I believe a member of this house can think it so. It is said why bring forward the proposition in that shape. The gentleman himself has shewn what must appear clearly, that the proposition does not stand in the same situation. He has said that it was unparliamentary to bring it forward in the same session; if it was in the same shape as at first, I should think it so. But when the whole of this business came forward in one bill, on which the houses differed, it could not be determined on which proposition either house adhered. We can not know that the senate will not adopt this bill. What then is the great difficulty—how can it be called an insult? The observations that have been made are founded upon a supposition that the senate will not agree to the present proposition. I shall readily agree, that with respect to the appointment of electors, the legislature may adopt what mode they please. And if the legislature declare that any individual man shall appoint them, it will be consistent with the constitution. In New-Jersey, they have left it to the governor and council;—in other states they have left it to the people; there may be a state where it is done by concurrent resolution; but the greater part of the states have adopted the mode that we now propose. Is there any constitutional ground for the senate to take, that they cannot come into the measure; I know of none. Even upon the conference the whole debate turned upon one point, the election of senators. It was there acknowledged, that as to the electors, any mode might be agreed to,

Mr. *Harrison*.—If there was any thing wanting to convince me of the propriety of those sentiments which I entertain upon the present occasion, the gentleman who was last on the floor has supplied the deficiency. He has clearly acknowledged that the provision of the state constitution, with regard to the election of delegates, does not apply to the subject under consideration, and that the legislature may adopt any mode for the appointment of electors which they shall think proper. Taking up the matter, therefore, in this point of view, it must appear evident to every gentleman of the committee, that this is not a question upon which we are obliged to be tenacious; and consequently that we may with propriety consult the inclinations and principles of the senate respecting it.

If this house, sir, is at liberty to adopt any mode of appointment which they may think proper, then there can be no *constitutional objection* to the mode which I propose. The only questions which will remain for our consideration are the two following, *which* of the two modes proposed by the bill and amendment is the most proper, and which is the most likely to succeed with the senate?

Sir, it is in vain for us to resolve on the mode which we shall think most proper, unless it is such as the other house can adopt.

The great constitutional question which has been agitated in this house during the present session, being out of sight upon this occasion, let us then contemplate which mode of appointing electors is most likely to meet the approbation of the senate. In considering this question we must remember that the mode proposed by the bill has already been decided upon in the senate, when it constituted a part of *that bill* for organizing the new government, which has unfortunately been lost. Upon that occasion, the senate have not only declared that the mode proposed by the bill was a mode which they disliked, but they have also declared that it was such a one as, in duty to their constituents, they were obliged to reject. It is a mode, Sir, to which we ought not to ask their concurrance; because, upon their principle, they can agree to none which does not secure to them *a perfect equality.* If this is the case, what good purpose will it answer to send them the proposition contained in the bill.

Sir, if the amendment is adopted, (and the gentleman admits that we may adopt it, if we please) then it is probable that we may meet the ideas of the senate; because the amendment holds out to them that perfect equality between the two houses for which *they* contend.

Sir, I do not pretend to say that the mode of appointing electors which I have proposed is the best that could possibly be devised. I am not particularly attached to it, if any other is brought forward in which the same principle is preserved; but at any rate, I wish the provision to be temporary, and that another legislature, coming forward with the sense of the people upon this subject, may determine whether the choice of electors should be referred to the people at large, or exercised by the legislature itself.

But, sir, if we examine even the other question, what reason have we to suppose that the proposition in the bill is the very best that can be framed? It is undoubtedly a mode by which this house can assume the sole appointment, whilst the senate have only the appearance of a voice. But this reason tho' it may appear conclusive to us, must have a different operation in the other branch of the legislature.

It is true, sir, that this house are the representatives of the people, and so are the senate also. Can we be certain that the people of this state would have chosen this house *alone* to appoint the electors? Is there any thing in the nature of their election which designates such an intention? If there is, I am totally unacquainted with it. I suppose that each branch of the legislature is equally trusted by the people and by the constitution; that the senate have as much the confidence of the people as the assembly; and that as the senate have derived their equality from the constitution they cannot possibly resign it.

On the question to agree to the amendment proposed by Mr. Harrison. . . .[4]

Mr. *Harrison.*—As it is possible that many gentlemen may have voted against the amendment from a wish to see some other mode adopted, I shall propose another amendment in hopes that it may be more acceptable than the one that has just been decided on. It is to expunge the whole of the first clause, and to substitute one to the following effect: "That —— be, and they are hereby appointed electors," &c. It is meant merely to be confined to the first election; let the future representatives of the people determine on any other mode that they may think proper.

Mr. *Gilbert.*—I shall just remark, that I suppose it is the object of every gentleman present that this bill should be productive of the end intended to be answered by it. It is clear that the constitution never contemplated electors, and that this is a matter of discretion in the legislature. I ask what could be the reasons that induced the gentleman to bring forward the bill as it stands, when he must be certain it will be rejected; and when he acknowledges that it might have been brought forward in some other way? Why, I say was this exceptionable mode again brought forward? Was it to compel the senate to come into our measures? Can we hope to succeed in such an attempt? Is it right to try to force them into our opinion for a particular mode, when it is admitted that both houses may exercise their discretion? I wish, sir, that this house would for a moment be calm, and reflect seriously upon what they are doing. If the bill is not amended, we shall spend our time and the public money to very little purpose.

Mr. *Jones.*—I did not intend to say any thing more on this subject, but I am compelled to justify, in some measure, the reasons for bringing forward the bill. It is asserted that the senate can not pass it; this argument has been urged more than once, and that they cannot depart from their opinions. I am really much at a loss to know from whence gentlemen get this information. The gentlemen should recollect that we went to the conference upon three distinct propositions, that the bill might have been lost from either house adhering to only one of them. We do not know that the senate will reject the mode contained in the bill; the gentlemen have no evidence that they will. Where then was the impropriety of bringing it forward? Sir, I think it the most proper mode, and bring it forward as such, not because another mode may not be adopted. With respect to the first proposition, would it be right to draw cuts for it—it would really be like casting lots. With respect to the second, what are we to do, not to prescribe a mode for choosing the electors, but to enact them; this I think equally improper with the first. I do not hold that we are bound in this instance either by the constitution of the state or the constitution of the United States. The electors are to be appointed by the legislature, they may do it in such way as they please. But it is proper when we legislate, that in all our laws, the result should be the effect of the thing intended; we must therefore devise such a mode for an election, as will ensure it. But if we make the appointment of electors or senators by law, each house may do their duty, and yet by differing in sentiment with each other, there may be no election at all; this then cannot be a proper mode. And this is the reason that I have brought forward the proposition in the shape that it stands in the bill. We ought not to contrast this business with what produced the conference; the great question there respected only the appointment of senators. This house held that they were bound by a mode prescribed by the state constitution; and the senate urging that by the adoption of the new constitution, the rule prescribed in the state constitution was of no effect, and that they were to enjoy an equality. There is a great distinction too—by the constitution the senators are to be chosen by the legislature, the electors are to be chosen in such manner as they shall prescribe. But let us in either case adopt a mode that shall produce the thing intended.

Mr. *Gilbert*.—The gentleman asks how do we know that the senate will oppose this mode. I answer, sir, that I get my information from the conference; did they not declare there that the same principles operated against the proposition respecting electors as the one respecting senators. Sir, to speak plain, I believe it must be sufficiently understood that this mode will not be agreed to.

Mr. *Harrison*.—It is undoubtedly an unfortunate circumstance, with respect to the human species that they are not only apt to draw different inferences from the same circumstances, but that they will differ as to the circumstances themselves. I am led to make this observation, before I address the committee on the subject matter before them, because I am surprized that a gentleman has given an account of the conference, so very different from what I should. Upon this occasion, I suppose we advert to different circumstances, and the natural bent of our dispositions may have given some bias to our minds. I say this, because I do not wish to arraign either the gentleman's veracity or candor; but, at the same time, I must appeal to the house, whether my account is not equally well founded. Sir, the gentleman has told us, that from the reasons urged at the conference by the senate, he concluded that they were of opinion, the appointment of electors was wholly discretionary, and that they were not bound to any system upon that occasion. Sir, in this respect, I must differ with the gentleman. If I have any recollection of what passed at the conference, the conferrees on the part of the senate substantially declared that the question respecting the electors depended upon the same principles as stated by the conferrees on the part of the senate, with respect to the choice of senators to the United States; and they reasoned nearly in this way—there is a power now to be exercised by both houses of the legislature—both houses by the constitution, possess an equality, except in such cases as are particularly specified. The senate, therefore, being possessed of a right to equality with the assembly, upon every occasion not excepted, consider that equal right as a trust which they can not give up by agreeing to a mode of appointment which will throw the whole power into the hands of the other branch of the legislature. This, sir, was my idea of the conference; such appeared to me to be the ideas of the senate on the subject now in debate; and from the declared principle of the senate I infer that unless a mode is fallen upon that will preserve that equality to the senate, to which they suppose themselves entitled, they cannot possibly accede to the bill. In this view of the matter, it appears to me, sir, to be a fruitless attempt to offer the senate the bill in its present shape. The same principles say they operate in both cases, which we have considered; it is not one to which a particular clause of the constitution applies, but it depends with us on the principles of equality in the two branches of the legislature, derived from the constitution. Such, sir, is the case with respect to the principles maintained by the senate. If I am wrong, the gentlemen who hear me will not be influenced by what I say upon the occasion; but if I am right, there is no probability that the senate will agree to the bill in its present form. It is our duty, therefore, to fall on some other mode that is likely to succeed. The committee, I hope, will excuse me if I make use of a familiar allusion to explain my ideas upon the present occasion—Sir, when with a view to the attainment of some important object, we are necessitated to undertake a long and fatiguing journey, it is natural for us to prefer that road which appears to be the best, the shortest, and capable of supplying the most eligible refreshments upon the cheapest terms. Such, sir, are the dictates of prudence in the common occurrences of life. But if we should meet with unexpected obstructions in the road we had embraced, what then would be our conduct? Sir, the same prudence which we had before consulted, should again govern our choice—we should turn a little to the right or to the left; we should forsake the road which we had at first selected, and pursue another free from the embarrassments which had before impeded us, and which, tho' not quite so pleasant or so direct as the first, might finally conduct us in safety to the end of our journey. Perhaps, sir, the gentlemen of the committee may think that the road pointed out for us by the bill is the best, the shortest, and the cheapest that we can possibly travel; but they must consider the obstructions that will certainly present themselves, and that we can not possibly pursue any route which is not sanctioned by the consent of the senate. Sir, these are the ideas with which I have brought forward the proposed amendment to the bill; but I am not for my own part convinced even that the mode of appointing electors held out in the bill is the best that could be adopted if we had time for the purpose, and I shall beg the indulgence of the committee while I give my sentiments upon that subject. Sir, my idea respecting the appointment of electors is, that they ought to be chosen by the people; and on a former occasion I was against removing a preamble which assigned the reasons why the legislature at this time were obliged to make the appointment. With these ideas, had I been the framer of the bill, I should have brought it forward merely for the present time; but the gentleman brings forward the bill as a perpetual one. I have no doubt he thought it proper; but my ideas are different from his. The amendment I bring forward is only a temporary provision. It is true difficulties may arise as to the names to be inserted in the bill; but I rather think both houses will concur in the appointment of such characters as appear worthy of their confidence. It is clear, from the mode in which the bill is brought forward, that the legislature may be both the persons to appoint the electors and the prescribers of the mode in which the appointment shall be made.—Sir, I am not tenacious on this point—if the gentleman means to oppose the motion because he thinks that it is not in truth an effectual way to prescribe the mode of appointment, I shall have no objection to substitute a clause declaring that the electors shall be chosen by concurrent resolutions of both houses. But, sir, I conceive that the actual appointment by the legislature is in fact prescribing a mode of election—the mode is, an act of the legislature. This may be a sufficient answer to all the arguments that rest upon the words of the new constitution.

But, sir, after all I have my doubts on the great question that I raised when I was first on the floor, whether we have a right at the present time to make any appointment of electors. I am certain that any attempt towards it must be considered as a mere experiment. And I feel a reluctance to try experiments at the expence of my constituents, unless they are rational in themselves, justified by the importance of the object, and not destitute of all probability of success: To such experiments I will not object, but I am certain that to employ our time in passing a bill, which beforehand we are apprised will not be agreed to by the senate, will be as idle an experiment as ever employed the attention and wasted the treasure of persons in search of the philosopher's stone, and who have vainly attempted, during a series of years, to convert the basest metals into pure gold.

Mr. *Lansing*.—So much has been said on this subject, that I did not intend to trouble the house. The proposition, however, now brought forward, it is supposed, ought to be adopted, as one probably that will surmount every difficulty, and ensure the concurrence of the senate; there is some weight in this observation; but, sir, with me the motion is as exceptionable as the one just rejected. It has been stated to the house, and it ought to have weight, that in the mode proposed, if even all parties are disposed to make an election, yet it may be prevented; for instances may arise in which no election will be had.

I differ, sir, with the gentleman, as to the expediency of leaving the rule to be laid down by future legislatures. I suppose it incumbent on us to adopt a rule, and that it ought to be such a one as will operate uniformly to promote the happiness of the people. I have on a former occasion mentioned my reasons for supposing that in the hands of the people this trust will be of no importance. But the state legislatures, having it in their hands, it will be in their power to secure their consequence. Sir, if the people are to determine who is to be the electors, the vote of the state will in most cases be lost, and the choice of president and vice president will either be left to chance or to cabal. Sir, I am therefore of opinion, that we ought to prescribe such a mode as will vest the power in the hands of the legislature. It unfortunately has happened that the two houses have differed; but in respect to the point in question, this proposition has not been sent to them alone; it was connected with two others; we do not know how it may be received. I am not therefore without hopes that it may succeed. If it fails, our time cannot be considered as mispent; for we shall be able to say that we have done our duty; that we submitted a bill to the senate, and that they did not concur; and it will be incumbent on them to convince their constituents that they were right in not concurring. Sir, notwithstanding the declaration of the conferees, who declare that the senate can not give up their equality, we have seen a solemn act of that body, which declares that if there was time they would submit the choice to the people. If they wish to leave it with the people, and there is not time for it, they certainly ought to permit that body of men who come nearest to the people, to make the choice. This conclusion is deducible from their own reasoning. It has been said that if a traveller has it in object to reach a certain point, and if he meets with obstructions in the direct road, that he must turn a little to the right or to the left; and thus, by avoiding the difficulties that were opposed to him, at length gains the end of his journey. A little change of this figure will turn the argument. The senate and assembly have the same object to accomplish; they are travelling the same road; the assembly say, we wish to press forward and follow the plain and direct road. The senate, they say no, we will take a by road, without knowing where it will come out, and which, if they pursue, may lead them into a labyrinth of difficulties. Sir, we may debate on a variety of propositions that might be offered, but I hold that the mode proposed in the bill, is the only safe and eligible one to be adopted by this house, and which I hope we may not depart from.

Mr. *Harrison.*—I must beg the indulgence of the committee while I say a few words in reply to the gentleman just up. He says that there is weight in the observation that we ought to adopt a mode that will ensure the appointment; for my part, I know no more effectual mode than the naming eight persons in the act, and passing it. But examine the matter upon the Gentleman's own principles, is it certain, that if the joint ballot is effected, the vote may not be divided. Sir, on an occasion like this we have only to adopt the most probable mode, for there is hardly one to be thought of, that objections may not be raised against. I say Sir that the joint ballot does not actually secure an election. Suppose the two houses make an even number, that number may be divided into two equal parts; what then becomes of the certainty of election. In the mode now proposed, there is no doubt but both houses will be so much under the guidance of reason, that if proper characters are proposed, that they will agree to them. The general course of reasoning has been directed by the principle that it was discretionary in the legislature and gentlemen who have been on the floor agree in opinion that the people would be the proper choosers, but the gentleman last up has ventured to give a sentiment of another kind, this sentiment was however, advanced on a former occasion, and at that time received a discussion. But Sir to take up the gentleman's principle that the electors ought to be appointed by the state legislatures; can they be said to come forward as the voice of the state governments; when only one branch chooses them. Sir they ought to speak the voice of the whole government; if the assembly chooses, they will speak the voice of that body; but Sir the house of assembly is only half, the senate have as much to say in the business as they have. And Sir with respect to the argument drawn from the assembly being persons nearest to the people, I say that we cannot say that they speak the sentiments of the people, on this occasion; it cannot be said that the people had it in view that their representatives were to choose electors: but Sir, is it not a strange argument that because the people trust the assembly in one sense, that they will trust them in every sense. Is it not more reasonable to suppose they have confidence in both branches; and that they chose the assembly in confidence that they would be under the check of the upper house. If we recur to the sense of the people, their constitution expresses this sentiment. It is in vain to say that coming immediately from the people, they are to be solely trusted with this power; because it does not appear that it was intended to be given to them. As I am for paying every deference to the sentiments of the people, I am for leaving this matter to them. If they should delegate the power to this house, I should have no objections to their exercising it. But I am unwilling that this house should assume those powers. I consider this house as no more the representatives of the people, than the senate. Both houses have an equal voice; and we ought to make such a proposition as to secure that equality.

On the question to agree to the motion. . . .[5]

Mr. Watts then moved for the following amendment: That the senate should nominate eight persons, and the assembly also to nominate eight; and each house should by ballot choose four out of the eight, so nominated by the other.

The question was taken upon this motion, without debate. . . .[6]

The question was then called on the first clause of the bill, as it stood. . . .[7]

The committee then proceeded in the bill, and having agreed to the same, rose and reported, when it was ordered to be engrossed.

1. *Daily Advertiser*, 13 and 14 February 1789. The debates were also printed, with minor variations, in the *Morning Post*, 14, 16, and 17 February; the *Daily Gazette* printed its own summary of the debates on 14 and 16 February. On 4 February the *Daily Advertiser* had printed a one-paragraph factual summary of the Assembly proceedings.

2. Although the newspaper printed "proportions," the word "propositions" was undoubtedly intended.

3. In New Jersey, Electors were chosen by the governor and Privy Council. In Delaware, Maryland, Pennsylvania, and Virginia the Electors were elected in general elections. The Connecticut legislature chose Electors by concurrent resolution.

4. For the roll call on this motion, which was carried in the negative, see Assembly and Senate Proceedings, 27 January 1789, immediately above.

5. For the roll call on this motion, which was carried in the negative, see Assembly and Senate Proceedings, 27 January 1789, immediately above. The proceedings list Kortz as voting in the negative; he is not listed as voting here, although this is certainly an omission as Kortz voted in every other roll call on this day.

6. For the roll call on this motion, which was carried in the negative, see Assembly and Senate Proceedings, 27 January 1789, immediately above.

7. For the roll call on this motion, which was carried in the affirmative, see Assembly and Senate Proceedings, 27 January 1789, immediately above.

The New York Election Law, 27 January[1]

An Act directing the times places and manner of Electing Representatives in this State, for the House of Representatives of the Congress of the United States of America.

~~Whereas it is necessary that Provision should be made, for electing Representatives to represent the People of this State in the Congress of the United States, in conformity to the Constitution of the United States, ratified by the People of this State, represented in Convention at Poughkeepsie on the twenty sixth day of July last, therefore~~

Be it enacted by the People of the State of New York, represented in Senate and Assembly, and it is hereby enacted by the Authority of the same, That this State shall be and hereby is divided into six Districts, as follows, that is to say, the Counties of Suffolk, Queens, Kings and Richmond shall be one District, and the City and County of New York and Westchester County except the Towns of Salem, North Salem, Courtlandt, York Town and Stephen Town—shall be one District, and the County of Dutchess and the Towns of Salem, North Salem, Courtlandt, York Town and Stephen Town—in Westchester County shall be one District, and the Counties of Ulster and Orange shall be one District, and the Counties of Columbia, Washington and Clinton with all the remaining part of this State lying on the East side of Hudsons River shall be one District, and that part of the County of Albany, which lies on the West Side of Hudsons River and the Counties of Montgomery and Ontario shall be one District; and that at every Election in each District for Representatives of the People of this State in the House of Representatives of the Congress of the United States, a person who shall have attained the Age of twenty five years, who shall have been seven years a Citizen of the United States, and who shall then be an Inhabitant of this State—shall be chosen by the People of such District, that is to say, by such Persons who are or shall be qualified to vote for Members of the Assembly of this State,[2] each of whom shall be entitled to vote for one person as such Representative, and the Person who shall have the greatest Number of votes in such District shall be the Representative; And all such Elections shall be held and conducted by such Persons and in the same manner as the Elections for Members of the Assembly of this State are by Law to be held and conducted;[3] and upon closing the Poll at every such Election the Poll books or Lists, shall after due examination and correction thereof be signed by the Inspectors attending the closing of the Poll books or Lists, and by the Clerks who shall have kept the same Poll books or Lists respectively; and the Box containing the Ballots shall then be opened, and the Ballots contained therein be taken out, and without being opened or inspected, shall, together with both the Poll books or Lists be immediately put up under Cover and enclosed, and the enclosure bound with Tape, and sealed in such manner as to prevent its being opened without discovery; and the Inspectors present at closing of the Poll shall then put their Seals and write their Names upon the same Enclosure; and one of the Inspectors then present, to be appointed for that purpose by a Majority of them, shall without delay and within five days thereafter, deliver the same Enclosure so sealed up as aforesaid, to the Sheriff of the County, who shall upon receiving the said Enclosures without opening or inspecting the same, or any of them, put the said Enclosures and every of them into one Box, which shall be well closed and sealed up by him; and he shall put his Seal and write his Name and the name of his County on the said Box, and shall within fourteen days thereafter either in person or by his sufficient Deputy, deliver the said Box without opening the same or the Enclosures therein contained, into the Office of the Secretary of this State where the same shall be safely kept by the Secretary of this State, or by his Deputy, unbroken and unopened, until the Meeting of the Committee herein aftermentioned and appointed to canvass and estimate the Ballots therein contained, when all the said Boxes shall be delivered unbroken and unopened to them; and for which Service the Sherifs of the respective Counties shall be allowed at and after the rate of one shilling per Mile for going to the Secretary's Office, to be computed from the Sherifs place of abode in each County, to the Secretary's Office, and to be paid on the Certificate of the Secretary, by the Treasurer of the State out of any Monies in his hands unappropriated.

And be it further enacted by the Authority aforesaid, That the Inspectors of the Elections in that part of the County of Albany, now called the District of Saraghtoga and the Inspectors at any future Election subsequent to the first day of April next, when the said District will become the Town of Saraghtoga, and the Town of Stillwater, shall at all Elections for such Representatives as aforesaid, take and keep the Votes and Poll Lists of the Electors on each side of Hudsons River, separately from each other, designating whether such Poll Lists are respectively made for that part of the said District or Towns, as the case may be, on the East or West side of the said River, and inclose them with the Ballots in separate Enclosures, and shall mention in Writing in such Poll Lists and on such Enclosures, on which side of Hudsons River the Voters respectively dwell.

And be it further enacted by the Authority aforesaid, That the Committee annually to be appointed by virtue of the Act entitled An Act for regulating Elections passed the 13th: day of February 1787, or the Major part of them,[4] shall, and hereby are authorized and required, to Canvass and Estimate the Votes to be taken as aforesaid for Members of the House of Representatives of the Congress of the United States; and shall on the third Tuesday in May next after every such Election, meet together at the Office of the Secretary of this State; and the said Committee or the Major part of them shall on the said day, and within so many days there after as shall be necessary for the purpose, proceed to Open the said Boxes one after the other and the Enclosures therein contained respectively, and canvass and Estimate the Votes therein contained, and as soon as they shall be able to determine upon such Canvass and Estimate who by the greatest number of Votes shall have been chosen a Member of the House of Representatives of the Congress of the United States, in each of the said Districts, and within fourteen days next after the said third Tuesday in May, they shall determine the same; and thereupon without delay make and Subscribe with their own proper Names and Hands writing, a Certificate of such Determination in a Book to be kept for that purpose, in the said Secretary's Office, there to remain of Record, and without delay deliver or cause to be delivered a true Copy thereof so subscribed as aforesaid, to each of the Persons so Elected respectively, and another Copy thereof so subscribed as aforesaid to the House of Representatives of the Congress of the United States, at their then or next Meeting; And that all and every Duty enjoined on the said Committee by this Act, shall and may be exercised by the Chancellor and Justices of the supreme Court, on the occasions, and in the manner, directed by the said Act.

And be it further enacted by the Authority aforesaid, That when a Majority of the said Committee shall meet at any time for the purpose of canvassing and estimating the Votes taken for any such Representative or Representatives, such Majority shall be and hereby are Authorized empowered and required, to proceed to such canvass and estimate; and all Questions which shall arise upon such Canvass and Estimate, or upon any of the proceedings therein, shall be determined according to the Opinion of the major part of the Committee so Met.

And be it further enacted by the Authority aforesaid, That the said Committee, or such of them as shall meet to make such Canvass and Estimate as aforesaid, shall, before they proceed to open any of the Boxes delivered by the Sherifs as aforesaid, severally take and Subscribe the Oath prescribed by the eleventh Section of the said Act, adding after the word *Senators* (in the said Oath) "and for Member or Members of the House of Representatives of the Congress of the United States," which Oath the said Committee or any of them are hereby authorized and required to Administer to each other; and the same shall be entered of Record by the said Secretary, or his Deputy, in the same book in which the Certificate of their Determination is to be recorded as aforesaid.

And be it further enacted by the Authority aforesaid, That the first Election in this State for such Representatives as aforesaid, shall begin on the first Tuesday in March next, and General Elections for such Representatives shall be held at the times following, that is to say, the first General Election next after that which is to be held on the first Tuesday in March next, shall be held on the last Tuesday in April One thousand Seven hundred and Ninety, and every subsequent General Election shall be held on the last Tuesday in April in every second year thereafter; And in case of any vacancy or vacancies, by Death or otherwise, in the said Office of Representatives, between any of the said General Elections, the Person Administering the Government of this State for the time being, shall by Proclamation give Notice thereof, and shall in such Proclamation signify out of what District or Districts the Person or Persons are to be Elected to fill—such vacancy or vacancies, and shall also appoint a day, not less than forty nor more than sixty days, from the day of the Publication of such Proclamation, for such Election, and cause a Copy of such Proclamation to be delivered to each Sherif within such Districts, and the respective Sheriffs—shall give Notice in writing of such Election to the Supervisors of the several Towns or Districts within their Bailiwyck within eight days after receiving such Proclamation; and Notices shall be published by the Supervisors to the People; and such Elections shall be held and conducted by such Persons and in the same manner as the General Elections for Representatives, are herein before directed to be held and conducted; and the Secretary of this State for the time being, shall within ten days after receiving the Boxes containing the Ballots taken at any such

Election, by special Messengers at the Expence of this State, give Notice thereof in Writing to each Member of the said Committee, and require his Attendance at the Secretary's Office at a certain day not less than twenty days nor more than thirty days from the date of the said Notice, to Canvass and Estimate the Votes taken at such Election; and such Canvass and Estimate shall be made by the said Committee, or a Majority of them, and in the same manner, and such Certificates of their Determination be made and given, as is and are herein before directed upon a General Election for Representatives, provided nevertheless, that the Canvass and Estimate of the Votes to be taken at the Election to be held on the first Tuesday in March next, shall be made on the first Tuesday in April next, at such place as the Person Administring the Government of this State for the time being, shall appoint; and if he shall not appoint the City of New York, he shall then give timely Notice to the Secretary of the State to attend either by himself or by his Deputy, with the Boxes at the place appointed.

And be it further enacted by the Authority aforesaid, That if any Person shall be guilty of Bribery or Corrupt Conduct at any such Election, or in any of the Duties required of him by this Act, or shall neglect or refuse to perform any of the Duties required of him by this Act, every such Person so offending, shall be liable to the same pains and penalties as are imposed for the like Offences in and by the Act entitled "An Act for regulating Elections," and to be recovered and applied in the manner therein directed.

And be it further enacted by the Authority aforesaid, That no Officer or other Person shall call or order any of the Militia of this State to appear or Exercise, on any day or at any time during any such Election, or at any time within twenty days before the Ordinary and Established days of Election, (except in cases of Invasion or Insurrection) on pain of Forfeiting the Sum of Two hundred pounds for every such Offence, to be recovered by any Person who will Sue for the same, with Costs, the one Moiety of such Penalty to his own use, and the other Moiety thereof to the People of this State.

And be it further enacted by the Authority aforesaid, That it shall not be lawful for any Officer or Minister of Justice, to serve any civil Process in any City or Town within this State, on any Person entitled, to vote at any such Election, between the day preceeding any Election, and the day subsequent to the closing of the Poll at such Election in such City or Town.

State of New York—In Assembly January 21st. 1789.
This Bill having been read a third Time,
Resolved that the Bill do pass.
By Order of the Assembly.
[signed] John Lansing Junr. Speaker.

State of New York—In Senate Januy. 15th: 1789
This Bill having been read a third time
Resolved that the Bill do pass.
By Order of the Senate.
[signed] Pierre Van Cortlandt Presdt.

1. DS, N. The law was printed as a broadside by state printers Samuel and John Loudon (Albany, 1789); copies are in the Broadside Collection, Rare Book Room, DLC, and at the New York State Library. The Council of Revision noted its approval on the back of the folded law: "In Council of Revision 27th January 1789[.] Resolved That it does not appear improper to the Council That this Bill.—Entitled 'An Act directing the Times, Places & manner of electing Representatives in

this State for the House of Representatives of the Congress of the United States of America' should become a Law of this State.—" It was signed "Geo: Clinton." The law was printed in the following New York newspapers: *Daily Advertiser*, 2 February 1789; *Daily Gazette*, 3 February; *Country Journal*, 3 February; *New York Packet*, 3 February; and *New York Journal*, 5 February.

2. Article VII of the state constitution states: "That every male inhabitant of full age, who shall have personally resided within one of the counties of this State for six months immediately preceding the day of election, shall, at such election, be entitled to vote for representatives of the said county in assembly; if during the time aforesaid, he shall have been a freeholder, possessing a freehold of the value of twenty pounds, within the said county, or have rented a tenement therein of the yearly value of forty shillings, and been rated and actually paid taxes to this State . . ." (Thorpe, V, 2630).

3. The most recent law, "An Act for regulating elections," passed 13 February 1787, extended voting by ballot to elections for state senators and assemblymen. Prior to that, the elections for those officeholders had been *viva voce*. The governor and lieutenant governor had been elected by ballot since 1778. Article VI of the state constitution encouraged "a fair experiment" to determine "which of those two methods of voting is to be preferred" (Thorpe, V, 2630).

4. The election act of 13 February 1787 states: "That a joint Committee shall be appointed yearly and every year, to canvass and estimate the votes for Governor, Lieutenant-Governor, and Senators, or such of them as are then to be chosen, which Committee shall consist of twelve members; that is to say, six to be appointed by the Senate out of their body, and six to be appointed by the Assembly out of their body; and such Committee shall be annually appointed by resolution of each body respectively. . . . *And further*, That in case no such Committee should be appointed, or if such Committee should not meet . . . the Chancellor and Justices of the Supreme Court: or the main part of them shall be, and hereby are in such case authorised and required to meet at the office of the Secretary of this State . . . [to] canvass and estimate the said votes" (*Laws of the State of New-York* [New York, 1787], 32–35).

Maryland Journal (Baltimore), 27 January

Extract of a Letter from New-York, to a Gentleman in this Place, dated January 16, 1789.

I suppose you are informed of the divided State of our Politics.—It is feared that the Disagreement between our Legislative Bodies will deprive us of that Influence in the first Debates of the New Congress, which now becomes so essentially necessary to secure to us the first grand Object, which we expect will occupy the Attention of Congress—that is—The *Twelve Miles square Business.* We are, however, doing all we can to give Congress the most favourable Reception in our Power. We have, in the first Place, built them a comfortable House, hoping that when once they sit down in it, they will not like to move into the Bush. We have also a few little Attractions, which make no great Noise in the political World, although their Powers are most sensibly felt—and excuse me when I say that most of your *young*, and a few of your *old* Southern Delegates are not the most insensible to them. We have strong Assurances that *all* the States to the Northward of us, will run in favour of New-York.—But we are much afraid that Pennsylvania will be joined by the greatest Part of the Southern Interest; if so, the Contest will be warm—and (pardon me when I say *I fear*) will terminate by fixing on a more central State than either; for, I believe, if we come to *centrality* of *Place*, or *Population*, your little State would carry the Palm. We hear that "the *Federals* give the *Antis* no Quarter in your State—and that your representation in Congress will be *Federal to a Man.*"—I wish we could say the same; but the British left and still retain a cursed Influence in our Politics here.[1]

1. This article was reprinted in the Philadelphia *Federal Gazette*, 2 February 1789; Boston *Herald of Freedom*, 13 February; Exeter, New Hampshire, *Freeman's Oracle*, 17 February; and Worcester *Massachusetts Spy*, 19 February. The Philadelphia *Independent Gazetteer* reprinted the article on 3 February with the editorial comment: "This letter-writer does not consider that almost all the rank and rigid TORIES (the avowed enemies of our freedom and independence) *to a man* in the city of New-York, particularly those who attached themselves to the *British* cause and army, during the late war, are professedly the most violent FEDERALISTS: so that his remark, 'the accursed influence of the British on our politics,' is more applicable to the *party* he seems to have espoused, than to *that* which he so unjustly censures and condemns."

Spectator, Herald of Freedom (Boston), 27 January

I was much surprised last evening to hear Mr. Bowdoin of Dorchester, son to our late worthy governour, assert, in the House of Representatives, that the Legislature of New-York wished to destroy the new federal Constitution. Unfortunately for that state, as well as the rest of the union, the two branches of their Legislature could not agree as to the mode of choosing their electors and Senators; and after a Committee of conference between the two Houses, on this subject, on which much ingenuity was displayed, the time passed, and the injury was of course irretrievable. This being the true state of the case, it appears the more astonishing that any gentleman should make such a round assertion on such very slender information. The Senate of that state is unquestionably federal, and their answer to the message of the governour of that Commonwealth, is at once a proof of their patriotism and discretion.[1] Nor does it ever appear, by any authentick documents—that their House of Representatives is opposed to the Constitution, unless wishing for amendments is to be considered as evidence, and, in that case, more than two thirds of the whole people of America are in the same way of thinking. This sort of official abuse had best be restrained, for it can have no other tendency than to irritate and mislead, without answering a single valuable purpose.

SPECTATOR.

1. For the Senate's answer to Governor Clinton's speech, see Senate Proceedings, 26 December 1788, above.

Tench Coxe to James Madison, New York, 27 January (excerpts)[1]

The State of New York still retain their impressions against the Constitution. They still decline to elect Senators upon legislative principles, and I think an absence of two of the Senate[2] is, from Appearances determined on to avoid the precedent of conceding their due legislative independence—They will have two antifdlts, and no Merchant on their Senate. . . . New York by her districts[3] will have two federalists & very able ones I hope—

1. RC, Madison Papers, DLC. Printed: Rutland, *Madison*, XI, 429–33. For other excerpts from this letter, see DHFFE, II, 397; Chapter XII, Part Five:I; and Chapter XIV.

2. State Senate.

3. For the House of Representatives.

Senate Proceedings, Wednesday, A.M., 28 January

A message from the Honorable the Assembly by Mr. Low and Mr. D'Witt, was received with the following resolution for concurrence, which was read. viz.

Resolved, (if the Honorable the Senate concur herein) that the Printer for this State be, and he is hereby directed forthwith to print seven hundred copies of the act entitled "An act for directing the times, places and manner of electing Representatives in this State for the House of Representatives of the Congress of the United States of America," and to deliver the same to His Excellency the Governor; and that His Excellency be requested to transmit so many of the copies of the same act, to the Clerks of the respective counties of this State, by special messengers, at the expence of the State, as he shall judge to be requisite, with directions to such Clerks respectively to forward the said copies immediately to the Supervisor or inspectors of elections, in each town or district within his county, in proportion to the number of inhabitants and extent of the towns respectively; and that the said Printer be further directed to publish the same act, in one of the newspapers to be published in his office.

Thereupon, *Resolved*, That the Senate do concur with the Honorable the Assembly in their preceding resolution.

Ordered, That Mr. Yates and Mr. Micheau, deliver a copy of the preceding concurrent resolution to the Honorable the Assembly.

[John Smith to Melancton Smith, Albany, 28 January][1]

I have to acknowledge your favour of the 10th Instant[2] since which the Assembly have passed a Bill which, in substance, is the same as that part of the Bill that was lost which respected Senators tho in other words[.] it has for a Recital that part of our State Constitution which relates to the choosing Delegates in Congress and inacts that senators be chosen in the same way[.] another for choosing Electors in like manner. what the Senate will do with these Bills there is various opinions[.] some suppose they will reject them others suppose they will make amendments similar to those made to the other Bill.

Notwithstanding the right which the Senate claim on this occasion and the injury they would do both their constituents and their Consciences if they should give it up I think it is easily to be seen from the Bills they have passed and the amendments they have made and proposed to make to others that it is Men they are contending for and not the Mode[.] this being true I would ask what we are to expect from such Men who to answer a particular purpose would be willing not only to violate our State Constitution but the General one also which if an Anti presumes to touch they roar aloud and cry out as demetrious and his men did of old when Paul declared they were no god which were made with hands[.] Great is Lion of the Ephesians for and if they dare say it this craft we have [- - -]

I am sorry to hear of your illness and hope by this time you are better but as you excuse yourself for writing a Long Letter on account of your indisposition [(]which did not need any excuse) I am led to believe that writing is an amusemen[t.] I therefore wish you would give the Public a short statement of the present Dispute between the Senate and Assembly on the present Question

1. FC?, Melancton Smith Papers, N. This draft of a letter is undated and unsigned, but it is in John Smith's handwriting, and the references to an earlier letter and the recipient's illness point to Melancton Smith as the recipient. John Smith was attending the Assembly in Albany. For the evidence for the dating, see [John Smith to Melancton Smith], c. 31 January 1789, below.

2. Printed above.

Assembly and Senate Proceedings, Thursday, A.M., 29 January

The Assembly

The engrossed bill entitled *An act for directing the manner of appointing Electors in this State, for choosing the President and Vice-President of the United States of America*, was read a third time.

Resolved, That the bill do pass.

Ordered, That Mr. Low and Mr. D'Witt deliver the bill to the Honorable the Senate and request their concurrence.

Mr. Jones from the committee appointed on the 22d. day of December last, to report an application to be made to the Congress of the United States, in the name and behalf of the Legislature of this State, for calling a Convention to revise the Constitution, ratified by the Convention of this State, on the 26th. day of July last, brought in the report of the said committee, which was read, and is in the words following, viz.

"*Resolved*, (if the Honorable the Senate concur herein,) That an application be made to the Congress of the United States of America, in the name and behalf of the Legislature of this State, in the words following, to wit;"

"The People of the State of New-York having ratified the Constitution, agreed to on the seventeenth day of September, in the year of our Lord one thousand, seven hundred and eighty-seven, by the Convention then assembled at Philadelphia, in the State of Pennsylvania, as explained by the said ratification, in the fullest confidence of obtaining a revision of several articles of the said Constitution, by a General Convention. In compliance therefore with the unanimous sense of the Convention of this State, who all united in opinion, that such a revision was necessary to recommend the said Constitution to the approbation and support of a numerous body of their constituents, and a majority of whom conceived the Constitution so exceptionable, that nothing but such confidence, and an invincible reluctance to separate from our sister States, could have prevailed upon a sufficient number to assent to it, without stipulating for previous amendments; and from a conviction that the apprehensions and discontents which those articles occasion, cannot be removed or allayed, unless an act to revise the said Constitution be among the first that shall be passed by the new Congress: WE, the Legislature of the State of New-York, DO, in behalf of our constituents, in the most earnest and solemn manner, make this application to the Congress, that a Convention of Deputies from the several States be immediately called, with full power to take the said Constitution into their consideration, and to report such amendments thereto, as they shall find best suited to promote our common interests, and secure to ourselves and our latest posterity, the great and unalienable rights of mankind."

Ordered, That the said report be committed to a committee of the whole House. . . .

A copy of a resolution of the Honorable the Senate, of yesterday, delivered by Mr. Yates and Mr. Micheau, was read, concurring with this House, in their resolution, of the 27th instant, for printing and distributing copies of the statute, entitled "An act for directing the times, places and manner of electing Representatives in this State, for the House of Representatives of the Congress of the United States of America."

The Senate

A message from the Honorable the Assembly, by Mr. Low and Mr. D'Witt, was received with a bill for concurrence, entitled *An act for directing the manner of appointing Electors in this State, for choosing the President and Vice-President of the United States of America*, which was read the first time, and ordered a second reading.

Tench Coxe to Benjamin Rush, New York, 29 January (excerpt)[1]

The Senators[2] of New York will lessen their majority of fedts. I think by two voluntary absences, and obtain by that method two Senators for Congress among whom there will be neither federalism nor mercantile knowlege most probably—

I think the cause appears in a good way—there will be a pretty large portion of federalists in the house of reps. This state I think will certainly have two fedts. and the chance is of more from the favorable mode of electing. It was strange in the Opposition to consent to this mode, but [Luem Jurdence?] &c—

1. RC, Rush Papers, PPL. For another excerpt from this letter, see DHFFE, I, 386–87.
2. State senators.

Alexander Hamilton to Theodore Sedgwick, New York, 29 January (excerpt)[1]

. . . New York from [her?] legisla[ture?] having by their contentions let slip the d[ay?] will not vote at all. For the last circumstance I am not sorry as the most we could hope would be to ballance accounts and do no harm. The Antifœderalists incline to an appointment notwithstanding, but I discourage it with the Fœderalists. Under these circumstances I see not how any person can come near Mr. Adams that is taking it for granted that he will unite the votes in [New?] Hampshire & Massachusetts. I expect that the fœderal Votes in Virginia if any will be in favour of Adams.

You will probably have heared that our Legislature has passed a bill for electing representatives—The houses continue to disagree about Senators, and I fear a compromise will be impracticable. I do not however intirely lose hope. In this situation you will perceive that we have much to apprehend respecting the seat of Government. The Pensylvanians are endeavouring to bring their forces early in the field—I hope our friends in the North will not be behind hand. On many accounts indeed it appears to be important that there should be an appearance of zeal & punctuality in coming forward to set the Government in motion.

I shall learn with infinite pleasure that you are a representative—As to me this will not be the case—I believe, from my own disinclination to the thing. We shall however I flatter myself have a couple of Fœderalists.

1. RC, Hamilton Papers, DLC. Printed: Syrett, V, 250–51. For another excerpt from this letter, see Chapter XIV.

Senate Proceedings, Friday, A.M., 30 January

The bill entitled *An act directing the manner of appointing Electors in this State, for choosing the President and Vice-President of the United States of America*, was read a second time, and committed to a committee of the whole.

Abraham B. Bancker to Peter Van Gaasbeek, Albany, 30 January[1]

Mrs. Bancker being upon her return, the most News I can at present give you is the Bill for choosing Representatives for the new Congress, which I here inclose—the Senate Bill hangs by the Eye lids upon which I expect a second Conference and the result will in my Opinion be similar to the first—another Bill for choosing Electors has also passed the Assembly and I shall this Morning give it a second reading in the Senate in Order for a Committment[2]—The Fœderal Gentry here have determined to hold up Judge Yates in opposition to our friend G. C—— but I expect more Candidates will be offered and thereby a Division of their Interest as well as our own will be the Consequence[.] It Stands with the Antifederal Interest to be firm as a Rock in the ensuing Election[3]—Judge Wynkoop is talked of among our Members of the Middle District for a Senator in the room of Judge Humfrey of Dutchess[4]—and I Expect our County will furnish the Representative for our District in the Congress of the United States—My friends are just getting ready to set out and I must away to the Senate—Schoonmaker would have wrote but concludes to defer it till something new shall offer—I am in haste—

1. RC, Peter Van Gaasbeek Papers, NHpR. The letter was addressed to Van Gaasbeek in Kingston, Ulster County. Abraham B. Bancker (1754–1806), of Kingston, was a lieutenant in the Continental Army during the Revolutionary War; clerk of the state Senate, 1784–1802; and secretary of the state Convention in 1788. He was the son of Evert (1721–1803), nephew of Adrian (1724–1792), and cousin of Abraham (1760–1832).

2. On 31 January 1789, Bancker relayed the same information about the bills for the elections of Representatives, Senators, and Electors to his father, Evert, in New York City (Albany, RC, Bancker Family Papers, NHi).

3. In the election for governor, 28 April 1789, the Federalists supported Robert Yates, an Antifederalist, against Governor George Clinton.

4. Dirck Wynkoop, Ulster County, served in the Assembly, 1780–1781, and in the state Convention in 1788, where he voted against ratification of the Constitution. Cornelius Humfrey (Humphrey), Dutchess County, represented the Middle District in the state Senate, 1787–1789.

[John Smith to Melancton Smith, Albany], c. 31 January[1]

I wrote you the 28th Instant[2] and promised when I had time to inform you more particularly of the State of Politics here and for fear that you are not sufficiently acquainted with the Proceedings of the Legislature at the opening of the session I will begin there and confine myself to the measures which have been taken with Respect to puting the General Government into operation.

The first business that the Senate did was to orginate a Bill for the appointment of Senators for the Congress in which they nominated General Schuyler and Judge Yates and another for the choosing of Electors for President and Vice President which enacted that Each House appoint four[.] these Bills were sent to the Assembly read committed and rejected[.] The Assembly had before them at the same time a Bill for both this purposes and that of Electing Representatives in the Congress which directed the choice for Senators and Electors to be made in the manner that is Prescribed by our Constitution for choosing Delegates in Congress and that Representatives be elected nearly in the same manner as the Law which has since past [– – –] which I Presume you have seen—This Bill was sent to the Senate and amended by them so that the Senators were to be appointed by Concurrent Resolution of both Houses and that Electors should be nominate[d] in the same manner that Deleg[a]tes were formirly choosen and those which were not agreed to by both Houses should be appointed by Concurrent Resolution[.] upon this Bill there was a Conference and it was lost—I think the Newspaper I sent you contained an exact Copy of a Bill which is before the Assembly for the Choosing senators which has been amended in the same way by the Senate as the former[.] this I expect will also produce a Conference and I expect will end in the same way[.] In all this business the Majority in Senate has been from one to three as the members happened to attend in the Assembly from 9 to 11—After this I believe I need not inform you that parties are warm—Mr. Havens Mr. Jones Mr: Schenk[3] and some of the Dutchess Members with myself live at A. Bloodgoods but not more agreeable to me than we did last winter[.] Parties run full as high with the inhabitants as in the Legislature and a Federalist rarly gives an Anti a Dinner—However I got one at Genl. Schuylers when I first came—

1. FC, John Smith of Mastic Papers, NHi. The letter is undated and unsigned, but it is in John Smith's handwriting. For evidence that the recipient was Melancton Smith, see Melancton Smith to John Smith, 10 January 1789, and [John Smith to Melancton Smith, 28 January 1789], both above.

2. Printed above.

3. Jonathan N. Havens (Suffolk County), Samuel Jones (Queens), and John Schenck (Queens), all members of the Assembly.

Senate Proceedings, Monday, P.M., 2 February

Mr. Morris from the committee of the whole, to whom was referred the bill, entitled *An act for directing the manner of appointing Electors in this State, for choosing the President and Vice-President of the United States of America*, reported, that upon reading a part of the enacting clause of the bill, in the words following, viz. "That the Electors to be appointed in this State, for choosing the President and Vice President of the United States of America, shall be appointed in the manner following, that is to say, *the Senate* and Assembly shall each openly nominate, as many persons as shall be equal to the whole number of the Electors to be appointed by this State, after which nomination, the Senate and Assembly shall meet together, and compare the lists of the persons by them respectively nominated; and those persons named in both lists shall be Electors, and out of those persons whose names are not in both lists, one half shall be chosen by the joint ballot of the Senators and Members of Assembly so met together as aforesaid." Mr. Duane, moved to expunge the whole after the words *the Senate*, and to substitute the following in its stead, viz. "Shall openly nominate eight persons, and shall transmit their nomination to the Assembly, that the Assembly upon receiving such nomination, shall in like manner nominate eight persons, and transmit their nomination to the Senate; that each House shall then choose out of the others list four persons to be Electors, and that the eight persons so chosen shall be the Electors." Debates arose upon the said motion, and the question being put thereon, it was carried in the affirmative, in manner following, viz.

FOR THE AFFIRMATIVE.

Mr. Philip Schuyler,	Mr. Vanderbilt,
Mr. Douw,	Mr. Roosevelt,
Mr. Micheau,	Mr. L'Hommedieu,
Mr. Peter Schuyler,	Mr. Duane,
Mr. Fonda,	Mr. Hoffman.

FOR THE NEGATIVE.

Mr. Yates,	Mr. Tredwell,
Mr. Hopkins,	Mr. Humfrey,
Mr. Williams,	Mr. Clinton,
Mr. Swartwout,	Mr. Hathorn.
Mr. Townsend,	

Mr. Morris further reported, that the comittee had gone through the bill, made an amendment thereto, and agreed to the same, which report he read in his place, and delivered the bill with the amendment in at the table, where they were again read; and Mr. President having put the question, whether the bill with the amendment shall pass, it was carried in the affirmative, by all the members who voted for the affirmative upon the last question, with the addition of *Mr. Morris*. Thereupon,

Resolved, That the bill with the amendment do pass.

Ordered, That Mr. Vanderbilt and Mr. Hopkins, deliver the bill with the amendment to the Honorable the Assembly, and inform them that the Senate have passed the bill with the amendment therewith delivered.

Tench Coxe to Benjamin Rush, New York, 2 February (excerpt)[1]

It appears next to certain New York will not appoint Electors. If they have Senators they will possess neither federalism nor mercantile talents, nor does it appear probable that they will have one mercantile man in their representation. Thus the execution of the plan of government shews that there is no danger in committing commercial Arrangements to a bare Majority.

1. RC, Rush Papers, PPL. The letter was addressed to Rush in Philadelphia. For another excerpt from this letter, see Chapter XIV.

An Observer, Daily Advertiser (New York), 2 February

Among the regrets which all parties feel at the unfortunate differences between the senate and assembly of this state, and which are likely so deeply to affect its immediate interests, it must afford no small consolation to the advocates for the new constitution to see the utility of a provision, which has been most complained of by its opponents, exemplified in the very out-set of the government;—I mean that which empowers the Congress to *make* and *alter* the regulations respecting the times, places and manner of electing senators and representatives. We perceive that to secure to a state its proper weight in the union, even against the effects of disagreement between the different branches of its own legislature, it is necessary there should be a COMMON UMPIRE.—Will not all reasonable men feel pleasure in the reflection that the interposition of Congress can, in the last resort, save us from the disagreeable and humilitating situation of being *governed* without being *represented*? How wise must every dispassionate man, now he has experience for his guide, acknowledge that provision to be, which secures the people from the possibility of so great an evil! Thus do the very measures which are supposed to flow from ill-will to the system, tend to illustrate its merits.

AN OBSERVER.

January 31.[1]

1. This article was reprinted in the Philadelphia *Federal Gazette*, 8 February 1789; Philadelphia *Pennsylvania Packet*, 9 February; Philadelphia *Pennsylvania Gazette*, 11 February; and Boston *Herald of Freedom*, 20 February.

Assembly and Senate Proceedings, Tuesday, A.M., 3 February

The Assembly

A message from the Honorable the Senate, . . . delivered by Mr. Vanderbilt and Mr. Hopkins, with the bill and amendment therein mentioned, was read, that the Senate have passed the bill, entitled *An act for directing the manner of appointing Electors in this State, for choosing the President and Vice-President of the United States of America*, with the amendment therewith delivered.

The bill and amendment were read.

The first paragraph of the enacting clause of the bill being again read, is in the words following, viz.

"Be it enacted by the People of the State of New-York, represented in Senate and Assembly, and it is hereby enacted by the authority of the same, That the Electors to be appointed in this State, for choosing the President and Vice-President of the United States of America, shall be appointed in the manner following, that is to say, the Senate and Assembly shall each openly nominate as many persons as shall be equal to the whole number of the Electors to be appointed by this State; after which nomination the Senate and Assembly shall meet together, and compare the lists of the persons by them respectively nominated; and those persons named in both lists shall be Electors; and out of those persons whose names are not in both lists, one half shall be chosen by the joint ballot of the Senators and Members of Assembly, so met together as aforesaid."

The amendment proposed by the Honorable the Senate is to obliterate from the words *that is to say*, to the end of the paragraph, and insert in the stead thereof, as follows, viz. "The Senate shall openly nominate eight persons, and shall transmit their nomination to the Assembly; that the Assembly upon receiving such nomination, shall in like manner nominate eight persons, and transmit their nomination to the Senate; that each House shall then choose out of the others list, four persons to be Electors, and that the eight persons so chosen shall be the Electors."

The said paragraph, as proposed to be amended by the Honorable the Senate, was read as follows, viz.

"Be it enacted by the People of the State of New-York, represented in Senate and Assembly, and it is hereby enacted by the authority of the same, That the Electors to be appointed in this State, for choosing the President and Vice-President of the United States of America, shall be appointed in the manner following, that is to say, the Senate shall openly nominate eight persons, and shall transmit their nomination to the Assembly; that the Assembly upon receiving such nomination, shall in like manner nominate eight persons, and transmit their nomination to the Senate; that each House shall then choose out of the others list four persons to be Electors, and that the eight persons so chosen shall be the Electors."

Mr. Speaker then put the question, whether the House did concur with the Honorable the Senate, in the said amendment, and it passed in the negative, in the manner following, viz.

FOR THE NEGATIVE.

Mr. Jones,	Mr. Griffen,
Mr. G. Livingston,	Mr. J. Smith,
Mr. Kortz,	Mr. D'Witt,
Mr. Frey,	Mr. Wisner,
Mr. Stauring,	Mr. Adgate,
Mr. Van Dyck,	Mr. Harper,
Mr. J. Van Rensselaer,	Mr. Havens,
Mr. Winn,	Mr. Schenck,
Mr. Duncan,	Mr. Cornwell,
Mr. Tearse,	Mr. Akins,
Mr. Savage,	Mr. E. Clark,
Mr. Webster,	Mr. Patterson,
Mr. M'Cracken,	Mr. Scudder,
Mr. Thompson,	Mr. Cantine,
Mr. Bay,	Mr. Bloom,
Mr. Schoonmaker,	Mr. Smith,
Mr. Tappen,	Mr. Veeder.

FOR THE AFFIRMATIVE.

Mr. B. Livingston,	Mr. Low,
Mr. Gilbert,	Mr. Bancker,
Mr. Seaman,	Mr. Vandervoort,
Mr. Barker,	Mr. Rockwell,
Mr. Harison,	Mr. Verplanck,
Mr. H. Van Rensselaer,	Mr. Giles,
Mr. Younglove,	Mr. Gardiner,
Mr. Watts,	Mr. Macomb.
Mr. Horton,	

Thereupon, *Resolved*, That this House do not concur with the Honorable the Senate in their amendment to the said bill.

Ordered, That Mr. Verplanck and Mr. Schenck deliver the bill, and a copy of the preceding resolution, to the Honorable the Senate.

The Senate

A message from the Honorable the Assembly, by Mr. Verplanck and Mr. Schenck, was received with the bill, entitled *An act for directing the manner of appointing Electors in this State, for choosing the President and Vice-President of the United States of America*, together with a resolution that they do not concur with the Senate in their amendment to the said bill.

The Senate having reconsidered their said amendment, Mr. Duane moved that the Senate do adhere to their said amendment, and Mr. President having put the question thereon, it was carried in the affirmative, in manner following, viz.

FOR THE AFFIRMATIVE.

Mr. Philip Schuyler,	Mr. Lawrance,
Mr. Douw,	Mr. Morris,
Mr. Micheau,	Mr. Roosevelt,
Mr. Peter Schuyler,	Mr. L'Hommedieu,
Mr. Fonda,	Mr. Duane.
Mr. Vanderbilt,	

FOR THE NEGATIVE.

Mr. Yates,	Mr. Townsend,
Mr. Hopkins,	Mr. Tredwell,
Mr. Williams,	Mr. Humfrey,
Mr. Van Ness,	Mr. Clinton,
Mr. Swartwout,	Mr. Hathorn.

Thereupon, *Resolved*, That the Senate do adhere to their amendment to the said bill, not concurred in by the Honorable the Assembly.

Ordered, That Mr. Hopkins and Mr. Williams deliver the bill, with a copy of the preceding resolution to the Honorable the Assembly.

The Assembly

A message from the Honorable the Senate, delivered by Mr. Hathorn and Mr. Philip Schuyler, with the bill and amendments therein mentioned, on the 28th ult. which were then read, and the consideration thereof postponed, was again read, that the Senate have passed the bill entitled *An act for prescribing the times, places and manner of holding elections for Senators of the United States of America, to be chosen in this State*, with the amendments therewith delivered.

The bill and amendments were read.

The first paragraph of the first enacting clause of the bill being again read, is in the words following, viz.

"Be it enacted by the People of the State of New-York, represented in Senate and Assembly, and it is hereby enacted by the authority of the same, that the Senators of the United States to be chosen in this State, shall be chosen in the same manner, that Delegates to represent this State in the General Congress of the United States of America, are directed to be appointed as aforesaid, by the Constitution of this State."

The amendment proposed to this paragraph, is to obliterate from the word *Senators* to the end of the paragraph, and to substitute as follows, viz. "to represent this State in the Senate of the Congress of the United States of America, to be chosen by the Legislature of this State, shall be chosen in the manner following, that is to say, the Senate and Assembly of this State shall, if two Senators are to be chosen, openly nominate two persons, and shall respectively give notice each to the other of such nomination; that if both Houses agree in the nomination of the same person or persons, the person or persons so nominated and agreed to, shall be the Senator or Senators, to represent this State in the Senate of the Congress of the United States. That if the nomination of either House does not agree in any of the persons nominated by the other, the Senate shall on the same day openly choose one of the persons nominated by the Assembly, and the Assembly shall on the same day openly choose one of the persons nominated by the Senate, and the two persons so chosen, shall be the Senators to represent this State in the Senate of the Congress of the United States. That in every case when two Senators are to be chosen, and both Houses agree only as to one in such nomination as aforesaid, and in every case where only one Senator is to be chosen, either of the two Houses of the Legislature may propose to the other a resolution for concurrence, naming therein a person to fill the office of Senator; and if the House receiving such resolution shall concur therein the person so named in such resolution, shall be the Senator; but if such resolution shall not be concurred in, either House may on that, or any future day, proceed to offer to the other a resolution for concurrence from time to time, until they shall agree upon a Senator."

The amendment proposed having been read and considered, and debates had thereon, *Mr. Speaker* put the question whether the House did concur with the Honorable the Senate therein, and it passed in the negative, in the manner following, viz.

FOR THE NEGATIVE.

Mr. Jones,	Mr. Tappen,
Mr. G. Livingston,	Mr. Griffen,
Mr. Kortz,	Mr. J. Smith,
Mr. Frey,	Mr. D'Witt,
Mr. Stauring,	Mr. Wisner,
Mr. Van Dyck,	Mr. Adgate,
Mr. J. Van Rensselaer,	Mr. Harper,
Mr. Veeder,	Mr. Havens,
Mr. Winn,	Mr. Schenck,
Mr. Duncan,	Mr. Akins,
Mr. Tearse,	Mr. E. Clark,
Mr. Savage,	Mr. Patterson,
Mr. Webster,	Mr. Scudder,
Mr. M'Cracken,	Mr. Cantine,
Mr. Thompson,	Mr. Bloom,
Mr. Bay,	Mr Smith,
Mr. Schoonmaker,	Mr. Carman.

FOR THE AFFIRMATIVE.

Mr. B. Livingston,	Mr. Low,
Mr. Gilbert,	Mr. Bancker,
Mr. Seaman,	Mr. Vandervoort,
Mr. Barker,	Mr. Rockwell,
Mr. Harison,	Mr. Verplanck,
Mr. H. Van Rensselaer,	Mr. Cornwell,
Mr. Younglove,	Mr. Giles,
Mr. Watts,	Mr. Gardiner,
Mr. Horton,	Mr. Macomb.

Thereupon, *Resolved*, That this House do not concur in the before mentioned amendment to the bill.

The recitals in the bill, and the amendment thereto proposed, were respectively again read; the said recitals are in the words following, viz.

"Whereas it is provided by the Constitution of this State, that Delegates to represent this State in the General Congress of the United States of America, be annually appointed as follows, to wit, the Senate and Assembly shall each openly nominate as many persons, as shall be equal to the whole number of Delegates to be appointed; after which nomination they shall meet together, and those persons named in both lists shall be Delegates; and out of those persons whose names are not in both lists, one half shall be chosen by the joint ballot of the Senators and Members of Assembly, so met together as aforesaid."

"And whereas by the Constitution of the United States of America, ratified and assented to by the Convention of this State, on the twenty-sixth day of July last, it is ordained and established that all Legislative powers therein granted, shall be vested in a Congress of the United States, which shall consist of a Senate and House of Representatives; and that the Senate of the United States shall be composed of two Senators from each State, chosen by the Legislature thereof for six years; and that the times, places and manner of holding elections for Senators and Representatives, shall be prescribed in each State, by the Legislature thereof."

The amendment is to add to the last recital, as follows, viz. "By reason whereof the before recited clause of the Constitution of this State, is become of no effect, and it is necessary that the Senators to represent this State, in the Congress of the United States of America, be chosen by the Legislature."

The last mentioned amendment having been read and considered, and debates had thereon, *Mr. Speaker* put the question whether the House did concur with the Honorable the Senate therein, and it passed in the negative, in the manner following, viz.

FOR THE NEGATIVE.

Mr. Jones,	Mr Schoonmaker,
Mr. Carman,	Mr. Tappen,
Mr. G. Livingston,	Mr. Griffen,
Mr. Kortz,	Mr. J. Smith,
Mr. Frey,	Mr. D'Witt,
Mr. Stauring,	Mr. Wisner,
Mr. Van Dyck,	Mr. Adgate,
Mr. J. Van Rensselaer,	Mr. Harper,
Mr. Veeder,	Mr. Havens,
Mr. Winn,	Mr. Schenck,
Mr. Younglove,	Mr. Akins,
Mr. Duncan,	Mr. E Clark,
Mr. Tearse,	Mr. Patterson,
Mr. Savage,	Mr. Scudder,
Mr. Webster,	Mr. Cantine,
Mr. M'Cracken,	Mr Bloom,
Mr. Thompson,	Mr. Smith.
Mr. Bay,	

FOR THE AFFIRMATIVE.

Mr. Gilbert,	Mr. Horton,
Mr. Seaman,	Mr. Low,
Mr. Barker,	Mr. Bancker,
Mr. Harison,	Mr. Vandervoort,
Mr. H. Van Rensselaer,	Mr. Verplanck,
Mr. Watts,	Mr. Cornwell,

Mr Giles,	Mr. Gardiner,
Mr. Rockwell,	Mr. Macomb.

Thereupon, *Resolved,* That this House do not concur with the Honorable the Senate, in either of their amendments to the bill entitled *An act for prescribing the times, places and manner of holding elections for Senators of the United States of America, to be chosen in this State.*

Ordered, That Mr. Giles and Mr. Akins deliver the bill, and a copy of the preceding resolution, to the Honorable the Senate.

The Senate

A message from the Honorable the Assembly, by Mr. Giles and Mr. Akins was received, with the bill, entitled *An act for prescribing the times, places and manner of holding elections for Senators of the United States of America, to be chosen in this State*; with a resolution that they do not concur with the Senate in their amendments to the said bill.

Ordered, That the re-consideration of the said amendments be postponed until to-morrow.

The Assembly

Mr. Webster, from the committee of the whole House, on the report of the committee appointed to prepare a draft of an application of the Legislature of this State, to the Congress of the United States of America, to call a Convention for revising the Constitution for the said United States of America, adopted by the Convention of this State, on the 26th day of July last, reported, that the said committee of the whole House had made some progress in the said report, and had directed him to move for leave to sit again.

Ordered, That the said committee of the whole House have leave to sit again. . . .

A copy of a resolution of the Honorable the Senate, delivered by Mr. Hopkins and Mr. Williams, with the bill therein mentioned, was read, that the Senate do adhere to their amendment to the bill entitled *An act for directing the manner of appointing Electors in this State, for choosing the President and Vice-President of the United States of America.* Thereupon,

Resolved, That a conference be held with the Honorable the Senate on their amendment to the said bill; and that such conference be held at four of the clock this afternoon, at such place as the Honorable the Senate shall be pleased to appoint for that purpose.

The House then pursuant to the fifteenth article of the Constitution of this State, proceeded to choose by ballot a committee to manage said conference on the part of this House, and on the ballots being taken, it appeared that Mr. Jones, Mr. G. Livingston, and Mr. Adgate, were duly elected for that purpose. Thereupon,

Resolved, That Mr. Jones, Mr. G. Livingston and Mr. Adgate, be a committee to manage the said conference, on the part of this House.

Ordered, That Mr. Havens and Mr. E. Clark deliver a copy of the two last preceding resolutions, to the Honorable the Senate.

The Senate

A message from the Honorable the Assembly, by Mr. Havens and Mr. E. Clark, was received with the following resolutions, which were read, viz. *Resolved,* that a conference be held with the Honorable the Senate on their amendment to the bill, entitled *An act for directing the manner of appointing Electors in this State, for choosing the President and Vice-President of the United States of America*, and that such conference be held at four of the clock this afternoon, at such place as the Honorable the Senate shall be pleased to appoint for that purpose.

Resolved, That Mr. Jones, Mr. G. Livingston and Mr. Adgate be a committee to manage the said conference on the part of this House. Thereupon,

Resolved, That the Senate will meet the Honorable the Assembly, at four of the clock this afternoon, at the Assembly-Chamber, to hold the conference proposed by that Honorable House, on the bill, entitled *An act for directing the manner of appointing Electors in this State, for choosing the President and Vice-President of the United States of America.*

Resolved, That Mr. Philip Schuyler, Mr. Duane and Mr. Morris, be a committee to manage the said conference on the part of the Senate.

Ordered, That Mr. Williams and Mr. Van Ness, deliver a copy of the preceding resolutions to the Honorable the Assembly.

Then the Senate adjourned until half past three of the clock in the afternoon.

The Assembly

A copy of resolutions of the Honorable the Senate, delivered by Mr. Williams and Mr. Van Ness, was read, that the Senate will meet this House at four of the clock this afternoon, in the Assembly-Chamber, to hold the conference proposed by this House, on the bill entitled *An act for directing the manner of appointing Electors in this State, for choosing the President and Vice-President of the United States of America.*

Then the House adjourned until four of the clock in the afternoon.

Assembly Debates, Tuesday, 3 February[1]

A message was received from the senate that they had passed the bill for appointing electors, with an amendment: On motion of Mr. Jones the house went immediately into consideration of the same.

The amendment proposed that the senate should nominate eight persons, and the assembly eight; and that each house should choose four out of the eight so nominated by the other.

Mr. Giles moved that the house do concur.

Mr. Jones.—I could wish the amendment was such as we could with propriety accede to. But, sir, this house cannot agree to it. Let us only examine into the proposition; each house is to nominate eight persons—is there any thing to prevent each house from nominating the same men? and then each house is to choose from out of those eight—and what is to prevent them from choosing the same persons?—So that it may happen that there may be only four, five, or six persons chosen. Now, sir, any mode that is liable to those defects I think we cannot agree to.

The division was then called for on the motion for concurring. . . .[2]

This business being over, on motion of Mr. Jones the house went into the consideration of the amendment of the senate to the bill for choosing senators.

The amendment being read (which was similar to the one proposed on a former occasion)

Mr. Harrison moved that the house concur; he supposed the subject had been so frequently discussed, that little debate was to be expected; gentlemen he supposed had made up their minds, for his part he confessed that he had not heard any thing to convince him that the senate were wrong; on the contrary he was more confirmed in the opinion that the amendment ought to be acceded to.

Mr. *Jones.*—I suppose that on the present occasion debate will be useless; but there is one remark that may be made: sir, the question varies from every other we have had before us; the senate have thought proper to insert a recital which declares that our constitution has become of no effect. For my part if I could concur with the proposition, I never can agree to the recital.

Mr. *Harrison.*—I take it for granted that the recital only respects that article of the constitution which relates to the appointment of delegates to Congress; it can have no other meaning.

Mr. *Jones.*—The words of it are so general that it goes against every part of the constitution.

The question being called for on the amendment to the first enacting clause. . . .[3]

The division was then called on a motion to concur with the recital proposed by the senate—"that the constitution of the state was of no effect." . . .[4]

A message was received from the senate that they adhered to their amendment to the bill for appointing electors.—Thereupon the house resolved to request a conference with the senate, and appointed Mr. Jones, Mr. G. Livingston, and Mr. Adgate, managers of the conference on the part of the assembly.

This resolution having been sent to the senate, an answer was returned that they would meet the assembly at four o'clock in the afternoon; and that they had appointed Mr. Duane, Mr. Schuyler, and Mr. Morris, conferees on the part of the senate.

The house then adjourned till four o'clock, P.M.

1. *Daily Advertiser*, 16 and 17 February 1789. The debates were also printed in the *Morning Post*, 19 February.

2. For the roll call, which was carried in the negative, see Assembly and Senate Proceedings, 3 February 1789, immediately above.

3. For the roll call, which was carried in the negative, see Assembly and Senate Proceedings, 3 February 1789, immediately above.

4. For the roll call, which was carried in the negative, see Assembly and Senate Proceedings, 3 February 1789, immediately above.

Joint Conference Committee Debates, Tuesday, 3 February[1]

Eodem Die, P.M.

The assembly met, and presently after the senate attended: The bill and amendments, which were the subject of the conference, being read.

Mr. G. Livingston rose,

Mr President said he, upon the second clause of the first section of the second article of the new constitution the bill is founded on which the conference is now held (he then read that part of the constitution) I say on this clause of the new constitution the assembly have originated and sent this bill which has been read by the clerk of the senate, and to which the senate has made the amendment that has likewise been read, and to which the assembly have not concurred. We are Mr. President exceeding sorry that the assembly cannot meet the senate on the amendment proposed. Sir, there is a principle laid down in our state constitution, on which elections with respect to the general government have ever been conducted, and from which we cannot deviate;

and Sir in practice has ever been found that the plan was founded in wisdom, then I would ask, why we ought to vary from what has been found to work well; there is a hazard in trying experiments; we may think of some new mode that has no apparent difficulty, but it is the lot of mankind to be liable to error. Sir in the amendment here proposed there is an insurmountable obstacle, the plan does not ensure the end proposed, and it is a restriction to the freedom of choice. The senate are to propose eight persons, which I will suppose to be the best men that are to be found in the state, what is to prevent the assembly from choosing the same men, if they should, then only four electors will be chosen, if both houses concur in sentiment as to the best four of these eight persons nominated. There is no provision against this contingency, which may happen. Does not this prove that there is hazard in making experiments. Sir I cannot but hope that the senate will see that the objection to their proposition is well founded, and that they will recede from it, so that this state may have a voice with her sister states in the election of that important officer, the first magistrate of the land.

Gen. *Morris*.—Mr. Speaker; as the gentleman who was last up has thrown no light on the subject, I shall not trouble the two houses with going over the old ground of argument; if any thing new is offered, I trust that those gentlemen who are to follow me, on the part of the senate, will take proper notice of it; and make a suitable reply.

Mr. *Adgate*.—Mr. President; the subject matter of this conference is similar to that on which the two houses have recently met. I believe Sir the arguments that were then used might with propriety be now recapitulated. Sir the difference between the two houses is the mode in which the electors are to be chosen; the assembly conceive it their duty to pursue that line of conduct pointed out by the state constitution; it appears to them to be the only one by which a choice can be effected; they are however of opinion that if circumstances would admit that it would be the duty of the legislature to refer the choice to the people, but if this cannot be done they conceive that next to the people is the whole body of the legislature; who by a joint ballot ought to make the choice; this is coming nearest to the choice by the people than any other mode. As Sir, the assembly conceive the liberty and privileges of the people better secured, the more general the election is; it is on that ground that they adhere to the mode pointed out in the bill. Much might be said, Sir, but it would be repeating what has been offered. I shall therefore leave further observations on the subject to the gentleman who is to come after me.

Gen. *Schuyler*.—Mr. Speaker,—I regret sir, that the two houses should have met to debate on the same subject, which was so lately before them; this would not have been the case had the hon. the assembly sent to the senate a bill differing in the mode, to that they had before rejected. It is with reluctance that I again enter on the business of advocating the principles of the senate; indeed there is nothing new that can be offered, and to repeat what has been said will be paying an ill compliment to the gentlemen of the assembly, as it will be supposing that they have forgotten the arguments which were advanced at the late conference. But I will trespass on their patience, by observing on what has been said by the hon. the conferees on the part of the assembly, just up. The gentleman first on the floor conceives that this is a constitutional question, and supposes that the mode in the bill must be adhered to on that ground. Sir, I do not see what the constitution of this state has to do in the business; it is sir, a mere blank letter. What says the constitution under which this appointment is to be made, not that a constitution which never contemplated a general government like the one soon to be put into operation shall give the rule, but that each state shall appoint the electors in such manner as the legislature may direct. And I agree with the gentleman last on the floor, that the appointment ought to be made by the people. It is of necessity however that the legislature should now proceed to the appointment themselves. The constitution says each state shall appoint the electors in such manner as the legislature shall direct; here a question presents itself. Who are the legislature! Certainly the assembly will not say that they are the legislature of the state of New-York. The senate I am persuaded are not; neither the one or the other are the legislature; but both of them form that body—both the creatures of the people. Is there any way for this legislature to express its will but by law, in which case each house has a negative. If the constitution of the state was binding, the assembly have gone beyond the line of their duty in proposing to pass an act where there was no necessity for it; the constitution should have been immediately recurred to, and the business done by resolution. But sir, the constitution of the United States under which we now act, gives a discretion to the legislature, we may direct the council of appointment, or any individual to make the appointment, and it would be valid.—As therefore the constitution of the state is out of the question with respect to this business, and the general constitution vests this matter in the legislature who are to exercise their discretion, the senate can only agree upon some mode which gives them that equality which they are bound to maintain. The superiority of numbers in the assembly gives them no legislative superiority; the senate possess equal powers; and it is their indispensible duty to see that they are not infringed. On the present occasion they do not like the assembly insist on a mode which lessens the influence of either house; they claim nothing more than what they are willing to give. The gentleman has further observed that the mode proposed by the assembly has worked well; but he has not produced instances. I believe we have been happy in the choice of delegates to Congress hitherto, tho' the mode has always worked in favor of the assembly; but we might on this occasion adduce a recent instance, where by this mode, not one of the candidates proposed by the senate was adopted by the assembly.[2] They had no choice in that appointment, the superior numbers of the assembly absorbed all their influence; however, that was a constitutional mode and they do not complain of it. But where the last act of the people permits a deviation from that rule, and gives an equality, the senate conceives it a right that they ought to be entitled to, and that this can only be preserved by giving each house a check on the other. Sir if the framers of the state constitution had not thought it salutary that the two houses should check each other, they would have dispensed with the expence that must attend two branches, and declared that one house should be the legislature; but happily for the people, and happily for these members who were of that convention and have immortalized their names by it, they have established two houses of the legislature, and given them equal powers, so that nothing should be binding without the consent of both of them. The senate conceive that their mode is most eligible as it squares most with the principles of the constitution of the state; these principles they conceive to be that each house shall check the other, and thus guard against that intemperance or folly which might occasionally exist in either; for sir, the legislature composed of frail mortals are ever liable to error; sir, there is a greater benefit that may result from this check, should your first magistrate ever worm himself into the favor of one or the other house thro' the influence of his office and from motives of ambition, create a party dangerous to the welfare of the state, the safety, nay the very existence of the liberties of the people will depend upon the check he may receive from the other. Hence sir, it is reasonable to suppose that the constitution meant in every act in which both Houses were to be concerned, that each should be a check on the other.

Sir, another gentleman, the one last up, says the mode proposed by the assembly is most eligible, as it comes nearest the people. This declaration can not be supported; the senate, Mr Speaker, feel themselves the representatives of the people, they are as much so as the assembly, there is no man so powerful but he is under their control—there is no one so insignificant but he is entitled to their protection; why it should be supposed that the assembly are nearer to the feelings of the people than the senate, the senate cannot conceive. They trust; they are persuaded that the hon. conferee on the part of the assembly must have been mistaken; it never could be the sentiments of the hon. house of assembly. Sir, perhaps too much has been said on a subject on which it is even doubtful whether a conference can be constitutionally held, as the bill is precisely in the words on which the last conference was held. It may be asked why the senate propose amendments to such a bill; they answer from a spirit of accommodation; from an expectation that the assembly would see the propriety of the principles that actuated the senate, and from a hope that their amendment would be acceded to.

Mr. *Jones*—Mr. President, the business of this conference being explained, I shall proceed to the consideration of the question. How far the constitution of the state may be obligatory or not, I shall not now consider; but suppose it has nothing to do with the question, in framing the bill it was necessary that the assembly should give their opinion—that they should examine the constitution of this state, and the United States. In doing this, it appeared to them prudent to pursue a mode pointed out in the constitution of this state for the election of officers of the general government—they adopted this mode, not more from the consideration I have mentioned, than that it appeared conformable to the constitution of the United States.

They do not, at least I trust there is none, who suppose that they can, or that they ought to control the negative of the senate, on laws or resolutions—that point has always been admitted; this very conference is a proof of it; but the question is, whether that negative shall extend to all cases, as in the election of officers. It has been doubted how far the conference on this business was strictly constitutional. I am sorry any thing of that kind should be mentioned in the present stage of the business. The senate, if they thought the bill improper, should have rejected it. But I think it perfectly consistent with the proceedings of the legislature. The assembly formed a bill to put the new constitution into operation, and which provided for the election of electors, senators and representatives. To this bill the senate made several amendments, and which, after a conference, ended in its rejection. Now what was there in the nature of things to prevent either house from originating separate bills for each of the objects that was intended by the one first brought in? The senate, sir, did originate one, and the assembly the other two. The bill in question is not the same in the title, nor the words; but substantially it is the same, because it is for the same thing. It is said that the senate are equally near to the people; and that they feel themselves the representatives of all the people, as much as the assembly. I am sorry we are obliged to make remarks on that ground; but let it be remembered, that the senate, though they are an equal branch; and though I hope they will enjoy that equality, yet they are representatives chosen by a part of the people; that is, the free-holders, and they are to hold their offices four years. The assembly are chosen by all descriptions of people in the state, and annually. They are therefore more recently from the people, and more likely to represent their feelings. I mention this as an answer to some observations which I wish had been spared. The assembly, sir, suppose, that what they proposed was within the strict line of their duty, and that it would have effected the end intended. But the mode proposed by the senate is such as they ought not to adopt under any situation whatever. It is a mode, in their opinion, that differs wholly from what is proper in an appointment, or choice, for it may happen, and probably it will happen, that they may proceed to a choice, and that no choice will be made. Each house is to name eight electors, but may they not name the same persons; the probability is that they will. If both houses do name the same persons, ought they not to be the electors. What then is to be done, should both houses agree in the nomination. The senate are to choose out of the list sent by the assembly—the assembly out of the list by the senate. Now it is a thousand to one that the whole eight will not be chosen. There may be four, five, six or seven; it is possible eight. Is this a proper mode to adopt. The assembly thinks it is not wise to accede to such a proposition.

Mr. *Duane*.—Mr. Speaker; as the subject now before us has taken up much of our time already, I shall be brief in offering my sentiments on the present occasion; and without descanting on the propriety of the present conference shall proceed to notice the arguments that have been offered by the conferees, on the part of the Hon. the assembly.

Sir the gentleman who was first up thinks it of importance that this state should join with her sisters in choosing the first magistrate of the land; the welfare of the state is concerned in it, and I beg gentlemen to believe that there is not a wish nearer to my heart than the accomplishment of that great and desirable end.

The point in dispute must turn on this question, what are the rights of the two houses? Will any one say that they do not possess an equality. If then they have equal rights, and the amendment of the senate has only in object to secure the right which they possess, are not the assembly bound by the constitution to agree to it? Sir, there can be no doubt on this subject. It has been even conceded by two of the conferees on the part of the assembly, that the state constitution, so far as it respects the mode, is out of the question on the present occasion, for have they not said that was there time it would be proper to refer this matter to the people. But peculiar circumstances renders it impossible, and the legislature are obliged to take upon themselves the exercise of that power. If then the legislature are to exercise that power, must it not be in their legislative capacity—each house acting independently and exercising its negative on the other? The principle held out in the bill sir, is truly fallacious. Can it be said that the two houses coming together and acting as one body, are a legislature? Does the constitution warrant such a thing? Can they do any legislative act in that situation? I appeal to the constitution. Sir, what I offer is fair reasoning, and I think it cannot be disputed. I might add that, with respect to the rule prescribed in the state constitution for the choice of delegates to Congress, as being applicable to the present case, that no argument is necessary to shew that the gentleman is mistaken. For no man can say that the electors were a class of officers ever contemplated by the state constitution. It is a mere blank letter, Sir; and all our authority on the question before us is derived from the general constitution of the United States, which vests this power in the state legislatures. These are the principles on which the senate founded their amendment to the bill, and I wish, considering the importance of the subject, that it might not have been opposed without some substantial reason. The reasoning of the senate with me is clear, and conclusive. And however they may be urged by inclination to adopt any measures which will promote the interest of the state, they must adhere to their duty, they cannot sacrifice principle to convenience; the ground therefore that they have taken cannot be departed from.

Sir, it has been said that the amendment proposed by the senate is defective; that it does not ensure an election of eight electors. Upon what ground does this rest? What does the amendment propose? The senate are to nominate eight persons, and send such nomination to the assembly; the assembly are then to nominate eight persons, and send such nomination to the senate; is it supposeable that the assembly being informed of the nomination made by the senate, will nominate the same persons? Sir, conjectures of this kind is straining the matter beyond all suggestion. The objection is really weak; it is ill founded. The amendment, if agreed to, will answer the end proposed; it will ensure an election. To talk of the numbers of the assembly, is improper; the constitution has not given that house any more power than the senate, tho' the one consists of 72 men, the other of 24; they possess, I say, equal powers. In consequence of which the senate may not agree to any act which does not in the most implicit manner acknowledge that principle. Sir, I wish we may consider this point seriously; we are at a crisis; and there is a vast difference in the situation of the two houses. The senate are not encroaching on the privileges of the assembly—they are only contending against an invasion of those rights which is vested in them by the constitution, and which has been handed down to them unimpaired by their predecessors, and which they are resolved to hand down in purity to those who may succeed them.

Sir, I shall not add any thing farther on the subject. I conceive it must be useless; the argument offered at the late conference can not be forgotten. The presumption is that they must yet have their influence.

The Senate then withdrew.

1. *Daily Advertiser*, 17 and 18 February 1789. The debates were also printed in the *Morning Post*, 19, 20, and 21 February, and *Daily Gazette*, 18 and 19 February.

2. See Assembly Debates, 17 December 1788, n. 3, and Abraham Bancker to [Evert Bancker], 20 December 1788, both above.

Assembly and Senate Proceedings, Tuesday, P.M., 3 February

The Senate

The Senate met pursuant to adjournment.

Mr. President left the chair, and with the members of the Senate, proceeded to the Assembly-Chamber, to meet the Honorable the Assembly, for the purpose of holding the conference agreed upon by both Houses; by their respective resolutions of this day; and after having held the said conference, the Senate returned to the Senate-Chamber, and Mr. President re-assumed the chair.

Mr. Philip Schuyler moved that the Senate do adjourn until to-morrow morning. Debates arose upon the said motion, and Mr. President having put the question thereon, it was carried in the affirmative, in manner following, viz.

FOR THE AFFIRMATIVE.

Mr. Philip Schuyler,	Mr. Vanderbilt,
Mr. Douw,	Mr. Lawrance,
Mr. Micheau,	Mr. Morris,
Mr. Peter Schuyler,	Mr. Roosevelt,
Mr. Fonda,	Mr. Duane.

FOR THE NEGATIVE.

Mr. Yates,	Mr. Van Ness,
Mr. Hopkins,	Mr. Swartwout,
Mr. Williams,	Mr. Townsend,

Mr. Tredwell,	Mr. Clinton,
Mr. Humfrey,	Mr. Hathorn.

The Senate being equally divided upon the question, Mr. President determined in the affirmative. Thereupon,

The Senate adjourned accordingly, until ten of the clock to-morrow morning.

The Assembly

Mr. Speaker left the chair, and with the House attended the Honorable the Senate in the Assembly-Chamber, pursuant to the resolutions of both Houses, for holding a conference on the amendment to the bill entitled *An act for directing the manner of appointing Electors in this State, for choosing the President and Vice-President of the United States of America*; and the said conference being ended, *Mr. Speaker* re-assumed the chair, and reported to the House, that a conference had been held in the presence of both Houses, on the amendment proposed to the said bill.

The House proceeded to the further consideration of the said bill and amendment, and the same were again read, and debates had thereon.

Mr. Speaker then put the question, whether the House did adhere to the said bill, and it was carried in the affirmative, in the manner following, viz.

FOR THE AFFIRMATIVE.

Mr. Jones,	Mr. Schoonmaker,
Mr. Carman,	Mr. Tappen,
Mr. G. Livingston,	Mr. Griffen,
Mr. Kortz,	Mr. J. Smith,
Mr. Frey,	Mr. D'Witt,
Mr. Stauring,	Mr. Wisner,
Mr. Van Dyck,	Mr. Adgate,
Mr. J. Van Rensselaer,	Mr. Harper,
Mr. Veeder,	Mr. Havens,
Mr. Winn,	Mr. Schenck,
Mr. Duncan,	Mr. Akins,
Mr. Tearse,	Mr. E. Clark,
Mr. Savage,	Mr. Patterson,
Mr. Webster,	Mr. Scudder,
Mr. M'Cracken,	Mr. Cantine,
Mr. Thompson,	Mr. Bloom,
Mr. Bay,	Mr. Smith.

FOR THE NEGATIVE.

Mr. B. Livingston,	Mr. Horton,
Mr. Gilbert,	Mr. Low,
Mr. Seaman,	Mr. Bancker,
Mr. Barker,	Mr. Vandervoort,
Mr. Harison,	Mr. Rockwell,
Mr. H. Van Rensselaer,	Mr. Verplanck,
Mr. Younglove,	Mr. Giles,
Mr. Watts,	Mr. Gardiner,
Mr. Livingston,	Mr. Macomb.

Thereupon, *Resolved*, That this House do adhere to their said bill.

Ordered, That Mr. Patterson and Mr. Scudder deliver the said bill, and a copy of the last preceding resolution, to the Honorable the Senate.

Federal Gazette (Philadelphia), 3 February

Every day's experience more clearly evinces the excellence of the new constitution, even of those parts of it which at first appeared objectionable to many. Does any person call for a proof of this? let him turn his eyes to the state of New-York, where the legislature, composed of two houses, a senate and assembly, lost to all sense of the duty they owe to their own state, and to the United States, lost to every feeling that warms the patriot-breast, and totally forgetting their own dignity, have been for some time past, playing at the *childish* amusement of *cross-purposes* with each other; and have not hesitated to sacrifice the interests of New-York and the union, at the accursed shrine of party spirit and political intrigue, Not able to agree among themselves, as to the manner of choosing electors of a president and vice-president of the United States, they have chosen—*none.* Differing in opinions with respect to the mode of electing federal senators, they have elected—*none*—nor is it likely that they will. And, in open defiance of the new constitution, they have infringed the rights of the people, by dividing the state into districts for electing federal representatives; so that no freeman is allowed to vote for more than *one* representative, tho' he *has a right* to vote for *six.* Surely every friend to America must exult in that part of the new constitution, which gives the general government the power of its own organization, and provides for its existence, independant of any state cabals, that may have a tendency to injure the interests of the union. Here the necessity of Congress having power to regulate elections, &c. appears, in a most convincing point of view. Were it in the power of New-York, or any other disaffected state, to destroy the very existence of Congress; or to baffle the most salutary measures of the union, as heretofore, we should be a truly despicable people indeed.[1]

1. This article was reprinted in the *Morning Post,* 10 February 1789.

Assembly and Senate Proceedings, Wednesday, A.M., 4 February

The Senate

A message from the Honorable the Assembly by Mr. Patterson and Mr. Scudder, was received with the bill, entitled *An act directing the manner of appointing Electors in this State, for choosing the President and Vice-President of the United States of America,* together with a resolution, that they do adhere to their said bill, which was read. Thereupon,

Mr. Tredwell moved that the Senate do recede from their amendment to the said bill, and Mr. President having put the question thereon, it passed in the negative, in manner following, viz.

FOR THE NEGATIVE.

Mr. Philip Schuyler,	Mr. Peter Schuyler,
Mr. Douw,	Mr. Fonda,
Mr. Micheau,	Mr. Vanderbilt,

Mr. Lawrance,	Mr. L'Hommedieu,
Mr. Morris,	Mr. Duane.
Mr. Roosevelt,	

FOR THE AFFIRMATIVE.

Mr. Yates,	Mr. Townsend,
Mr. Hopkins,	Mr. Tredwell,
Mr. Williams,	Mr. Humfrey,
Mr. Van Ness,	Mr. Clinton,
Mr. Swartwout,	Mr. Hathorn.

Thereupon, *Resolved*, That the Senate do adhere to their amendment to the said bill.

Ordered, That Mr. Van Ness and Mr. Swartwout, deliver a copy of the preceding resolution, to the Honorable the Assembly.

The Assembly

A copy of a resolution of the Honorable the Senate, delivered by Mr. Van Ness and Mr. Swartwout, was read, that the Senate do adhere to their amendment to the bill entitled *An act for directing the manner of appointing Electors in this State, for choosing the President and Vice-President of the United States of America.*

Mr. B. Livingston, made a motion for a resolution in the words following, viz.

"*Resolved*, (if the Honorable the Senate concur herein) that be, and they hereby are appointed Electors on the part of this State, for choosing the President and Vice-President of the United States of America; that the said Electors shall meet together at the City-Hall of the city of Albany, on the first Wednesday in February, in the year of our Lord 1789, and then and there proceed to vote by ballot for two persons, as mentioned in the first section of the second article of the Constitution of the United States, in the manner and agreeable to the directions therein contained; and further to do and perform all other the duties enjoined on them by the said Constitution."

That Mr. Adgate, as an amendment made a motion, that the first part of the resolution proposed by the motion of Mr. B. Livingston, whereby it is intended that the Electors should be named therein, be obliterated, and the following substituted in its stead, viz.

"*Resolved*, (if the Honorable the Senate concur therein) that eight persons be appointed Electors of the President and Vice-President of the United States of America, in the same manner as Delegates are chosen to represent this State, in the United States in Congress assembled; and that this House will immediately proceed to the nomination of eight persons as aforesaid."

Debates arose on the amendment proposed by the motion of Mr. Adgate, and the question being put whether the House did concur therein, it was carried in the affirmative.

The said resolution being amended and agreed to by the House, is in the words following, viz.

"Resolved, (if the Honorable the Senate concur therein) That eight persons be appointed Electors of the President and Vice-President of the United States of America, in the same manner as Delegates are chosen to represent this State, in the United States in Congress assembled, and that this House will immediately proceed to the nomination of eight persons as aforesaid: That the said persons shall meet together at the City-Hall of the city of Albany, on the first Wednesday in February, in the year of our Lord 1789, and then and there proceed to vote by ballot for two persons, as mentioned in the fifth section of the second article of the Constitution of the United States, in the manner, and agreeable to the directions, therein contained; and further to do and perform all other the duties enjoined on them, by the said Constitution."

Ordered, That Mr. Cantine and Mr. Carman deliver a copy of the last preceding resolution, to the Honorable the Senate.

Mr. Webster, from the committee of the whole House, on the report of the committee appointed on the twenty-second day of December last, to prepare a draft of an application of the Legislature of this State, to the Congress of the United States of America, to call a Convention for revising the Constitution for the said United States, adopted by the Convention of this State, on the 26th day of July last, reported, that after the said report of the committee, as entered on the journal of this House of the 29th ultimo, had been read, and debates had thereon, Mr. B. Livingston made a motion that the same should be rejected, and a resolution substituted in its stead, in the words following, viz.

Resolved, (if the Honorable the Senate concur herein) That an application be made to the Congress of the United States of America, in the name and behalf of the Legislature of this State, in the words following, to wit:

Whereas, the Convention of the good People of the State of New-York, on the 26th day of July last past, assented to and ratified the Constitution proposed on the 17th day of September, in the year of our Lord 1787, by the Convention then assembled at Philadelphia, in confidence nevertheless, "that the amendments which might be proposed to the said Constitution would receive an early and mature consideration:["] And whereas the said Convention, at the same time agreed to sundry amendments, and in the name and behalf of their Constituents, enjoined it upon their Representatives in Congress, to exert all their influence, to obtain a ratification of the same, in "the manner prescribed in the said Constitution:" Therefore, we the Representatives of the People of the State of New-York, in Senate and Assembly convened, in compliance with the sense of our Convention, and anxious that the necessary amendments may be introduced as soon as possible, do earnestly and in the most solemn manner, call upon the Congress of the United States, to take the amendments recommended by our Convention, and by those of our sister States, into their "early and mature consideration," and to take effectual measures to obtain a ratification of such of them, as may be deemed necessary to induce a general confidence in the Government; either by proposing the same to the Legislatures of the different States, or by calling a Convention to meet at a period not far remote, agreeable to the manner prescribed by the fifth article of the Constitution aforesaid, as the one or the other mode of ratification may to them appear best calculated to promote the peace and welfare of the Union.

That debates ensued on the resolution proposed by the motion of Mr. B. Livingston, and that the question having been put whether the committee did agree to the same, it passed in the negative, in the manner following, viz.

FOR THE NEGATIVE.

Mr. Jones,	Mr. Harison,
Mr. Gilbert,	Mr. Hoffman,
Mr. G. Livingston,	Mr. Veeder,
Mr. Kortz,	Mr. Winn,
Mr. Frey,	Mr. H. Van Rensselaer,
Mr. Stauring,	Mr. Younglove,
Mr. SPEAKER,	Mr. Duncan,
Mr. J. Van Rensselaer,	Mr. Tearse,

Mr. Savage,
Mr. M'Cracken,
Mr. Thompson,
Mr. Bay,
Mr. Schoonmaker,
Mr. Tappen,
Mr. Griffen,
Mr. Carpenter,
Mr. J. Smith,
Mr. Low,
Mr. Bancker,
Mr. D'Witt,
Mr. Wisner,
Mr. Vandervoort,
Mr. Adgate,
Mr. Harper,
Mr. Havens,
Mr. Rockwell,
Mr. Schenck,
Mr. Akins,
Mr. E. Clark,
Mr. Patterson,
Mr. Scudder,
Mr. Gardiner,
Mr. Cantine,
Mr. Bloom,
Mr. Smith.

FOR THE AFFIRMATIVE.

Mr. B. Livingston,
Mr. Seaman,
Mr. Barker,
Mr. Watts,
Mr. Horton,
Mr. Verplanck,
Mr. Cornwell,
Mr. Giles,
Mr. Macomb.

That the first paragraph of the said draft of an application to Congress, being again read, is in the words following, viz.

The People of the State of New-York, having ratified the Constitution agreed to on the seventeenth day of September, in the year of our Lord one thousand seven hundred and eighty-seven, by the Convention then assembled at Philadelphia, in the State of Pennsylvania, as explained by the said ratification, in the fullest confidence of obtaining a revision of the several articles of the said Constitution, by a general Convention.

That the said paragraph having been read, *Mr. Speaker* made a motion that an addition be made to the said paragraph, in the words following, viz.

"And in confidence, that certain powers in and by the said Constitution granted, would not be exercised until such revision should have taken place."

That the question having been put whether the House did concur in the amendment proposed by the motion of *Mr. Speaker*, it was carried in the affirmative, in the manner following, viz.

FOR THE AFFIRMATIVE.

Mr. Jones,
Mr. Carman,
Mr. G. Livingston,
Mr. Kortz,
Mr. Frey,
Mr. Stauring,
Mr. Speaker,
Mr. J. Van Rensselaer,
Mr. Veeder,
Mr. Winn,
Mr. Duncan,
Mr. Tearse,
Mr. Savage,
Mr. M'Cracken,
Mr. Bay,
Mr. Schoonmaker,
Mr. Tappen,
Mr. Carpenter,
Mr. J. Smith,
Mr. D'Witt,
Mr. Wisner,
Mr. Adgate,
Mr. Harper,
Mr. Havens,

Mr. Schenck,	Mr. Scudder,
Mr. Akins,	Mr. Cantine,
Mr. E. Clark,	Mr. Bloom,
Mr. Patterson,	Mr. Smith.

FOR THE NEGATIVE.

Mr. B. Livingston,	Mr. Low,
Mr. Gilbert,	Mr. Bancker,
Mr. Seaman,	Mr. Vandervoort,
Mr. Barker,	Mr. Rockwell,
Mr. Harison,	Mr. Verplanck,
Mr. Hoffman,	Mr. Cornwell,
Mr. H. Van Rensselaer,	Mr. Giles,
Mr. Watts,	Mr. Gardiner,
Mr. Livingston,	Mr. Macomb.
Mr. Horton,	

That the committee had made further progress in the said draft of an application to the Congress of the United States, and had directed him to move for leave to sit again.

Ordered, That the said committee have leave to sit again.

The Senate

A message from the Honorable the Assembly, by Mr. Cantine and Mr. Carman, was received with the following resolution, which was read, viz.

Resolved, (if the Honorable the Senate concur herein) That eight persons be appointed Electors of the President and Vice-President of the United States of America, in the same manner as Delegates are chosen to represent this State, in the United States in Congress assembled; and that this House will immediately proceed to the nomination of eight persons for Electors as aforesaid: That the said Electors shall meet together at the City-Hall of the city of Albany, on the first Wednesday in February, in the year of our Lord one thousand, seven hundred and eighty-nine; and then and there proceed to vote by ballot for two persons, as mentioned in the first section of the second article of the Constitution of the United States, in the same manner and agreeable to the directions therein contained: And further, to do and perform all other the duties enjoined on them by the said Constitution.

Mr. Philip Schuyler thereupon moved that the Senate do not concur in the said resolution. Debates arose, and Mr. President having put the question on the motion, it was carried in the affirmative, in manner following, viz.

FOR THE AFFIRMATIVE.

Mr. Philip Schuyler,	Mr. Lawrance,
Mr. Douw,	Mr. Morris,
Mr. Micheau,	Mr. Roosevelt,
Mr. Peter Schuyler,	Mr. L'Hommedieu,
Mr. Fonda,	Mr. Duane,
Mr. Vanderbilt,	Mr. Hoffman.

FOR THE NEGATIVE.

Mr. Yates,	Mr. Williams,
Mr. Hopkins,	Mr. Van Ness,

Mr. Swartwout,	Mr. Humfrey,
Mr. Townsend,	Mr. Clinton,
Mr. Tredwell,	Mr. Hathorn.

Thereupon, *Resolved*, That the Senate do not concur with the Honorable the Assembly in their preceding resolution.

Mr. Philip Schuyler then moved for the following resolution; on which debates arose, and upon Mr. President putting the question thereon, was carried in the affirmative, in the same manner as upon the last question. Thereupon,

Resolved, (if the Honorable the Assembly concur therein) That the Electors on the part of this State, for choosing the first President and Vice-President of the United States of America, shall be appointed in manner following, that is to say; the Senate of this State shall forthwith choose openly four persons, and send a list of the persons so chosen to the Assembly, and thereupon the Assembly shall choose four other persons in like manner; and the eight persons so chosen shall be the Electors, and shall meet together at the City-Hall of the city of Albany, on the first Wednesday in February, in the year of our Lord one thousand, seven hundred and eighty-nine, and then and there proceed to vote by ballot for two persons as mentioned in the first section of the second article of the Constitution of the United States, in the same manner and agreeable to the directions therein contained: And further, to do and perform all other the duties enjoined on them by the said Constitution.

Ordered, That Mr. Morris and Mr. Roosevelt, deliver a copy of the two preceding resolutions to the Honorable the Assembly.

The Assembly

A copy of two resolutions of the Honorable the Senate, delivered by Mr. Morris and Mr. Roosevelt, were read; by the first of which said resolutions it appears that the Senate do not concur with this House, in their resolution of this day, for the appointment of Electors to choose a President and Vice-President, of the United States of America.

The other of the said resolutions, is in the words following, viz.

"*Resolved*, (if the Honorable the Assembly concur herein) that the Electors on the part of this State, for choosing the first President and Vice-President of the United States of America, shall be appointed in the manner following, that is to say, the Senate of this State shall forthwith choose openly, four persons, and send a list of the persons so chosen to the Assembly; and thereupon the Assembly shall choose openly four other persons in like manner; and the eight persons so chosen, shall be Electors, and shall meet together at the City-Hall of the city of Albany, on the first Wednesday in February, in the year of our Lord, 1789, and then and there proceed to vote by ballot for two persons, as mentioned in the first section of the second article of the Constitution of the United States, in the manner and agreeable to the directions therein contained; and further to do and perform all other the duties enjoined on them, by the said Constitution."

The last mentioned resolution having been read and considered, *Mr. Speaker* put the question, whether the House did concur with the Honorable the Senate therein, and it passed in the negative, in the manner following, viz.

FOR THE NEGATIVE.

Mr. Carman,	Mr. Frey,
Mr. G. Livingston,	Mr. Stauring,
Mr. Kortz,	Mr. J. Van Rensselaer,

Mr. Veeder,	Mr. D'Witt,
Mr. Winn,	Mr. Wisner,
Mr. Duncan,	Mr. Adgate,
Mr. Tearse,	Mr. Harper,
Mr. Savage,	Mr. Schenck,
Mr. Webster,	Mr. Akins,
Mr. M'Cracken,	Mr. E. Clark,
Mr. Bay,	Mr. Patterson,
Mr. Schoonmaker,	Mr. Scudder,
Mr. Tappen,	Mr. Cantine,
Mr. Griffen,	Mr. Smith,
Mr. Carpenter,	Mr. Jones.
Mr. J. Smith,	

FOR THE AFFIRMATIVE.

Mr. B. Livingston,	Mr. Bancker,
Mr. Gilbert,	Mr. Vandervoort,
Mr. Seaman,	Mr. Havens,
Mr. Harison,	Mr. Rockwell,
Mr. Hoffman,	Mr. Verplanck,
Mr. H. Van Rensselaer,	Mr. Cornwell,
Mr. Younglove,	Mr. Giles,
Mr. Watts,	Mr. Gardiner,
Mr. Livingston,	Mr. Macomb,
Mr. Horton,	Mr. Bloom.
Mr. Low,	

Thereupon *Resolved*, That this House do not concur with the Honorable the Senate in the said resolution.

Ordered, That Mr. Bloom and Mr. Smith deliver a copy of the last preceding resolution, to the Honorable the Senate.

Mr. Watts then made a motion, for a resolution [in] the words following, viz.

"*Resolved*, (if the Honorable the Senate concur therein) that a committee of five persons from each House be appointed, who shall immediately meet and confer together, for the purpose of nominating eight Electors, for the election of a President and Vice-President of the United States of America, and such committee shall, without delay report such nomination to the Assembly and Senate; and such eight persons, if approved of by the Senate and Assembly, shall be the Electors as aforesaid."

The resolution proposed by the motion of Mr. Watts, having been read and considered, *Mr. Speaker* put the question, whether the House did agree to the said resolution, and it passed in the negative, in the manner following, viz.

FOR THE NEGATIVE.

Mr. Jones,	Mr. Winn,
Mr. Carman,	Mr. Duncan,
Mr. G. Livingston,	Mr. Tearse,
Mr. Kortz,	Mr. Savage,
Mr. Frey,	Mr. Webster,
Mr. Stauring,	Mr. M'Cracken,
Mr. J. Van Rensselaer,	Mr. Bay,
Mr. Veeder,	Mr. Schoonmaker,

Mr. Tappen,
Mr. Griffen,
Mr. Carpenter,
Mr. J. Smith,
Mr. D'Witt,
Mr. Wisner,
Mr. Adgate,
Mr. Harper,
Mr. Schenck,
Mr. Akins,
Mr. E. Clark,
Mr. Patterson,
Mr. Scudder,
Mr. Cantine,
Mr. Smith.

FOR THE AFFIRMATIVE.

Mr. B. Livingston,
Mr. Gilbert,
Mr. Seaman,
Mr. Harison,
Mr. Hoffman,
Mr. H. Van Rensselaer,
Mr. Younglove,
Mr. Watts,
Mr. Livingston,
Mr. Horton,
Mr. Bancker,
Mr. Vandervoort,
Mr. Havens,
Mr. Rockwell,
Mr. Verplanck,
Mr. Cornwell,
Mr. Giles,
Mr. Gardiner,
Mr. Macomb,
Mr. Bloom.

The Senate

The Senate proceeded to the re-consideration of their amendments proposed to the bill, entitled *An act for prescribing the times, places and manner of holding elections for Senators of the United States of America, to be chosen in this State*, and which were not concurred in by the Honorable the Assembly.

Mr. Tredwell thereupon moved, that the Senate do recede from their said amendments, and Mr. President having put the question thereon, it passed in the negative, in manner following, viz.

FOR THE NEGATIVE.

Mr. Philip Schuyler,
Mr. Douw,
Mr. Micheau,
Mr. Peter Schuyler,
Mr. Fonda,
Mr. Vanderbilt,
Mr. Lawrance,
Mr. Morris,
Mr. Roosevelt,
Mr. L'Hommedieu,
Mr. Duane,
Mr. Hoffman.

FOR THE AFFIRMATIVE.

Mr. Yates,
Mr. Williams,
Mr. Van Ness,
Mr. Swartwout,
Mr. Tredwell,
Mr. Humfrey,
Mr. Clinton,
Mr. Hathorn.

Thereupon, *Resolved*, That the Senate do adhere to their amendments to the said bill, not concurred in by the Honorable the Assembly.

Ordered, That Mr. Roosevelt and Mr. Townsend deliver the bill, with a copy of the preceding resolution to the Honorable the Assembly.

A message from the Honorable the Assembly, by Mr. Bloom and Mr. Smith, was received, with a resolution that they do not concur with the Senate, in their resolution of this day, prescribing the mode of appointing Electors on the part of this State, for choosing the first President and Vice-President of the United States of America, which was read.

Assembly Debates, Wednesday, 4 February[1]

A message was received from the senate that they adhered to their amendments to the bill for appointing electors.

Mr. B. Livingston then proposed a resolution upon the principles of the senate, that the two houses should each nominate eight, and then choose one half of those nominated by the other house.

Mr. Adgate moved as an amendment, that they be chosen by joint ballot; this amendment was carried, and the resolution sent in that form to the senate.

A message was shortly after received from the senate, that they had rejected the resolution; and proposing the same mode that had been proposed by Mr. B. Livingston.

The question was then put, whether the house would agree to the resolution of the senate, it was carried in the negative.—31 to 21.

Mr. Watts then proposed a resolution that a committee of five be appointed from each house to make a nomination of eight electors, which eight persons if approved of, should be the electors; this motion was *negatived* 31 to 20.

The house then went again into committee on the draft of an application to Congress to call a convention to revise and propose amendments to the new constitution.

Mr. Webster in the chair.

The following draft of an application to Congress was read.

Resolved (if the honorable the senate concur herein) that an application be made to the Congress of the United States of America in the name and behalf of the legislature of this state, in the words following, to wit

The people of the state of New York having ratified the constitution agreed on the 17th September, 1787, by the convention then assembled at Philadelphia, as explained by the said ratification, in the fullest confidence of obtaining a revision of the several articles of the said constitution by a general convention. In compliance, therefore, with the unanimous sense of the convention of this state, who all united in opinion, that such a revision was necessary to recommend the said constitution to the approbation and support of a numerous body of their constituents, and a majority of whom conceived the constitution so exceptionable that nothing but such confidence, and an invincible reluctance to separate from our sister states could have prevailed upon a sufficient number to assent to it without stipulating for previous amendments, and from a conviction that the apprehensions or discontents which those articles occasion, cannot be removed or allayed, unless an act to revise the said constitution be among the first that shall be passed by the new Congress: WE, the legislature of the state of New-York, DO, in behalf of our constituents, in the most earnest and solemn manner, make this application to the Congress, that a convention of deputies from the several states be immediately called, with full power to take the said constitution into their consideration, and to report such amendments thereto as they shall find best suited to promote our common interests, and secure to ourselves and our latest posterity the great and unalienable rights of mankind.

Mr. *B. Livingston*—I do not rise, Mr. Chairman, to oppose an application to Congress for a revision of the new Constitution, but to state my objections to its being made in the form of the resolution now under consideration. I must, however, be indulged in declaring that when I give my assent to making any application to Congress upon this subject, it is not from a conviction that any amendments whatever are necessary. I consider the constitution as perfect as we could reasonably have expected it from the hands of men. But as a revision of the system will have a tendency to render it more universally acceptable, it may not be improper to take some measures on our part to obtain it in a constitutional way. It is with us to determine in what mode this revision should be had, so as to promote the salutary ends we all have in view.

Sir, the constitution of the United States provides that amendments may be obtained either by Congress proposing them to the legislatures of the different states, or by calling a new convention for the purpose. Will it not then be prudent to leave it to the discretion of Congress to determine which of these two modes will be best calculated to answer the end the resolution has in view, and not to insist on their calling a convention immediately?

Conventions are assemblies which should as seldom as possible be resorted to, where the ordinary administration is adequate to the object. Here the government are vested with powers expressly comprehending the present case. Is there any danger that these powers will not be called into exercise if the public good requires it? Of whom will Congress be composed? Are not the senators chosen by the different state legislatures, and the other branch by the people themselves? Will they not be acquainted with the sentiments and wishes of their constituents? Will they not feel every obligation, as well as inclination, to pursue such measures as will best accord with those sentiments and wishes? From an assembly thus constituted, may we not expect that the proper amendments will be proposed as soon as possible after their first meeting? To whom are those amendments to be submitted? To the legislatures of the several states, who will doubtless ratify such of them as in their estimation will be acceptable to their constituents. This mode of proceeding is attended with fewer embarrassments, and will take up much less time, than what must necessarily elapse before a convention can be assembled; the result of whose deliberations (should they ever agree) must undergo the same discussion as those which may be proposed by Congress. Should Congress believe a majority of the people wish for amendments, it is probable that the legislature of this state, at their very next meeting, may be employed in deliberating on some of their proposing—while, from the time that must unavoidably transpire in the summoning and meeting of a convention, the advocates for amendments can scarcely flatter themselves with a speedy revision of the system in that way.

But delay is not the only inconvenience attendant on a new convention. Dangers of a more serious nature are to be apprehended. It is well known that this state, as well as some others, are divided into two parties, federal and antifederal. These terms are not used with a view of casting an odium on the one or the other; but because I do not recollect any other term that is so generally applied, or is better understood. Gentlemen have been blamed for mentioning that parties exist in the state; but when the notoriety of the fact renders concealment impossible, and when pertinent arguments may be drawn from the present situation of the country, where can be the impropriety in taking notice of it. If then parties exist, what will be their conduct in the case of a convention? Will not federalists choose federalists; and those of an opposite character, send members possessing the same sentiments with themselves? Will members thus chosen feel all that independence of sentiment so essential to a cool and dispassionate consideration of the constitution they are to revise? Will a body composed of such heterogeneous materials, be likely to accord in any one amendment? Will not the same spirit of party which influenced their election, continue to actuate the different members of the convention, until they are compelled to return home, without effecting any alteration in the new system of government? Should this be the case, will all those who desire amendments feel disposed to acquiesce in that disappointment? We might indeed have expected that this would have been the case, had not an honorable gentleman, who was one of the managers in a late conference between the two houses, declared in the presence of both, that he hoped his constituents would never rest satisfied until they had obtained the amendments they desired.[2] This, sir, is going much farther than our convention have gone, and it is to be sincerely hoped that the gentleman may be mistaken in the sentiments he entertains of his constituents. Should these, however, be the real intentions of so respectable a part of the community, and should pains be taken to disseminate them still farther, what are we to expect in case of the convention's rising without proposing amendments, but a civil war? The gentleman who made this declaration may have familiarised himself to such an event. His nerves may be sufficient to meet it, and to carry him through without emotion; but, for my own part, I cannot, while the devastations of the late war are fresh in my memory, but tremble at the idea of a repetition of them.

Having stated some objections to the immediate calling of a convention, I shall offer a resolution by way of amendment to the one which has just been read, by which Congress are left at liberty to call a convention, or to propose amendments in the other way, as they shall think best. The resolution is as follows:

Resolved, (if the honourable the senate concur herein) that an application be made to the Congress of the United States of America, in the name and behalf of the legislature of the state, in the words following, to wit,

Whereas the convention of the good people of the state of New-York, on the 26th day of July last past, assented to and ratified the Constitution proposed on the 17th day of September, in the year of our Lord 1787, by the Convention then assembled at Philadelphia, in confidence nevertheless, "*that the amendments which might be proposed to the said constitution, would receive an early and mature consideration*"

And whereas the said convention at the same time agreed to sundry amendments, and in the name and behalf of their constituents, "*enjoined it upon their representatives in Congress to exert all their influence to obtain a ratification of the same in the manner prescribed in the said constitution.*" Therefore, we the representatives of the people of the state of New-York, in senate and assembly convened, in compliance with the sense of our convention, and anxious that the *necessary amendments* may be introduced as soon as possible, do earnestly and in the most solemn manner call upon the Congress of the United States, to take the amendments recommended by our convention, and by those of our sister states, into their "*early and mature consideration*," and to take effectual measures to obtain a ratification of such of them as may be deemed necessary to induce a general confidence in the government, either by proposing the same to the legislatures of the different states, or by calling a convention to meet at a period not far remote, agreeable to the manner prescribed by the fifth article of the constitution aforesaid, as the one or the other mode of ratification may to them appear best calculated to promote the peace and welfare of the union.

After reading the resolution Mr. Livingston proceeded.

Sir, In framing this resolution I have followed as nearly as possible the sentiments of our convention as expressed in their instrument of ratification. In one place they express a confidence that the amendment which might be proposed, would receive an early and mature consideration, but are silent as to the mode in which that consideration was to be had; in another part, they enjoin it upon their representatives in Congress, to exert all their influence to obtain a ratification of certain amendments in the manner prescribed in the constitution. Here again, nothing is said of a convention.

I am aware it will be mentioned, that by their circular letter, they have recommended the calling of a convention to all the other states. But, Sir, notwithstanding the respect we entertain for the honorable gentlemen who composed that convention; notwithstanding the gratitude we must all feel for their having ratified a form of government which cannot fail of producing the most solid advantages to our country, yet I trust we shall not think ourselves precluded by the advice contained in this letter, further than as it corresponds with our own ideas of propriety. Far be it from me to censure those who signed that letter, yet to prevent its having an undue influence, I shall stand excused for reminding the committee that our convention were chosen for the sole purpose of taking into consideration the new constitution. If we recur to the resolutions under which they acted, we shall find no other authority delegated to them; whatever, therefore, they have done beyond ratifying the constitution, and particularly this letter, must be considered in the light of advice, which we are at liberty to follow or not, as the same may appear expedient or otherwise.

Upon the whole, the amendment which is brought forward is so unexceptionable, that I cannot but hope it will meet with the approbation of the committee.

Mr. *Jones.*—I am not a little surprized at what I have heard. The arguments appear to me to be extraordinary. We are told, in the first place, that it would be improper to call a convention immediately, because there are parties in the states, and that the persens chosen to go to the convention will be the representatives of those parties. But, the representatives to be chosen in the several states, to represent them in Congress, are not to be men of party; they are to be divested of all those prejudices which have been created since the new constitution has been the subject of political speculation and party rage. Sir, is there not a contradiction in this reasoning? Will not these parties have as much influence in the choice of members of Congress, as in the choice of members of convention? Can this be doubted? Why then are we to look to Congress, as a body in whom party heats and prejudices will be unknown? It is said too, that it is too soon to call a convention—that bad consequences will follow from it, in case they do not come to a happy result; and yet, if we leave it to the new government to propose amendments, notwithstanding every thing will be new to them, and it will be a long time before they get organized, and can take up the subject; yet it is said we shall probably be deliberating on amendments that they shall propose, before even a convention can be called. Really, sir, these arguments have no weight in them—they are fallacious. Again, it is said that the convention of the state did not request that a convention should be called immediately. But, sir, this sentiment is expressed in the ratification; if the gentleman will recur to it, he will find the proposed application conformable thereto. Sir, we need not apprehend that a convention will be called too soon—it will take a long period of time for the new government to get organized; and tho' I have not the smallest doubt of two thirds of the states in the union making an application, yet two years at least will elapse before an act can be passed, and a convention called. Sir, the arguments of the gentleman, as it respects the ratification of the convention, is not fair; the inference he draws from it is not just. The convention could not, in the instrument of ratification, insist upon the calling of a convention; but if they could, it would not have been prudent in them to have attempted it. But they could express their sentiments in a circular letter, and it is well known that they did this, and unanimously recommended the calling a convention; how far they had a right to do this I submit to the committee, and to the world. And I have not a doubt but their conduct is approved of. Sir, the convention of this state never would have ratified the constitution, if they had not been persuaded that their sister states in the union would have consented to call a convention, and if the circular letter had not been agreed to by both parties. Indeed this may be considered as a condition on which the constitution was ratified. Can it then be expected of us that we will submit to the general government to make the amendments? Was it ever known that the rulers themselves would say, you have trusted us with too much power, we therefore beg of you to take back a part of it? That they may want more power is highly probable; but it is not in the nature of man to suppose that too much confidence is reposed in them; they are never disposed to contemplate an abuse of power which they hold in their own hands. Shall we, therefore, trust to our own rulers to make amendments for us? The reason why there are two modes of obtaining amendments prescribed by the constitution I suppose to be this—it could not be known to the framers of the constitution, whether there was too much power given by it or too little; they therefore prescribed a mode by which Congress might procure more, if in the operation of the government it was found necessary; and they prescribed for the states a mode of restraining the powers of the government, if upon trial it should be found they had given too much. In my opinion, therefore, we ought to call for a convention as the proper line chalked out by the constitution for the people to obtain such amendments as to them appear essential to their happiness.

I am sorry that the sentiments of an individual, who he is I do not know, should be taken up as the sentiments of the people. The sentiments of the convention ought to have the preference; and we ought to pay deference to that sentiment only. The convention have declared a convention of the states to be necessary—even if no amendments are made; it will certainly quiet the apprehensions of a great number of people, and thereby give additional spirit to the new government itself. And, sir, I believe that peace will never be perfectly restored to the United States, until a convention is called, and they either declare that no amendments are necessary, or propose some.

But, sir, with respect to the existence of parties, it is natural, and is to be expected as a consequence resulting from freedom. There are parties in all free governments—at least, I have no knowledge of any in which party did not exist. One will sometimes be strongest—sometimes the other: In our country, which ever may prevail, I hope they will always pursue the great rights of mankind.

Mr. *Lansing*. In discussing this business, I shall pay some attention to the remarks of the gentleman who has brought forward the amendment; and I believe I can convince the committee that it would be improper to adopt it, unless they hold the same ideas as the gentleman himself. If agreed to, it would appear, instead of urging to Congress the necessity of calling a convention, that we did it barely in compliance with the recommendation of the late convention, and that it is repugnant to our own sentiments. The resolution as reported by the committee who were appointed to essay it, declares that the people of the state of New-York wish a convention called to revise the new system of general government. Sir, we are to believe that the resolution reported by them is the sense of the people, in as much as it is conformable to the unanimous sentiment of the late convention, who were elected by the people for the special purpose of giving their sentiments on that subject—and further, sir, I believe it speaks the sense not only of this house, but of the legislature, and a very great majority of the people of the state. As the convention I say were called to express the sense of the people on the new constitution, we ought to respect their opinion. That convention adopted the constitution, not because they approved of it, but because the pressure of circumstances, and the ratification of it by a number of our sister states, had an influence on a majority of the members of that body. Sir, when the subject was under their consideration, men of all parties—of all descriptions—and all views, united in the opinion that a convention of the states, and the immediate revision of the system was necessary; indeed the unanimity which prevailed in the convention on the subject of the circular letter, is the strongest proof of the sentiments of the people. I am not apprehensive therefore that the sense of our constituents can be conveyed in too strong terms. This being my sentiment, it can not be supposed that I shall advocate the amendment proposed by the gentleman—for it will not in my opinion convey the sentiments of the people of the state. Is it probable that a revision will take place in the mode prescribed by the gentleman? the national government will be a long time making the necessary arrangements—for it is yet to be organized—and they will have a variety of important objects to pay immediate attention to; indeed much more than they can accomplish in two or three years. We are not to suppose that they will abandon all the national objects that will be before them to decide on the different amendments that have been proposed—After all this time expires, and Congress do propose amendments, then they are to go to the states, where another considerable period of time must elapse before three-fourths of the states agree to them. In the one instance we submit the propriety of making amendments to men who are sent, some of them for six years, from home, and who lose that knowledge of the wishes of the people by absence, which men more recently from them, in case of a convention, would naturally possess. Besides, the Congress, if they propose amendments, can only communicate their reasons to their constituents by letter, while if the amendments are made by men sent for the express purpose, when they return from the convention, they can detail more satisfactorily, and explicitly the reasons that operated in favour of such and such amendments—and the people will be able to enter into the views of the convention, and better understand the propriety of acceding to their proposition.

The hon. gentleman who has brought forward the amendment is fearful that the convention will be called at too early a day; for my part, I wish it was possible to anticipate the business; for the sooner amendments are made, the better. I should have preferred calling a convention before the meeting of Congress, was it practicable.

Sir, we have heard the word party too often mentioned. I suppose there is a material difference in what is now termed party, than that which originates in particular attachments to particular men—the present division of the people, arising from constitutional causes. One part of them supposing the new constitution a good one and the other supposing it dangerous to their happiness; this is the opinion of the majority of our constituents, as is evidenced by the complexion of this house. The reason why a different sentiment prevails in the senate may be accounted for from this cause; that that branch of the legislature is composed of men not so recently elected by the people; they were most of them chosen at a time when the present political dispute was unthought of; but, sir, this house speaks the sentiments of the people; for the majority of the members have been elected under that influence which is opposed to the new government. I am pained when I make these observations; but I do it to explain the distinctions that prevail at present, and they are such as are founded on fact. But, sir, it is insinuated, that if we do not leave this power with Congress, it will be supposing them not trustworthy. Sir, this is not a fair supposition, for it is impossible for any member to entertain such opinions without knowing of what characters Congress may be composed. But, sir, it is reasonable to expect that Congress will be unwilling to relinquish any of the powers that are given. Mankind are not disposed to give up advantages that they possess; it is easier to give power than to reclaim it. The contest between the two houses clearly proves this principle.

Mr. *B. Livingston.*—I shall be very short in my reply to the remarks of the two gentlemen who were last on the floor. In opposition to the proposed resolution, it is said that

Congress will be too much embarrassed by a variety of important business, during their first session to attend to the subject of amendments. In answering this objection it may be asked, whether any more important object can claim their attention than the revision of the very system by which they are constituted, nor will this subject require as much time or avocation from their other concerns, as is apprehended. All the amendments which have been proposed by the different states, will lay before them. From these may be selected and recommended to the different legislatures such as may be deemed the most salutary: But should Congress be of opinion that a majority of their constituents are satisfied with the constitution in its present form, they will certainly act wisely not to recommend any innovations until experience shall have evinced the necessity of them.

Again, it is said, that a majority of the good people of the United States, and of this state in particular, are solicitous for the immediate assembling of a new convention. Was I satisfied of this being the fact, averse as I feel to this mode of obtaining amendments, I should think it my duty to give it every support, But I am yet to be convinced that this is the case: Several states, have unanimously ratified the new constitution, others have done it by very large majorities, without saying a syllable upon the subject of amendments, or a new convention; whence then is it to be inferred, that a major part of the people are anxious for this measure. It is by no means certain that a majority of our immediate constituents think it expedient.

One other remark which escaped those gentlemen ought not to pass unnoticed. They both observed that the new constitution would probably not have been adopted by our convention, unless the gentlemen who had from the first advocated this measure, had consented to sign the circular letter. If this information be true, (and it certainly is, for it comes from two gentlemen who had the honor of being members of that convention) it militates much against the attention which ought otherwise to be paid to a proceeding which had the appearance of being adopted with so much unanimity. If I say this letter was the result of compromise or compassion, surely as much credit is not due to it, as if every member had signed it voluntarily and without any other consideration than a conviction of its being an eligible step. This was so far from being the case, that several gentlemen, whose names appear to that letter, from the information which has been given the committee, seem to have been placed in such a situation as to have no alternative but that of signing the letter or losing the constitution. They preferred the former as the least of the two evils. The respect we were all ready to pay to the unanimous recommendation of our convention, must be much weakened now we are informed by what means this unanimity was effected.

I shall make but one observation more. The proposed resolution goes much farther than the circular letter of our convention. By the latter it is recommended that a convention meet at *a period not far remote*. By the application before us, we desire a convention may be assembled *immediately*. There is a very great and manifest difference between these terms. From this guarded expression of our convention we may conclude, that while they wished measures might be immediately taken to *call* a convention to satisfy a part of their constituents, they did not judge it expedient that this convention should assemble until experience had pointed out the defects of the new system, and therefore fixed the time of their meeting to *a period not far remote*

Mr. *Jones*.—With respect to the circular letter, I have no recollection if I said they were compelled to sign it. I think that I did not say so. The fact is, they were not compelled to sign it. The friends of the constitution dictated it themselves. There are some of the members in both houses who were of that convention—let them declare the fact.

Mr. *Lansing*.—If I conveyed an idea that there was compulsion in the framing of the circular letter, it was what I did not intend—nor do I believe I did express a sentiment of the kind. Sir, I said that the change that took place between the time of election and the time of ratification, had an influence on a majority of the convention to ratify the constitution—tho' it did not alter their sentiments in respect to the merits of it. The question then was, how were they to shew the disapprobation of the state on the subject?—and all parties agreed in the measure of writing a circular letter, inviting our sister states to join with us to effect a revision of the system;—the better to secure the liberties of the people.

Mr. *Gilbert*.—I think a great deal of what has been said, is foreign to the subject; the only question before the committee is, whether we shall apply to Congress to call a convention, or whether we shall leave it to them to exercise their discretion in either calling a convention, or proposing amendments. We are to answer this question, in my opinion, by asking another—Are the proceedings of the convention binding?—if they are binding, are they so in the whole, or in part? For my part I think them binding in the whole; if so, we are bound to respect them, and we have no discretion on the present question—we must vote for calling a convention.

Mr. *Harrison*.—I feel myself peculiarly circumstanced upon the present occasion. I could wish to have remained silent—but it may be necessary that I give the committee my ideas. I am in sentiment opposed to the amendment offered by the gentleman from New York;—and yet I differ with the gentlemen who oppose it. I shall not however, enter into any argument on the subject, as my sense of amendments to the new constitution will appear on the journals of the convention—and I have hitherto seen no reason to alter my opinion. I think that if the amendments which were proposed in that body were adopted, that it would defeat the constitution by rendering it useless. But as a member of that convention, when I considered the situation of the state, and the sentiments that prevailed among a great number of the people, and the heats that had taken place, I was induced to think that every measure which could allay the apprehensions of the people, and prevent mischiefs which were then contemplated, ought to be adopted. Under these impressions I signed the circular letter. I was willing that the constitution should be submitted to a convention; not doubting but the good sense of the citizens of America would not rashly make such alterations as would impair its beauty—or enervate any of its essential parts; and that they would weigh well all that could be said for and against it. I am not unwilling, sir, to trust my countrymen; if I am mistaken in my opinion, I will submit to their's. And tho' the constitution is in my opinion as good as can be expected, yet I do not consider it so perfect as not to want improvement; if therefore a convention can point out any alterations tending to promote the happiness of the people, I shall think it my duty to acquiesce. And I must confess that I think the calling of a convention, the only means to restore peace and harmony to our country, and to destroy those parties that exist amongst us;—under this impression I shall vote against the amendment.

Sir, I can not think it right that any invidious comparisons should be drawn between the two houses. I consider both of them as the representatives of the people, with whose sentiments I suppose them equally acquainted. We do not, sir, know what may be the sense of the people, in respect to the proceedings of this legislature; but to the bar of the public the two houses will have to appeal; where, if the conduct of the one or the other is approved of, they will again be sent forward as their representatives. Sir, gentlemen in either house may maintain opposite principles; but it is cruel to suppose they do not originate in pure motives. We are to suppose that both houses act conscientiously.

Mr. *Lansing*—I believe, sir, that the gentlemen of the committee will recollect the expressions I made; and what I said cannot be construed into an invidious distinction. I stated facts, and they can not be contradicted. I say, that the last year, when an election was had, that throughout the state, it took a complexion from the sentiments of the people, as they respect the new constitution; and the consequence is, that in this house we have a majority for amendments. I say, too, that the senate, having been elected at an earlier period, do not entertain the same sentiments, and that this difference in the two houses, arises from the senate not having come so recently from the people. When I state these facts, I disclaim any intention of injuring the feelings of the senate.

On the question to agree to the amendment proposed by Mr. B. Livingston. . . .[3]

The committee then rose and asked for leave to sit again.

1. *Daily Advertiser*, 18, 19, 21, and 23 February 1789. The *Morning Post* printed virtually the same account on 21, 23, 24, and 25 February.

2. See Gilbert Livingston's speech in Joint Conference Committee Debates, 5 January 1789, above.

3. For the roll call, which was carried in the negative, see Assembly and Senate Proceedings, 4 February 1789, immediately above.

Samuel Miles to Tench Coxe, Philadelphia, 4 February (excerpt)[1]

I have Noticed the difference of sentiments in the Senate and House of Representatives, of York State, and cannot help entertaining a sacred wish that they may not unite, as I think the want of a full Representation from that State, will be a strong induc[e]ment to Congress to remove else where. This sentiment, I acknowledge, is too interested.—but I cannot help it.—[2]

1. RC, Tench Coxe Papers, PHi. Miles (1739–1805) was a member of Pennsylvania's colonial assembly, 1772 and 1775; served as a brigadier general in the Pennsylvania militia during the Revolution; was elected to the Pennsylvania Supreme Executive Council in 1788, Philadelphia alderman in 1789, and mayor of Philadelphia in 1790.

2. Others with an interest in moving the federal capital expressed similar sentiments. On 21 March 1789 Richard Bassett wrote to George Read: "N. York It seems is not likely to be Represented at all, the Quarrels are great and run very high—It would seem as if there would be a warm push for an immediate removal of Congress, as soon as they are Competent to the Transaction of business" (New York, RC, Rodney Collection, DeHi).

Comte de Moustier to Comte de Montmorin, New York, 4 February (excerpt)[1]

The tranquility that the United States is enjoying at this moment is only an appearance; waiting for the new government to form, the parties are daily assuming more consistency. Those of New York do not cease to irritate themselves with pin-pricks, frequently juvenile and always inconsequential. The cause of Antifederalism has become personal to the governor and to his supporters; there is now no argument, except for the men. The Federalists are continually in the minority; no occasion has been missed to humiliate them and the Senate struggles in vain against the petulance of the Assembly composed almost entirely of men of the people. One endeavors to wait for the overthrow of the governor who is at the head of this majority, and never before has there been seen in the United States more activity, animosity, and hate than seen there today to return this odious officer to the multitude.

1. RC (translated from French), Correspondance Politique, Etats-Unis, Vol. 34, ff. 19–22, Archives du Ministère des Affaires Etrangères, Paris, France. Comte de Montmorin was the French Minister of Foreign Affairs.

Assembly and Senate Proceedings, Thursday, A.M., 5 February

The Assembly

Mr. Webster, from the committee of the whole House, on the draft of an application by the Legislature of this State to the Congress of the United States of America, to call a Convention for revising the Constitution for the said United States, adopted by the Convention of this State, on the 26th day of July last, reported, that after the said draft had been this day read in the committee, a paragraph thereof was again read, in the words following, viz.

"We, the Legislature of the State of New-York, do, in behalf of our Constituents, in the most earnest and solemn manner, make this application to the Congress, that a Convention of Deputies from the several States be immediately called, with full powers to take the said Constitution into their consideration, and to propose such amendments thereto, as they shall find best calculated to promote our common interests, and secure to ourselves and our latest posterity, the great and unalienable rights of mankind."

That the said paragraph having been read, Mr. Livingston made a motion, that the word *immediately* be obliterated, and the words *at a period not far remote*, inserted after the word *called.*

That the question having been put, whether the committee did agree to the amendment proposed by the motion of Mr. Livingston, it passed in the negative in the manner following, viz.

FOR THE NEGATIVE.

Mr. Jones,	Mr. M'Cracken,
Mr. G. Livingston,	Mr. Thompson,
Mr. Kortz,	Mr. Bay,
Mr. Frey,	Mr. Schoonmaker,
Mr. Stauring,	Mr. Tappen,
Mr. SPEAKER,	Mr. Carpenter,
Mr. Van Dyck,	Mr. J Smith,
Mr. J. Van Rensselaer,	Mr. D'Witt,
Mr. Veeder,	Mr. Wisner,
Mr. Winn,	Mr. Adgate,
Mr. Duncan,	Mr. Harper,
Mr. Tearse,	Mr. Havens,
Mr. Savage.	Mr. Schenck,

Mr. Akins,	Mr. Cantine,
Mr. E. Clark,	Mr. Bloom,
Mr. Patterson,	Mr. Smith.
Mr. Scudder,	

FOR THE AFFIRMATIVE.

Mr. Carman,	Mr. Low,
Mr. B. Livingston,	Mr. Bancker,
Mr. Gilbert,	Mr. Vandervoort,
Mr. Seaman,	Mr. Rockwell,
Mr. Harison,	Mr. Verplanck,
Mr. Hoffman,	Mr. Cornwell,
Mr. Watts,	Mr. Giles,
Mr. Livingston,	Mr. Gardiner,
Mr. Horton	Mr. Macomb.

That Mr. Macomb then made a motion, that the word *immediately* be obliterated, and the words *as early as possible*, inserted after the word *called.*

That the question having been put, whether the committee did agree to the amendment proposed by the motion of Mr. Macomb, it was carried in the affirmative, in the manner following, viz.

FOR THE AFFIRMATIVE.

Mr. Jones,	Mr. Low,
Mr. Carman,	Mr. Bancker,
Mr. Gilbert,	Mr. Vandervoort,
Mr. Seaman,	Mr. Havens,
Mr. Kortz,	Mr. Verplanck,
Mr. Stauring,	Mr. Schenck,
Mr. Harison,	Mr. Cornwell,
Mr. Hoffman,	Mr. Giles,
Mr. Savage,	Mr. Gardiner,
Mr. Thompson,	Mr. Macomb,
Mr. Livingston,	Mr. Cantine,
Mr. Horton,	Mr. Smith,
Mr. Tappen,	Mr. Watts,
Mr. J. Smith,	Mr. B. Livingston.

FOR THE NEGATIVE

Mr. G. Livingston,	Mr. Carpenter,
Mr. Frey,	Mr. D'Witt,
Mr. SPEAKER,	Mr. Wisner,
Mr. Van Dyck,	Mr. Adgate,
Mr. J. Van Rensselaer,	Mr. Harper,
Mr. Veeder,	Mr. Akins,
Mr. Winn,	Mr. E. Clark,
Mr. Duncan,	Mr. Patterson,
Mr. M'Cracken,	Mr. Scudder,
Mr. Bay,	Mr. Bloom.
Mr. Schoonmaker,	

That Mr. Livingston then made a motion for an amendment, to obliterate the words, *the said Constitution*, and instead thereof to insert the words, *amendments proposed by this or the other States*, whereby that part of the said paragraph, would be in the words following, viz.

"We, the Legislature of the State of New-York, do, in behalf of our Constituents, in the most earnest and solemn manner, make this application to the Congress, that a Convention of Deputies from the several States be called as early as possible, with full powers to take *the amendments proposed by this or other States*, into their consideration."

That the question having been put, whether the committee did agree to the amendment proposed by the motion of Mr. Livingston, it passed in the negative, in the manner following, viz.

FOR THE NEGATIVE.

Mr. Jones,	Mr. J. Smith,
Mr. Carman,	Mr. Bancker,
Mr. G. Livingston,	Mr. D'Witt,
Mr. Kortz,	Mr. Wisner,
Mr. Frey,	Mr. Vandervoort,
Mr. Speaker,	Mr. Adgate,
Mr. Van Dyck,	Mr. Harper,
Mr. J. Van Rensselaer,	Mr. Havens,
Mr. Harison,	Mr. Schenck,
Mr. Hoffman,	Mr. Akins,
Mr. Veeder,	Mr. E. Clark,
Mr. Winn,	Mr. Patterson,
Mr. Savage,	Mr. Scudder,
Mr. M'Cracken,	Mr. Gardiner,
Mr. Thompson,	Mr. Macomb,
Mr. Bay,	Mr. Cantine,
Mr. Schoonmaker,	Mr. Bloom,
Mr. Tappen,	Mr. Smith.
Mr. Carpenter,	

FOR THE AFFIRMATIVE.

Mr. B. Livingston,	Mr. Watts,
Mr. Gilbert,	Mr. Livingston,
Mr. Seaman,	Mr. Low,
Mr. H. Van Rensselaer,	Mr. Verplanck,
Mr. Duncan,	Mr. Giles.

That the resolution and application reported by the committee appointed for that purpose, being amended, is in the words following, viz.

"*Resolved*, (if the Honorable the Senate concur therein) that an application be made to the Congress of the United States of America, in the name and behalf of the Legislature of this [state], in the words following, to wit:

The People of the State of New York, having ratified the Constitution agreed to on the seventeenth day of September, in the year of our Lord, 1787, by the Convention then assembled at Philadelphia, in the State of Pennsylvania, as explained by the said ratification, in the fullest confidence of obtaining a revision of the said Constitution, by a General Convention; and in confidence that certain powers in and by said Constitution granted, would not be exercised, until a Convention should have been called and convened, for proposing amendments to the said Constitution. In compliance therefore, with the unanimous sense of the Convention of this State, who all united in opinion, that such a revision was necessary to recommend the said Constitution, to the approbation and support of a numerous body of their Constituents; and a majority of the members of which, conceived several articles of the Constitution so exceptionable, that nothing but such confidence, and an invincible reluctance to separate from our sister States, could have prevailed upon a sufficient number to assent to it, without stipulating for previous amendments: And from a conviction, that the apprehensions and discontents which those articles occasion, cannot be removed or allayed, unless an act to revise the said Constitution be among the first that shall be passed by the new Congress: WE, *the Legislature of the State of New York,* DO, in the behalf of our Constituents, in the *most earnest and solemn manner,* make this application to the Congress, that a Convention of Deputies from the several States be called as early as possible, with full powers to take the said Constitution into their consideration, and to propose such amendments thereto, as they shall find best calculated to promote our common interests, and secure to ourselves and our latest posterity, the great and unalienable rights of mankind."

That the said resolution and application having been read, the question was put whether the committee did agree to the same, and that it was carried in the affirmative, in the manner following, viz.

FOR THE AFFIRMATIVE.

Mr. Jones,	Mr. Tappen,
Mr. Carman,	Mr. Carpenter,
Mr. Gilbert,	Mr. J. Smith,
Mr. G. Livingston,	Mr. Low,
Mr. Kortz,	Mr. Bancker,
Mr. Frey,	Mr. D'Witt,
Mr. Stauring,	Mr. Wisner,
Mr. SPEAKER,	Mr. Vandervoort,
Mr. Van Dyck,	Mr. Adgate,
Mr. J. Van Rensselaer,	Mr. Harper,
Mr. Harison,	Mr. Havens,
Mr. Hoffman,	Mr. Rockwell,
Mr. Veeder,	Mr. Schenck,
Mr. Winn,	Mr. Akins,
Mr. Duncan,	Mr. E. Clark,
Mr. Savage,	Mr. Patterson,
Mr. M'Cracken,	Mr. Scudder,
Mr. Thompson,	Mr. Gardiner,
Mr. Livingston,	Mr. Cantine,
Mr. Bay,	Mr. Bloom,
Mr. Schoonmaker,	Mr. Smith.
Mr. Horton,	

FOR THE NEGATIVE.

Mr. B. Livingston,	Mr. Watts,
Mr. Seaman,	Mr. Verplanck,
Mr. Barker,	Mr. Giles,
Mr. H. Van Rensselaer,	Mr. Macomb.

That it was thereupon *Resolved*, that the committee did agree to the said resolution and application, which he was directed to report to the House; and he read the report in his place, and delivered the said draft of a resolution and application in at the table; where the same were again read, and agreed to by the House. Thereupon,

Resolved, (if the Honorable the Senate concur therein) That an application be made to the Congress of the United States of America, in the name and behalf of the Legislature of this State, in the words following, to wit:

THE PEOPLE OF THE STATE OF NEW-YORK, having ratified the Constitution agreed to on the seventeenth day of September, in the year of our Lord one thousand seven hundred and eighty seven, by the Convention then assembled at Philadelphia, in the State of Pennsylvania, as explained by the said ratification, in the fullest confidence of obtaining a revision of the said Constitution, by a General Convention; and in confidence, that certain powers in and by the said Constitution granted, would not be exercised, until a Convention should have been called and convened, for proposing amendments to the said Constitution. In compliance therefore, with the *unanimous* sense of the Convention of this State, who all united in opinion, that such a revision was necessary to recommend the said Constitution to the approbation and support of a numerous body of their Constituents; and a majority of the members of which, conceived several articles of the Constitution so exceptionable, that nothing but such confidence, and an invincible reluctance to separate from our sister States, could have prevailed upon a sufficient number to assent to it, without stipulating for previous amendments: And from a conviction, that the apprehensions and discontents which those articles occasion, cannot be removed or allayed, unless an act to revise the said Constitution, be among the first that shall be passed by the new Congress: WE, *the Legislature of the State of New-York,* DO, in behalf of our Constituents, in the *most earnest and solemn manner*, make this application to the Congress, that a Convention of Deputies from the several States be called, as early as possible, with full powers to take the said Constitution into their consideration, and to propose such amendments thereto, as they shall find best calculated to promote our common interests, *and secure to ourselves and our latest posterity, the great and unalienable rights of mankind.*

Ordered, That Mr. Jones and Mr. Carman deliver a copy of the preceding resolution, to the Honorable the Senate.

A message from the Honorable the Senate, delivered by Mr. Roosevelt and Mr. Townsend, with the bill therein mentioned was read, that the Senate do adhere to their amendments to the bill entitled *An act for prescribing the times, places, and manner of holding elections for Senators of the United States of America, to be chosen in this State*, which were not concurred in by this House.

Thereupon *Resolved*, That a conference be held with the Honorable the Senate, on their amendments to the said bill, which were not concurred in by this House; and that such conference be held on Monday next, at eleven of the clock in the forenoon, at such place as the Honorable the Senate shall be pleased to appoint for that purpose.

The House then pursuant to the fifteenth article of the Constitution of this State, proceeded to choose by ballot, a committee to manage the said conference on the part of this House; and the ballots being taken, it appeared that Mr. Jones, Mr. G. Livingston and Mr. Bay, were duly elected for that purpose. Thereupon,

Resolved, That Mr. Jones, Mr. G. Livingston and Mr. Bay, be a committee to manage said conference, on the part of this House.

Ordered, That Mr. Jones and Mr. Carman, deliver a copy of the two last preceding resolutions, to the Honorable the Senate.

The Senate

A message from the Honorable the Assembly, by Mr. Jones and Mr. Carman, was received with the following resolution for concurrence, which was read, viz. . . .[1]

Thereupon,

Ordered, That the consideration of the said resolution be postponed.

With the same message was received, the following resolutions, which were read, viz.

Resolved, That a conference be held with the Honorable the Senate, on their amendments to the bill, entitled *An act for prescribing the times, places and manner of holding elections for Senators of the United States of America, to be chosen in this State*, and that such conference be held on Monday next, at eleven of the clock in the forenoon, at such place as the Honorable the Senate shall be pleased to appoint for that purpose.

Resolved, That Mr. Jones, Mr. G. Livingston and Mr. Bay, be the conferees to manage the said conference on the part of this House. Thereupon,

Resolved, That the Senate will meet the Honorable the Assembly on Monday next, at eleven of the clock in the forenoon, at the Assembly-Chamber, to hold the conference proposed by that Honorable House on the bill, entitled *An act for prescribing the times, places and manner of holding elections for Senators of the United States of America, to be chosen in this State.*

Resolved, That Mr. Duane, Mr. L'Hommedieu and Mr. Philip Schuyler, be the conferees to manage the said conference on the part of the Senate.

Ordered, That Mr. Townsend and Mr. Tredwell, deliver a copy of the two last preceding resolutions to the Honorable the Assembly.

1. For the text of the second convention resolution, see Assembly Proceedings, immediately above.

New York Journal, 5 February

We learn, by yesterday's stage, that another conference was to take place between the senate and assembly on the bill for choosing senators to the new Congress; and that it was the current opinion at Albany that neither house would recede from their first principles.[1]

1. This article was reprinted in the *Country Journal*, 10 February 1789; Philadelphia *Federal Gazette*, 13 February; Philadelphia *Pennsylvania Packet*, 13 February; and Philadelphia *Pennsylvania Mercury*, 14 February.

Federal Gazette (Philadelphia), 6 February

Extract of a letter from New-York, dated 2d inst.

You complain much in Pennsylvania of the virulent party spirit that prevails among you; but never have the effects of party contests been so disgraceful in that state as in this. For with you who have a single legislative body, a majority rules; but with us one branch of the legislature counteracts the proceedings of the other, and the utmost dissentions have for some time past subsisted between the two houses. In consequence of this New-York will have no vote in the choice of a president and vice-president of the United States; so that governor Clinton has no chance of being chosen. And what is still worse, it is to be feared that this state will have no senators in Congress at their first meeting when the great question of "where shall Congress reside?" will be warmly agitated; so that it is generally apprehended that after all our expence in preparing for their reception we must inevitably lose their company, as the southern states seem very clamorous for their removal to a more central situation. Such, my friend, are the deplorable effects to be dreaded from dissentions among ourselves![1]

1. This article was reprinted in the Philadelphia *Pennsylvania Packet*, 7 February 1789; Philadelphia *Independent Gazetteer*, 10 February; *Morning Post*, 12 February; Boston *Herald of Freedom*, 20 February; *Providence Gazette*, 28 February; and *Pittsburgh Gazette*, 21 March.

Assembly and Senate Proceedings, Saturday, A.M., 7 February

The Senate

The Senate proceeded to the consideration of the resolution from the Honorable the Assembly, of the 5th instant, respecting an application to Congress, to call a Convention for the purpose of considering the amendments proposed to the new Constitution. Debates arose thereon, and Mr. President having put the question, whether the Senate do concur with the Honorable the Assembly, in their said resolution, it was carried in the affirmative, by all the Members present, excepting *Mr. Douw* and *Mr. Lawrance.*

Thereupon, *Resolved*, That the Senate do concur with the Honorable the Assembly, in their said resolution.

Ordered, That Mr. Tredwell and Mr. L'Hommedieu, deliver a copy of the preceding concurrent resolution to the Honorable the Assembly.

The Assembly

A copy of resolutions of the Honorable the Senate, delivered by Mr. Townsend and Mr. Tredwell, with the bill therein mentioned, was read, that the Senate will meet this House on Monday next, at eleven of the clock in the forenoon, at the Assembly-Chamber, to hold a conference on the bill entitled *An act for prescribing the times, places and manner of holding elections for Senators of the United States of America, to be chosen in this State*; and that Mr. Duane, Mr. L'Hommedieu and Mr. Philip Schuyler, be a committee to manage the said conference, on the part of the Senate. . . .

A copy of a resolution of the Honorable the Senate, delivered by Mr. Tredwell and Mr. L'Hommedieu, was read, concurring with this House in their resolution, and an application of the Legislature (as inserted in the Journal of this House on the fifth day of February instant) to the Congress of the United States of America, that a Convention of Deputies be called, for a revision of the Constitution of the said United States.[1]

1. The second convention resolution was printed in many newspapers, beginning with the *Daily Advertiser*, 12 February 1789. On 27 February the Assembly resolved to "request" the governor to transmit the resolution to Congress and to send copies to the governors of the other states (for transmittal to their legislatures). A motion to kill the provision for sending copies to the governors of the other states was defeated on a roll call vote of 28 to 15. The Senate concurred with the Assembly resolution on 3 March.

David Brearley to Tench Coxe, Trenton, 7 February[1]

I was honoured with your Letter of the 31st. ult. on thursday last for which I am extremely obliged to you.—it contained much necessary information and I can only regret that it did not arrive a day earlier.[2]

With regard to Mr. Adams I think that there can be no doubt but that he will be the Vice President, even if he should not have a majority of the whole number of votes, which I apprehend he will, yet he will certainly have by far the largest number of votes, except General Washington, which will unquestionably secure him the office.

You appear to be of opinion that New York may yet appoint Electors of a President, as the Resolution accompanying the Constitution is considered not to be binding.—The resolution is a temporary matter, and therefore is perhaps no part of the Constitution, but the constitution itself settles this business, I apprehend, beyond a controversy. In the 1 sec. of the 2 Art. are these words, "The Congress may determine the time of choosing the Electors, and the day on which they shall give their votes; *which day shall be the same throughout the united States.*" It appears to me that upon the present occasion the day of election is past.

1. RC, Tench Coxe Papers, PHi. Brearley, a presidential Elector in New Jersey, had—along with the other Electors—voted for President on 4 February. Coxe's letter of 31 January has not been located. For a biographical sketch of Brearley, see Chapter XII.

2. "Thursday last," 5 February 1789, was the day after the balloting for President.

Abraham B. Bancker to Evert Bancker, Albany, 8 February (excerpt)[1]

Tomorrow we shall have a third Conference on the Senates Amendments to the Bill for choosing Senators, the Majority in the one House differing in Sentiment with the Majority of the other[.] I Expect the Bill will fall through unless one or two of the Senators should change in their Votes- more on the Subject of Election when I write again

1. RC, Bancker Family Papers, NHi. The letter was addressed to Evert Bancker in New York City.

Joint Conference Committee Debates, Monday, 9 February[1]

Agreeable to the resolution of the two houses, the senate attended, when the conferrence was opened—the subject being read.

Mr. *G. Livingston.*—Mr. President, the bill which has just been read, on which the present conferrence is held, respects the election of senators, to represent this state in the Congress of the United States.—The house of assembly have during this present sessions, passed a bill for putting into operation the new government, wherein was contained provision for appointing electors to chuse a president and vice-president—for chusing senators—and for the election of representatives. This bill, Sir, was lost after a conferrence had thereon, between the two houses of which this legislature is composed—the senate adhering to amendments to the said bill, which the house of assembly did not suppose they could constitutionally agree to: Since the loss of the bill above mentioned, a separate bill for the election of representatives has passed both houses, and has become a law: A bill only providing for the appointing electors, has likewise passed the house of assembly—and after passing through the like process with the bill first above mentioned, for the same reasons was likewise finally lost: Besides those before mentioned, two bills have been sent to the house of assembly, from the honorable the senate, the one providing for the appointment of electors—the other for appointing senators; these bills were brought while the bill first above mentioned was under consideration, and just before it passed. By the common mode of doing business, the assembly went into committee on these bills, and finding them drawn on principles which (they conceived) contravened the spirit as well as the letter of the state constitution not only, but also the spirit of the new constitution (and consonant to which, the amendments which came from the honorable the senate to the bill first mentioned, were likewise made)—they were therefore both rejected. The bill now before us must be the last which can at this sessions come under consideration on this subject. Here again by the amendments proposed the old controversy turns up. The assembly, sir, suppose their allegiance to the state constitution not dissolved, and therefore, in electing members to represent this state in the general government of the United States, that they are bound by the mode for that purpose inserted therein: The bill, sir, is introduced by two recitals, the first is, of the clause from the state constitution which provides for the appointment of members of Congress, by joint ballot of the two houses, where there may be any difference in the nomination: The second is of the clause in the new constitution, which directs the chusing of senators to represent each state in the Congress of the United States—to the last of these recitals the honorable the senate have proposed an amendment, which expressly declares, that "the before recited clause of the constitution of this state is become of no effect;" to this declaration the house of assembly have great objections.—Tho' they grant that the new constitution supercedes the old one, yet they hold, that this must be expressly done, or that the state constitution still binds with its full force. With permission, sir, I will endeavor to contrast them, by which we will see the propriety of our still adhering to our bill, and with it to the state constitution.

I would ask—

1st. Who are to be chosen?

The answer is—Representatives of this state, as a state.

2d. In what government are they to exercise their powers?

Answer—In a general government of the confederated states of America.

3d. By whom are they to be appointed or chosen?

Answer—By the legislature of this state.

4th. By what name are those representatives called?

Answer—Members of the Congress of the United States of America.

Suppose, sir, that no such instrument or compact, as that of the constitution of this state, ever to have existed, and the same questions put, (as those I have just now mentioned) on the articles of the new constitution, respecting the chusing of senators. The same answers, will be as just and true in the one case, as they are in the other. Do not these questions and their answers contain the whole essence, spirit, and effect of the clauses under consideration in each of the constitutions? Are they not therefore, not only consistent with each other, but do they not perfectly agree, in each of the particulars just mentioned? This I think, sir, candor must grant—Then, sir, to what will it tend to hold up an idea, that the part of the state constitution now under consideration, is virtually repealed by the new one? I know of no other answer, than that the more of it is done away, the less strength will remain to resist any attempt which hereafter may be made to fritter away the privileges we now enjoy under it.

At present I conceive there is no essential difference either in the mode of election, the body which elect, or the object to which the persons are elected, under the several clauses in the respective constitutions—and (in my opinion) the only difference which *caution* itself can apprehend, is this, that the first provided for electing representatives in a *free state*—but this may not long be the case under the second.

The 3d section of the 1st article of the new constitution, directs that "The senate of the United States shall be composed of two senators from each state, chosen by the legislature thereof." Sir, it is agreed on all hands, that this clause is binding on us, since the adoption of the new constitution.—Now, sir, what is the duty of the legislature, under the clause just mentioned? The answer is easy—We are to chuse two senators. Another question arises, which is—How is this choice to be made? The 4th sect. of the said 1st article directs, that "the times, places, and manner of holding elections for senators, &c. shall be prescribed in each state by the legislature thereof." Now, sir, does the amendment proposed by the honorable the senate, contain a *manner* for holding this *election*, which will answer the purposes required in the articles of the general government before mentioned? I will concisely examine it, and I trust the result will answer this question in the negative.

Every plan which is founded in wisdom, should be efficient, that is, it should contain principles and directions, which if pursued, will infallibly in the event, produce the end or effect desired. The amendment directs "that in every case where two senators are to be chosen, and both houses agree as to one, in such nomination as aforesaid, and in every case when only one senator is to be chosen, either of the two houses of the legislature *may* propose to the other a resolution for concurrence, naming therein a person to fill the office of a senator, and if the house receiving such resolution *shall concur therein*, the person so named in such resolution shall be the senator: *but if such resolution be not concurred in*, either house *may* on that or any other future day, proceed to offer to the other a resolution for concurrence *from time to time*, until they shall agree upon a senator." I have recited only such part of the amendment as respects the choice of only one senator—That part which respects the choice of two, I shall consider when I examine our right of adopting the mode proposed, in any case whatever. Now, sir, does not the amendment suppose a non-concurrence to the resolution which may be sent from one house to the other?—And does it not expressly provide, that either house *may from time to time* offer other resolutions for concurrence, until they shall agree upon a senator? Here we find that either house may; but it is not said they *shall* ever originate new resolutions—but, sir, had the amendment gone so far, as to *oblige* the houses, or one of them, to have originated new resolutions, yet the house to which the resolution may be sent, is not, and perhaps ought not, to be obliged to concur—nay, very possibly *would not* give their assent to the person proposed. This, sir, from the present complexion of things, is *at least a supposeable case*—Where is this to end? Is the legislature to spend a whole sessions in resolving and non concurring: I hold it right of matters of the kind, and of the importance of the one now under consideration, that every supposeable case ought to be supposed: Certainly it cannot be wise or politic to lay the foundation of a government, (which from the many predictions concerning it, is to last to ages far distant) on a base so tottering—so sandy—as that a shower of dissention, and a gale of party, between the two branches of the legislature, may sap the very foundation-stone of the strongest pillar, which is to support the grand expanded arch of this sumptuous temple—and thus lay prostrate in the dust, the *desire* and expectation of its friends and admirers. This might well happen, for if it is right, and the best mode in this state; it will be so in others—and if so, we must suppose it will be adopted—In that case, the calamitous disaster I just mentioned, is at least to be dreaded as a consequence, which possibly might follow the adoption of such a plan, as that proposed in the amendment. This objection, and the consequence which may result from it, I am confident the honorable the senate did not contemplate, or they would not have adopted a system, an attempt to execute which, may endanger the very existence of this sumptuous edifice, they would certainly have secured its very ground work better. We, sir, the house of assembly, in sentiment with the honorable the convention of this state, which adopted it, have an equal wish, that such measures may be followed, as well with respect to its beginning as its progress, as that this pile may rise fair and strong, that the foundation of it may be fixed on the rock of wisdom, and the pieces of marble of which its pillars shall be composed, may be united by a cement, the chief ingredient of which, will be equal liberty, and that the key stone of its principal arch may be *merited public confidence.* Against a building thus founded, and thus reared, party and dissention will rage in vain. We look forward with pleasure at the prospect, that our posterity, for ages yet to come, may be sheltered, secured and defended (by its expanding, yet impenetrable roof) against the assaults of tyranny, whether in the shape of wide deluging torrents, or by its rays collected in a more irresistable manner into a focus of oppression.

I think, sir, that I have sufficiently shewn that the clauses before mentioned, in each of the constitutions, perfectly harmonize; if this be true, it certainly follows, that the mode of election pointed out in the state constitution is binding on us in its full force. But, sir, if this was not the case, the new constitution itself, in our apprehension, equally determines us against adopting the amendment, or any part of it—this directs that the senators shall be "chosen" (which means the same thing as to be *elected*) now if the two houses in their separate political capacity, are to make a choice, or hold an election, they are and must be considered in the same situation, with two individuals holding an election, and all the reasoning which will apply, in the one case, will be true in the other.

Let us consider how this will operate; suppose two men are to hold an election: If A votes for the man he thinks best qualified to fill the office, and proposes him to B, he, not having the same opinion of the candidate as A has, cannot agree in the election. B proposes a second to A, under the same circumstances as the first, this one is likewise rejected. They may proceed thus, proposing and rejecting, till the time perhaps elapses, in which the business is to be performed, by the officer to be chosen; or some other incident happens, which may be fatal to the end proposed; or if they chose at all, it may be the effect of accommodation, wherein perhaps only A has his choice, or more probably, neither A or B appoint the man which either of them best approve.

This, sir, I think is sound reasoning, and tends to shew, that the proper idea of an election, by a legislature composed of two houses, is totally distinct from the one held up in the amendment proposed by the honorable the senate, but that it is essentially necessary, for the purpose of an *election*, that the members of the two houses, be considered in their individual capacity, as members of the legislature only, without respect to either of the houses in particular; and this, sir, will bring us to the solid, safe, and efficient ground on which the bill is formed, to wit, that of the state constitution, where a joint ballot always has, and ever will, give us the object required.—I have endeavoured, Mr. President, to state my objections, and which I take to be, at least a part of the objections (of the house I have the honor to represent) to the amendments now under consideration, and if I have the happiness to be understood, and if the reasoning urged has the same weight with the honorable the senate, as it has with us, the amendments will be receded from, and on the old tried mode of the state constitution, a choice will be rendered certain.

I would here just remark, that the members of convention, which founded the newly adopted plan of government, were chosen in this manner; then why not proceed in the same way to ensure its continuance. This, sir, is the third conference the two houses have had on the subject of putting the new government into operation.

It is really something extraordinary that though both houses have appeared as desirous that this event might take place, as the children of Israel were to have a change in their government, and to have a king appointed over them, like their neighbouring nations, the severe, repeated and pointed admonitions and warnings of *Samuel*, notwithstanding; yet so it has happened in the course of events, as that this state has not had the honor of a voice in electing the head of the new government; this ruler, who is to go in and out before the people. This calamitous circumstance notwithstanding, I still hope that we shall be so happy as to participate with our sister states in all the salutary consequences, which we all, with eager expectations, look for, from this great and sudden revolution. And I farther hope, that we shall not, in *like manner*, lose our representation in so important a branch, in this new government, as that of the senate of the United States.

Upon the whole, sir, we of this house think we stand on firm ground; first, because our foundation is constitutional with respect to the new government, as well as that of our own state; and secondly, because our mode is efficient, and will infallibly produce an election, whereas the amendment proposed, we conceive is not conformable at least to the spirit of either constitutions, but might, and probably would (if adopted) be a *felo de se.*

Mr. *L'Hommedieu.*—Mr. Speaker, it cannot be expected that any thing new can be offered on a subject so lately discussed at a former conference. This bill except the preamble, with the amendments, were contained in the bill which was lost at a conference lately held between the two houses. The amendment to the preamble is in some measure expressive of the reasons which induced the senate not to concur with the honourable assembly in their bill, and to return the same with the like amendment, which was returned with their former bill relative to the choice of senators.

The senate are of opinion, that the clause in the constitution of this state, recited in the preamble of this bill, when applied to the choice of senators, is become of no effect; because the only authority by which they can be appointed, is derived from the constitution of the United States, which being the last act of the people, is superior to any law or constitution of the state (in every case where their provisions vary.) This constitution directs that the choice of senators shall be made by the *legislature of the state*—this legislature by the state constitution is declared to consist of two distinct & separate bodies of men, the one called the assembly, and the other the senate.—By the same constitution this senate and assembly are vested with equal powers, and equal negative in all cases except where the same is otherwise directed. The consequence is, that in this case the senate are not at liberty to agree to the bill of the honourable the assembly for the choice of senators by joint ballot, without violating the constitution by which the people, for the security of their liberties vested in the senate, (though inferior in numbers,) equal powers and an equal negative with the honourable assembly.

How far the state constitution as to the election of delegates, after the ratification of the *confederation* was binding, or whether the legislature could not have directed the *election* to be made by the people at large, is a question which, (perhaps) at present is unnecessary to discuss—that *confederation* directed, that delegates should be annually appointed in such manner as the legislature of each state should direct, by which the election was not confined to any particular body of men, it might have been made by the people at large, or in such other manner as the legislature should direct—But the constitution of the United States, confines the choice of senators, and directs that the choice be made, not in such manner as the legislature may direct, not by the people at large, not by the senate and assembly by joint ballot in their individual capacity, but by *the legislature of the state.*

In every point of view in which this question has been considered by the senate, they are of opinion, that the article of the state constitution, respecting the election of delegates, and recited in the preamble of this bill, is become of no effect when applied to senators, (whose powers are in every respect different from delegates elected under the confederation) and is no more a rule or obligatory on the legislature in this case, than the mode pursued by any other state for the election of their delegates: And that the legislature of this state have the same liberty in directing the mode for the choice of their senators, as they might have had in case that article in the state constitution respecting the election of delegates, had never been made or put in practice; even the originating this bill suggests the idea, that a doubt at least must have arisen whether that clause in the constitution was of any effect, when applied to the choice of senators, for whence the necessity of fixing the mode of that choice by law, which requires the concurrence of both houses, when it is contended that the mode of choosing, to be enacted by the law, is binding without the law, upon this principle the bill would be unnecessary except as to the time and place.

The only question now remaining, in the opinion of the senate, is which is the best mode for making the choice of senators by the legislature.

The senate are not tenacious of any particular mode, provided the same is warranted by the constitution which gives them equal powers, and an equal negative, with the honourable assembly, which equal powers and equal negative, could not be designed to be impaired or abridged by the constitution of the United States, directing the choice to be made by the legislature; and if a choice of senators can be made by the legislature, or in other words, by the senate and assembly in their legislative capacity, and not by joint ballot (as individuals) then the article of the constitution of the United States, directing the choice of senators to be made by the legislature, and the constitution of this state, vesting equal powers in the two branches of the legislature are perfectly consistent, and is the only mode by which such choice can constitutionally be made.—Such choice can be made; and it is to be presumed; will be made in the mode proposed by the amendment to the bill, if the same is agreed to by the honourable assembly; senators have been chosen in other states in a mode similar to the one proposed by the amendment, and in one at least where their constitution directed the election of their delegates by joint ballot of both houses;[2] and why cannot the choice of senators be made in like manner by the legislature in this state? Has that mode ever failed where it has been tried? It has not. Has not a treasurer been annually appointed by a rule in the constitution, by which the negative of the senate is preserved? Are we alarmed lest a treasurer might not be elected? We are not. Nor ought we to distrust the legislature's doing their duty in the choice of senators. It ought always to be presumed, and it is presumed by every state, that the legislature will perform every necessary act required of them by the constitution of the United States, and of their own state; and if part of that time which has been lost in originating bills and holding conferences upon the mode proposed by this bill, had been applied in making a choice in such mode that the equal rights of both houses would be preserved, 'tis probable, that long before this time, senators would have been chosen to the satisfaction of the senate and assembly.

It is said that the mode prescribed by the bill insures a choice with greater certainty and dispatch than the one proposed by the amendment; but will it follow, if we admit it, that it is the best mode—that the liberties of the people are best secured—or that the senate are at liberty to consent to such mode without violating that constitution which gives them equal rights with the honorable the assembly, and which they hold themselves obliged to support and maintain for the liberties of the people.

The principal of the objection against the equal powers and equal negative of the senate, in their opinion, goes too far: by the same reasoning it applies to the passing of all necessary laws—to the appointment of necessary commissions—and especially to the appointment of a treasurer.

On a former conference on this subject, it was observed on the part of the senate, that the inference which was made against the equal rights of the senate (for which they contended) from the words *chosen* and *election* being used in the constitution of the United States, directing the choice of senators, could not be just; when by the clause in the constitution of this state, directing the appointment of a treasurer, the words *appoint* and *elected* are used, altho' he must be appointed by act of the legislature, in which the senate have a negative.

The senate equally regret with the honorable the assembly, the unhappy difference of sentiment which has subsisted between the two houses on this subject, and deprecate the evils which may ensue.

They are equally anxious with the honorable assembly that the legislature should be represented in the senate of the United States, and are sincerely disposed to accommodate, by every means in their power, to the views of the honorable assembly, if it can be done without violating the rights of either house. But at the same time they cannot, consistently with the duty they owe to their country, and the solemn obligations they are under not to sacrifice the rights of the people, committed to them by the constitution, concur in this bill for the election of senators, in such manner that the senate might only be solemn witnesses to the choice of the honorable assembly.

Mr. *Jones*—Mr President, little can be said that will be new; indeed it cannot be expected, as we have so recently held two conferences, in which the same arguments were brought forward, that may be, and I suppose will be applied, to the present occasion.

It is to be regretted, that any thing is contested but the mode; the question however as it stands on constitutional ground, must again be brought into view; as on a former occasion we were told that the legislature might exercise their discretion; and it is now said that the senate must adhere to a principle from which they cannot deviate. In framing the bill for electing the senators of the United States, to be chosen in this state, the assembly examined both the constitution of their own state, and the constitution of the United States, in that of their own state, they find an article which points out the mode of electing members of the General Government of the United States, and they find that that mode is still a constitutional mode in this state—their reasoning is this, the constitution of the state of New York was formed before the confederation, in it there is an article which declared that the delegates to the general government, should be chosen in such manner as the *legislature* of the state should direct. It is well known that in carrying into execution that confederation no difficulty was found; the legislature proceeded in the mode directed by the constitution of the state. It appears therefore to the assembly, on a full investigation of the matter, that that article of the constitution of the state of New York, was formed with a view to a general government, and intended to apply to any general government, however modified, in which the state, as a state, was to be represented. This they conceive a fair and just construction of the constitution; and this doubtless was the reasoning of the legislature, when they applied it to the confederation.—Might not the senate at that time, have come forward, and said, here are new powers given, the duration of the delegate is fixed, the number to be chosen is fixed, they may be recalled, &c. might they not I say, as well have come forward with pretensions, that these things were not contemplated by the state constitution, that therefore it was of no effect. Is there not a similarity of situation, between the senate that existed at that day, and the present senate. In my mind sir, the constitution of the state bears the same relation to that of the United States, as it did with the confederation. There is no doubt but the same arguments will apply to both cases. But what was the language of the legislature at that day, sir they conceived it their duty to observe those directions contained in the constitution of the state, and have practiced upon them ever since. The reasons that weighed with them, ought to have their influence now.

The arguments of the senate in favor of their amendment, that the new constitution, being the last act of the people must be adhered to, proves nothing, for the constitution of the state where it is not expressly repealed, or does not clash with the general government, must also be adhered to. The words of the new constitution are, two senators shall be chosen in each state, by the legislature thereof; does it follow that each branch shall have a negative?—Is it not more rational to say, that it shall be done in that mode of choice pointed out by the constitution of the state; and which mode has always been followed, and which has always been productive of a choice? But it is said that in that mode the senate will lose their negative, and that they are entitled to it by the constitution. Sir, their negative, as it respects laws has never been disputed; but is there no distinction between laws and elections? Is there any thing either in the state constitution, or the constitution of the United States, that gives the senate a negative in elections? For my part, I am at a loss to know whence the power is to be derived. Why should we deviate from our constitution? Why search for principles to alter that mode? It is no where said that both houses shall have a negative. Indeed it would be improper that such a negative should exist in cases of election; because it may destroy the very constitution itself. The whole weight of the argument rests on one word of the new constitution. The senate claim their right to a negative, because the choice is to be made by the legislature; and insists on its being done in the usual way that laws are passed; if the assembly conceive that this mode is not the one intended by the general government, and is contrary to the constitution under which they act, and cannot be adopted without invading these rights they are sent here to maintain. In order to determine what meaning the words shall have, we ought to examine the whole instrument in which they stand; and they are to receive an explication agreeable to the whole context. We are told that the treasurer of the state may be *appointed* by act of the legislature, but that he shall not be elected out of the legislature. Let us examine whether the article of the constitution of the state, which speaks of a treasurer, and that part of the constitution of the United States, which speaks of the election of senators, and the inferences drawn from the one to the other can apply. The article of the constitution declares that the treasurer shall be appointed by act of the legislature; but that he shall not be *elected* out of the legislature; what now is meant by election? Shall we take the word there in the appropriate sense, a choice by a number of individuals? It cannot mean that, because it is declared before, that the treasurer shall be *appointed*; the word *elected*, therefore, can mean no more than that he shall not be *taken* out of the legislature; it cannot mean an election by a plurality of voices, as an election in the appropriate use of the word[.] The terms in which the senate are spoken of in the constitution of the United States, shew clearly what kind of an election is to be held; they are to be *chosen* by the legislature of each state. If the meaning of this choice can be determined, then that question is in some measure decided. How are the legislature to choose? Are they to do it by law, to go through the ordinary forms of legislation? Is that a mode that will comport with the next direction of the constitution, that the time, place and manner of holding elections for senators, shall be prescribed in each state by the legislature thereof? The assembly cannot conceive how the time, place and manner of passing an act can be defined; the manner of doing it is fixed by the constitution; the legislature cannot vary it. The time cannot be fixed, when an act is to be passed, and yet the legislature to exercise their discretion. If the mode proposed by the bill is adopted, there will be an immediate election; if the amendment is agreed to, there may be none; for if each house retains its negative, they may conscientiously do their duty, and yet they may never agree in the choice of any two persons. The assembly suppose, therefore, that if the question was taken up on the single ground of the new constitution, that policy would direct the adoption of the mode proposed by the bill; because it is a mode that will produce the effect.—It is a principle that ought never to be forgotten; it is one on which the government must rest; it can never be prudent to put it in the power of the minority to defeat the intentions of the majority. By the amendment it may be in the power of thirteen, nay, sometimes seven individuals, to defeat any election—Can this be right? Ought not a law to carry the government of the United States into operation, to be so framed, as that it will keep that government in motion. Nothing can prevent an election on the plan proposed by the assembly;—on that proposed by the senate it never can be certain. If my information is right, it has been tried in some states, and accommodation at last produced the election. In Massachusetts it was tried in the choice of senators, and being found inconvenient, in that of electors, they recurred to the joint ballot.[3] To be brief, sir, the assembly conceive that they are bound by the constitution of the state, and the constitution of the United States, not to adopt the amendment of the senate—as departing from the principles they hold will be betraying the rights of their constituents—and perhaps defeat the general government itself.

The assembly are not a little surprised at the declarations made by the senate, that that article of the constitution is of no effect:—They cannot find when, nor by whom it has been repealed: They are astonished that the legislature should have acted on that article in the present session, and supposed it in full operation—and that now the assembly should be asked to accede to a proposition that it has become of no effect. Let what will be the consequence, they never can agree to such a recital; it would in their opinion be a repeal of the constitution by an act of the legislature. How far it would be right—how far it would be reasonable for them to agree to the amendment, under this view of the matter, they submit to the senate, hoping they will re-consider that recital, and ask themselves whether they can expect that the assembly can accede, or whether it is right for the senate to maintain such a principle. I will just remark on the impropriety of the bill as it will stand if the amendment is agreed to—It will then stand, that the senate and assembly may propose resolutions to each other from [time] to time, till they shall agree upon a senator or senators—and yet in the same bill it will be declared that they shall be appointed within ten days after passing the act: Sir, the bill will be at war with itself. Taking all these circumstances into consideration, the assembly never can agree to the proposition of the honorable the senate.

Mr *Duane*.—Mr. Speaker, It is assigned to me to close the business of this day, and I confess, after so much time has been fruitlessly spent, I feel some embarrassment in choosing the path which I ought to pursue. Besides the frequent and animated debates which have engrossed the attention of both houses in their separate deliberations, this is the third public conference which has taken place in the space of a few days, not indeed upon exactly the same point, but upon the very same principle. An event so novel and inauspicious must long be remembered with regret—while a practice has been introduced, highly detrimental both to dispatch of public business, and the harmony which ought to subsist between the different branches of the legislature. The senate most earnestly hope that this example will never be imitated!

Indeed, sir, the promptitude with which the honorable assembly rejected the two bills respecting senators and electors, sent by us for their concurrence—the transmission of others from their house on an opposite system, subversive of our constitutional rights, and the total inefficacy of both the conferences which ensued, precluded the prospect of conciliation[.] Unless our sincerity was distrusted, nothing could succeed but a modification consistent with that equality for which we had so strenuously contended, and so solemnly declared, could not be yielded up without the violation of a trust which we held sacred.

Under these impressions, it was little expected that a controversy, which had already been carried to an unexampled length; should again be revived by a third bill, cloathed indeed in a garb something different, to save appearances; but in principle, substance and effect, altogether the same as the former.

Those feelings, sir, which are natural to every upright heart could not but be excited at an operation so unusual. They were suppressed from an earnest solicitude on our part, that this state should have every chance, however remote of a representation in the general government: The feeblest ray of hope on a subject so deeply interesting, was thought a sufficient inducement to prefer an amendment to a rejection.

Thus, sir, dispensing with all exceptions against the regularity of these proceedings, we are once more brought forward in effect to vindicate our constitutional rights, as an independent branch of the legislature.

But, Mr. Speaker, how shall I proceed to perform the task assigned to me in a manner acceptable to the honorable assembly, or consistent with my own sense of propriety? Shall I repeat the arguments which have been so frequently labored to refute objections which already stand fully refuted? Shall I waste the time in enforcing constitutional principles, against which the honorable assembly have twice given judgment? Shall I hazard the charge of indecency, by supposing that what we so lately had the honor to submit to your consideration was not understood, or that it has already vanished in oblivion? Or shall I sit down in silence and suffer it to be implied, that the elaborate efforts of your honorable conferrees deserve no notice?

My repugnance, sir, to resume the debate shall yield to my respect for the honorable assembly who have been pleased to require this conference; and however I may be censured for vain repetitions, or a waste of time, on a subject so generally understood, I shall proceed to a reply, hoping for that indulgence to which the circumstances give me some claim.

He then went on to reply to the observations of the gentlemen who had spoke on the part of the assembly: This made it necessary for him to repeat those arguments which had been advanced at a former conference, and which again required to be brought into view, as an answer to those observations. In the course of this reply, he spoke in a clear, explicit and animated manner, and urged with great earnestness the necessity of moderation, and a cool and dispassionate decision of the question. But as there was little room for novelty, as nothing new had been advanced by the opposite party, it may be unnecessary therefore to detail the minute and ample answers that were given by him, especially as the arguments on this subject must be fresh in the memory of most of our readers.

[Gen. Schuyler being indisposed, did not attend the conference; in consequence of which Mr. Bay, who was one of the managers on the part of the assembly remained silent][4]

The Senate then withdrew.[5]

1. *Daily Advertiser*, 24 and 25 February 1789. The *Morning Post* printed virtually the same account on 27 and 28 February and 2 March.

2. Massachusetts chose its Senators with each house of the General Court retaining a negative on the nominations of the other. Massachusetts had elected delegates to the Confederation Congress by joint ballot (see DHFFE, I, 511–28).

3. With much difficulty, Massachusetts chose its Senators by joint resolution. The Massachusetts Election Resolutions, written before Senators were chosen, stipulated a joint session of the legislature, in combination with a popular vote, for choosing Electors (see DHFFE, I, 508–20).

4. These brackets are in the original newspaper printing.

5. This newspaper account concluded with the roll call by which the Assembly adhered to its bill (34 to 21), and with the notation that the Senate adhered to its amendments, "in consequence of which the bill was lost." For the roll call, see Assembly and Senate Proceedings, 9 February 1789, immediately below.

Assembly and Senate Proceedings, Monday, A.M., 9 February

The Senate

Mr. President left the chair, and with the Members of the Senate proceeded to the Assembly-Chamber, and met the Honorable the Assembly, for the purpose of holding the conference agreed upon by both Houses, by their respective resolutions of the fifth day of February instant, and after having held the said conference, the Senate returned to the Senate-Chamber, and Mr. President re-assumed the chair.

The Assembly

Mr. Speaker then left the chair, and with the House attended the Honorable the Senate, in the Assembly-Chamber, pursuant to the resolutions of both Houses, for holding a conference on the amendments to the bill entitled *An act for prescribing the times, places and manner for holding elections for Senators of the United States of America, to be chosen in this State*; and the said conference being ended, *Mr. Speaker* reassumed the chair, and reported to the House, that a conference had been held in the presence of both Houses, on the amendments proposed by the Honorable the Senate, to the said bill.

The House then having reconsidered the said bill and amendments, *Mr. Speaker* put the question, whether the House did adhere to the said bill, and it was carried in the affirmative, in the manner following, viz.

FOR THE AFFIRMATIVE.

Mr. Jones,	Mr. Tappen,
Mr. Carman,	Mr. Griffen,
Mr. G. Livingston,	Mr. Carpenter,
Mr. Kortz,	Mr. J. Smith,
Mr. Frey,	Mr. D'Witt,
Mr. Stauring,	Mr. Wisner,
Mr. Van Dyck,	Mr. Adgate,
Mr. J. Van Rennsselaer,	Mr. Harper,
Mr. Veeder,	Mr. Havens,
Mr. Winn,	Mr. Schenck,
Mr. Duncan,	Mr. Akins,
Mr. Tearse,	Mr. E. Clark,
Mr. Savage,	Mr. Patterson,
Mr. Webster,	Mr. Scudder,
Mr. Thompson,	Mr. Cantine,
Mr. Bay,	Mr. Bloom,
Mr. Schoonmaker,	Mr. Smith.

FOR THE NEGATIVE.

Mr. B. Livingston,	Mr. Horton,
Mr. Gilbert,	Mr. Low,
Mr. Van Cortlandt,	Mr. Bancker,
Mr. Seaman,	Mr. Vandervoort,
Mr. Barker,	Mr. Rockwell,
Mr. Harison,	Mr. Verplanck,
Mr. Hoffman,	Mr. Cornwell,
Mr. H. Van Rensselaer,	Mr. Giles,
Mr. Younglove,	Mr. Gardiner,
Mr. Watts,	Mr. Macomb.
Mr. Livingston,	

Thereupon *Resolved*, That this House do adhere to their said bill.

Ordered, That Mr. G. Livingston and Mr. Seaman deliver the bill, and a copy of the preceding resolution, to the Honorable the Senate.

The Senate

A message from the Honorable the Assembly, by Mr. G. Livingston and Mr. Seaman, was received, with the following resolution, which was read, viz.

Resolved, That this House do adhere to their bill, entitled *An act for prescribing the times, places and manner of holding elections for Senators of the United States of America, to be chosen in this State.*

Mr. Roosevelt thereupon moved, that the Senate do adhere to their amendments to the last mentioned bill.

Mr. Tredwell, as an amendment to the last motion moved, that the question on Mr. Roosevelt's motion be postponed until to-morrow, and Mr. President having put the question thereon, it passed in the negative by more than two thirds of the members.

Mr. President, then put the question on the first motion, viz: Whether the Senate do adhere to their amendments to the last mentioned bill, and it was carried in the affirmative, in manner following, viz.

FOR THE AFFIRMATIVE.

Mr. Philip Schuyler,	Mr. Lawrance,
Mr. Douw,	Mr. Morris,
Mr. Micheau,	Mr. Roosevelt,
Mr. Peter Schuyler,	Mr. L'Hommedieu,
Mr. Fonda,	Mr. Duane,
Mr. Vanderbilt,	Mr. Hoffman.

FOR THE NEGATIVE.

Mr. Yates,	Mr. Townsend,
Mr. Hopkins,	Mr. Tredwell,
Mr. Williams	Mr. Humfrey,
Mr. Van Ness,	Mr. Clinton,
Mr. Swartwout,	Mr. Hathorn.

Thereupon, *Resolved,* That the Senate do adhere to their amendments to the bill, entitled *An act for prescribing the times, places and manner of holding elections for Senators of the United States of America to be chosen in this State.*

Ordered, That Mr. L'Hommedieu and Mr. Duane, deliver a copy of the preceding resolution to the Honorable the Assembly.

Comte de Moustier Journal, 9 February[1]

Several days ago the New York Assembly again tried to agree on the form for the election of Senators. Accordingly they named deputies to go into conference, but since each party had resolved in advance not to bend, this conference was as fruitless as the preceding ones. According to the new Constitution, it will thus rest with the new Congress to determine the manner in which this election ought to take place.

1. MS (translated from French), Extraits du Journal de M. de Moustier, in Extraits des Papiers de la Légation de France aux Etats-Unis, I, Part II (Cahier 4), 5–6, Benjamin Franklin Collection, CtY.

Assembly Proceedings, Tuesday, A.M., 10 February

A copy of a resolution of the Honorable the Senate, delivered by Mr. L'Hommedieu and Mr. Duane, was read, that the Senate do adhere to their amendment to the bill entitled *An act for prescribing the times, places and manner of holding elections for Senators of the United States of America, to be chosen in this State.*

James Clinton to [William Cross], Albany, 13 February (excerpt)[1]

I havnt time to write you About Pollliticks[.] the Antes have A Large Majority in the Assembly[.] the Federals has A Majority of two in the Senate So that the Publick Business goes on Slowly As far as it Relates to the New Government we have not Chosen any Electors to Chose A President And Vice President Nor are we Likely to Chuse Senators for the Same[.] the Assembly wants to Chuse them Agreable to the Mode that the State Choose their Delegates for Congress Agreable to the State Constitution[.] the Senate wants A New Method As they say the Majority of both House's are Antes and of Consequence if that Mode is Adopted they can put in who they please[.] There is many Candidates for Govr. the Ensuing Election[.] the Federals first proposed Judge Morris and has Made Interest for him but Doubting his Interest would not do, they have fixed on Judge Yates in order to Devide the Govrs Interest but in that they will be Mistaken As Judge Yates friends are all Determined to Oppose his Election at this time As they know the Designs of the Federals. The Lieut Govr has taken Umbrage At their Preferring Judge Morris & Yates before him therefore he has Advertised himself for A Candidate in Case the People should Incline to Change the present Govr. The Antes has had A Meeting and are Unanimous to make no Change the Next Election in their Govr or Lt Governor[2]

1. RC, George and James Clinton Papers, DLC. The address page of the letter is missing, but written beneath Clinton's signature, in a different handwriting, is the notation: "To Wm Cross."

2. Prominently mentioned as candidates for governor were Richard Morris, Robert Yates (Chief Justice and justice of the state supreme court, respectively), and lieutenant governor Pierre Van Cortlandt.

James Monroe to Thomas Jefferson, Fredericksburg, Virginia, 15 February (excerpt)[1]

Your favor of the 9th. of August last has been recd.—before this I doubt not mine of a date subsequent to those you acknowledge has reach'd you. It gave you a detail of the proceedings of the convention of this State. Since which the eleven that have adopted the govt. under the act of Congress that was necessary to put them in motion have taken the necessary measures for its organization; except New York whose operations have been retarded, by some misunderstanding between the Senate & the other branch of the government. This obstacle will however I doubt not be remov'd since I have reason to believe, it has on neither side any other object in view than some arrangment suited to the prejudices of the pre-existing parties of that State. The publick papers say it respects the mode of appointing representatives.

1. RC, Jefferson Papers, DLC. Printed: Boyd, XIV, 557–59. For another excerpt from this letter, see DHFFE, II, 347. For a biographical sketch of Monroe, see DHFFE, II, 419.

Edward Carrington to Henry Knox, Richmond, 16 February (excerpt)[1]

It is a disagreable thing for difficulties to arise between the two Branches of a Legislature, but yet I cannot help rejoicing that the wild antifederalism of the lower House in New York has met with so firm a Check from the Senate—there is no doubt but that in a Combined vote of the whole together, the Senate would have had no influence in any choice which might have been made, and none but anti's would have come in. I hope the expected compromise did not issue in such a Manner as to blend the two Bodies in the business of voting.

1. RC, Knox Papers, MHi. For other excerpts from this letter, see DHFFE, II, 402–3, and Chapter XV. Knox (1750–1806), of Massachusetts, was secretary at war for the Confederation Congress. For a biographical sketch of Carrington, see DHFFE, II, 411.

John Lansing, Jr., to John Lamb, Albany, 18 February[1]

I was honored with Yours of the 4th Instant which [should] not have remained a Moment unanswered had I not wished particularly to ascertain the Opinion of our Friends on its subject Matter.

Sincerely disposed to take every Measure necessary to promote the common Cause, we have to regret that in this part of the State few very few have both Inclination & Ability to make any Advances to effect it—Hence the Burthen on those who actually contribute is as much as they can bear—In Addition to the ordinary Calls we have a press which as we were oblidged to force we can only retain by almost daily Expenditures to enable it to support itself, to which its productions afford little Aid as its recent Establishment unavoidably render the Receipts in it extremely trifling—These Circumstances render us unable to give that Assistance to Mr. Greenleaf which he may require—I shall however try in another Mode than an Application to our Friends jointly which has proved fruitless to procure the necessary Sum and if I succeed will apprise you of it by the next Stage. Greenleaf ought not to be permitted to sink—It is of too much Consequence to the common Cause to permit it and his Exertions must warmly recommend him to the support of every Republican.[2]

My Time is so entirely engrossed by Business that I have scarcely a Moment exempt from it—this prevents me from writing Colonel Willet[3]—I will thank you to make any Compliments to that Gentleman & to inform him that the Intimation he was so oblidging to give respecting the Intention of the Anti-Republicans in their Election for Governor was of Service and will be improved on.

The Senate and Assembly have a few Days since appointed an informal Committee of both Houses to devise a Mode of electing Senators—but as neither appeared disposed to depart from the principles adopted by their Houses it [pro?]duced Nothing.[4]

The Session draws to a Close & the next Week will probably terminate it—In the mean Time if Senators should be elected I think it probable Judge Yates & Judge Smith will be the Men[5]—tho' some of our Friends are not convinced that either of them is *Orthodox*—Be so good to communicate this last Sentiment to Mr Smith

1. RC, Lamb Papers, NHi. The letter was addressed to Lamb in New York City.

2. For the Antifederalists' efforts to establish a newspaper in Albany, see Abraham G. Lansing to Abraham Yates, Jr., 3 August 1788, Part One. Thomas Greenleaf's *New York Journal*, published in New York City, was one of the leading Antifederalist newspapers in the country.

3. Marinus Willett (1740–1830), a wealthy merchant and landowner, served in the army throughout the Revolutionary War, rising to the rank of lieutenant colonel. He was sheriff of New York City and County, 1784–1787 and 1791–1795. In 1788 he was defeated as an Antifederalist candidate for a seat in the New York Convention. Willett was mayor of New York City, 1807–1808.

4. It was probably this "informal" committee that gave rise to the many rumors that the legislature had finally agreed to elect Senators. On 23 February 1789, for example, the *Daily Gazette* reported: "Letters received by the last Albany post communicate the happy and long expected account of the two houses having agreed to appoint Senators to represent the State in Congress; and that a Committee was appointed for that purpose." The item was reprinted in the *Weekly Museum*, 24 February; *Morning Post*, 24 February; and at least seven out-of-state newspapers. Similarly, on 24 February the *New York Packet* reported: "A correspondent who has just received accounts from Albany has informed us, that the Senate and Assembly have actually come to a perfect reconciliation on a late contested business; and that we shall certainly have our representation in the Senate of the United States. It is reported that John Lawrance, Esq. will be held up." This report was reprinted in the *Country Journal*, 3 March, and in at least eleven out-of-state

newspapers. For more details about the informal committee, see Abraham Bancker to Evert Bancker, 25 February, below.

5. Robert Yates and William Smith.

William Bingham to Tench Coxe, Philadelphia, 23 February (excerpt)[1]

I am much indebted to you for the Information conveyed in your favor of the 15th Inst—

I concur in opinion with you that the Legislature of New York will not appoint Senators, for I believe the predominant Party are averse to the Residence of Congress being fixed in New York, from a Persuasion that it will give great Weight & Consideration to their Antagonists, who will be more intimately connected with that Body—

1. RC, Tench Coxe Papers, PHi. For other excerpts from this letter, see DHFFE, I, 404, and Chapter XIV. For a biographical sketch of Bingham, see DHFFE, I, 413.

Daily Advertiser (New York), 24 February

Accounts from Albany assure us, that we may yet expect that this state will be represented in the senate of the United States.[1]

1. This report was reprinted in the Philadelphia *Federal Gazette*, 2 March 1789; Philadelphia *Pennsylvania Packet*, 2 March; Philadelphia *Pennsylvania Gazette*, 4 March; and *Carlisle Gazette*, 11 March.

New York Packet, 24 February

Extract of a letter from Albany, dated Feb. 15.

There have been no great political points in agitation since the conference of the Legislature on the bill for electing federal Senators. That bill shared the unhappy fate of the former on the same subject. I am suspicious, that some Federalists will censure the Senate for not receding from their amendments; but, the Senate will be justified by all impartial men. That respectable body required no more than an *equal* right in the election of Senators. As an independent branch of the Legislature, they had an undoubted right to it, since the proposition for chusing Senators was transmitted to them in the form of a *Bill*—a right they could not yield, without establishing a precedent, which might eventually destroy, or greatly diminish that balance of power, which the Constitution has wisely appointed to each House.[1]

1. This article was reprinted in the *Country Journal*, 3 March 1789; Philadelphia *Pennsylvania Gazette*, 4 March; Worcester *Massachusetts Spy*, 5 March; and *New Haven Gazette*, 5 March.

Abraham Bancker to Evert Bancker, Albany, 25 February (excerpt)[1]

I have to lament, that the Prospect of obtaining a Representation in the Senate of the United States, is still [– – –], As the last Resource, an informal Committee has been appointed consisting of several Members from either House, who have met and conferred on the Subject, two several Times, without coming to any decision. They have adjourned to meet again, if their Chairman shall be disposed to convene them.[2]

We, Yesterday came to a Resolution of adjourning on Saturday next, if the Senate shall concur. It was deli[vered?] to the Senate, and they have thought proper to postpone the Con[sidera?]tion of it, for a few days. We make great Progress, but Notwit[hstand?]ing, should we take up and pass on every thing that Offers, We may continue sitting a Year and a day, and then not have finished, for believe me, we have near a Bagfull of Petitions already, and their Numbers are daily increasing—

1. RC, Bancker Family Papers, NHi. The letter was addressed to Evert Bancker in New York City.

2. For rumors that developed from the meeting of this committee, see John Lansing, Jr., to John Lamb, 18 February 1789, n. 4, above.

New York Daily Gazette, 25 February

The expence, with which the dispute between the two houses (says a correspondent) is attended, ought to give us but little concern. Both, without doubt, conceive the welfare of the State involved in the contest; and are therefore tenacious of their rights. As patriotism is indisputably their guide, who can suppose them under the influence of petulance, avarice or ambition? Men of sense, as they unquestionably are, can never be suspected of opposition, unless on very substantial grounds; and although the sum total of the expence may be considerable, his share of emolument will be but a trifle to each individual. With respect to ambition, it cannot be supposed, that they aim at gratifying that passion by this altercation, because they must be convinced that the people (the only ladder of ambition in this country) take but very little notice of the matter at present; although no doubt it will be remembered in due season,[1] and proper measures taken for preventing the gentlemen from quarrelling again on the same subject.

"When great men fall out (says an ancient writer) the people are the sufferers." What an obstinate fellow is *truth*, who will not accommodate himself to times, places, and circumstances! He has long been banished from courts for his want of politeness; and, if he does not mend his manners, he will shortly be insulted and proscribed even in a republic.

1. The legislative deadlock over election of presidential Electors and Senators became an issue in the gubernatorial election in late April, as each party blamed the other for the impasse. See, for example, "Junius," *New York Journal*, 2 April 1789; "H.G.," *Daily Advertiser*, 7 April; "Marvel," *Daily Advertiser*, 7 April; "Cato," *Country Journal*, 14 April and 12 May; and "Junius," *Country Journal*, 28 April.

Daily Advertiser (New York), 2 March (excerpt)[1]

Extract of a letter from Albany, dated Feb. 25. . . .

To-morrow the assembly are to fix on the place to which they will adjourn, but it is expected the anties will oppose the consideration of this question, merely to render nugatory a resolution we have already passed to adjourn on Saturday. Some of the senate have imprudently declared that they will go home on Monday at all events—the policy of the assembly will be, therefore, to protract the sessions a week longer, in hopes of carrying two antifederal senators.[2]

1. For another excerpt from this article, see Part Three, District 2. The article was reprinted in the *Daily Gazette*, 3 March 1789, and Philadelphia *Federal Gazette*, 5 March.

2. On 6 March 1789, William Maclay, a Senator from Pennsylvania, wrote Thomas Mifflin: "Governor Clinton is returned from Albany, and the Assembly of this State have broke up without having appointed Senators. This was contrary to the present Expectation" (New York, RC, Division of Public Records, Records of the Supreme Executive Council, PHarH).

Alexander White to [Mary] Wood, New York, 8 March (excerpt)[1]

The States of N. York and New Jersey were carrying on their Elections at and after the time appointed for the Meeting of Congress—and matters are so conducted that the Returns of the N. York Elections cannot be made till after the 10th of April—the two Houses of Assembly of that State have differrent with Respect to the choice of Senators and adjourned so that they will have no share in that Branch of the Federal Government—The City of N. York have made wonderful exertions in erecting a Building for our reception, it is nearly finished and will when completed contain some of the most elegant appoi[n]tments[.] this some say is intended as a Trap to catch us Southern Men—

1. RC, L. W. Smith Collection, NjMoW. The letter was addressed to "Mrs Wood" in Winchester, Virginia. For a biographical sketch of White, a Representative from Virginia, see DHFFE, II, 422–23. Mary Wood was White's mother-in-law.

Country Journal (Poughkeepsie), 24 March

From a CORRESPONDENT.

He observes that much hath been said to urge the necessity of making amendments to many parts of the new constitution: among which, the power vested in the national government to regulate elections, hath ever been esteemed one of the most exceptionable; but will not a very small degree of attention serve to convince every rational mind; and will not every honest, unprejudiced man confess the absolute necessity of those powers being vested in the general government at this early period of its operation? Do we not see the necessity in respect to the interest of the state of New-York, as to the times and manner of electing senators in this state to serve in the Congress of the United States, agreeable to the first article and fourth section of the constitution of the United States? Have the legislature of this state agreed on passing a law as to the time when, or manner how senators are to be appointed or elected in this state to serve in the general Congress? If not, it becomes necessary for the national government to interpose—or is this state to be unrepresented in the senate of the United States, when matters of the greatest moment are to come under consideration; such as laying the foundation of the national government (of which we are or ought to be a respectable part) establishing its courts of justice; regulating its revenues—its commerce, &c. &c.—which in its operation will no doubt interfere in some instances with the local interest of this state:—Is it even supposable that the freemen of this state in the present relation to the union (which may God continue) will or can sit down easy and contented without a full representation in that august assembly, at the most interesting moment that can possibly arrive? Are we to be bound by law in all cases of a national concern, and our taxes to be proportioned without our proper consent—for no other reason but because the heats of party in the legislature appeared to them (if we may judge by events) to be of more importance than the interest of the union? Will not Congress rather as the supreme rulers of a republican nation, agreeable to the powers vested in them, direct the time and manner in which the legislature of this state shall proceed in the choice of those important members in the national government? Can any one presume in future to say that the powers vested in the national government in that instance are either unnecessary to the purposes of government, or dangerous to the liberties of the people, when it is the only thing that can insure to them a representation in the general government amidst the heats of party, where their most worldly interests are depending?—There are other obvious reasons why that particular power ought to be vested in the national government also.—Some unforeseen occurrence is as likely to take place in future in this or in some other state in the union, as what hath already taken place in this state, which might make the exertions of Congress as necessary in a future day as at the present, and that it is now necessary for Congress to interpose in behalf of this state is self-evident; which I think cannot be denied on the ground of truth.—What man in this state, or in the union, that doth not possess the spirit of a tyrant or the meanness of a slave, that would not prefer the regulating power of Congress to be exerted in those respects, than to remain unrepresented dupes of party, or the passive instruments of revenge in the hands of those whose tender mercies are cruelty, and in the end will but prey upon their vitals?—[1]

1. This article was reprinted in the Boston *Herald of Freedom*, 14 April 1789.

Jeremiah Hill to George Thacher, Biddeford, Maine, 25 March (excerpt)[1]

It would be no hazard in me to guess what views the Assembly of New York had in not concuring with their Senate in adopting any mode for choosing their federal Senators for it appears to me that the Congress as soon as it is form'd or as soon as there is a quorum convened, may adopt a mode for them, and as I can see no reason for their conduct I will hazard a guess, that it is the effects consequential of original Sin. I acknowledge I don't know the prevailing Religion of that State, if I had perhaps I should not have conjectured the above reason for the Assembly's conduct—

1. RC, Thacher Papers, MB. The letter was addressed to Thacher in New York City, where he represented the Maine counties of Massachusetts in the House of Representatives. For another excerpt from this letter, see DHFFE, I, 581–82n. Hill (1747–1820), a Biddeford merchant, was an officer during the Revolutionary War and town clerk of Biddeford, 1780–1788. He was a United States collector of customs in Maine from 1789 to 1809. For a biographical sketch of Thacher, see DHFFE, I, 760.

James Madison to Thomas Jefferson, New York, 29 March (excerpt)[1]

I omitted to mention that a dispute between the Senate of this State, which was federal, and the other branch, which was otherwise, concerning the manner of appointing Senators for the Congress, was so inflexibly persisted in that no appointment was made during the late session, and must be delayed for a considerable time longer, even if the dispute should on a second trial be accommodated. It is supposed by some that the superintending power of Congress will be rendered necessary by the temper of the parties. The provision for the choice of electors was also delayed until the opportunity was lost; and that for the election of Representatives so long delayed that the result will not be decided till tuesday next. It is supposed that at least three out of the six will be of the federal party. In New Jersey, the inaccuracy of the law providing for the choice of Representatives has produced an almost equal delay, and left room for contests, which, if brought by the disappointed candidates into the House, will add a disagreeable article to the list of its business.

1. William C. Rives and Philip R. Fendall, eds., *Letters and Other Writings of James Madison* . . . (4 vols., Philadelphia, 1865), I, 457–61. Also printed in Rutland, *Madison*, XII, 37–40. For another excerpt from this letter, see DHFFE, II, 408.

Junius, Country Journal (Poughkeepsie), 31 March (excerpt)

To the ELECTORS *of the Counties of*
Dutchess *and* Ulster.

. . . If we contemplate the conduct of the majority of the federal party, even from the first dawn of the new constitution, we cannot help suspecting that their apparent views in effecting the operation of that system, originated more in a lust for power and dominion, or personal aggrandisement or emolument, than in the laudable desire to promote the welfare of the community. What must we think of the proceedings of the federalists in the last session of the legislature at Albany, in their persevering opposition and final obstruction of the appointment of Senators to the general government, notwithstanding the visible delay their opposition in this respect would operate to the other business before the houses, and the additional expence which would accrue to the state by such opposition? Their transactions on this occasion evidently favoured the most flagrant and daring attempt, to undermine one of the grand pillars of republican government, viz. the privilege of electing representatives of the people by a majority. The whole of their views in this matter plainly subserved the intention and desire of placing men to represent you in the general Congress, who possessed political sentiments similar to their own, and like themselves renounced the idea of amendments, as of no consequence, or as an affair in which the people ought to have no agency. When such bold stretches are made to rob us of the dear privileges on which our liberty and safety is hinged, I think it is high time that every citizen of the state should open his eyes, and join hands with his neighbours to ward off if possible, the latent evils with which artful and designing men repeatedly threaten us.[1]

1. The major portion of this article was an appeal for the reelection of George Clinton as governor. "Cato" (*Country Journal*, 14 April 1789, in an article dated 2 April), in a reply to "Junius," defended the Senate's conduct: "The Senate declared positively that they were actuated by a serious regard to the constitution of the State, which they could not deviate from without abusing the confidence the people had reposed in them through the constitution—that the federal constitution directs that the Senators should be chosen by the state legislatures—the state constitution gives the Senate equal powers with Assembly; and therefore the Senate have equal power with the Assembly in the choice of federal Senators. This, if it is not just, it is at least plausible reasoning, and deserves a more serious refutation than vague and general declamation." "Cato" called for the defeat of Governor Clinton and expressed the hope that "the late unhappy political controversy

has fortunately arrived at a conclusive point; and the most wise & moderate part of the community wish to bury in oblivion all dissentions of party, that the name of Federal and Anti-federal may no more be known among us—"

In the *Country Journal*, 28 April, "Junius" dismissed "Cato's" arguments as ignorant. He repeated his support for Clinton and charged that the Federalists, in the legislative dispute over the election of Senators, had attempted to abolish the clause in the state constitution which provided for the election of delegates to Congress.

Virginia Gazette (Winchester), 1 April

Our accounts from New-York, received by the last post, are to the 17th ult. at which time Congress had not commenced business, owing to the reasons mentioned in the following letter.

Extract of a letter from a gentleman, Delegate of the new Congress from this State,[1] *to a gentleman in this town, dated New-York, March* 12, 1789.

"It is with real regret I am under the necessity of observing, that we have no addition to our numbers since last Thursday, when they amounted only to eighteen Representatives and twelve Senators. This circumstance induced all the members present to agree to write to their absent colleagues, urging their immediate attendance; and as there were no members from Maryland, I was requested to write to the gentlemen of that State, as well as my own, which I have done.

"This extraordinary delay may, in part, be attributed to the badness of the roads, and the impracticability of crossing the rivers, but it is principally owing to the misconduct of the States of New-York and New-Jersey, respecting their elections; the former, from pure principles of antifederalism, have failed to appoint Senators, and have so ordered the election of Representatives, that the returns cannot be examined till the 10th of April; and the latter actuated by state faction, keep open the polls in some counties, and threaten to do so till the Assembly sits, to pass a law for closing them. It is somewhat remarkable, that circumstances should so soon arise, to prove the propriety of that part of the Constitution which gives to Congress the power of regulating elections; these instances shew, that without it, the general government might, and probably would be, done away by the machinations of wicked men in the particular States. I am much fatigued with the task imposed on me, and therefore conclude, that I am your's, &c."

1. The author was undoubtedly Alexander White, who represented Virginia in the House of Representatives. In a letter dated 24 March 1789 to Adam Stephen of Berkeley County, Virginia, White expressed some of the same ideas contained in this letter. For excerpts from the letter to Stephen, see Part Three: Representatives Election Commentary, and Chapter XII, Part Six.

H.G., Daily Advertiser (New York), 7 April[1]

LETTER XII.

March 8, 1789.

Dear Sir,

The seventh of the circumstances enumerated in proof of his Excellency's enmity to the Union is,[2] That he has continued his opposition to the new constitution even since its adoption by this state.

There are two kinds of opposition, direct and indirect. The Governor must have been an ideot to have rendered himself chargeable with the first kind. It would have brought the resentment of the whole community upon him, and frustrated the very object he had in view. Indirect methods were the only ones that could be practised with safety, or with any prospect of success. To embarrass, not to defeat the operation of the government was, of necessity the plan of a man who wished ill to it.

The adversaries of the constitution in Virginia have furnished a striking specimen of this species of policy. The last legislature, in which they were predominant, made no difficulty about organising the government. The act of the people was of course to be obeyed in appearance. But its efficacy was to be destroyed by throwing obstacles in the way of the administration of the system. For this purpose an act has been passed, declaring it incompatible for any officer of the state to perform official functions under the authority of the United States.[3]

This act, *if valid* would *oblige* the United States to have a complete set of officers for every branch of the national business, judges, justices of the peace, sheriffs, jail keepers, constables, &c. which could not fail to render the government completely odious. This may serve as a sample of the means by which it may be distressed and counteracted.

The friends of the Governor tell us that after the adoption of the constitution, he declared in convention that he should conceive himself bound to maintain the public peace, and to concur in putting the system *into operation*. This was saying as little as possible. Luckily, the public peace was in no danger, and his Excellency with all his hardihood would not dare to refuse an official co-operation in putting the government established by the people *in motion*. I attended the debates of the convention, and I could not forbear remarking, that the Governor, in the speech alluded to, seemed carefully to confine his assurances to a mere *official compliance*. The impression made upon my mind by the *two* last speeches he delivered was this, that he would as Governor of the state, in mere official transactions *conform* to the constitution, but that he should think it expedient to keep alive the spirit of opposition in the people, until the *amendments proposed*, or another convention (I am not certain which) could be obtained. In this impression I am not singular; there were others who understood him in the same sense.

No reasonable man can doubt that such a sentiment was an unjustifiable one. The United States are to determine on the propriety of amendments, and on the expediency of a convention. Both must be referred to their judgment. If they think both improper, or unnecessary, it is the duty of a particular member to acquiesce. This is the fundamental principle of the social compact. To threaten the continuance of an opposition therefore till either of those purposes was accomplished, was in every view intemperate and unwarrantable. That there will be a reconsideration of parts of the system, and that certain amendments will be made, I devoutly wish and confidently expect. I have no doubt that the system is susceptible of improvement, and I anxiously desire that every prudent means may be used to conciliate the honest opponents of it. But I reprobate the idea of keeping up an opposition to the government upon principles, which derogate from those, on which the union is, and must necessarily be supported. I reprobate the idea of one state giving law to the rest.

But even the official compliance promised by the Governor, has hitherto been afforded in a very ungracious and exceptionable manner; in such a manner as indicates secret hostility, and a disposition to have the government considered in an unimportant and inferior light. On the 13th of Sept. 1788, the act for organising the government was passed by Congress, and it is presumable, was communicated without delay. We know that it immediately appeared in the public papers. But it was not until the 13 of October following, that the Governor issued his proclamation for convening the legislature, and the time appointed for their meeting was less than a month from that which was fixed for the appointment of electors to choose the President and vice President. This procrastination appeared at a time extraordinary to every body, and wore the aspect of *slight and neglect* at least. The Governor asserts, that it was impracticable to convene the legislature sooner, but he has not told us why it was so; and I scruple not to affirm that if a reason is ever assigned, it will be found so flimsy a one, as to discover the insignificant light in which his Excellency was disposed to view and treat the national government. *Neglects* and *slights* calculated to lessen the opinion of the importance of a thing and bring it into discredit, are often the most successful weapons by which it can be attacked.

But this is not the only view in which the delay in convening the legislature is to be considered as reprehensible. It had the effect of depriving the legislature itself of the exercise of a right vested in them by the national constitution, and hazarded an undue postponement of our representation in Congress, which has actually happened. As to the first, the constitution of the United States leaves the mode of appointing electors to the discretion of the state legislatures. They may therefore refer them to the choice of the people if they think proper. This has been done in several of the states, and is, in my opinion, a privilege which it is of great importance should be in the hands of the people. Making the usual allowances for want of punctuality in meeting, disagreement in opinion, difficulties in framing new and untried regulations, it may be safely pronounced that the legislature was assembled too late to refer the choice of electors to the people; whereby they were deprived of an opportunity of exercising a constitutional discretion, and *the people* of a chance of exercising a privilege of very considerable moment to their interests. May it not be justly said in this instance that the Governor *undertook to think* for the legislature?

But this is not all; the state of the parties in the legislature was understood long before they met; and it was to have been foreseen, that there would have been a diversity of views, in regard to the mode of appointing our national representatives, and consequently delays in agreeing upon any. By not calling the legislature early enough to allow time for overcoming these impediments, it happens that in a matter, in which the two houses did finally agree, to wit, the manner of choosing members of the national house of representatives, the execution has been so greatly procrastinated, that it must be more than a month from the time appointed for the meeting of the body, before it can be even ascertained who our representative are.

There is a further circumstances in which the Governor's conduct subjects him to the suspicion of an intention[4] to embarrass the measures relating to the constitution.

The senate having in very gentle terms intimated a wish that the legislature had been more early convened, the Governor in a very petulant and indecent reply, considering that it was the executive speaking to a branch of the legislature, made himself a party on the side of the assembly, in the controversy between the two houses, and thereby furnished a motive of obstinacy to the one, and of irritation to the other. It is well known that in that controversy, one of the reasons on which the assembly had chiefly relied, in insisting upon the joint ballot, was, that *it approached more nearly to an election by the people*, while the senate held that they were entitled to an equal voice, and that as being the *peculiar representative*, by our constitution, of the *great body of the freeholders*, they were bound by a regard to the interests of that class as well as to own their rights, as a branch of the legislature, to insist upon the equality they claimed.

The senate in their speech had observed that if there had been time they would have been for referring the choice of electors to the people. The Governor answers, that it was impracticable to convene the legislature in time for that object, and intimates a persuasion that the senate will see the propriety of pursuing their principle as far as circumstances would permit, by adopting such mode of appointment as should appear *most nearly to approach an election by the people*, adverting to the ground which had been taken by the majority in the assembly. This intimation of the Governor could not be understood in any other light than as advocating their principle, and could not have failed to have had the effect of confirming them in it, and alienating the senate who were indelicately treated still more from it. There are circumstances which render a hint as intelligible as the most precise and positive expressions.

This species of interference in a question between the two branches of the legislature was very unbecoming in the Chief Magistrate—and bespoke much more the intemperate partizan than the temperate arbiter of differences prejudicial to the state.

And the inference from the whole of what I have stated, is, that the Governor since the adoption of the constitution in this state, has manifested the *reverse* of a disposition to afford it a cordial support.

I remain,

With great regard,

Yours, &c.

H—— G——.

To —— ——. Esq.
Suffolk County.

1. "H.G." was undoubtedly Alexander Hamilton. Sixteen "H.G." letters were printed in the *Daily Advertiser* between 10 March and 11 April 1789, all sharply anti-Clinton and designed to defeat the governor for reelection. For evidence of Hamilton's authorship, see Syrett, V, 262.

2. In "Letter VI" (*Daily Advertiser*, 18 March 1789), "H.G." presented eight "facts" to prove that Governor Clinton was "an enemy" of the Union: "I. That while he has acknowleged the insufficiency of the old government, he has strenuously opposed the principal measures devised by the joint councils of America for supporting and strengthening it. II. That he has treated Congress, as a body, in a contemptuous manner. III. That his behaviour towards the individuals composing that body, has been of a nature calculated to give them just cause of disgust. IV. That he disapproved of the very first step taken towards the effectual amendment of the old confederation. V. That he prejudged and condemned the new constitution before it was framed. VI. That he opposed it after it appeared, with unreasonable obstinacy. VII. That he has continued his opposition to it even since its adoption by this state. And VIII. That he is unfriendly to the residence of Congress in this city."

3. For the Virginia Disabling Act, approved by the Virginia legislature on 6 December 1788, see Hening, XII, 694–95.

4. The newspaper printed "inattention"; it obviously meant "intention."

Benjamin Rush to John Adams, Philadelphia, 4 June (excerpt)[1]

I find you, & I must *agree, not* to *disagree*, or we must cease to discuss political questions. I could as soon believe that the British parliament had once a right to tax America, as believe that a major part of the citizens of New York were *federal*, or that many of the federal minority were so, from proper motives.—I know from good authority that some of the leading federalists of New York pressed the Senate at Albany to relinquish the power of appointing federal senators, to the Assembly, rather than risk the loss of the residence of Congress in New York.

1. RC, Adams Papers, MHi. Printed: Butterfield, *Rush*, I, 513–15. For another excerpt from this letter, see Chapter XIV.

PART THREE

THE ELECTION OF REPRESENTATIVES

Only five weeks were available for campaigning between passage of the election law for Representatives on 27 January 1789 and the opening of the polls on 3 March. During this time nominating meetings were held in many counties, their proceedings published, and circular letters concerning the nominations passed around the districts. All this could be accomplished in the short time available for two reasons: New York already had two well-established, distinct political parties, and the parties were already geared up for the gubernatorial election to be held in April.

The elections for Representatives clearly took second billing to the gubernatorial election. The Federalists, realizing that their chances of electing a Federalist governor were very slim, nominated Robert Yates, an Antifederalist, to oppose George Clinton, running for his fifth three-year term. But when the Federalists met to nominate candidates for Representatives, they chose Federalists. Antifederalist leaders, still struggling to close ranks following their sharp differences and defeat in the state Convention the previous year, nominated Antifederalists for Representatives in the four northern districts, and they expected them to win. In the two southern districts the Antifederalists kept a low profile.

The efficiency of the political party apparatus is evident in the fact that there were usually no more than two candidates, one from each party, nominated in each congressional district. Except for the election in District 2, the candidates' stand for or against amendments to the Constitution usually was the only important campaign issue. Reports of the public nominating meetings are the principal published information about the elections; these reports also list the gubernatorial and state Assembly and Senate nominees.

The Antifederalists expected to do well in the balloting, and thus Federalist victories in four of the state's six districts were a severe disappointment to them. To Federalists, their surprising strength signaled growing public acceptance of the Constitution.

The documents printed immediately below in "Representatives Election Commentary" discuss the elections for Representatives in general terms or give details about the elections in more than one district. Documents which deal with the election in a single district are printed below under that district's heading.

Representatives Election Commentary

New York Packet, 20 January 1789

In nothing, says a correspondent, are we so inconsistent with ourselves as in panting after enjoyments which we imagine would certainly confer happiness if attained; yet we generally find these objects of our wishes incapable, when possessed, of affording the blessings we expected; or we neglect to cultivate them. In nothing can this be better exemplified then in our anxious solicitude for the preservation of civil liberty, to which freedom of election, or government by the representatives of our choice, is deemed absolutely essential. How do the vassals of Europe pant for this darling prerogative! Through what deluges of blood have Americans waded to secure this first privilege of free citizens! And yet (shameful to be told) how many of them suffer it to lie dormant! and how few exercise this boasted right! How will every foreigner be struck with astonishment, when he hears we are so lost to a sense of freedom, that not more than a *fourth*, in some Instances, not a *tenth*, of us think worth while to assist in the choice of legislators, &cc. and this too on the most important occasions. Oh, Americans, why do you thus prove yourselves unworthy of freedom!

While the unhappy people of Europe, says a correspondent, are involved in all the horrors of war, and are sacrificed by thousands at the shrine of regal pride and ambition, the citizens of America enjoy all the blessings of domestic tranquility, and are calmly preparing for a revolution in their government, such as the astonished world never before was witness to; a revolution which has not been brought about by force of arms, by the artful machinations of ambitious men, nor by tumultuous risings of the people, wherein order and government are generally given up a prey to the dæmon of anarchy, till some ruffian, more hardy or artful than the rest, becomes their tyrant, and gives them laws at the point of the bayonet; but a revolution wherein the people have voluntarily formed and ratified an energetic Constitution, wisely calculated to establish order and good government on the ruins of anarchy and licentiousness. O happy Americans! singularly favored of Heaven! go on with the glorious work. Let the love of your country always predominate in your bosoms. Wisely seize the present favorable moment to extend your commerce, to encourage your agriculture, to cultivate the arts and sciences, to establish useful manufactories; and, in fine let nothing be neglected that may encrease your own and your country's good. This is a time pregnant with circumstances peculiarly favourable, such as ages may not again produce: You have just emerged from the calamities of a tedious war, in defending your liberties, and after having experienced the disadvantages both of a tyranific and licentious government, you are now presented with a happy mean between the two extremes; you may now profit by the follies and the madness of the European nations; and taught, as you have been, in the school of national adversity, you must now be careful of discerning the true interests of your country. From all these circumstances, it is evident, that the 'present tide,' if wisely improved, cannot fail to waft you to happiness and glory.

Massachusetts Centinel (Boston), 21 February

The Hon. Mr. HAMILTON will be held as a Candidate for Representative for New-York district,[1] and EZRA L'HOMMEDIEU, Esq. for Long [and] Staten Islands.

1. On 4 March 1789 the *Massachusetts Centinel* informed its readers that Hamilton had declined to be a candidate, and that "it is said" that Rufus King would be nominated in his place. That report was reprinted in the *Salem Mercury*, 10 March, and Portsmouth *New Hampshire Gazette*, 11 March.

Richard Platt to Jeremiah Wadsworth, New York, 22 February (excerpt)[1]

We are told we shall have senators, by compromize, one Federalist & one Anti—Our Hall will be ready for the reception of Congress next week. We are in the midst of Electioneering—i.e. our Committees meet twice or thrice a Week—Yeates we hold up for Governor & Laurance for our representative—Floyd is the man from Long & Staten Islands: & Benson we hope will get in for Dutchess County[2]—Mr Griffin[3] dined at Club with us yesterday & shewed a Return of Representatives of Six Federalists from Virginia & the prospect is in favor of more—Madison is one of the Number—and what adds to the singularity of his appointment is, that he was chosen from a District comprizing 7 Counties, six of which were antifederal.

Trumbull[4] & you must live with me till other arrangements are made—I hope to see you both next Week at farthest—

1. RC, Wadsworth Papers, CtHi. The letter was addressed to Wadsworth in Hartford. Platt (1754–1830), a New York City businessman, was a member of the Federalist committee of correspondence for the city. Wadsworth had been elected to the House of Representatives from Connecticut; for a biographical sketch, see DHFFE, II, 59.

2. Wadsworth later reported from New York City that New York would elect "two certain probably three federalists" (to [Peter Colt?], 29 March 1789, RC, Wadsworth Papers, CtHi).

3. Cyrus Griffin of Virginia, last president of the Confederation Congress.

4. Jonathan Trumbull, Jr., another Representative from Connecticut; for a biographical sketch, see DHFFE, II, 58.

Tench Coxe to John Adams, New York, 1 March (excerpt)[1]

There seems no doubt that John Lawrence Esqr. and Ezra L Homidieu Esqr. will represent the two Southern districts of this state, tho it is uncertain whether any other person, friendly to the constitution will be carried in the other four Districts—Our last Advices render it doubtful whether the legislature will concur in any mode of electing Senators, but tis probable you will have later Advices than ours from Albany.

1. RC, Adams Papers, MHi. For other excerpts from this letter, see Chapter XII, Part Five:I, and Chapter XIV.

Country Journal (Poughkeepsie), 3 March

This day comes on the election for Representatives of this state to serve in the Great Congress of the United States—and to-morrow is the day appointed for their first meeting, at the City Hall of the city of New-York.—There being but one day's difference between the election of our Representatives (and no senators apointed) will make it from the length of time given to return those elected Representatives, near the middle of April before this state will be represented at all in that important body.

Cassius, Country Journal (Poughkeepsie), 3 March

To the PEOPLE of the STATE of
NEW YORK.

The next Election will perhaps be as important to the general interests of America, as any that ever have been or will be held in this country; for it may greatly depend upon them, whether the new constitution is to continue in its present form, or to receive such amendments as have been proposed by many of the State Conventions, and are anxiously desired by so great a proportion of the citizens of these United States. That the leaders of the federal party, th[r]oughout these States, are opposed to those amendments, which we consider as the most essential, I believe is now beyond a doubt. Their conduct in all the legislatures whose proceedings we have had any account of, the sentiments held out by their writers in the public papers, and the indefatigable pains taken to get in those who call themselves federalists at the ensuing election for State and Continental Representatives, establish this truth in my opinion beyond all contradiction—for if they are not opposed to the amendments, why are they opposed to our having such persons to represent us, as we may be assured will use their endeavours to obtain them? I defy any one to give a satisfactory answer to this question, (for it is clear that the highest or farthest object which the warmest opponent to the new constitution can now have in view, is to have the amendments take place which are so generally esteemed to be necessary for the security of our State governments, and of the inestimable rights of freemen.) We may easily see from this, if we wish for the amendments, the absolute necessity of exerting ourselves to get into the elective offices, both of our own, and of the general government, persons possessed of the same wishes. We cannot suppose any one to be a sincere friend to amendments who shall advise us to trust those of a contrary character to obtain them; the absurdity of such a supposition would be too glaring not to strike the most common observer. It is a favorite sentiment with the federal writers, to postpone amending, till we experience the defects in the system by its operations; which is as much as to say, bow your unwilling necks to the yoke, till the experiment can be fairly tried, whether the people cannot be goaded into a tame submission to this system without alterations. Is this the language of those who wish for amendments? Surely not. For the sake of every thing which is dear to freemen, let us not suffer ourselves to be deceived upon this occasion by *artful* and insidious professions; but let us be fully impressed with this important truth, established by the invariable experience of ages, that if we wait till the fetters are fairly and completely rivetted on, nothing but steel will be able to file them off. The people of these States have it yet in their power, by proper and judicious elections, to retrieve and establish their liberties on a sure and permanent foundation.

Every scheme and artifice which can be devised are now using, and will be used to oust our present Governor at the next election, for no other reason but because he is a whig, a republican, a friend to the liberties of the common people, and a professed enemy to aristocracy; which he and all writers and thinkers upon the subject, justly esteem to be the most oppressive kind of government on earth. They can justly find no fault with his character, none with his public administration; and I believe that no one who is acquainted with the history of his life, will dare to accuse me of partiality, when I say I believe him to be one of the best public characters on the continent. From his (legal) infancy he has been in our assembly an able and steady asserter of the rights of the people, until the commencement of the late war, through which, amidst innumerable difficulties, he has defended them with equal activity, abilities and firmness in the field. Nor was his merit less conspicuous, in the peace and good order which immediately took place upon our taking possession of the southern district of this State, between the jarring elements which came together upon that occasion. When resentments ran so high as to threaten the destruction of part of the community, the peace was preserved, the dignity of government kept up, and the authority of the laws prevailed.—And what is now peculiar to his character, and distinguishes it from most of the shining ones of the time, is, that he does not ask, he does not wish, as a reward for his services, a surrender of those rights into his own hands, but still remains the same steady and sincere friend to the liberties of his country, and the same determined opposer of tyranny, whether it comes in the shape of a royal Prerogative, an act of Parliament, or in one less alarming, and consequently more dangerous.

Some time ago, at a meeting of near forty of the members of the Legislature, friends to amendments, it was by a unanimous ballot, determined to hold up at the ensuing election his excellency George Clinton, Esquire, for Governor, and the honorable Pierre Van Cortlandt, Esquire, for Lieutenant-Governor. It would be highly imprudent if not dangerous to make any great changes in the officers of government at this time, when the cold water which is thrown upon the amendments to the new constitution, will probably prove as oil to the fire of discontent already kindled throughout this continent, by that system of government, which, in its present form, is justly looked upon to be so very defective and dangerous. It would be unwise to dismiss from the helm of government, a pilot of experienced skill, courage and integrity, at a time when the political horizon lowers so heavily.

The friends of freedom in our sister states, at present overpowered by the arts, deceptions, and influence of their great men, turn their eyes to us from every part of the continent with the most anxious solicitude and concern, depending chiefly upon the active exertions of this state and Virginia, and the still, but powerful influence arising from the determination of North-Carolina and Rhode-Island, not to adopt the system in its present form, to support the cause of amendments, on which depends the liberties of America.

The Conventions of Massachusetts, New-Hampshire, New-York, Virginia and South-Carolina, and a respectable and virtuous minority in the convention of Pennsylvania, have declared to the world in the most unequivocal manner, by the amendments they have proposed to this system, that they look upon it as dangerous to liberty: And the states of North Carolina and Rhode-Island, have still more forcibly, though not more clearly, expressed the same sentiment, by their refusing to adopt it. What then, my fellow citizens, must we think of those, who are endeavouring to persuade us, that the amendments are matters of no consequence, that the government will not abuse its powers; that we ought to sit still, and not seek for any alterations, until, like the rest of the nations of the world, we *feel* ourselves enslaved and oppressed (should they not add) and like them unable to resist or shake off the tyranny? What must we think of those who are endeavouring, by insidious and malicious insinuations, and the most low and despicable falsehoods, to destroy our confidence in those whose fidelity we have sufficiently proved, by their having long enjoyed that confidence, and having never abused or betrayed it, who have steadily opposed foreign and open attempts upon the liberties of their country, and as steadily refuted the more artful, sly and concealed encroachments of domestic tyranny? What can we think of those who vilify that excellent mode of trial by jury, and thereby shew an inclination to persuade us to give up that invaluable privilege? Is it possible we can suppose that they are friends to our liberties? May Heaven forbid so fatal an infatuation!—It is high time to open our eyes to our true situation. Is not the declared sense of so many respectable public bodies of the defects and dangers in that constitution sufficient to awaken our attention? Is it not a ground that will justify at least some small degree of jealousy concerning the design of those who are opposed to the amendments; especially when we look round and observe who they are? are they not generally the rich, the powerful, the great, the well born and the upstart, the governors (except our own) the senators and the high officers of government? Is it not sufficient to evince the necessity at least of our being cautious whom we trust with power, until the necessary amendments to the new constitution shall be obtained, whereby the powers of the government may be clearly defined and limited, the rights of the state governments (most of them sufficiently extensive for free ones) properly ascertained & established, every idea of their consolidation erased (an idea I will be bold to say, never contemplated by Congress, or one of the state legislatures, or by the people of any of these states) and the rights and privileges of freemen permanently secured to us and our late posterity?—Let us upon this occasion convince the world that we have the good sense to guard those rights, which we have so lately had the courage to defend.

CASSIUS.[1]

1. Some passages of this article were printed in the *Federal Herald*, 30 March 1789, as "Extract of a letter from Albany."

Temperance, New York Packet, 3 March

Messieurs PRINTERS,

This is the day[1] in which every good citizen should come forward with an unprejudiced mind, and be strictly on his guard against all those artifices which are usually practiced at elections, for the insiduous purpose of misleading the understanding, and creating divisions. How happy should we be, if we could stand firm against every current of faction? The day of trial is now at hand; we are brought into an uniformity of opinion concerning the necessity of an efficient government—The names of whig and tory that were once deemed incompatible, are at length lost in the general unanimity which prevails, the bulk of both parties being really united in principles of liberty! We sincerely wish that now may be the happy time when those odious distinctions of whig and tory, federal and antifederal may be no more remembered. We have all one interest to attend to, from which the same obligations arise to every man, to these principles let us inviolably adhere. It is now the duty of every free citizen to maintain and improve the union so happily begun, and to bless God for disposing the temper of the people almost universally to it.

TEMPERANCE.

1. The polls opened for the election of Representatives on 3 March 1789.

Henry Knox to Edward Carrington, New York, 8 March (excerpt)[1]

By the post of last evening I had the pleasure to receive your favors of the 16th and 18th ultimo—The Elections of representatives in Virginia have verified your predictions that the people would change their sentiments.—The effects will be happy for the Country

The legislature of New York have risen without appointing Senators—the senate were inflexible and evinced a considerable degree of magnanimity—hazarding a local injury by the removal of Congress, which possibly may be effected for want of the senators from this State, rather than embarrass the general government with two antifederals for a great length of time[.] The elections are making for representatives—Laurence will be elected for this district, and Floyd for Long Island and Staten Island—It is possible that Benson may be elected for Dutchess but not probable[2]

1. RC, Henry Knox Letters, ViHi.

2. In a letter written the following day, Knox told George Washington that it was "probable there will be 4 Opposers, and 2 supporters of the Government" elected as Representatives from New York (9 March 1789, New York, RC, Washington Papers, DLC).

Proclamation by Governor George Clinton, 11 March[1]

By his Excellency GEORGE CLINTON, Esq. GOVERNOR of the STATE of NEW-YORK, &c.

Pursuant to the authority vested in the person administering the government of this State, in and by an act of the Legislature, entitled 'an act directing the times, places and manner of electing Representatives in this State for the House of Representatives of the Congress of the United States of America;' passed the 27th day of January last—The Secretary's Office of the said State, in the city of New-York, is, by these presents, appointed the place to canvass and estimate the Votes taken at the Election on the first Tuesday in March last, of which all persons concerned are to take notice and govern themselves accordingly.

Given under my hand, at the city of New-York, this eleventh day of March, in the thirteenth[2] year of the Independence of the said State, 1789.

GEO. CLINTON.

1. *New York Packet*, 13 March 1789. The *Packet* printed the proclamation again on 17 March (see n. 2, below), and it was also printed in the *Daily Gazette*, 14 March; *Daily Advertiser*, 14 March; *Morning Post*, 16 March; *New York Journal*, 19 March; *Country Journal*, 24 March; and *Albany Journal*, 30 March.

2. The *New York Packet*, 13 March, printed "eleventh" here, but corrected it to "thirteenth" on 17 March.

Abraham Yates, Jr., to Melancton Smith, Albany, 18 March[1]

Your favour, not being one of the Committe I have Laid before them who will answer you that part[.] I just now Leave Connely in order to write this in answer to the other part of your Letter. By the Information you, Conely and Others ~~give~~ Matters Stand with you better then I have expected. It has all along been my opinion that the patriotic Cause has suffered in New York for want of decision and I am not without my apprehension that Many will get Embarrassed by Concessions; that they will not Insist upon all the amendments—The Leaders on the federal side will often confess in Conversation that they are for amendments but not for all; in order to extract from the others that he will do so too, and when once that Concession is extorted then to Dispute wither they shall give over some of the material or the Immaterial

The publications from this place you will have an opportunity to see at Greenliefs who is constant[ly] Receiving Barbers Paper[2]—Connelly will be able to tell you more then I can write about our Politicks here—I believe Renselaer and Edgate have succeeded[3]—But the Governours Election is the main point: I am sanguin in my expectations of his Carrying the Election: But that is Not all we are to Look to; this Election, Being General the Event of it will Carry with it; an Aspect so as to shew, the proportion for or against the Constitution in its present form: and therefore the greater the Number for Clinton the Better And the more Determined it will shew the disposition of the People; and it is of great Consequence that we get the majority in the Governours favour in the City of New York[.][4] My Compliments to the friends for all the amendments I Remain Sir your very Humble Sevt

1. RC, Roberts Autograph Collection, PHC. The letter was addressed to Smith in New York City.

2. Thomas Greenleaf published the *New York Journal*; Robert Barber, the *Albany Register*.

3. Jeremiah Van Rensselaer and Matthew Adgate, candidates for Representative in districts 6 and 5, respectively. Van Rensselaer was elected; Adgate was defeated.

4. In the election begun on 28 April 1789, Robert Yates received 833 votes to George Clinton's 385 in New York City and County.

James Madison to George Washington, New York, 19 March (excerpt)[1]

On our arrival here we found that the number of Representatives on the spot had been stationary from the second day of the meeting. Mr. Page, Mr. Lee, & myself raised it to 21, and Mr. S. Griffin and Mr. Moore have been since added.[2] The number of attending Senators continues at 8. When a quorum will be made up in either House, rests on vague conjecture, rather than on any precise information. It is not improbable I think that the present week will supply the deficiency in one, if not in both of them. The States most convenient, are among the defaulters. It will not be known, I am told, in this State, who the Representatives are till some time next month. The federal party calculate on an equal division of the six: Mr Laurence for the City district, Mr. Floyd for the Long Island district, and Mr. Benson for a third.

1. RC, Washington Papers, DLC. Printed: Rutland, *Madison*, XII, 22–23. For another excerpt from this letter, see Chapter XII, Part Five:I.

2. John Page, Richard Bland Lee, Samuel Griffin, and Andrew Moore, along with Madison, were Representatives from Virginia.

Alexander White to Adam Stephen, New York, 24 March (excerpt)[1]

The Assembly of New York have adjourned without appointing Senators—and so ordered the Election of representatives, that they cannot take their Seats till late in April, the Commissioners who are to examine their returns not being to meet till the tenth of that month—this is ascribed to the prevalence of Antifederalism—

1. RC, Adam Stephen Papers, DLC. The letter was addressed to Stephen in Berkeley County, Virginia. For further elaboration of White's views, see the Winchester *Virginia Gazette*, 1 April 1789, Part Two; for another excerpt from this letter, see Chapter XII, Part Six. Stephen (1730–1791), a military veteran of the French and Indian War and a major general in the Continental Army during the Revolutionary War, represented Berkeley County, Virginia, in the Virginia House of Delegates, 1780–1784. He voted to ratify the Constitution in the Virginia Convention in 1788.

New York Daily Gazette, 7 April

A committee of both houses of the Legislature appointed at the last session, are to assemble at the Secretary's Office this day, to canvass and estimate the votes given in for Representatives of this State, in the House of Representatives of the Congress of the United States. We hope in a few days to present our readers with the names of the gentlemen elected to the honorable office.[1]

1. This item was reprinted in the Philadelphia *Independent Gazetteer*, 14 April 1789.

Fisher Ames to [John?] Lowell, New York, 8 April (excerpt)[1]

Col John Lawrence of this City took his Seat for New York to day. Egbert Benson is also elected. His rival, one Bailey, had more votes—but some were rejected for irregularity. A Mr. Floyd is also said to be chosen for Long Island.

1. RC, PPRF. The address page of the letter is missing; at the bottom of the last page the addressee is listed as "Hon Mr Lowell." This was probably John Lowell (1743–1802), a prominent Boston lawyer and politician. From 1784 to 1789 he was a judge of the Massachusetts Court of Appeals; in 1789 he became a federal judge for the District of Massachusetts. Ames was in New York City representing Massachusetts in the House of Representatives; for a biographical sketch, see DHFFE, I, 743.

Official Canvass of the Votes for Representatives, New York, 11 April[1]

State of New York, to wit, We the Subscribers, being the major Part of the Joint Committee appointed by the Senate and Assembly of the State of New York by Virtue of the Act entitled "an Act for regulating Elections" to canvas and estimate the Votes to be taken at the next Election for Governor Lieutenant Governor and Senators, having met at the Office of the Secretary of this State in the City of New York on the first Tuesday of April Instant for the Purpose of canvassing and estimating the Votes taken at the last Election in this State for Members of the House of Representatives of the Congress of the United States of America pursuant to the Act entitled "An Act directing the Times Places and Manner of electing Representatives in this State for the House of Representatives of the Congress of the United States of America," did there on that Day and the three next succeeding Days canvas and estimate the Votes taken at the said last Election in this State for Members of the House of Representatives of the Congress of the United States of America; And we do upon the said Canvass and Estimate determine and declare and hereby Certify That William Floyd Esquire was by the greatest Number of Votes at the said last Election in the District comprehending the Counties of Suffolk, Queens, Kings and Richmond chosen a Member of the House of Representatives of the Congress of the United States; And that John Lawrance Esquire was by the greatest Number of Votes at the said last Election in the District comprehending the City and County of New York and Westchester County except the Towns of Salem, North Salem, Courtlandt, York Town and Stephen Town, chosen a Member of the House of Representatives of the Congress of the United States; And that Egbert Benson Esquire was by the greatest Number of Votes at the said last Election in the District comprehending the County of Dutchess and the Towns of Salem, North Salem, Courtlandt, York Town and Stephen Town in Westchester County chosen a Member of the House of Representatives of the Congress of the United States; And that John Hathorn Esquire was by the greatest Number of Votes at the said last Election in the District comprehending the Counties of Ulster and Orange chosen a Member of the House of Representatives of the Congress of the United States; And that Peter Silvester Esquire was by the greatest Number of Votes at the said last Election in the District comprehending the Counties of Columbia, Washington and Clinton with all the remaining Part of this State lying on the East Side of Hudson's River chosen a Member of the House of Representatives of the Congress of the United States; And that Jeremiah Van Rensselaer Esquire was by the greatest Number of Votes at the said last Election in the District comprehending that Part of the County of Albany which lies on the West Side of Hudson's River and the Counties of Montgomery and Ontario chosen a Member of the House of Representatives of the Congress of the United States.

Given under our Hands at the said office of the Secretary of this State in the City of New York the Eleventh Day of April in the thirteenth Year of the Independence of this State and in the Year of our Lord one thousand Seven hundred and Eighty nine.

[signed] Samuel Jones
John Watts Junr.
Christr. Tappen
Gilbert Livingston
John Smith

Jas. Duane
Isaac Roosevelt
Lewis Morris

1. DS, James Duane Papers, NHi. No official vote counts are extant; the February 1787 state election law required "that immediately upon making such determination as aforesaid, all the poll-books, or lists and ballots, or tickets . . . shall be destroyed by the said joint Committee" (*Laws of the State of New-York* [New York, 1787], 34).

Richard Bland Lee to Leven Powell, New York, 13 April (excerpt)[1]

The Returns for members to represent this state in the house of Representatives have been examined in the course of the past week—and four uniform friends to the Government out of six have been elected. Strange that the sense of the poeple in this state should also be contrary to that of their Legislature.[2]

1. RC, Leven Powell Papers, DLC. Printed: *John P. Branch Historical Papers of Randolph Macon College*, 1st ser., no. 3 (1903), 219–20. The letter was addressed to Powell in Middleburg, Loudoun County, Virginia. Lee was representing Virginia in the House of Representatives; for a biographical sketch, see DHFFE, II, 416. Powell (1737–1810), a Virginia Federalist, represented Loudoun County in the Virginia House of Delegates, 1779, 1787–1788, and 1791–1792.

2. Virginia Federalists repeatedly asserted that the Antifederalist-controlled Virginia legislature was out of touch with the sentiments of their constitutents.

Massachusetts Centinel (Boston), 18 April

FROM NEW-YORK.

APRIL 9. . . .

It is pretty certain, that FOUR of the six General Representatives chosen by this State, are Federalists. A gentleman from Albany says, that in the counties near that city, Judge YATES' friends are very numerous.[1]

1. This item was reprinted in the Portland, Maine, *Cumberland Gazette*, 23 April 1789. No printing of this item in a New York newspaper has been located.

Peter Waldron Yates and Richard Lush to Jonathan Lawrence, Albany, 19 April (excerpt)[1]

our late disappointments in the Election for continental Representatives, so far as respects Adgate and Bailey, ought to awaken and spur us on to more vigorous Exertions—[2]

1. RC, Lamb Papers, NHi. The letter was addressed to Lawrence, "Chairman of the republican Committee," in New York City. Yates (1747–1826), an Albany lawyer, served in the Assembly, 1784–1785, and in Congress in 1786. He was a nephew of Abraham Yates, Jr. Lush was Albany County clerk from 1790 to 1808 and county surrogate from 1811 to 1813. He was a founding director of the New York State Bank in Albany, which was organized in 1803.

2. This excerpt is part of a long letter outlining developments in the gubernatorial election and urging Antifederalists to unite and work hard for the reelection of George Clinton.

Massachusetts Centinel (Boston), 22 April

FROM NEW-YORK.

APRIL 16. . . .

The six Representatives of this State are chosen, and behold, FOUR of them are staunch federalists.[1]

1. No printing of this item in a New York newspaper has been located.

DISTRICT 1

Both Antifederalist and Federalist public nominating meetings held in District 1 in mid-February 1789 chose Ezra L'Hommedieu, a Federalist, as their candidate for Representative. Yet as early as 22 February, Richard Platt, of the New York City Federalist committee of correspondence, reported that William Floyd was the Federalist candidate for the district (to Jeremiah Wadsworth, Representatives Election Commentary, above). L'Hommedieu may have voluntarily stepped aside in favor of Floyd, his brother-in-law, perhaps because he preferred election to the Senate rather than to the House of Representatives (see [Robert Troup] to Alexander Hamilton, [12 July], Part Four). In post-election speculation as to who the winner in District 1 would be, only Floyd is mentioned (Henry Knox to Edward Carrington, 8 March, and James Madison to George Washington, 19 March, both Representatives Election Commentary, above). Floyd was probably acceptable to the Antifederalists, who apparently did not nominate an opposition candidate. In early 1788 Jonathan N. Havens, a Suffolk County Antifederalist, called the idea that Floyd was an Antifederalist "comical," but still put Floyd on his slate of candidates for the state Convention (St. Patrick [Jonathan N. Havens] to John Smith, 5 April 1788, RC, John Smith of Mastic Papers, NHi).

Except where another location is indicated, the documents referred to above are printed below. There are additional documents concerning the election in District 1 printed in Representatives Election Commentary, above.

Daily Advertiser (New York), 9 February 1789

We are informed, from good authority, that Ezra L'Hommedieu, Esq. will be held up as the federal candidate for representative in Congress, for the district of Long and Staten-Islands.[1]

1. This article was reprinted in the *New York Packet*, 10 February 1789; *Federal Herald*, 16 February; and at least five out-of-state newspapers from Baltimore northward.

Kings County Nominating Meeting, 13 February[1]

At a numerous and respectable meeting of Freeholders and Farmers of Kings county at Flatbush, on Friday the 13th instant, it was unanimously agreed to support at the ensuing Election his Excellency *George Clinton* Esq. the present governor again as governor, and the Hon. Pierre Van Cortlandt, Esq. as Lieut. governor.

At the said meeting it was also unanimously agreed to support the Hon. Ezra L'Hommedieu Esq. as a representative at the ensuing Election for a representative to represent the district of the counties of Kings, Queens, Suffolk and Richmond, in the house of representatives of the Congress of the United States.

By order of the meeting,
PHILIP NAGEL, Chairman.

Flatbush, Feb. 13, 1789.

1. *Daily Advertiser*, 16 February 1789. The proceedings were reprinted in the *New York Packet*, 17 and 20 February; *New York Journal*, 26 February; and *Albany Journal*, 2 March; and printed in slightly different form in the *Federal Herald*, 2 March.

Richmond County Nominating Meeting, 14 February[1]

At a meeting of the most respectable inhabitants of the county of Richmond, on Saturday the 14th inst. EZRA L'HOMMEDIEU, Esq. was unanimously agreed to be voted for as representative to serve in Congress for the district to which that county belongs.

1. *Daily Advertiser*, 17 February 1789.

Daily Advertiser (New York), 17 February

Mr. CHILDS,

An inhabitant of King's county, would wish to enquire from the Chairman of the meeting at Flat-Bush,—who were the numerous and respectable Farmers & Freeholders of that county that composed the meeting?[1] There is good reason to suppose, that instead of its being a general, it was only a partial and interested one, made up chiefly of people under obligations to the present Governor, or of people in expectations of appointments, should the governor succeed in the ensuing election.—It certainly has the appearance of a stolen meeting, and sent abroad with a *brazen* countenance.[2]

1. See Kings County Nominating Meeting, 13 February 1789, above.
2. For a reply, see "A Spectator," *Daily Advertiser*, 18 February 1789, immediately below.

A Spectator, Daily Advertiser (New York), 18 February

Mr. CHILDS,

To satisfy the inhabitant of Kings county, who through the channel of your paper wishes to inquire from the chairman of the meeting held in the said county, on the 13th instant—"who were the numerous and respectable farmers and freeholders of that county which composed the said meeting?"[1] Please to inform him, that the meeting was composed of the Judges of the court of common pleas for the said county, the High Sheriff, county Clerk and some other civil magistrates, Supervisors, all the field officers commanding the regiment of militia in the said county, and some of the commissioned officers of the regiment, every person who has had the honour of being elected and served as a member to represent the county in the legislature of this state, since the revolution, except those members now actually attending the legislature at Albany, together with a number of respectable freeholders and inhabitants of the said county. The Kings county inhabitant might have fully informed himself at home and satisfied his curiosity without going abroad to another county for information, but as it appears his manner of inquiry is intended to deceive the public by holding forth, "that this meeting has the appearance of a stolen one," if he is still dissatisfied let him come forward with his name openly, and the facts above alledged respecting, the persons composing this meeting, shall be proved to his facc.

A Spectator at the Meeting Abovementioned.

Kings County, Feb. 17.

1. See *Daily Advertiser*, 17 February 1789, immediately above.

Daily Advertiser (New York), 19 February

Mr. CHILDS,

The Inhabitant of King's County feels himself highly obliged by the very *full* information which *Mr. Spectater of the Meeting at Flatbush* has given him.[1] He has never entertained a doubt but his honor the chief judge, with his colleagues of the court of common pleas, the high sheriff, county clerk, *some* other civil magistrates, the field officers of the militia, with *some* of the commissioned officers, and *every member* who has served in the legislature since the peace, gave a sanction to the meeting: But still he will support his assertion that the meeting was a partial and an interested one, and that the inhabitants throughout the county were not generally summoned for the purpose for deliberating upon so important a subject as that of nominating a Chief Magistrate.—He is still dissatisfied with Mr. Spectator's information, for the whole suit of his honor, his colleagues, high sheriff, county clerk, some magistrates, and even the *two* members who have served us since the peace, however high they sound, will make but a small part of the inhabitants of the respectable county of King's; and instead of intending to deceive, it was, and is only his intention to undeceive; he therefore again asserts at any risk (if Mr. Spectator pleases) that it was a partial and interested meeting, obtained by the influence of some great men of our county, whose views he is well acquainted with.

He would wish, however, to observe, that it is not intended to apply generally to the individuals who composed the meeting, for he is sensible that many of them, upon cooly considering the matter, will think with him, and see the necessity there is for changing the Chief Magistrate—He only means to apply his observations to the influence that brought the meeting forward.

February 18.

1. See "A Spectator," *Daily Advertiser*, 18 February 1789, immediately above.

Queens County Nominating Meeting, 19 February[1]

At a respectable Meeting of a number of the freeholders from the townships of North Hempstead, Jamaica, Flushing, and Newtown,

Colonel JOSEPH ROBINSON, Chairman.

Letters from the committee of Kings county, on the subject of electing a representative for the district of Long Island and Staten-Island, to serve this state in the Congress of the United States, was read. Also an address from the committee of the city of New-York, on the subject of electing a new governor for this state.[2]

On motion, Agreed that the hon. EZRA L'HOMMEDIEU, Esq. be nominated as a candidate for this district the ensuing election, for a representative in the Congress of the United States.

It is further agreed that this meeting coincide in sentiment with the meeting of the inhabitants of New-York, in holding up as candidate ROBERT YATES, Esq. as governor; and PIERRE VAN CORTLANDT. Esq. as lieutenant governor for this state.

The following gentlemen were appointed a committee to correspond with the other committees in the several counties in this district, on the subject abovementioned, viz.

Doctor Isaac Ledyard, Robert Furman, James D'Peyster, Doctor Daniel Monema, Francis Lewis, jun. Doctor William Lawton, Andrew Onderdonck, and John M. Smith.

By Order of the Meeting,
JOSEPH ROBINSON, Chairman.

Jamaica, Feb. 19, 1789.

1. *Daily Advertiser*, 23 February 1789. Reports of this meeting were reprinted in the *Daily Gazette* and *New York Packet*, both 24 February.

2. See Queens County Committee of Correspondence to New York City Federalist Committee of Correspondence, 19 February 1789, n. 4, immediately below.

Queens County Committee of Correspondence to New York City Federalist Committee of Correspondence, 19 February[1]

The Committee appointed by the Meeting at Bardin's Tavern, on the 11th inst[2] have received the following communication from Queens County.

A. HAMILTON, Chairman.

Gentlemen, *Jamaica, Feb.* 19, 1789.

This day a meeting was held in Jamaica of a number of respectable electors and freeholders from the towns of Flushing, North Hempstead, Jamaica, and Newtown.[3]

At the meeting it was agreed to nominate and support EZRA L'HOMMEDIEU, Esq. for representative in Congress. Letters from some members of your committee, enclosing your address,[4] were laid before the meeting, whereupon they agreed to nominate and support the Hon. ROBERT YATES, and PIERRE VAN CORTLANDT, Esqrs. as governor, and lieutenant governor. They then proceeded to choose a committee of correspondence to promote the measures agreed upon by the meeting. The proceedings of this meeting we have the honor to enclose,[5] and are, gentlemen, with great respect, your obedient humble servants,

Isaac Ledyard, Dan. Menema, John M. Smith, Francis Lewis, jun. Andrew Onderdonk, William Lawton, Robert Furman.

To the Committee of Corres-
pondence of New-York.

1. *Daily Advertiser*, 23 February 1789. This letter and the proceedings of the Queens County Nominating Meeting, 19 February 1789, immediately above, were reprinted in the *Daily Gazette* and *New York Packet*, both 24 February.

2. On 11 February 1789, New York City Federalists met at Bardin's Tavern to choose a candidate to oppose Governor George Clinton's reelection. They nominated an Antifederalist, Robert Yates, in an effort to divide Clinton's support, and appointed a committee of correspondence headed by Alexander Hamilton to publicize Yates's nomination throughout the state (see the account of "a numerous and respectable meeting of Citizens at Bardin's tavern on Wednesday the 11th instant," *Daily Advertiser* and *Daily Gazette*, both 13 February, and Alexander Hamilton "To the Supervisors of the City of Albany," 18 February, in the *Daily Advertiser* and *Daily Gazette*, both 20 February).

3. See Queens County Nominating Meeting, 19 February 1789, immediately above.

4. On 18 February 1789, Alexander Hamilton, chairman of the New York City Federalist committee of correspondence, addressed a circular letter to the supervisors of the city of Albany, supporting the candidacy of Robert Yates for governor. Both the *Daily Advertiser* and *Daily Gazette*, which printed the letter on 20 February, reported that the committee intended to send the letter to town supervisors throughout the state.

5. See Queens County Nominating Meeting, 19 February 1789, immediately above.

Queens County Committee of Correspondence to the Suffolk County Electors, 19 February[1]

Gentn.

The Electors of ye County of Queens having recd a Letter from the County of Kings[2] who had met and agreed upon Mr L Homadieu to be held up at ye ensuing Election for Representative of this District in ye House of Representatives in ye Congress of ye United States[3] and another Letter from a Committee appointed by ye Citizins of ye County of New York requesting the concurrence of this County with them in holding up ye Honble Robt. Yates Esquire at ye ensuing Election for Govr. of ye State of N York.[4] A number of respectable Electors & Freeholders of the Towns of Jamaica, North Hamstead, Flushing & New Town met at Jamaica and agreed with the County of Kings in holding up Ezra L Homadieu Esquire as a Member of ye House of Assembly of the Congress of the United States & having duly & seriously considered the weighty reasons contained in the address of ye Citizens of N York & other reasons at that time urged, did think it a Duty highly incumbent upon them both as Citizens of this State & of ye United States to nominate ye Honble Robt. Yates Esquire for Governor of this State.

We shall have the honor to forward to you a number of ye Addresses herein aluded to, and now enclose you the proceedings of ye Meeting at Jamaica.[5] We as a Committee of this Meeting have it in Charge to assure you that nothing but a real sense of Duty as well-wishers to their County induced to ye measures then taken & hope that the people of Suffolk will see it right to concur with them.

We have the honor to be with
great Respect Gentn.
Your Obedt. & very humble
Servts.

Jaimaica 19th Feby. 1789
To ye Electors of ye County of Suffolk

Francis Lewis Junr
Andrew Onderdonk
Robert Furman
John M Smith
Isaac Ledyard
Danl Menema
William Lawton

1. *Long Island Historical Society Quarterly*, I (1939), 20.
2. See Queens County Nominating Meeting, 19 February 1789, above.
3. See Kings County Nominating Meeting, 13 February 1789, above.
4. See Queens County Committee of Correspondence to New York City Federalist Committee of Correspondence, 19 February 1789, n. 4, immediately above.
5. See Queens County Nominating Meeting, 19 February 1789. above.

Daily Advertiser (New York), 9 April (excerpt)

On Tuesday[1] the committee appointed by the legislature to canvass and estimate the votes given in the different districts for representatives to Congress, met at the secretary's office in this city, and proceeded to the execution of their duty. . . .

In the district comprehending Long-Island and Staten-Island, the hon. William Floyd was found to have a majority of votes and was declared duly elected.

1. 7 April 1789.

New York Journal, 9 April (excerpt)

On Tuesday last the committee of both houses of the legislature of New-York (appointed for the purpose at the late session) began to canvass and estimate the votes for representatives from this state to the Congress of the United States, at the secretary's office.—This committee, last evening, had finished counting the ballots from three districts.

By this estimation it appeared, that WILLIAM FLOYD, Esq. had 894 votes, and was elected by the district composed of Long and Staten islands.[1]

1. Essentially the same report was reprinted in the *New York Packet*, 10 April 1789; *Weekly Museum*, 11 April; *Albany Journal*, 13 April; *Federal Herald*, 13 April; *Country Journal*, 14 April; *Hudson Weekly Gazette*, 14 April; and New Haven *Connecticut Journal*, 15 April. Beginning in mid-April the names of all the winners were printed in newspapers throughout the country.

District 2

The most publicized contest for Representative in the state took place in District 2. The dispute was not essentially between Antifederalists and Federalists, however, since New York City and adjacent areas were overwhelmingly Federalist. Rather, the election centered on whether a lawyer or merchant should represent the district. John Laurance, a lawyer, was nominated at a public meeting on 23 February, but shortly thereafter support developed for merchant John Broome, president of the New York City Chamber of Commerce. New York City Antifederalists generally supported Broome.

Among the interested spectators of the contest were members of the first federal Congress, then assembling in New York City for their first session.

There are additional documents concerning the election in District 2 printed in Representatives Election Commentary, above.

Daily Advertiser (New York), 7 February 1789

The Inspectors of the ensuing Election, are requested to meet on Monday evening 6 o'clock, at Simmons's Tavern in Wall-street.

John Lamb to John Smith, New York, 11 February (excerpts)[1]

As this seems to be a time for speculating in Election business, I wish our Friends (from the different Counties) who are Members of the Legislature would go in for, a Plan for the government [– – –] the Anti's, in the Southern District[2] by which we might be enabled to bring our force to a point and counteract the designs of our opponents.

This Evening the Feds, are to have a grand Meeting at the City Tavern, to form their Arrangement for the ensuing Elections; what System they will form I do not know but I dare to say, they will take their measures so as to secure (if possible) their Election, for Governor and Representatives.[3]

You will see by Child's Paper of this date that Judge Morris's Friends, are offended at the Junto's dropping him and taking up Judge Yates.[4]—I hope that his standing a Candidate, will divide their interest. . . .

Mr. Gelston and some more of our Friends are now at my House to consult on proper measures to be pursued, so as to form a Union of sentiment, with our Friends in Westchester County; and to fix on some proper Character to run against any person whom they may think proper to hold up in this District as a Candidate to represent us in the New Government.

1. RC, John Smith of Mastic Papers, NHi. The letter was addressed to Smith in Albany.

2. The southern senatorial district of New York consisted of Kings, New York, Queens, Richmond, Suffolk, and Westchester counties.

3. See Queens County Committee of Correspondence to New York City Federalist Committee of Correspondence, 19 February 1789, n. 2, District 1, above. City Tavern was also known as "Bardin's Tavern," after its owner, Edward Bardin. The New York City Federalists did not nominate a candidate for Representative until 23 February, when John Laurance was nominated.

4. Lamb's comment makes it clear that Federalist leaders had determined to reject Federalist Chief Justice Richard Morris in favor of Robert Yates as a candidate for governor even before

the meeting at Bardin's Tavern on 11 February—a decision not all of Morris's supporters accepted. On the same day Yates was nominated, the *Daily Advertiser* began printing a notice that stated that "the Friends of Chief Justice MORRIS, in this city, . . . are now happy in being able to assure the Public, that he will be offered at the ensuing Elections as a Candidate" for governor.

An Elector, New York Daily Gazette, 19 February

Mr. M'LEAN,

I have frequently, in different companies, heard AARON BURR, Esquire, mentioned as a proper person for Representative in Congress for this District; having seen no person yet publicly announced as a Candidate, I beg leave, through your paper, to hold the Name of that Gentleman.

AN ELECTOR.

New-York, February 19, 1789.[1]

1. This item was reprinted in the *Daily Advertiser*, 20 February 1789.

New Hampshire Spy (Portsmouth), 20 February

Extract of a letter from a gentleman in New York, dated February 8th, 1789.

The legislature of this state are yet in session at Albany. They have passed an act for choosing Representatives to the new Congress; but, by the last accounts, it was quite uncertain, whether they would agree on a mode for appointing Senators. We have no late accounts from Georgia. South-Carolina have chosen Gen. Sumter, Judge Burke, Dr. Tucker, D. Huger, and William Smith, Esquires, for Representatives, the last of which (only) is said to be federal. [*Melancholy fact.*][1] Am not informed respecting their Senators.—No particulars from Virginia, but fear their Representatives will be mostly Anties. The appointments in Maryland, Delaware and Pennsylvania, are chiefly federal. New Jersey has not decided—great interest is making there for the appointments, but suppose they will all be federalists. Mr. Hamilton would be chosen a Representative for the district in which this city is included, but it is said he declines it,[2] and there is some talk of putting up Mr. King[3]—but the choice of Representatives, in this state will not be determined until the first Tuesday in April.

There is not a Congress at present. It is expected there will be a sufficient number of members in town next week. It seems to be the earnest desire of the friends to the new government, that all the Senators and Representatives appointed, may be here on the day affixed for their meeting, as it will require considerable time to put the wheels in motion, and the interest of the Union *suffers much for want of government.*

1. The brackets are in the original printing.
2. As early as 29 January 1789, Hamilton wrote of "his own disinclination" to be a Representative (to Theodore Sedgwick, Part Two). Later, Tristram Lowther, a New York and North Carolina lawyer, wrote to James Iredell of North Carolina that "the popularity of Col: Hamilton has been hurt by his declining to represent this District in Congress[.] it is supposed he looks up to be financier general for which he has been preparing himself or to be appointed a foreign ambassador for either of which he is extremely well qualified, he is said & believed to be a man of such

extraordinary powers as to be able to render himself master of any subject in a week" (New York, 9 May 1789, Tr, Charles E. Johnson Collection, Nc-Ar).

3. It is unlikely that Rufus King was being seriously considered; he had only moved permanently to New York City from Massachusetts a few months before. However, the Boston *Massachusetts Centinel* reported on 4 March 1789 that "it is said" that King would be a candidate; it also noted that Hamilton had declined. The *Centinel* article was reprinted in the *Salem Mercury*, 10 March, and Portsmouth *New Hampshire Gazette*, 11 March. In late April 1789, King was elected to represent New York City and County in the Assembly.

A Federalist, Daily Advertiser (New York), 21 February

Mr. CHILDS,

Through the channel of your useful paper, I beg leave to recommend JOHN LAWRENCE Esq. to the suffrages of his Fellow Citizens as a fit person to represent this district in Congress.—His integrity and abilities in discharging the duties of the several important stations, to which he has been called by the voice of his country, prove him to be worthy of the public confidence; and besides bidding fair to combine in his favor, the influence of the various classes of citizens in this city, it is certain that he will be decidedly supported by his numerous Friends in West-Chester County.

A FEDERALIST.[1]

1. This announcement was also printed in the *Daily Gazette* on the same date.

New York City Nominating Meeting, 23 February[1]

At a very numerous and respectable Meeting of the Inhabitants of this City, convened at Bardin's Tavern, on the 23d Inst.—

Thomas Randall, Esq. in the Chair.

It was unanimously agreed, That JOHN LAWRENCE Esq. be supported as Representative for this District in the Congress of the United States.

And the Sense of the Meeting having been taken on the Nomination made by the Meeting assembled on the 11th Inst. of the Hon. ROBERT YATES, Esq. as Governor, and the Hon. PIERRE VAN CORTLAND, Esq. as Lieutenant Governor, the same was unanimously approved and confirmed.

And it was further agreed, that the Committee then appointed, should be a Committee for the foregoing purposes.[2]

By order of the Meeting,
THOMAS RANDALL, Chairman.

1. *Daily Gazette*, 24 February 1789. The *Daily Gazette* reprinted this item six times between 25 February and 4 March; the *Daily Advertiser* printed it six times between 24 February and 5 March. It also appeared in the *Morning Post*, 25 February; *New York Journal*, 26 February; *Weekly Museum*, 28 February; *Albany Journal*, 2 March; and *New York Packet*, 3 March.

2. The committee consisted of Alexander Hamilton (chairman), Robert Troup, William Duer, William Constable, John Murray, Richard Platt, Isaiah Wool, Robert Browne, Aaron Burr, John Meyer, George Gosman, James Robinson, and Daniel Hitchcock (*Daily Advertiser* and *Daily Gazette*, both 13 February 1789).

New York City Federalist Committee of Correspondence, Election Circular, c. 25 February[1]

Sir

As it will evidently be of great use in the ensuing election to have some Gentlemen of activity in each ward to superintend the business and promote activity among the electors the Committee appointed to forward the election of John Laurence Esquire will be much obliged by your assistance for those purposes, in the ward to which you belong, and request the same accordingly. With this view they will be happy to see you at Bardin's on Monday Evening next[2] at seven oClock to concert the preparatory arrangements.

I am Sir Your Obedient & hum servant A H[3]

By Order of the Committee

1. Syrett, V, 268–69. Syrett transcribed the document from a privately owned "Autograph Draft Signed," but notes that the initials "A H" have been crossed out on this draft. Syrett dates the document "[February 23–28]."
2. 2 March 1789, the day before the elections for Representatives began.
3. Alexander Hamilton was chairman of the committee of correspondence.

Westchester County Nominating Meeting, 26 February[1]

At a meeting of a number of the Freeholders and Inhabitants of the Towns in the County of West-Chester annexed to the City and County of New-York, as a district, held at the White Plains, on the 26th of Feb. 1789.

Joseph Browne, Esq; in the chair.

It was agreed that JOHN LAWRENCE, Esq; be supported as Representative for this district in the Congress of the United States, at the ensuing election.

It was further agreed that this meeting be adjourned to the Court House at Bedford on the 19th day of March next, for the purpose of then nominating Governor, Lt. Governor, and a Senator for the Southern District; and also Members of Assembly for the County at the ensuing election.

By order of the meeting,
JOSEPH BROWNE, Chairman.

1. *Daily Advertiser*, 3 March 1789. The *Advertiser* reprinted the report on 4 and 5 March; the *Daily Gazette* printed a similar item on 4 March. On 2 March the *Advertiser* had prepared its readers for the report by noting: "We are informed that at a meeting of the inhabitants of Westchester county, they have determined to support the election of JOHN LAWRENCE Esquire."

New York Journal, 26 February

A correspondent assures us, that a number of merchants, traders, mechanics, and others, are determined to give their votes at the ensuing election for a representative for this district to the general government in favor of JOHN BROOME, Esq. that information of the same is already sent to a number of influential gentlemen in West-Chester county and there is not a doubt but that he will have a majority of votes in that part of the district.

A Federal Merchant and an Elector, New York Daily Gazette, 26 February

To the MERCHANTS *of the City of New-York.*

Gentlemen,

In the operations of the intended government of the United States, the interests of the mercantile part of this State will be deeply affected, and as a Merchant, I feel myself extremely hurt by the proceedings of a late meeting for a nomination of a representative for this district to the general government,[1] especially as it is notoriously known, that a reputable Merchant was *hiss'd* for attempting to shew the necessity of the person to be elected, being taken from the body of Merchants; and as there was little prospect of being treated with decency at that meeting, unless in sentiment with the *Lawyers*, I have taken this method of proposing to you a few queries and observations.—

Can it be possible that of so very respectable a body of men as the Merchants of this city, not one gentleman can be found possessed of sufficient abilities to represent this great and respectable metropolis in the general government?

Is there no Merchant whose knowledge extend beyond his *counting-house?*—And is the mercantile interest of the State to be represented by none but *Lawyers*, &c.

There certainly are among the Merchants of this City many men of learning and extensive knowledge, although they are not acquainted with the *quibbling* and chicanery of law. Indeed I have only to mention the President of the Chamber of Commerce, *John Broome*, Esq. a gentleman of sound understanding, excellent judgment, and great mercantile knowledge, and as it has been urged to be of great importance to have a person elected who will be competent to determine on the *judiciary* part of the new government, Mr. Broome will be fully capable to judge of its merits and defects, he having been intended for the bar,[2] and received a suitable education for it.

Should you determine to support this gentleman at the ensuing election, it is believed that both the *federal* and *antifederal* mechanics and farmers of the city and county, will show, by their suffrages, that as they look up to the Merchant for encouragement and support, he will be a more proper Representative for a great commercial community, than a *Lawyer*; and from the information received from some respectable persons of that part of Westchester County comprised in this District, I am confident that a gentleman of Mr. Broome's known integrity and probity, will have a majority of the votes of the yeomanry of that part of the District.

A Federal Merchant and an Elector.

1. See New York City Nominating Meeting, 23 February 1789, above. John Laurance, a lawyer, was nominated for Representative at that meeting.

2. Before becoming a merchant, John Broome had studied law for a time with William Livingston of New Jersey.

Daily Advertiser (New York), 26 February

A number of respectable Merchants, Traders, and Mechanics of this city, are of opinion that the public good, and especially the interest of this city, requires that the Representative from this District to the Congress, should be a Merchant: As it is not probable that any gentleman of that class will be returned from any of the other

Districts, they therefore invite such of their fellow citizens as concur with them in opinion, to meet THIS EVENING, at Six o'clock, at the Merchants Coffee-House, to consult upon a proper mercantile character as a candidate.[1]

1. This item was also printed in the *Daily Gazette* and *New York Journal* on the same date. For a report about the meeting, see Chairman of the Coffee House Meeting to the Citizens of New York City, 26 February 1789, immediately below.

Chairman of the Coffee House Meeting to the Citizens of New York City, 26 February[1]

In consequence of an advertisement which appeared in the public papers of this day, inviting the citizens to meet at the Coffee-House, at 6 o'clock in the evening,[2] *to consult upon a proper mercantile character as a candidate to represent this district in the Congress of the United States*—a number of gentlemen convened, but finding that there was not sufficient room to contain the whole who attended upon the occasion, it was unanimously voted to adjourn until to-morrow evening, at 6 o'clock, to meet at the City Tavern—and that public notice thereof should be given to the citizens.

By Order of the Meeting,
W. MALCOM, Chairman.[3]

1. *Daily Advertiser*, 27 February 1789. This item was also printed in the *Daily Gazette*, 27 February 1789, and paraphrased in the *New York Packet*, 27 February.
2. See the *Daily Advertiser*, 26 February 1789, immediately above.
3. William Malcolm (1750–1791) was a New York City merchant and founding member of the city's chamber of commerce. He was a brigadier general in the state militia during the Revolution and in the militia of New York and Richmond counties in 1789. Malcolm was a New York City assistant alderman in 1785 and represented the city in the Assembly in 1784, 1786, and 1787.

New York City Federalist Committee of Correspondence to Their Fellow Citizens, 26 February[1]

The Committee appointed by the Meeting at Bardin's Tavern, on Monday Evening, for the purposes of carrying into execution the Views of the Meeting respecting the Election of Mr. JOHN LAWRENCE, as a Representative of this District in Congress, having understood that a Meeting was held this Evening at the Coffee-House in opposition to that Nomination, which has been adjourned till To-morrow Evening, at Bardin's Tavern, and thinking it of importance to the Union of the City that the intended Meeting should be a full one, beg leave to recommend the general attendance of their fellow Citizens upon that occasion.

By Order of the Committee,
ALEXANDER HAMILTON,
Chairman.

1. *Daily Gazette*, 27 February 1789. This notice was also printed in the *Daily Advertiser* on the same date.

New York City Nominating Meeting, 27 February[1]

The Citizens who upon an adjournment Assembled at the City Tavern this Evening—upon Motion of Colonel Robert Troup, by a very great Majority, did confirm the Proceedings of a Meeting held at the same place on Monday the 23d Inst. and Voted that the same should be Published.

By order of the Meeting,
WM. MALCOM, Chairman.

Upon Motion, it was Resolved, that the unanimous Thanks of the Meeting be voted to Gen. Malcom for his impartial Conduct in the Chair.

New-York, Feb. 27.

1. *Daily Gazette*, 28 February 1789. This item was also printed in the *Daily Advertiser*, 28 February and 3 March, and *New York Packet*, 3 March.

A Friend to Truth, New York Daily Gazette, 27 February

A person who addresses the Merchants of this city, under the signature of *A Federal Merchant and an Elector*,[1] has asserted, that at the meeting at Bardin's on Monday last, a very reputable Merchant was hissed "*for attempting to shew the necessity of the person to be elected being taken from the body of the Merchants.*" This is a gross misrepresentation of the fact. It is true, that very unfortunately a very respectable Merchant was hissed at that meeting, by part of the persons present. But it is not true that it was for the cause alledged. It was for asserting in direct terms, that *it would be a disgrace to the city to be represented by any but a Merchant*; a position neither just in itself, nor to be countenanced by any other class of the community. It is therefore more to be regretted than to be wondered at, that it should have produced such a mark of indignation in a mixed assembly. And I have even been informed that the hiss originated with some of the mercantile part of the meeting. In making these remarks, it is not meant to justify the *thing*, but to correct misrepresentation.

Being one of the meeting, I was a witness of what passed, and can appeal to every gentleman present for the truth of the above statement.

Though shocked at the declaration which produced it, I was sorry to see it occasion any thing like intemperance or indecorum; and sincerely felt for the gentleman concerned, from a belief, that though he had uttered a most exceptionable sentiment, his expressions imported more than he intended.

A FRIEND TO TRUTH.

1. See the *Daily Gazette*, 26 February 1789, above.

The Gubernatorial Campaign and the New York City Nominating Meetings, 11, 23, and 27 February

The Bardin's Tavern nominating meetings on 11, 23, and 27 February and the city's method of nominating a federal Representative played important roles in the gubernatorial campaign between Robert Yates and George Clinton. Federalists frequently referred to the nominating meetings to prove that Yates had been freely chosen at open public meetings, and that he therefore represented the views of a majority of the city's voters. Antifederalists retold the story of the meetings time and again to prove that Yates had been nominated by audiences that had been deliberately packed with Federalists, and that these meetings were not a true indication of Yates's support. (In the election in New York City and County in late April, Yates outpolled Clinton, 833 to 385.)

The following four documents are from campaign broadsides and newspaper essays that appeared between 9 March and 8 April, during the gubernatorial election campaign. Each throws additional light on the nominating meetings and the city's nomination of a federal Representative.

Federal Herald (Lansingburgh), 9 March

Abstract of a letter from a gentleman at
New-York, to his friend in Albany.

I wrote you fully by the last post of our situation and prospect—The friends to governor Clinton since that, have been endeavoring to play upon the feelings of the merchants with a view of exciting a scism in this city, in hopes of turning it to advantage in the election for governor—In that design they caused a meeting to be held at the Coffee-house, on Tuesday evening,[1] which was adjourned to Friday evening, at Bardin's tavern. The *pretended* object was to promote the election of a *merchant* to represent this district, in the house of representatives of the Congress; the *real one* to sow division. The committee immediately convened and published an invitation to the citizens. The consequence was a very numerous meeting indeed. General Malcolm (who had presided at the meeting at the Coffee-house) was continued in the chair, and the friends of governor Clinton were so effectually combated, that, though their whole strength was collected, when the question came to be taken, they had not more than from 12 to 20 hands in their favor. The result has been, that Gen. Malcolm has subscribed, not only to the nomination of Mr. LAWRENCE, for representative but, to that of judge YATES for governor. The victory was complete, and has confirmed the unanimity of the city against Mr. Clinton. The accounts we receive from other parts of the district are perfectly agreeable to our wishes, and there is great reason to believe that judge Yates will prevail, Kings county is not satisfied with the nomination of Mr. Clinton, and as soon as Mr.   arrives, a meeting will be held there. Judge Morris has resigned his pretentions, and the friends of Lt. governor Cortlandt will urge him to do the same.[2]

New York City Federalist Committee of Correspondence to the Electors of New York, 1 April (excerpt)[3]

To the independent and patriotic Electors
of the State of New-York. . . .

Three successive mixed and numerous meetings of the inhabitants of this city, have concurred in the nomination of Judge Yates, and in the appointment of us to forward the success of that nomination. The first of these meetings was held on the 11th of Feb. last. Of the intention of holding this meeting, besides free and unreserved verbal communications, a previous notification was fixed up in the coffee-house, a place of constant resort by the merchants in general. Some hundreds of respectable citizens of different classes attended, and were unanimous in the nomination of Judge Yates. Of this meeting Mr. William Constable, a respectable merchant and freeholder, was chairman.

On the 23d of February, a second meeting was had upon like previous notification, considerably more numerous than the former. At this meeting, which was also a mixed one, the great body of the merchants were present. The original purpose of it was to nominate a representative of the district in Congress; but it was thought advisable to take the sense of this meeting also on the subject of the election for governor. The result was the same as at the former. It was agreed unanimously, or with not more than from six to twelve dissenting votes at the most, to support Judge Yates. Of this meeting Mr. Thomas Randal, an ancient and very respectable burgher, was chairman.

The third meeting was had on the 27th February.

The circumstances attending this meeting, afford conclusive evidence of the sense of this city. They were briefly these.—Some persons dissatisfied, probably from various motives, with the nomination of the representative in Congress, made at the preceding meeting, called, through the channel of the newspapers, another meeting for the purpose of making a different nomination. At this meeting, several, if not all of those who compose the committee of which Mr. Jonathan Lawrence is chairman,[4] were present. Mr William Malcom, one of them, was placed in the chair. This meeting adjourned for want of room, till the next evening, to a different place; which was announced the day following in the public prints.

We, on our part, published the day following, a general invitation to the citizens, to attend at the time and place appointed.[5] This we did, in order to obtain the more full and complete sense of the city, and prevent the success of an attempt, which we considered as calculated to produce a division, in respect to the election of a representative, which might be turned to account in that of governor.

A meeting was held according to adjournment; there was a greater concourse of the citizens upon this occasion, than there had been upon either of the former; comprehending as before the principal part of the merchants, and a large number of other very respectable inhabitants. Mr. William Malcom was again placed in the chair. A free and fair course was allowed to debate on both sides. Mr. Melancton Smith, and Mr. Marinus Willet, two other members of the adverse committee, spoke repeatedly and largely. The result was, that the former nomination, not only of the person to be representative, but of Mr. Yates as Governor, was confirmed by an almost unanimous vote. We express ourselves thus, because out of several hundred persons, of whom the meeting consisted, we are confident there were not above forty, (if so many) who dissented from what was done. And we can with the utmost truth add, that from every appearance, there is great reason to believe, that pains were taken to collect the friends of Governor Clinton upon the occasion. But be this as it may, we trust it must be apparent to every candid man, from the circumstances attending this last meeting as stated, that the inhabitants of this city are almost unanimous in their preference of Judge Yates to Governor Clinton. . . .

By order of the Committee,
ALEXANDER HAMILTON, Chairman,

New-York, April 1, 1789.

New York City Committee to Reelect Governor Clinton to the Electors of New York, 7 April (excerpt)[6]

To the Unbiassed & Independent
ELECTORS
OF THE
STATE OF NEW-YORK. . . .

We now beg leave to make a few remarks on the evidence which our opponents bring forward to prove, that the great body of the freeholders of this city and county favor the election of Judge Yates.—It is said, that three successive and numerous meetings held in this city, concurred in his nomination—The first of these was held for the express purpose of deliberating on the choice of Governor. We believe that a notification thereof was fixed upon the Coffee-House, on the day preceding it but very few of the burghers of the city, except those who generally frequent the Coffee-House, and who are but a small proportion of the qualified electors, knew any thing of the matter, until after the proceedings were published. It is said, that free and verbal communications were unreservedly given, of the intended meeting, but we cannot learn, that any of the friends of Governor Clinton were made acquainted with it.

The second meeting was intended to nominate a Representative to the Congress of the United States—Very few of the citizens, who favored the re-election of Governor Clinton, interested themselves in this business.

The third, and last meeting, was held in consequence of an invitation, published in the newspapers, inviting such persons as were of opinion, that it was proper to choose a mercantile character to represent this district in the house of representatives of the Congress of the United States, to nominate one for that purpose; for want of room, this meeting was adjourned to Bardin's tavern, to assemble on the following evening. It is well known, that the gentlemen, who promoted this meeting had nothing in view but to support the election of a merchant, as the most suitable character to represent this commercial city, and to fix upon the person proper to be held up as the candidate. It is a fact, notorious to the whole city, that this meeting was diverted from the object for which it was originally called, and decided upon a question totally unconnected with the one upon which they were invited to assemble. We forbear to make any remarks upon the artifice made use of to bring about this event; we cannot help, however, observing that the room was filled before the hour appointed for the meeting; that there were as many persons without the room as there were in it; and that a very great majority, it is presumed, of those who voted, were not electors.

Our opponents assert, that at this meeting a free and fair course was admitted to debate on both sides; we appeal to every candid person who attended, whether the gentlemen who spoke in favor of a mercantile character, did not suffer great and frequent interruption, so as not to be heard at any considerable distance. It is further to be remarked, that no debate whatever was had, respecting the election of Governor. It is a very vague and uncertain method of ascertaining on which side a majority of such a city as this lies, from the determination of a meeting like the one held at Bardin's. Many of the most respectable citizens are averse to assemblies of that kind, and seldom, if ever, attend them. On such occasions many persons appear, and are the most zealous, who have no votes; and the minds of a number are influenced by the address of public speakers, to decisions, of which, in their cooler moments, they are convinced of the impropriety. We will not undertake to determine what proportion of the electors will give their suffrages in favour of Governor Clinton: we are sensible that this must, in a great measure, be a mere matter of opinion on both sides, and that the sentiments of men, on subjects of this nature, are apt to accord with their wishes; of this, however, we are confident, that no such unanimity exists, as our opponents seem to suppose, and would induce you to believe. It is not our wish to deceive our fellow citizens by misrepresentations; and we pledge ourselves to them, that the friends to the Governor, in this city, are respectable, both in point of character, and number.

By Order of the Committee,
JONATHAN LAWRENCE,
CHAIRMAN.

New-York, April 7, 1789.

Philanthropos, Daily Advertiser (New York), 8 April (excerpt)

To the Independent and patriotic Electors of the State of New-York.

. . . I beg leave

First, To call your attention to those persons, with whom the opposition to Governor Clinton in favor of Judge Yates, originated, this naturally begs a question or two. Does not the opposition owe its birth to the landed interest in the state? Yes: And is not the same backed by the characters high in power, legislative, judicial and executive, all of whom I trust are the wealthy and great? If this is the fact which no one can doubt, the one idea is true, and that the other is so also, I will observe,

Secondly, That whoever attended the meeting alluded to by Mr. H—n on the 27th February, wherein the business of former meetings was ratified, must be easily convinced, that the majority of the people then convened in the great room, at Bardin's tavern, came clearly within the second class, and that one of the champions of the night was known to be at the head of them; if these are facts, wherein does inconsistency exist? I trust no where. And that they are facts, no one will deny. At this meeting let me observe, for your satisfaction, that the greater number of those who have a right to vote for Governor in this city, who attended the meeting for the purposes the same was called, had not an opportunity to hear the debates, owing to the rooms being filled with school-boys, merchants, lawyers and mechanic's apprentices, before the business could be fairly opened; and that one of those gentlemen, Mr. Smith,[7] who is said to have spoken repeatedly and largely at the meeting—it was with great difficulty he could force his way through a throng of the above description to a place from whence he could be heard, and when there, I deny that either he or the other gentlemen entered upon the subject of the choice of Governor. No, it was foreign to the business for which they met. The only question was, which of the two characters, a lawyer or a merchant was the most suitable to represent this district in the general government, and that their speeches were confined to that subject, the truth of it I submit to those who were present. This accounts for the smallness of the minority of that meeting, and I have also above accounted to you for the method pursued by the Governor's friends to ascertain their number in this city. Which every candid person will think with me under those circumstances was the most eligible. The friends of the Governor want not to deceive you by misrepresentations—No gentlemen—nor have they ever had an idea of the kind—They know you have been grossly abused hitherto in that way—but fortunately the reverse effect is already experienced from that intended by the enemies of the governor, they are now convinced of this, and wish they had directed their malice in a different channel from that hitherto pursued. . . .

PHILANTHROPOS.

1. The meeting was held on Thursday, 26 February 1789.

2. This letter was reprinted in the Fredericksburg *Virginia Herald*, 26 March 1789.

3. Broadside, MiU-C. This broadside was also printed in the *Daily Advertiser*, 2 April 1789, and *New York Packet*, 3 April.

4. Jonathan Lawrence (1737–1812), a New York City merchant and state senator for the Southern District, 1777–1783, was chairman of the city's committee for the reelection of George Clinton as governor.

5. See New York City Federalist Committee of Correspondence to Their Fellow Citizens, 26 February 1789, above.

6. Broadside, NHi. This broadside was also printed in the *Daily Advertiser*, 14 April 1789; *New York Packet*, 14 April; and *New York Journal*, 16 April. The *Journal*, 9 April, had informed its readers that the broadside was received too late to be printed in the issue of that date; it would be printed in the next issue.

7. Melancton Smith.

Daily Advertiser (New York), 27 February

The Votes and Interest of the Electors of this District, are requested in favor of JOHN BROOME, Esq to represent them in the Congress of the United States.—He is a Gentleman of great Mercantile Knowledge, sound Judgment, and firmly attached to the Constitution—Altho' a Merchant, he is a Man of Letters, and well acquainted with Law.[1]

1. The *Daily Advertiser* printed this notice again on 28 February and 4 March 1789.

Brutus, Daily Advertiser (New York), 28 February

To the free Electors of this District.

GENTLEMEN,

Being at a very large and respectable meeting of the citizens held at Bardin's tavern, on the 23d inst. at which a very large proportion of the merchants were present—after cool deliberation, it was unanimously resolved to hold up JOHN LAWRENCE, Esq. as representative for this district, in the Congress of the United States. I was not a little surprised to see in the paper of yesterday, a meeting called at the Coffee-House, to consult upon a proper mercantile character to represent this district. I felt that anxiety which every good citizen must feel when the state is likely to be distracted and split into factions by the influence of ambitious men. I conjectured that it was a *deep laid plan*, which the bare view of the meeting, *the chairman, the principal speakers*, confirmed. To be plain, my fellow citizens, it is a Cl—t—n—n[1] faction. It is done with a design to disturb that unanimity which has so happily prevailed among the inhabitants of this city, in hopes that by sowing the seeds of discord at present among us, they will grow up against that day when the election of a chief magistrate is to be held. Forbid it my countrymen! Let not those tools of unlimited ambition blind you. Remember that it is owing to our firmness and unanimity on a former occasion, that the state is at this day a member of the United States under the new constitution.—Remember that the same persons who advised and counselled you then, advise you at present. Those very persons who have managed our affairs during the late gloomy prospect; and, in spite of the opposition of a man, whose high office, during a *long* administration, has rendered him very influential, have, by their integrity and perseverance, placed them in the happy situation they now are,—advise and entreat you to be unanimous in perfecting what you have been so far successful in. United we continue respectable in the eyes of our fellow citizens of the other states. Divided we become contemptible. But pray what is the cause of this division? Because the person held up as a proper person to represent us in the United States, is not of a *particular* class of citizens. Is this fair? Is it proper that one class of citizens, in a city where there are such a number of different professions and employments, should (even permitting that class to be more numerous than any other class) say, that they are entitled to have a member of their class sent to the Congress to represent all the rest, and that it would be a *disgrace* for the district to be represented by one of any other profession. Is this reasonable? Is it acting like republicans? No, I hope every good citizen and I am sure the greatest part of the merchants are so, will spurn at so illiberal an idea. Let us consider the man and his qualities, not his profession. For my own part, were there a merchant and a lawyer both equally well qualified, though I have no particular attachment nor aversion to any profession whatever, I should give my suffrage for the former, in order to promote that harmony among my fellow citizens which is so much to be wished for at this *critical juncture*; but when I am conscious that this is not the case, I feel myself bound by a regard to my own welfare, by the duty I owe to this state in particular, and to the United States in general, to prefer him who is best qualified, who has the knowledge requisite, and what is equally important, the gift of communicating it. The gentleman unanimously agreed upon to be held up by a large proportion of the citizens, tho' he has the *misfortune* to be a lawyer, is a man of known integrity and firmness, possessed of the qualities requisite for the office, and tho' no merchant, has perhaps more of that abstracted and speculative mercantile knowledge requisite for forming commercial treaties, and planning out an extensive system of commerce, than merchants infinitely better acquainted with the practical part of merchandise; and if he should be at a loss for any thing in that respect, he can at all times have the information of the merchants, to whom he no doubt will recur, and consult upon every occasion, when their interests are concerned. The mercantile gentleman, *for whom the votes of the electors are requested*, was to be sure a very high character in the *newspapers*. I confess I have not so perfect a knowledge of him as this gentleman, who holds him up, seems to have; but from the little I have, I am apt to think that he has viewed his qualifications and abilities through a magnifier. There are among that respectable class of citizens, the merchants, a great number of persons much better qualified for such an office than he is. Not to mention more, is not Wm. Seton, Esq.[2] infinitely better qualified in every respect? As to the gentleman's law knowledge, of which we are informed, I believe it is not very extensive. It is not that knowledge of the laws of nations, and of the several commercial treaties of different nations, as well as that extensive knowledge of the boundaries and limits of the different courts of judicature, so necessary for a representative. As to his integrity, his COUNTRY, before whom he had the honor to come when A—d—m—n, can best attest that.[3] But he is the properest person for the objects of those, who wish to make him a tool for distracting the city in the same manner as their beloved *head* has done the country. He is said to be firmly attached to the new system of government; if he is really so, he will not suffer himself to be held up to serve so base a purpose as its enemies design. He will not be the cause of dividing his fellow citizens, and of disturbing that harmony so happily subsisting to the great mortification of those who are afraid it will be the means of turning out of office a magistrate, whom, when virtuous, his fellow citizens loved and honored, but now, when ambitious without limits, they must degrade and despise.

BRUTUS.

New York, Feb 27.

1. Clintonian.
2. Seton was a New York City merchant.
3. John Broome was an alderman for New York City's East Ward, 1783–1784 and 1785–1786. During his last term on the city council, the aldermen were accused of extortion; the case was never brought to trial (see *Daily Advertiser*, 29 April 1786).

John Randolph to St. George Tucker, New York, 1 March (excerpt)[1]

There has been a terrible ado a few Days since in this Town concerning a Representative to be sent from this District, and likewise with Regard of turning out the Governor & substituting Judge Yates in his Place—The Words *party Tory, Anti & Federalist* compose the greatest Part of the Conversation of this Place.—

1. RC, St. George Tucker Papers, DLC. The letter was addressed to Tucker in Williamsburg, Virginia. Randolph (1773–1833), a stepson of Tucker, was attending Columbia College in New York City in 1789. He later represented Virginia in the House of Representatives, 1799–1813, 1815–1817, 1819–1825, and 1827–1829, and in the United States Senate, 1825–1827; he was known as "John Randolph of Roanoke." Tucker (1752–1827), a Virginia lawyer, had become a judge of the Virginia General Court in 1788.

Hugh Williamson to James Iredell, New York, 2 March (excerpt)[1]

There has been a considerable debate among the citizens of New York whether a Lawyer or Merchant, both Federalists, shall represent this District in the new Congress. The election comes on soon: it seems to be at length agreed to support the Lawyer. Gov. Clinton will be hard run: a moderate Antifed is started against him, &c.

1. Griffith J. McRee, *Life and Correspondence of James Iredell* . . . (2 vols., New York, 1857–1858), II, 255.

Lynceus, Daily Advertiser (New York), 2 March

To the Federal Electors of this District.

Gentlemen,

The unanimity of so large a meeting as that held at the city tavern on Friday evening,[1] where there were almost a 1000 citizens present, and not forty dissenting voices, plainly shews the intention of those who called the meeting at the coffee house, and who had the assurance to say that it was the wish of a large proportion of the merchants, a class of citizens no less noted for their attachment to the beneficial system of government lately adopted, than for their firmness and steadiness on all occasions, and who with one voice disapproved of altering the nomination of the 23d ult.—But the persons who called this meeting have different views from the merchants, whose sole object must be the prosperity of the country. They wish for a division of sentiments among the citizens—they find that unanimity in promoting the public welfare is inimical to ambitious men—Had a merchant been proposed, and had the citizens thought that it would have been most for their interest to hold him up, they then would not have been for a lawyer.—Their conduct on Saturday as well as their obstinacy on Friday evening fully demonstrates the truth of this assertion; after finding that the citizens who met that evening were almost unanimously of opinion that, considering all circumstances, John Lawrence, Esq was the properest person to represent them, ought not, then, the few who differed from the citizens at large, in political sentiments, acquiesced in the opinion of so great a majority, and like good citizens remained quiet till the day of election, and then, if they thought proper, come up to the poll and vote according to their sentiments? but their conduct is very different. Finding that their address to the pride of the merchants was too shallow an artifice to escape the discernment of so enlightened a body, they now attack another class of respectable citizens—I mean the mechanics. They have been endeavouring ever since, both by themselves and their emissaries, to infuse into their minds a jealousy against the lawyers, by using the three following arguments: 1st, that they endeavour to engross all the offices of the state—Every citizen of the least discernment must see that this is a misrepresentation, that they neither wish, and that if they did, they could not engross more than their proportion, that in general they are an accommodating set of men—That if a survey is made of the different offices in the state, it will be found that each class of citizens have a pretty equal share—that there are not more of them filled with gentlemen of the bar than the public welfare requires; and that those offices, which that class of citizens have filled, have been discharged with integrity. 2d, They have advanced, and endeavour to persuade the mechanics that this class of citizens in particular wished to prevent any of them from being elected aldermen at the last election. There is only one gentleman of that profession who is an alderman, and he was elected to that office, vacant by the resignation of his predecessor, by the unanimous suffrages of the electors of that ward, a very small proportion of whom are of his profession. There was only one other law character who was held up as a candidate, partly by the mechanics, to divide a certain interest, in order to promote the election of that worthy mechanic who now fills the office. I believe it is pretty generally known that several of the gentlemen of the bar were very instrumental in promoting the election of the mechanics. The last argument, and the most useful for the purpose, is that it is owing to the lawyers that the citizens have so large a tax imposed on them for the repairs of the city-hall[2]—A strange assertion indeed! But are the sacred walls of truth sufficient to confine those men who, forgetting the true interests of their country, have devoted themselves to support an ambitious man, in whose downfall is involved the annihilation of their own consequence? To what lengths will they not go to secure unto him the power of bestowing the rewards promised to his successful servants? Will they not throw every obstacle in the way of that system of government under which his power and influence will be lessened the man of merit alone rewarded and promoted, and those little meteors who shine by reflected light, rendered invisible. But, my fellow-citizens, to blame the lawyers for this, is ungenerous—they were not the cause of it, as you all, who have read the journals of the assembly must well know. Nor is it a matter for which any one deserves censure. On the other hand, they are worthy of praise. The design of laying out this money, which certainly has been all given to the mechanics, was to accommodate the congress in such a manner as might induce them to fix the seat of the federal government for some time here, a thing which will be very beneficial for every class of citizens, more particularly the mechanics, and will very amply reward them for the very small portion of tax that will fall to their share. But why, it may be asked, tax this city, and not the whole state? For want of a man of public spirit at the head of it. A man who would endeavour impartially to promote the interest of the whole, and not that of a party; at whose head he has placed himself, and to whose good alone he is attentive. My fellow citizens it is owing to the influence of that man, whose *junto* in this city, endeavours to prejudice you against your best friends, in order that they may take an advantage of the division to re-elect him to rule over you. They declared at the public meeting on Friday evening, that they thought the representative from this district ought to be a man early, firmly, and uniformly attached to the new government, they *gild the pill in order that it may appear the more agreeable.* They hold up a man whose attachment to this system was long suspected, and who never declared for it till he saw that the current in this city run strongly that way. But he is a friend of their bosom friend, he is a man who, if they can promote him, will, they think, assist them in their design. Is it for nothing that they have been so active in endeavoring to carry his election ever since he was first mentioned? Is it because they think the interest of the district will be materially served by preferring him to the other candidates, that one of their party set out early on Saturday morning to Westchester to try to carry his election there, if not, at least to make a division, which I hope they cannot make here. Can any one say, that he is a man fit to lead the representation of the state? Is he one of sufficient influence to be of service to the city, in preventing the removal of the seat of government from this place, if it should come to be agitated in Congress? Has he sufficient abilities to produce the most forcible arguments against it? Every one who knows the man will answer, if he is candid, in the negative. But for want of these qualities they would prefer him. It is not their wish that Congress should stay here; Why? Because their champion wishes to see no man within the state so great as himself; and because he is afraid, as he is of so hospitable a disposition, that from the numerous entertainments he will then have an opportunity of giving, that the generosity of his heart may get the better of the prudence of his head. But my fellow citizens, as it is your wish and interest as well as mine to endeavor to keep the Congress here, now is the time to put in a man to represent us who has influence and abilities equal to the task. Let us all then unite in supporting that candidate held up by so great a majority of our fellow citizens at two very large meetings. Let us, like eagles watching their prey, be attentive to the motions of those factious men, whose sole design is either to carry a man friendly to their views, or to divide the happy unanimity of sentiment which prevails in the city; having discovered the plot, let us be on our guard against it, by remembering that happy motto, *One and All.*

LYNCEUS.

1. See New York City Nominating Meeting, 27 February 1789, above.
2. This refers to efforts by the city to renovate city hall in preparation for the first federal Congress.

Portius, Daily Advertiser (New York), 2 March

Mr. CHILDS,

Like BRUTUS, your paragraphist of last Saturday,[1] I was present at the meetings lately held for the purpose of holding up a fit person to represent us in the Congress of the

United States. Like him I went to hear argument, and to listen to whatever should be offered worthy of discreet men's notice; and like him too I was well satisfied with the result of the *first* deliberation at the City-Tavern.[2] Two reasons induced my hearty concurrence. 1st. Because the business was conducted with temper, and because there was explicit and substantial arguments urged by a gentleman to whom this city owes infinite obligations, and because those arguments were succeeded with a ready acquiescence, and with a vote uncommonly unanimous—2d. Because I was convinced that the sentiments which prevailed in the assembly room last Monday, very generally agreed with the voice of the people of the county at large.—Though I believe this to be a fact, yet I am displeased, (I beg Brutus' pardon 'tis of no great consequence) with the unhandsome reflections he takes occasion to insinuate as to the *characters and sources* of opposition to the decision of Monday last—Brutus has not done well in ascribing the whole management of opposition and the meeting at the Coffee-House to the agency of Clintonian tools—(I beg his pardon if I have misunderstood him and filled up the blanks improperly.) It is a truth that a merchant would have been very acceptable to many worthy citizens of different classes who are alike friends to the new government, but in the attempt to get such a representative it was very unfortunate that a few mercantile characters of more zeal than judgment took the lead in the business in such a manner, that had it not been checked in time might have essentially disturbed the political harmony of our city.—Had a merchant of acknowledged abilities come forward, I am sure he would have received the support of the city at large—but that discerning class of men saw (and many of the principal among them I heard frankly confess) that they really had no one in view whom at the *present* conjuncture they thought sufficiently fit for the office, and therefore I am confident have universally withdrawn their opposition. It is very certain that some intemperate federalists would have hazarded the advantages which union *here* on several important occasions has procured us, it is also true that there would not be men wanting who would assist in "troubling the waters," but in the present instance it is unfair to direct the whole strength of public indignation against the *chairman and principal speakers*.—General Malcom, tho' a decided antifederalist, and a decided friend to the governor, as far as he appeared in the late business behaved well—He contended for nothing while in the chair but order, and took the sense of both meetings in a way, that entitled him to what at the conclusion of the business he received, a unanimous vote of thanks!

I confess I dislike the view that Brutus gives us of the quondam A—n for whom the votes of the electors was requested.[3]—That gentleman is a merchant of character and respectability, and the side-glance at his conduct while a magistrate is very improper. No judgment was qiven in that case to substantiate guilt, and when after investigation no punishment is inflicted, 'tis an honorable presumption to believe there was no crime.[4] Upon the whole I acknowledge that Brutus has done well in warning his fellow citizens to beware of combinations calculated to produce disunion, but ambitious men will not be the less restless by being improperly accused, and I believe it will be found that moderation in politics, like moderation in religion, is the only rational way to make converts.

PORTIUS.

1. "Brutus," *Daily Advertiser*, 28 February 1789, above.
2. See New York City Nominating Meeting, 23 February 1789, above.

3. John Broome, who was an alderman for New York City's East Ward, 1783–1784 and 1785–1786.

4. During Broome's last term on the city council, the aldermen of New York City were accused of extortion; the case was never brought to trial (see *Daily Advertiser*, 29 April 1786).

Daily Advertiser (New York), 2 March (excerpt)[1]

Extract of a letter from Albany, dated Feb. 25.

"The exertions that our fellow citizens in your part of the state are making in favor of Judge Yates, are very pleasing to a great majority of citizens in these northern counties: God grant it may prove successful, as the peace and prosperity of the state depends on it.

There has lately been a very numerous meeting of inhabitants from Albany, Columbia, and Montgomery counties, at Lansingburgh, when they agreed to support Judge YATES at the ensuing election.[2]

I am thoroughly satisfied that our political enemies have nothing in view but a total subversion of the new government, and that it is of the utmost importance to have as many of its firm friends in it as possible;—it behoves you therefore to return a decided and unequivocal character in your district. Considering this matter in its most important light, I think good policy dictates that Mr. Lawrence should be supported at the ensuing election; he is a determined federalist, and will be a useful member. Beware of divisions! . . ."

1. For another excerpt from this article, see Part Two. The article was reprinted in the *Daily Gazette*, 3 March 1789, and Philadelphia *Federal Gazette*, 5 March.

2. See Albany, Columbia, and Montgomery Counties Nominating Meeting, 10 February 1789, District 5, below.

Daily Advertiser (New York), 2 March

We are informed that at a meeting of the inhabitants of Westchester county, they have determined to support the election of JOHN LAWRENCE Esquire.[1]

1. This item was reprinted in the *Daily Gazette*, 3 March 1789.

New York Daily Gazette, 2 March

A Numerous Body of the Citizens, Merchants, Mechanics and others, are determined to give their suffrages for JOHN BROOM Esq. as a Representative to the Congress, at the Election to be held on Tuesday next; notwithstanding the determination of the Meeting at Bardin's Tavern, on Friday last.

It must be apparent to every candid Citizen, that the interest of every class of men in the district, is intimately concerned in having a man of mercantile information to represent them; especially in the first Legislature, who are to form the whole system of commercial regulations.

The prosperity of the farmer, the landholder and the mechanic, as well as the merchant, are all connected with the prosperity of trade.

It is obvious that the sentiments of a great majority of the inhabitants of this city are decidedly in favour of a mercantile character to fill this important station. The gentleman who is proposed as a candidate, is of respectable character and abilities. He is President of the Chamber of Commerce, which is an evidence that he is highly esteemed in his profession; and has been, from the beginning, a decided and uniform friend to the New Constitution.

The free Citizens, it is hoped, will come forward, and give their votes on this occasion, according to the dictates of their own judgments, uninfluenced by the opinions or conduct of any man or set of men.

We are assured from undoubted authority from Westchester county, that Mr. Broom will be held up and supported there.

Curtius, Daily Advertiser (New York), 3 March

To the Electors of this District.

FELLOW CITIZENS,

It is with a degree of painful solicitude that I address you. When I contemplate but the bare possibility of your dividing into parties at this momentous period, all those anxious sensibilities press upon my mind that are natural to the man who makes your political happiness one of the constant and warmest wishes of his heart.

It is this sentiment solely that shall now govern my pen. Having no interested object in view, I am entitled to your hearing, and can boldly claim your confidence. I have never held any office in government, nor do I hold any such honor in expectation. I am neither a merchant nor a lawyer. Having received with my first breath the free air of America, I should disdain to hold any political opinion which I durst not publicly avow, and I have no other desire to be concealed from your view, than what diffidence dictates.

Union is the gift of heaven, and the spirit of it, is the glory of federalism. Hitherto this city has distinguished herself for this spirit, and thus been able, in the most astonishing manner, to defeat the schemes of its enemies. Then let us be careful how we disgrace this character, by suffering vulgar prejudices to sway our councils. Shall we, in the most wanton manner, banish from our district, the happy train that attend on concord and unanimity? Shall we welcome, in their place, discord and ungenerous suspicion, with all their baneful influences? Can it be possible that any of our merchants will give themselves up to be led by men who have uniformly opposed their political interests? Will they become the dupes to promote their consequence? Shall the poison be gorged, merely because it is handed in the cup of professional pride? And are we to receive the great council of the nation, in the midst of our feuds and contention, and at the very moment of our debasement?

I was a warm advocate for a merchant as the representative of this city, until I became the spectator of the second meeting of the citizens, held at the coffee-house.[1] There I beheld, for the first time, that serpent *Anti*, who heretofore had kept concealed under the grass, now raising his head, and under the fair guise of moderation, patriotism, and candour, insidiously winding himself into consequence, to triumph over your weakness and the destruction of your prosperity. To have proposed or supported an anti-federal candidate would at once have ruined his plan. *Dissention* was the golden, the promising object—To succeed in this, a worthy citizen was to be upheld; a man worthy our confidence; a man of known abilities and integrity; this man they have since cruelly, unjustly, but artfully, thought fit publicly to insult, in a piece signed Brutus,[2] doubtless with a view to blow up the flame they had kindled.

But all their plots and flames, I trust, will vanish into stench and darkness.—Let the friends, then, of the national constitution be firm and united. The person who has been agreed upon by two large meetings of the citizens, one of which was composed almost entirely of merchants, is not only versed in the theoretical part of commerce, but he possesses tried virtue, eminent integrity, and talents for the defence of that constitution. He will be able to detect every attempt to make that constitution less perfect than it is at present, and when real amendments are proposed, he will be able to enforce them. Let us then unite, not only as citizens, but in unison with our friends in Westchester; nor leave them an opportunity justly to charge us with fickleness, capriciousness, or the want of good faith.

At the last meeting, before mentioned, all the speakers in favor of disunion and discord were known antifederalists. At first they had a strong party. As the debates went on, such, upon good minds, is the resistless power of truth and eloquence combined, that the veil was removed—honest federalists deserted them—the victory was complete—their person respected, but their designs defeated and detected.—They stood alone—thus evidencing, as strongly as when the federal ship sailed through this city, that the characteristic of all *true born Americans*, is the love of order, moderation, union, and *freedom of debate* and sentiment.

CURTIUS.

1. By "second meeting," "Curtius" probably means the meeting held on 26 February at the Coffee House (see *Daily Advertiser*, 27 February 1789, above), which was adjourned to 27 February, at Bardin's Tavern (see New York City Nominating Meeting, 27 February, above).

2. See "Brutus," *Daily Advertiser*, 28 February 1789, above. John Broome was denigrated by "Brutus."

Mercator, Daily Advertiser (New York), 3 March[1]

To the Free Electors of this District.

Gentlemen,

I observed an illiberal publication in Mr. Childs' paper of this day, under the signature of Brutus;[2] this writer imputes the calling of the meeting at the Coffee-House to consider of a proper mercantile character to represent the district in Congress, to the designs of a faction, which he designates by the name Cl—t—n—n.[3] This gentleman is mistaken—this meeting accorded with the wishes of a large and respectable number of citizens of every order, and the object it aimed to effect, is conformable to the desires of a great majority of the electors of the district; it was to agree on a proper mercantile character to propose as a candidate for our representative. The insidious art, by which the meeting was prevented from deliberating upon that question, many of you were witnesses to.

What evidence has this writer adduced to prove this assertion? His reasons are an insult upon your good sense; the suggestion is reproachful to the characters of many respectable merchants and inhabitants, who have been as decided friends to the new government as himself. There were many, and still are a great number, who are in favor of a mercantile man for a representative; the great body of the merchants and mechanicks are of that opinion: does he mean to call these a Cl—t—n—n faction? I trust he does not. Can he mean that those are influenced by a faction? This is equally disgraceful; but what proof does he adduce to support his assertion—why truly this, that the appearance of the meeting, the chairman, and principal speakers confirmed his suspicion that it was a deep laid plan of a faction.

This writer well knows how it happened that one of the faction he speaks of was placed in the chair. This was part of a deep laid plan that this writer and the junto with whom he is connected laid, to prevent the citizens from deliberating and deciding upon the question for which they assembled, it was done to give color to a suspicion which never existed, save in the brains of this writer and his party, that this was an antifederal scheme, intended to divide and effect another election; as to the speakers, two of them only were antifederalists; the gentleman who spoke most largely is and has been as decided a federal character as any in the city;[4] how has he been treated for delivering his opinion as becomes a free and independent man? He has been charged with being influenced by the unworthy motives of private resentment—was repeatedly interrupted in an indecent manner, and has been lampooned by a scurrilous rhymer; but what in the name of common sense has this question to do with the dispute between the federalists and antifederalists—all agree that a federal character ought to be supported; the question is, shall this character be one of mercantile knowledge and information, or a lawyer; and are the citizens of New-York to be persuaded to refuse their support to a merchant, tho' four-fifths of them are of opinion that he is the most proper person to represent them; because it happens that a few antifederal characters join with them in this sentiment; because the antifederalists were wrong in their opinion on the subject of the new constitution, does it follow that they are never right in any thing? Can this writer suppose that the free electors of New-York are so bereft of reason as not to see the absurdity of such kind of reasoning; to urge such arguments afford strong presumptive proof that the party who support a lawyer are convinced that their nomination cannot be supported upon its own merits.

This writer expresses his anxiety at the prospect of a division of sentiment in the citizens at the election. To prevent it let him join in the opinion of a majority of the citizens, and choose the mercantile character proposed. How ridiculous is it to urge this as a reason against voting for a merchant? is it not a notorious fact that a division of sentiment does exist? That a majority of the citizens are of opinion that a mercantile character ought to be chosen. Under these circumstances to request persons not to oppose the gentleman of the law, who is in nomination, is to ask them to vote contrary to the conviction of their own minds, or which is nearly as inconsistent, not to vote at all. Is this the kind of union that this gentleman would recommend? a union subversive of all freedom of thinking and acting, for the sake of gratifying the views of an inconsiderable part of the community. Besides, Mr. Broome will be held up as a candidate, he will be voted for both here and in Westchester county: It cannot be prevented. The consequence therefore of the friends to a mercantile character remaining inactive, or giving their suffrages in favor of the gentleman of the law, who is the other candidate, will be, that an election will be carried against the opinion of a majority of citizens merely for want of their exertions. This writer asks, what is the cause of this division?—and represents it to be, that the person held up is not of one particular class of citizens. This he says is not fair: There are numerous classes and professions, and one should not be preferred to the other. The person and qualities, not the profession, (he says) ought to be considered. The people at the election are not to decide upon the merits of different professions, but in determining upon the person proper to represent them, they must take into consideration his profession, for that is one of his qualities—In short, the dispute is not whether a lawyer, a merchant, a mechanic, or any other profession, are to be the stated representatives of this district; but who is the proper person to represent it on the present occasion? There is a great uniformity of opinion that an essential qualification is, that he should possess mercantile information. The reasons are plain—the commerce of the union is placed under the direction of the general government; on its success the interest of the farmer, mechanic, and every other order of men in this district are connected. It is true a knowledge of commerce is not all that is requisite—other important concerns are committed to the government, but one man cannot be eminent in every art or science. It is to be hoped, when the legislature is collected, there will be found men of respectable talents, with competent knowledge on all the subjects which will come before them: There is no danger of the want of law knowledge, for there will be more of that profession in the legislature than of any other:—There are many from the other states, and several stand candidates, in this, besides the one held up for this city. This writer next contrast the qualities of the candidate; the one who has the good *fortune* to be a lawyer, he represents as a man of known integrity and firmness, possessed of the qualities requisite for the office; and though no merchant, has perhaps more of that abstracted speculative mercantile knowledge, necessary for forming commercial treaties, and planning extensive systems of commerce, than merchants infinitely better acquainted with the practical part of merchandize.

The mercantile character he confesses, he has not so perfect a knowledge of as the gentleman who holds him up seems to have; but from the little he has, he suspects his abilities have been viewed through a magnifier. As his opinion of his abilities is founded on conjecture, it deserves no confidence. My opinion is, that the mercantile gentleman knows more of the principles of the law, than the gentleman of the law does of the abstract speculative principles of commerce—that the merchant candidate is much better acquainted with the theory of trade than the lawyer, and in addition, is well versed in the practical knowledge of it—that in point of integrity and firmness, he is at least his equal; and that he is as capable of communicating his ideas with precision and perspicuity as the former. The illiberal insinuation against the integrity of the mercantile gentleman is unworthy my notice. To attempt to vindicate the moral character of a gentleman, who has for a long course of years lived in reputation in this city, from the aspersions of a nameless writer, is not necessary; his fellow citizens know his character. As to the insinuation that he will not suffer himself to be held up as a candidate—if he be a friend to the new system of government, it needs no reply; the free electors of the district know, that he is and has uniformly been attached to the new government; and the question between the advocates of the two candidates, has no manner of relation to the dispute respecting the new constitution: both are equally attached to it. Observations of this kind, as well as such as relate to the choice of a new chief magistrate, are only intended to mislead. The sole question is, which of the two gentlemen is the most suitable to represent you. Act in this respect as becomes the characters of free and independent electors—Come forward and give your suffrages agreeably to your own sentiments.

MERCATOR.

New York, 28th February.

1. The *Daily Advertiser* had printed a brief note on 2 March 1789 stating that the "Mercator" article had been received too late and was too lengthy to be printed on that date; it would be printed the next day.

2. See "Brutus," *Daily Advertiser*, 28 February 1789, above.

3. Clintonian.

4. The two Antifederalist speakers were Melancton Smith and Marinus Willett; the Federalist was possibly Moses Rogers. The other Federalists who were reported to have spoken, Alexander Hamilton and William Duer, supported John Laurance for Representative (see "A Spectator," *New York Packet*, 3 March 1789, below).

A Federalist, Daily Advertiser (New York), 3 March

Mr. CHILDS,

Although the necessity of close union among the federalists of this city has lately at two very respectable public meetings been very ably and very clearly demonstrated; yet this subject appears to me of such infinite consequence to our prosperity and happiness, that I hope to be excused in an attempt to impress it again upon the minds of my fellow citizens. Sir, I am neither a lawyer nor a merchant—I am unconnected with any party, unplaced, unpensioned, and without hope of either—but I have been a citizen from my infancy, and am now the father of a family, who I expect to succeed me in the enjoyment of the little earnings of a life of industry—from affection therefore and interest, I am anxiously solicitous for the prosperity of this city; and I have lived to see more than one instance in which its best interests have been sacrificed to party spirit, and have again been restored by concord and unanimity: Of the latter a more recent or important instance cannot be given, than the success which attended the federal ticket for representatives to the late convention. I conceive that it is of the utmost consequence, that the representative we shall send to the general assembly of the United States, as well as those we send to the assembly of our own state, shall at all times be the representative, and speak the sentiments of the whole city; that they may possess that weight and consequence in either house, which the great importance of this flourishing city, when united, will always command. With how much more attention will our representative be heard, and how much more weight will his arguments carry with them, when it is known that in him we all speak; and that to slight or disregard him, is to contemn the united voice of the city of New-York. If possible therefore I could wish that the very shadow of division should be done away. The important question now before us does not so much regard col. Lawrence, or Mr. Broom, a lawyer or a merchant, or whether a man of either profession should represent us; we are not so deficient in merit, but that good and fit men may be found in all professions;—but the question is, shall our representative truly represent the city? Shall we be united in choosing him? If we are, that very unanimity will give him consequence; and especially while the United States remain in this city, there is no fear that he will want information upon any subject which shall come before them, and in which we shall be particularly interested. If these are just sentiments, then surely all contention, under the present state of things, will cease. Col. Lawrence has been nominated at two very respectable meetings of the inhabitants, and the generality of those who were present at those meetings, conceive themselves pledged to him and to their fellow citizens to support him; there can then be no doubt, but that he will obtain the majority of suffrages; and if the majority, why not the whole? What end can a feeble opposition answer, but to manifest our disunion, and give an opportunity to our antifederal opponents to rejoice in the success of their schemes. The time for contest is at the previous meetings called to determine on our men; at which meetings let every man speak his sentiments with freedom, and be heard with candor; but after a fair discussion, having once pitched upon our representative, let all opposition cease; let the minority like good republicans yield to the voice of the majority; and from that moment giving up private opinions, and private interests, let us unite as one man in the choice of our representative, and by that unanimity give him all the importance in our power, that he may do us all the good in his.

A FEDERALIST.

March 1st, 1789.

Brutus, Daily Advertiser (New York), 3 March

Mr. CHILDS,

Portius[1] wishes to appear a man of great moderation. I hope he is so. I sincerely agree with him that moderation, both in politics and religion, are best calculated to make converts. I am no friend to a man that is immoderate about either, more particularly the *latter*. If I appeared warm, when I warned my fellow citizens of danger, it was love for my country that made me so.[2] That I did not mistake the source of the late opposition, this day, as well as the preceding has done, will shew. I have as high an opinion of general Malcom as Portius has, but I dislike his politics, tho' I believe him to be moderate. I agree with Portius also, "That when after investigation, no punishment is inflicted, it is an honorable presumption that there was no crime;" but when an indictment is *quashed* for not being brought in a proper court, I suppose he will agree with me, that this is not getting off on the *merits* of the cause. It is my decided opinion, that in a republic, the very first misconduct in a public officer should be discountenanced, and after a person has been once accused of mal practice or extortion, unless he clears himself upon the merits of the cause, he should never be held up for any office. I believe it is a safe rule—a rule which the wisest nations have observed. I will also inform Portius, that whenever I see any danger to my country, I shall be ready to give the alarm. But as I hope that Portius is no friend of Cesar's, and he says he is of the same sentiments as I am with regard to the candidate proposed, enough is said. Wishing us success in this and every other undertaking calculated for the good of our country and prosperity of our fellow citizens, I remain

BRUTUS.

1. See "Portius," *Daily Advertiser*, 2 March 1789, above.
2. See "Brutus," *Daily Advertiser*, 28 February 1789, above.

Daily Advertiser (New York), 3 March

This day comes on the election of a Representative of this district in the Congress of the United States.

The poll in the East-Ward will be opened at the Coffee-House.

In the North-Ward, at Aorson's Tavern, in Nassau street.

In the West-Ward, at the City-Tavern.

In Montgomery-Ward, at Rawson's.

In the Out-Ward, at the Bull's Head.

In the Dock-Ward, at Mr. Francis', No. 3, Great Dock street.

In South-Ward, at the Exchange.

Daily Advertiser (New York), 3 March

A correspondent takes the liberty of informing his fellow citizens, that every male inhabitant, of full age, who has resided in this county for six months past, and possesses a freehold of the value of twenty pounds, or rents a tenement of the yearly value of forty shillings, in this county, and has been rated, and has actually paid taxes to this state—is entitled to vote at the election this day, to be held for the choice of a representative of this district in Congress. The above qualifications are the same which entitle a person to vote for members of the assembly of this state.[1]

1. This item was also printed in the *Daily Gazette* on the same date.

New York City Federalist Committee of Correspondence, Daily Advertiser (New York), 3 March

To the ELECTORS of the CITY and COUNTY of NEW-YORK.

Fellow-Citizens,

Having been appointed by two different, and very numerous meetings of the inhabitants of this city, among other purposes, for that of forwarding the election of John Lawrence, Esq. as the representative of this district in Congress—we think it our duty to state to such of you as may not have been present at those meetings, what we understand to have been the motives to his nomination, and the circumstances which have attended it.

It appeared, from the particular situation of this state in regard to the new constitution, to be peculiarly necessary to use great care in the choice of the person who was to represent this district. In proportion as there was reason to apprehend that such a choice as we should not approve, was likely to be made in most of the other districts, it became important that our immediate representative should be of a character, which united in a considerable degree all the qualifications requisite to the due support of the credit and interest of the state, and to the advancement of the particular interests of the district; that he should be of a character calculated to acquire a proper degree of weight with his colleagues, and to induce, on their part, a co-operation in such measures as the public good should require. And in addition to the rest, that he should be of a character which afforded complete security that he would be disposed to withstand every attempt to *destroy* or *weaken* the national government.

To these ends, it was conceived that he ought to be a man of integrity, of sense, of information, of *early* and *decided* attachment to the federal constitution, and of *tried firmness* of temper. The two last qualifications were considered as not less important than any of the former; because, though the constitution for the United States has been ratified by a very great majority of the people, it cannot yet be regarded as entirely out of danger. It is a truth which we mention with reluctance, but which ought not to be lost sight of, that many of its most powerful adversaries, so far from relinquishing their hostility to it, seem still to meditate its destruction, in the plausible, but insidious shape of amendments. And on this account it is of serious moment, that as far as depends on us, no man should be entrusted with its administration in the outset, whose attachment to it has been either tardy or equivocal, who does not possess decision or firmness of temper sufficient to resist attempts to injure it, or who is under any influence or bias, which in any possible combination of circumstances, might incline him to yield to the artifices of its enemies.

Among the other qualifications which were taken into consideration, that of a talent for public speaking was not unattended to; and though this was not deemed an indispensable one, it was yet regarded as *one* which could not fail to contribute in a material degree to the usefulness of the candidate.

Taking all circumstances into consideration, it was conceived that Mr. Lawrence united the requisite qualifications in such a degree as to render him, upon the whole, and in the present state of things, a more eligible candidate than any other proposed.—It did not pass unnoticed, that he might be deficient in the article of mercantile knowledge; but it was supposed that a man of information, accustomed to political enquiry could easily supply that deficiency, by consulting such of his constituents as were capable of advising him on the subject; and the known disposition of Mr. Lawrence left no reason to doubt that he would always take care to avail himself of this resource.

It was also considered that commercial arrangements were not the only matters which required our care. The preservation of the government itself, in its due force and vigor, is an object of the first consequence—and the establishment of the temporary residence of Congress in this city is another point in which we are deeply concerned. It must, doubtless, therefore be of great importance, from among the persons presented to our choice, to select the man in whose hands the general interest and our immediate interest, in those two points, are least likely to suffer, and most likely to be advanced.

The foregoing were some of the reasons which appear to us to have prevailed upon the first meeting to nominate Mr. Lawrence, and upon the last to confirm it.

We perceive, with regret, that notwithstanding those meetings have furnished the strongest evidence of the general sense of the city, there are still persons who persist in holding up Mr. Broome as a candidate, and endeavor to have it believed that the body of merchants concur in his favor.

To guard against the influence of such a misrepresentation, we think it necessary to assure you, and we doubt not their conduct in the election will evince it, that the great body of the merchants coincide in Mr. Lawrence's nomination. We assert this, because they very generally attended the two meetings, and at each gave their assent to the nomination.

We infer from this, and there are appearances which strengthen the inference, that other motives than the desire of having a mercantile character to represent us, operate with many of those who are most active in promoting Mr. Broome's election—Nothing can be better suited to the policy of those who differ in their sentiments from the inhabitants of this city, than to sow divisions among us. They know that if they can set different classes of men against each other, dissentions may spring up among us, which they may hereafter turn to their own purposes. Against this worst of evils we trust our fellow citizens will be on their guard. We have experienced the happy effects of union among ourselves, and we cannot be too watchful against every thing that may lead to disunion.

It is asserted that Mr. Broome will have extensive support in Westchester. Of this, at least, we can assure you, that the federalists in that county will generally vote for Mr. Lawrence. We have received an authentic account that at a meeting held at the White Plains, on Thursday last,[1] with a view to the election of a representative, Mr. Lawrence was agreed upon. In his support, we beg leave to recommend to our fellow citizens UNANIMITY and EXERTION.

By Order of the committee,
ALEXANDER HAMILTON, Chairman.[2]

1. See Westchester County Nominating Meeting, 26 February 1789, above. The account of the Westchester meeting was printed immediately below this article.

2. Hamilton was chairman of the committee of correspondence chosen by the Federalists at Bardin's Tavern on 11 February.

A Mechanic, Daily Advertiser (New York), 3 March

A CARD.

The following fact is submitted by a well wisher to the community, for the consideration of the citizens. Mr. Broom, on an application made to him by a gentleman of this city to lend his *credit only* for the small pittance of twenty pounds for the purpose of raising money to defray the expence of Federal Hall—*refused to comply, tho' earnestly solicited.*

Has he even contributed, my fellow labourers, towards our support? Did he shew an attachment to the federal cause? Is he worthy of a seat in that house to which he would not contribute? If his poverty was the cause of his refusal, he may be open to corruption. If party spirit prevented, it will be at least unsafe to trust him. Think well then before you give such a man your suffrages.

A MECHANIC.

One and All, New York Daily Gazette, 3 March

The True Federal Representative
John Lawrence, Esq.

Friends and Fellow Citizens,

Be not deceived by those who pretend that a *Lawyer*, or a *Merchant*, is the present object of contest—It is, whether the New Constitution shall stand, or be destroy'd; whether, the present Governor, the Champion of Antifederalism, shall plunge the State into anarchy, and distress—or give way to a more moderate, and virtuous citizen. Hence arises the pretended zeal, his partizans shew for the commercial interest of the city. As little founded is the declaration they impudently made, that the great body of the Merchants are for supporting Mr. Broome: 'Tis *not so*—They have at repeated meetings declared their determination to support Mr. LAWRENCE. Shew therefore, by a numerous Poll, and your firmness in supporting that Gentleman—that you are not unmindful of your old and successful motto, ONE AND ALL.[1]

1. This article was reprinted in the *Daily Advertiser*, 4 and 5 March 1789.

Locke, New York Daily Gazette, 3 March

To the Citizens of New-York.

GENTLEMEN,

It is very much to be lamented, that a few artful and designing characters are daily endeavouring to sow dissention and discord among us. On the great federal question, the persons who now come forward as the champions of the mercantile interest, were opposed to it. Instead of being the advocates of commerce, they were the instruments of dissention. Every considerate Merchant will believe, that that union by which our common interests have been hitherto promoted, ought more especially to be preserved at this critical period. An enlightened Merchant is the honor of his country. As such, he will not be led away by the artful, the designing, or the ambitious. It is insinuated that the Lawyers arrogate to themselves all abilities. Is it possible to suppose, that any profession of men would be so hardy as to presume that abilities resided only with them. The true reason why Mr. Lawrence was held up, was, not because he was a Lawyer, but because he was conceived to be, in general, better calculated than any other man then held up to promote the common interests of the community. I enter not into a discussion of Mr. Broome's character. But as men of honour, we have pledged ourselves, and therefore cannot recede. As politicians, we see the danger of disunion, and therefore ought not to recede. I wish to treat the gentlemen who, by every means in their power, endeavor to foment this business, with decency: But, at the same time, I warn the mercantile interest to beware of being made the tools of their pretended friends. Be not deceived, evil communications corrupt good manners.

LOCKE.

A Spectator, New York Packet, 3 March

Messrs. LOUDON,

Being present at the meeting which was held last Friday evening, at Bardin's tavern, I could not avoid making a few cursory observations, which are at your service.

The gentlemen who spoke, were Colonels Hamilton, Duer,[1] and Willet,[2] Melancton Smith, Esq. and Mr. M. Rogers[3]—Each of whom took the opportunity of clearing themselves and their friends, from every groundless charge of partial proceeding, which might have been reported through the city, with insiduous views of creating divisions and discontents among the people at so critical a time as the eve of an election.

Col. Willet and Mr. Smith contended for a mercantile character, as being the most proper to represent the city of New-York, in the Congress of the United States. They used the most powerful arguments that could be invented, to support their cause, and at the same time that they confessed their former disapprobation of the new-Constitution, they declared their firm resolution, that as it was now adopted, they would be the last men in the world to oppose its operations. They wished for a *Federal Merchant*, and notwithstanding they spoke often, they never once droped a word like personality against any man or set of men.

They were answered by Colonels Hamilton and Duer, in every point; who persisted in the idea of confirming the proceedings of the former meeting, and disclaimed against any change in the nomination then agreed to.

It would be a difficult task to follow the elegant and animated oratory of Colonel Duer, and no less presumtuous to attempt doing justice to the clear argumentative and finished powers of Col. Hamilton. Suffice it to observe, that the former proved himself a generous advocate, and despised every means of carrying his point that could be construed into *unfair* reasoning. The latter challenged the confidence of every spectator, and gained it. He said, 'that as the residence of Congress would doubtless be esteemed a matter of some import to the city of New-York, and as it would certainly be contended for—*Our representative* should be a man well qualified in oratory to prove, that this city is the best station for that honorable body. That Mr. Lawrence was well acquainted with the mercantile laws, and closely attached to the real interest of his commercial fellow citizens.—Therefore a very proper person to represent us.'

A SPECTATOR.[4]

1. William Duer (1747–1799), a wealthy New York City merchant and financier, was an active patriot during the Revolution and a delegate to Congress, 1777–1778. He played a major role in the founding of the Bank of New York in 1784; represented New York City and County in the Assembly in 1786; was secretary of the congressional Board of Treasury, 1786–1789; and was assistant secretary of the Treasury under Alexander Hamilton, 1789–1790.

2. Marinus Willett.

3. Moses Rogers was a New York City merchant.

4. This article was reprinted in the *Federal Herald*, 16 March 1789.

New York Packet, 3 March

We have every reason to assure the public, that Mr. Lawrence will run well in Westchester. Indeed whoever considers, that, not many years ago, he was a representative in Assembly for that county,[1] will easily believe he must then have had some political influence. Mr. Lawrence's political career since that time, has not disgraced him in the eyes of his former constituents—They view him, as he is, a man firm, a federalist, and one who will with all his might seek and promote the common welfare.[2]

1. Laurance represented Westchester County in the Assembly in 1782–1783.

2. This paragraph was preceded by a republication of the accounts of the New York City nominating meetings at Bardin's Tavern on 23 and 27 February 1789, at which Laurance was endorsed for Representative.

Tom Hatchway, New York Packet, 3 March

Messmate Loudon,—Please to tell all the *writers* of Brutus, Cato, &c. to *avast jawing* about the Captain and Mate's *Birth* of the *State's Brig*—I would not give a *marlinspike* to have either the *old ones* in or out of *station.* But I would advise *all hands* to work *double tides,* to get the *Congress Ship under sail,* with a good *crew* on board: For until this is done let who will be Captain or Mate, we shall never be able to *steer* our *course.*

Tom Hatchway.

A Federal Elector, 4 March[1]

THE Friends of Mr. JOHN BROOME have discovered, during the progress of the Poll, that Mr. PELL, and not Mr. BROOME, is the candidate held up by the Antifederals in the county of Westchester; and that while the same party in this city, under an affected zeal for the mercantile interest, hold up Mr. Broome, they are secretly balloting for Mr. PELL.

They have therefore determined, in order to prevent a division of the Federal interest to join heart and hand with their fellow citizens, in supporting Mr. JOHN LAWRENCE.

A Federal Elector.

March 4.

1. Broadside Collection, Rare Book Room, DLC. This broadside was also printed in the *Daily Advertiser* and *Daily Gazette* on the same date.

One and All, 4 March[1]

New-York preserved, or the Plot discovered.

WHILST the leaders of the antifederal junto in this city are raising a hue-and-cry electing a Lawyer, as a Representative for this district, their adherents in Westchester county are supporting with all their zeal, Mr. PELL, ANOTHER LAWYER, AND A RANK ANTIFEDERALIST, in opposition to Mr. LAWRENCE. Nor is this all; many of the same party in this city are secretly ballotting for Mr. Pell, whilst they are duping Mr. Broome, and those who adhere to him, with professions of support. For shame! for shame! Such Federalists as have been deluded with the idea that the present contest was only betwixt a lawyer and a merchant, ought to open their eyes; and those who have not been deluded, ought to redouble their exertions to bring out every vote to defeat the artifices of a party whose real object is to destroy the present Constitution, and to remove the residence of Congress from this city.

March 4. ONE and ALL.

1. Broadside Collection, Rare Book Room, DLC. This broadside was also printed in the *Daily Advertiser* on the same date.

Brutus, Daily Advertiser (New York), 4 March

MR. CHILDS,

Mercator's publication in your paper,[1] is such a jargon of unconnected reasoning, that I should not have taken any notice of it had it not been that I wish once more to intreat my fellow citizens to be unanimous. His conclusions drawn from false premises are such as might have been expected from one whom nothing but ignorance could have induced to espouse so bad a cause. The persons who were the cause of calling the meeting at the coffee house, and the intention with which they did it, are now well known. Their conduct has shewn, that the suspicion, which this writer is pleased to say, in the language of enraged disappointment, first existed in my brain, had a good foundation. His assertion that four-fifths of the citizens are of opinion, that Mr. Broome is the properest person to represent them, is such a *barefaced* misrepresentation that there is no danger of any bad consequences from it. As to his quere whether the antifederalists are ever right in any thing, I can assure him they are wrong at present, and that they do not wish to do right. Their attempt in the Out-Ward of this city, to carry Mr. Pell of Westchester,[2] plainly shews that their intention was, by attacking the pride of Mr. Broome, to use him as a tool to divide the citizens here, and then uniting with the antifederalists in Westchester to carry Pell. This at the same time that it points out to the citizens the necessity of guarding against divisions, may afford this useful lesson to Mr. Broome, not to believe that he is possessed of those qualities he never had an opportunity of acquiring, and by that means become the dupe of a set of men whose sole intention is to destroy our political harmony, to answer their own views. However, this, like all other antifederal schemes, has failed; and if we are unanimous they will all fail, and antifederalism itself will soon be subverted by the downfall of

George.[3] I would recommend it to Mercator, that when he has any *great, huge* antifederal scheme, the production of the wise men of the council of the great *Sachem*, to keep in with probability, as he has declared open war with truth.

BRUTUS.

March 3.

1. "Mercator," *Daily Advertiser*, 3 March 1789, above.
2. Pell received no votes in the Out Ward.
3. George Clinton.

A True Antifederalist, and No Lawyer, Daily Advertiser (New York), 4 March

BEWARE OF LAWYERS!!!

Of the men who framed that monarchical, aristocratical, oligarchical, tyrannical, diabolical system of slavery, the *New Constitution, one half* were Lawyers—!

Of the men who represented, or rather misrepresented, this city and county in the late convention of this state, to whose wicked arts we may chiefly attribute the adoption of that abominable system, *seven* out of the *nine* were Lawyers—!

This same class of men will do all they can to establish and confirm that nefarious system, and as long as they are blindly trusted by the people, we shall never be able to succeed in our virtuous attempts to destroy it.

And what crowns the wickedness of these wicked Lawyers is, that a great majority of them throughout the state, are violently opposed to our GREAT and GOOD HEAD, and never failing friend of the city and city interests, the PRESENT GOVERNOR. That aspiring party are the worst enemies of his and our VIRTUOUS ASPIRINGS.

We warned you against them at the election for convention men; we now warn you against them again.

Beware, beware, beware of Lawyers!

A true Antifederalist, and
NO LAWYER.

March 3.[1]

1. This article was also printed in the *Daily Gazette*, 4 March 1789; the *Daily Advertiser* reprinted it on 5 March.

Nestor, New York Daily Gazette, 4 March

Advice to the Federalists.

Fellow Citizens!

Be not inactive—when you are contending for a Federal Representative in opposition to one who is Antifederal; the least degree of inactivity would be highly criminal. Mr. Broom is not the man whom the Antifederalists support or wish to succeed. By authentic advices brought yesterday afternoon from Westchester county, it is certain, that the Antifederalists there are pressing the Election of Mr. Pell, a LAWYER in that county, with all their force. From some tickets which were accidentally discovered yesterday at one of the polls,[1] it cannot be doubted that Mr. Pell is also the real object of the

Antifederalists in this city. It is well known that Mr. Pell ever has been warmly opposed to that government which you so justly suppose to be the great rock of your political salvation. To carry his election it is good policy in the Antifederalists to make use of Mr. Broome as one of their instruments to divide your votes. Suffer not this manuvre to produce the effect intended by it. Despise the illiberal tales which are circulated about the federal lawyers. Remember their upright, firm, and judicious conduct upon all interesting subjects which have come before the legislature of this state since the peace.—Call to mind their efforts in the late election of men to represent you in the state convention.—Examine the debates and votes of that convention, and after laying your hands upon your hearts, ask yourselves whether the federal lawyers have in a single instance deceived you, or betrayed the sacred trusts you have confided to them? What reasons can you have to presume that upon the present important occasion, they are endeavouring to mislead you? Who are their accusers? Let the pretended advocates of Mr. Broome at the City Tavern on Friday night last, and their adherents answer these questions. The truth is, my Fellow Citizens, that the scheme for dividing you is a trap set by the Antifederalists to catch you, that they may disgrace you with an Antifederal Representative in Congress. Under this conviction I conjure you, as you value your honor and dearest interests, to turn out this day, and unanimously give your suffrages for Mr. LAWRENCE. Every man who neglects to vote for his representative in a free country, is unworthy of the blessings of freedom.

NESTOR.

1. This was probably the Out Ward; see "Brutus," *Daily Advertiser*, 4 March 1789, above. This is the first mention of "tickets" in the election.

A Federal Shop Keeper, Daily Advertiser (New York), 5 March[1]

Mr. CHILDS,

The unmerited and scurrilous abuse with which the papers for some days past have teemed against an old and very respectable merchant[2] and that numerous body of citizens who wish him to represent this district induces me as one of that number, and as a decided federalist [(]to which character liberality belongs) to enter my protest against such indecent and ungenerous proceedings. Notwithstanding the positive and dogmatical assertions of these railers, it is a well known fact that the *unbiassed*-sense of a great majority of this city would decide without hesitation, in favor of a merchant. How it has happened that a contrary determination by two meetings has been procured, cannot be matter of enquiry or surprise to those who attended them and observed the insidious stratagems employed to obtain those determinations; I presume it is not necessary with those who observe, think, and act for themselves, to enter into a particular detail of this unfair business. On the opposite description of men it could have no effect—their passions (and their passions, not their reason) govern their conduct, are already enlisted to serve under the standard of their aspiring rulers; I shall therefore consign them over to the vile drudgery and humble devotion which they have *so honorably* chosen. I cannot however, forbear to remark generally that the object of the merchants in the first meeting who went there, determined almost unanimously, I believe, to support the nomination of a merchant, was defeated by the rhetorick, rather than the logic, of a gentleman, to whom I cheerfully and most gratefully confess that this country in general, and this city in particular, are highly indebted, and whose superior talents (however our sentiments may differ on particular occasions) I shall always admire, and by the brow-beating and over-bearing manner of another gentleman who exerted his talents in that way with much assurance and success;[3] perceiving, however, by the advertisement calling a meeting of those who were disposed to elect a merchant, that their spirit had been stunned but not destroyed, they determined to muster their forces, attend the meeting, tho' uninvited, and repeat the blow. This was manifested in the beginning of the evening by the choice they made to fill the chair, intending, if they could gain a decision in their favor, to mortify and wound the feelings of the gentleman they placed in it[4] (knowing his sentiments to be opposed to their's) by forcing him to sanction their proceedings by his signature, and if it went against them, to stamp them with the odious brand of antifederalism; their conduct in the last meeting accorded perfectly with their behavior in the first, by ungenerously availing themselves of the late political character of two gentlemen who appeared,[5] and very impoliticly, I think, in behalf of the merchants, as they might readily have forseen the undue advantage that would be taken of them, and by transferring passion honestly and usefully excited on a late very important question, into one that has not the most remote connection with it, and in the event, by turning the attention of the meeting to an object altogether foreign from its original one, they obtained their object. From the clearest conviction of the necessity of a firmer union of the states, and of a strong energetic general government, I took an active part in the late controversy, and as far as my humble situation and talents afforded me the means, exerted my utmost industry to promote the federal cause, and could I now discover that it is at all mingled with the present question, I should not hesitate one moment to vote for the man who would most effectually promote it. But after a careful examination I cannot perceive the smallest relation between the two questions, the rival candidates are and have been equally federal, they are both men of talents and integrity; the question then in my mind resolves itself into this simple query—is it most proper to send a lawyer or a merchant from this district, considering the disproportion there is like to be in the general government between legal and commercial knowledge, and that unless we send a merchant from this city there probably will not be one gentleman of that description in it from this state! Viewing this question on its real merits, few I think can be long at a loss how to determine it.

As a man of moderation, and whose single object is the good of his country, I was much pleased to see in the circular letter of our committee, a sentiment to this effect, that as the constitution is now adopted, and the controversy thereby settled, we all ought to unite in striving to banish party heats and distinctions from among us, that they may give place to the more mild and agreeable sensations of social intercourse and affection.[6] Sentiments like this I wish should be cherished, and I confess it has been with the utmost regret that I have been a witness to the violent, but causeless, (at least as far as the public good is concerned) efforts which have been made to plunge us again into factious virulence; for what other purpose do we hear hourly trumpeted in our ears the sounds of *federal, antifederal, tricks, snares,* the *Trojan horse, and horrible plots,* as if the question between lawyer and merchant had any thing to do with these tragic and obsolete things; the truth is, that antifederal tricks and snares can have no more connection with the present dispute, than the Trojan horse, they being equally (as far as this business is concerned) the ingenious fictions of sportive imagination. The imputation of being the tool of the present governor, or of any his friends on this or any other occasion, I despise, as the insult of men more artful than liberal; and the only answer I shall condescend to give it is, that I shall, with equal independence of mind, guard against the undue influence of any other man, however highly I may respect his character, for all are liable to err, and almost all are biassed by particular interest.

Federalism is, thank God, established on a rock that cannot be shaken, and that deformed monster, his opponent, humbled to the dust and quite lifeless. Why then endeavor to disturb our imaginations by conjuring up her frightful spectre?—These necromantic arts may intimidate old women and children, but must be considered by all who are free from *political enthusiasm*, as mere trifling, and slight of hand tricks.

These observations have been extended much beyond what I intended when I took up my pen: I shall therefore only add, that I have too high an opinion of the understanding and independence of my fellow citizens to believe they will be convinced that they are the tools of a very few characters who have little or no influence in any way & (who now are doing penance for their former antifederalism) merely because they are most unreasonably charged with being so, by which charge they and common sense have been mutually and equally insulted.

A Federal Shop keeper.

March 4.

1. The *Daily Advertiser* printed a brief note on 4 March stating that the "Federal Shopkeeper" article had been received too late to be printed on that date; it would be printed the next day.
2. John Broome.
3. Alexander Hamilton and William Duer, respectively.
4. William Malcolm chaired the meeting.
5. Antifederalists Melancton Smith and Marinus Willett.
6. This sentiment is expressed in a circular letter of the New York City Federalist committee of correspondence to the supervisors of the city of Albany, 18 February 1789. The *Daily Advertiser* and *Daily Gazette*, which published the letter on 20 February, reported that the committee intended to send the letter to town supervisors throughout the state.

Daily Advertiser (New York), 5 March

Yesterday afternoon the poll in the Eastward was closed, after having taken in 336 votes.

A Parting Blow, Daily Advertiser (New York), 5 March

The exertions of the Federal Electors in supporting the election of that truly federal Representative

John Lawrence, Esq.

And their discernment in detecting the artifice of the opposers of the Constitution, who at the time they were raising a cry against Lawyers were supporting, for this district, Mr. PELL of Westchester, an *antifederal Lawyer*, entitle them to the grateful remembrance, not only of their fellow citizens, but of the friends of the Constitution in every part of the state. The polls already taken very nearly amount to the number given in for the late Convention—and one day's more exertion will crown the glorious work. Let us, therefore, deem nothing done whilst any thing remains to be done, but defeat every attempt of the antifederal party to destroy the union of this city, by giving them this day

A PARTING BLOW.

March 5, 1789.

N.B. The Polls are still open in the Out-Ward, Montgomery Ward, South Ward, North-Ward.[1]

1. This article was also printed in the *Daily Gazette* on the same date.

New York Journal, 5 March

Last Tuesday, in conformity to the directions of an act, entitled, "An act directing the times, places, and manner of electing representatives in this state, for the house of representatives of the Congress of the United States of America," passed the 27th of January last—the election was held in this district, composed of the city and county of New-York, and the county of Westchester, except the towns of Salem, North-Salem, Cortlandt, York-Town, and Steven-Town, in Westchester county.

The poles were opened in this city, in the forenoon, and are not yet all closed.

The true state of the poles will be given as soon as possible, as well from this district as the other five.[1]

1. This item was reprinted in the Philadelphia *Pennsylvania Packet*, 10 March 1789, and Philadelphia *Pennsylvania Journal*, 11 March.

A Federalist and No Lawyer, New York Journal, 12 March

Mr. GREENLEAF,

A Friend of Mr. V— W—k's[1] desires to be informed what number of Federal tickets for JOHN LAWRENCE, Esq. he disposed of during the late election for a Representative to Congress from this district.

A Federalist and no Lawyer.

March 9, 1789.

1. Possibly Dorus Van Wyck, a New York City merchant.

H. H., New York Journal, 2 April

Qualem commendes etiam atque etiam adspice, ne mox
Incutiant aliena tibi pecata pudorem.

HORACE.

In a land of freedom, where the legislator owes his dignified station to the suffrages of his fellow citizens, the people can never be too careful of their rights and privileges, nor look with too jealous eyes upon the conduct of any man who uses unfair means to jockey them out of their votes, either for himself, or in favor of his tools and partizans. It is true, that in all republics there are certain leading characters, by whom the people are naturally influenced: while such men appear to have the public good at heart, and will act, as well as reason, fairly, they are certainly entitled to praise; but when a man, to accomplish a favorite design, endeavors, by every artifice that low cunning can suggest, to acquire an undue influence, his ambition should be checked.

These reflections arise from an impartial review of the conduct of a couple of men in this city, who have taken upon them to govern elections since the peace, and for that purpose have, in some of the wards, a set of bullies and agents to bear down opposition by intimidating some with threats, and cajoling others with ready manufactured tickets. In this manner have a brace of Creoles,[1] with no other merit than what may possibly be derived from the most consummate impudence, and a redundancy of what is vulgarly called slack jaw, given us assembly-men, senators, and convention-men, ever since the peace, and are now endeavoring to palm a Governor of their own making upon us in spite of our teeth.[2]—Nor do they stop here; they have it in agitation, also, to cram a senator upon us from another state,[3] as if New-York did not possess an individual of abilities and merit sufficient for that important station.

The methods recently taken to bear down all opposition, at a late election, must fill every good man with just indignation. Not satisfied with the tricks they played upon the merchants, by stealing a march upon them;[4] how many lies were fabricated, and published in hand-bills, to deceive the ignorant, and take in the unwary.

For my part I am easily led, but I will not be driven, or bamboozled, if I can help it. I think the two Creoles have reigned long enough in the business of elections, and I sincerely hope, that my fellow citizens will not be biassed by their sophistry, or intimidated by their champions, at the ensuing election, but unite in giving their votes to such men as they conceive best qualified to serve them, without paying a servile homage to the decisions of Tom S—t and his overbearing fraternity.

April 28, 1789.[5] H—— H——.

1. This probably refers to Alexander Hamilton, who was born in the British West Indian colony of Nevis, and to William Duer, who had lived in Dominica prior to settling in New York in the mid-1770s.

2. The Federalists were promoting Robert Yates for governor.

3. Rufus King, who had recently moved to New York from Massachusetts, was being supported by Hamilton for Senator.

4. When a group of merchants called a public meeting in New York City to nominate a merchant for Representative, the city's Federalist committee countered by urging the supporters of John Laurance, a lawyer, to attend the meeting.

5. The date should undoubtedly be 28 March 1789.

New York City Federalist Committee of Correspondence to the Electors of New York, c. 7 April (excerpt)[1]

TO THE INDEPENDENT AND PATRIOTIC ELECTORS OF THE STATE OF NEW-YORK. . . .

In our first address we advanced this sentiment, that all should join "in the support of the constitution established by the people of the United States, and that all should join in the reconsideration of the parts which have been the subject of objection."[2] On this point we are charged with inconsistency, and it is asserted, that there is every reason to believe, that the principal opponents to the governor do not wish to see *any* amendments to the constitution and are averse to a *reconsideration* of it. As far as we are concerned we affirm that the charge is destitute of truth, and we defy those who make it to produce any thing like proof of its being well founded.

It is true, that on the occasion of the election of a representative of this district in Congress, we most of us contended for the propriety of choosing a person attached to the constitution; but this certainly has nothing to do with a disinclination to amendments or to a reconsideration of the system; nor will it in any candid mind appear to militate against the sincerity of the desire, which we profess to have, of reconciliation and union, between the different parties in the state. It was not to be doubted, that in other parts of this state every effort would be made, by those who opposed the constitution, to choose for representatives men of sentiments similar to their own, and it could not reasonably be expected, under such circumstances, that its friends in a friendly district would not be equally strenuous for representatives of their own sentiments. Could it be expected that we should abandon the distinctions which actually exist, previous to a foundation being laid for a reciprocal renunciation of them? This is the desireable object at which we and our fellow citizens now aim. Nor can a better proof be given of it, than in the disposition manifested to support a man of political opinions different from those generally entertained by them and by us.[3] And we strongly flatter ourselves, that the desireable end in contemplation will be attained, by the co-operation of all those throughout the state who wish to see the spirit of faction and dissention extinguished. . . .

By Order of the Committee,
ALEXANDER HAMILTON.
Chairman.

1. Broadside, MiU-C. Printed: Syrett, V, 317–29. Alexander Hamilton sent a copy of this broadside to the *New York Journal* on 7 April 1789 (see *New York Journal*, 9 April), thus the c. 7 April dating here. In the bulk of this twelve-page broadside, Hamilton outlined the reasons why Governor Clinton should not be reelected. Among other things, Hamilton accused Clinton of fomenting "the spirit of party" that had "attained an alarming and pernicious height in the state," and which was responsible for New York's lack of representation in Congress. The broadside was also printed in the *New York Journal*, 9 April 1789; *New York Packet*, 10 April; and *Country Journal* (supplement), 21 April.

2. See Alexander Hamilton's address "To the Supervisors of the City of Albany," in the *Daily Advertiser*, 20 February 1789.

3. The Federalists were supporting Robert Yates, an Antifederalist, for governor.

Daily Advertiser (New York), 9 April (excerpt)

On Tuesday[1] the committee appointed by the legislature to canvass and estimate the votes given in the different districts for representatives to Congress, met at the secretary's office in this city, and proceeded to the execution of their duty.

In the district comprehending the city and county of New-York, and part of West-Chester county, the votes stood as follow:

	JOHN LAWRENCE.	JOHN BROOME.	PHILIP PELL.
City and County of New York.			
East ward	280	51	2
Montgomery ward	567	95	
North ward	284	34	

	JOHN LAWRENCE.	JOHN BROOME.	PHILIP PELL.
City and County of New York. (cont.)			
Out ward	330	33	
West ward	494	26	
Dock ward	80	30	
South ward	216	11	
West-Chester County.			
Town of West-Chester	15	5	
White Plains	10	4	1
Poundridge	4	4	16
North Castle	12		14
East-Chester	8	15	
Mount Pleasant	31	11	
Rye	10	11	
New Rochelle	9	8	
Pelham		7	
Mamorconcek	5	13	
Bedford	31	1	
Yonkers	9	6	
Greenbush	23	7	
	2418	372	33

Mr. Lawrence having been declared duly elected, yesterday attended and took his seat in Congress.

1. 7 April 1789.

2. The *Daily Gazette*, 9 April 1789, and *New York Packet*, 10 April, printed election returns for New York City and County that differ somewhat from the ward figures printed in the *Daily Advertiser*. But the returns in the *Gazette* and *Packet* do not correctly add up to the totals given in those newspapers, although they do agree with the *Advertiser* as to the total votes cast (2,531) in New York City and County. Thus it appears that the *Advertiser*'s numbers, which do add up correctly, are correct for New York City and County. The *New York Journal*, 9 April, immediately below, and *New York Packet*, 10 April, reported that Laurance had 291 votes in Westchester County, which is 124 more votes than the *Advertiser* reported.

New York Journal, 9 April (excerpts)

On Tuesday last the committee of both houses of the legislature of New-York (appointed for the purpose at the late session) began to canvass and estimate the votes for representatives from this state to the Congress of the United States, at the secretary's office.—This committee, last evening, had finished counting the ballots from three districts. . . .

That JOHN LAWRENCE, Esq. had 2251 votes, in the city and county of N. York, and 291 in Westchester, and was elected by the district of New-York and the southern part of Westchester. . . .

The hon. JOHN LAWRENCE yesterday took his seat in the house of representatives—[1]

1. Essentially the same report was printed in the *New York Packet*, 10 April 1789; *Weekly Museum*, 11 April; *Albany Journal*, 13 April; *Federal Herald*, 13 April; *Country Journal*, 14 April; *Hudson Weekly Gazette*, 14 April; and New Haven *Connecticut Journal*, 15 April. Beginning in mid-April the names of all the winners were widely printed in newspapers throughout the country.

A Freeman, New York Packet, 28 April (excerpts)

. . . all the great objects of commerce are now transferred to the august Councils of the Union; while the Legislature still retains the power to encourage domestic manufactories. Impressed with this idea the mechanics did not come forward in the late election for a representative in Congress to urge their peculiar interests. No antifederalist was heard to bawl out a mechanic! a mechanic! a mechanic!—No! the federalism of the mechanic body was too well known to suffer even an attempt to be made to mislead them, by so flimsy a conceit as the vulgar prejudice against lawyers.

That was the victory of public spirit, liberality and union over prejudice, pride, and deep laid design!—The mercantile discernment penetrated the vail, and it is hoped they will perceive it to be as absurd to reject a candidate now, because he is a *mechanic*, as it would have been then, because he was a lawyer.

It is the diffident opinion of the citizen who addresses you, that the distinctions at present held up are unwise and improper. Hereafter they will perhaps unavoidably grow out of a circumstance which has already been alluded to—at present they are premature and dangerous. If the merchants list was withdrawn, the other might be termed the federal ticket, and all good citizens unite in its support.

Federal and anti-federal are epithets that will soon probably become obsolete, but continue as yet to convey important distinctions. When once a complete representation of this State is obtained, and the authority of Congress officially recognized throughout its extensive jurisdiction—Then, but not till then, let present distinctions, like those of whig and tory, be utterly forgotten! . . .

Hitherto a spirit of union has existed among us, which has done honor to the patriotism of this city, and been productive of the happiest consequences. A spirit of union which has precluded every division into parties, which could be turned into mischievous purposes by the enemies of the Federal Constitution. It is still wished, that conciliatory measures might put an end to all impolitic and invidious distinctions.—No good purpose can be answered by opposing the favorite object of the mechanic body—It is obvious, that at present many ill ones may.

A FREEMAN.[1]

1. In the remainder of the article, "A Freeman" deplored the fact that candidates for the state legislature were running on competing mechanic and merchant "tickets." He urged voters to choose the best candidate, irrespective of label.

District 3

The election campaign in District 3 revolved around the positions of the two candidates on calling a convention to amend the Constitution. This focus reflected the make-up of the district and public attitudes toward ratification of the Constitution: Dutchess County had sent seven Antifederalists to the state Convention less than a year earlier, whereas Westchester County's six delegates were all Federalists. Moreover, Melancton Smith, a Dutchess delegate, had played a major role in fashioning the compromises in the Convention that coupled ratification of the Constitution with a circular letter calling for a second constitutional convention. The "second convention" issue was, therefore, still very much alive in the district.

Egbert Benson, the Federalist candidate, was an experienced politician with an extensive record of local, state, and national service. Antifederalist Theodorus Bailey, by contrast, was a decade younger than Benson and a relative newcomer to politics.

There are additional documents concerning the election in District 3 printed in Representatives Election Commentary, above.

Country Journal (Poughkeepsie), 10 February 1789

A Meeting is requested by a number of the Citizens of Dutchess county, at the house of John Adriance, Esq; at Hopewell, on Thursday the 19th day of February instant, of those of the Electors of the District consisting of the county of Dutchess, and the towns of Salem, North-Salem, Courtlandt, York-Town and Stephen-Town, in the county of Westchester, who can conveniently attend, and who are in favor of a speedy revision of the new Constitution by a general Convention of the States, in order to agree on a Person to be proposed as a Candidate at the ensuing election in the said District, to represent the People of this State in the House of Representatives of the Congress of the United States.

February 6th, 1789.[1]

1. The *Country Journal* printed the announcement again on 17 February 1789. It was reprinted in the Boston *Herald of Freedom*, 20 February, and *Salem Mercury*, 24 February.

Country Journal (Poughkeepsie), 17 February

A very great number of the Electors of Dutchess County, and of the Towns of Salem, North-Salem, Courtlandt, York-Town and Stephen-Town, in the county of Westchester, are fully apprised of the importance of electing a proper person to represent them in the House of Representatives of the Congress of the United States, and have decidedly made up their minds on the subject. The long-tried patriotism—the great abilities—the moderation, and integrity of the Honorable EGBERT BENSON, Esq. mark him as the MAN OF THE PEOPLE. A man, highly qualified to fill a station where the greatest confidence must necessarily be placed, and where there is a moral certainty it will not be abused.

Hopewell Nominating Meeting, 19 February[1]

At a meeting of a respectable number of Freeholders and Inhabitants of the county of Dutchess, held at the house of John Adriance, Esq; of Hopewell, in pursuance of a notice published the 6th day of February instant,[2] it was unanimously agreed, to hold up at the ensuing Election, his Excellency GEORGE CLINTON, Esquire, as Governor, and the Honorable PIERRE VAN CORTLANDT, Esquire, as Lieutenant Governor—

and *Isaac Bloom, Matthew Patterson, Jonathan Aikins, Peter Tappen, Thomas Mitchel, Barnabas Paine, and Henry Schenk,* as Members of Assembly for this county.

At the same meeting it was unanimously agreed to hold up THEODORUS BAILEY, as a Candidate in the District consisting of the county of Dutchess, and the towns of Salem, North Salem, Courtlandt, York-Town and Stephen-Town, in the county of Westchester, to represent this State in the House of Representatives of the Congress of the United States, at the ensuing Election, to commence on the 3d day of March next. It is an object of great importance in the opinion of the meeting, that the person who shall be elected as a Representative to the Congress, should be in favor of amendments to the new Constitution.—The gentleman proposed is decidedly in that sentiment, and may be confided in to use his endeavours to procure them. All who concur in opinion that it is necessary to the security of the public liberty, that amendments be made, will perceive the importance of uniting in the choice of a person who from principle and inclination will exert himself to obtain them.

Published by order of the meeting,
JAMES S. SMITH, Clerk.

February 20th, 1789.

1. *Country Journal,* 24 February 1789. Abbreviated accounts of the meeting were printed in the *New York Journal,* 26 February, and *Daily Advertiser,* 27 February.
2. See *Country Journal,* 10 February 1789, above.

Endorsement of Hopewell Nominating Meeting, 20 February[1]

Poughkeepsie, 20*th February,* 1789.

Sir, One of the most important elections is soon to take place that can possibly engage the attention of a free people. It is for Governor, Lieutenant-Governor, a Continental Representative, and members of Assembly.

We have in the election of last spring, exerted ourselves in favor of such persons as were for obtaining amendments to the new Constitution; and we conceive it necessary at this time to pay particular attention to the same object. We are apprehensive that our political opponents will attempt every measure to divide us, in order to effect their purposes. You have we suppose, before now been informed of the candidates by them proposed.

At a late meeting at the house of John Adriance, Esq; at Hopewell,[2] of a large number of citizens, it was unanimously agreed to hold up the following persons as candidates at the ensuing election. *George Clinton,* Governor, *Pierre Van Cortlandt,* Lieutenant-Governor, *Theodorus Bailey,* Continental Representative; for members of Assembly, *Isaac Bloom, Peter Tappen, Barnabas Paine, Jonathan Akins, Thomas Mitchell, Mathew Paterson,* and *Henry Schenck*; in whose favor we entreat you to exert yourselves; and we by all means recommend unanimity, as on this the success of our cause in a great measure depends. As the election of the Continental Representative is of the utmost importance, and will commence on the 3d of March next, immediate exertions ought to be made in his behalf. We are, with the greatest respect,

Your humble servants,

Zephaniah Platt, Murry Lester, John Davis, Ezekiel Cooper, William Emott, Daniel Duffee, Nathaniel Platt, Isaac Balding, junior, James Rogers, Stephen Hendrickson, James Cooper, Ebenezer Badger, James Pritchard, Robert Hoffman, John M'Coun, Israel Smith, David Carpenter.

1. *Country Journal*, 10 March 1789. This "printed address" is part of a longer article by "An Impartial Citizen." "Citizen" included the address, "in its own words," as an example of the party spirit which characterized the election campaign for governor and other officials and which he deplored: "Upon the whole I submit it to the public, with becoming deference to the gentlemen who subscribed that circular address, whether it does not contain very imprudent and unjustifiable assertions, and whether the *party spirit* which it discovers, is not calculated to widen rather than to heal those unhappy divisions, which have too long agitated and disturbed the good sense of this state. Such conduct I always contemplate with tender regret; especially when I observe it to come from men who are respectable and useful. It is now high time for our countrymen of all descriptions, to endeavour to subdue the spirit of party, lest hereafter it become too encorrigible to be corrected. Faction has ever been dreaded by virtuous and discerning citizens, as incompatible with the harmony and good order of Society. It may be denominated *the evil genius* of republican governments, and has in all ages too unhappily for the cause of freedom, shaded, if not totally eclipsed the lustre of their progress."

2. See Hopewell Nominating Meeting, 19 February 1789, immediately above.

An Impartial Citizen, Country Journal (Poughkeepsie), 24 February

There are two Candidates which have been publicly proposed in this district for the Representative in Congress. I observe that one of them has been proposed by a meeting assembled in consequence of a notification to those who were for a speedy revision of the new constitution, by a general Convention of the States. It is to be presumed that the nomination was made with a view to such a general convention, because the meeting was called expressly on that principle. I apprehend that many of the electors must be under some mistake as to the means of obtaining a general convention. It is not improbable that they suppose the Representatives in Congress are to be the authors of the measure. This is an obvious mistake.—The members of Congress in their public capacity, can exercise no discretion in the business. The constitution directs, that when the legislatures of two thirds of the several states concur in an application to Congress for a general convention, the Congress *shall* call one. In that case they are obliged to call one, whether it is or is not agreeable to their wishes. If two-thirds of the state legislatures do not make an application for that purpose, Congress have themselves no authority to call a convention. It would be a violation of the constitution if they should do it. These observations are self-evident to those who have attended to that article in the new constitution, which points out the path for amendments. It is therefore perfectly immaterial who we send to Congress, if our object is a general convention. Congress is only a passive instrument in the hands of the state legislatures: They, and they only, are the agents who are to produce the convention. We are therefore led to this conclusion, and I submit it to the public, whether it is not a perfectly just conclusion—That in fixing on a candidate to Congress, we are solely to attend to the competency of the individual; and that the policy or necessity of a speedy revision of the constitution by a general convention of the states, is a consideration which does not come in question. I have made these observations because I have some reason to suppose that many people who are not able, or who have not curiosity to inform themselves; and who, therefore, receive their information on trust, have been mistaken on the subject.

It cannot have escaped the good sense of this district, that the trust to be reposed in the representatives, at the first commencement of this government especially, will be immensely arduous. The laws which will be requisite to give this constitution a more perfect organization, and which will be requisite to regulate and establish on permanent principles, the judicial, the revenues, the commerce, the public burthens and the general security of the union, are objects of primary magnitude to the welfare of America.

An Impartial Citizen.

Country Journal (Poughkeepsie), 24 February

Several Persons from the different parts of the County assembled occasionaly in this place during the late Circuit Court, unanimously agreed to vote for EGBERT BENSON as Representative in Congress, and to recommend him to the choice of the other electors in the district.

Poughkeepsie, Feb. 20, 1789.[1]

1. This item was reprinted in the *Daily Advertiser*, 27 February 1789.

Rhinebeck Nominating Meeting, 26 February[1]

At a numerous and respectable meeting of the Electors in Rhinebeck precinct,[2] held at the house of George Sharp, on the 26th day of February 1789;[3]

A List of persons proposed as Candidates for the suffrages of the people at the next general election, and agreed to at a meeting held at Hopewell on the 19th instant, having been communicated to this meeting,[4] and it being unanimously conceived that it will not meet the approbation of the generality of the electors in the county, a meeting therefore of such of the electors as can conveniently attend, and who are of opinion that a preferable list can be formed, is requested at the house of Timothy Beadle, in the Nine-partners, on Tuesday the 10th day of March next, at 10 o'clock in the forenoon of said day.

At the same time a committee of nine persons was appointed with particular instructions, to communicate to the said meeting, to be held at the house of Timothy Beadle as aforesaid, the unanimous sense of this meeting in favor of the nomination of the hon. Robert Yates, Esq; as candidate for the office of Governor, and the hon. Pierre Van Cortlandt, Esq; for Lieutenant-Governor, at the ensuing general election.[5]

By order of the Meeting,
PETER CANTINE, jun. Chairman.

1. *Country Journal*, 3 March 1789.
2. In Dutchess County.
3. In the *Country Journal*, 7 April 1789, "A Dutchess County Freeholder" claimed that only about 25 to 40 people (accounts varied) attended the meeting, that it was "uncertain" how many of them were electors, and that only persons likely to support Robert Yates for governor were notified of the meeting in advance. He further asserted that, with one or two exceptions, the Antifederalists present were either "connexions" of Yates or under his "powerful influence."
4. See Hopewell Nominating Meeting, 19 February 1789, above.
5. Although this Rhinebeck meeting did not specifically object to the nomination of Theodorus Bailey for Representative, the circular letter that resulted from this meeting stated that Egbert Benson had been unanimously nominated for Representative (see Rhinebeck Circular Letter, 27 February 1789, immediately below).

Rhinebeck Circular Letter, 27 February[1]

Rhinebeck precinct, Feb. 27, 1789.

Gentlemen,

We yesterday had a meeting of the most respectable electors of this precinct on the subject of the ensuing general election, as well the election of a representative in Congress for this district—The nomination of Judge Yates as governor, Pierre Van Cortlandt lieutenant-governor, and Egbert Benson as representative in Congress, was unanimously agreed to by the meeting.—At the same time we were appointed a committee to correspond with such gentlemen in the different parts of the county as we should suppose would be in favor of this nomination, and to request that their exertions may be united with those of the people of this precinct in its support:—We therefore take the liberty to address you on the subject, trusting that you will join with us in the opinion that a change of measures, and for that purpose a change of men is necessary in the government of this State. The reasons on which this opinion is founded, would open too copious a field for discussion at this time—We therefore shall content ourselves for the present with referring you to a circular letter lately published by a committee of correspondence appointed by a meeting held in the city of New-York: In it are contained the greater part of those reasons which have influenced our conduct on the present occasion.[2]—With respect to the representative in Congress, as the election is so nigh at hand we would beg your immediate exertions:—The time before the general election for governor, lieutenant governor, &c. will afford a better opportunity to use your influence in favor of the gentlemen proposed, should you agree with us in the choice.

You will perceive by a notification which will appear in the Poughkeepsie paper on Tuesday next;[3] that our meeting in this precinct, also resolved to request a meeting of such gentlemen in the county as can conveniently attend, at the house of Timothy Beadle in the Nine-partners, on Tuesday the 10th day of March next, with a view to concert measures respecting the above nomination of governor and lieutenant-governor, and also to form a list of candidates for senate and assembly, differing from the one lately made at Hopewell,[4] and more acceptable we trust to the electors of the county in general, at which time and place we beg your attendance, and wish that you would invite such other gentlemen in your precinct as you imagine will approve the object of the meeting.

We shall be glad also if you should be in sentiment with us, that you would write to such gentlemen in the county of your acquaintance as you shall think proper, and urge the necessity of giving success to the measures we have taken.

We are gentlemen, with sentiments of esteem, your most obedient servants,

Goldsbrow Banyar,
Robert Sands,
Wm. Wheeler,
Cornelius I. Elmendorph,
Jacob Radclift.

1. *Country Journal*, 7 April 1789. The circular letter was quoted in an essay by "A Dutchess County Freeholder." No copy of the original circular letter has been located.

2. On 18 February 1789, Alexander Hamilton, chairman of the New York City Federalist committee of correspondence, addressed a circular letter to the supervisors of the city of Albany, supporting the candidacy of Robert Yates for governor. Both the *Daily Advertiser* and *Daily Gazette,*

which printed the letter on 20 February, reported that the committee intended to send the letter to town supervisors throughout the state.

3. See Rhinebeck Nominating Meeting, 26 February 1789, immediately above. The account of the meeting was printed in the *Country Journal*, 3 March.

4. See Hopewell Nominating Meeting, 19 February 1789, above.

John Jay to George Washington, New York, 1 March (excerpt)[1]

It is still doubtful whether Senators will be appointed for this State—but our accounts from the Country afford Reason to hope that a greater number of fœderal characters will be sent to the lower House, than was expected. our attorney General, Mr Benson, a very worthy man will probably be one of them—

1. RC, Washington Papers, DLC.

Country Journal (Poughkeepsie), 10 March

Wednesday[1] the pole closed at this place for a Representative of this district in the general Congress—and we are happy to add that that party spirit which on such occasions for some time past has raged through this county, seemed to have almost wholly subsided.[2]

1. 4 March.

2. This article was reprinted in the *Morning Post*, 16 March 1789; Philadelphia *Pennsylvania Packet*, 18 March; and *New York Journal*, 26 March.

James Kent to Simeon Baldwin, Poughkeepsie, 26 March (excerpt)[1]

we are very much agitated in this Country with our approaching trienniel Election for Governor—A new Candidate is proposed in opposition to Clinton—It is Judge Yates one of the Judges of our Supreme Court & altho he has been decidedly opposed to the new Constitution yet he is considered upon the whole as a much more virtuous, more independent & more advisable Man for our Chief Magistrate than the other. I am one of that part of the Community who are in faver of the Change & I have some Hopes of Success.

This district to which I belong have sent *it is supposed* a delegate to Congress who is against the Constitution—the Ticketts are not yet counted but it is believed they are in faver of the antifederal Candidate—this Candidate is my next Neighbour & brother in Law Mr. Bailey[2] an amiable man but who in my Opinion has wrong Notions on the Subject of national Policy.

We are turning our attention here very much to New York—the assembling of the new Congress opens a different & a pleasing Scene to our thoughts. There is a very elegant & commodious Building prepared for their Reception & the Citizens of that town are warm & sincere in their wishes for the Honor of Congress & for the Utility of their administration.—

1. RC, Simeon E. Baldwin Collection, CtY. Kent (1763–1847), a Poughkeepsie lawyer, represented Dutchess County in the Assembly, 1791 and 1792–1793. He later was a professor of law at Columbia College, 1794–1798 and 1824–1825; an assemblyman from New York City and County, 1796–1797; a justice of the state supreme court from 1798 until he became Chief Justice in 1804 (serving until 1814); and chancellor of the state, 1814–1823. Baldwin (1761–1851), a New Haven, Connecticut, lawyer, was a son-in-law of Roger Sherman; he served in the United States House of Representatives, 1803–1805.

2. Kent was married to Elizabeth Bailey, Theodorus Bailey's sister.

Margaret Beekman Livingston to Robert R. Livingston, Clermont, April 1789 (excerpt)[1]

I had yesterday the pleasure of Receiving your Letter by Mr Jones[.] Gaurdoque & North[2] are here and talk of Leaving us tomorrow—I am Very Sorry you have not kept to your intention of being here at the Election as Cockburn Informs me your Tenants are for the old Govr.[3]—I was so unsuccessful in my applications Among your Tenants when I last applyed to them that I have givin up all thoughts of going among them however I shall send Cockburn to do what he can among them[.] Woodstock cant avail as they have no Leases, so that nothing can come from that Quarter—your not being here may give C—— the majority, as I think I have been the means of geting in Benson by my Exertions—

1. RC, Robert R. Livingston Collection, NHi. The letter was addressed to Livingston in New York City. "Clermont" was the Livingston family manor in Dutchess County. Mary Beekman Livingston was Robert R. Livingston's mother.

2. Don Diego de Gardoqui (1735–1798) was the Spanish minister to the United States; William North (1755–1836) was an aide-de-camp to Baron von Steuben during the Revolution and an assemblyman from Albany City and County, 1792 and 1794–1796, and from Schenectady County, 1810. He was married to Mary Duane, daughter of James Duane.

3. George Clinton.

Daily Advertiser (New York), 9 April (excerpts)

On Tuesday[1] the committee appointed by the legislature to canvass and estimate the votes given in the different districts for representatives to Congress, met at the secretary's office in this city, and proceeded to the execution of their duty. . . .

The committee yesterday went through the examination of the votes for the district comprehending Dutchess and the northern part of West-Chester counties. In this district the hon. Egbert Benson, was found to have a majority of 10 votes, and was declared duly elected.[2] As Mr. Benson is now in town, it is expected he will take his seat this day.

1. 7 April.

2. On 8 April 1789, Fisher Ames reported that Theodorus Bailey had received more votes than Benson, but that "some were rejected for irregularity" (to [John?] Lowell, Representatives Election Commentary, above).

New York Journal, 9 April (excerpts)

On Tuesday last the committee of both houses of the legislature of New-York (appointed for the purpose at the late session) began to canvass and estimate the votes for representatives from this state to the Congress of the United States, at the secretary's office.—This committee, last evening, had finished counting the ballots from three districts. . . .

That EGBERT BENSON, Esq. had 584 votes, in the district of Dutchess county, and the northern part of Westchester, and was elected.

THEODORUS BAILEY, Esq. had 574 votes, as competitor to Mr. Benson.

. . . and, we are informed, that EGBERT BENSON, Esq. will take his seat in that honorable body this day.[1]

1. Essentially the same report was printed in the *New York Packet*, 10 April 1789; *Weekly Museum*, 11 April; *Albany Journal*, 13 April; *Federal Herald*, 13 April; *Country Journal*, 14 April; *Hudson Weekly Gazette*, 14 April; and New Haven *Connecticut Journal*, 15 April. Beginning in mid-April the names of all the winners were printed in newspapers throughout the country.

DISTRICT 4

The Federalists apparently did not nominate a candidate in District 4. Both men mentioned as candidates, John Hathorn and Cornelius Schoonmaker, were steadfast Antifederalists. The district had been strongly Antifederalist during the ratification contest: delegates from Orange and Ulster counties had voted 8 to 1 against final ratification of the Constitution in the state Convention. Governor George Clinton's home was in Ulster County.

Peter Van Gaasbeek to Abraham B. Bancker, Kingston, 26 February 1789[1]

When I returned home from Albany I found that Mr Sherif Dumond[2] Captn. Hend-[– – –] Schoonmaker and myself were regularly elected Deputies from this town to meet at Montgomery[3] with Ulster and Orange—And we accordingly attended on the 24th. Instant. But did not find so general a deputation from Orange as we had reason to have expected. Among the first objects that took up our attention was that of a Continental representative—A party from Orange were obstinate for the nomination of Genl. Hathorn to the important office—Others were equally strenuous for Cornelius C. Schoonmaker Esqr. and I think from our present political situation in respect to our maintaining our weight (and if possible a ballance in the Senate) the latter disposition was by far most consistent with the public weal—It was observed that we did not mean to hold entirely to Mr. Schoonmaker, but were willing and ready to unite upon any other person in whose integrity we could confide—However in order to prevent any open rupture, we unanimously agreed to hold up both these gentlemen to the people as Candidates worthy of so high a trust—This however with us was solely expediency; for reason whereof I took on myself to give a particular account of the conversation we had last Saturday Evening at Hiltons, and of Genl. Hathorns declaration to me—I also declared I had the fullest confidence in the integrity and partriotism of Genl.

Hathorn, but on this occassion for the reasons mentioned I could not think it prudent or politic to determine in his favor—We unanimously agreed on John Cantine and Joseph Carpenter Esqrs.[4] as Senators from this District—The last and perhaps the most important of our decisions was our unanimity to support George Clinton as Governor and Pierre Van Courtlandt as Lt. Governor at the ensuing Election—I send this by express; and if Genl. Hathorn should be willing to signify his intention by Letters I will endeavour to have them published before the Election

N.B. Colo. Hamilton's Letters as Chairman of the corresponding federal Committee in New-York, made their appearance at our meeting, but were ordered to be thrown under the Table, which was accordingly done[5]

1. RC, Bancker Family Papers, NHi.

2. Egbert Dumond was sheriff of Ulster County, 1778–1781 and 1785–1789.

3. The town of Montgomery in Ulster County.

4. Cantine (1735–1808) was Marbletown town clerk, 1763–1781; an Ulster County assemblyman, 1777–1778, 1779–1781, 1784–1785, and 1787–1789; and a state senator for the Middle District, 1789–1797. He voted against ratification of the Constitution in the state Convention in 1788. Carpenter represented the Middle District in the state Senate, 1789–1793.

5. The postscript and the sentence supporting Clinton and Van Cortlandt were printed in the *Federal Herald*, 9 March 1789, and *Albany Gazette*, 13 March; the *Albany Register*, 6 April, reported only the treatment Hamilton's messages received at the Ulster meeting. Hamilton's "Letters" also received a hostile reception elsewhere. For their treatment in New Windsor, Ulster County, see New Windsor Election Meeting, 4 March, below. In Chester (Goshen Precinct, Orange County), "a large body of respectable freeholders" voted unanimously on 18 March that the papers sent by the New York City Federalist committee of correspondence "should be cast under the table as fraught with scurrility" (*Goshen Repository*, 24 March).

Christopher Tappen to Peter Van Gaasbeek, Albany, 27 February[1]

Yours directed to Mr. Bancker[2] was read to the Members of the Counties of Ulster and Orange.[3]—General Hathorn was requested to answer the part respecting him—he told us that it was too delicate a matter for him to determine in so short a Time, that he might displease his Friends who wish to promote his Interest—in Short Sir his answer is as such a one as I expected notwithstanding his Declarations to you, General Clinton[4] & several other Gentlemen—his determination is in my Opinion to use all his Exertions to Obtain that Office—the Legislature have Resolved to rise tomorrow—if this shall take place I hope to have the pleasure to Act with you and our Friends in Support of the Gentm. you hold up for Ulster—In haste—

1. RC, Peter Van Gaasbeek Papers, Senate House Museum, Kingston, N.Y. The letter was addressed to Van Gaasbeek in Kingston. Tappen (1742–1826), of Kingston, was a major during the Revolution and represented Ulster County in the provincial congresses, 1775–1777. He also represented Ulster in the Assembly, 1788–1790, and the Middle District in the state Senate, 1796–1797 and 1798–1799; was deputy county clerk of Ulster (under County Clerk George Clinton), 1760–1812; and county clerk, 1812–1821. Tappen was a brother-in-law of George Clinton.

2. See Peter Van Gaasbeek to Abraham B. Bancker, 26 February 1789, immediately above.

3. Presumably the assemblymen from Ulster and Orange counties; Tappen was representing Ulster in the Assembly.

4. James Clinton, Governor George Clinton's brother.

New Windsor Election Meeting, 4 March[1]

GOSHEN, *March* 11,

At a meeting of many of the respectable inhabitants of the township of New-Windsor, held on the 4th inst. for the purpose of chusing a representative for the general government, it was proposed (after the business of the day was closed) that the proceedings of a committee held in the city of New-York, should be publicly burnt, they being esteemed no better than a lible against our present Governor, and the proposing of Judge Yates for that office only a party scheme,—Colonel George Denniston was then chosen chairman, and the proceedings of the aforesaid committee being read to the audience, it was accordingly burnt on an elevated pole, and the business concluded by three unanimous huzza's for Governor Clinton.

1. *Weekly Museum*, 21 March 1789. This article was reprinted in the *New York Journal*, 26 March; Philadelphia *Independent Gazetteer*, 27 March; Baltimore *Maryland Gazette*, 3 April; and *Albany Gazette*, 24 April.

Daily Advertiser (New York), 10 April (excerpt)

The committee appointed to canvass and estimate the votes for representatives to Congress, yesterday went through the counting of the votes from the district composed of Orange and Ulster counties: in which the hon. JOHN HATHORN, Esq. had a majority of votes, and was declared duly elected.

District 5

The victory of Federalist Peter Silvester over Antifederalist Matthew Adgate in District 5 was the major upset of the Representatives elections in New York. Delegates from the district (Clinton, Washington, and Columbia counties, and Albany County east of the Hudson River) had voted unanimously against the Constitution in the state Convention. But there had always been a visible minority of Federalists among the large manor owners in Columbia and Albany counties.

There are additional documents concerning the election in District 5 printed in Representatives Election Commentary, above.

Albany, Columbia, and Montgomery Counties Nominating Meeting, 10 February 1789[1]

At a meeting of a number of respectable citizens of the city and county of Albany, from the districts of Saratoga, Stillwater, Halfmoon, Ballstown Schaghticoke, Hosac, Cambridge, Stephentown, East Manor of Rensselaer, West Manor of Rensselaer, Great Imbagt, city of Albany and town of Lansinghburgh, together with some gentlemen from the counties of Columbia and Montgomery, convened (at Platt's inn, in the town of Lansinghburgh, on Tuesday the tenth instant) for the purpose of consulting upon proper persons to be nominated as candidates at the ensuing elections.

Brigadier general Abraham Ten Broeck, in the chair.

Resolved, That Mr. William Van Ingen be appointed clerk of this meeting.

Resolved, That the following persons be recommended to the electors of the city and county of Albany and the counties of Columbia and Montgomery for their suffrages at the ensuing election, to wit, at the election to be held the first Tuesday in March next.

ABRAHAM TEN BROECK, Esq. as a representative to congress from Montgomery county, and that part of the county of Albany that lies on the west side of Hudson's river.

PETER SILVESTER, Esq. as a representative to congress from the counties of Columbia, Washington, Clinton and that part of the county of Albany which lies on the east side of Hudson's river.

At the election to be held on the last Tuesday in April next.

ROBERT YATES, Esq. Governor.

PIERRE VAN CORTLANDT, Esq. Lieut. Gov.

PHILLIP SCHUYLER,
VOLKERT P. DOUW, } Esqrs. Senators.

Stephen Van Rensselaer,
Richard Sill,
John Younglove,
Henry K. Van Rensselaer,
Cornelius Van Vechten,
James Gordon,
Leonard Bronck, } Esqrs. Assemblymen.

Resolved, That Leonard Gansevoort, Daniel Hale, Francis Nicoll, Jacob Cuyler and Volkert Van Vechten be appointed a committee to notify the above candidates of this nomination, and to cause the proceedings of this meeting to be published.

A true copy of the minutes,

Attest, William Van Ingen, clerk.

Leonard Gansevoort,
Jacob Cuyler,
Francis Nicoll,
Volkert Van Vechten,
Daniel Hale, } Committee.

1. *Hudson Weekly Gazette*, 24 February 1789. The proceedings of the meeting were reprinted in the *Albany Journal*, 2 March; *Federal Herald*, 2 March; *Daily Advertiser*, 3 and 4 March; and *Daily Gazette*, 4 and 5 March.

Peter Van Schaack to Henry C. Van Schaack, Kinderhook, 22 February (excerpt)[1]

I was made happy with your Letter of the 15–18th instant by yesterday's Stage—and thank you for your Communications in the political Line and hope your Presages respecting the Residence of Congress will be verified—I look forward to the important Event of the Organization of the fœderal Government with sincere Pleasure, and unless I egregiously mistake my own Heart, it is a Pleasure derived from the Love of my Country. Whether we shall in Fact derive all those salutary Effects which we hope for from the new Government and which the Theory of it, I think, so well justifies, is yet a Matter of Speculation—if we have Virtue in the Execution of it equal to that which I verily believe animated the Framers of it, there wod be nothing to fear. But alas! instead of Men who will *endeavor to* act up to its Spirit and to give it a fair and liberal Experiment, it is much to be feared that many will come within those Walls for the very Purpose of defeating or embarassing it. Let me recommend to you to attend closely to every Proceeding of this great Assembly. Read over & over again the Constitution, especially any Clauses which may be the Subject of Argument and Diversity of Opinions, and you shod revolve in your Mind what passed at the Convention at Poghkeepsie, where your Attendance was certainly not for the Sake of Amusement only.[2] Mr Silvester is held up as a Candidate; he signified his Wishes to the contrary, but at the same Time declared that he conceived it the Duty of every Citizen to give up his own Inclinations to the Voice of the People. If he succeeds in this Antifederal District, I shall be much deceived, tho he will have many Votes this Year which he had not the last. I was talked of, but very early declared in explicit Terms that I wod *not* be held up. Indeed I returned to my Country with a fixed Determination to keep out of public Life—the Instance of last Spring was an Exception to the Rule not an Infraction of it—it was a peculiar Case and justified by the *Occasion.* I am persuaded that as a private Citizen I can do more good than I cod do in any official Character. As to contested Elections, my Experience in England as well as in my native Country has given me an Abhorrance of them. In this State where the Mode of Ballot is established by the Constitution, the Iniquity practised in Elections is a shocking Violation of the very Principles upon which that Species of Voting is founded. I could dilate this Subject by a Train of Reasoning, and a Detail of Facts which fully convince my Mind.

1. RC, Van Schaack Collection, NNC. The letter was addressed to Henry C. Van Schaack in New York City. Peter Van Schaack (1747–1832), a Kinderhook, Columbia County, lawyer, had lived in England, 1778–1785, after cooling to the patriot cause early in the Revolution. The state of New York allowed Van Schaack to return in 1785; he was readmitted to the bar in 1786; and he practiced and taught law thereafter. He was defeated as a Federalist candidate for the state Convention from Columbia County in 1788. He was Peter Silvester's brother-in-law. Henry C. Van Schaack (1769–1797), Peter Van Schaack's son, was admitted to the Columbia County bar in 1791.

2. Henry C. Van Schaack attended the state Convention as an observer (Henry C. Van Schaack, *The Life of Peter Van Schaack, LL.D.*, . . . [New York, 1842], 426–27).

An Elector, Hudson Weekly Gazette, 24 February

Mr. Stoddard,

The approaching election for a representative to congress, being of importance, and the electors being considerably divided upon the character for that station, I shall give you my sentiments, submitting them at the same time to the consideration of the public, who must determine their propriety.

The proper character for a representative, I conceive to be this.—A man of upright principles—of considerable political information—who knows the real interest of the people, who has that kind of general knowledge necessary to make him respectable, and who is capable of delivering his sentiments in a manner becoming his cause, respectful to his station and honorable to his constituents.—Whose information in the system of finance, in commerce, manufactures and husbandry, will enable him to judge rightly of regulations in either of these points, and will thereby be enabled to enforce such alterations as shall be necessary, and whose legal information will enable him to judge of the necessary regulations for the federal court. These are the requisites for a representative to congress. The objects of congressional inquiry are of such important and general concern, that local prejudices must give way to them. A man, therefore, tolerably qualified for the state legislature, will find himself ill qualified for congress.

The next object for our inquiry is, where shall we find a man, who possesses the confidence of the people, and the qualifications already mentioned. I believe there are many, who have the necessary qualifications, but who either possess a small share of public confidence, or whose private business will not permit them to attend at all times to their duty. The election law enables us to choose a person from any part of the state, but while persons are to be found within our district, I think we ought not to choose one out of it. Nor will there be an attempt for it. But I fear the attempt will be to elect an improper person in the district—it is this apprehension which induces me to give my opinion to the public in this manner, which I should not have done, had I not been fearful that the misapprehension of the people to their own interest, will mislead them.

The hon. Peter Silvester, and Matthew Adgate, esquires, are the two persons held up by different persons for the federal representative. Notwithstanding I respect Mr. Adgate, and really think him a man of considerable abilities, I cannot think him any way equal to Mr. Silvester. He has neither the legal nor political knowledge adequate to the task. Yet for a member of assembly of this state, I think him a proper character. Mr. Silvester's legal knowledge, his eloquence, his political abilities, and his honest impartiality, proclaim him worthy of the confidence and suffrages of the people. He will be supported, I believe, by many of both parties, and my sincere hope, arising from a disinterested regard for the honor and interest of the state, is that he will be elected.

Should Mr. Adgate relinquish his pretensions and support Mr. Silvester, and should he offer himself a candidate for the assembly of this state, where I think he will shine, better than in congress, I will support him with pleasure. I therefore most seriously recommend it to my fellow citizens to be watchful of their interest, nor let a misguided zeal lead them from the proper object of their political happiness. I wish them to step forth on this occasion and support Mr. Silvester, a man, as I said before, every way qualified to serve the real interest of the people.

An ELECTOR.

Hudson Weekly Gazette, 24 February

We are fully authorised to assure the public, that

The Honorable Peter Silvester, Esq.

notwithstanding he declined being held up a candidate for representative to congress, at a late meeting at the house of Lawrence Hogeboom, Esq. has complied with the request of his friends and will accept of that office, if he has the suffrages of the people. It is therefore expected that he will meet with the support of the electors of this district at the ensuing election—as from his reputation for abilities and integrity, it is presumed that no person will more carefully attend to the general interest of the union, or the particular and local interests of this state.

Alexander Coventry Diary, 6 March (excerpts)[1]

Hudson, 6 March, 1789. Warm and pleasant to-day, with considerable high south wind. Thawed a considerable in the P.M. Clouded up about sunset. . . . Went to Hudson with Mr. Van Alstine, with my horses, and his slay, to vote for a representative to Congress, this being the last day of the poll. This State sends 6. and is divided into 6 districts for that purpose: and of which Columbia and Washington Counties, with the rest of the land lying between, forms one District.[2] Adgate and Silvester are held up here. The Federal party vote for Silvester, who is a man of unblemished character; and the Antifederalists for Adgate. A Col. Williams is held up in Washington Co. Van Alstine and I voted for Silvester.

1. Tr, NHi. Coventry (1766–1831), a Hudson physician, was born in Scotland and emigrated to America in 1785. About 1790 he left Hudson for the Utica area, where he was active in both agricultural and medical societies.

2. Clinton County was also in District 5.

Henry Van Schaack to Theodore Sedgwick, [Pittsfield], 9 March (excerpts)[1]

Immediately after our town meeting on the 3d. Instant[2] I went over to Kings District and attended their polling for three days—I conclude from what passed that Silvester had about half the Votes[.][3] In the Districts of the two lower manors the upper manor Kinderhook and Claverack[4] the majority will be 5 to one—. . .

A late publication from New York containing the Sense of the Citizens of that metropolis upon the subject of electing an other Governor carried such strong marks of Conviction that a change must take place in favor of judge Yates—It is signed by Colo. Hamilton and is addressed to the Supervisors in the different Districts.[5] Never was any thing read with more avidity and with greater success—The necessity of a change is almost in every bodys mouth.

Why cant you and Mrs. S make us a visit before the snow goes off? The Slaying will do for a jaunt of pleasure. I have neglected so much business by the different Elections, that I cannot call to see you. Besides if I cod. go to Stockbridge you cannot fill my bags with good potatoes my pockets with good apples nor my belly with good Cyder all which I can do—besides you and I can hammer over Politics and arrange matters for matters to take place in future. I shall expect to see you here—Sorry very sorry I was indeed that I was from home when you called here—But this may be in part remedied if you will accept of my Invitation.

1. RC, Sedgwick Papers, MHi. The letter's dateline only gives "Massachusetts" as the place of origin, but Van Schaack lived in Pittsfield, Massachusetts. The letter was addressed to Sedgwick in Stockbridge, Massachusetts. For another excerpt from this letter, see DHFFE, I, 698. Van Schaack (1733–1823) was born at Kinderhook and lived in Albany from about 1756 to 1769. He held many local offices (including justice of the peace and postmaster at Albany) before the Revolution. Van Schaack was a loyalist during the Revolution, after which he moved to Berkshire County, Massachusetts, remaining there until about 1806, when he retired to Kinderhook. He represented Pittsfield in the Massachusetts House of Representatives in 1787.

2. The third election for Representative in the Hampshire-Berkshire District of Massachusetts took place on 2 March; Sedgwick ran a close second in the election (he eventually won in the fifth election, on 11 May). The district was adjacent to New York's District 5.

3. Matthew Adgate defeated Peter Silvester, 249 to 108, in Kings District, Columbia County.

4. These were all locations in Columbia County.

5. On 18 February 1789, Alexander Hamilton, as chairman of the New York City Federalist committee of correspondence, had addressed a circular letter to the supervisors throughout New York, supporting the candidacy of Robert Yates for governor. The address was published in both the *Daily Advertiser* and *Daily Gazette* on 20 February.

Killian K. Van Rensselaer to Samuel Blachley Webb, [Claverack], 2 April[1]

I received your polite letter pr. Stage for which I sincerely thank you—I shall be with you about the 20th. of this Month, and will communicate a *thousand* things that I cannot for want of leasure, advise you of at present—The objict of my dropg. these lines to you is with a View, to obtain from N York as early as possible the news, who is declared Representative in Congress for Columbia district &c—Judge *Silvester* and Mat. *Adgate* were the two Candidates—I will be much obliged to you when the *Canvassors* next Tuesday meet at the Secretary's Office to *obtain* an exact account how many Votes have been taken in the great district to which Columbia belongs, and in particular the 8. districts in this County and how the Votes are divided[.] let me know if you please, who are appointed to represent the other districts in this State

I send you love *from one* & sincere & cordial good wishes from many

1. RC, Webb Papers, CtY. The letter was addressed to Webb in New York City; an endorsement on the address page gives Claverack as the place of writing. Van Rensselaer (1763–1845) practiced law in Claverack and Albany; he served in the House of Representatives, 1801–1811. Webb (1753–1807), a colonel during the Revolutionary War, was the New York City agent of a Boston merchant in 1789. He moved to Claverack sometime in 1789.

Daily Advertiser (New York), 10 April (excerpts)

The committee appointed to canvass and estimate the votes for representatives to Congress, yesterday went through the counting of the votes. . . .

In the district composed of the counties of Columbia, Washington, and Clinton, and that part of Albany county on the East side of Hudson river; the Hon. PETER SYLVESTER, Esq. had a majority of votes, and was declared duly elected.

The votes in this district were divided between Mr. Sylvester and Mr. Matthew Adgate.

For Mr. Sylvester,	1628
Mr. Adgate,	1501
Majority	127

Hudson Weekly Gazette, 28 April

Statement of the votes taken in the district composed of Columbia, Washington, and Clinton and that part of Albany county lying on the east side of Hudson's river, for a representative to congress.

	Mr. Silvester.		Mr. Adgate.		Mr. Williams.	
Columbia county.						
Hudson	221		2			
Kinderhook	216		84			
Manor of Livingston	123		45			
Clavasack	82		155			
Kings	108		249			
Hillsdale	125		174			
Clermont	68		4			
East Camp	11	954	10	723		
Washington county.						
Argyle	52		24		2	
Kingsbury	4		37		5	
Salem	34		87		1	
Hebron	7		53			
Granville	10		30			
Hampton	1		17			
Westfield	39	147	0	248	6	14
Clinton county.						
Wilksburgh	23		0			
Plattsburgh	0	23	0		36	36
Albany county.						
Hosick	36		49			
Stephentown	88		55			
Saratoga, E.H.R.	44		71			
Cambridge	37		101			
Rensselaerwyck	268		155			
Schaghticoke	31	504	99	530		
Mr. Silvester		1628		1501		50
Mr. Adgate		1501				
Majority in favor of Mr. Silvester		127				

District 6

The contest in District 6 was between two prominent public figures: Antifederalist Jeremiah Van Rensselaer and Federalist Abraham Ten Broeck. A major campaign issue was the Antifederalists' continuing demand for amendments to the Constitution and the election of a candidate sympathetic to that cause. (Delegates from the counties which comprised the district had voted unanimously against ratification of the Constitution in the state Convention in 1788.) But here—as elsewhere in the state—the election of a Representative appears to have been overshadowed by the developing gubernatorial election.

For an additional comment about the election in District 6, see Abraham Yates, Jr., to Melancton Smith, 18 March 1789, Representatives Election Commentary, above.

City of Albany Political Meeting, 7 February 1789[1]

ALBANY, February 7th, 1789

At a numerous and respectable Meeting of Citizens of the city of Albany:

ABRAHAM TEN BROECK, Esq. Chairman.

WHEREAS it has been represented to this Meeting, that proposals are circulated through the several Districts in the city and county of Albany, for a County Meeting, to be held in the town of Lansingburgh, on Tuesday next, for the purpose of nominating proper Persons as Candidates to be held up at the ensuing Election.[2] And whereas, the purpose of the proposed Meeting is perfectly agreeable to us, and we hope will conduce to promote that *Unanimity* so ardently desired.

Resolved, That *Abraham Ten Broeck, Daniel Hale, Jacob Cuyler, Leonard Gansevoort, Henry I. Bogert, Thomas Barret*, and *William Van Ingen*, be appointed to meet such Persons as shall attend at said Meeting, from the different parts of the county, and that they report their Proceedings to this Meeting, on Saturday, the 14th instant.

1. Broadside, Howard Townsend Collection, NAlI. The broadside also included an account of the nominating meeting on 14 February 1789 and an appeal, dated 20 February, for support of the candidates nominated (see City and County of Albany Nominating Meeting and Circular Letter, 14 and 20 February, below).

2. See Albany, Columbia, and Montgomery Counties Nominating Meeting, 10 February 1789, immediately below.

Albany, Columbia, and Montgomery Counties Nominating Meeting, 10 February (excerpt)[1]

Resolved, That the following persons be recommended to the electors of the city and county of Albany and the counties of Columbia and Montgomery for their suffrages at the ensuing election, to wit, at the election to be held the first Tuesday in March next.

ABRAHAM TEN BROECK, Esq. as a representative to congress from Montgomery county and that part of the county of Albany that lies on the west side of Hudson's river.

1. *Hudson Weekly Gazette*, 24 February 1789. For a complete account of the meeting at Lansingburgh, see Albany, Columbia, and Montgomery Counties Nominating Meeting, 10 February 1789, District 5, above. The meeting included representatives from, and nominated candidates for, both the fifth and sixth districts.

City and County of Albany Nominating Meeting and Circular Letter, 14 and 20 February[1]

SATURDAY EVENING, *February* 14*th*, 1789.

ISAAC VAN AERNAM, Chairman.

THE Gentlemen appointed to attend the Meeting held at Lansingburgh, on Tuesday last,[2] Reported, That the Meeting had agreed to the following Nomination, to wit,

ABRAHAM TEN BROECK, Esq.

Representative to the Congress of the United States, from the District of which the city of Albany forms a part.

ROBERT YATES, Esq. Governor.

Pierre Van Cortlandt, Esq. Lt. Governor.

Philip Schuyler,
Volckert P. Douw, } Esqrs. Senators.

STEPHEN VAN RENSSELAER,
RICHARD SILL,
JOHN YOUNGLOVE,
HENRY K. VAN RENSSELAER, } Esquires, ASSEMBLY-MEN.
CORNELIUS VAN VEGHTEN,
JAMES GORDON,
LEONARD BRONCK,

The Committee, further reported, That the Meeting was very respectable, and consisted of 47 Persons—and, that all the above Nominations were unanimous, except, two dissenting votes, to Robert Yates, Esq. as Governor.

Resolved unanimously, That this Meeting concur in the above Nominations.

Resolved, That *Cornelius Glen, Daniel Hale, John H. Wendell, John D. P. Ten Eyck, Leonard Gansevoort, John Boyd, David Groesbeeck, Thomas Barret, Henry I. Bogert, Jacob Cuyler, James Caldwell* and *Thomas L. Witbeeck* be appointed a Committee, to promulgate the said Nominations, in such manner as they shall deem most expedient.

A true state of the proceedings,

Leonard Gansevoort, Chairman.
of the COMMITTEE.

ALBANY, February 20, 1789.

FROM the preceding publication, you will perceive, that we have been appointed to promulgate the Nominations (made by a numerous and respectable Meeting of Gentlemen, from the different parts of the city and county of Albany) of Persons to be held up as Candidates, at the ensuing Election.

We flatter ourselves, that no reasonable objections can be offered to the Characters of the Gentlemen nominated, and therefore cheerfully execute the Duty assigned us, by diffusing the Recommendation of the County Meeting—and, as we trust that it will meet with general Approbation, we hope it will receive your Support.

WE ARE, VERY RESPECTFULLY,
YOUR OBEDIENT HUMBLE SERVANTS,
By ORDER *of the* COMMITTEE,
Leonard Gansevoort, Chairman.

1. Broadside, Howard Townsend Collection, NAll. The broadside also included an account of the political meeting in Albany (see City of Albany Political Meeting, 7 February 1789, above).

2. See Albany, Columbia, and Montgomery Counties Nominating Meeting, 10 February 1789, immediately above.

Circular Letter Supporting the Election of Abraham Ten Broeck, 14 February

ALBANY, February 14, 1789.

AT a Meeting of a Number of Citizens from most of the Districts in the County of Albany, and some Gentlemen from Montgomery, General *ABRAHAM TEN BROECK* was *unanimously* nominated, as a Candidate for the Office of REPRESENTATIVE to CONGRESS, from the District formed of the County of Montgomery and that Part of Albany which lies on the West Side of Hudson's River; of this Nomination, we, as a Committee, are directed to advise you: And as the Gentleman nominated, has discharged a Variety of public Offices, with Honor to himself and Advantage to the Public—and as his Conduct in Life, has invariably evinced him a Man of strict Integrity, and attentive to the Rights and Liberties of his Fellow-Citizens, and strongly impressed with that Spirit of Conciliation, which tends to promote the Peace and Welfare of Society, we trust his Nomination will meet with general Approbation and Support—*we hope for yours*: And, as the Day for Election, which is to be on Tuesday, the Third Day of March next, is so near at Hand, we intreat you to circulate this Nomination, without Delay, to the Citizens in your Neighborhood.

We are,

Your very humble Servants,

PHILIP SCHUYLER,
JELLES FONDA,
PETER SCHUYLER,
PETER GANSEVOORT, jun.
DAVID GROESBECK,
ROBERT M'CLALLEN,
ISAAC VAN AERNAM,
JOHN D. P. TEN EYCK,
HENRY GLEN,
DANIEL HALE,
LEONARD GANSEVOORT.

1. Broadside Collection, NHi. This particular copy of the broadside, addressed to John Saunders, Schenectady, carried the following handwritten postscript: "Relying upon your Zeal to promote the Object of the foregoing Letter we beg leave to Solicit your Attendance at the Poll, with Ballots to furnish such Persons as come unprepared with them—"

City and County of Albany Circular Letter, 19 February[1]

Albany, 19th February, 1789.

GENTLEMEN,

ONE of the most important Elections is soon to take place, that can possibly engage the attention of a free people—it is for a Governor, Lieutenant-Governor, a Continental Representative, State Senators, and Assembly-Men. We have in the Election of last spring, exerted ourselves in favor of such persons as were for obtaining Amendments to the New Constitution; and we conceive it necessary, at this time, to pay particular attention to the same object.

We are apprehensive that our political opponents will attempt every measure to divide us, in order to effect their purposes. You have we suppose, before now, been informed of the Candidates by them proposed.

At a late Meeting in this city, of near forty Members of the Legislature, they have unanimously agreed to recommend GEORGE CLINTON, as Candidate for the Government, and PIERRE VAN CORTLANDT, for Lieutenant-Governor, at the ensuing Election.

A Number of our Friends, from several districts of this county, have also had a Meeting in this city, and unanimously agreed and concluded to hold up the following persons as Candidates:

GEORGE CLINTON, Governor;
PIERRE VAN CORTLANDT, Lieutenant-Governor;
JEREMIAH VAN RENSSELAER, Continental Representative;
HENRY OOTHOUDT, } Senators;
JOHN LANSING, jun. }

In whose favor we entreat you to exert yourselves. As the Election of the Continental Representative is of the utmost importance, and near at hand, immediate exertions ought to be made in his behalf.

After the Election of the Continental Representative (which is to be held on the first Tuesday of March next) it is proposed to convene a full Meeting of one or more of our Friends from the several districts in this county, in order to concert the necessary measures to promote the Election of Members of Assembly.

We are, with the greatest respect,
your most humble servants,

JACOB C. TEN EYCK,	MATTHEW VISSCHER,	
JACOB LANSING, jun.	ARIE LEGRANGE,	
ABRAHAM YATES, jun.	JACOBUS WYNKOOP,	
ABRAHAM CUYLER,	PETER W. YATES,	
GERRIT LANSING, jun.	VOLKERT A. DOUW,	
BASTEJAN T. VISSCHER,	ABM. G. LANSING,	
JOHN PRICE,	JACOB H. WENDELL,	
HENRY TEN EYCK,	JACOB ROSEBOOM,	
CORNELIUS WENDELL,	WILLIAM I. HILTON,	
W. MANCIUS,	ABRAHAM I. YATES.	
P. W. DOUW,		
GYSBERT MARSELUS,	CHRIS. P. YATES,	Represen-
ABRAHAM TEN EYCK,	VOLKERT VEEDER,	tatives in
RICHARD LUSH,	HENRY STARING,	Assembly
JOHN W. WENDELL,	WILLIAM HARPER,	of Mont-
JACOB G. LANSING,	JOHN FREY,	gomery
D.B.V. SCHOONHOVEN,	JOHN WINN.	county.

P. S. The original letter (of which this is a copy) is in possession of Abraham G. Lansing, Esq.

1. Broadside, Rare Book Room, DLC. This broadside was also printed in the *New York Journal*, 26 February 1789; *Daily Advertiser*, 27 February; and *Albany Gazette*, 13 March. The *Daily Advertiser* reported that the broadside had been "circulated in the county of Albany." A few words that were obscure on the original broadside have been obtained from the *New York Journal*.

New York Daily Gazette, 27 February

Extract of a letter from a gentleman of information and character, dated Albany, February 22.

In Montgomery county the contending parties nominated a joint committee to determine on candidates. They all agreed in Judge Yates as Governor, Pierre Van Cortland, Esq. as Lieutenant Governor, General Schuyler and Mr. Dowe, as Senators; three Antifederalists and as many Federalists as members of the Assembly:—And that the Representative in Congress for the District, should be left to the discretion of each party.[1]

1. This article was reprinted in the *Weekly Museum*, 28 February 1789; Philadelphia *Pennsylvania Packet*, 6 March; Boston *Massachusetts Centinel*, 11 March; and York *Pennsylvania Herald*, 18 March.

Albany Journal, 2 March

The piece signed An Elector, on the comparative merit of Abraham Ten Broeck and Jeremiah Van Rensselaer, Esquires, Candidates for the office of Representative to the Federal Congress, has been received; but, as the character of the former gentleman is too well known to require a publication of it, and the conduct of the latter with respect to the New Constitution, having been made known to the public, by a letter, signed T.V. in the Gazette of Thursday last,[1] *the printers have thought proper to suppress it.*

1. No "T.V." article has been located.

An Amendment Man, Albany Gazette, 13 March

To Jacob C. Ten Eyck, Jacob Lansing, jun. Abraham Yates, jun. Abraham Cuyler, Gerrit Lansing, jun. Bastejan T. Visscher, Henry Ten Eyck, W. Mancius, Gysbert Marselus, Matthew Visscher, Arie Legrange, Jacobus Wynkoop, Peter W. Yates, Volkert A. Douw, John Price, Cornelius Wendell, P. W. Douw, Abm. G. Lansing, Abraham Ten Eyck, Richard Lush, John W. Wendell, Jacob G. Lansing, D. B. V. Schoonhoven, Jacob H. Wendell, Jacob Roseboom, William I. Hilton, Abraham I. Yates, Chris. P. Yates, Volkert Veeder, Henry Staring, William Harper, John Frey, and John Winn, Esquires.

Gentlemen,

A Number of printed copies of a letter signed by you[1] have been directed and sent to several persons in this town and district, and I am informed, that has also been the case in other districts in this and the neighboring counties; in which letter, you remind the people of their exertions at the election last spring, to put such members in the *state convention*, as were for *amendments to the new constitution*; and exhorting them to pay particular attention to the same object at the ensuing election; you then hold up GEORGE CLINTON, for Governor, JER. VAN RENSSELAER, for Continental Representative, &c. The citizens in this quarter recollect with pleasure, their exertions at that time, and are generally of opinion, that the same object should be attended to in chusing a Continental Representative; but there are very few, or none who can discover, what the amendments to the new constitution have to do, or how they are in the least connected with the election for Governor?—If you had pointed it out in your letter, it would have been rather better received. From the good opinion I and many others have *hitherto*, entertained of many of you we are unwilling, *at present*, to think you meant to deceive us, but rather that most of you have not duly considered the construction of your letter; for this you may be assured, that there are hundreds, in this and other districts, who were as much opposed to the new Constitution, before it was adopted by this state, and are now as much in earnest, to obtain amendments to it, as any of you, that differ very widely with you in respect to the *re-election* of GOVERNOR CLINTON; holding it to be a good republican principle, that, the greatest security the people have, is a rotation, in those offices which possess great powers. Don't you remember, one of the amendments we wish to the new Constitution, is, that the same person shall not be *more than twice successively* elected President? and Mr. Clinton has already been *four times* successively chosen governor of this state; and you now want to put him in a fifth time—whatever may be really your ideas, it would be well at least to have the appearance of consistency. Your's, &c.

An Amendment Man.

Schenectady, 28th Feb. 1789.[2]

1. See City and County of Albany Circular Letter, 19 February 1789, above.
2. This article was reprinted in the *Hudson Weekly Gazette*, 17 March 1789.

Daily Advertiser (New York), 11 April

JEREMIAH VAN RENSELAER, Esq. is elected a representative to the Congress of the United States, for the district, including that part of Albany county lying West of Hudson river, and the counties of Montgomery and Ontario.

For Jeremiah Van Renselaer,	1456
Abraham Ten Broeck,	1215
Majority	241

In the county of Albany, Mr. Ten Broeck had a majority of 36.[1]

1. This article was reprinted in the *New York Packet*, 14 April 1789.

PART FOUR

THE ELECTION OF SENATORS

In the April 1789 elections for the state Assembly and Senate, Federalists won enough seats to hold majorities in both houses. Thus when Governor George Clinton called the legislature into special session at Albany on 6 July to elect United States Senators, it was virtually certain that Federalists would be elected.

The parties nevertheless continued to spar over the method by which the Senators were to be chosen. The Antifederalists, although now in the minority in both houses, continued to advocate a joint vote by the Assembly and Senate, while the Federalists attempted to keep the two houses autonomous. The Federalists prevailed, but the Council of Revision rejected the resulting bill as "inconsistent with the Public good" (Council of Revision Proceedings, 15 July). The legislature then decided to appoint Senators by concurrent resolution.

In an effort "to consolidate their strength to prevent division" ([Robert Troup] to Alexander Hamilton, [12 July]), the Federalists had caucused early in the legislative session and chosen Philip Schuyler and James Duane as their candidates. But Ezra L'Hommedieu and Lewis Morris spoiled the Federalists' unanimity; each announced he would be a candidate for Senator despite the caucus vote. The division among the Federalists, as well as the Antifederalist opposition to Duane, resulted in "subtle parliamenteering" (Abraham Bancker to [Evert Bancker], 16 July) before Schuyler and Rufus King were appointed Senators.

The documents referred to above are printed in this part.

Hudson Weekly Gazette, 21 April 1789 (excerpts)

Copy of a letter circulating through the western district of the state of New-York; particularly handed to the freeholders of said district.

Albany, 7th April, 1789.

From a persuasion that the same principles actuate you, which formerly induced you to contend for amendments to the new constitution, previous to its adoption, we take the liberty again to address you on the subject of the next election.

We are aware that it has been said, that the election of governor, senators and representatives of assembly cannot influence the measures to be pursued for obtaining amendments to the new constitution; but, as two senators for the new government will probably be chosen by the legislature, it is of great importance that such state officers be elected, as will be decidedly in favor of amendments, and will be disposed to favor the calling of a general convention for the purpose, and against which convention many of those who call themselves federal are opposed. It is an undoubted truth, that several of those who are for preserving the new constitution in all its parts, have publicly declared, that the next election will decidedly discover the opinion of the people on that occasion; and hence, if you join in giving your votes in favor of those candidates who are opposed to amendments, you will either appear to confess that you have been mistaken in the measures you have formerly taken in favor of amendments, or that you are not anxious to obtain them. . . .[1]

We are, Your most obedient, humble servants,
By order of the Republican Committee, lately called the Anti-Federal Committee,
Jer. Van Rensselaer, Chairman.
Mat. Visscher, Secretary.

1. In the remainder of the letter the writer urged support for George Clinton as governor.

Proclamation by Governor George Clinton, 4 June[1]

L.S. By GEORGE CLINTON,

Governor of the State of New-York, General and Commander in Chief of all the Militia, and Admiral of the Navy thereof.

A PROCLAMATION.

Whereas, an occasion exists, which renders it necessary that the Legislature should be convened at an earlier day than that appointed by law for their annual meeting:

I have therefore thought fit to issue this, my PROCLAMATION, hereby requiring the SENATE and ASSEMBLY to meet at the City-Hall in the city of Albany, on Monday the sixth day of JULY next; of which, all concerned, are to take notice, and govern themselves accordingly.

Given under my Hand and the Privy Seal, at the city of New-York, this fourth day of June, in the thirteenth year of the Independence of the said State, 1789.

GEO. CLINTON.

1. *New York Packet*, 6 June 1789. This proclamation was also printed in at least seven other New York newspapers during June.

James Duane to Philip Schuyler and Volkert P. Douw, New York, 5 June[1]

I enclose for each of you an original certificate of the result of the canvass for Governor, Lieut. Governor and Senators at the late Election.[2] The great change in the House of Assembly will give you pleasure. I estimate 42 Feds against 22 Antis at the same time that both your elections are honorably secured.[3] In the Senate we retain a majority of two if Savage should Join and Webster continue in the opposition points in which I am not clear.[4] The Governor has convened the Legislature for the 4th July. I flatter myself we shall all promptly attend and confine ourselves to the immediate occasion of this Session and that every thing will soon be concluded according to our conceptions of the publick good for which we have so strenuously contended. It is a most pleasing reflection that contrary to the expectation of our opponents our conduct has met with publick approbation and the Federal Government with a sanction that must rejoice every man who wishes it prosperity and stability.

1. FC, Duane Papers, NHi. The Duane Papers also contain an earlier draft of this letter. Douw (1720–1801), of Albany, was a judge of the Court of Common Pleas, 1759–1770; recorder of the city of Albany, 1750–1760; a member of the colonial assembly, 1757–1759, and provincial congresses, 1775–1777; and a state senator from the Western District, 1786–1793.

2. Duane was a member of the joint committee appointed by the legislature (six members from each house) to canvass and count the votes from the state elections held in late April 1789.

3. Schuyler and Douw had both been reelected state senators from the Western District.

4. Edward Savage and Alexander Webster, representing the Eastern District in the state Senate, had usually voted with the Antifederalists in the balloting for United States Senators during the 1788–1789 session. They continued to do so at the July session.

Richard Bland Lee to Leven Powell, New York, 12 June (excerpt)[1]

You will have heard that Mr: Clinton succeeded in his election by a majority of 400 only. The Legislature elected at the same time are decidedly friendly to the Constitution and are summoned to meet in Albany on the 6th. of July when the appointment of Senators to Congress from this state will certainly be made—and men of proper political characters chosen.

1. RC, Leven Powell Papers, ViW. Printed: *John P. Branch Historical Papers of Randolph Macon College*, 1st ser., no. 3 (1903), 222–23. The letter was addressed to Powell in Middleburg, Loudoun County, Virginia.

Memorandum by Rufus King of a Conversation with Governor George Clinton, New York, 12 June[1]

Govr. Clinton called on me yesterday—the servant denied me and he left his Compliments—Today I called on him—After observing that he had called on me once or twice, and to avoid ceremony had not left a card, he remarked that he shd. have called the Legislature to meet on the first of July, but was apprehensive that the week might be lost from the celebration of the 4th. of July—that he did not think the Legislature wd. have Occasion to be together more than one week, as their only business wd. be the Choice of senators—He remarked that the controvercy of last Winter on the part of the Feds was probably grounded on a desire of particular men for the Office—on the other hand he suggested the idea of the Antis having conscientious Scruples concerning the manner of the Choice, and that they were not united in their men, could they have even regulated the manner of Choice—That Mr. Lansing[2] wd. not have served, and that Melancton Smith had disgusted many of the Antifeds by acceeding to the Ratification of the Constitution—that therefore his Choice wd. have been difficult—The Govr. asked who were spoken of as Candidates—I observed that I had never conversed with any Member of Assembly on the Subject and knew nothing more than the loose conversation of unimportant politicians—that I had heard the names of Genl. Schuyler, Judge Yates, Mr. Lansing, Mr. Duane, Judge Morris & the Chancellor[3] mentioned but I knew nothing of the private opinion of influential men—the Govr. observed, that Mr. Lansing wd. not serve if elected, that his prospects were good in his profession, and that he owed it to a numerous young family, not to go into public life[4]—that he thought it an important Question, whether any Gentleman in the State Judiciary ought to take a share in the national Legislation, that this might be Confounding the judiciary and Legislative Departments—besides that it had uniformly been his Opinion that the Offices of Great power shd. not all be concentered in a certain party, or family association—that their abilities and wealth already gave them great influence, and that the addition of great offices to the entire exclusion of other Characters might endanger the public Liberty—That he was desirous that they shd be allow'd their reasonable share according to their abilities, and that he wd. pay a proper consideration to their property, but that such allowance shd. be a distinct thing from a monopoly of the public Offices—He observed that Mr. Duane had considered it as his right to be appointed a senator—but that it was not a right of any man; Mr. Duane had said in some conference as to the manner of choice "that he wd. not give up *his* right"—a member criticising the expression, Mr. D. observed that he meant his right as a member of the senate, which Br. ought to have a negative in the Choice—The Govr. added that some persons had thought that there shd. be a mercantile character in the Senate, but that it was a little difficult to find one, in all points suitable; That he had heard my name mentioned, but that I was not a mercantile man—I here observed that it had been mentioned to me but not by any member of the Assembly, besides that I was but lately an Inhabitant of the State, that probably many of the old and very respectable Citizens wd. claim it as their right, and that I had no Disposition to enter into any Controversy on the subject—the Govr. observed that the novelty of my Inhabitancy could be no Objection—that I was a member of the Assembly, and that he had ever considered that appointment as sufficient authority for him to appoint any person to an Office for which he might in his Judgement appear capable—that as to the expectations of any Gentlemen that they had a right to the Office &c he repeted his former Observations—with this addition, that formerly there were two great families or Parties namely Delancys & Livingstons—That from their Opposition they kept so constant a watch on each other, that neither dared any measure injurious to the mass of the people—that the case was now different, the Delancy party was extinct by the Revolution; and all the great & opulent families were united in one Confederacy—That his politicks were to keep a constant eye to the measures of this Combination, and he thought the people shd. be on their guard against their active Efforts—He observed that he had not heard my name mentioned by any of the members of the City, but by some Gentlemen from the Country—he added that he thought there shd. be an understanding among the members of Assembly previous to yt. meeting as to the individuals of their Choice—

Concerning the removal of the Legislature to this City he observed, that it had been forced from this place by the indiscretion of the City members—that the Country members were men of sound Judgement, but not used to public Speaking—that they were ridiculed and their Speeches improperly taken & published by Childs[5]—that a remonstrance presented to the Legislature at a certain Time, he believed it concerned the emission of the paper money, had placed in a ridiculous view some part of a Speech of a Mr. Taylor a member from Albany,[6] that from that moment he foresaw that Taylor wd. attempt, and succeed in it, to remove the Legislature to Albany—That if the City members had been prudent and wd. have gratified the Country members with meeting some Times for a short Session (for example) at Poughkeepsie or Esopus they never wd have thought of a removal—

1. MS, King Papers, NHi.

2. John Lansing, Jr.

3. Philip Schuyler, Robert Yates, John Lansing, Jr., James Duane, Richard Morris, and Robert R. Livingston.

4. Lansing had a successful law practice and was mayor of Albany.

5. Francis Childs published the *Daily Advertiser*.

6. John Tayler (1742–1829), a merchant, represented Albany City and County in the Assembly, 1777–1779, 1780, and 1786–1787, and the Eastern District in the state Senate, 1804–1813. He was a judge of Albany County, 1797–1803, and lieutenant governor of New York, 1813–1822.

Massachusetts Centinel (Boston), 20 June

The Legislature of New-York are to meet at Albany the 6th July—there does not remain a doubt but that this State will be represented in the Federal Senate in next month.

New York Daily Gazette, 22 June

ALBANY, June 15.[1]

The principal reason for calling together the Legislature early in July, is said to be for the appointment of gentlemen, on the part of this state, to the Senate of the United States; in which Hon. body we are at present without any representation. As this was the only business of any importance left unfinished at the close of the last session, and nothing of consequence, as far as we can learn, has since occurred to occasion the present call, it is reasonable to conclude that the next will be a short session.[2]

1. No printing of this item in an extant Albany newspaper has been located.

2. This article was reprinted in the *New York Packet*, 23 June 1789; Philadelphia *Federal Gazette*, 24 June; *New York Journal*, 25 June; Philadelphia *Pennsylvania Mercury*, 25 June; and Philadelphia *Pennsylvania Packet*, 25 June.

Morgan Lewis to Alexander Hamilton, Rhinebeck, 24 June[1]

I am informed the Inhabitants of New York have it in Contemplation to make Mr King one of our Senators. Under this Persuasion I have thrown it out in Conversation to several of the Country Members & have found it very generally disapproved of, so much so, that I am satisfied it cannot at present be accomplished. I am afraid too, it would interfere with the appointment of Genl. Schuyler, in this Way. Many Persons think we are bound to support Judge Yates, in Order to convince the public, that our only Object in pushing him for the Government, was not merely the removal of Mr. Clinton. This may operate with many as a Reason for supporting the Judge against the General.[2] How will it answer to try the old Chief[3] for the Southern District—This I immagine will give pretty general Satisfaction.—The old Gentleman will be provided for, and Judge Yates satisfied with stepping into the Chief Justice's Chair. Give me your Sentiments upon this subject; and also upon the Mode most proper to be adopted in the Appointment of Senators—

1. RC, Hamilton Papers, DLC. The letter was addressed to Hamilton in New York City. Lewis (1754–1844) held many public offices, including assemblyman from New York City and County, 1789–1790, and from Dutchess County, 1792; state attorney general, 1791–1792; a justice of the state supreme court, 1792–1801; Chief Justice of New York, 1801–1804; and governor, 1804–1807.

2. The Federalists had backed Robert Yates for governor against George Clinton in the April elections.

3. Richard Morris, Chief Justice of the state supreme court.

Massachusetts Centinel (Boston), 4 July

FROM NEW-YORK.

JUNE 28. . . .

A majority of the *Legislature* of this *State* are federalists. They are to meet to-morrow week at Albany. The first business will be, the election of *Federal Senators.*

William Smith to Edward Rutledge, [New York], 5 July (excerpt)[1]

The Legislature assemble at Albany tomorrow, for the sole purpose of electing Senators—the Candidates are Genl. Schyler, Duane, Judge Yates—King—the Chancellor—Morris.[2] Schyler & Yates have the best prospect of success—many speak of L'Hommedieu as having a good chance.—King is a member of the Legislature from this City—He has been admitted at the Bar here by unanimous consent, agst. the rules of the Court[3]—& has the Interest of Hamilton on this occasion, but he is too young in the Country in the opinion of a great many.

1. RC, William Loughton Smith Papers, ScHi. Printed: *South Carolina Historical Magazine*, LXIX (January 1968), 10–13. Smith was representing South Carolina in the House of Representatives; for a biographical sketch, see DHFFE, I, 225.

2. Philip Schuyler, James Duane, Robert Yates, Rufus King, Robert R. Livingston, and Lewis Morris.

3. In early 1789 the state supreme court admitted King to the New York bar, waiving the requirement in the law of 20 February 1787 that judges examine candidates for the bar (Robert Ernst, *Rufus King: American Federalist* [Chapel Hill, N.C., 1968], 141).

Assembly and Senate Proceedings, Monday, 6 July

The Assembly

A message from the Honorable the Senate was delivered by Mr. Yates and Mr. Peter Schuyler, that the Senate are met, and ready to proceed on business.

Ordered, That Mr. Livingston and Mr. Van Cortlandt, wait on his Excellency the Governor, and inform him that this House is met, and ready to proceed on business.

Ordered, That Mr. Gordon and Mr. Giles, wait on the Honorable the Senate, and inform them that this House is met, and ready to proceed on business.

Mr. Livingston reported, that pursuant to the order of the House, Mr. Van Cortlandt and himself had waited on his Excellency the Governor, with the message from this House, and that his Excellency was pleased to say, that he would send a message to the House immediately.

Mr. Gordon reported, That Mr. Giles and himself had waited on the Honorable the Senate, with the message from this House.

A message from his Excellency the Governor, was delivered by his private Secretary, that his Excellency requires the immediate attendance of this House in the Assembly Chamber.

Mr. Speaker left the chair, and with the House, attended accordingly, and His Excellency the Governor, and the Honorable the Senate, who had also attended, having respectively retired, Mr. Speaker reassumed the chair, and reported to the House, that

His Excellency had been pleased to make a speech to both Houses of the Legislature, and to deliver him a copy thereof. The same being read, is in the words following, viz.

Gentlemen of the Senate, and of the Assembly,

I CONCEIVED it to be my duty to convene you at this early period, that the Legislature might again have an opportunity of choosing Senators to represent this State in the Congress of the United States: and I flatter myself that an occasion so important and interesting will command an approbation of the measure.

I am sensible, however, that should your session be protracted at this season, it would be injurious, as well as inconvenient to many of the members. Impressed with this idea, and as nothing extraordinary hath taken place in the recess, I shall not attempt to call your attention to any other object. Our circumstances require unremitted industry, and the strictist economy; and I have a confidence that this consideration alone will be a sufficient motive with you to give as much dispatch to the public business as may be consistent with safety.

Gentlemen,

WHILST the distresses experienced by the failure of the last years crops, particularly in the exterior settlements, and by the poorer class of people, are contemplated with anxiety; the unmerited favors daily conferred on us by Almighty God, and especially the kind interposition of his Divine Providence in so ordering the seasons as to afford a prospect of relief from the approaching harvest, cannot fail to inspire us with sentiments of unfeigned gratitude and thankfulness.

Albany July 6, 1789. GEO. CLINTON. . . .[1]

Resolved, That His Excellency the Governor's speech, and the several matters which accompanied the same, be committed to a committee of the whole House.

Ordered, That His Excellency's speech be forthwith printed.

The House resolved itself into a committee of the whole House on His Excellency the Governor's speech, and the several matters which accompanied the same, and after some time spent thereon, Mr. Speaker reassumed the chair, and Mr. Livingston, from the said committee reported, That the committee had agreed to a resolution, which he was directed to report to the House, in the words following, viz.

Resolved, That it is the opinion of this committee, that a committee be appointed to prepare and report a draft of a respectful address to His Excellency the Governor, in answer to his speech.

Mr. Livingston, from the said committee further reported, That the committee had made progress in the speech of His Excellency the Governor, and the papers which accompanied the same, and had directed him to move for leave to sit again.

Ordered, That the said committee have leave to sit again.

Resolved, That a committee be appointed to prepare a draft of a respectful address to His Excellency the Governor, in answer to his speech, and that Mr. Jones, Mr. King, and Mr. Sill, be a committee for that purpose.

The Senate

Ordered, That Mr. Clinton and Mr. L'Hommedieu wait on His Excellency the Governor, and inform him that the Senate are met, and ready to proceed on public business.

Ordered, That Mr. Yates and Mr. Peter Schuyler wait on the Honorable the Assembly with the like message.

Mr. Clinton reported that Mr. L'Hommedieu and himself had, agreeable to the order of the Senate, waited on His Excellency the Governor with their message, when His

Excellency was pleased to say, that as soon as he should receive a message from the Honorable the Assembly, that they were also met and ready to proceed on business, he would send a message to the Senate.

Mr. Yates reported, that Mr. Peter Schuyler and himself had, agreeable to the order of the Senate, waited on the Honorable the Assembly with their message.

A message from the Honorable the Assembly, by Mr. Gordon and Mr. Giles, was received, informing that they were met, and ready to proceed on public business.

A message from His Excellency the Governor, by his private Secretary, was received, requiring the immediate attendance of the Senate in the Assembly Chamber.

Mr. President accordingly left the chair, and with the members of the Senate attended His Excellency in the Assembly Chamber, and being returned, reassumed the chair, and informed the Senate, that His Excellency the Governor had made a speech to the Legislature, of which he had obtained a copy, which being read, is in the words following, viz. . . .[2]

Ordered, That his Excellency's Speech, with the papers accompanying the same, be committed to a committee of the whole.

The Senate accordingly resolved itself into a committee of the whole on His Excellency's Speech and the papers accompanying the same; after some time spent thereon, Mr. President[3] reassumed the chair, and Mr. Duane reported, that it was the opinion of the committee that a special committee be appointed to prepare and report a respectful answer to His Excellency's Speech, and that the committee had directed him to move for leave to sit again: Thereupon,

Ordered, That Mr. Duane, Mr. L'Hommedieu and Mr. Roosevelt, be a committee to prepare and report a respectful answer to his Excellency's Speech.

Ordered, That the committee have leave to sit again.

1. Clinton's speech was widely printed in New York newspapers. For a signed, manuscript copy of the speech, see Letters to and by George Clinton, 1777–1798, N.Y. MSS E, WHi.

2. For Clinton's speech, see Assembly Proceedings.

3. Lieutenant Governor Pierre Van Cortlandt was president of the Senate.

Assembly and Senate Proceedings, Tuesday, A.M., 7 July

The Assembly

Mr. Jones, from the committee appointed to prepare a draft of a respectful address to His Excellency the Governor, in answer to his speech, reported, That the committee had prepared a draft accordingly; and he read the draft in his place, and delivered the same in at the table, where it was again read.

Ordered, That the said draft of an address be committed to a committee of the whole House. . . .

The House resolved itself into a committee of the whole House, on the draft of a respectful address to His Excellency the Governor, in answer to his speech, and after some time spent thereon, Mr. Speaker reassumed the chair, and Mr. Gordon from the said committee reported, that the committee had gone through the said draft without amendment, which he was directed to report to the House; and he read the report in his place, and delivered the said draft in at the table, where the same was again read, and agreed to by the House.

Ordered, That the said draft of a respectful address be engrossed. . . .

The engrossed address to His Excellency the Governor, in answer to his speech at the opening of the session, was read, and is in the words following, viz.

To His Excellency George Clinton, Esquire, Governor of the State of New-York, General and Commander in Chief of all the militia, and Admiral of the navy of the same.

The respectful address of the Assembly, in answer to His Excellency's speech.

WE the Representatives of the People of the State of New-York, in Assembly convened, impressed with the high importance of a complete organization of the Government of the United States of America, do in the fullest manner, approve of your Excellency's having convened the Legislature at this period, for the purpose of appointing Senators to represent this State in the Senate of the United States.

We are, with your Excellency, sensible of the inconvenience of a session of the Legislature at this particular season, and are therefore anxious to confine our deliberations to those objects which shall appear absolutely necessary to the public happiness.

At the same time that we lament the distresses to which many of our fellow citizens in the exterior settlements of the State have been exposed, from a scarcity of some of the necessaries of life, we unite with your Excellency in rendering our fervent thanks to Almighty God, for the frequent interpositions of his Providence in our favor, and more especially for the prospects which we enjoy of relief and plenty from the approaching harvest.

Assembly-Chamber, July 7th, 1789.

Ordered, That Mr. Speaker subscribe the said address on behalf of the House.

Ordered, That the said address be presented to His Excellency the Governor by the whole House.

Ordered, That Mr. King and Mr. Jones, wait on His Excellency the Governor, and request to be informed when he will be pleased to be attended by this House, with their respectful address. . . .

Mr. King reported, that pursuant to the order of the House, Mr. Jones and himself had waited on his Excellency the Governor, to know when he would be pleased to be attended by this House, with their respectful address; and that his Excellency had been pleased to appoint to-morrow, at eleven of the clock in the forenoon, for that purpose.

The Senate

Mr. Duane, from the committee for that purpose appointed, reported an answer to his Excellency the Governor's Speech, which he read in his place, and delivered the same in at the table, where it was again read, and agreed to by the Senate: Thereupon,

Ordered, That the same be engrossed. . . .

The engrossed answer to His Excellency's Speech was read and agreed to.

Ordered, That the same be signed by Mr. President in behalf of the Senate.

Ordered, That Mr. Roosevelt and Mr. Micheau wait on his Excellency the Governor to know when and where he will be pleased to receive the Senate with their answer to his Speech.

The answer of the Senate to His Excellency's Speech is in the words following, viz.

The respectful Answer of the Senate of the State of New-York, to the Speech of His Excellency George Clinton, Esq. Governor of the said State, General and Commander in Chief of all the Militia and Admiral of the Navy of the same.

SIR,

WE the Senate in Legislature convened, return your Excellency our thanks for your Speech.

A full participation in the exercise of the national government, we consider as an object of great moment, and we therefore entirely approve of your Excellency's convening the Legislature at so early a period for the important purpose of choosing Senators to represent this State in the Congress of the United States.

It gives us pleasure to learn from your Excellency that nothing extraordinary hath taken place in the recess, which will require the protraction of the present meeting at a season inconvenient to many of our members, and we shall endeavor to bring it to a conclusion with all the dispatch which may be consistent with the public good.

Among the numberless blessings which demand our pious gratitude to the Almightly Ruler of the Universe, we view the approach of a more favorable harvest than from human observation we had reason to expect; and this impresses us the more sensibly as it promises a speedy relief to the distresses which some of our fellow citizens in the exterior settlements have experienced.

By order of the Senate,

Senate-Chamber, July 7, 1789. PIERRE VAN CORTLANDT, *President.*

Assembly and Senate Proceedings, Wednesday, A.M., 8 July

The Assembly

Mr. Speaker left the chair, and with the House attended his Excellency the Governor with their respectful address, according to his appointment; and being returned he reassumed the chair, and reported, that the House had attended his Excellency the Governor with their respectful address, and that his Excellency had been pleased to return an answer, and deliver a copy thereof, in the words following, viz.

Gentlemen,

PERMIT me to render you my cordial thanks for this polite address.

The approbation which you have been pleased to express of my conduct in convening the Legislature on the present occasion, affords me much pleasure; and I am persuaded that your punctual attendance on the public business, particularly at this season, cannot fail of being highly acceptable to your constituents.

GEO. CLINTON.

Albany, 8th July, 1789.

Ordered, That the respectful address of this House to his Excellency the Governor, and his Excellency's answer, be forthwith printed. . . .

Mr. Childs moved for leave to bring in a bill directing the manner of electing Senators to represent this State in the Senate of the United States.

Ordered, That leave be given accordingly.

Mr. Childs, according to leave, brought in the said bill, entitled *An act directing the manner of electing Senators to represent this State, in the Senate of the United States*, which was read the first time, and ordered a second reading.[1]

The Senate

Mr. Roosevelt reported that Mr. Micheau and himself had, agreeable to the order of the Senate of yesterday, waited on his Excellency the Governor, with their message, when His Excellency was pleased to appoint twelve of the clock this day, at his Chamber, to receive the Senate with their answer to his Speech. . . .

Mr. President left the Chair, and, with the members of the Senate, proceeded to wait on His Excellency the Governor, with their answer to his Speech, and being returned he reassumed the Chair, and informed the Senate that upon delivering their answer, His Excellency had been pleased to make a reply and furnish him with a copy; the same was read in the words following, viz.

Gentlemen,

IT is with great satisfaction, I discover in the Senate so perfect a coincidence in sentiment with me on the propriety of convening the Legislature at this time; and I entreat you to be assured that the obliging manner in which you have been pleased to communicate your approbation affords me the highest pleasure.

GEO. CLINTON.

Albany, 8th July, 1789.

1. See Assembly Draft Bill for the Election of Senators, 8 July 1789, immediately below.

Assembly Draft Bill for the Election of Senators, 8 July[1]

An act directing the manner of electing Senators to represent this State in the Senate of the United States.

Be it enacted by the people of the state of New-York, represented in Senate and Assembly, and it is hereby enacted by the authority of the same, that the Senators of the United States to be chosen in this state, shall be chosen in the manner following, that is to say, the Senate and Assembly of this state, shall, if two Senators are to be chosen, openly nominate and appoint two persons, and shall respectively give notice each to the other of such nomination, that if both houses agree in the nomination of the same person or persons, the person or persons so nominated and agreed to, shall be the Senator or Senators to represent this state in the Senate of the United States; that if the nomination of either house does not agree in any of the persons nominated by the other, the Senate shall without delay openly choose one of the persons nominated by the Assembly, and the Assembly shall without delay openly choose one of the persons nominated by the Senate, and the two persons so chosen shall be the Senators to represent this state in the Senate of the United States; that in every case where two Senators are to be chosen, and both houses agree only as to one in such nomination as aforesaid, and in every case where only one Senator is to be chosen, either of the two houses of the legislature may propose to the other a resolution for concurrence, naming therein a person to fill the office of Senator, and if the house receiving such resolution shall concur therein, the person so named in such resolution shall be the Senator, but if such resolution shall not be concurred in, either house may on that or any future day proceed to offer to the other a resolution for concurrence, naming therein the same or any other person, from time to time, until they shall agree upon a Senator.

1. *Daily Advertiser*, 16 July 1789. The bill was also printed in the *Daily Gazette*, 17 July, and *Gazette of the United States*, 18 July. The bill was introduced into the Assembly by Francis Childs and read for the first time on 8 July. It was read a second time, debated, and amended on 9 July.

Abraham B. Bancker to Evert Bancker, Albany, 8 July (excerpt)[1]

Early last Sunday morning I left Arrietta and the Children in good health and in Company with the Governor Miss Tappen & Mc:Kesson[2] arrived here by Land about 10 oClock on Monday Morning, when the Corporation received his Excellency at the Ferry under a Salute of 13 Cannon and as many Vollies from a Light Infantry Corps then proceeded to the Court House where refreshing Liquors were prepared upon the Occasion, immediately after which both Senate and Assembly having a Quorum (the Members being quallified) the Assembly chose Gulian Verplanck Esquire their Speaker when his Excellency Opened the Session with the Recommendation of Choosing Senators for Congress;—and after appointing the usual Committees, both Houses Adjourned for the day when our Company from Kingston Dined with his Worship the Mayor of this City[3]—As nothing more will remain to be done at this Meeting I Expect after fixing upon Senators an Adjournment will follow in the course of a few days—

1. RC, Bancker Family Papers, NHi. The letter was addressed to Evert Bancker in New York City.
2. John McKesson, clerk of the Assembly.
3. John Lansing, Jr.

Assembly Proceedings, Thursday, A.M., 9 July

The bill entitled *An act directing the manner of electing senators to represent this State in the Senate of the United States*, was read a second time, and committed to a committee of the whole House. . . .

The House by unanimous consent resolved itself into a committee of the whole House on the bill, entitled *An act directing the manner of electing Senators to represent this State in the Senate of the United States*; after some time spent therein Mr. Speaker reassumed the chair, and Mr. Gordon from the said committee reported, that after the said bill had been read through in the Committee the first paragraph was again read in the words following, viz.

"BE IT ENACTED by the people of the State of New-York, represented in Senate and Assembly, and it is hereby enacted by the authority of the same, That the Senators of the United States to be chosen in this State, shall be chosen in the manner following, that is to say, the Senate and Assembly of this State shall, if two Senators are to be chosen, openly nominate and appoint two persons, and shall respectively give notice each to the other of such nomination, that if both Houses agree in the nomination of the same person or persons, the person or persons so nominated and agreed to, shall be the Senator or Senators to represent this State in the Senate of the United States."

That the said paragraph having been read, Mr. King made a motion, that the same should be obliterated, and a paragraph there inserted in the words following, viz.

"BE IT ENACTED by the people of the State of New-York, represented in Senate and Assembly, and it is hereby enacted by the authority of the same, That the Senators to be chosen by the Legislature of this State to represent the State in the Senate of the United States, shall be chosen in the manner following, that is to say, the Senate and Assembly of this State shall respectively openly nominate one or two persons, as the case may be, and shall immediately afterwards give notice each House to the other, of such nomination; and if both Houses agree in the nomination of the same person or persons, the person or persons so respectively nominated and agreed to, shall be the Senator or Senators to represent this State, in the Senate of the United States."

That Mr. Schoonmaker, as a farther amendment, made a motion, that the said first paragraph of the bill which was before read, together with the next ensuing paragraph, which is in the words following, viz. "That if the nomination of either House does not agree in any of the persons nominated by the other, the Senate shall without delay openly choose one of the persons nominated by the Assembly, and the Assembly shall without delay, openly choose one of the persons nominated by the Senate, and the two persons so chosen shall be the Senators to represent this State in the Senate of the United States," should respectively be obliterated; and that a paragraph be substituted in their stead in the words following, viz.

"BE IT ENACTED by the people of the State of New-York, represented in Senate and Assembly, and it is hereby enacted by the authority of the same, That the Senators to be chosen in this State for the United States, shall be chosen as follows, that is to say, the Senate and Assembly of this State, shall each openly nominate as many persons as shall be equal to the whole number of Senators to be chosen by this State, after which nomination the Senate and Assembly shall meet together, and compare the lists of persons by them respectively nominated; and those persons named in both lists, shall be Senators for the United States; and out of those persons whose names are not in both lists, one half shall be chosen by the joint ballot of the Senators and Members of the Assembly, so met together as aforesaid; and the copies of the resolutions of the Senate and Assembly, testifying the said choice, shall be thereupon delivered to each of the persons so chosen a Senator for the United States."

That the question having been put on the amendment proposed by the motion of Mr. Schoonmaker, it passed in the negative, in the manner following, viz.

FOR THE NEGATIVE.

Mr. Speaker,	Mr. Barker,
Mr. King,	Mr. Crane, jun.
Mr. Clarkson,	Mr. Livingston,
Mr. Will,	Mr. Myers,
Mr. Post,	Mr. Crane,
Mr. Childs,	Mr. Arndt,
Mr. S. Van Rensselaer,	Mr. Watts,
Mr. Sill,	Mr. Lewis,
Mr. Van Rensselaer,	Mr. Van Veghten,
Mr. Cornwell,	Mr. Bronck,
Mr. Vandervoort,	Mr. Younglove,
Mr. Giles,	Mr. Haight,
Mr. Winant,	Mr. Converse,
Mr. Bancker,	Mr. Morgan,
Mr. Van Cortlandt,	Mr. Talman,
Mr. J. Brown,	Mr. Hitchcock,
Mr. Rockwell,	Mr. J. Livingston,
Mr. Seaman,	Mr. Gilbert,
Mr. Horton,	Mr. Tillotson.

FOR THE AFFIRMATIVE.

Mr. Randall,	Mr. Landon,
Mr. J. Smith,	Mr. Tappen,

Mr. Schoonmaker,
Mr. Clark,
Mr. Smith,
Mr. Bruyn,
Mr. Clowes,
Mr. Jones,
Mr. Carman,
Mr. Marvin,
Mr. M'Master,
Mr. Carpenter,
Mr. Griffen,
Mr. Rowan,
Mr. Savage,
Mr. Scudder,
Mr. Havens,
Mr. Coe,
Mr. Sickles,
Mr. Bloom,
Mr. Veeder.

That the question having been put on the amendment proposed by the motion of Mr. King, it was carried in the affirmative,[1] and the bill amended accordingly.

That in proceeding farther in the bill, and the last paragraph of the draft of the bill having been read, the latter part of the said paragraph was again read in the words following, viz.

"But if such resolution shall not be concurred in, either House may on that or any future day, proceed to offer to the other a resolution for concurrence, from time to time, until they shall agree upon a Senator."

That the said part of a paragraph having been read, and debates had thereon, Mr. Lewis, as an amendment, made a motion that the same should be obliterated, and a paragraph inserted instead thereof, in the words following, viz.

"But if such resolution shall not be concurred in, or when only one Senator is to be chosen, each shall nominate one candidate, of whom one shall be elected by a majority of fifteen electors, to be chosen in manner following, that is to say, the Senate shall by ballot elect from among the members of the Assembly seven electors, and the Assembly shall also by ballot elect from among the members of the Senate eight electors, which electors when so chosen, shall immediately, in presence of both Houses, elect by ballot one of the persons so nominated, and the person so elected shall be the Senator."

That debates were had on the amendment proposed by the motion of Mr. Lewis; and that the question having been put, whether the committee did agree to the same, it passed in the negative, in the manner following, viz.

FOR THE NEGATIVE.

Mr. Speaker,
Mr. King,
Mr. Clarkson,
Mr. Will,
Mr. Randall,
Mr. Post,
Mr. Childs,
Mr. S. Van Rensselaer,
Mr. Van Rensselaer,
Mr. J. Smith,
Mr. Landon,
Mr. Tappen,
Mr. Schoonmaker,
Mr. Clark,
Mr. Smith,
Mr. Bruyn,
Mr. Clowes,
Mr. Cornwell,
Mr. Jones,
Mr. Carman,
Mr. Vandervoort,
Mr. Giles,
Mr. Winant,
Mr. Bancker,
Mr. Van Cortlandt,
Mr. J. Brown,
Mr. Rockwell,
Mr. Seaman,
Mr. Horton,
Mr. Marvin,
Mr. Crane, jun.
Mr. M'Master,

Mr. Livingston,	Mr. Rowan,
Mr. Myers,	Mr. Savage,
Mr. Crane,	Mr. Scudder,
Mr. Arndt,	Mr. Havens,
Mr. Watts,	Mr. Coe,
Mr. Van Veghten,	Mr. Bloom,
Mr. Bronck,	Mr. Talman,
Mr. Younglove,	Mr. Veeder,
Mr. Haight,	Mr. Hitchcock,
Mr. Carpenter,	Mr. Livingston,
Mr. Griffen,	Mr. Gilbert,
Mr. Converse,	Mr. Tillotson.
Mr. Morgan,	

FOR THE AFFIRMATIVE.

Mr. Sill,	Mr. Lewis.
Mr. Barker,	

That the whole of the last paragraph of the original draft of the bill, was again read, in the words following, viz.

"That in every case when two Senators are to be chosen, and both houses agree only as to one, in such nomination as aforesaid, and in every case when only one Senator is to be chosen, either of the two Houses of the Legislature may propose to the other a resolution for concurrence, naming therein a person to fill the office of Senator; and if the House receiving such resolution shall concur therein, the person so named in such resolution, shall be the Senator; but if such resolution shall not be concurred in, either House may on that or any future day, proceed to offer to the other a resolution for concurrence, from time to time, until they shall agree upon a Senator."

That the question having been put, whether the committee did agree to the said paragraph, it was carried in the affirmative, in the manner following, viz.

FOR THE AFFIRMATIVE.

Mr. Speaker,	Mr. Horton,
Mr. King,	Mr. Barker,
Mr. Clarkson,	Mr. Crane, jun.
Mr. Will,	Mr. Livingston,
Mr. Post,	Mr. Myers,
Mr. Childs,	Mr. Crane,
Mr. S. Van Rensselaer,	Mr. Arndt,
Mr. Sill,	Mr. Watts,
Mr. Van Rensselaer,	Mr. Lewis,
Mr. Cornwell,	Mr. Van Veghten,
Mr. Vandervoort,	Mr. Bronck,
Mr. Giles,	Mr. Younglove,
Mr. Winant,	Mr. Haight,
Mr. Bancker,	Mr. Converse,
Mr. Van Cortlandt,	Mr. Morgan,
Mr. J. Brown,	Mr. Savage,
Mr. Rockwell,	Mr. Talman,
Mr. Seaman,	Mr. Hitchcock,

Mr. J. Livingston,	Mr. Tillotson,
Mr. Gilbert,	

FOR THE NEGATIVE.

Mr. Randall,	Mr. Marvin,
Mr. J. Smith,	Mr. M'Master,
Mr. Landon,	Mr. Carpenter,
Mr. Tappen,	Mr. Griffen,
Mr. Schoonmaker,	Mr. Rowan,
Mr. Clark,	Mr. Scudder,
Mr. Smith,	Mr. Havens,
Mr. Bruyn,	Mr. Coe,
Mr. Clowes,	Mr. Bloom,
Mr. Jones,	Mr. Veeder.
Mr. Carman,	

That the committee had gone through the bill, made amendments, added a clause,[2] and altered the title; that the altered title is, *An act prescribing the manner of holding elections for Senators to represent this State, in the Senate of the United States.*

That the amended bill, clause added and altered title having been again read, the question was put, whether the committee did agree to the same; and it was carried in the affirmative, in the manner following, viz.

FOR THE AFFIRMATIVE.

Mr. Speaker,	Mr. Crane, jun.
Mr. King,	Mr. Livingston,
Mr. Clarkson,	Mr. Crane,
Mr. Will,	Mr. Arndt,
Mr. Post,	Mr. Watts,
Mr. Childs,	Mr. Lewis,
Mr. S. Van Rensselaer,	Mr. Van Veghten,
Mr. Sill,	Mr. Bronck,
Mr. Van Rensselaer,	Mr. Younglove,
Mr. Cornwell,	Mr. Haight,
Mr. Vandervoort,	Mr. Converse,
Mr. Giles,	Mr. Morgan,
Mr. Winant,	Mr. Savage,
Mr. Bancker,	Mr. Hitchcock,
Mr. J. Brown,	Mr. J. Livingston,
Mr. Rockwell,	Mr. Gilbert,
Mr. Seaman,	Mr. Tillotson,
Mr. Horton,	Mr. Talman,
Mr. Barker,	Mr. Myers,

FOR THE NEGATIVE.

Mr. Randall,	Mr. Bruyn,
Mr. J. Smith,	Mr. Clowes,
Mr. Landon,	Mr. Jones,
Mr. Tappen,	Mr. Carman,
Mr. Schoonmaker,	Mr. Marvin,
Mr. Clark,	Mr. Carpenter,
Mr. Smith,	Mr. Rowan,

Mr. Scudder,	Mr. Bloom,
Mr. Havens,	Mr. Veeder,
Mr. Coe,	Mr. M'Master.

Mr. Gordon read the report in his place, and delivered the bill, amendments and clause in at the table, where the same were again read, and agreed to by the House.

Ordered, That the bill, amendments and clause be engrossed.

1. The *Daily Advertiser*, 16 July 1789, reported that Rufus King's amendment was "agreed to without opposition." The *Daily Gazette*, 17 July, made the same comment.

2. The clause was probably proposed by Morgan Lewis. In its report on the Assembly proceedings for 9 July 1789, the *Daily Advertiser*, 16 July, noted: "On motion of Col. Lewis, a clause was added to the bill directing the manner in which the senators were to receive the certificates of their appointment, to wit, that the certificate should be signed by the President of the senate, and the speaker of the house of representatives, after which it shall be exemplified under the great seal of the state." The *Daily Gazette*, 17 July, carried the same account.

Richard Platt to Winthrop Sargent, New York, 9 July (excerpt)[1]

Clinton you have heard is re-elected Governor, & the moment his Election was declared, he called our Legislature together & they are now in Session at Albany, with a Majority in both Houses of Fœderal Members—a strange alteration this, to be made in one year, in the minds of the people of the State; for last year at this time we could not send more than 19 fœderal Members to the Convention or Legislature, out of 65—and now we have an handsome majority. (This promises us fœderal Senators, & checks the rascallity of Clinton[)] Rufus King is one of our City Members, & is to be our Premier in the Assembly & the Chance is in his favor of being a Senator, with Genl. Schuyler.

1. RC, Sargent Papers, MHi.

Abraham Bancker to Evert Bancker, Albany, 10 July (excerpt)[1]

I just inform you that the House of Assembly have been in Committee on a Bill directing the Manner of electing Senators to represent this State in the Senate of the United States. That it has been ordered to be engrossed from the Report. That this morning, in all probability, it will pass the House and be transmitted to the Senate for concurrence—Two thirds of the Assembly are federal. In the Senate 11 to 9—Anti-federal Schemes prove abortive. The Face of Affairs is entirely changed, and wears now a pleasing Appearance—

The Senate have passed a Bill for releasing Abraham Lott from Confinement.[2] Our house will take it up this day. We shall have an extremely short Session. Probably shall adjourn early in the ensuing week, and shall strive for New York as the place of our next Meeting. The federal Senators to be supported are Genl. Schuyler and Mr: Duane, who has agreed, if elected to resign his Mayoralty[3] as it is found incompatible to hold both Offices at the same time

1. RC, Bancker Family Papers, NHi.

2. Abraham Lott (c. 1726–1794), colonial treasurer of New York, 1767–1776, was a loyalist during the Revolution. He was jailed in the late 1780s for failure to settle his colonial accounts

with the state; on 14 July 1789 the legislature passed a law releasing Lott from prison on condition that he settle the accounts and pay the state the money due it.

3. Of New York City.

Assembly and Senate Proceedings, Friday, 10 July

The Assembly, A.M.

The engrossed bill entitled *An act prescribing the manner of holding elections for Senators to represent this State, in the Senate of the United States,* was read a third time.

Mr. Speaker put the question whether the bill shall pass, and it was carried in the affirmative, in the manner following, viz.

FOR THE AFFIRMATIVE.

Mr. King.	Mr. Crane, jun.
Mr. Clarkson,	Mr. Livingston,
Mr. Will,	Mr. Myers,
Mr. Post,	Mr. Crane,
Mr. Childs,	Mr. Arndt,
Mr. S. Van Rensselaer,	Mr. Watts,
Mr. Sill,	Mr. Lewis,
Mr. Gordon,	Mr. Van Veghten,
Mr. Van Rensselaer,	Mr. Bronck,
Mr. Cornwell,	Mr. Younglove,
Mr. Vandervoort,	Mr. Haight,
Mr. Giles,	Mr. Converse,
Mr. Winant,	Mr. Morgan,
Mr. Bancker,	Mr. Savage,
Mr. Van Cortlandt,	Mr. Talman,
Mr. J. Brown,	Mr. Hitchcock,
Mr. Rockwell,	Mr. J. Livingston,
Mr. Seaman,	Mr. Gilbert,
Mr. Horton,	Mr. Tillotson.
Mr. Barker,	

FOR THE NEGATIVE.

Mr. Randall,	Mr. M'Master,
Mr. J. Smith,	Mr. Carpenter,
Mr. Landon,	Mr. Griffen,
Mr. Tappen,	Mr. Rowan,
Mr. Schoonmaker,	Mr. Scudder,
Mr. Clark,	Mr. Havens,
Mr. Smith,	Mr. Coe,
Mr. Bruyn.	Mr. Sickles,
Mr. Clowes,	Mr. Bloom,
Mr. Jones,	Mr. Veeder.
Mr. Carman,	

Thereupon, *Resolved*, That the bill do pass.

Ordered, That Mr. J. Livingston and Mr. Bloom, deliver the bill to the Honorable the Senate, and request their concurrence.

The Senate, P.M.

A message from the Honorable the Assembly, by Mr. J. Livingston, and Mr. Bloom, was received with a bill for concurrence, entitled *an act prescribing the manner of holding elections for Senators to represent this State in the Senate of the United States*, which was read the first time, and by the unanimous consent of the Senate, was also read a second time, and committed to a committee of the whole.

Senate Proceedings, Saturday, P.M., 11 July

Mr. Hoffman, from the committee of the whole, to whom was referred the bill entitled *an act prescribing the manner of holding elections for Senators to represent this State in the Senate of the United States*, reported, that in proceeding to consider the bill by paragraphs, the first paragraph was read in the words following, viz. "BE IT ENACTED by the People of the State of New-York, represented in Senate and Assembly, and it is hereby enacted by the Authority of the same, That the Senators to be chosen by the Legislature of this State, to represent the State in the Senate of the United States, shall be chosen in the manner following—*that is to say*, the Senate and the Assembly of this State shall respectively openly *nominate* one or two persons, as the case may be, and shall immediately afterwards give notice, each House to the other of such nomination; and if both Houses agree in the nomination of the same person or persons, the person or persons so respectively nominated and agreed to, shall be the Senator or Senators to represent this State in the Senate of the United States." Mr. Williams thereupon moved, that the latter part of the said paragraph be expunged from the word *nominate*, and the following substituted in its stead, viz. "as many persons as shall be equal to the whole number of Senators to be chosen by this State, after which nomination the Senate and Assembly shall meet together, and compare the lists of the persons by them respectively nominated, and those persons named in both lists, shall be Senators for the United States, and out of those persons whose names are not in both lists, one half shall be chosen by the joint ballot of the Senators and members of the Assembly so met together as aforesaid, and copies of the resolutions of the Senate and Assembly, testifying the said choice, shall be thereupon delivered to each of the persons so chosen a Senator for the United States." Debates arose upon the said motion, and the question being put thereon, it was carried in the negative in the manner following, viz.

FOR THE NEGATIVE.

Mr. Duane,	Mr. L'Hommedieu,
Mr. Roosevelt,	Mr. Philip Schuyler,
Mr. Micheau,	Mr. Livingston,
Mr. Vanderbilt,	Mr. Douw,
Mr. Morris,	Mr. Peter Schuyler.

FOR THE AFFIRMATIVE.

Mr. Townsend,	Mr. Williams,
Mr. Clinton,	Mr. Swartwout,
Mr. Yates,	Mr. Carpenter,
Mr. Webster,	Mr. Van Ness.
Mr. Savage,	

That Mr. Williams then moved, "that the bill be so amended as that the elections may be conducted by ballot." Debates arose on the said motion, and the question being put thereon, it was carried in the negative in the same manner, as on the last preceding question.

That Mr. L'Hommedieu then moved to expunge after the words *that is to say*, in the aforesaid paragraph, the words "the Senate and Assembly of this State shall respectively openly nominate one or two persons," and to substitute the following in their stead, viz. "each person of the Senate and Assembly of this State shall in their separate Houses, ballot for one or two persons, as the case may be, who shall be the person or persons in nomination for Senator or Senators, and out of which number in each House respectively, shall by a majority of voices be chosen a Senator or Senators." Debates arose upon the said motion, and the question being put thereon, it passed in the affirmative in manner following, viz.

FOR THE AFFIRMATIVE.

Mr. Townsend,	Mr. Savage,
Mr. L'Hommedieu,	Mr. Williams,
Mr. Clinton,	Mr. Swartwout,
Mr. Yates,	Mr. Carpenter,
Mr. Webster,	Mr. Van Ness.

FOR THE NEGATIVE.

Mr. Duane,	Mr. Philip Schuyler,
Mr. Roosevelt,	Mr. Livingston,
Mr. Micheau,	Mr. Douw,
Mr. Vanderbilt,	Mr. Peter Schuyler.
Mr. Morris,	

Mr. Hoffman further reported that the committee had gone through the bill, made several amendments thereto,[1] and agreed to the same; which report he read in his place, and delivered the bill, with the amendments, in at the table, where they were again read. Mr. Yates thereupon moved, that the bill be rejected, and Mr. President having put the question on the said motion, it was carried in the negative in the manner following, viz.

FOR THE NEGATIVE.

Mr. Duane,	Mr. Philip Schuyler,
Mr. Roosevelt,	Mr. Livingston,
Mr. Micheau,	Mr. Douw,
Mr. Vanderbilt,	Mr. Peter Schuyler,
Mr. Morris,	Mr. Webster,
Mr. Townsend,	Mr. Hoffman.
Mr. L'Hommedieu,	

FOR THE AFFIRMATIVE.

Mr. Clinton,	Mr. Swartwout,
Mr. Yates,	Mr. Carpenter.
Mr. Savage,	Mr. Van Ness.
Mr. Williams,	

Mr. President then put the question, Whether the bill with the amendments should pass, and it was carried in the affirmative. Thereupon

Resolved, That the bill with the amendments do pass.

Ordered, That Mr. Morris and Mr. Townsend, deliver the bill with the amendments to the honorable the Assembly, and inform them that the Senate have passed the bill with the amendments therewith delivered.

1. Although the Assembly and Senate journals refer to Senate "amendments" to the Senators bill, only the content of L'Hommedieu's amendment is discussed in the sources ([Robert Troup] to Alexander Hamilton, [12 July 1789], and Assembly and Senate Proceedings, 13 July 1789, both below). The *Daily Advertiser*, 20 July 1789, in its report of the Assembly proceedings for 13 July, gives the impression that the Senate's only amendment was that proposed by L'Hommedieu (Assembly and Senate Proceedings, 13 July, n. 1, below). All but one of the Senate amendments were rejected by the Assembly on 13 July. A comparison of the draft bill with the final approved bill suggests that the Senate amendment accepted by the Assembly was not substantive.

[Robert Troup] to Alexander Hamilton, [Albany, 12 July][1]

I arrived here on Friday night[.] I can do no business with the court of error so anxious is the Legislature to adjourn[.][2] It is generally thought that the appointment of Senators will be completed tomorrow or next day at farthest afterwhich nothing will keep the members together except some Indian business which has just turned up.[3] When our friends met it seems they judged it most prudent to consolidate their strength to prevent division—A general meeting took place—It was agreed unanimously to make Judge Yates the offer of a seat in the Federal Senate without any condition whatever annexed to it and a committee of two was appointed to wait upon him with the offer. The Judge received them with great cordiality & requested a night to consider of the offer. The next day he returned for answer that he felt himself infinitely obliged by the kind attention of his friends but that he declined the offer under a persuasion that it would be most prudent for him to continue in his present office. Genl. Schuyler I hear also waited upon him & begged him to accept of an appointment to the Senate & declared that if he would consent to be a candidate for the appointment that no federalist in the northern district of the State would stand in opposition to him; but the Judge it appeared had inflexibly resolved to decline a change of situation. I mention these circumstances to shew you that the Judge has been treated with every possible delicacy and that instead of being displeased he is highly gratified with the notice which has been taken of him—This with me is a great point gained—Yates is unquestionably [warm?] to us—They have on the other side offered him lately some very gross insults which have not made very slight impressions upon his mind to their prejudice—Judge Yates having declined to be a candidate for the senate our friends determined to ballot for the two Senators under an engagement to support totis viribus the two who had the majority—Upon the ballot Schuyler I understand was unanimously voted for—Duane had 24 votes and King 20. The latter instantly declined all opposition to Duane—said he was ashamed of being opposed to him &c and the matter was settled—L.Hommedieu and Genl. Morris both declared that they would not be bound by the ballot—The reason is obvious—They are both extremely anxious for their own appointment. Immediately after the ballot was finished a bill was brought into the assembly upon the old federal principles exactly—The bill passed without much opposition—Our majority is large enough in all conscience—Yesterday the bill passed the Senate with an amendment that the nomination in the first place in each house should be by ballot & that afterwards the appointment should be viva voce—This is the idea I have from several of the members—I have not seen the bill or amendment—Great efferts were made by Yates, Williams[4] &c to have the whole business determined by ballot instead of viva voce. The design was obvious—L.Hommedieu & Morris were ashamed to go fully with them into the balloting system but have concluded that they might safely agree to divide it—Phil. Livingston thinks it cannot injure as it now stands—I have not been able to talk with any other senator about it. If it were not for the defection of L.Hommedieu & Morris Schuyler and Duane would be appointed without difficulty—at present it is by no means certain that Duane will succeed—It is thought the opposition is to Duane only & not to Schuyler—Our friends in the Assembly remain & are likely to remain an unbroken phalax. Randall[5] has joined the Antifederalists with a sort of puritannical rage for liberty &c[.] He is an object of pity—He made a thundering—incoherent—and disgusting speech to all parties respecting the principles of the bill for the appointment of senators urging the joint ballot system—It had no effect—He has been often found crying since & is really thought to be disordered in his mind. He is treated under this idea with great delicacy by every body but has not the weight of a feather with anybody—All our other members behave as near to be wished—our King is as much followed & attended to by all parties as ever a new light preacher was by his congregation—He has acquired & will maintain an entire ascendency in the house. He is happy in his manner—his language his reasoning & his choice of subjects to speak upon—Nothing but delicacy to Duane as an old inhabitant has prevented King from being unanimously supported by all the members of the Southern district except L Hommedieu & Morris—Duane has engaged to resign his Mayoralty if he becomes a Senator—The Chancellor declined being a candidate. The Council of appointment[6]

1. RC, Hamilton Papers, DLC. The letter has no date or signature. Hamilton attributed the information he received in this letter to Robert Troup (see Hamilton to Rufus King, 15 July 1789, below). The dating is based on internal evidence. Troup (1757–1832), a New York City lawyer, was a lieutenant colonel in the Continental Army during the Revolution, an assemblyman from New York City and County in 1786, and a federal judge for the District of New York, 1796–1798.

2. The Court of Errors was made up of the Senate, lieutenant governor, chancellor, and the judges of the supreme court.

3. Surveyors in Montgomery County, surveying land that the state had recently bought from the Cayuga, Oneida, and Onondaga Indians, were being threatened and attacked by some dissident Indians. Both the Assembly and Senate passed resolutions requesting Governor Clinton to take measures to quiet the disorders.

4. Abraham Yates, Jr., and John Williams, both Senate Antifederalists.

5. Robert R. Randall, who represented New York City and County in the Assembly, 1789–1790.

6. The remainder of the letter is missing.

Assembly and Senate Proceedings, Monday, 13 July

The Assembly, A.M.

A message from the Honorable the senate, delivered by Mr. Morris and Mr. Townsend, with the bill and amendments therein mentioned, was read, that the Senate have passed the bill entitled, *An act prescribing the manner of holding elections for Senators to represent this State, in the Senate of the United States*, with the amendments therewith delivered.[1]

The bill and amendments were read.

The first part of the enacting clause of the bill being again read, is in the words following, viz.

"BE IT ENACTED by the People of the State of New-York, represented in Senate and Assembly, and it is hereby enacted by the authority of the same, That the Senators to be chosen by the Legislature of this State, to represent the State in the Senate of the United States, shall be chosen in manner following, that is to say, the Senate and Assembly of this State, shall respectively openly nominate one or two persons, as the case may be."

The first amendment being again read, is to strike out the words, "The Senate and Assembly of this State, shall respectively openly nominate one or two persons;" and instead thereof to substitute the following words, viz. "Each person of the Senate and Assembly of this State, shall in their separate houses, ballot for one or two persons, as the case may be, who shall be the person or persons in nomination for Senator or Senators, and out [of] which number in each House respectively, shall by a majority of voices be chosen a Senator or Senators."

The said proposed amendment having been read and considered, *Mr. Speaker* put the question, whether the House did concur with the Honorable the Senate therein, and it passed in the negative, in the manner following, viz.

FOR THE NEGATIVE.

Mr. King,	Mr. Seaman,
Mr. Clarkson,	Mr. Barker,
Mr. Will,	Mr. Crane, jun.
Mr. Post,	Mr. Livingston,
Mr. Childs,	Mr. Myers,
Mr. S. Van Rensselaer,	Mr. Crane,
Mr. Sill,	Mr. Arndt,
Mr. Gordon,	Mr. Watts,
Mr. Van Rensselaer,	Mr. Lewis,
Mr. Cornwell,	Mr. Van Veghten,
Mr. Carman,	Mr. Bronck,
Mr. Vandervoort,	Mr. Younglove,
Mr. Giles,	Mr. Haight,
Mr. Winant,	Mr. Talman,
Mr. Bancker,	Mr. J. Livingston,
Mr. J. Brown,	Mr. Gilbert.
Mr. Rockwell,	

FOR THE AFFIRMATIVE.

Mr. Randall,	Mr. Marvin,
Mr. J. Smith,	Mr. M'Master,
Mr. Landon,	Mr. Carpenter,
Mr. Schoonmaker,	Mr. Griffen,
Mr. Clark,	Mr. Converse,
Mr. Smith,	Mr. Morgan,
Mr. Bruyn,	Mr. Rowan,
Mr. Clowes,	Mr. Savage,
Mr. Jones,	Mr. Scudder,
Mr. Van Cortlandt,	Mr. Havens,
Mr. Horton,	Mr. Coe,

Mr. Bloom,	Mr. Hitchcock.
Mr. Veeder,	

The several other amendments being respectively read, the last was concurred in, and the others were not concurred in by the House.[2] Thereupon

Resolved, That this House do concur with the Honorable the Senate in their last amendment, and do not concur in the other amendments to the said bill.

Ordered, That Mr. Havens and Mr. Younglove deliver the said bill, and a copy of the preceding resolution to the Honorable the Senate.

The Senate, P.M.

[The Senate received the Senators bill and the Assembly resolution.]

The Senate proceeded to reconsider their said amendments not concurred in by the Honorable the Assembly, the first being the amendment proposed by Mr. L'Hommedieu on Saturday,[3] which being read, Mr. Roosevelt moved, that the Senate do recede from their said amendment, and Mr. President having put the question on the said motion, it was carried in the affirmative in manner following, viz.

FOR THE AFFIRMATIVE.

Mr. Duane,	Mr. Philip Schuyler,
Mr. Roosevelt,	Mr. Livingston,
Mr. Micheau,	Mr. Douw,
Mr. Vanderbilt,	Mr. Peter Schuyler,
Mr. Morris,	Mr. Hoffman.
Mr. L'Hommedieu,	

FOR THE NEGATIVE.

Mr. Townsend,	Mr. Savage,
Mr. Clinton,	Mr. Williams,
Mr. Yates,	Mr. Swartwout,
Mr. Webster,	Mr. Carpenter.

The Senate having also receded from their several other amendments, Thereupon

Resolved, That the Senate do recede from their amendments not concurred in by the Honorable the Assembly.

Ordered, That Mr. L'Hommedieu and Mr. Philip Schuyler, deliver the bill, with a copy of the preceding resolution to the Honorable the Assembly.

The Assembly, P.M.

[The Assembly received the Senators bill and the Senate resolution.]

Ordered, That the bill be amended agreeable to the amendment concurred in by this House; and the same was amended accordingly.

Ordered, That Mr. Griffin and Mr. Savage deliver the bill to the Honorable the Senate, and inform them that the bill is amended, agreeable to the amendment concurred in by this House.

The Senate, P.M.

[The Senate received the Senators bill and the Assembly message.]

The said bill having been examined,

Ordered, That Mr. Philip Schuyler and Mr. Livingston, return the bill to the Honorable the Assembly.

The Assembly, P.M.

[The Assembly received the Senators bill from the Senate.]

Ordered, That Mr. Giles and Mr. Clarkson, deliver the bill to the Honorable the Council of Revision.

1. The *Daily Advertiser*, 20 July 1789, in its report of the Assembly proceedings for 13 July, noted: "A message was received from the Senate, that they had passed the bill prescribing the manner of holding elections for Senators to represent this state in the Senate of the United States, with an amendment to the following purport—That previous to the openly voting for Senators, a nomination of candidates should be made by ballot." The same report was printed in the *Daily Gazette*, 21 July.
2. See Senate Proceedings, 11 July 1789, n. 1, above.
3. See Senate Proceedings, 11 July 1789, above.

Bill for the Election of Senators, 13 July[1]

The ACT *prescribing the manner of holding Elections for Senators to represent this State in the Senate of the United States.*

Be it enacted by the people of the State of New-York, represented in Senate and Assembly, and it is hereby enacted by the Authority of the same, That the Senators to be chosen by the Legislature of this state to represent the state in the Senate of the United States, shall be chosen in the manner following, that is to say: The Senate and Assembly of this state shall respectively openly nominate one or two persons, as the case may be, and shall immediately afterwards give notice, each House to the other of such nomination; and if both houses agree in the nomination of the same person or persons, the person or persons so respectively nominated and agreed to, shall be the Senator or Senators to represent this state in the Senate of the United States. That if the nomination of either House does not agree in any of the persons nominated by the other, the Senate shall without delay openly choose one of the persons nominated by the Assembly, and the Assembly shall without delay openly choose one of the persons nominated by the Senate, and the two persons so chosen shall be the Senators to represent this state in the Senate of the United States. That in every case when two Senators are to be chosen, and both Houses agree only as to one in such nomination as aforesaid, and in every case when only one Senator is to be chosen, either of the two Houses of the legislature may propose to the other, a resolution for concurrence, naming therein a person to fill the office of Senator; and if the House receiving such resolution shall concur therein, the person so named in such resolution shall be the Senator; but if such resolution shall not be concurred in, either House may, on that or any future day proceed to offer to the other, a resolution for concurrence from time to time, naming therein the same or any other person, until they shall agree upon a Senator. That whenever the choice of a Senator or Senators shall be made, the President of Senate and Speaker of the Assembly, shall certify the name of the person or persons so appointed Senator or Senators, to the person administering the government of this state for the time being, who shall thereupon exemplify such certificate under the great seal of this state, and deliver or cause the same to be delivered to the Senator so chosen, or when two are chosen, to each of them.

State of New-York, in Assembly, July 10th, 1789. This bill having been read a third time, resolved, that the bill do pass.

By order of the Assembly,
GULIAN VER PLANCK, Speaker.

State of New-York, in Senate, July 11th, 1789. This bill having been read a third time, resolved, that the bill do pass.

By order of the Senate,
PIERRE VAN CORTLANDT, President.

1. *Poughkeepsie Journal*, 28 July 1789. The *Journal* printed the bill under the Assembly proceedings for 15 July; the legislature completed action on the bill and sent it to the Council of Revision on 13 July. The *Poughkeepsie Journal*, first published under that title on 14 July 1789, was a direct continuation of the *Country Journal*.

Council of Revision Proceedings, Monday, P.M., 13 July

The Council of Revision met at the Chamber of his Excellency the Governor in the City of Albany on Monday the 13th day of July 1789 at three oClock in the Afternoon—

Present His Excellency Governor Clinton
The Hone. Mr. Justice Yates
The Hon Mr. Justice Hobart. . . .

Mr Giles and Mr Clarkson from the Honorable the Assembly brought up to the Council a bill about to be passed into a Law by the Legislature entitled An Act prescribing the Manner of holding Elections for Senators to represent this State in the Senate of the United States. which being read was committed to Mr. Justice Yates and Mr. Justice Hobart.

The Council then adjourned—

Poughkeepsie Journal, 14 July

We are informed that the Legislature of this State formed a quorum of both Houses on the day appointed for their meeting—and that they have passed a law establishing a mode for the appointing Senators. They are to be appointed by concurrent resolutions of both houses.—And we are further informed, that General Schuyler and Mr. Duane, Mayor of New-York, will be proposed as the Senators, and it is expected will be agreed to. The mail from Albany had not arrived when this paper was put to press—but in our next we shall be able, we hope, to furnish our readers with more particulars.

Council of Revision Proceedings, Wednesday, 15 July

At a Meeting of the Council of Revision at the Chambers of his Excellency the Governor the 15th day of July 1789—

Present His Excellency Governor Clinton
The Honore Mr. Chancellor Livingston
The Honore Mr. Justice Yates.

Mr Justice Yates one of the Committee to whom was referred the bill entitled An Act prescribing the Manner of holding Elections for Senators to represent this State in the Senate of the united states reported certain objections thereto which being read and amended and the said bill again read and considered

The Council object against the said bill becoming a Law of this State as inconsistent with the Public good—

1st Because the Constitution of the United States directs that the Senators be chosen from each State by the Legislature thereof[.] If by the Legislature is intended the Members of the two houses not acting [in] their Legislative Capacity no Law is necessary to prescribe the Mode of Election Concurrent Resolutions extending in this Case as well to the mode of election as to the Choice of Persons

And the bill as far as it goes operates as a restriction upon the Constitutional Rights of the Two Houses.—If the Legislature are only known in their Legislative Capacity the Senators can constitutionally be appointed by Law Only and no considerations arising from Inconvenience will Justify a deviation from the Constitution of the United States.

2dly Because this bill when two senators are to be chosen enacts that in Case of the Disagreement of the two Houses—In the Nomination Each house shall out of the nomination of the Other chuse One and that such Persons shall be the Senators to represent this State and thus by compelling each House to choose one of two Persons neither of whom may meet with their Approbation establishes a Choice of Senators by the separate Act of each Branch of the Legislature in direct Opposition to the Constitution of the United states which in the 3d section of the first Article declares that they shall be chosen by the Legislature

Ordered that the said bill with a Copy of the preceeding Objections thereto signed by his Excellency the Governor be delivered to the Honorable the Assembly by Mr. Justice Yates.

Assembly and Senate Proceedings, Wednesday, 15 July

The Assembly, A.M.

A message from the Honorable the Council of Revision, was delivered by the Honorable Mr. Justice Yates, with the bill and objections therein mentioned, "That he was directed by the Council, to deliver a copy of their objections to the bill entitled, *An act prescribing the manner of holding elections for Senators to represent this State, in the Senate of the United States.*"

The said objections being read, are in the words following, viz. . . .[1]

The said objections of the council of revision having been read and considered, and the said bill reconsidered, Mr. Speaker put the question, whether the bill, notwithstanding the objections of the Honorable the Council of Revision to the same, shall be a law of this State;[2] and it passed in the negative, in the manner following, viz.

FOR THE NEGATIVE.

Mr. King,	Mr. Bruyn,
Mr. Clarkson,	Mr. Cornwell,
Mr. Will,	Mr. Jones,
Mr. Randall,	Mr. Carman,
Mr. Post,	Mr. Vandervoort,
Mr. J. Smith,	Mr. Winant,
Mr. Landon,	Mr. Bancker,
Mr. Tappen,	Mr. Van Cortlandt,
Mr. Schoonmaker,	Mr. J. Brown,
Mr. Clark,	Mr. Marvin,
Mr. Smith,	Mr. M'Master,

Mr. Carpenter,	Mr. Sickles,
Mr. Griffen,	Mr. Bloom,
Mr. Converse,	Mr. Veeder,
Mr. Rowan,	Mr. Hitchcock.
Mr. Savage,	Mr. J. Livingston,
Mr. Scudder,	Mr. Gilbert.
Mr. Coe,	Mr. Morgan,

FOR THE AFFIRMATIVE.

Mr. Childs,	Mr. Crane, jun.
Mr. S. Van Rensselaer,	Mr. Livingston,
Mr. Sill,	Mr. Myers,
Mr. Gordon,	Mr. Watts,
Mr. Van Rensselaer,	Mr. Lewis,
Mr. Giles,	Mr. Van Veghten,
Mr. Rockwell,	Mr. Bronck,
Mr. Seaman,	Mr. Younglove,
Mr. Horton,	Mr. Haight,
Mr. Barker,	Mr. Talman.

Thereupon *Resolved*, that the said bill be not a law of this State.

Mr. Lewis then made a motion for a resolution in the words following, viz.

"*Resolved*, If the Honorable Senate concur therein, that Philip Schuyler and James Duane, Esquires, be, and they are hereby chosen by the Legislature of this State, Senators to represent this State, in the Senate of the United States."

Mr. Jones, as an amendment, made a motion for a resolution in the words following, viz.

"*Resolved*, (if the Honorable the Senate concur therein) that the Senators to represent this State, in the Senate of the Congress of the United States of America, shall be chosen in the same manner that Delegates to represent this State, in the United States in Congress assembled, are directed to be chosen by the Constitution of this State; and that the Senate and Assembly will on elect two persons for Senators to represent this State, in the Senate of the Congress of the United States."

The question being put, whether the House did concur in the resolution proposed by the motion of Mr. Jones, it passed in the negative, in the manner following, viz.

FOR THE NEGATIVE.

Mr. King,	Mr. Van Cortlandt,
Mr. Clarkson,	Mr. J. Brown,
Mr. Will,	Mr. Rockwell,
Mr. Post,	Mr. Seaman,
Mr. Childs,	Mr. Horton,
Mr. S. Van Rensselaer,	Mr. Barker,
Mr. Sill,	Mr. Crane, jun.
Mr. Gordon,	Mr. Livingston,
Mr. Van Rensselaer,	Mr. Myers,
Mr. Cornwell,	Mr. Watts,
Mr. Vandervoort,	Mr. Lewis,
Mr. Giles,	Mr. Van Veghten,
Mr. Winant,	Mr. Bronck,
Mr. Bancker,	Mr. Younglove,

Mr. Haight,
Mr. Converse,
Mr. Talman,
Mr. Hitchcock,
Mr. J. Livingston,
Mr. Gilbert.

FOR THE AFFIRMATIVE.

Mr. J. Smith,
Mr. Landon,
Mr. Tappen,
Mr. Schoonmaker,
Mr. Clark,
Mr. Smith,
Mr. Bruyn.
Mr. Jones,
Mr. Carman,
Mr. Marvin,
Mr. M'Master,
Mr. Carpenter,
Mr. Griffen,
Mr. Morgan,
Mr. Rowan,
Mr. Scudder,
Mr. Havens,
Mr. Coe,
Mr. Sickels,
Mr. Bloom,
Mr. Veeder.

Mr. Lewis, with leave of the House, withdrew his motion for the resolution thereby proposed; and Mr. Sill made a motion that the House would agree to a resolution in the words following, viz.

"*Resolved*, (if the Honorable the Senate concur herein) That be, and he is hereby chosen by the Legislature of this State, one of the Senators to represent this State in the Senate of the United States," which resolution was concurred in by the House.

Mr. Sill then made a motion that the name of Philip Schuyler, Esquire, should be inserted in the blank, in the said resolution.

Mr. Schoonmaker, as an amendment, made a motion that the name of Rufus King, Esquire, should be inserted in the blank, in the said resolution.

The question being put on the amendment proposed by the motion of Mr. Schoonmaker, it passed in the negative in the manner following, viz.

FOR THE NEGATIVE.

Mr. King,
Mr. Clarkson,
Mr. Will,
Mr. Post,
Mr. Childs,
Mr. S. Van Rensselaer,
Mr. Sill,
Mr. Gordon,
Mr. Van Rensselaer,
Mr. Cornwell,
Mr. Vandervoort,
Mr. Giles,
Mr. Winant,
Mr. Bancker,
Mr. Van Cortlandt,
Mr. J. Brown,
Mr. Rockwell,
Mr. Seaman,
Mr. Horton,
Mr. Barker,
Mr. Crane, jun.
Mr. M'Master,
Mr. Livingston,
Mr. Myers,
Mr. Watts,
Mr. Lewis,
Mr. Van Veghten,
Mr. Bronck,
Mr. Younglove,
Mr. Haight,
Mr. Converse,
Mr. Morgan,
Mr. Savage,
Mr. Talman,
Mr. Hitchcock,
Mr. J. Livingston,
Mr. Gilbert.

FOR THE AFFIRMATIVE.

Mr. J. Smith,	Mr. Carpenter,
Mr. Landon,	Mr. Griffen,
Mr. Tappen,	Mr. Rowan,
Mr. Schoonmaker,	Mr. Scudder,
Mr. Clark,	Mr. Havens,
Mr. Smith,	Mr. Coe,
Mr. Bruyn,	Mr. Sickels,
Mr. Jones,	Mr. Bloom,
Mr. Carman,	Mr. Veeder.
Mr. Marvin,	

The question being then put on the motion of Mr. Sill, it was carried in the affirmative. Thereupon

Resolved, (if the Honorable the Senate concur therein) that Philip Schuyler, Esquire, be, and he is hereby chosen by the Legislature of this State, one of the Senators to represent this State, in the Senate of the United States.

Ordered, That Mr. Van Rensselaer and Mr. Carman deliver a copy of the preceding resolution to the Honorable the Senate.

Mr. Seaman then made a motion, that the House would agree to a resolution in the words following, viz.

"*Resolved*, (if the Honorable the Senate concur herein) That   be, and he is hereby chosen by the Legislature of this State, one of the Senators to represent this State, in the Senate of the United States," which resolution was concurred in by the House.

Mr. Seaman then made a motion, that the name of James Duane, Esquire, should be inserted in the blank in the said resolution.

Mr. J. Smith, as an amendment, made a motion that the name of Rufus King, Esquire, should be inserted in the said blank.

Mr. Jones, as a farther amendment, made a motion, that the name of Ezra L'Hommedieu, Esquire, should be inserted in the said blank; and

Mr. Schoonmaker, as a farther amendment, made a motion, that the name of Lewis Morris, Esquire, should be inserted in the said blank.

The question being put, whether the name of Lewis Morris, Esquire, proposed by the motion of Mr. Schoonmaker, should be inserted in the said blank, it passed in the negative.

The question being put whether the name of Ezra L'Hommedieu, Esquire, proposed by the motion of Mr. Jones, should be inserted in the said blank, it passed in the negative, in the manner following, viz.

FOR THE NEGATIVE.

Mr. King,	Mr. Van Rensselaer,
Mr. Clarkson,	Mr. Cornwell,
Mr. Will,	Mr. Vandervoort,
Mr. Post,	Mr. Giles,
Mr. Childs,	Mr. Winant,
Mr. S. Van Rensselaer,	Mr. Bancker,
Mr. Sill,	Mr. Van Cortlandt,
Mr. Gordon,	Mr. J. Brown,

Mr. Rockwell,	Mr. Bronck,
Mr. Seaman,	Mr. Younglove,
Mr. Horton,	Mr. Haight,
Mr. Barker,	Mr. Converse,
Mr. Crane, jun.	Mr. Morgan,
Mr. Livingston,	Mr. Savage,
Mr. Myers,	Mr. Talman,
Mr. Watts,	Mr. Hitchcock,
Mr. Lewis,	Mr. J. Livingston,
Mr. Van Veghten,	Mr. Gilbert.

FOR THE AFFIRMATIVE.

Mr. J. Smith,	Mr. M'Master,
Mr. Landon,	Mr. Carpenter,
Mr. Tappen,	Mr. Griffen,
Mr. Schoonmaker,	Mr. Rowan,
Mr. Clark,	Mr. Scudder,
Mr. Smith,	Mr. Havens,
Mr. Bruyn,	Mr. Coe,
Mr. Jones,	Mr. Sickels,
Mr. Carman,	Mr. Bloom,
Mr. Marvin,	Mr. Veeder.

The question being put, whether the name of Rufus King, Esquire, proposed by the motion of Mr. J. Smith, should be inserted in the said blank, it passed in the negative, in the manner following, viz.

FOR THE NEGATIVE.

Mr. King,	Mr. Seaman,
Mr. Clarkson,	Mr. Horton,
Mr. Will,	Mr. Barker,
Mr. Post,	Mr. Crane, jun.
Mr. Childs,	Mr. Livingston,
Mr. S. Van Rensselaer,	Mr. Myers,
Mr. Sill,	Mr. Watts,
Mr. Gordon,	Mr. Lewis,
Mr. Van Rensselaer,	Mr. Van Veghten,
Mr. Cornwell,	Mr. Bronck,
Mr. Vandervoort,	Mr. Younglove,
Mr. Giles,	Mr. Haight,
Mr. Winant,	Mr. Converse,
Mr. Bancker,	Mr. Talman,
Mr. Van Cortlandt,	Mr. Hitchcock,
Mr. J. Brown,	Mr. J. Livingston,
Mr. Rockwell,	Mr. Gilbert.

FOR THE AFFIRMATIVE.

Mr. J. Smith,	Mr. Clark,
Mr. Landon,	Mr. Smith,
Mr. Tappen,	Mr. Bruyn,
Mr. Schoonmaker,	Mr. Jones,

Mr. Carman,
Mr. Marvin,
Mr. M'Master,
Mr. Carpenter,
Mr. Griffen,
Mr. Rowan,
Mr. Savage,
Mr. Scudder,
Mr. Havens,
Mr. Coe,
Mr. Sickels,
Mr. Bloom,
Mr. Veeder.

The question being then put whether the name of James Duane, Esquire, proposed by the motion of Mr. Seaman, should be inserted in the said blank in the proposed resolution, it was carried in the affirmative, in the manner following, viz.

FOR THE AFFIRMATIVE.

Mr. King,
Mr. Clarkson,
Mr. Will,
Mr. Post,
Mr. Childs,
Mr. S. Van Rensselaer,
Mr. Sill,
Mr. Gordon,
Mr. Van Rensselaer,
Mr. Cornwell,
Mr. Vandervoort,
Mr. Giles,
Mr. Winant,
Mr. Bancker,
Mr. Van Cortlandt,
Mr. J. Brown,
Mr. Rockwell,
Mr. Seaman,
Mr. Horton,
Mr. Barker,
Mr. Crane, jun.
Mr. Livingston,
Mr. Myers,
Mr. Arndt,
Mr. Watts,
Mr. Lewis,
Mr. Van Veghten,
Mr. Bronck,
Mr. Younglove,
Mr. Haight,
Mr. Converse,
Mr. Talman,
Mr. Hitchcock,
Mr. J. Livingston,
Mr. Gilbert.

FOR THE NEGATIVE.

Mr. Landon,
Mr. Tappen,
Mr. Schoonmaker,
Mr. Clark,
Mr. Smith,
Mr. Bruyn,
Mr. Jones,
Mr. Carman,
Mr. Marvin,
Mr. Carpenter,
Mr. Griffen,
Mr. Rowan,
Mr. Scudder,
Mr. Havens,
Mr. Coe,
Mr. Sickels,
Mr. Bloom,
Mr. Veeder,
Mr. J. Smith.

Thereupon, *Resolved*, (if the Honorable the Senate concur herein) that James Duane, Esquire, be, and he is hereby chosen by the Legislature of this State, one of the Senators to represent this State, in the Senate of the United States.

Ordered, That Mr. J. Livingston and Mr. Veeder deliver a copy of the preceding resolution, to the Honorable the Senate.

The Senate, A.M. and P.M.

[The Senate received the Assembly resolutions nominating James Duane and Philip Schuyler for Senators.]

Ordered, That the consideration of the said two resolutions be postponed.

Then the Senate adjourned until four of the clock in the afternoon.

IV o'C L O C K.

The Senate met pursuant to adjournment. . . .

The Senate proceeded to the consideration of the two resolutions received from the Honorable the Assembly in the forenoon, the first of which was read in the words following, viz.

Resolved, (if the Honorable the Senate concur herein) That James Duane, Esq. be and he is hereby chosen to represent this State in the Senate of the United States.

Mr. Livingston thereupon moved, That the Senate do concur with the Honorable the Assembly in their said resolution.

Mr. Williams as an amendment moved, That the Senate would adopt the following resolution as a substitute for the last preceding resolution, viz.

"*Whereas* there is a necessity of a speedy appointment of Senators to represent this State in the Senate of the United States. Therefore,

Resolved, (if the Honorable the Assembly concur herein) That the Senate and Assembly will to-morrow morning at ten of the clock, proceed to nominate and appoint two Senators to represent this State in the Senate of the United States in manner following: that is to say, The Senate and Assembly shall each openly nominate two persons and shall respectively give notice each to the other of such nomination, after which the Senate and Assembly shall meet together and compare the lists of the persons by them respectively nominated, and the person or persons named in both lists, shall be the Senator or Senators for the Senate of the United States, and out of the persons not named in both lists, a Senator or Senators shall be chosen by the joint ballot of the Senators and members of the Assembly so met together as aforesaid; and copies of the resolutions of the Senate and Assembly, testifying such choice shall be thereupon delivered to each of the persons so chosen a Senator to the Senate of the United States." The same being read, Mr. President put the question on the said motion, and it passed in the negative in manner following, viz.

FOR THE NEGATIVE.

Mr. Duane,	Mr. Philip Schuyler,
Mr. Roosevelt,	Mr. Livingston,
Mr. Micheau,	Mr. Douw,
Mr. Vanderbilt,	Mr. Peter Schuyler,
Mr. Morris,	Mr. Hoffman.
Mr. L'Hommedieu,	

FOR THE AFFIRMATIVE.

Mr. Townsend,	Mr. Williams,
Mr. Clinton,	Mr. Swartwout,
Mr. Yates,	Mr. Carpenter,
Mr. Webster,	Mr. Van Ness.
Mr. Savage,	

Mr. President then put the question on Mr. Livingston's motion for concurring in the said resolution, and it passed in the negative in manner following, viz.

FOR THE NEGATIVE.

Mr. Townsend,	Mr. Savage,
Mr. L'Hommedieu,	Mr. Williams,
Mr. Clinton,	Mr. Swartwout,
Mr. Yates,	Mr. Carpenter.
Mr. Webster,	Mr. Van Ness.

FOR THE AFFIRMATIVE.

Mr. Roosevelt,	Mr. Livingston,
Mr. Micheau,	Mr. Douw,
Mr. Vanderbilt,	Mr. Peter Schuyler,
Mr. Morris,	Mr. Hoffman.
Mr. Philip Schuyler,	

Thereupon, *Resolved*, That the Senate do not concur with the Honorable the Assembly in their said preceding resolution.

Ordered, That Mr. Peter Schuyler and Mr. Yates deliver a copy of the preceding resolution of non-concurrence to the Honorable the Assembly.

The second resolution was then read in the words following, viz.

Resolved, (if the Honorable the Senate concur herein) That Philip Schuyler, Esq. be and he is hereby chosen to represent this State in the Senate of the United States.

Mr. Vanderbilt thereupon moved, That the Senate do concur with the Honorable the Assembly in their said resolution, and Mr. President having put the question on the said motion, it was carried in the affirmative in manner following, viz.

FOR THE AFFIRMATIVE.

Mr. Duane,	Mr. Douw,
Mr. Roosevelt,	Mr. Peter Schuyler,
Mr. Micheau,	Mr. Webster,
Mr. Vanderbilt,	Mr. Savage
Mr. Morris,	Mr. Williams,
Mr. L'Hommedieu,	Mr. Hoffman.
Mr. Livingston,	

FOR THE NEGATIVE.

Mr. Townsend,	Mr. Swartwout,
Mr. Clinton,	Mr. Carpenter,
Mr. Yates,	Mr. Van Ness.

Thereupon, *Resolved*, That the Senate do concur with the Honorable the Assembly in their said preceding resolution.

Ordered, That Mr. Peter Schuyler and Mr. Yates deliver a copy of the preceding concurrent resolution to the Honorable the Assembly.

Mr. Williams then moved, That the Senate would adopt the following resolution which was read, viz.

Resolved, (if the Honorable the Assembly concur herein) That Ezra L'Hommedieu, Esquire, be and he is hereby chosen to represent this State in the Senate of the United States.

Mr. Livingston then moved as an amendment to the last motion, to expunge the name of Ezra L'Hommedieu in the said resolution, and to substitute the name of Rufus King, and Mr. President having put the question thereon it passed in the negative in manner following, viz.

FOR THE NEGATIVE.

Mr. Morris,	Mr. Webster,
Mr. Townsend,	Mr. Savage,
Mr. Clinton,	Mr. Williams,
Mr. Douw,	Mr. Swartwout,
Mr. Peter Schuyler,	Mr. Carpenter,
Mr. Yates,	Mr. Van Ness.

FOR THE AFFIRMATIVE.

Mr. Duane,	Mr. Vanderbilt,
Mr. Roosevelt,	Mr. Livingston,
Mr. Micheau,	Mr. Hoffman,

The President then put the question on the resolution as proposed by Mr. Williams' motion, and it was carried in the affirmative in manner following, viz.

FOR THE AFFIRMATIVE.

Mr. Morris,	Mr. Williams,
Mr. Townsend,	Mr. Swartwout,
Mr. Clinton,	Mr. Carpenter.
Mr. Yates,	Mr. Van Ness,
Mr. Webster,	Mr. Hoffman.
Mr. Savage,	

FOR THE NEGATIVE.

Mr. Duane,	Mr. Livingston,
Mr. Roosevelt,	Mr. Douw,
Mr. Micheau,	Mr. Peter Schuyler.
Mr. Vanderbilt,	

Therefore, *Resolved*, (if the Honorable the Assembly concur herein) That Ezra L'Hommedieu, Esq. be and he is hereby chosen to represent this State in the Senate of the United States.

Ordered, That Mr. Peter Schuyler and Mr. Yates, deliver a copy of the preceding resolution to the Honorable the Assembly.

1. For the objections of the Council of Revision, see Council of Revision Proceedings, 15 July 1789, immediately above.
2. A two-thirds majority of the members present, in both houses, was required to override a veto by the Council of Revision.

Alexander Hamilton to Rufus King, [New York], 15 July[1]

I received your letter by the last Post but one. I immediately sat about circulating an idea, that it would be injurious to the City to have Duane elected—as the probability was, that some very unfit character would be his successor.[2] My object was to have this sentiment communicated to our members—But a stop was put to my measures, by a letter received from Burr,[3] announcing that at a general meeting of the Fœderalists of both houses Schuyler and Duane had been determined upon in a manner that precluded future attempts.—I find however by a letter from General Schuyler received this day that L'hommedieu and Morris may spoil all. . . .[4] Troupe tells me that L'hommedieu is opposed to you[5]—He made our Friend Benson[6] believe that he would even relinquish himself for you—What does all this mean?[7]

Certain matters here, about which we have so often talked, remain in statu quo.

1. RC, King Papers, NHi. The letter was addressed to King in Albany.
2. Duane was mayor of New York City, 1784–1789.
3. Aaron Burr.
4. The ellipses are in the original.
5. See [Robert Troup] to Alexander Hamilton, [12 July 1789], above.
6. Egbert Benson.
7. Hamilton had earlier been accused of attempting "to cram a senator upon us from another state" (see "H.H.," *New York Journal*, 2 April 1789, Part Three, District 2).

Assembly and Senate Proceedings, Thursday, 16 July

The Assembly, A.M.

A copy of a resolution of the Honorable the Senate, delivered by Mr. Peter Schuyler and Mr. Yates, was read, that the Senate do not concur with this House in their resolution that James Duane, Esquire, be chosen to represent this State, in the Senate of the United States.

A copy of a resolution of the Honorable the Senate, delivered by Mr. Peter Schuyler and Mr. Yates, was read, that the Senate do concur with this House in their resolution, that Philip Schuyler, Esquire, be chosen to represent this State, in the Senate of the United States.

A copy of a resolution of the Honorable the Senate, also delivered by Mr. Peter Schuyler and Mr. Yates, was read, and is in the following words, viz.

Resolved, (if the Honorable the Assembly concur herein) that Ezra L'Hommedieu, Esquire, be, and he is hereby chosen to represent this State, in the Senate of the United States.

Mr. Speaker put the question, whether the House did concur with the Honorable the Senate in the said resolution, and it passed in the negative, in the manner following, viz.

FOR THE NEGATIVE.

Mr. Clarkson,	Mr. Barker,
Mr. Will,	Mr. Crane, junior,
Mr. Post,	Mr. Livingston,
Mr. Childs,	Mr. Myers,
Mr. S. Van Rensselaer,	Mr. Crane,
Mr. Sill,	Mr. Arndt,
Mr. Gordon,	Mr. Watts,
Mr. Van Rensselaer,	Mr. Lewis,
Mr. Giles,	Mr. Van Veghten,
Mr. Winant,	Mr. Bronck,
Mr. Bancker,	Mr. Younglove,
Mr. J. Brown,	Mr. Haight,
Mr. Rockwell,	Mr. Converse,
Mr. Seaman,	Mr. Morgan,
Mr. Horton,	Mr. Savage,

Mr. Tallman,	Mr. J. Livingston,
Mr. Hitchcock,	Mr. Gilbert.

FOR THE AFFIRMATIVE.

Mr. Randall,	Mr. Vandervoort,
Mr. J. Smith,	Mr. Marvin,
Mr. Landon,	Mr. M'Master,
Mr. Tappen,	Mr. Carpenter,
Mr. Schoonmaker,	Mr. Griffen,
Mr. Clark,	Mr. Rowan,
Mr. Smith,	Mr. Scudder,
Mr. Bruyn,	Mr. Havens,
Mr. Clowes,	Mr. Coe,
Mr. Cornwell,	Mr. Sickles.
Mr. Jones,	Mr. Bloom,
Mr. Carman,	Mr. Veeder.

Thereupon *Resolved*, That this House do not concur with the Honorable the Senate, in their last mentioned resolution.

Ordered, That Mr. Childs and Mr. Talman, deliver a copy of the last preceding resolution to the Honorable the Senate.

Mr. Giles then made a motion, that the House should agree to a resolution, in the words following, viz.

"*Resolved*, (if the Honorable the Senate concur herein) that Rufus King, Esquire, be, and he is hereby chosen to represent this State, in the Senate of the United States."

Mr. J. Brown, as an amendment, made a motion, that the name of Rufus King, in the resolution proposed by the motion of Mr. Giles be obliterated, and that the name of Lewis Morris, Esquire, be inserted in its stead.

The question being put on the motion of Mr. J. Brown, it passed in the negative, in the manner following, viz.

FOR THE NEGATIVE.

Mr. Clarkson,	Mr. Barker,
Mr. Will,	Mr. Crane, jun.
Mr. Randall,	Mr. Livingston,
Mr. Post,	Mr. Myers,
Mr. Childs,	Mr. Crane,
Mr. S. Van Rensselaer,	Mr. Arndt,
Mr. Sill,	Mr. Watts,
Mr. Gordon,	Mr. Lewis,
Mr. Van Rensselaer,	Mr. Van Veghten,
Mr. J. Smith,	Mr. Bronck,
Mr. Clark,	Mr. Younglove,
Mr. Smith,	Mr. Haight,
Mr. Clowes,	Mr. Griffen,
Mr. Cornwell,	Mr. Converse,
Mr. Vandervoort,	Mr. Morgan,
Mr. Giles,	Mr. Rowan,
Mr. Bancker,	Mr. Savage,
Mr. Rockwell,	Mr. Havens,
Mr. Marvin,	Mr. Coe,

Mr. Sickels,
Mr. Talman,
Mr. Veeder,
Mr. Hitchcock,
Mr. J. Livingston.

FOR THE AFFIRMATIVE.

Mr. Landon,
Mr. Tappen,
Mr. Schoonmaker,
Mr. Bruyn,
Mr. J. Brown,
Mr. Seaman,
Mr. Horton,
Mr. M'Master,
Mr. Carpenter,
Mr. Scudder,
Mr. Bloom,
Mr. Gilbert.

The question being then put on the motion of Mr. Giles, it passed unanimously in the affirmative. Thereupon

Resolved, (if the Honorable the Senate concur herein) That Rufus King, Esquire, be, and he is hereby chosen to represent this State, in the Senate of the United States.

Ordered, That Mr. J. Livingston and Mr. Havens deliver a copy of the preceding resolution to the Honorable the Senate.

The Senate, A.M.

A message from the Honorable the Assembly, by Mr. Childs and Mr. Tallman, was received, with a resolution that they do not concur with the Senate in their resolution of yesterday for choosing Ezra L'Hommedieu, Esquire, to represent this State in the Senate of the United States. . . .

Another message from the Honorable the Assembly, by Mr. Livingston and Mr. Havens was received with the following resolution for concurrence, which was read, viz.

"*Resolved*, (if the Honorable the Senate concur herein,) That Rufus King, Esquire, be and he is hereby chosen to represent this State in the Senate of the United States."

Mr. Duane thereupon moved, That the Senate do concur with the Honorable the Assembly in their said resolution, and Mr. President having put the question on the said motion, it was carried in the affirmative in manner following, viz.

FOR THE AFFIRMATIVE.

Mr. Duane,
Mr. Roosevelt,
Mr. Micheau,
Mr. Vanderbilt,
Mr. Morris,
Mr. Philip Schuyler,
Mr. Livingston,
Mr. Douw,
Mr. Peter Schuyler,
Mr. Swartwout,
Mr. Hoffman.

FOR THE NEGATIVE

Mr. Townsend,
Mr. Clinton,
Mr. Yates,
Mr. Webster,
Mr. Savage,
Mr. Williams,
Mr. Carpenter,
Mr. Van Ness.

Thereupon, *Resolved*, That the Senate do concur with the Honorable the Assembly in their preceding resolution.

Ordered, That Mr. Yates and Mr. Webster, deliver a copy of the preceding concurrent resolution to the Honorable the Assembly.

The Assembly, A.M.

A copy of a resolution of the Honorable the Senate, delivered by Mr. Yates and Mr. Webster, was read, concurring with this House in their resolution of this day, choosing Rufus King, Esquire, to represent this State, in the Senate of the United States.

Resolved, (if the Honorable the Senate concur therein) that the concurrent resolutions of this House, and of the Honorable the Senate, choosing Philip Schuyler and Rufus King, Esquires, Senators to represent this State, in the Senate of the United States, be subscribed by the Speaker of this House, and by the President of the Senate respectively, and be deposited in the office of the Secretary of this State; and that his Excellency the Governor be requested to cause the same to be exemplified under the great seal of this State, and that such exemplification be delivered to each of the persons so chosen.

Ordered, That Mr. Bancker and Mr. Post, deliver a copy of the preceding resolution to the Honorable the Senate.

The Senate, P.M.

[The Senate received the Assembly resolution.]

Resolved, That the Senate do concur with the Honorable the Assembly in their preceding resolution.

Ordered, That Mr. Savage and Mr. Williams deliver a copy of the preceding concurrent resolution to the Honorable the Assembly.

The Assembly, P.M.

A copy of a resolution of the Honorable the Senate, delivered by Mr. Savage and Mr. Williams, was read, concurring with this House in their resolution of this day, as to the subscribing, filing, and exemplifying the concurrent resolutions of this House, and of the Honorable the Senate, choosing Philip Schuyler and Rufus King, Esquires, Senators to represent this State, in the Senate of the United States.

Daily Advertiser (New York), 16 July

Our last accounts from Albany inform us, that senators to Congress are NOT yet appointed: but we hear from good authority, that JAMES DUANE and PHILIP SCHUYLER. Esqrs. will be elected.

New York Journal, 16 July

The latest accounts from Albany state, that the bill for the appointment of Senators to the Congress of the United States, had passed the house of assembly, and was sent to the senate for concurrence.—That Philip Schuyler and James Duane, Esquires, were in nomination, and had been *informally* agreed upon. From this circumstance it was expected, that those gentlemen would be chosen.[1]

1. There were many inaccurate newspaper reports of the election of Senators. Several newspapers confused nomination of Senators by one house with election. For example, on 15 and 16 July 1789 the *Gazette of the United States* and *Daily Gazette*, respectively, reported that Schuyler and Duane

had been elected, an error that was widely repeated in newspapers from New Hampshire to South Carolina (see, for example, Portsmouth *New Hampshire Gazette*, 23 July, and Charleston *City Gazette*, 5 August). Another erroneous report had L'Hommedieu and King elected (Baltimore *Maryland Journal*, 28 July).

The extent of the confusion is demonstrated in the following report from the Philadelphia *Federal Gazette*, 22 July: "The accounts from New-York respecting the election of Federal Senators by the Legislature of that state, are vague and contradictory. Sometime ago we heard that Mr. Schuyler and Mr. Duane were chosen. One paper of this morning mentions Schuyler and King—another says L'Hommedieu and King. The post to-morrow, in all probability, will determine this question."

At least twenty newspapers eventually reported, correctly, that Schuyler and King were elected Senators.

Abraham Bancker to [Evert Bancker], 16 July (excerpt)[1]

The Bill for electing Senators to represent this State in the Senate of the United States is lost, by reason of the Council's disapproving the Mode therein designated. One Objection, the latter one I mean, has great weight with it, and on due Consideration, a Majority agreed with the Council—

The Mode of concurrent Resolution has been since adopted, and after repeated Attempts, and subtle parliamenteering, we have got in to represent us, Philip Schuyler & Rufus King Esquires.—

1. RC, Bancker Family Papers, NHi. Although the address page is missing, the addressee is undoubtedly Evert Bancker, Abraham's uncle. Abraham signed the letter as "Your Affectn. Nephew."

Christopher Gore to Rufus King, Boston, 26 July (excerpt)[1]

Last evening I was just prepar'd for sleep, a boy rapped at the door & offrd Fenno's gazette—this paper I always view with curiousity—I read the debates of Congress—Mr Ledyards death—Tablet &c &c—on the last sheet, right Constitution of a free Common wealth examind—*Albany*—attracted my notice[2]—but having before read in our papers that Genl Schuyler & Mr Duane were chosen senators;[3] I read that sketch, as I generally do advertisements; till I met, with a paragraph announcing the appointment of Rufus King, a senator for the state of New York—to you, who know my wish for the best admin— of the federal government, and that those who are most capable from their abilities & inclination shoud administer it, I need not express the pleasure I receiv'd—it was unalloy'd—it afforded me all the delight that any public event coud produce in my mind—

1. RC, King Papers, NHi. Gore (1758–1827), a Massachusetts Federalist and close friend of King, was a member of the Massachusetts Convention; United States district attorney for Massachusetts, 1789–1796; commissioner under terms of the Jay Treaty and Chargé d'Affaires in London, 1796–1804; state senator, 1806–1807; governor, 1809–1810; and United States Senator, 1813–1816.

2. John Fenno's *Gazette of the United States*, 22 July 1789, contained articles entitled "The Tablet—No. XXIX" and "The Right Constitution of a Commonwealth Examined." Under the heading "Albany," a sketch of the proceedings of the New York Assembly, 13–16 July, was published. Rufus King's election was reported in the proceedings for 16 July.

3. The Boston *Massachusetts Centinel*, 22 July 1789, and Boston *Independent Chronicle*, 23 July, both erroneously reported Duane's election.

Henry Jackson to Henry Knox, Boston, 26 July (excerpt)[1]

I am pleased that Mr. King is chosen a Senator by the State of New York, this must be very flattering to him—many here will be mortified as it will place him far beyond what they wish him to be—Envy has great favor in the mind—

1. RC, Knox Papers, MHi. The letter was addressed to Knox, Secretary at War, in New York City. Knox, appointed secretary at war by the Confederation Congress in 1785, continued in that post in the Washington administration; he retired in 1794. Jackson (1747–1809), of Massachusetts, was a close friend and business associate of Knox. He was a colonel in the Continental Army during the Revolution; a major general of the state militia, 1792–1796; and treasurer of the Massachusetts Society of the Cincinnati, 1783–1809.

Credentials of the New York Senators, 27 July[1]

The People of the State of New York, by the Grace of God Free and Independent. *To all* to whom these presents shall come send Greeting: *Know Ye* that We having inspected the Records remaining in our Secretary's Office do find there on file a certain concurrent Resolution of our Senate and Assembly in the Words and Figures following, to Wit, "*State* of New York, In Assembly July 16th. 1789, *Resolved*, if the Honorable the Senate concur herein that Rufus King[2] Esquire be and he is hereby chosen to represent this State in the Senate of the United States, By Order of the Assembly Gulian Verplanck Speaker—*State* of New York, In Senate July 16th. 1789 *Resolved* that the Senate do concur with the Honorable the Assembly in their preceding Resolution, By order of the Senate Pierre Van Cortlandt Presdt. .["] *All which* we have caused to be Exemplified by these presents: *In Testimony* whereof We have caused these our Letters to be made patent and the Great Seal of our said State to be hereunto affixed *Witness* our Trusty and well beloved *George Clinton* Esquire Governor of our said State General and Commander in Chief of all the Militia and Admiral of the Navy of the same, at New York, this Twenty seventh day of July[3] in the Year of our Lord one Thousand seven hundred and Eighty nine, and in the fourteenth year of our Independence—

[signed] Geo: Clinton

[SEAL]

1. DS, RG 46, DNA.
2. The name of Philip Schuyler was substituted for that of Rufus King in the other copy of the credentials, under Assembly and Senate dates of 15 July.
3. King left Albany for New York City on 23 July 1789, and presented his credentials to the Senate and took his seat on 25 July, even though Governor Clinton did not prepare his official credentials until 27 July. Schuyler presented his credentials and took his seat on 27 July (DHFFC, I, 91).

Abraham B. Bancker, Senate clerk, explained the delay in issuing King's credentials: "In respect to Mr. King not being able to take his Seat when Papa wrote on the 24th. July, I shall only Observe that he was furnished with a Resolution of his Appointment under the Hand of Mr. McKesson and myself before he left Albany, but a Commission could not issue before the Governors Arrival with the Seal" (to Evert Bancker, Kingston, 29 August 1789, RC, Bancker Family Papers, NHi). John McKesson was clerk of the Assembly.

George Lux to George Read, Baltimore, 28 July (excerpt)[1]

We have just got the account of the great changes in the House of Delegates of N York, the late one, being 2 Antis to 1 Federal, & the present ones 5 Federals to 3 Antis, in consequence of which, Senators are chosen, & very good ones, I know they are, although from the character I have heard of Mr. King, I could rather have wished to see him in the House of Delegates, his eloquence being better adapted to a popular than a select branch—I am also happy to learn, that Governour Clinton has abandoned his virulent opposition to the New Government, & become moderate & dispassionate—I have ever wished to see staunch Federals placed in the Senate, & that barrier to popular caprice being secured, I am for calling forth the ablest men into the House of Delegates, without reference to their political opinions—

1. RC, Rodney Collection of Read Papers, DeHi. The letter was addressed to Read in New York City, where he was attending the United States Senate. Lux (c. 1754–1797), a Federalist, was a Baltimore merchant. He was related to Read through marriage. For a biographical sketch of Read, see DHFFE, II, 97.

Thomas Hartley to Jasper Yeates, New York, 29 July (excerpt)[1]

The Collection Bill has passed both Houses and will be soon ratified by the President—in other respects we are going on rapidly—and have a reasonable prospect of an adjournment some Time in September—

A Contest will arise about the Place to which we shall adjourn—I fear that the New Yorkers will prevail—

In order to secure the Eastern Influence.—they have elected Rufus King senator—if Mr. Hamilton[2] intends to be here when the Business of adjournment will be agitated—about the first week in September will be his Time—

1. RC, Yeates Papers, PHi. The letter was addressed to Yeates in Lancaster, Pennsylvania. Yeates (1745–1817), a Lancaster lawyer, was a justice of the Pennsylvania Supreme Court, 1791–1817. In 1787 he voted to ratify the Constitution in the Pennsylvania Convention. For a biographical sketch of Hartley, who was representing Pennsylvania in the House of Representatives, see DHFFE, I, 417.

2. William Hamilton of Philadelphia, who was advocating Lancaster, Pennsylvania, where he owned much land, as the site for the new federal capital.

William Wetmore to Rufus King, Boston, 29 July (excerpt)[1]

Can we now safely congratulate you on your appointment to the Senatorship? I was at Portland when the paper arrived with ye names of Schuyler & Duane—then came the notice appointing Schuyler & Coriolanus[2] and who says the *Egotist*, can Coriolanus be? Do you not know Rufus Coriolanus? It cannot be him—they never would appoint him; but they have done it already—It is impossible; but when a thing takes place it is no longer impossible—It is mere newspaper intelligence, but it is Fenno's paper[3]—I am not satisfied with the account; Ay, that we all know—How many faces have gathered blackness on this event! what chagrin! what mortification! what disappointment! I wish you were here & at N.[4] for a moment to see with your own eyes. Your friends rejoyce that N.Y. has done you that Justice which the people here were ready to offer but were prevented by the vile & secret, tho successful artifices, of three or four vipers[5]—But enough upon this subject—and I will only add at present that your good fortune, cannot afford more real pleasure to any man, than to your Faithful Friend And Most Obedient

1. RC, King Papers, NHi. Printed: King, *Life*, I, 364–65. Wetmore (1749–1830), a Massachusetts and Maine lawyer, had represented Salem in the Massachusetts House of Representatives, 1777, and was an associate justice of the Massachusetts Circuit Court of Common Pleas, 1811–1821.

2. Coriolanus, Gaius (or Gnaeus) Marcius, legendary Roman hero of the fifth century, B.C., acquired the name "Coriolanus" for his courage against the Volsci at the siege of Corioli (493 B.C.). Later exiled from Rome, he commanded the Volscian army against Rome.

3. John Fenno's *Gazette of the United States* reported King's election on 22 July 1789.

4. Probably Newburyport, Massachusetts, where King had made his home before moving to New York.

5. King had been frequently mentioned as a candidate for Senator from Massachusetts, but he received no votes in the balloting by the Massachusetts General Court. See DHFFE, I, 511–28.

Massachusetts Centinel (Boston), 29 July

NEWS FROM NEW YORK.

JULY 25. In one of my last letters, I mentioned that Messrs. SCHUYLER and DUANE were elected Federal Senators for this State—This was a mistake.—Mr. DUANE was chosen by the House but the Senate did not concur therein.—The second choice was concurred in, and the persons chosen to represent this State in the Senate of the United States, are—the

Hon. PHILIP SCHUYLER,
Hon. RUFUS KING, Esq'rs.[1]

On the appointment of the latter gentleman I particularly congratulate your State—as it is certainly confering a great honour on it, by electing a person whom they so lately sent to Congress—and who has resided with us but a short time. He was unanimously chosen in the House, and by a large majority in the Senate.

1. Up to this point this article was reprinted in the Boston *Independent Chronicle*, 30 July 1789.

John Adams to William Tudor, New York, 18 September (excerpt)[1]

Other States reward their Benefactors. King, only for manœuvring Congress out of their design to go to Philadelphia has been nobly rewarded.[2]—But a Man may drudge forever for Massachusetts and die a beggar; nay what is worse die in disgrace. God forgive them.[3]

1. RC, Tudor Papers, MHi. The letter was addressed to Tudor in Boston. Tudor (1750–1819), a Boston lawyer, had studied law with Adams.

2. In April 1787 advocates of moving Congress from New York City to Philadelphia believed

they had enough votes in Congress to effect the move. However, when the question was raised, Rufus King, representing Massachusetts, managed to have the move defeated through parliamentary maneuvering and by convincing one member to change his vote (Kenneth R. Bowling, "Wigwam of Empire: The Location and Idea of the United States Capital," unpublished manuscript, Chapter VII, 5).

3. Earlier in this letter Adams had complained that Massachusetts was to blame for what Adams considered the very low salary that Congress set for the Vice President. Adams accused Massachusetts of being ungrateful.

NEW YORK CANDIDATES

Adgate, Matthew (1737–1818), Candidate for Representative, District 5

Born in Norwich, Connecticut, Adgate was the son of a farmer. After 1767 he moved to Canaan, Albany County, where he was a farmer and a mill owner. In 1775 Adgate served on the Albany committee of correspondence and safety and in 1776 on the Albany committee of inspection. He was supervisor for Canaan, 1777–1780 and 1787–1788. He represented Albany City and County in the provincial congresses, 1775–1777, and in the Assembly, 1780–1785. After Columbia County was created from Albany County in 1786, Adgate represented that county in the Assembly, 1788–1789, 1791, and 1792–1795. He was a Columbia County justice of the peace, 1786–1804. As a Columbia delegate to the state Convention in 1788, Adgate voted against ratification of the Constitution.

Bailey, Theodorus (1758–1828), Candidate for Representative, District 3

Born near Fishkill, Dutchess County, Bailey was admitted to the New York bar in 1778 and established a law practice in Poughkeepsie. During the Revolution he served as an adjutant in the New York militia; after the war, he attained the rank of brigadier general before retiring in 1805. Bailey served in the House of Representatives, 1793–1797 and 1799–1803, and he represented Dutchess County in the Assembly in 1802. In 1803 he was elected to the United States Senate, but he served only until early 1804, when he was appointed postmaster of New York City. Bailey was postmaster until his death.

Benson, Egbert (1746–1833), Elected Representative, District 3

Born in New York City, Benson graduated from Kings College (Columbia) in 1765. He studied law with John Morin Scott, was admitted to the New York bar in 1769, and practiced law in New York City and Dutchess County. In 1775 Benson was a Dutchess County delegate to the provincial convention, and in 1777 the provincial congress appointed him to the New York council of safety. He became attorney general of New York in 1777 and filled that post until elected to the House of Representatives in 1789. He represented Dutchess County in the Assembly from 1777 to 1781, and he served in Congress in 1784, 1787, and 1788. In 1786 Benson and Alexander Hamilton represented New York at the Annapolis Convention. Benson served in the Assembly again in 1788 and in the House of Representatives, 1789–1793. In 1794 he was appointed an associate justice of the New York Supreme Court, a position he held until 1801, when he was named a United States Circuit Court judge by President John Adams, in one of the "midnight appointments." When this judgeship was nullified in 1802, Benson retired from public life. He was elected to the House of Representatives again in 1813, but served only a few months.

Benson served on numerous committees to settle New York border disputes in the 1780s and 1790s. He was a member of the board of regents of the University of the State of New York from 1784 to 1802. Benson was the first president of the New-York Historical Society, 1805–1815, and he received honorary law degrees from Dartmouth, Harvard, and Union colleges.

Broome, John (1738–1810), Candidate for Representative, District 2

Born on Staten Island, Broome studied law with William Livingston of New Jersey. About 1762 he abandoned the law and joined his brother, Samuel, in a partnership importing British goods. Broome represented New York City and County in the provincial congresses, 1775–1777 (where he served on the committee that drafted the state constitution). When the British occupied New York City during the Revolution, he moved to Connecticut, where he outfitted privateers to harass British vessels. When the British evacuated the city, Broome was elected an alderman; he represented the East Ward in the City Council, 1783–1784 and 1785–1786. He was also city treasurer in 1784. From 1785 to 1794 Broome was president of the New York City Chamber of Commerce, a time when Broome's business firm was engaged in trade with India and China. From 1800 to 1802 he represented New York City and County in the Assembly. In 1804 he was elected to the state Senate to represent the Southern District and served on the Council of Appointment. The same year Broome was elected lieutenant governor, an office he held until his death.

Duane, James (1733–1797), Candidate for Senator

Born in New York City, Duane was the son of a prosperous merchant who had emigrated from Ireland shortly after 1700. He studied law with James Alexander and was admitted to the New York bar in 1754. He developed a large and prestigious New York City law practice, and in 1767 was attorney general for New York. In 1774 he was the colony's Indian commissioner. Duane was a member of the New York committee of correspondence in 1774, and later that year the committee appointed him to Congress, where he served in every session until 1783. He represented New York City and County in the provincial convention, 1775, and provincial congresses, 1775–1777. In 1781 the Philadelphia *Freeman's Journal* accused Duane of loyalism, but influential friends defended him, and the New York legislature expressed continued confidence in him. He represented the Southern District in the state Senate, 1782–1785 and 1788–1790. In 1784, following the British evacuation of New York City, Governor George Clinton appointed Duane mayor of the city, a position he held until 1789. Duane was also a member of the first board of regents of the University of the State of New York in 1784. In 1788 he was a member of the state Convention, where he voted to ratify the Constitution. He resigned as mayor when President George Washington appointed him a federal judge for the district of New York. He retired in 1794 and moved to Schenectady, where he lived until his death. Throughout his career Duane was involved in land development, especially in the Mohawk Valley, where he owned almost all of Duanesburg. He was married to Mary Livingston, daughter of Robert Livingston, Jr.

Floyd, William (1734–1821), Elected Representative, District 1

Born in Brookhaven, Long Island, Floyd was the son of a wealthy landowner. He had a limited education, but he inherited, at the age of eighteen, an estate from his father. He was a colonel in the Suffolk County militia during the Revolution (commissioned a major general at war's end), but saw little military action. He was appointed to Congress in 1774, and served from 1774 to 1776 and again from 1779 to 1783. He was a signer of the Declaration of Independence. Floyd was a Suffolk County delegate to the New York provincial convention in 1775 and to the council of safety in 1777, and he represented the Southern District in the state Senate, 1777–1788. In 1787 he was a member of the Council of Appointment. He served one term in the House of Representatives and was defeated for reelection. He was appointed a presidential Elector in 1792, 1800, 1804, and 1820, although he did not attend the 1820 Electors meeting. In 1801 he represented Suffolk in the state constitutional convention. Floyd moved to Oneida County in 1803, where he farmed, and in 1808 he represented the Western District in the state Senate.

Hathorn, John (1749–1825), Elected Representative, District 4

Born probably in Wilmington, Delaware, Hathorn moved to Philadelphia, where he completed his schooling. A surveyor and schoolteacher, Hathorn moved to Warwick, Orange County, prior to 1770 to assist in establishing the border between New York and New Jersey. In Warwick he farmed and operated a store and an iron forge. Hathorn was a colonel in the New York militia during the Revolution, after which he continued to serve in the militia and attained the rank of major general. He represented Orange County in the Assembly, 1777–1778, 1779–1780, 1781–1785, 1795, and 1804–1805, serving as Speaker in 1784. He represented the Middle District in the state Senate, 1787–1789 and 1800–1803. He was a member of the Council of Appointment in 1787 and 1789. In December 1788 Hathorn was appointed to the last Confederation Congress, but he did not attend. Hathorn served in the House of Representatives, 1789–1791 and 1795–1797, losing bids for reelection in 1791, 1793, and 1797. In 1804 he was supervisor for Warwick.

King, Rufus (1755–1827), Elected Senator

Born in Scarborough, Maine, the son of a merchant and farmer, King graduated from Harvard College in 1777. He studied law with Theophilus Parsons of Newburyport, Massachusetts, was admitted to the Massachusetts bar in 1780, and practiced law in Newburyport. He was elected to the Massachusetts House of Representatives in 1783, 1784, and 1785. From 1784 to 1787 he was a delegate to Congress. In 1787 he was a member of the Constitutional Convention and in 1788 of the Massachusetts Convention (where he voted to ratify the Constitution). In 1786 King had married Mary Alsop, daughter of Joseph Alsop, a wealthy New York merchant. In 1788 he moved permanently to New York City after failing to win election to either the United States Senate or House of Representatives from Massachusetts.

In April 1789 King was elected to the New York Assembly. Later in the year he was elected to the United States Senate, where he drew a six-year term. He was reelected in 1795. In 1791 King was chosen a director of the Bank of the United States. He resigned from the Senate in 1796 to become minister to Great Britain. He returned to the United States in 1803 and the following year unsuccessfully ran for Vice President on the Federalist Party ticket with Charles Cotesworth Pinckney. They again ran unsuccessfully in 1808. In 1813 King was again elected to the United States Senate, where he served until 1825. In 1816 he was the Federalist Party's last presidential candidate. In 1825 he was again appointed minister to Great Britain, but returned to New York in failing health the following year.

Laurance, John (1750–1810), Elected Representative, District 2

Born in Cornwall, England, Laurance (often spelled "Lawrence") emigrated to New York City in 1767. He studied law with Lieutenant Governor Cadwallader Colden and was admitted to the New York bar in 1772. He was a second lieutenant in the First New York Regiment of the Continental Army in 1775 and was promoted to brigadier general in 1776. From 1777 to 1782 he was the judge advocate general on General George Washington's staff. He was a founding member of the Society of the Cincinnati. In 1784 Laurance was appointed to the board of regents of the University of the State of New York, on which he served until 1787. In 1784 he was also elected to the Assembly, where he represented New York City and County for one term, 1784–1785. He attended Congress, 1785–1787, and then represented the Southern District in the state Senate, 1788–1789. He was also a New York City alderman, representing the East Ward, 1788–1789. Laurance served in the House of Representatives, 1789–1793. In 1794 President Washington appointed him a federal judge for the district of New York. He resigned his judgeship in 1796 when elected to the United States Senate, where he served until his retirement in 1800. He was a member of the New York Manumission Society. Throughout his career, Laurance was a very successful speculator in New York lands. He was married to Elizabeth McDougall, daughter of Alexander McDougall.

L'Hommedieu, Ezra (1734–1811), Candidate for Senator

Born in Southold, Long Island, L'Hommedieu was the son of a merchant and sea captain. He graduated from Yale College in 1754, studied law with Robert Hempstead, and practiced law in Southold. He represented Suffolk County in the provincial congresses, 1775–1777, and he also served on the New York committee of safety. From 1777 to 1783 L'Hommedieu represented Suffolk County in the Assembly. He served in Congress, 1779–1783 and 1788; in the state Senate, representing the Southern District, 1784–1792 and 1794–1809; and on the Council of Appointment, 1784 and 1798. He was Suffolk County clerk every year from 1784 until his death except 1810. L'Hommedieu was a principal force behind the organization of the University of the State of New York; he served on the university's first board of regents in 1784 and from 1787 until his death. In 1801 he represented Suffolk County in the state constitutional convention. L'Hommedieu was a founding member of the Agricultural Society of the State of New York, and he wrote extensively on agricultural topics. He was married to Charity Floyd, sister of William Floyd.

Morris, Lewis (1726–1798), Candidate for Senator

Born on the family estate of "Morrisania" in Westchester County, Morris was the grandson of New York's Chief Justice and New Jersey's first royal governor. He was educated at Yale College, although he left school just before graduating in 1746; he was not awarded his degree until 1790. He spent most of his early years farming on the family estate. In 1760 he was appointed a judge of the Court of Admiralty and served until 1774. He was a member of the colonial assembly in 1769. In 1775 Morris represented Westchester County in the provincial convention, which appointed him to Congress, where he signed the Declaration of Independence and served until 1777. In 1776 he was commissioned a brigadier general in the Westchester militia. Morris served in the provincial congresses, 1775–1777, and in 1777 he was a county judge and on the committee on detection of conspiracies. He represented the Southern District in the state Senate, 1777–1778, 1779–1781, and 1784–1790, and on the Council of Appointment, 1786. In 1784 he was appointed to the first board of regents of the University of the State of New York; he was appointed again in 1787. Morris was a delegate from Westchester County to the New York Convention in 1788, where he voted to ratify the Constitution. He was a presidential Elector in 1796. Morris was a half-brother of Gouverneur Morris.

Pell, Philip (1753–1811), Candidate for Representative, District 2

Born at Pelham Manor, Westchester County, Pell graduated from Kings College (Columbia) in 1770 and received a master's degree in 1773. He was admitted to the New York bar in 1774, and practiced law in Westchester County and New York City. Pell was a lieutenant in the New York militia, 1776; a deputy judge advocate in the Continental Army, 1777; and judge advocate general for the army, 1781–1783. He represented Westchester County in the Assembly, 1779–1781 and 1784–1786. He was appointed to the first board of regents of the University of the State of New York in 1784. From 1787 to 1800 he served as surrogate of Westchester County; he was sheriff of the county, 1787–1788. In December 1788 Pell was appointed to the last Confederation Congress, which he attended in early 1789.

Schoonmaker, Cornelius C. (1745–1796), Candidate for Representative, District 4

Born in Shawangunk (now Wallkill), Ulster County, Schoonmaker was a surveyor and farmer. During the Revolution he served as Ulster County coroner and as a member of the county committee to detect conspiracies. He was supervisor for Shawangunk, 1778–1779 and 1784. Schoonmaker represented Ulster in the Assembly, 1777–1781, 1782–1790, and 1795. As a delegate from Ulster to the state Convention in 1788, he voted against ratification of the Constitution. Schoonmaker served in the House of Representatives from 1791 to 1793.

Schuyler, Philip (1733–1804), Elected Senator

Born in Albany, the son of an Albany alderman and merchant who died in 1741, Schuyler was educated by a private tutor in New Rochelle. He inherited large land tracts in the Mohawk Valley and along the Hudson River and an estate near West Troy. On these lands Schuyler lumbered and developed waterpower for his saw, grist, and flax mills; he also established a fleet of ships on the Hudson. In 1755 Schuyler married Catherine Van Rensselaer, daughter of John Van Rensselaer of Claverack. He served as a captain, 1755–1757, and then as a major, 1758–1761, in the British army during the French and Indian War; although he did see some military action in western New York, Schuyler's main responsibility was provisioning the troops.

Schuyler was elected to the colonial assembly in 1768, where he served until the demise of that body in 1775–1776. He was a member of the provincial convention in 1775, which elected him to Congress. He served in Congress, 1775, 1777, and 1779–1780. In 1775, at the outset of the Revolution, Schuyler was named one of four major generals under General George Washington. As head of the Continental Army's Northern Department, Schuyler was blamed for the surrender of Fort Ticonderoga in 1777, and was replaced by General Horatio Gates. Schuyler requested a court martial to judge his conduct, and the court completely exonerated him. He resigned his commission in 1779. Schuyler was surveyor general of New York from 1781 to 1784, and he was a founding member of the Society of the Cincinnati.

Schuyler resumed his political career in 1780 when he was elected to represent the Western District in the state Senate; he served from 1780 to 1784 and from 1786 to 1790. He also served on the Council of Appointment in 1786, 1788, 1790, and 1794. In 1787 he was appointed to the board of regents of the University of the State of New York. He was elected to the United States Senate in 1789, drew a two-year term, and was defeated for reelection in 1791. He returned to the state Senate in 1792, where he served until 1797, when he was again elected to the United States Senate. Poor health forced his resignation from the Senate the following year. Schuyler's daughter, Elizabeth, was married to Alexander Hamilton.

Silvester, Peter (1734–1808), Elected Representative, District 5

Born on Shelter Island, near Long Island, Silvester was admitted to the New York bar in 1763, and established a law practice in Albany. He married Jane Van Schaack, daughter of Cornelius Van Schaack, and moved in about 1766 to an estate in Kinderhook he had acquired through marriage. He was a member of the city of Albany common council in 1772 and the Albany committee of safety in 1774. He represented Albany in the provincial congresses, 1775–1777. When Columbia County was created from Albany County in 1786, Silvester became a judge of the Court of Common Pleas for Columbia. He represented the county in the Assembly, 1788, 1803, and 1804–1806, and the Middle District in the state Senate, 1796–1800. Silvester served in the House of Representatives, 1789–1793. He was appointed to the board of regents of the University of the State of New York in 1787.

Ten Broeck, Abraham (1734–1810), Candidate for Representative, District 6

Born in Albany, the son of the city's mayor, Ten Broeck served an apprenticeship in the countinghouse of his brother-in-law, Philip Livingston, in New York City. Upon completion of his apprenticeship, he returned to Albany and established himself as a merchant. He represented the Manor of Rensselaerwyck in the colonial assembly, 1761–1775, and served as an Albany County judge of the Court of Common Pleas, 1773–1775. Ten Broeck represented Albany City and County in the provincial convention in 1775 and in the provincial congresses, 1775–1777 (serving as president in 1777). During the Revolution he served first as a colonel (1775–1778) and then as a brigadier general (1778–1781) in the state militia. He was mayor of Albany and represented the Western District in the state Senate from 1779 to 1783. He served one year on the Council of Appointment, 1780–1781. In 1781 he was appointed a county judge of the Court of Common Pleas and served until 1794. He was a director and the first president of the Bank of Albany, 1792–1798. In 1796 he was a presidential Elector. Ten Broeck was mayor of Albany again from 1796 to 1798. He was married to Elizabeth Van Rensselaer, daughter of Stephen Van Rensselaer.

Van Rensselaer, Jeremiah (1738–1810), Elected Representative, District 6

Born probably at "Rensselaerwyck" in Albany County, Van Rensselaer graduated from the College of New Jersey (Princeton) in 1758. An heir to "Rensselaerwyck," he also owned land in the lower manor of Claverack. He supplemented his income from his estates by land surveying. An early supporter of the Revolution, he was a member of the Albany Sons of Liberty and the Albany committee of safety. During the Revolution, Van Rensselaer served as a paymaster and a lieutenant in New York units of the Continental Army, and he was a founding member of the Society of the Cincinnati. The only Antifederalist member of his family, he was chairman of the Albany Republican Committee from 1787 to 1789; this committee drew up a list of objections to the adoption of the federal Constitution in 1787. Van Rensselaer represented Albany City and County in the Assembly, 1788–1789. He served in the House of Representatives until 1791, when he was defeated for reelection. A member of the first board of directors of the Bank of Albany in 1792, he was the bank's president, 1798–1806. Van Rensselaer was a presidential Elector in 1800 and lieutenant governor from 1801 to 1804. Philip Schuyler was his brother-in-law.

Williams, John (1752–1806), Candidate for Representative, District 5

Born in Barnstable, England, Williams studied medicine at St. Thomas Hospital in London and served briefly as surgeon's mate on an English warship. In 1773 he emigrated to New Perth, Charlotte County (later Salem, Washington County), where he practiced medicine. At the outset of the Revolution, Williams sided with the patriots and served as a surgeon and colonel in the New York militia. He represented Charlotte County in the provincial congresses, 1775–1777. He was elected to represent the Eastern District in the state Senate in 1777, but he rarely attended and was ultimately expelled in 1778 for defrauding the militia of pay. He represented Charlotte in the Assembly, 1781–1782, and the Eastern District in the state Senate, 1782–1795. In 1789 he served on the Council of Appointment. In 1784 he was appointed to the first board of regents of the University of the State of New York. In 1788 Williams represented Washington County in the state Convention, where he voted against ratification of the Constitution. He was a member of the House of Representatives, 1795–1799. Although Williams served extensively in state and national offices, he continued to practice medicine in Salem and to serve in local offices, such as county judge and supervisor for Salem. He was also involved in land speculation and development and was the largest landowner in Washington County. Williams was an early promoter of the Erie Canal.

Index

There are two major subdivisions within the index, corresponding to the elections in the two states (New Jersey and New York) that comprise this volume. Subjects that pertain only to an individual state are indexed under that state. Relevant entries for the elections of presidential Electors, Representatives, and Senators are indexed under the state headings and in the general index. Topics which pertain to both states are indexed in the general index.

All names of persons are indexed except the names of state legislators that appear only in legislative roll calls and the names of persons that are mentioned only incidentally in the documents. The abbreviation "*id.*" following a name precedes the page or pages wherein the individual is identified.